THE OXFORD HANDB

TOPIC THEORY

THE OXFORD HANDBOOK OF

TOPIC THEORY

Edited by

DANUTA MIRKA

OXFORD

UNIVERSITY PRESS

OXFORD
UNIVERSITY PRESS

Oxford University Press is a department of the University of Oxford.
It furthers the University's objective of excellence in research, scholarship,
and education by publishing worldwide.

Oxford   New York
Auckland   Cape Town   Dar es Salaam   Hong Kong   Karachi
Kuala Lumpur   Madrid   Melbourne   Mexico City   Nairobi
New Delhi   Shanghai   Taipei   Toronto

With offices in
Argentina   Austria   Brazil   Chile   Czech Republic   France   Greece
Guatemala   Hungary   Italy   Japan   Poland   Portugal   Singapore
South Korea   Switzerland   Thailand   Turkey   Ukraine   Vietnam

Oxford is a registered trade mark of Oxford University Press
in the UK and certain other countries.

Published in the United States of America by
Oxford University Press
198 Madison Avenue, New York, NY 10016

Library of Congress Cataloging-in-Publication Data
The Oxford handbook of topic theory / edited by Danuta Mirka.
pages cm
Includes bibliographical references and index.
ISBN 978–0–19–984157–8 (hardcover : alk. paper); 978–0–19–061880–3 (paperback : alk. paper)
1. Music—18th century—History and criticism. I. Mirka, Danuta.
ML196.O84 2014
780.9'033—dc23
2014003819

CONTENTS

SECTION V LISTENING TO TOPICS

Acknowledgments

....

I wish to express my thanks to Suzanne Ryan for coming up with the idea of this handbook and for inviting me to become its editor. I learned a lot in the process of preparing it for publication and will benefit from this experience in my further research. I am most grateful to the authors of individual chapters for accepting my invitations, for their excellent contributions, and for bearing with the editor. I am also grateful to three anonymous reviewers at Oxford University Press for their comments, which resulted in significant improvements of some parts of the manuscript. My special thanks to Mary Ann Smart and Richard Taruskin for sharing the manuscript of Wye J. Allanbrook's posthumous book *The Secular Commedia: Comic Mimesis in Late Eighteenth-Century Music* with me and my contributors.

Most musical examples in this collection were set by Kathryn Puffett, whom I thank for her reliability and flexibility in adjusting to the schedules of individual authors and in accommodating their different wishes and needs. I thank further Danielle Sutcliffe for her help with bibliographic references, Sylvia Cannizzaro for copyediting the manuscript, and the editors at Oxford University Press—especially Lisbeth Redfield and Adam Cohen—for safely shepherding it through various stages of the publication process. Emilia Maggio found the cover image with a *commedia dell'arte* scene including dancers, musicians, and—unavoidably—a dog!

LIST OF CONTRIBUTORS

Kofi Agawu is professor of music at Princeton University. His research focuses on analytical issues in selected repertoires of Western Europe and West Africa. He is the author of *Playing with Signs: A Semiotic Interpretation of Classic Music* and *Music as Discourse: Semiotic Adventures in Romantic Music*, among other books. He has also published articles in *Critical Inquiry, Music Theory Spectrum, Journal of Music Theory, Ethnomusicology, Music Theory Online, Music Analysis*, and the *Journal of the American Musicological Society*. He is a corresponding fellow of the British Academy.

Tom Beghin is associate professor at the Schulich School of Music of McGill University and an internationally active performer on historical keyboards. His recording of Joseph Haydn's complete solo keyboard music (Naxos) marked a remarkable fusion of historical performance practice with the newest research in recording techniques. With classicist Sander Goldberg he coedited *Haydn and the Performance of Rhetoric*, winner of the 2009 Ruth Solie Award from the American Musicological Society. His monograph *Haydn at the Keyboard: A Performer's Paradox* is forthcoming. He is currently focusing his artistic research on the piano works of Ludwig van Beethoven.

Vasili Byros is assistant professor of music theory and cognition at the Northwestern University. He won the Patricia Carpenter Emerging Scholar Award from the Music Theory Society of New York State in 2006 and the TAGS Essay Prize from the Society for Music Analysis in 2008. His research focuses on the cultural and psychological foundations of style in music of the long eighteenth century. His articles about Beethoven's "Eroica," the *le–sol–fi–sol* schema, historical modes of listening, and the intersections among syntactic and semantic structures have appeared in *Music Analysis, Eighteenth-Century Music, Musica Humana*, and *Theory and Practice*.

William E. Caplin is James McGill Professor of Music Theory at the Schulich School of Music, McGill University, specializing in the theory of musical form and the history of harmonic and rhythmic theory in the modern era. His book *Classical Form: A Theory of Formal Functions for the Instrumental Music of Haydn, Mozart, and Beethoven* won the 1999 Wallace Berry Award from the Society for Music Theory and forms the basis of his recent textbook *Analyzing Classical Form*. A former president of the Society for Music Theory, he has presented many keynote addresses, guest lectures, and workshops in North America and Europe. He recently completed a two-year leave supported by a Killam Research Fellowship from the Canada Council of the Arts on the project "Cadence: A Study of Closure in Tonal Music."

Keith Chapin is senior lecturer in music at Cardiff University. He has also taught at Fordham University and at the New Zealand School of Music. He specializes in critical theory, music aesthetics, and music theory in the seventeenth through twentieth centuries, focusing on issues of counterpoint and the sublime. He has been coeditor of *Eighteenth-Century Music* and associate editor of *19th-Century Music*. He coedited the essay collections *Speaking of Music: Addressing the Sonorous* and *Musical Meaning and Human Values*, and his articles have appeared in such journals as *Music and Letters, Eighteenth-Century Music, 19th-Century Music*, and *The International Review of the Aesthetics and Sociology of Music*.

Sarah Day-O'Connell is associate professor in the Department of Music at Knox College and was research fellow at the Institute for Advanced Studies in the Humanities at the University of Edinburgh in 2009–10. Her work focusing on English song and the visual, material, and popular scientific culture of the late eighteenth century has appeared in *Eighteenth-Century Music* (receiving the 2011 Pauline Alderman Award for outstanding scholarship on women and music), *Coll'astuzia, col giudizio: Essays in Honor of Neal Zaslaw*, and *Zyklus und Prozess: Joseph Haydn und die Zeit*. She is coeditor, with Caryl Clark, of the forthcoming *Cambridge Haydn Encyclopedia*.

Joel Galand is associate professor of music theory and director of graduate studies at Florida International University. He won the Society for Music Theory's Young Scholar Award in 1996, is a past editor of the *Journal of Music Theory*, and has contributed articles and reviews pertaining to eighteenth-century music and Schenkerian theory to the *Journal of Music Theory, Music Theory Spectrum, Intégral, Notes, Current Musicology*, and the *Schenkerian Studies* book series. He also writes on the music of Kurt Weill. He has been a volume editor for the Kurt Weill Edition and serves on its editorial board.

Sheila Guymer is a fortepianist and chamber musician with research interests in the performance practices of the First Viennese School, Schubert, Schumann, and Brahms. In Australia, she has held academic and performance teaching positions at the Universities of Melbourne, Sydney, Victoria, and New England. In 2011 she was awarded the F.F.I. Freda Bage Fellowship to undertake a Ph.D. in Music, supervised by Nicholas Cook at the Faculty of Music, University of Cambridge.

Andrew Haringer is a teaching fellow in humanities at Quest University, Canada. His research focuses on political and religious issues in the music of Franz Liszt, topic theory, and broader questions relating to Romantic pianism. He has book chapters in *Liszt: A Chorus of Voices, "Grandeur et Finesse": Chopin, Liszt and the Parisian Musical Scene*, and *Liszt Legacies*. He has written book reviews for *Current Musicology, L'analyse musicale*, and *Music and Letters*.

Robert S. Hatten is professor of music theory at University of Texas at Austin and author of *Musical Meaning in Beethoven: Markedness, Correlation, and Interpretation*, which was corecipient of the Wallace Berry Award from the Society for Music Theory in 1997. His second book, *Interpreting Musical Gestures, Topics, and Tropes: Mozart, Beethoven,*

Schubert, helped launch the book series Musical Meaning and Interpretation, for which he serves as general editor. He has completed terms as vice president of the Society for Music Theory and president of the Semiotic Society of America.

Matthew Head is reader in music at King's College, University of London. His research focuses on music and literature in the German- and English-speaking eighteenth century. He is the author of two books: *Orientalism, Masquerade and Mozart's Turkish Music* and *Sovereign Feminine: Music and Gender in Eighteenth-Century Germany*. His current project explores music, sound, and vibration through notions of "touch," feeling, and sensation.

Julian Horton is professor of music and head of the Music Department at the University of Durham. His research focuses on the analysis and reception of nineteenth-century instrumental music, with special interests in the music of Anton Bruckner and first-movement form in the early nineteenth-century piano concerto. He is the author of *Bruckner's Symphonies: Analysis, Reception and Cultural Politics* and the editor of *The Cambridge Companion to the Symphony*. His articles have appeared in many publications including *Music and Letters, The Musical Quarterly*, and *Music Analysis*. He is the president of the Society for Music Analysis.

Mary Hunter is A. Leroy Greason Professor of Music at Bowdoin College. She is the author of *Opera Buffa in Mozart's Vienna: A Poetics of Entertainment* and *Mozart's Operas: A Companion* and coeditor, with James Webster, of *Opera Buffa in Mozart's Vienna* and, with Richard Will, of *Engaging Haydn: Culture, Context, and Criticism*. She has contributed articles on opera buffa, Mozart, Haydn, and the history of performance to such journals as *Cambridge Opera Journal* and *The Journal of the American Musicological Society* and to many edited collections.

John Irving is an academic and performer specializing in the music of Mozart and in performance practice of the eighteenth century. Formerly professor of music at Bristol University and director of The Institute of Musical Research, School of Advanced Study, University of London, he now divides his time between performance as a fortepianist and academic work as reader in historical performance at Trinity Laban Conservatoire of Music and Dance. His publications on Mozart include *Understanding Mozart's Piano Sonatas, Mozart's Piano Concertos*, and a biography *The Treasures of Mozart*. His CD recordings include solo and chamber discs of works by Mozart, Beethoven, and their Viennese contemporaries. He is an associate fellow of the Institute of Musical Research and serves as vice president of The Royal Musical Association.

Roman Ivanovitch is associate professor of music theory at Indiana University, Bloomington. His research concerns issues of form, style, and aesthetics in the eighteenth century, particularly with respect to classical-era variation and sonata form. His principal focus is the music of Mozart, on which he has published articles in *Music Theory Spectrum*, the *Journal of Music Theory*, and *Music Analysis*. The *Music Analysis* article "Mozart's Art of Retransition" won the Marjorie Weston Emerson Award from the

Mozart Society of America for the best English-language article on Mozart published in 2010–11.

Melanie Lowe is associate professor of musicology at Vanderbilt University's Blair School of Music. Author of *Pleasure and Meaning in the Classical Symphony* and coeditor of the forthcoming *Rethinking Difference in Musical Scholarship*, she has widely published on Haydn and other eighteenth-century subjects, topic theory, music in American media, and music history pedagogy.

Elizabeth Hellmuth Margulis is professor of music and director of the Music Cognition Lab at the University of Arkansas. Her research uses theoretical, behavioral, and neuroimaging methodologies to investigate the dynamic, moment-to-moment experience of listeners without special musical training. She is the author of *On Repeat: How Music Plays the Mind*. Her articles have appeared in diverse publications ranging from *Music Theory Spectrum, Journal of Music Theory, Music Perception, Journal of New Music Research,* and *Psychology of Music* to *Human Brain Mapping, Frontiers in Psychology,* and *Journal of Cognitive Neuroscience.*

Catherine Mayes is assistant professor of musicology at the University of Utah. Her research focuses on exoticism and national styles in music of the late eighteenth and early nineteenth centuries, with particular attention to Viennese representations of Hungarian-Gypsy music. Her articles pertaining to this topic have appeared in *Eighteenth-Century Music* and *Music and Letters.*

Clive McClelland is associate professor of music at the University of Leeds. His book *Ombra: Supernatural Music in the Eighteenth Century* is the standard text on the subject. Other recent and forthcoming publications include chapters on Schubert's supernatural lieder in *Schubert the Progressive: History, Performance Practice and Analysis* and on Spohr's *Faust* in *The Oxford Handbook of Faust in Music* and an article on Elgar's "dark saying" for the *Musical Times.*

Eric McKee is associate professor of music theory at the Penn State University. His book *Decorum of the Minuet, Delirium of the Waltz* investigates the social contexts and bodily rhythms of the two most important dances of the eighteenth and nineteenth centuries. His current research, for which he was awarded a fellowship from the American Council of Learned Societies, focuses on the influence of the dance in Chopin's music. His articles have appeared in such journals as *Music Theory Spectrum, Music Analysis, In Theory Only,* and *Theory and Practice.*

Danuta Mirka is reader in music at the University of Southampton. She is the coeditor, with Kofi Agawu, of *Communication in Eighteenth-Century Music.* Her books include *The Sonoristic Structuralism of Krzysztof Penderecki* and *Metric Manipulations in Haydn and Mozart: Chamber Music for Strings, 1787–1791,* which won the 2011 Wallace Berry Award from the Society for Music Theory. Her articles have appeared in many publications including *The Journal of Musicology, Journal of Music Theory, The American Journal of Semiotics, Musical Quarterly,* and *Eighteenth-Century Music.*

Stephen Rumph is associate professor of music history at the University of Washington. He is the author of *Beethoven after Napoleon: Political Romanticism in the Late Works* and *Mozart and Enlightenment Semiotics*, both published by the University of California Press. His articles have appeared in the *Journal of the Royal Musical Association, Eighteenth-Century Music, 19th-Century Music, Music and Letters*, and *Beethoven Forum*.

Elaine Sisman is the Anne Parsons Bender Professor of Music at Columbia University. The author of *Haydn and the Classical Variation*, the Cambridge Handbook *Mozart: The "Jupiter" Symphony*, and editor of *Haydn and His World*, she has published numerous essays on music of the eighteenth and nineteenth centuries that interweave history, biography, aesthetics, and analysis. She has been awarded the Alfred Einstein Award of the American Musicological Society for best article by a younger scholar, serves on the boards of international Haydn and Mozart societies as well as *The Musical Quarterly* and *The Journal of Musicology*, and completed a term as president of the American Musicological Society, which elected her to Honorary Membership in 2011.

W. Dean Sutcliffe is associate professor in the School of Music at the University of Auckland, and coeditor of *Eighteenth-Century Music*. His research interests are focused on the eighteenth century, and publications have covered composers such as Domenico Scarlatti, Gyrowetz, Boccherini, Mozart, Scarlatti's Spanish contemporary Sebastián de Albero, Manuel Blasco de Nebra, and, above all, Haydn. He was awarded the Dent Medal for 2009 by the Royal Musical Association. He is vice president of the Society for Eighteenth-Century Music, a member of the Committee of Honour of the Haydn Society of Great Britain, a member of the Advisory Board of the Haydn Society of North America, and serves on the Council of the American Musicological Society.

Lawrence M. Zbikowski is associate professor of music and the humanities and Deputy Provost for the Arts at the University of Chicago. His principal research interests involve applying recent work in cognitive science to various problems confronted by music scholars, with a particular focus on music theory and analysis. He is the author of *Conceptualizing Music: Cognitive Structure, Theory, and Analysis*, which won the Society for Music Theory's 2004 Wallace Berry Award. His articles have appeared in such scholarly journals as *Music Perception, Music Analysis, Music Theory Spectrum, Music Theory Online*, and *Journal of the Royal Musical Association*.

Note on Sources and Musical Examples

⋯⋯⋯⋯⋯⋯⋯⋯⋯⋯⋯⋯⋯⋯⋯⋯⋯⋯⋯⋯⋯⋯⋯⋯⋯⋯⋯⋯⋯

This book contains numerous references to German, French, and Italian sources related to eighteenth-century music theory, aesthetics, and criticism. Many of these sources have not been translated into English and are quoted here in the authors' translations. Except for passages quoted from existing English translations, the original text is provided alongside the translation. For block quotations, it occurs after the translation. For quotations within the main text, the original is given in an endnote or, for brief quotations, it is enclosed in round brackets after the translation.

Unless otherwise specified, the texts of musical examples from Haydn, Mozart, and Beethoven are based on *Joseph Haydn Werke* (Henle), *Neue Mozart Ausgabe* (Bärenreiter), and *Beethoven Werke* (Henle). When other editions are used for reasons related to the authors' arguments, they are identified in the course of the accompanying discussions.

ABOUT THE COMPANION WEBSITE

www.oup.com/us/ohtt

Oxford has created a website to accompany *The Oxford Handbook of Topic Theory*. Material that cannot be made available in a book, namely the audio and video examples accompanying Chapters 14 and 21 as well as the appendices to Chapters 18 and 21, are provided here. The reader is encouraged to consult this resource in conjunction with reading the chapter. Examples available online are signaled with Oxford's symbol ⏵.

THE OXFORD HANDBOOK OF

TOPIC THEORY

INTRODUCTION

DANUTA MIRKA

THE concept of topics was introduced into the vocabulary of music scholars by Leonard Ratner. In his seminal book *Classic Music: Expression, Form, and Style*, which promises the reader "a full-scale explication of the stylistic premises of classic music" (1980: xiv), Ratner defines topics as "subjects for musical discourse" (9) and divides them into "types" and "styles." The former group embraces dances and marches. The latter includes such styles as Turkish, military, or hunting. The inventory of types and the fact that they "appear as fully worked-out pieces" implies that they are equivalent to genres. By contrast, styles are "progressions within a piece" but, as Ratner points out, "the distinction between types and styles is flexible; minuets and marches represent complete types of composition, but they also furnish styles for other pieces" (9). The further course of his discussion makes clear that it is their deployment in other pieces and mixtures with other styles that turns styles into topics. Some of them are derived from popular and functional music. Others form cross-references between artistic styles and genres. Before Ratner such cross-references went largely unnoticed. His insight that classical masterpieces were full of references to eighteenth-century soundscape transformed their reception by modern listeners as the discovery that the Parthenon was painted transformed the reception of monumental ruins of classical antiquity. To modern spectators of monochromatic marble it revealed that the uniformity of color was due only to time. For inhabitants of Athens in the fifth century BC the marble appeared full of colors, which adorned the metopes of gods, heroes, and centaurs. Similarly, for listeners in eighteenth-century Vienna the musical repertoire of the time presented a colorful gallery of characters known from everyday musical life. As the repository of stylistic knowledge shared by composers and listeners, Ratner's topics constituted a source of meaning and means of communication in eighteenth-century music. Today they allow one to gain access to its meaning and expression in a way that can be intersubjectively verified.[1]

This might be why topics are so attractive. By now they have become part of the common vocabulary of music scholars and have been applied to a wide range of musical repertoires. Topic theory was developed from Ratner's seminal insight by Wye Allanbrook,

Kofi Agawu, Robert Hatten, Raymond Monelle, and others, who explored its epistemological implications and furnished tools for analysis, but in the process the concept of topics has lost its sharp profile.[2] Allanbrook's study of *topoi* in Mozart's operas (1983) explored the meanings of dances and marches—Ratner's types—but in his later article Ratner suggested that a topic could be not only "a style" or "a type" but also "a figure, a process or a plan of action" (1991: 615). Other authors have expanded this concept ever further. The Universe of Topic outlined by Agawu (1991: 30) supplements Ratnerian topics with an affect (*amoroso*) and melodic figures (sigh motive, Mannheim rocket). In the most recent version (2009: 43–44) it comes up to sixty-one items and includes further affects (pathetic, tragic), melodic figures (military figures, hunting fanfares, horn calls, *Lebewohl*), and accompanimental patterns (Alberti bass, murky bass, *Trommelbass*). The ultimate expansion of the Topical Universe takes place in Allanbrook's posthumous book (2014: Chapter 3), where the concept of topics subsumes styles and genres, affects, accompanimental patterns, melodic and rhetorical figures, harmonic schemata (cadence)—even meters (4/4). In light of these discrepancies, the fundamental question of topic theory is: What are musical topics? To be sure, they are conventions, but do they form a "trusty umbrella" (Allanbrook 2014: 117) for all kinds of musical conventions or do they represent a special kind? In this volume we propose that it is useful to distinguish topics from other conventions in order to see how they interact with each other. Consequently, we return to Ratner's original concept of topics and define them as *musical styles and genres taken out of their proper context and used in another one*. Other conventions, subsumed under this concept by other authors, are not topics, even if some of them are related to topics on the grounds of this definition: melodic or accompanimental figures are musical characteristics of topics insofar as they allow one to recognize a style or genre; affects form part of topical signification. Rhetorical figures and harmonic schemata are unrelated to topics but can combine with them into more or less stable amalgamates that are conventional in their own rights.

The definition of topics adopted in this volume has implications for the historical basis of topic theory. Securing this basis was of utmost importance for Ratner, who coined the concept of topics as part of his larger project "to approach the music and musical precepts of the 18th century in much the same way a listener of that time would have done" (1980: xvi). Accordingly, his discussion of topics is prefaced with a historical survey of eighteenth-century ideas of expression and the discussions of individual topics are full of references to historical sources. Further references were culled by Allanbrook (1983: 1–70) and Agawu (1991: 26–30), but their validity was questioned by Monelle (2000), who critically reviewed Ratner's sources, accused him of their problematic selection and odd translation, and concluded that "contemporary writers are no good as buttresses of topic theory" (2000: 33). This verdict undermined the credentials of topic theory in the age of authenticity. The fact that the concept of topics did not exist in the eighteenth century and Monelle's suggestion that it had no basis in eighteenth-century sources discredited it in the eyes of those for whom historical pedigree of theoretical concepts featured high on the agenda. As a result, topic theory has not been integrated into the field of historically informed music theory, although the advances of this field in the last three decades were stimulated by Ratner's project. But the reserved attitude toward stylistic cross-references, represented by topics, does not account for the basic premise of eighteenth-century music aesthetics, according to which all dimensions of musical structure stand in service of affect and character, which, in their turn, are closely related to styles and genres. If topics are styles and genres used out of their proper context, the question of the historical basis of topic theory splits into two different but interrelated questions: first, whether or not a given style or genre was recognized by contemporary writers; second, whether or not it was recognized in other contexts, when mixed with other styles and genres. I will deal with these questions in section 1 of this introduction. I will then try to find a place for topics in eighteenth-century music aesthetics (section 2). This will take me on a journey during which I explore the connection between music and affect and relate Ratnerian topics to Sulzer's concept of characters. This relation bears on the scope and semiotic status of topical signification, as I show in section 3. In section 4 I revisit and reaffirm the distinction between topics and pictorialism, blurred by Monelle (2000). In section 5 I address the thorny issue of their relation to rhetoric. The final section of the introduction reviews further questions emerging from critical reception of topic theory, explains the structure of the volume, and opens the floor for other authors.

1. STYLES AND GENRES

The concept of style emerged in seventeenth-century music theory to become an object of special attention in the first half of the eighteenth century. The oldest stylistic division was that into *stilo antico* and *stilo moderno*. Derived from Claudio Monteverdi's distinction between *prima* and *seconda prattica* by Giovanni Battista Doni (1635), it was adopted in Germany by Christoph Bernhard and continued in the eighteenth century under the names of the strict and free (or galant) styles. Another stylistic division originated with Marco Scacchi (1649), who distinguished between the church style (*stylus ecclesiasticus*), theatrical style (*stylus theatralis*), and chamber style (*stylus camerae*). This classification was combined by Johann Mattheson with a set of stylistic categories devised by Athanasius Kircher (1650): *stylus ecclesiasticus, canonicus, motecticus, phantasticus, madrigalescus, melismaticus, hyporchematicus, symphoniacus,* and *recitativus*. In *Das beschützte Orchester* (1717) Mattheson subsumes Kircher's *species stylorum* under Scacchi's *genera stylorum*. He retains this stylistic system in *Kern melodischer Wissenschaft* (1737) and *Der vollkommene Capellmeister* (1739).[3]

Yet another classification was proposed by Johann Adolph Scheibe (1745). Although Scheibe accepts the division into the church, theatrical, and chamber styles, he subordinates it to the division into the high, middle, and low styles. As he points out, each of these "good" styles "can and must be used for church music as well as theatrical and chamber pieces,"[4] even though it has to be properly modified. Mattheson makes the same observation, but for him the need of modification is not a proof that the church, theatrical, and, chamber styles are subordinated to the high, middle, and low styles but, on the contrary, that the high, middle, and low styles should be subordinated to the church, theatrical, and chamber styles, which he calls the "main" styles: "For any and all expressions [*alle und iede Ausdrücke*], though they may comprehend something elevated [*erhabenes*], moderate [*mäßiges*], or lowly [*geringes*], must inevitably and without exception conform in all respects to the above-mentioned three most important genera [*Geschlechtern*] of writing style with all thoughts, inventions and strengths, as servants to their masters" (Mattheson 1739: 69; Harriss 1981: 190, translation modified). While the distinction between the high, middle, and low style became obsolete in the second half of the eighteenth century (see Forkel 1788: 44; Koch 1802: col. 1455), the division into the church, theatrical, and chamber style persisted into the nineteenth. As noted by Heinrich Christoph Koch (1802: col. 1452), it overlaps with the division into the strict and free style because the former has its privileged place in church music. Since it is difficult to draw a borderline—based on technical criteria—between the theatrical and chamber styles (col. 1455), these two styles fall into one. As a result, "one could divide the musical style into religious and profane or, as the elders used to say, in the sacred and secular."[5] On the other hand, the three main styles could be grouped into public (church, theatrical) and private (chamber) (Sulzer 1792–94, 1: 441). Some authors develop the stylistic division into church, theatrical, and chamber styles by adding further branches or subdivisions. Mattheson considers the possibility of a separate martial style:

> Heretofore I thought that the categories of these styles would some day be increased: for, whoever only would want could spread not only the secondary branches quite a bit; but also other branches would appear, among which especially the field or martial style would be of no small consideration. For though marches and such many melodies belong to the hyporchematic style; still the martial music itself has, in many respects, things which are somewhat peculiar to it which might be worth investigating. (Mattheson 1739: 93; Harriss 1981: 225)

Christian Friedrich Daniel Schubart (1806) posits a *pantomimischer Styl*, which includes dance music, and supplements the classification with a *populärer Styl*, including popular music and folk songs. In the eighteenth century the division into church, theatrical, and chamber styles coexists with other stylistic divisions. The styles of vocal and instrumental melodies were described by Mattheson (1739: 203–10; Harriss 1981: 418–29). The concept of national styles reached back to Kircher (1650: 543–45). The most important among them were the French and the Italian, but other national styles were frequently mentioned: Mattheson (1713: 200–31) singles out English and German; Scheibe (1745: 145–50) German and Polish. By the end of the eighteenth century the German style reaches an international position on a par with the styles of French and Italian music.

In all these classifications the emphasis lies on differences between styles and the purpose of their discussion is to teach composers how to use them in their proper contexts. Instances of using styles in other contexts or mixing them with other styles are only infrequently mentioned. If they receive any comments, evaluations of such mixtures are invariably negative. Mattheson continues his deliberations as follows:

> These were my thoughts heretofore; now however, after considering everything carefully, I am a little worried, namely that as time goes by only a few or even perhaps not a single one of these styles and their categories might remain unadulterated and with distinguishing characteristics. For there is already such a mishmash [*Mischmasch*] to be found in the styles of many self-instructed composers, as if everything were deteriorating into a formless mass. And I believe that one would find many, who, upon inquiry as to the style in which this or that piece was set, would be embarrassed for an answer. (Mattheson 1739: 93; Harriss 1981: 225)

Scheibe grants mixtures of styles a separate place in his stylistic system, in which the "good" styles—high, middle, and low—are contrasted with their "bad" counterparts: the pompous style (*die schwülstige Schreibart*), the disorderly or uneven style (*die unordentliche oder ungleiche Schreibart*), and the flat or mean style (*die platte oder niederträchtige Schreibart*). He describes the disorderly style as follows:

> One has written one line in high, another in middle, yet another in low style. Here stand French, there Italian passages. First goes a theatrical phrase, then one which belongs to the church. Everything is so chaotically mixed together that one cannot find a dominant style or a proper expression.
>
> Furthermore, one mixes particular characteristics of certain compositions. For instance, one writes overtures in the manner of symphonies or concertos, or one inserts such passages into symphonies and concertos which properly belong to overtures. The melody of an aria sounds like a recitative but recitative turns into an aria. Generally, one pulls together several kinds of pieces, throws them on one heap, and writes at whim the first name above it which comes to mind.... This unevenness arises also when one throws together the characters of French, Italian, German, or other compositions without considering the fact that each composition requires its own elaboration. The style also becomes uneven when one mixes the expression of different moral characters or mixes up the expression of one character with the other.... Am I not right when I call this lumpy, bumpy, and disorderly style the worst of all? Yes, it is this style that covers music with the greatest dishonour since it suppresses the beautiful and natural to the greatest extent. And yet it occurs in most musical works.

> Man hat in einer Zeile hoch, in der andern mittelmäßig, und in der dritten endlich gar niedrig geschrieben. Hier stehen französiche, dort aber italienische Stellen. Bald zeigt sich ein theatralischer Satz, bald auch ein anderer, der sich in die Kirche schickte. Ja, alles ist so bunt und so kraus durch einander gemischet, daß man keinesweges eine herrschende Schreibart, oder einen gehörigen Ausdruck der Sachen finden wird.
>
> Man vermischet ferner die besondern Eigenschaften gewisser Stücke, indem man in Ouverturen synphoniemäßig und concertenmäßig schreibet, oder auch in die Symphonien und Concerten solche Stellen einrücket, die in die Ouverture gehören. Die Melodie der Arie wird oft recitativmäßig, das Recitativ aber zur Arie gemacht. Ueberhaupt aber wirft man vielerley besondere Arten einzelner Stücke in einen

Haufen, und schreibt nach Belieben einen Namen darüber, welcher dem erfahrenen Componisten am ersten einfällt.... Diese Ungleichheit wird auch verursachet, wenn man die Charactere der französischen, italienischen, deutschen oder anderer Stücke, unter einander wirft, ohne zu bedenken, daß jedes Stück seine eigene Ausarbeitung erfordert. Auch wird die Schreibart ungleich, wenn man den Ausdruck verschiedener moralischen Charactere vermischet, oder auch den Ausdruck des einen mit dem andern verwechselt.... Werde ich nun wohl unrecht haben, wenn ich diese höckerische, holprichte und unordentliche Schreibart die allerschlechteste nenne? Ja, diese ist es eben, die der Musik am meisten zu Schande gereichet: weil sie am meisten das Schöne und Natürliche verhindert und unterdrücket, dennoch aber sich in den meisten musikalischen Stücken befindet. (Scheibe 1745: 134–36)

The works condemned by Scheibe for their disorderly style represented the new Italian style of instrumental music gaining the upper hand in the first half of the eighteenth century. As the popularity of this style increased in the second half, subsequent generations of German critics continued to raise the charges of "mishmash" (*Mischmasch*) and "disorder" (*Unordnung*) against younger generations of Italian and Italianate composers.[6]

The reason for this criticism was related to the fact that different styles were associated with different affects. The division into the high, middle, and low style was based on the dignity of affect. Scheibe equates this dignity with strength. For instance, "the magnanimity, the majesty, thirst for power, the splendour, the arrogance, the wonder, the anger, the horror, the fury, the vengeance, the rage, the despair...can be expressed in no other style than the high one."[7] By contrast, for Mattheson the dignity of an affect depends not on its strength but moral value. He polemically raises this issue in his debate with Scheibe:[8]

Among those affections which one commonly attributes to the high style are many which do not deserve to be called high at all, in the good sense. For, what can be lower than anger, fear, vengeance, despair, etc. Beating, boasting, snoring is indeed not true nobility. Arrogance is itself only an inflating of the soul, and actually requires more bombast than nobility for expression: now the most haughty are again unfailingly the most angry, in their feelings one debility after another takes the helm. (Mattheson 1739: 71; Harriss 1981: 194)

The division into the church, theatrical, and chamber style is based on venue but it, too, has affective implications because different venues call for different affects.[9] This is why high, middle, and low styles are modified by their use in church, theatrical, or chamber styles. These stylistic divisions intersect because they bring about alternative ways of grouping affects. The affects of the church style can be high, middle, or low, but not every high, middle, or low affect can be used in this style:

Divine majesty, heavenly splendor, rapture and magnificence, together with the elevated style of writing [*hohen Schreib-Art*] naturally required for it, are subordinated to the sacred main style [*dem geistlichen Haupt-Styl unterworffen*]. Devotion, patience [*Geduld*], etc., together with their appropriate middle style of writing correctly belong there, too, namely, in the church, i.e., in the service of God. Repentance, supplient entreaties, etc., in their appropriate low style similarly stand under the same banner, and these three types of characteristics must together be at the disposal of the church style as well as the dramatic and domestic ones, each in its own way. (Mattheson; 1739: 70; Harriss 1981: 191, translation modified)

Affects were also associated with genres. If styles encompass broad affective zones, genres composed in these styles are related to specific affects. This concerns, in particular, the instrumental genres that Mattheson called "small *Pieçes*" and took the pride of first describing in *Das Neu-Eröffnete Orchestre* (1713: 189–90). When he returns to them in *Kern melodischer Wissenschaft* and *Der vollkommene Capellmeister*, each genre receives its typical affect. For example, the affect of the allemande is one of a "contented or satisfied spirit," of the bourrée "contentment and pleasantness," of the courante "sweet hopefulness," of sarabande "ambition," of the rigaudon "trifling jocularity," of the passepied "frivolity," of the gavotte "exalting joy," of the gigue "passionate and volatile ardour," of the canarie "eagerness and swiftness," of the angloise "stubbornness," and of the minuet "moderate gaiety" (Buelow 1983: 406–7). Affective characters of larger pieces are less specific. In symphonies, which form introductions to operas or church or chamber music, "the expression of affects ... would have to conform to those passions which predominate in the work itself" (Mattheson 1739: 234; Harriss 1981: 467). In sonatas and concerti grossi affects are "manifold and various" (Mattheson 1739: 234; Harriss 1981: 467).

While Mattheson relishes in this variety and does not try to constrain it, subsequent generations of German critics insist that various affects of larger instrumental pieces should be unified by a single character. The concept of character entered eighteenth-century discourse about music through the writings of Scheibe, who inherited it from his teacher, Johann Christian Gottsched. In *Versuch einer critischen Dichtkunst* (1730) Gottsched explains that character embraces the entire disposition of a given person, which consists of natural inclinations and acquired habits and manifests itself in feelings, deeds, and words. This disposition bears traces of life and descent: "the nature and its creator, the country where one was born, the parents and ancestors, the gender and age, the wealth and status, the education, the times in which one lives, the good and bad luck, the persons with whom one mixes and so on."[10] A poet should be at pains that his characters be plausible in light of such circumstances. Above all, he should avoid furnishing them with contradictory features. "A self-contradictory character is a monster which does not occur in nature: therefore a greedy man must be greedy, a proud man proud, a hot-headed man hot-headed, a faint-hearted man faint-hearted— and so he must remain."[11]

Scheibe applies this concept of character to persons represented in operas as well as oratorios, cantatas, church music, and songs. As he points out, characters of such persons consist of outer (or general) and inner (or particular) characters. The outer character is determined by their social status. The inner character can be called the character proper. Taken together, the outer and the inner character condition the strength of affects experienced by a given person: "The character of persons softens or strengthens the passions.

The joy, the sadness, the horror, the fear, the hate, the love etc. are not equally violent, medium, or weak in all persons. We have certain degrees which the characters of persons forbid us to exceed."[12] Although a given person can experience a wide range of affects, they are unified by the character. "It should therefore be noted as a basic rule that, when the composer observes the characters of persons, he will never transgress against affects."[13] When he "mixes the expression of different moral characters or mixes up the expression of one character with the other," the composer ends up in an uneven or disorderly style.

The concept of character was further developed by Johann Georg Sulzer. If Scheibe applies it to vocal music, Sulzer extends it to vocal and instrumental genres:

> Every composition, whether it is vocal or instrumental, should possess a definite character and be able to arouse specific sentiments in the minds of listeners. It would be foolish of the composer to begin composing without having established the character of his work. He must know whether the language he will set down is that of a man who is proud or humble, courageous or timid, pleading or commanding [*eines Bittenden oder Gebietenden*], tender or tempestuous. Even if he stumbles upon his theme by chance, or he arbitrarily selects it, he must still examine its character carefully so that he can sustain it while composing. (Sulzer 1792–94, 1: 273; Baker and Christensen 1995: 53, translation modified)

In the article "Charakter" from the *Allgemeine Theorie der schönen Künste* Sulzer declares that characters of persons are the most important objects of fine arts (Sulzer 1792–94, 1: 454). Since passions and actions spring from the character of a given person like fruits from a tree, mixing features of different characters is as unnatural as mixing features of different species:

> Just as the painter must obey nature, for instance, by attributing to each tree the leaves and fruits which are natural to it and placing them only on those branches on which they really grow, and not at arbitrarily selected places; so also the poet must deal with expressions of emotion, which are as natural effects of the character as leaves and fruits are effects of the particular nature of a tree.

> Wie der Mahler sich lediglich an die Natur halten, und z. E. jedem Baume, nicht nur die Art der Blühte oder Frucht zueigen muß, die ihm natürlich ist, sondern sie auch nur an denjenigen Arten der Zweige, an denen sie würklich wachsen, nicht aber an willkührlichen Stellen, anbringen darf; so muß es auch der Dichter mit jeder Aeußerung des Gemüths halten, die eben so natürliche Würkungen des Charakters sind, als Blühten und Früchte Würkungen der besondern Natur eines Baumes. (Sulzer 1792–94, 1: 456)

The same holds for the composer. Incoherent mixtures of sentiments in larger instrumental pieces, such as symphonies, sonatas, or concerti, are aesthetically and morally suspect because they resemble "people who in their deeds and way of thinking show no definite character; they are like weathercocks, which can take any turn and position, and thus let themselves to be dragged along in any direction."[14] Since, under normal circumstances, contrasting affects are not experienced in quick succession, sudden contrasts of affects suffer under the lack of verisimilitude (*vraisemblance*), a fundamental principle of neoclassical aesthetics.

To be sure, contrasting affects can be experienced under exceptional circumstances. Such circumstances are frequently portrayed in tragedies, where characters are tossed between contrasting affects by series of dramatic events, but there the events are explained by the text. The role of the text in explaining context of affects determined the superiority of vocal over instrumental music in eighteenth-century aesthetics and inspired the apology of instrumental genres undertaken by Johann Abraham Peter Schulz and Koch. In the articles "Sonate" and "Symphonie" written for Sulzer's *Allgemeine Theorie*, Schulz compares the sonata to a cantata and a symphony to a chorus. Koch picks up on these comparisons in the *Versuch einer Anleitung zur Composition* (1782–93) and goes on to question Sulzer's negative verdict about the concerto by comparing it with an ancient tragedy in which the "actor expressed his feelings not towards the pit, but to the chorus" (Koch 1983: 209; see also 1802: col. 354).[15] But the stylistic and affective mixtures characteristic of the southern style of instrumental music sustained no comparison to tragedy. Rather, they resembled the Viennese comedy, a theatrical genre modeled on the Italian *commedia dell'arte*. Ultimately, the charge of "disorder" and "mishmash" raised against the new instrumental style was a charge against its comic spirit.[16] Indeed, as critics point out, the incompatible affects par excellence are the serious and the comic. Schulz, who praises the freedom of sonatas to "assume any character and every expression" (Sulzer 1792–94, 4: 425; Baker and Christensen 1995: 103), faults Italian sonatas for their "bizarre sudden changes in character from joy to despair, from the pathetic to the trivial" (Sulzer 1792–94, 4: 425; Baker and Christensen 1995: 104). Johann Christoph Stockman brandmarks "the strange mixture of comic and serious, of the trifling and the moving" (Heartz 1995: 349), and Johann Adam Hiller warns composers of instrumental music "of that strange mixture of the comic and the serious, the happy and the sad, the elevated and the lowly, that will remain tasteless as long as it is unnatural to laugh and cry at the same time" (Hosler 1981: 7). For him, such contrasts do not resemble affective torments of noble heroines and heroes but "vulgar antics" of Hans Wurst, the stock character of Viennese comic scene.[17]

To be sure, the North-German critics correctly recognized the origins of the new instrumental style in comedy and its musical counterpart: opera buffa. What prevented them from appreciating this style on its own terms was the difference between their aesthetic theory and the compositional practice of Italian and South-German composers. Whereas the critics, formed by the Lutheran tradition, insisted on the moral function of music, the composers, exposed to commercial demands of the musical market, relished in its function as entertainment. Since their style did not develop its own aesthetics, in its days it received no adequate critical appraisal. The topic theory, concerned with cross-references between styles and genres, can be considered a theory of this style, and *The Oxford Handbook of Topic Theory* will go some way toward reconstructing its aesthetic underpinnings—but it will not start from scratch. Rather, it will build on premises of North-German music aesthetics. As we will see, South-German composers were committed to them, even if they used them *a rebours*.

2. MUSIC AND AFFECTS

Undoubtedly, the basic premise of eighteenth-century music aesthetics was the con-nection between music and affects. The belief that music had the power to arouse and appease emotions went back to antiquity and permeated the Middle Ages. After the Reformation it continued in both Lutheran and Catholic traditions. Luther was enthusiastic about music's effects on the soul, illustrating them with the biblical story of David and King Saul.[18] In the seventeenth century his views were frequently reiter-ated by German authors (Otto 1937) and the "wonderful effects of music" (Hosler 1981: 37) described in terms of affects or affections. Derived from Latin *affectus* and equivalent to Greek *pathos*, this concept was synonymous to passion (*Leidenschaft*) and remained in use until the end of the eighteenth century, but if before the connection between music and affects was supported by theological speculation, now it invited sci-entific explanation.

The first attempt to explain the affective power of music was undertaken by Mattheson. This explanation, contained in Part One of *Der vollkommene Capellmeister* and frequently—if improperly—called the doctrine of affections (*Affektenlehre*),[19] stipulates that the connection between music and affect is based on similarity between musical motion (*Bewegung*) and emotion or, as Mattheson calls it, "motion of the soul" (*Gemüthsbewegung*). His account of the latter motion relies on the theory of emotion adopted by Athanasius Kircher in *Musurgia universalis* (1650), according to which affects are caused by the so-called animal spirits flowing in nerves and stimulating physiological processes such as blood circulation. Kircher discusses eight affects—love, sorrow, joy, anger, compassion, fear, insolence, and wonder—the first three of them being the most important. Mattheson calls them the main affects (*Haupt-Affekte*), dis-tinguishes them from subsidiary affects (*Nebenaffekte*), and construes other affects as combinations of *Haupt-* and *Nebenaffekten*. As he explains, each affect is characterized by a specific motion of the animal spirits, which can be represented by music.[20]

> Since, for example, joy is felt [*empfunden*] as an expansion of our animal spirits [*Lebens-Geister*], thus it follows reasonably and naturally that I could best express this affect by large and enlarged [*erweiterte*] intervals. Instead, if one knows that sad-ness is a contraction of these subtle parts of our body, then it is easy to see that the small and smallest intervals are the most suitable for this passion [*Leidenschaft*]. If we further consider that love is in fact essentially a diffusion of the spirits [*Geister*], then we will rightly conform to this in composing, and use similar relationships [*gleichför-migen Verhältnissen*] of sounds (*intervallis n. diffusis & luxuriantibus*). (Mattheson 1739: 16; Harriss 1981: 104–5, translation modified)

If, initially, Mattheson concentrates on affective qualities of intervals, this is because they were discussed by Kircher and Christoph Raupach *alias* Veritophilus in a treatise about affective power of music that Mattheson edited and prefaced (1717), but his further discussion in Part Two of *Der vollkommene Capellmeister* makes clear that all musical parameters have affective qualities. Paramount among them is rhythm. Mattheson demonstrates this in an experiment in which he transforms affects of melodies by changing their rhythmic patterns. As a result, he turns five chorales into dances—a minuet (Example 0.1A), a gavotte (Example 0.1B), a sarabande, a bourrée, and two polonaises—and two dances—a minuet and an angloise—into chorales.[21] In each case the change of rhythmic pattern causes a change of meter. Affective qualities of meter are not discussed in *Der vollkommene Capellmeister*, but Mattheson refers the reader back to his first treatise, *Das Neu-Eröffnete Orchestre* (1713: 76–89), where meters are assigned different affects and related to different genres. In the same treatise Mattheson discusses affective qualities of keys (231–53). Although his discussion is specific and detailed, he admits that key characteristics are surrounded by controversies and explains differences of opinions about them in terms of differences between temperaments, so that "for someone with a

EXAMPLE **0.1** Mattheson, *Der vollkommene Capellmeister* (1739), 161: (A) chorale *Wenn wir in höchsten Nöthen* turned into a minuet and (B) chorale *Wie schön leuchtet* turned into a gavotte.

sanguine temperament a key may seem lively and merry, but for someone who is phlegmatic, it will seem complaining and troubled etc." (Buelow 1983: 402).[22]

For Scheibe and the next generation of North-German critics the connection between music and emotion was based on the doctrine of mimesis. According to this doctrine, derived from Aristotelian poetics by the French neoclassicism and propagated in Germany by Gottsched, the function of arts was imitation of nature but, while fine arts imitate the physical world, music should imitate the world of human passions as they express themselves in inarticulate cries and sighs as well as accents and inflections of articulated speech. One of the first to propose this notion of imitation was Abbé Jean-Baptiste DuBos in *Réflexions critiques sur la poësie et sur la peinture* (1719): "Just as the painter imitates the forms and colours of nature so the musician imitates the tones of the voice—its accents, sighs and inflections. He imitates in short all the sounds that nature herself uses to express the feelings and passions" (Le Huray and Day 1981: 18). This notion was further developed by Charles Batteux in *Les Beaux Arts réduits à un même principe* (1746). If DuBos introduced it in reference to vocal music, Batteux applied the principle of imitation to vocal and instrumental music but allowed instrumental music to imitate unimpassioned sounds. Drawing on the parallel with painting, he thus distinguished two kinds of music based on "the same" (*un même*) principle:

> The one merely imitates unimpassioned sounds and noises and is equivalent to landscape painting. The other expresses animated sounds and relates to the feelings. This corresponds to portrait painting. The musician is no freer than the painter: he is continuously subject in every way to comparison with nature. In depicting a storm or little stream or a gentle breeze, the sounds come from nature, and from nature alone must he take them. (Le Huray and Day 1981: 49)

Batteux's treatise—translated by Gottsched in 1751—further consolidated the influence of the French neoclassic aesthetics into Germany, but this aesthetics met with resistance from advocates of a new taste in German literature and Gottsched's position was undermined by the controversy with the Swiss critics Johann Jacob Bodmer and Johann Jacob Breitinger, whose ideas strongly influenced Sulzer. Indeed, although he uses the word "imitation" (*Nachahmung*) and accepts DuBos's notion that music imitates accents of passionate speech, Sulzer rejects the principle of imitation formulated by Batteux. As he emphasizes in the article "Nachahmung," "only the fine arts seem to have arisen from imitation of nature. But eloquence, poetry, music, and dance have arisen from the fullness of animated sentiments and from the desire to express them, [and] to maintain them in ourselves and in others. Indubitably, the first poets, singers, and dancers expressed their own real—not merely imitated—sentiments."[23] As well as his reaction against Batteux, Sulzer's position indicates the influence of Jean-Jacques Rousseau. Rousseau's ambivalence about the concept of imitation is reflected in *Essai sur l'origine des langues, où il est parlé de la mélodie et de l'imitation musicale*. As the subtitle makes clear, Rousseau did not discard the concept of imitation, but his take on this concept was different from Batteux's. If for Batteux music is "the artificial portrait of the human passions" (Le Huray and Day 1981: 46)—"nothing about them is true; everything is artificial" (48)—for Rousseau musical imitation reaches beyond its artifice and back to its origins in real passions.

> By imitating the inflections of the voice, melody expresses plaints, cries of suffering or of joy, threats, moans; all the vocal signs of the passions fall within its province. It imitates the accents of [various] languages as well as the idiomatic expressions commonly associated in each one of them with given movements of the soul; it not only imitates, it speaks; and its language, though inarticulate, is lively, ardent, passionate, and a hundred times more vigorous than speech itself. This is where musical imitation acquires its power, and song its hold on sensitive hearts. (Rousseau 1986: 282)[24]

Through written between 1755–61, *Essai sur l'origine des langues* was published in 1781, after the first edition of Sulzer's *Allgemeine Theorie der schönen Künste* (1771–74), but the step from imitation to expression was taken by Rousseau in *Dictionnaire de musique* (1768) and his earlier novels.[25] In *Julie, ou la nouvelle Héloïse* (1761), which went through countless editions and reached enormous popularity on the wave of sentimentalism, the male protagonist Saint Preux explains to Julie his experience of listening to an opera:

> During the brilliant passages, full of strong expression, through which the disorder of violent passions is at once depicted and aroused, I completely lost any idea of music, song, and imitation. I believed I was hearing the voice of pain, fury, and despair itself; I thought I heard lamenting mothers, betrayed lovers, and furious tyrants, and I could hardly remain in my place due to the great shock which I felt.

> Bey den glänzenden Stellen, voll eines starken Ausdrucks, wodurch die Unordnung heftiger Leidenschaften gemahlt, und zugleich würklich erregt wird, verlor sich bey mir die Vorstellung von Musik, Gesang und Nachahmung gänzlich. Ich glaubte die Stimme des Schmerzens, des Zorns, der Verzweiflung selbst zu hören; ich dachte, jammernde Mütter, betrogene Verliebte, rasende Tyrannen zu hören, und hatte Mühe, bey der großen Erschütterung, die ich fühlte, auf meiner Stelle zu bleiben. (Sulzer 1792–94, 3: 432–33)

This passage is quoted by Sulzer in the article "Musik" as a proof of music's power to arouse passions. In fact, Saint Preux's account of his listening experience makes clear that Rousseau goes beyond the doctrine of mimesis as regards not only the origin of musical imitation but also its goal. For him, the process of imitation does not stop at the recognition of passions by the listener. Rather, their recognition results in arousal of these passions by way of sympathy or compassion (*la pitié*). Sulzer adopts the concept of sympathy from Rousseau. In the article "Theilnehmung" he explains that "the good effect of the most important works of art is based on the characteristic of the human soul which makes us quite often feel moved by good or bad fate of other people as by our own and thus capable of true and heartfelt sympathy with them."[26] But, if Rousseau goes beyond Batteux's concept of imitation, Sulzer goes beyond Rousseau's concept of sympathy in that the listener's passions may be aroused not only by sympathy with others but also by sympathetic vibration.

This acoustic phenomenon was known from the seventeenth century and is described by Mattheson (1739: 12–13; Harriss 1981: 100) but plays no role in his discussion of affects.

The idea that emotion can be accounted for in terms of vibration emerged in the further course of the eighteenth century with the rise of a new theory of emotions based on nerves and nervous system. To be sure, nerves played an important role in the old theory of emotions adopted by Mattheson from Kircher but they were thought to be hollow channels that enabled the flow of animal spirits. In the new theory nerves were solid and susceptible to vibrations.[27] This view, advanced by Isaac Newton, was adopted by John Locke in *An Essay Concerning Human Understanding* (1690), but Locke did not describe the operations of nerves in any detail, which explains why Mattheson did not refer to them, although he was the first German music theorist to embrace Locke's sensualism. Only with the rise of experimental physiology in the 1740s did vibrations of nerves become part of common knowledge. Consequently, vibration of the air transmitted to the ear by the sound (*Schall*) was thought of to incite sympathetic vibration of nervous fibers. This common knowledge is assumed by Sulzer in his commentary on the words of Saint Preux:

> One knows that the animation of sentiments depends on the play of nerves and the fast speed of blood circulation. It cannot be denied that music has an effect on both. Since it depends on the movement of the air, which stimulates the most sensitive nerves of hearing, it affects the body; and how could it fail to do this, if it even shakes inanimate matter—not just thin windows but solid walls?

> Man weiß, daß die Lebhaftigkeit der Empfindungen von dem Spiel der Nerven, und dem schnellen Laufe des Geblütes herkommet; daß die Musik würklich auf beyde würke, kann gar nicht geläugnet werden. Da sie mit einer Bewegung der Luft verbunden ist, welche die höchst reizbaren Nerven des Gehörs angreift, so würket sie auch auf den Körper; und wie sollte sie dieses nicht thun, da sie selbst die unbelebte Materie, nicht blos dünne Fenster, sondern sogar feste Mauern erschüttert? (Sulzer 1792–94, 3: 433)

The epistemology of sensualism and aesthetics of sentimentalism led Sulzer to update his terminology for emotions. Although he uses the word *Affekt* and retains the German synonym for passion (*Leidenschaft*), his term of choice is *Empfindung*, which can mean either sentiment or sensation. Thus, it implies that music's power to arouse passions results from the sensual effect of the sound (*Schall*) on the nervous system. As Sulzer observes, "sound can carry tenderness, good will, hate, anger, despair, or another passionate expression of a soul. Therefore one soul can become sensible to the other through sound."[28]

The twofold manner of arousing sentiments—indirectly by way of sympathy and directly through sympathetic vibration—suggested to Sulzer two ways in which composers can learn the art of musical expression. On the one hand, they should observe others in order to become familiar with *outer* expressions of passions, in particular, their vocal expressions:

> Every passion must be seen not simply in respect to its idea, but in respect to its particular character: tone of voice [*Ton der Stimme*], register, tempo, and accent of the speech [*den Accent der Rede*]....Joy speaks [*spricht*] with full tones, a tempo that is not rushed, and moderate gradations of dynamics and pitch. Sadness expresses itself

in slower speeches [*in langsamen Reden*]; it wells up from deep within the breast and with subdued tones. Every sentiment has something special that distinguishes it in speech [*in der Sprache etwas eigenes*]. (Sulzer 1792–94, 1: 272; Baker and Christensen 1995: 51–52, translation modified)

On the other hand, composers should feel the passions within themself in order to observe their *inner* effect on the soul. In this regard Sulzer's advices for composers are similar to Mattheson's (1739: 16–17; Harriss 1981: 105–7). The difference between them lies in the fact that, for Sulzer, the motion of the soul is not a motion of animal spirits but

a series of moving impressions. This is already revealed by the phrase we use to express passion: the movement of emotions [*Gemüthsbewegung*]. There are passions in which impressions flow evenly like a gentle brook. There are other passions which flow onward faster and with more turbulence. In a few, the succession of impressions rush forward as if a raging stream whose banks are swollen after a heavy rain, sweeping away everything that stands in its way. Sometimes the feelings caused by these impressions are like the wild sea crashing before the shore, retreating back only to surge forth again with renewed strength. (Sulzer 1792–94, 1: 272; Baker and Christensen 1995: 52)

In the further course of the article "Ausdruck," from which this quote is excerpted, Sulzer makes clear that this movement can be portrayed by all musical parameters. Consequently, all musical parameters are means of expression.

These means are: (1) The basic progression of harmony without regard to meter....; (2) Meter, by which the general character of every kind of movement may be imitated; (3) Melody and rhythm, which are themselves capable of portraying the language of all emotions; (4) Changes in the dynamics of notes, which may contribute much to expression; (5) The accompaniment and particularly the choice and mixture of accompanying instruments; And finally, (6) Modulation to, and digression in, foreign keys. (Sulzer 1792–94, 1: 272–73; Baker and Christensen 1995: 52–53)

Sulzer extends this list in other articles. In the article "Musik" he supplements it with key. In the article "Singen" with ornamentation. In the article "Melodie" he adds tempo, articulation, register, and phrase rhythm. He follows this discussion with an experiment that demonstrates "how the same series of pitches can acquire quite different characters through changes of meter, rhythm, and phrase rhythm."[29] This experiment is clearly inspired by Mattheson in that the affective quality of the melody is transformed by its temporal arrangement (Example 0.2).

Near the end of the article "Musik" Sulzer discloses that the content of this and other articles about music is indebted to Johann Philipp Kirnberger and announces the forthcoming publication of the second volume of Kirnberger's *Die Kunst des reinen Satzes in der Musik*, which "will undoubtedly become the most important work about the theory" of this art.[30] Indeed, in the first section of this volume, published 1776, Kirnberger

EXAMPLE **0.2** Sulzer, *Allgemeine Theorie der schönen Künste* (1792–94), vol. 3, 379.

undertakes the task of describing all musical parameters in so far as they contribute to expression. In Chapter 1 he elaborates on Sulzer's discussion of harmony—the first point on the previously quoted list of parameters in the article "Ausdruck"—and describes four methods of harmonizing a melody with regard to the intensity of expression. He points out that the same melody can acquire different expression through different harmonization and demonstrates this with a series of twenty-six harmonizations of the chorale *Ach Gott und Herr, wie gross und schwer sind mein begangne Sünden!* (Example 0.3). Once again, this demonstration is strikingly similar to the experiments carried out by Mattheson and Sulzer, but the fact that the parameter singled out for attention is not rhythm but harmony stands in marked contrast to the suppression of harmony by the earlier authors. Of course, this change of focus reflects the influence of Jean-Philippe Rameau, whose theory of harmony Kirnberger embraced in the first volume of *Die Kunst des reinen Satzes* (1771).[31] In the following chapters of the second volume Kirnberger discusses key characteristics (Chapter 2), melodic progressions (Chapter 3), tempo, meter, and phrase rhythm (Chapter 4). The most interesting—and modern—aspect of Kirnberger's discussion is his emphasis on the interdependence of musical parameters and their mutual modification of each other's expression. For instance, his unique attempt to define expression of all—ascending and descending—melodic intervals is qualified by the remark that this expression can be changed by other parameters:

> Much depends here on what precedes and follows and, in general, on the totality of the melodic phrase in which these progressions occur; it also depends on the position of the intermingled minor and major seconds of the scale or mode, and above all on the beat of the measure on which they are used and on the harmony that is placed under them. Every melodic progression can acquire a different shade of expression from the harmony. (Kirnberger 1776: 104; 1982: 374)

Similar remarks are made about tempo, meter, rhythm, and key, explaining—in a new way—the controversies around key characteristics, noted by Mattheson.

Even though Sulzer's concept of sentiments has different physiological foundations and philosophical implications than Mattheson's affects, it should be clear from the foregoing discussion that the description of musical parameters with regard to expression, undertaken by Sulzer and Kirnberger, forms a continuation of Mattheson's doctrine of affections. For them, as for Mattheson, all musical parameters have affective qualities. All states of such parameters and their configurations can express affects. Consequently, music is comparable to the "unfathomable sea" (*unergründlichen Meer*) of affects described by Mattheson in *Der vollkommene Capellmeister* (1739: 19): an inexhaustible source of expression and boundless resource for infinitely nuanced representation of emotional states. The difference between Mattheson's affects and Sulzer's sentiments is that affects are static and distinct from each other while sentiments are dynamic and fluid. The ebb and flow of sentiments means that each of them is always in danger of sliding into others.[32] This fluctuation of sentiments is reflected in the fluidity of parametric reconfigurations and mutual modifications described by Sulzer and Kirnberger. Still, some states and configurations of musical parameters are more stable

EXAMPLE 0.3 The last six harmonizations of the chorale *Ach Gott und Herr, wie gross und schwer sind mein begangne Sünden!* from Kirnberger, *Die Kunst des reinen Satzes in der Musik* (1771–79), vol. 2, section 1, 28–29.

than others. In this regard, they are comparable not so much to sentiments as, rather, to characters. This brings us back to the concept of character discussed in the previous section. For Sulzer the difference between a character and a sentiment is equivalent to that between *ethos* and *pathos* (1792–94, 3: 237).While the latter is a fleeting passion, the former refers to a constant disposition of a given person. At the same time, characters are closely related to sentiments. On the one hand, they determine the strength

EXAMPLE 0.3 (Continued)

of sentiments a person can perceive in relation to other persons and objects. (It is this function of characters, described in section 2, that safeguards affective unity of musical pieces.) On the other hand, sentiments have influence on characters if they are consolidated by repetition. "A feeling that through constant repetition and reinforcement becomes the cause of certain inner or external actions" is called by Sulzer sentiment "in a moral sense" and is distinguished by him from sentiments "in a psychological sense."

Moral sentiments are "the sentiments that in their differing mix and strengths determine the moral character of men" (Sulzer 1792–94, 2: 54; Baker and Christensen 1995: 28).[33] Consequently, these sentiments can stand for the character as such. When Sulzer writes about characters of men who are "proud or humble, courageous or timid, pleading or commanding, tender or tempestuous," he describes them with adjectives derived from their moral sentiments.

This close relation between characters and sentiments makes possible musical representation of characters. Although characters are the most important objects of arts, Sulzer admits that music can represent them only insofar as they express themselves in sentiments.

> Since the differing degrees of animation of individual men and the way they express their emotions have the greatest influence upon their moral character, music can often be used to express the morality of such men and entire people, in so far as they may be sensed. So indeed are national songs and dances a true reflection of morality. They can be as sprightly or serious, tender or tempestuous, refined or coarse, as the morals of the people themselves. (Sulzer 1792–94, 3: 425; Baker and Christensen 1995: 84)

Their connection with moral characters explains why national songs and dances attract Sulzer's attention. His discussions of dances in *Allgemeine Theorie der schönen Künste* draw on Mattheson's discussions of small compositions in *Der vollkommene Capellmeister*, but what Mattheson called "affect" now turns into "character." That this last term is used by Sulzer in the sense of a "moral character" is clear from his entries on the sarabande, the musette, and the rigaudon—dances that he relates to different characters in ballets. The sarabande can be used "for serious characters who appear with great dignity or majesty" (*zu den ernsthaften Charakteren, die mit großer Würde, oder mit Majestät verbunden sind*; 4: 128); the musette suits "both noble pastoral and lowly peasant characters" (*sowol zu edlen Schäfercharakteren, als zu niedrigen bäuerischen*; 3: 421); and the rigaudon can be applied to a "serious as well as humorous and lowly character" (*sowol zum ernsthaften, als zum scherzhaften und niedrigen Charakter gebraucht*; 4: 106). Apart from dances, characters are ascribed by Sulzer to two other genres: festive entrées (*Aufzüge*) and military marches.

By contrast to small compositions, larger compositions have no determined characters. This does not mean that they have no characters at all—every composition must have a character that safeguards its affective unity—but their characters are defined by the composer rather than by genre. To this category belong overtures, symphonies, sonatas, and concerti. The freedom of composers in selecting characters of these genres is not equal, though, but more or less limited by their function. The character of overtures, whose function is similar to entrées, is most closely determined (3: 643). The character of church and theatrical symphonies, which serve to prepare the listener for the subsequent piece, is determined by this piece (4: 479–80). The character of a chamber symphony is free from this limitation but it should harmonize with the expression of "the grand, the festive, and the sublime" (*des Großen, des Feyerlichen und*

Erhabenen; 4: 478). Sonatas can assume "any character and every expression" (4: 425; Baker and Christensen 1995: 103), whereas concerti are criticized by Sulzer on account of the fact that their composers—who, for the most part, are also their performers—are not in the business of representing characters but of highlighting their technical skills (1: 573).[34]

Sulzer's distinction between small compositions of determined character and larger compositions of undetermined character is adopted by Koch. As he explains in *Versuch einer Anleitung zur Composition* (1782–93), small compositions—to which he counts dances and marches—"aim to arouse only one feeling," whereas in larger compositions "different kinds of feelings follow one another" (Baker and Christensen 1995: 147). Koch retains this distinction and retraces Sulzer's discussions of small compositions in *Musikalisches Lexikon* (1802). It is this distinction that makes room for topics in eighteenth-century music aesthetics. From my discussion it follows that small compositions of determined character are equivalent to Ratner's types. As such, they are the source of his core musical topics. By contrast, larger compositions "of undetermined character" (*von unbestimmtem Charakter*), that is, such "which can acquire every character" (*die jeden Charakter annehmen können*; Koch 1802: col. 314), are the genres that create opportunities for topics to mix together. In other words, they are the field of topical play in eighteenth-century music.[35] The play, too, was recognized by Sulzer. When, in the article "Vortrag," he recommends performers to practice "dance pieces of different character and expression" (*Tanzstücken von verschiedenem Charakter und Ausdruck*; 1792–94, 4: 711) in order to learn how to express characters in other genres, he motivates this advice with the remark that "the dance pieces contain most, if not all, of what our good and bad pieces of every art contain: the latter are different from the former only in that they combine several dances put together into a more or less coherent whole."[36] Whether the whole is "more or less coherent" depends on the character of the dances in relation to one another and to the character of the larger composition selected by the composer. The requirement of coherence is the hallmark of North-German aesthetics, but Sulzer's remark indicates that—coherent or not—by the late eighteenth century topical mixtures were the bread and butter of instrumental music in the North and the South.

3. AFFECTS AND TOPICS

The discussion of the connection between music and affects helps us to clarify the relation between affects and topics. To be sure, this relation lies at the heart of topic theory. Ratner's discussion of topics in *Classic Music* fills in the first part of his book, devoted to expression, which, as he emphasizes from the outset, "was an ever-present concern in 18th-century musical thought and practice" (1980: 1). Agawu treats "the concept of topic as key to expression" (1991: 128) and links it to this term of the dichotomy between "expression" and "structure." The status of topics as expressive signs, first posited by Agawu, was consolidated by Robert Hatten (1994, 2004) and Raymond Monelle (2000, 2006) in their studies framing topics within the field of music semiotics. The fact that Ratnerian topics have their source in small compositions that, in turn, are related by Sulzer to characters confirms the intimate link between topics and expression of eighteenth-century music but it suggests that topical signification stands in relief from affective signification and differs from it in two respects: the scope and semiotic status.

3.1. Scope

Insofar as small compositions form stable configurations of musical parameters that, like moral sentiments, are consolidated by repetition, the scope of topical significa-tion is more restricted than the scope of affective signification, which embraces all states of musical parameters and their configurations. It follows that some passages of eighteenth-century music may display no topics.

So far the right of eighteenth-century music to contain topically neutral passages has not been acknowledged by representatives of topic theory. Agawu questions it on the basis of the provisional status of the Universe of Topic: "Theoretically, UT is open, since it continues to expand as more and more topics are uncovered; UT can only attain clo-sure on the last day of research" (Agawu 1991: 128). This means that "references to an area of 'neutral' topical activity indicate not necessarily the absence of topic, but, rather, the absence of an appropriate label within the restricted domain of our topical universe" (49). This opinion is further radicalized by Allanbrook, who explicitly denies the exis-tence of topically neutral passages in Classic music:

> Expression saturates this music; it is never *not* a parameter, even if a particular *topos* does not have a convenient style name or obvious historical association. The *topoi* do appear with varying degrees of markedness: we can say of one passage that it is a military march or a sarabande, while of another only that it is legato or lyrical. But "legato" or "lyrical" are *topoi* simply by virtue of being juxtaposed to passages that are staccato or that clearly mimic orchestral rather than vocal procedures. No moment is ever "expressively neutral": when it ceases to be A, it must be B or C or D. *Topoi* articulate each other's differences in the same way as modern linguists understand phonic units as delimiting each other: by juxtaposition and opposition, by rubbing shoulders, "jostling each other about." (Allanbrook 2002: 214)[37]

To be sure, "the *topoi* do appear with varying degrees of markedness" or, to put it more properly, some topics are more salient than others.[38] This is, first, because topics form sets of characteristics derived from higher or lower numbers of musical parameters. For instance, the military march is described by Sulzer (1792–94, 3: 363–65) in terms of its major key (especially B flat, C, D, or E flat), 4/4 or ¢ meter, uniform pace, dotted rhythms, slower or faster but "pathetic" tempo, orchestration featuring trumpets and horns, and a phrase rhythm consisting of two-measure incises or pairs of one-measure incises that start either with downbeats or quarter-note upbeats and combine into four-measure phrases. This topic is thus more salient than the sarabande, which is in slow tempo, 3/2 or 3/4 meter, and starts with the downbeat (Sulzer 1792–94, 4: 128).[39] Second, some topics can occur without some of their characteristics. For instance, the topic of military march can dispense with trumpets and horns when it is played by a string quartet. But from the fact that some topics are less salient than others it does not follow that all eighteenth-century music is topical. In terms of modern linguistics, invoked by Allanbrook, musical characteristics of topics can indeed be compared to distinctive features of phonemes ("phonic units") and sorted out through oppositions[40]—the opposition between "legato" and "staccato" being one of them—but such characteristics are not topics, and not every configuration of musical characteristics is a topic of eighteenth-century music, just as not every configuration of distinctive features is a phoneme of English language. Some passages may share characteristics of several topics, while some others may represent no specific topic. In other words, expression saturates eighteenth-century music without necessarily being A, B, C, or D.

Clearly, Allanbrook can jump from the premise that "no moment is ever expressively neutral" to the conclusion that every moment is topical because she equates topics with expression, but this equation has no foundation in eighteenth-century sources. What these sources suggest is, instead, that *topics are islands of affective signification emerging from the sea of eighteenth-century music*. In fact, Allanbrook's description of topics "rubbing shoulders" and "jostling each other about" resembles Johann Nikolaus Forkel's description of the "sea of affects," which arguably forms the apex of the doctrine of affections developed before him by Mattheson, Sulzer, and Kirnberger. Like those authors, Forkel conceives of emotion in terms of motion (*Bewegung*) but gives this concept a new twist. Rather than the motion of animal spirits, described by Mattheson, or the series of moving impressions, evoked by Sulzer, he identifies it with modification or "modulation" of sentiment, that is, its intensification and deintensification.

> No sentiment, which should last for some time—not just be aroused but also sustained—remains the same from the beginning until the end. It increases and decreases through infinite and indiscernible degrees of intensity. This growth and decline of sentiment is called "modification" but it could equally well or even better be called "modulation," which word is taken from the technical vocabulary of music. Not only is the process of musical modulation perfectly equivalent to the tiny and gradual transitions of sentiment between greater or lesser degrees of intensity but it also gives us a hint that the modulation of sentiment can be best expressed and imitated through the modulation of tones. Even if a sentiment can express itself in many ways, it is easy to note that only at one point is it exactly itself and differs from any other sentiment; all other points and degrees of this sentiment border on sentiments of some other sort—which are more or less distant from another main sentiment—and can serve the definition of these sentiments as much as they served the definition of the original sentiment as soon as their relations to each other are changed.

> Keine Empfindung, die anhaltend seyn, oder durch irgend ein Mittel nicht nur geweckt, sondern auch unterhalten werden soll, ist sich, vom Anfang ihrer Entstehung an bis ans Ende, gleich. Sie nimmt nach und nach durch unendliche

und unbegreifliche Grade von Stärke und Schwäche an und zu. Dieses Wachsen und Abnehmen der Empfindung nennt man gewöhnlich Modification; es könnte aber eben so füglich, und vielleicht noch füglicher mit einem Worte bezeichnet werden, welches wir in der musikalischen Kunstsprache moduliren nennen; denn das musikalische Moduliren entspricht den feinen allmähligen Uebergängen der Empfindung zur Stärke oder Schwäche nicht nur vollkommen, sondern giebt auch gleichsam einen kleinen Wink, daß die Modulation der Leidenschaft durch die Modulation der Töne am besten auszudrücken, und nachzuahmen sey. So vielartig aber auch immer eine Leidenschaft sich äußern kann, so ist doch leicht zu bemerken, daß sie nur auf einem einzigen Punkte genau diejenige Empfindung sey, die sie von allen andern unterscheidet; alle andere Punkte oder Grade derselben gränzen auf eine oder die andere Art, mehr oder weniger entfernt an eine andere Hauptempfindung, und dienen zur genauern Bestimmung derselben ebensowol, wie sie zur Bestimmung der ersten dienten, sobald ihre Verhältnisse, oder ihre Beziehungen unter einander verändert werden. (Forkel 1788: 8)

For Forkel, it is sentiments that delimit each other "by juxtaposition and opposition." Modulation of sentiments and transitions between them are engineered by reconfiguration of musical parameters. The same state of a given parameter can express different sentiments if it is combined with different states of other parameters. In order to illustrate this occurrence, Forkel singles out harmony and demonstrates how it can change expression of the same melody. This demonstration builds on Kirnberger's experiment with different harmonizations of the chorale and develops his remark that "every melodic progression can acquire a different shade of expression from the harmony," which determines its tonal context and, therefore, scale degrees represented by its pitches within a given (major or minor) key. Forkel's brief melody (Example 0.4a) is harmonized in four different keys—C major, G major, E minor, and A minor (Example 0.4b)—"and has a different meaning in each of these four tonal contexts" (*und hat unstreitig in jeder dieser vier Beziehungen eine andere Bedeutung*; Forkel 1788: 13). In this way, harmony is elevated by him to the status of the musical parameter that defines finest subtleties of human feeling.

3.2. Semiotic Status

The rise of topic theory in the 1980s coincided with the rapid growth of semiotics, which developed from an arcane discipline to an all-embracing theory of signs aspiring to redefine the terms of human knowledge. As a source of meaning and expression, topics yielded themselves to this theory and the study of topics became the foremost branch of music semiotics. So far the semiotic status of topics has been framed in terms of modern semiotics developed by twentieth-century authors such as Charles Sanders Peirce, Ferdinand de Saussure, Roman Jakobson, and Umberto Eco, but the eighteenth century possessed its own theory of signs that imbued music aesthetics.[41] It will be necessary to

EXAMPLE 0.4 Forkel, *Allgemeine Geschichte der Musik*, vol. 1 (1788), 13–14: (a) melody and (b) its harmonizations in four different keys.

turn to eighteenth-century semiotics in order to explain the difference between affective and topical signification of eighteenth-century music.

The fundamental distinction drawn by eighteenth-century authors was that between natural and arbitrary signs. It was based on the origin of the sign–object relation. In natural signs this relation is given in nature, because "natural signs precede, follow upon (or are co-present with) the things they signify" (Wellbery 1984: 26). In terms of Peircian semiotics, a natural sign is thus an *index*: "a sign that is related to its object through co-occurrence in actual experience" (Turino 1999: 227). Natural signs produced by man include postures, gestures, facial expressions, unarticulated sighs, and cries as well as vocal accents and inflections of articulated speech. By contrast, arbitrary signs are instituted by human beings. Consequently, they correspond to Peircian *symbols*: signs related to their objects by convention and, most characteristically, represented by words.

The distinction between natural signs and arbitrary signs was the touchstone of musical mimesis. When Abbé DuBos points out that "the musician imitates the tones of the voice—its accents, sighs and inflections," he adds:

> All these sounds … have a wonderful power to move us because they are the signs of the passions that are the work of nature herself, from whence they have derived their energy. Spoken words, on the other hand are only arbitrary symbols of the passions. The spoken word only derives its meaning and value from man-made conventions and it has only limited geographical currency. (Le Huray and Day 1981: 18)

Insofar as music imitates the signs of passions, it is an *icon*. This term "refers to a sign that is related to its object through some type of resemblance between them" (Turino 1999: 226). Translated into terms of Peircian semiotics, affective signification of music posited by the doctrine of mimesis involves two levels of signification: musical sounds are *icons* of natural sounds, which are *indices* of emotional states. But, in the French Enlightenment, the category of imitative signs (*icons*) was not cleanly distinguished from expressive signs (*indices*). Consequently, music was subsumed under natural signs and contrasted with language (Wellbery 1984: 29–30).[42]

The collapse of two levels of musical signification—*icon* and *index*—into one natural sign was facilitated by Rousseau. At the same time as he takes the contrast between music and language to extremes, he traces them back to their common origin in songs sung by southern nations at the fountains where men and women came to fetch water for their herds and households:

> Around the fountains which I have mentioned, the first speeches were the first songs: the periodic and measured recurrences of rhythm, the melodious inflections of accents, caused poetry and music to be born together with language; or rather, all this was nothing other than language itself in those happy climates and those happy ages when the only pressing needs that required another's collaboration were needs born of the heart. (Rousseau 1986: 276)

This myth of the origin explains how imitation and expression are united in Rousseau's aesthetics. Though the concept of imitation is not banned from it, music does not imitate speech but, rather, itself: eighteenth-century operatic recitatives and airs imitate the first songs of passion. Embracing Rousseau's aesthetics, Sulzer adopts his theory of signs:

> The individual sounds that comprise song are the expressions of animated sentiments, since man expresses pleasure, pain, or sadness through sounds, and the sentiments aroused demand to be expressed, even if against one's will, by the sounds of song, not speech. Thus the elements of song are not so much the invention of man as of nature herself. Rather than calling these the extracted sounds from the sentiments of man, we will simply call them passionate tones [*leidenschaftliche Töne*]. The sounds of speech are drawing tones [*zeichnende Töne*], which originally served to awaken images of things which produce such or similar sounds [*Vorstellungen von Dingen zu erweken, die solche oder ähnliche Töne hören lassen*]. Now most such sounds are indifferent tones [*gleichgültige Töne*] or arbitrary signs [*willkührliche Zeichen*], while the passionate tones are natural signs [*natürliche Zeichen*] of sentiment. A succession of arbitrary sounds designates speech, a succession of passionate tones, song. (Sulzer 1792–94, 2: 369; Baker and Christensen 1995: 93, translation modified)

For Sulzer, thus, language is a system of arbitrary signs, while music consists of natural signs. Insofar as the listener is affected by sympathy, that is, through recognition of natural signs of affections, the arousal of passions by music is a semiotic process.

At the same time, however, arousal of passions can be unmediated by signs, if it is caused by sympathetic vibration. The idea that emotions consist in vibration of nerves and can be induced by sound (*Schall*) formed an uneasy match with Rousseau's aesthetics. Instead, it aligned with Rameau's theory of *corps sonore*. Since Rameau's example of *corps sonore* was the monochord, vibration of strings became an image for the vibration of nerves and the listener's body was thought of as a *corps sonore* on which music can play like on a clavichord. A follower of Rameau, Michel Paul Gui de Chabanon, declared that "man is only an instrument" and the arousal of passions by music is a purely sensual effect that takes place "without the mediation of the soul" (Chua 1999: 101).[43] This sensual effect of music was vigorously opposed by Rousseau. In fact, the myth of song proposed by him as an account of the origins of music and language was an alternative to Rameau's theory of *corps sonore*, which Rousseau rejected on the grounds that it substitutes sentiments with sensations:

> As long as sounds continue to be considered exclusively in terms of the excitation they trigger in our nerves, the true principles of music and of its power over men's hearts will remain elusive. In a melody, sounds act on us not only as sounds but as signs of our affections, of our sentiments; that is how they arouse in us the motions which they express and the image of which we recognize in them. (Rousseau 1986: 283)

The fact that Sulzer embraces Rousseau's aesthetics while accepting aesthetic ideas inspired by his main opponent may create an impression of eclecticism, but to call him eclectic does not do justice to Sulzer. For one thing, he could not have read the above-quoted passage, excerpted from the *Essai sur l'origine des langues*. In *Dictionnaire de musique*, which Sulzer consulted, Rousseau admits that music has an effect "on the ear and on the soul" (Thomas 1995: 126 n. 110).[44] When Sulzer follows the passage from *La nouvelle Héloïse* with remarks about vibration of the air "which stimulates the most sensitive nerves of hearing," he does not contradict Rousseau but implies that music has an effect on Saint Preux's soul and body.[45] Sulzer's comments on the circulation of blood—alongside "the play of nerves"—point toward Mattheson, and his further remarks about therapeutic effects of music parallel those with which Mattheson precedes his discussion of music's affective power in *Der vollkommene Capellmeister* (1739: 14–15; Harriss 1981: 102–3). In fact, a close reading of Sulzer's articles about music in *Allgemeine Theorie der schönen Künste* suggests that he attempted a synthesis of the French doctrine of mimesis, anthropologically inflected by Rousseau, with the German doctrine of affections inherited from Mattheson and filtered through the sensualist epistemology.[46] The common denominator of both doctrines is the concept of emotion as motion of the soul. For Mattheson this motion (*Gemüthsbewegung*) should be emulated by musical motion. For DuBos, Batteux, and Rousseau music should imitate motions of the soul (*mouvements de l'âme*) as they express themselves in vocal accents of passionate speech. Such accents are expressive signs (*indices*) but, at the same time, they are similar to "the motions which they express" due to the similarity between causes and effects. Such similarity was posited by Alexander Gottlieb Baumgarten and his pupil Georg Friedrich Meier in connection with the concept of "essential signs" (*wesentliche Zeichen*) whose relation to objects is based on similarity (Wellbery 1984: 29–30).

Essential signs are equivalents of Peirce's *icons*, but the idea that effects are similar to causes means that there is no significant difference between iconic signs and indexical signs caused by their objects.[47] Just as imitative signs (*icons*) produced by the composer are expressive (*indices*), so also expressive signs of emotion (*indices*) produced by nature are imitative (*icons*).[48] By imitating accents of passionate speech, as stipulated by the doctrine of mimesis, the composer imitates "the motions which they express"—be they the motions of animal spirits or vibrations of nerves—but he can also represent these motions by similar motions along any number of musical parameters, as stipulated by the doctrine of affections. In both doctrines music consists of icons.

If affective signification of music takes an important place in the system of eighteenth-century semiotics, topical signification—based on cross-references between styles and genres—does not easily fit in it. The only text that has been invoked as a proof of its eighteenth-century recognition comes from Chabanon, who denies that music can imitate anything else than other music:

> Imitation in music is not truly sensed unless its object is music. In songs one can successfully imitate warlike fanfares, hunting airs, rustic melodies, etc. It is only a question of giving one song the character of another. Art, in that case, does not suffer violence. When one moves away from this, however, imitation grows weaker, actually because of the insufficiency of means which music can employ. (Allanbrook 1983: 6)

Although this passage is inspired by Chabanon's insistence on the sensual basis of music and his rejection of the doctrine of mimesis, Allanbrook used it to frame topics within this doctrine. According to Allanbrook, topics form a kind of musical mimesis that consists in imitation of "simpler music which men use to accompany their daily activities and amusements" (Allanbrook 1983: 6). Classic music is "a musical language created out of the ordinary materials of its own musical life" (Allanbrook 1996: 75). In other words, it is "music made out of music" (Allanbrook 2014: 114). With this last remark Allanbrook echoes Sulzer's opinion that larger compositions are made out of small compositions: "The dance pieces contain most, if not all, of what our good and bad pieces of all kinds consist."

Although Allanbrook is not concerned with semiotics, her references to the doctrine of mimesis help us clarify the semiotic status of topics. For Allanbrook the first step of topical signification is the recognition of a style or genre imitated in a given passage of Classic music. "Eighteenth-century listeners were fully familiar with this musical vocabulary. They encountered it in its basic forms daily, so recognition would have been instant and enjoyable" (Allanbrook 2014: 111). But topical signification does not stop at this recognition: it extends, on the one hand, to associations of styles and genres with affects, and, on the other hand, to their associations with social contexts. For instance, dances raise associations with ballrooms and social status of dancers; military marches with parades or battlefields; church music with religious rituals; pastoral music with the countryside; hunting calls with hunts. According to Allanbrook, this is how Classic music is mimetic not just of other music but "of the world of men, their habits and actions" (1983: 3). Again, she could have supported her insistence on the role of social context in the definition of topics with Sulzer's remarks about small compositions. In the article "Instrumentalmusik" Sulzer observes that such compositions need no text in order to explain objects of sentiments, since these objects are explained by context and function of such compositions in everyday life: "One can easily dispense with vocal music for dancing, festive entrées [*Aufzügen*] and military marches, since instruments alone are sufficient to arouse and sustain the appropriate sentiments for such occasions" (Sulzer 1792–94, 2: 677; Baker and Christensen 1995: 95, translation modified). This observation is reiterated by Koch, whose article "Instrumentalmusik" in *Musikalisches Lexikon* draws on Sulzer's: "If instrumental music … is meant to awaken and maintain specific feelings, then it must be involved in such political, religious, or domestic circumstances and actions as are of pronounced interest for us, and in which our heart is predisposed to the expression of the sentiments that it [the instrumental music] is supposed to awaken and maintain."[49] While she leaves out Sulzer, Allanbrook quotes Koch's words (1988: 11; 2014: 107) but turns them against Koch. As she points out, "he fails to realize that the 'political, religious, or domestic' associations that topoi carry with them will complement the indeterminate feelings aroused naturally by the textless music alone, supplying a context out of context" (2014: 107). Accordingly, she questions the further course of Koch's argument:

> If, however, it [music] should undertake to stimulate in us feelings for which the situation in which we find ourselves offers no occasion, feelings to which our hearts are not open, it lacks the means to make these feelings interesting to our hearts through the unarticulated tones of instrumental music. It cannot under these circumstances make comprehensible to us why it wants to transport us into gentle or sad, exalted or happy, sentiments; it cannot awaken in us either the images of that good whose enjoyment is to delight us, or the images of that evil that is to cause fear or distress. To sum up, it can infuse into our hearts no interest in the sentiments which it expresses.

> Wenn sie [die Musik] es aber unternehmen soll, in uns Gefühle anzufachen, wozu in der Lage, in welcher wir uns befinden, keine Ursache vorhanden, wofür unser Herz nicht aufgeschlossen ist, so fehlt es ihr, wenn es bloß durch die unartikulirten Töne der Instrumentalmusik geschehen soll, an Mitteln, unsern Herzen diese Gefühle interessant zu machen. Sie kann uns unter diesen Umständen nicht begreiflich machen, warum sie uns in sanfte oder traurige, in erhabene oder fröhliche Empfindungen versetzen will; sie kann in uns weder die Bilder desjenigen Gutes, dessen Genuß uns ergötzen, noch die Bilder desjenigen Uebels darstellen, welches Furcht oder Betrübniß veranlassen soll. Kurz, sie kann unsern Herzen kein merkliches Interesse an den Empfindungen, die sie ausdrückt, einflössen. (Koch 1802: cols. 792–93)

Koch concludes that, in order to arouse such interest, music needs text that "prepares the listener, helps him to the intended frame of mind, and gives interest to the feelings to be expressed."[50] He uses this argument to proclaim the superiority of vocal over instrumental music, but Allanbrook rejects this claim and uses topics as the springboard for an apology of instrumental music: "There was no reason why instrumental music, granted the direct reference due to its intimate connection with human occasions, could not provide its particular blend of instruction and pleasure for audiences outside the venues that originally supplied it with these meanings" (Allanbrook 2014: 108). For her, such music needs no text to have a context. Rather, the context is supplied by topics. Because "topoi bear their contexts with them like a snail traveling in its shell" (107), they take over the role of text and explain the feelings expressed by instrumental music. This is how topic theory writes the unwritten aesthetics of South-German instrumental music in North-German terms.

The foregoing discussion brings to light a number of differences between affective and topical signification of eighteenth-century music, which are summarized in Figure 0.1. Solid arrows in this figure represent sign–object relations. Affective signification of music is represented by the lower horizontal arrow. As this arrow suggests, all states of musical parameters and their configurations have affective qualities and carry affective signification. Some of these configurations are characteristic of topics. This is indicated by the dashed vertical arrow. Topics refer to styles and genres from which they are derived. This first step of topical signification is represented by the upper horizontal arrow. Further steps arise from associations of styles and genres with social contexts and functions (upward vertical arrow) and from their associations with affects (downward vertical arrow). Ultimately, topical signification thus reaches affects but, if affective signification of music rests on a direct *iconic* relation between music and affect—so direct, in fact, as to risk losing its semiotic status and turning into "a pure form of sentient communication" (Chua 1999: 118)[51]—affective signification of topics is indirect because it arises from their similarity (*icon*) to genres or styles that, in their turn, are associated (*index*) with specific affects or affective zones. As a result, this signification is more stable than affective signification of music posited by the doctrine of mimesis and the doctrine of affections. Whereas affective signification posited by these doctrines is susceptible to fluctuations of parametric configurations and therefore cannot be detached from actual music, topical signification can be cued by names of styles or genres in absence of any actual music.[52] This justifies the comparison of topics to words, implied by terms such as "thesaurus" or "vocabulary,"[53] and their relation to Sulzer's characters represented by moral sentiments. Just as moral sentiments form a subset of psychological sentiments that have been consolidated by repetition, topics form a subset of all configurations of musical parameters consolidated by their associations with styles and genres and affects represented by topics form a subset of all affects that can be expressed by music. Recognition of these affects is based on the listener's recognition of styles or genres. Nonetheless, topically marked musical passages contain both types of signification. Even if the listener does not recognize a given topic, she can perceive the affect of this topic by virtue of musical motion characteristic of it.

The differences between affective and topical signification, gleaned from eighteenth-century semiotics and Allanbrook's discussion, feed back into the semiotic status of topics in modern semiotics. The route of topical signification in Figure 0.1 resembles the semiotic model put forward by Raymond Monelle, shown in Figure 0.2, but his figure strays from mine in one important respect: whereas in Figure 0.1 the relation of topics to

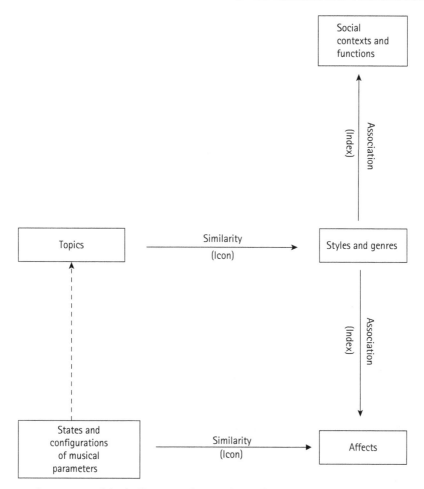

FIGURE **0.1** Semiotic model of affective and topical signification.

styles and genres is iconic, in Figure 0.2 the relation of musical item to object is indexical. Indeed, for Monelle,

> many topics are in the first place not iconic, but indexical; the dance measures listed
> by Ratner and Allanbrook, the "fanfare" motive, the topics of "French overture" and
> "Turkish music" do not signify by virtue of resemblance, but because they reproduce
> styles and repertoires from elsewhere. Insofar as the slow movement of the "Jupiter"
> Symphony is in sarabande meter, it presents the dance measure itself rather than an
> imitation of it, and thus signifies indexically. (2000: 17–18)

Ironically, Monelle goes on to substantiate this view by quoting Chabanon's words
cited by Allanbrook without taking into account that Chabanon writes about imitation—not reproduction—of styles and repertoires and that such imitation seldom replicates all musical parameters. "In songs" that Chabanon describes, "warlike fanfares"

FIGURE 0.2 Semiotic model of indexical topics, after Monelle, *The Sense of Music* (2000), 18, fig. 2.1.

or "hunting airs" are played not by hunting horns or military trumpets but by the keyboard; the same instrument can imitate the orchestral timbre of French overture and Turkish music, as testified by the introduction of Beethoven's "Pathetique" and Mozart's "Rondo alla Turca." Even in orchestral music the sound of Turkish instruments used in Janissary bands is imitated by a set of winds and percussion detailed by Monelle (2006: 117–19).

Of course, Monelle is aware that topics do not "reproduce" all aspects of styles or repertoires from which they are derived. This is why he qualifies his original statement in the second sentence, when he writes that the slow movement of the "Jupiter" Symphony "presents" the sarabande "measure" rather than the sarabande. But "presentation" of selected qualities is not a "reproduction" and, in semiotic terms, it does not qualify as an *index* but an *icon*. The fact that Monelle bases his interpretation of "indexical topics" on the concept of reproduction indicates that he treats these topics as "samples" of genres and styles that have been "torn out" of their objects and incorporated into other styles or genres. The relation of a sample to its objects is based on "contiguity," which belongs to the definition of indexical signs (Monelle 2000: 17), but one can only speak of a sample if it reproduces all qualities of the object save its shape and size. A sample that reproduces some qualities of the object while omitting others is not a sample but an imitation—like Chinese imitations of fashion products by Giorgio Armani.[54] This issue touches on the debate about iconic signs, which rolled through the semiotic circles in the 1970s. In Eco's (1976: 191–217) account, Peirce defined an icon as a sign that represents "its object mainly by its similarity" (195) but failed to explain the notion of similarity as such. This task was left to his followers. According to Charles Morris, an "iconic sign . . . is any sign which is similar in some respects to what it denotes" (192). But, as Eco points out, "the problem lies first of all in the meaning given to the expression 'in some respects': if an iconic sign is similar to the thing denoted *in some respects*, then we arrive at a definition which satisfies common sense, but not semiotics" (193). His own solution, in a nutshell, is that "one decides to recognize as similar two things because one chooses certain elements as pertinent and disregards certain others" (196). As Eco emphasizes, the choice of pertinent elements is dictated by conventional rules that have been culturally accepted and coded.[55] His notion of similarity inspired Naomi Cumming's definition of a musical icon. Drawing on Peirce and Eco, Cumming proposes that X is an icon of Y if "certain characteristics of Y may be heard in X" (2000: 89). That is what can be said about the sarabande (Y) in the slow movement of the "Jupiter" Symphony (X). Consequently, this movement is an icon of the sarabande.[56]

4. Topics and Pictorialism

Whereas the route of topical signification in Figure 0.1 strays from Monelle's model of *indexical topics* (Figure 0.2), it is equivalent to his model of *iconic topics* (Figure 0.3). For Monelle, this group of topics includes such "musical items" as *pianto* or "noble horse." Iconic topics feature an *iconic* relation between the sign and its object and an *indexical* relation between the object-as-a-sign and its signification.

What may have induced Monelle to introduce the concept of iconic topics is Ratner's ambivalence about the relationship between topics and pictorialism. At the beginning of his chapter about topics Ratner divides them into types and styles but at the end he includes a section on pictorialism and in the first sentence of this section he writes: "Given the wealth of available topics, 18th-century composers at times could easily take a further step and become frankly pictorial in their music" (1980: 25). Whether this step would lead them into another group of topics or take them beyond the field of topics into a different realm is not clearly stated. Throughout the book Ratner never uses the concept of topics in reference to pictorialism, and pictorial effects are not subsumed under this concept by Allanbrook and Agawu.[57] Monelle justifies his decision to subsume them under topics with the fact that "topics may be glimpsed through a feature that seems universal to them: a focus on *the indexicality of the content*, rather than the content itself" (2000: 17). This "indexicality of the content" is represented by the right-hand-side arrows in Figures 0.2 and 0.3. It is a common feature of indexical and iconic topics and it marks the difference between iconic topics and *musical icons*. In the former the object of the iconic relation arouses further associations with culturally prescribed meanings, whereas in the latter such associations do not arise. The structure of musical icons is thus reduced to the iconic relation between musical item and signification (Figure 0.4). For Monelle, "the commonest musical icons" are "portrayals of waves, clouds, storms, horses" (17).[58] As a border case, he considers the cuckoo's call. "If it is culturally prescribed that the imitation of a cuckoo by an orchestral instrument *inevitably signifies the heralding of spring*, then this icon has been transformed into a topic. It is not at all clear that this is the case; the cuckoo must be considered a prototopic" (17).

Even if subsuming pictorialism under the concept of topics raises no logical problems, it is historically problematic insofar as musical imitation of other music was unrelated to pictorialism in the eighteenth century. If the former was absent from the doctrine of mimesis, the latter had its firm place in this doctrine, though more modest than musical imitation of human voice. DuBos distinguished imitation of passionate utterances

FIGURE 0.3 Semiotic model of iconic topics, after Monelle, *The Sense of Music* (2000), 18, fig. 2.1.

FIGURE 0.4 Semiotic model of musical icons, after Monelle, *The Sense of Music* (2000), 18, fig. 2.2.

from imitation of natural sounds of inanimate objects (Le Huray and Day 1981: 19–20). Batteux drew an equivalent distinction between musical "portrait painting" and "landscape painting" but he considered "landscape painting" an inferior type of musical imitation. Rousseau and Sulzer criticized tone painting on the grounds that it compromises the aim of music, which is expression of sentiments.

> Using only tone [*Ton*] and movement [*Bewegung*], it is possible to imitate wind, thunder, the roar of the ocean, or the gurgles of a brook, a flash of lightning, and other such things. Even the most learned and skilled composers can be found doing this. But such [tone] painting violates the true spirit of music, which is to express the sentiments of feeling, not to convey images of inanimate objects. (Sulzer 1792–94, 2: 357; Baker and Christensen 1995: 90, translation modified)

Ultimately, tone painting entered the edifice of eighteenth-century music aesthetics through the back door opened by Johann Jakob Engel. In his essay *Über die musikalische Malerey* (1780) Engel distinguished three types of tone painting. The first type, which can be called "tone painting" proper, consists in imitation of sonic impressions. The second type includes sonic analogues of other sensory impressions. The third type arises when the composer represents "not a part or a property of the object itself, but the impression that this object tends to make on the soul" (1998: 222).[59] This last category was inspired by Rousseau, who insisted that the composer should "not directly represent things, but excite in the soul the same movement which we feel in seeing them" (Barry 1987: 10). Engel echoes Rousseau when he emphasizes that

> the composer should always paint feelings rather than objects of feelings; always the state into which the soul and with it the body are conveyed through contemplation of a certain matter and event, rather than this matter and event itself. . . . So in the kind of storm symphony that appears in various operas, it is always better to paint the inner movements of the soul in a storm than the storm that occasions these movements. (Engel 1998: 225)

The means of painting these movements listed by Engel—mode, key, melody, tempo, rhythm, harmony, register, instrumentation, and dynamics—correspond to those called on by Mattheson, Sulzer, and Kirnberger. One could thus argue that the third type of tone painting is the doctrine of affections in disguise. But this doctrine itself makes room for pictorialism. While it stipulates that music should represent movements of the soul (*Gemüthsbewegungen*), these movements may be similar to physical movements. As we have seen, Sulzer compares emotion to the motion of a gentle brook, a raging stream, or a wild sea. If physical motion and emotion display the same pattern, the difference between them disappears. Consequently, a musical passage may represent (1) a storm, (2) a feeling caused by storm, or (3) a stormy feeling. This line of argument is pursued by Koch in the article "Malerey" from the *Musikalisches Lexikon* (1802). At first, Koch follows in Sulzer's footsteps and condemns tone painting but then he draws consequences from Sulzer's comparison between physical motion and emotion and justifies pictorial effects when they depict feelings:

> When certain sounds and motions out of inanimate Nature, such as the rolling of thunder, the tumult of the sea, the rustle of the wind and such, are imitated in music, this is called tone painting....However, occasionally there are instances in which such tone paintings are immediately related to the state of the soul or where they can express the stirring of sentiments. An example will explain this. When the composer takes recourse to a restless and wavering movement of tones in the aria from Wieland's *Alceste*—My life wavers / Between fear and hope / Like a skiff which moves between rocks / in the rage of swollen rapids—then this kind of movement is an artistic means of expressing the emotion. Here one should not think that the composer's intention is to paint a skiff thrown back and forth in swollen rapids or the swollen rapids themselves. Rather, the wavering and restless movement of tones represents the heart struggling between fear and hope and, therefore, the nature of the sentiment itself.[60]

> Wenn in einem Tonstücke gewisse Bewegungen oder Töne aus der leblosen Natur nachgeahmt werden, wie z. B. das Rollen des Donners, das Brausen des Meeres, oder das Säufeln des Windes u. d. gl. so nennet man eine solche Nachahmung eine Malerey oder ein Gemälde....Es kommen aber auch zuweilen Fälle vor, wo sich solche Tongemälde unmittelbar auf die Schilderung des Seelenzustandes selbst beziehen, oder wo sie Ausdruck der Bewegung der Empfindungen sind. Ein Beyspiel wird dieses deutlicher machen. Wenn der Tonsetzer sich z. B. bey der Arie aus Wielands Alceste: Zwischen Angst und zwischen Hoffen / Schwankt mein Leben; wie im Rachen / Der empörten Flut ein Nachen / Aengstlich zwischen Klippen treibt—einer gewissen unruhigen und schwankenden Bewegung der Töne bedient, so ist diese Art der Bewegung eines derjenigen Kunstmittel, diesen Seelenzustand auszudrücken. Hier muß man also nicht glauben, als sey die Absicht des Tonsetzers durch diese unruhige und schwankende Bewegung ein Gemälde eines Nachens darzustellen, welcher in empörten Fluten hin und her geworfen wird, oder die empörte Flut selbst zu malen; sondern hier ist die schwankende und unruhige Bewegung der Töne auf das genaueste mit dem zwischen Angst und Hoffnung kämpfenden Herzen, und also mit der Natur der Empfindung selbst, verwandt. (Koch 1802: cols. 924–25)

When Beethoven insists that his "Pastoral" Symphony (1806), including a depiction of storm, is "more expression of sentiments than tone painting" (*mehr Ausdruck der Empfindung als Mahlerey*), he takes recourse to Koch's argument and uses Koch's vocabulary.

From the perspective adopted in this volume, Monelle's "iconic topics" are not topics because they do not form cross-references between musical styles or genres. Instead of dividing musical topics into iconic and indexical, it will be more appropriate to distinguish between two classes of musical signs based on imitation (Figure 0.5): musical

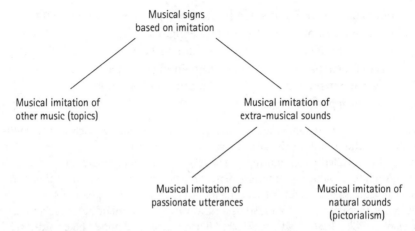

FIGURE 0.5 Classification of musical signs based on imitation.

imitation of other music (topics) and imitation of extra-musical sounds. The second class can be further subdivided into two types: imitation of passionate utterances and imitation of natural sounds (pictorialism). The former type of imitation was preferred by the doctrine of mimesis; the latter was recognized but not preferred by this doctrine. Musical imitation of other music—Ratner's topics—lay outside the doctrine of mimesis in the eighteenth century but was subsumed under this doctrine in the twentieth. Note that Monelle's "iconic topics" not only blur the distinction between the two classes of signs based on imitation—including, respectively, topics and pictorialism—but also conflate two historically distinct types of musical imitation subsumed under the second class. Whereas the topic of *pianto* (sigh motive) is an imitation of passionate utterance (sigh), the topic of "noble horse" is an imitation of a natural sound (gallop).

Although the signs in Figure 0.5 refer to different kinds of objects, they have the same structure of signification, shown in Figure 0.3, within which different sign–object relations receive different emphasis. In the second group, embracing imitation of passionate utterances and pictorialism, the emphasis falls on the *iconic* relation between the musical item and its object. If the sign–object relation between the musical item (sigh motive) and the object (sigh) is recognized, the listener can associate the idea of sigh with a range of contexts and situations without misinterpreting the musical sign. The same holds for the topic of "noble horse" in relation to gallop. It follows that the *indexical* relation between object and signification is less important and the difference between iconic topics and musical icons, based on this relation, less crucial than suggested by Monelle. (Incidentally, it is contentious that the signification of the "cuckoo" is less "culturally prescribed" than the signification of the "noble horse.") By contrast, in the case of Ratner's topics, the iconic relation between a musical item (sarabande-as-a-topic) and its object (sarabande-as-a-genre) is trivial because both of them belong to the musical realm. Instead, signification of topics hinges on the *indexical* relation between the object (sarabande-as-a-genre) and its affect, which Monelle describes, quoting Ratner, as a dance of "a deliberate, serious character which represented the high style" (2000: 18).

He adds that "it was thought to have had a Spanish origin (Koch 1802, column 1289); perhaps it made people think of the Spanish court, and thus of lofty decorum. Mozart's signification in the 'Jupiter' is *seriousness* and *decorum*, not merely 'sarabande'" (2000: 17–18). The distinction drawn by Monelle between the seriousness and the decorum of the sarabande hinges on the distinction between affects and social contexts of styles and genres represented, respectively, by the downward and upward arrows on the right-hand side of Figure 0.1. The downward arrow represents seriousness as an affective association of the sarabande. The upward arrow represents its decorum, which relates to further associations of this dance with its social function at the Spanish court. Koch took the information about Spanish origins of the sarabande from Sulzer (1792–94, 4: 128), who in turn took it from Mattheson (1713: 187). The culturally prescribed signification of the sarabande in the "Jupiter" Symphony thus reached Mozart's audience through the lineage described in section 2.

If, occasionally, the distinction between topics and pictorialism becomes obliterated, this is not because some pictorial effects are topics but, rather, because some topics originate in pictorial effects that have turned into styles or genres. For instance, frequent musical imitations of storm turned into the style of storm scenes in opera seria. Taken out of its proper context and used in other genres, the style of such scenes gave rise to the topic called by Ratner *Sturm und Drang*. The *ombra* topic, introduced by Ratner and discussed by Clive McClelland (2012), features tremolo effects and dotted rhythms that imitate trembling and irregular heartbeat as indexical signs of fear at the appearance of ghosts in *ombra* scenes. "Sigh" motives originate in imitation of sigh as an index of grief in vocal music but they turned into an attribute of the eighteenth-century culture of sensibility (*Empfindsamkeit*) in vocal and instrumental music. In each case, the signification of topics arises from their similarity to genres or styles rather than from direct musical imitation of nonmusical sounds. Although such styles were not clearly recognized in their own times, they can be included in the list of eighteenth-century topics, even if their topical status is different—and, admittedly, more fragile—than that of the sarabande, the minuet, or the march.

5. TOPICS AND RHETORIC

As we have seen, the contrast between music and language was the hallmark of eighteenth-century aesthetics. But, as much as it emphasized the distinction between natural and arbitrary signs, the eighteenth century drew on the parallel between music and language. If the contrast was stressed by semiotics, the parallel was pursued by musical rhetoric.

After the surge of interest in rhetoric, its influence on eighteenth-century music theory and aesthetics came to be questioned by many authors. Some of them established an opposition between rhetoric and semiotics, but the main actors of my discussion so far—whether or not involved in the business of semiotics—were all committed to the rhetorical enterprise.[61] The most prominent champion of musical rhetoric was, of course, Mattheson. His discussion of the compositional process in terms of invention, disposition, elaboration, decoration, and execution draws on five stages of rhetoric—*inventio, dispositio, elocutio, memoria*, and *pronuntiatio*—and his division of musical composition into six parts—*exordium, narratio, propositio, confutatio, confirmatio*, and *peroratio*—was based on its analogy to speech.[62] Analogies between music and rhetoric were commonplace in neoclassical aesthetics. Scheibe's *Critischer Musikus* (1745) was informed by Gottsched's *Versuch einer Critischen Dichtkunst* (1730) and *Ausführliche Redekunst* (1736), and Scheibe frequently refers to the "sister disciplines" of music, rhetoric, and poetry. Batteux distinguishes fine arts from eloquence but he compares poetry, music, and dance to rhetoric (Le Huray and Day 1981: 50) and encourages the union of these arts with Quintilian's remark about the unity of words (*verba*), voice (*vox*), and gesture (*gestus*) in the delivery of oration (Le Huray and Day 1981: 53–54). For Rousseau the common origins of music and language justify their parallel functions in the society, which are to speak, respectively, to heart and reason. In the *Essai sur l'origine des langues* he calls for the recovery of society through restoration of "the public rhetoric of oratory," which is "the language of liberty"; and "the more private rhetoric of vocal melody," which is "the language of feeling" (Barry 1987: 68). The function of music as the language of passions (*Sprache der Leidenschaften*) or sentiments (*Sprache der Empfindungen*) was reiterated by Sulzer, Koch, and Forkel, as was the connection of music with heart and language with reason. Sulzer and Koch turn back to the idea of musical rhetoric when they describe the process of composition in terms of invention, disposition, elaboration, and execution.[63] Forkel distinguishes between musical grammar and rhetoric, and his account of music history is predicated on the parallel development of music and language "from the very beginning until the highest perfection" (*vom ersten Anfang an bis zur höchsten Vollkommenheit*; 1788: 2).

The influence of rhetoric on eighteenth-century music theory and aesthetics extends to the concepts directly related to musical topics. The division of musical styles into high, middle, and low corresponds to three rhetorical styles (*tria modi dicendi*)—*sublimis, mediocris*, and *humilis*—to be selected by the orator so as to suit the occasion, the status of persons, and the importance of matters to be discussed in the oration (Scheibe 1745: 139–40). The division into the church, theatrical, and chamber styles—Mattheson's *genera stylorum*—corresponds to the division into three rhetorical genres (*tria genera dicendi*): *deliberativum, iuridiciale*, and *demonstrativum*. In the modern era these *genera* were further subdivided into different genres of oration. The classification of musical genres, undertaken by Mattheson in *Kern melodischer Wissenschaft* (1737) and *Der vollkommene Capellmeister* (1739), parallels Gottsched's classifications of rhetorical and poetic genres in *Versuch einer Critischen Dichtkunst* (1730) and *Ausführliche Redekunst* (1736).[64] The goal of music to move the listener is equivalent to one of three rhetorical functions (*tria officia dicendi*): *docere, movere, delectare*. The concept of affect (*pathos*), fundamental for the doctrine of affections, was derived from one of three methods of rhetorical persuasion: *ethos, pathos*, and *logos*. The requirement that music should imitate passionate accents of human voice, essential for the doctrine of mimesis, was based on the authority of Cicero, who asserted that "every motion of the soul has by nature a certain countenance, sound, and gesture" (*omnis motus animi sum quemdam a natura habet vultum, at sonum, at gestum*).[65]

Given that Ratner defined topics as "subjects for musical discourse," thus framing them with the metaphor of music as language, it is not surprising that he labeled them with a rhetorical concept. In Classical rhetoric topics—Greek *topoi* or Latin *loci communes* (common places)—were categories of arguments and thus methods of finding materials for speeches. As such, they were discussed by Aristotle and Cicero as tools of invention. Cicero's discussion in *Topica* became canonical for later authors, and his list of sixteen topics persisted in rhetorical textbooks into the eighteenth century. It includes arguments from the whole and parts, from genus and species, from similarities and contraries, from adjuncts, and so on. Clearly, these categories can subsume any number of arguments, depending on circumstances of a given case: they are containers that can hold any content. As noted by Stephen Rumph, Ratner's topics are not equivalent to rhetorical topics nor do they align with their applications to music in the eighteenth century. Rumph further points out that, as tools of invention, topics were disdained by eighteenth-century authors. He thus concludes that "Ratner's types and styles violate both the letter and the spirit of the classical *ars topica*" (2012: 83).[66] Allanbrook retraces Rumph's line of argument, revisits his sources, and confirms his conclusion. She suggests that Ratner may have adopted the concept of topics from *Music in the Baroque Era* published in 1947 by his mentor, Manfred Bukofzer. "Unfortunately, Bukofzer harbored a fundamental confusion about the nature of these *loci topici*, which he identified with the treasure house of the *Affektenlehre*" (2014: 91). Even more importantly, Allanbrook notes the similarity between Ratner's musical topics and literary topics discussed by Ernst Robert Curtius in *European Literature and the Latin Middle Ages* (1953) but she points out that Curtius's topics are no "common places" but "commonplaces"—a collection of themes and plots for literary discourse. "Common places and commonplaces are not the same" (97).

Rumph and Allanbrook are right that Ratner's musical topics are not equivalent to rhetorical topics, but it is worth reviewing the relation of the former to the latter in order to explain the role of topics in musical invention. In the era when composers were expected to compose new pieces on daily basis, the problem of invention was of enormous practical importance and was frequently raised in composition handbooks. Although their authors stress that invention is a matter of genius and thus cannot be learned,[67] they come up with advice on how to stimulate it. The most important tools of musical invention are *ars combinatoria* and *loci topici*.[68] These tools are first mentioned by Johann David Heinichen in the preface to *Gründliche Anweisung zur Erlernung des General-Basses* (1711). The former is treated by him with disdain. Changing the order of notes is of little use in finding materials for compositions because "the tenderness or the soul of music cannot be found in such wooden notes" (*die Tendresse oder Seele der Music unmöglich bey solchen hölzern Noten zu finden ist*; 12–13). By contrast, *loci topici* are the main source of invention because they pursue "the true goal of music" (*den wahren Endzweck der Musik*) which is "to move the listener's affections" (*die Gemüther der*

Zuhörer zu bewegen; 10). For Heinichen, this goal should be achieved through expression of affects contained in the text of vocal music. The prospect of inexhaustible riches awaiting composers in the domain of expression fills him with awe: "What an unfathomable sea we still have before us in the expression of words and the affects in music!"[69]

Out of the sixteen *loci topici*, Heinichen uses only one, the *locus adjunctorum*, which he subdivides, after Cicero, into *antecedentia*, *concomitantia*, and *consequentia*. The "adjunct" to music is its text while the antecedents, concomitants, and consequents are the words of the text occurring before, during, and after a given musical passage. In his early treatise he applies this tool of invention to the aria "Bella donna e che non fá?" In the expanded and revised version of his preface from *Der General-Bass in der Composition* (1728), he takes four other texts and shows incipits of sixteen arias. Although his concept of topics is different from Ratner's, Heinichen's application of *loci topici* in these arias takes recourse to Ratner's topics: the "heroic decision" (*heroische Entschließung*; 39) of Metilde in the third aria is represented with the fanfare (Example 0.5a), the tenderness of Aminta for his shepherdess in the ninth aria with the siciliana (Example 0.5b), and their "sighing love" (*seuffzende Liebe*; 64) with *Seufzer* (sighs), emblems of *Empfindsamkeit* (Example 0.5c). Heinichen explicitly names the siciliana and describes it as a "kind of composition which has something languid to it,"[70] thus linking its affect to genre.

Mattheson's discussion of *loci topici* in Part Two of *Der vollkommene Capellmeister* uses the full list of Cicero's topics.[71] The "unfathomable sea of affects" (*Affektenmeer*) is just one of them but the most noble of all. For Mattheson musical representation of affects is "the richest source, indeed, in my humble opinion, the most reliable and essential guide to invention" (1739: 127; Harriss 1981: 290). Since he does not constrain them to

EXAMPLE 0.5 Heinichen, *Der General-Bass in der Composition* (1728): (a) 39, fanfare; (b) 62, siciliano; (c) 64, *Seufzer*.

(Continued)

EXAMPLE **0.5** (Continued)

affects of the text, he subsumes this source not under *locus adjunctorum*, as Heinichen, but under *locus descriptionis*, thus emphasizing the function of music to represent or "describe" affects. As he points out, "because of the very quantity and nature of such abundant and multifarious passions, this description-locus cannot possibly be given as many clear and specific rules as the preceding [*locus notationis*]" (1739: 127; Harriss 1981: 290) but he sends the reader back to his discussion of affects in Part One, where he first broaches the idea of affects as tools of invention, employs Heinichen's metaphor of the "sea of affects" and refers to the discussion of *loci topici* in Heinichen's treatises.

The associations of affects with genres, which Mattheson discusses in the further course of *Der vollkommene Capellmeister*, could have led him to the conclusion that representation of affects can be accomplished by emulation of small compositions. Consequently, he could have realized that specific rules of *locus descriptionis* can be derived from the study of dances and marches. This conclusion is not reached by Mattheson but it is drawn by Sulzer and Kirnberger. While Sulzer dismisses rhetorical *loci communes*, he approvingly refers to Mattheson's discussion of musical invention in the article "Erfindung" (Sulzer 1792–94, 2: 90), and his remarks about invention in instrumental music, scattered in other articles, imply that invention of larger compositions is more challenging than invention of small ones. Apparently, the challenge is the greater, the greater the composer's freedom in defining the character of a composition. From the fact that the overture and the symphony have more closely determined characters it follows that in these genres the composer has "something by which to base his invention, since his music must express the main character [*Hauptcharakter*] of the play," but "the invention of a concerto, trio, solo, sonata, and the like…is left almost entirely to chance" (Sulzer 1792–94, 2: 678; Baker and Christensen 1995: 96). By contrast, invention of small compositions is facilitated by their characters, "and the composer has a plumb-line as to their character by which he may proceed in its composition" (Sulzer 1792–94, 2: 678; Baker and Christensen 1995: 96). Although Sulzer does not formulate any advices for composers, his advice for performers, quoted earlier, to practice dances in order to learn how to express characters of larger compositions is based on the assumption that larger compositions are made out of small compositions and it implies that small compositions can be used by composers as tools of musical invention outside their own genres.

The role of dances as tools of musical invention was explicitly noted by Kirnberger. In the preface to the second volume of *Die Kunst des reinen Satzes* (1776) he promises to "aim above all at determining the true character of the various commonly accepted dance melodies, since a thorough knowledge of them greatly facilitates the invention of melodies that have a definite expression of some sentiment or passion" (1982: 279). Kirnberger did not fulfill this promise due to his illness and death but filled this gap in his treatise with *Recueil d'airs de danse caractéristiques* (1777), whose aim, specified in the subtitle, was "to serve as models for young composers and exercises for those who play the keyboard." Kirnberger's unfulfilled promise sheds light on the relation between musical and rhetorical topics. The suggestion that small compositions facilitate invention and the fact that they form the source of Ratner's topics indicates that musical topics—though not equivalent to rhetorical ones—are related to them. As islands of affective signification emerging from the sea of eighteenth-century music, they find their place in Heinichen's *locus adjunctorum* and Mattheson's *locus descriptionis*. If rhetorical topics are "common places" where one can find materials for speeches, musical topics are "commonplace" materials found at one "common place."

One more peculiarity of musical topics should be noted. If the concept of topics is related to the first part of rhetoric (*inventio*), the definition of musical topics as "styles and genres taken out of their proper context and used in another one" suggests their relation to the third part of rhetoric (*elocutio*). This relation was discussed in section 1. It follows that, by contrast to rhetorical topics, musical topics are associated with two different parts of rhetoric—invention (*inventio*) and style (*elocutio*).[72] This is reflected in the remark by Kirnberger's pupil, Peter Schulz, in the article "Schreibart; Styl" of Sulzer's *Allgemeine Theorie der schönen Künste*, that "it is difficult to decide what belongs to the ideas of a musical work and what to its style."[73] The reason for this difficulty is that, unlike language, music lacks the distinction between the content of an utterance (*res*) and its expression (*verba*), on which the distinction between *inventio* and *elocutio* is founded. In language, which is a system of arbitrary signs, sign and object can be easily separated. In music, which consists of natural signs, similarity between sign and object means that they merge together. Even if topics are comparable to words, their associations with affects emerge from affective signification of music based on similarity between musical motion and emotion.[74] This brings us back from rhetoric to semiotics. Ultimately, the difference between musical and verbal rhetoric hinges on the semiotic difference between music and language.

6. TOPICS OF THIS VOLUME

If it has not yet become clear from my discussion, it is time to explain that this volume is dedicated to eighteenth-century musical topics. The focus on one research field justifies its inclusion in the series of *Oxford Handbooks* but, unlike other *Oxford Handbooks*, this handbook does not summarize the state of art in the field but establishes it and lays foundations under its future development. Although the study of musical topics has been conducted for more than three decades, it has been wrought with discrepancies that have prevented it from displaying its full potential. The aim of this volume is to clear away these discrepancies in order to turn topic theory into an efficient tool of analysis and interpretation.

Section I, "Origins and Distinctions," traces the origins of cross-references between styles and genres of eighteenth-century music to transformations of eighteenth-century musical life. The new function of music as entertainment stimulated the quest for popularity and the need for recognizable musical materials. The ease and enjoyment of their recognition and association with familiar styles and genres were conducive to commercial success of compositions. This reality of music production and consumption left its mark on the genre of opera buffa, examined by Mary Hunter (Chapter 1). The author considers the practice of mixing popular materials—derived from other contexts of musical life—in this genre and identifies buffa topics that consist of materials endemic to opera buffa, whether or not they were imported (or importable) to other styles and genres. The following chapters discuss the emergence of topical mixtures in instrumental genres. Elaine Sisman (Chapter 2) writes about the transfer of this phenomenon from operas to symphonies. Further transfer of this practice to chamber music, discussed by Dean Sutcliffe (Chapter 3), was fostered by keyboard transcriptions of operas and symphonies and by chamber performances of orchestral works. Given the function of symphonies to introduce theatrical plays and operas, it was only natural for them to borrow their materials from the world of theater. Sisman shows how stylistic contrasts were inscribed in eighteenth-century views of the genre and how the symphony developed its own repertoire of topical markers derived from orchestral sonority. Sutcliffe uses the concept of chamber music in its modern sense constrained to domestic genres for one player per part—solos, duos, trios, quartets, and so forth—which in the eighteenth century fell under the definition of sonata. While they did not develop topics of their own, Sutcliffe finds that these genres absorbed a wider spectrum of topics, combined them with a greater versatility, and changed them at a quicker rate than any other genres of eighteenth-century music.

Section II, "Contexts, Histories, Sources," documents historical reality of individual topics or groups of topics on the basis of eighteenth-century sources to music theory, aesthetics, and criticism. The first two chapters are devoted to dance topics. Whereas minuets and new German dances reigned in the ballrooms of the late eighteenth-century Vienna, French Baroque dances were no longer danced but in ballets and operas. The distinction between current and historical dances is of consequence for signification of dance topics and their effects on listeners. If references to current dances aroused associations with familiar environments and relied on familiarity of their step patterns, historical dances were voices of the past coming from distant locations—be it Arcadia or Versailles. Differences between these groups of dances are elucidated by Lawrence Zbikowski (Chapter 4) and Eric McKee (Chapter 5). Zbikowski uses his concept of "sonic analog" to account for different degrees of correlation between music and dance. McKee supplements his earlier work on minuets (2005, 2012) with detailed discussion of less known but more popular repertoires of contredanses, *Ländler*, and *Waltzer*. Hunt, military, and pastoral topics were explored by Monelle (2006). If Monelle questioned Ratner's sources, Monelle's sources are questioned by Andrew Haringer (Chapter 6), who reveals a number of eighteenth-century documents not considered by Monelle and shows how they can enrich and refine Monelle's discussion. Catherine Mayes (Chapter 7) discusses Turkish and Hungarian-Gypsy styles. While the labels *alla turca* and *all'ongherese* were interchangeable and the styles denoted by them have similar musical characteristics (signifiers), they carry different meanings (signifieds) and perform different functions in eighteenth-century musical repertoire. Sarah Day-O'Connell (Chapter 8) lays foundation under the future investigation of the singing style: a vast topical field with multifarious signifiers derived from an array of vocal genres and with complex signifieds including categories such as beauty, innocence, simplicity, and, especially, comprehensibility. Matthew Head (Chapter 9) reconsiders the stylistic categories of fantasia and *Empfindsamkeit*. Regarding the former, he problematizes the fantasia topic by demonstrating that eighteenth-century fantasias were characterized not by a single style but a mixture of styles. Regarding the latter, sensibility was not a style but a broad aesthetic category. Even if Head identifies materials of fantasia that can serve as signifiers of the fantasia topic and finds idiomatic musical expressions of sensibility, his account of both topics is far more restricted—and clearly defined—than Ratner's. Another problematic topic is *Sturm und Drang*. The name, derived from a pre-Romantic trend in German literature, has been criticized as anachronistic in reference to music. Clive McClelland

(Chapter 10) replaces it with *tempesta*, which hints at the origins of this topic in depictions of storms, earthquakes, and other devastations. Since such cataclysms were usually caused by wrath of gods, *tempesta* is a counterpart of *ombra*, a topic derived from scenes involving supernatural beings. The two topics have parallel psychological effects of terror and horror and parallel sets of musical characteristics. Keith Chapin (Chapter 11) delves into the complexities of the learned style. As he demonstrates, the aura of learnedness surrounded a high number of styles reaching from *stile antico* to galant counterpoint. Chapin reviews the various concepts that governed this stylistic field, along with their technical and aesthetic implications, examines the origins of learned styles in various source genres and styles, and discusses their functions and signification. He also considers the aesthetic ambivalence of these styles: representing dignity and elevation due to their associations with church music and an elite professional tradition, admired for the display of technical prowess yet despised for their scholastic pedantry and the air of classroom exercises. Roman Ivanovitch (Chapter 12) identifies the source of the brilliant style in display episodes of instrumental concerti. Such display easily turned into quasi-theatrical play of the performer in front of the audience and could be emulated by the composer persona in other musical works. Like buffa topics in opera buffa and symphonic topics in the symphony, the brilliant style is a concerto topic in the concerto but can be transferred to other styles and genres.

Section III, "Analyzing Topics," relates topic theory to music analysis. The fact that Ratner subsumed topics under the rubric of expression encouraged his followers to use them as tools of interpretation, but their musical characteristics are imbricated in various dimensions of musical structure and therefore have implications for analysis. For the North-German critics, all dimensions of musical structure stood in service of expression, but the contributors to this section show that the interaction between structure and expression can take both directions. On the one hand, the choice of meter, key, rhythmic figures, melodic gestures, or harmonic progressions can be motivated by topics. On the other hand, selection and succession of topics can be governed by structural demands. Danuta Mirka (Chapter 13) concentrates on the relation of topics to meter. Given the expressive qualities of meters in the eighteenth century and their associations with genres, the choice of meter and its changes in the course of a given piece are frequently conditioned by topics. At the same time, eighteenth-century peculiarities of metric notation are of consequences for topical identification. Vasili Byros (Chapter 14) dwells on the relation between musical topics and harmonic schemata— two different types of eighteenth-century conventions. While schemata can be dressed in different topics, certain topics combine with some schemata more frequently than others. Analysis of the correlation between the *ombra* topic and the *le–sol–fi–sol* schema in Beethoven's "Eroica" leads Byros to a fresh interpretation of this masterpiece in light of Beethoven's troubled biography. William Caplin (Chapter 15) pursues a special case of a topic inextricably linked with a single schema: the lament. He examines the structure of the schema and, building on his earlier study (2005), surveys the full range of formal function enacted by the topic. Joel Galand (Chapter 16) explores the role of topics in tonal processes shaped by eighteenth-century composers. Given that some topics are associated with specific keys, the course of such processes can be influenced by topics. Galand establishes conditions under which an influence of topics on tonal processes can be asserted and considers cases when their coordination with tonal processes can be assumed, even if it cannot be proven. The enterprise of relating topics to form was first undertaken by Kofi Agawu (1991). In his contribution to this volume Agawu (Chapter 17) provides a close reading of the relation between musical topics and form in the first movement of Mozart's String Quintet in E flat major, K. 614, surveyed by Ratner (1980: 237–45). The analysis demonstrates how topics enhance our experience of the sonata form on the one hand and thematic contrasts or affinities on the other. Stephen Rumph (Chapter 18) starts off by comparing topics to words only to draw attention to what he calls topical figurae: musical characteristics of topics comparable to distinctive features of phonemes. Since figurae articulate multiple topics and forge structural links between them, figural analysis accounts for the succession of topics in terms of distinctive features running beneath the topical surface. Robert Hatten (Chapter 19) develops the concept of topical tropes introduced in his earlier books (1994, 2004). He proposes a set of criteria to evaluate the effect of tropes based on the compatibility of topics, their dominance or subordination, interaction with surrounding materials, and influence on the expressive trajectory of a given work. It is tempting to draw parallels between the last two analytical approaches and two most influential streams of eighteenth-century music aesthetics discussed in this introduction. Rumph's approach can be thought of as a modern version of the doctrine of affections in its final phase represented by Forkel, in which transitions between sentiments are engineered by reconfigurations of characteristics derived from different musical parameters. Hatten's approach has its origin in the doctrine of mimesis favored by neoclassical aesthetics: his references to an internal agent as the subject of expressive states evoked by topics recall the efforts of North-German critics to account for the variety of affects in terms of a unifying character.

Analysis remains the focus of attention in the last two sections of this volume, but the analytical perspective shifts from composers to performers and listeners of eighteenth-century music. Section IV, "Performing Topics," explores the potential of topical analysis for historically informed performance practice. The three chapters in this section are devoted to keyboard music, "a quintessential locale for the play of a topic" (Ratner 1991: 616). John Irving (Chapter 20) explains how topics can help performers to enliven their musical experience by detecting and enacting stylistic opportunities comprised in eighteenth-century repertoire. Tom Beghin (Chapter 21) draws the distinction and connections between topics and rhetorical figures. He examines the topical reading of the first movement of Mozart's Piano Sonata in F major, K. 332, by Allanbrook (1992) in light of the rhetorical reading by Friedrich August Kanne and the experience of performing this piece on historical keyboards. Sheila Guymer (Chapter 22) holds up for inspection the other Mozart sonata discussed by Allanbrook—K. 333—and recounts experiences of two other fortepianists, Robert Levin and Bart van Oort, which corroborate the relation between topics and characters established in this introduction.

Section V, "Listening to Topics," rounds off the volume by linking back to Section I. If the use of topics by eighteenth-century composers was motivated by demands of eighteenth-century listeners, what did the listeners make of them? Melanie Lowe (Chapter 23) argues that topics were the springboard for understanding of musical structure and the construction of meaning by amateurs (*Liebhaber*). Consequently, she speculates that the way of handling topics was an important factor in commercial success or failure of musical works. She illustrates this point with Mozart's, Haydn's, and Pleyel's string quartets, which make different demands on the topical competency of their consumers and differently fared in the musical marketplace. Elizabeth Hellmuth Margulis (Chapter 24) suggests that topics may be responsible for different affective responses to surprise. She conducts an empirical study in which the same surprising event—general pause—occurs in different topical contexts and finds that it causes momentary intensification of different affects. Her results indicate that topic theory may become an ally of expectancy theory in solving the problem of affective differentiation. Julian Horton (Chapter 25) takes the concept of topics into the nineteenth century. Although old topics acquire new meanings and new topics emerge, the way of handling them remains key to the apprehension of musical forms by both amateurs (*Liebhaber*) and connoisseurs (*Kenner*) and bold topical mixtures continue to offend musical critics. Max Kalbeck's comparison of Bruckner's Seventh Symphony to "an impromptu comedy with stock characters" echoes Hiller's complaints about Hans Wurst springing into the middle of eighteenth-century works. Stylistic cross-references remain important factors in twentieth-century music, but the spectrum of such references and complexity of their sociocultural meanings exponentially increases. In the last decade the study of musical topics has extended from the eighteenth to the nineteenth and twentieth centuries, but explanation of their place in changed aesthetic environments and investigation of their function in postclassical repertoires lies beyond the scope of this volume. It is to be hoped that further music theorists and historians will take up the gauntlet thrown by the volume's contributors and turn topic theory into a fruitful mode of inquiry into music of the nineteenth, twentieth, and twenty-first centuries.

Notes

1. About the role of topics as means of communication between composers and listeners, see Mirka (2008).
2. It is not my intention to survey the development of topic theory in this introduction. For such surveys, see McKay (2007) and Agawu (2008).
3. Mattheson's appropriation of Kircher's categories is based on the entry "*Stilo*" from Sébastien de Brossard's *Dictionnaire de musique* (1703), whose German translation is included by Mattheson in *Das beschützte Orchester* (1717). Brossard modifies Kircher's system by dropping *stylus canonicus* and advancing *stylus choraicus* to the rank of a species. For Kircher this style, including social dances, was one of two subspecies of *stylus hyporchematicus*, the other being *stylus theatricus* including theatrical dances in operas and ballets. Mattheson undertakes further modifications: he reintroduces *stylus canonicus* and replaces *stylus ecclesiasticus* with one of its subspecies (*stylus ligatus*) including compositions with *cantus firmus*. The genesis and evolution of Mattheson's stylistic classification is discussed by Katz (1926) and Palisca (1983).

4. "Man kann und muß also, so wohl zu Kirchenmusiken, als zu theatralischen oder Kammerstücken die hohe, die mittlere, oder die niedrige Schreibart anwenden" (Scheibe 1745: 388).

5. "Man könnte überhaupt den musikalischen Styl, in den *religiösen* und *profanen*, oder wie es die Alten zu thun pflegten, in den geistlichen und weltlichen Styl eintheilen" (Schubart 1806: 343).

6. The criticism of the Italian style of instrumental music in Germany is summarized by Hosler (1981: 1–30).

7. "Die Großmuth, die Majestät, die Herrchsucht, die Pracht, der Hochmuth, das Erstaunen, der Zorn, das Schrecken, die Raserey, die Rache, die Wuth, die Verzweiflung … können in keiner andern Schreibart, als in der hohen, ausgedruckt werden" (Scheibe 1745: 127).

8. The debate is recounted by Schmidt (1981: 14–15), who illustrates it with the same quotations.

9. Mattheson (1739: 69; Harriss 1981: 191) emphasizes that the church, theatrical, and chamber styles retain their functions even if the music is performed in other venues. Ultimately, their affective implications are determined by functions—not by venues as such.

10. "Alles trägt zur Gemüthsart eines Menschen etwas bey; die Natur und ihr Urheber, das Land, da man gebohren ist, die Aeltern und Vorfahren, das Geschlecht und Alter, das Vermögen und der Stand, die Auferziehung, die Zeiten, darinn man lebt, die Glücks- und Unglücksfälle, die Personen, mit denen man umgeht, u. a. m." (1751: 499).

11. "Ein widersprechender Character ist ein Ungeheuer, das in der Natur nicht vorkömmt: daher muß ein Geiziger geizig, ein Stolzer stolz, ein Hitziger hitzig, ein Verzagter verzagt seyn und bleiben" (Gottsched 1751: 619).

12. "Der Charakter der Personen mildert oder stärket die Leidenschaften. Die Freude, die Traurigkeit, das Schrecken, die Furcht, der Haß, die Liebe u. d. gl. sind nicht bey allen Personen gleich heftig, mittelmäßig, oder schwach. Wir haben gewisse Stufen, welche zu überschreiten, die Charaktere der Personen uns ausdrücklich verbieten" (Scheibe 1745: 94–95).

13. "Es ist dahero als ein Grundsatz anzumerken, daß, wenn ein Componist die Charaktere der Personen beobachtet, er nimmermehr wider die Gemüthsbewegungen verstoßen kann" (Scheibe 1745: 309).

14. "Es giebt Menschen, die in ihren Handlungen, und in ihrer Art zu denken, gar keinen bestimmten Charakter zeigen, die einigermaßen den Wendfahnen gleichen, die für jede Wendung und Stellung gleichgültig sind, und sich also nach allen Gegenden gleich herumtreiben lassen" (Sulzer 1792–94, 1: 455).

15. These ideas are reflected in Jérome-Joseph de Momigny's analysis of Mozart's String Quartet in D minor, K. 421, from the *Cours complet d'harmonie et de composition* (1806), where Momigny provides the first movement with the text of Dido's lament, thus turning it into a cantata (Irving 1998: 75–76). Grétry proposes to underlay Haydn's symphonies with texts (1978: 183; see Geck 1995: 310 n. 14).

16. This conclusion is drawn by Allanbrook (2014). In this paragraph I follow Allanbrook's discussion in Chapter 1 and make use of her quotations.

17. "Nowadays we hear so many concertos, symphonies, etc., that in their measured and magnificent tones allow us to perceive the dignity of music; but before one suspects it, in springs Hans Wurst, right into the middle of things; and the more serious the emotion that had immediately preceded his arrival, the more he arouses our sympathy with his vulgar antics" (Sisman 1997: 22).

18. Luther's views on music and their influence on eighteenth-century German music aesthetics are discussed by Hosler (1981: 36–42).

19. Mattheson applies the term *Affektenlehre* to affections as such, not to their emulation by music. For the criticism of this term and its problematic uses by modern authors, see Buelow (1983).

20. It has been taken for granted by several authors (Hosler 1981; Schmidt 1981; Buelow 1983; Neubauer 1986) that Mattheson's discussion of affects relies on *Les passions de l'âme* by René Descartes (1649). In fact, Mattheson mentions Descartes's treatise as a good read about the theory of temperaments (1739: 15) but he does not adopt the six elementary passions listed by Descartes (Wonder, Love, Hatred, Desire, Joy, and Sadness) and deviates from Descartes's account of the motion of animal spirits. Apart from the reasons mentioned in the main text, my suggestion that Mattheson's theory of affects comes from Kircher is supported by the fact that Kircher's theory forms the basis of Christoph Raupach's *Veritophili deutliche Beweis-Gründe* (1717), which Mattheson prepared for publication and mentions on the same page as the Descartes treatise.

21. Mattheson affirms that "the experiment is new" (1739: 161; Harriss 1981: 345), but in fact it is based on Friedrich Erhard Niedt's experiment from the second volume of *Musikalische Handleitung*, edited and published by Mattheson in 1721, where Niedt changes the rhythm of the same bass line and harmonic progression, turning it into a series of dances: allemandes, courantes, sarabandes, minuets, and gigues.

22. A summary of affective qualities ascribed by Mattheson to musical parameters can be found in Schmidt (1981: 28–38). Neubauer (1986: 51–59) critically reviews Mattheson's discussion.

23. "Die zeichnenden Künste scheinen die einzigen zu seyn, die aus Nachahmung der Natur entstanden sind. Aber Beredsamkeit, Dichtkunst, Musik und Tanz sind offenbar aus der Fülle lebhafter Empfindungen entstanden, und der Begierde, sie zu äußern, sich selbst und andere darin zu unterhalten. Die ersten Dichter, Sänger und Tänzer haben unstreitig würkliche, in ihnen vorhandene, nicht nachgeahmte Empfindungen ausgedrückt" (Sulzer 1792–94, 3: 487–88).

24. This and other excerpts from Rousseau's *Essai* in Victor Gourevitch's translation appear in Thomas (1995).

25. In any case, the concepts of "imitation" and "expression" form a false dichotomy for music. As Hosler (1981: xiv–xviii) points out, the terms "expression," "imitation," "depiction," "painting," and "representation" were used interchangeably by eighteenth-century authors. See note 48.

26. "Die gute Würkung der wichtigsten Werke des Geschmaks gründet sich auf die Eigenschaft des menschlichen Gemüthes, der zufolge wir gar oft von dem Guten und Bösen, das andern Menschen begegnet, wie von unserm eigenen gerührt werden, und deswegen einen wahren und herzlichen Antheil daran nehmen" (Sulzer 1792–94, 4: 531).

27. My discussion in this paragraph is indebted to Barker-Benfield (1992: 3–9).

28. "In dem Schalle kann Zärtlichkeit, Wohlwollen, Haß, Zorn, Verzweiflung und andre leidenschaftliche Äußerung einer gerührten Seele liegen. Darum kann durch den Schall eine Seele der andern empfindbar werden" (Sulzer 1792–94, 3: 91).

29. "Wir wollen hier nur noch einige besondere Beyspiele anführen, an denen man fühlen wird, wie ein und eben dieselbe Folge von Tönen, durch Verschiedenheit des Metrischen und Rhythmischen, ganz verschiedene Charaktere annimmt" (Sulzer 1792–94, 3: 378–79).

30. "Das wichtigste Werk über die Theorie wird ohne Zweifel das seyn, was der Berlinische Tonsetzer Hr. Kirnberger unternommen hat, wenn erst der zweyte Theil desselben wird an das Licht getreten seyn" (Sulzer 1792–94, 3: 439).

31. In fact, his demonstration that harmony changes expression of melody flies in the face of the superiority of melody over harmony, claimed (in defiance of Rameau) by Mattheson and endorsed (under Rousseau's influence) by Sulzer. The "unresolved tension between (Sulzer's) endorsement of melodic expressiveness and (Kirnberger's) defense of harmony" in the article "Harmonie" is noted by Christensen (Baker and Christensen 1995: 14).

32. This is why the goal of music is not just to express sentiments but to maintain them. For Sulzer music is a sequence of tones "which have the power to maintain and strengthen the sentiment" (*die Kraft haben, die Empfindung zu unterhalten und zu stärken*; Sulzer 1792–94, 3: 424). Should music have no other goal than expression and arousal of sentiments, it would not differ from cries of fear or joy (3: 423).

33. A useful discussion of Sulzer's concept of character is provided by Schmidt (1981: 46–50), but this author is unaware of the origins of this concept in Gottsched's and Scheibe's aesthetics.

34. Characters of these instrumental genres are discussed by Schmidt (1981: 51–54) and Hosler (1981: 163–68).

35. Connection between topics and characters is drawn by Agawu (1991: 26–27) but rejected by Matthew Pritchard (2012: 77): "Characters at this period were *not* topics—not limited associative nodes, activated and manipulated semiotically and thus publicly interchangeable with corresponding verbal signs." The reason of Pritchard's position is that he refers to the concept of character by Christian Gottfried Körner, who further develops Sulzer's distinction between character and sentiment. If for Sulzer musical representation of characters is possible insofar as they express themselves in sentiments, for Körner character cannot be directly represented by music. The character "could be read only by close and prolonged observation of the individual's moods or individual states of mind, states that music already had the means to depict" (71).

36. "Die Tanzstücke enthalten das mehreste, wo nicht alles, was unsere guten und schlechten Stücke aller Arten in sich erhalten: sie unterscheiden sich von jenen blos darin, daß sie aus vielen zusammengesetzte Tanzstücke sind, die in ein wol [*sic*] oder übel zusammenhängendes Ganze gebracht werden" (Sulzer 1792–94, 4: 711).

37. This passage is split into two parts and paraphrased by Allanbrook in her posthumous book (2014: 120, 123).

38. Although Allanbrook borrows the term "markedness" from Hatten (1994), her remark that topics "appear with varying degrees of markedness" indicates that she does not use this term in his sense. For Hatten "markedness" refers to asymmetrical relations between opposite musical characteristics such as major and minor mode. Thus it does not depend on "appearance" and has no "degrees"—a term of an opposition is either marked or unmarked. As Hatten explains, "markedness is not equivalent to salience" (this volume, note 4 on page 534).

39. Interestingly, Sulzer does not mention second-beat emphasis singled out by Allanbrook (1983: 38) as a distinctive feature of the sarabande.

40. This comparison is elaborated by Stephen Rumph (2012 and this volume) but his conclusions align with mine. The continuity of the linguistic analogy and the difference between the conclusions drawn from it by Allanbrook and Rumph are noted by Mirka (2014).

41. The first author to frame the concept of topics within Enlightenment semiotics was Stephen Rumph (2012). For a comprehensive assessment of Rumph's discussion, see Mirka (2014) and below.

42. The failure of Enlightenment semiotics to distinguish between indices and icons reflects an inherent property of iconic and indexical signs recognized by modern semiotics. Naomi Cumming explains that indices can be embedded in icons and illustrates this with a vocal expression of an emotional state: "Consider Peirce's further example of a shriek (CP 2), a sound that causes hearers to look immediately for the source of someone's pain or distress. It 'indexes' an intrusion on the body, or a confronting violation of someone's personal space and momentary expectations. At the same time it 'presents' (makes an aural icon of) distress . . . . In both the 'live' and recorded settings, an 'index' to a physical state of the body (and indirectly to a confronting circumstance) may be heard within the sound, as an 'icon' of distress. In less extreme circumstances of vocal production, the indexing of a physical state in a quality of voice remains evident, but ceases to be of concern in itself, an interest is focused on the affective state alone" (Cumming 2000: 90). See note 47.

43. Chabanon's ideas were echoed by Johann Gottfried Herder: "Music performs on the clavichord within us, which is our own inmost being'" (Chua 1999: 118).

44. The development of Rousseau's reaction against Rameau between the articles for *Encyclopédie*, their revised versions in the *Dictionnaire de musique* and the *Essai sur l'origine des langues* is discussed by Thomas (1995). As he concludes, the conceptions developed in the *Essai* "indicate a desire to formulate a coherent theory of music, constructed in opposition to Rameau" (126 n. 110).

45. In a footnote Sulzer refers to the article "Musique" from Rousseau's *Dictionnaire* for an account of physical effects of sound.

46. To be honest, Mattheson's doctrine of affections is not perfectly filtered through the sensualist epistemology. Apart from remarks on blood circulation, Sulzer includes references to animal spirits—ghosts of the old theory of emotions. His careful study of Mattheson's writings was motivated by the insistence on music's moral function, which Sulzer shared with Mattheson (Baker and Christensen 1995: 12 n. 20).

47. Far from being a regressive feature of Enlightenment semiotics, similarity between causes and effects has been observed in modern semiotics as a factor that blurs the distinction between iconic and indexical signs. "It is obvious that a photograph can be understood as similar to its subject or as caused by its subject" (Lidov 1999: 93). A recording of a shriek (see note 42) illustrates the same phenomenon in relation to an acoustic sign. In both examples, it is a physical reproduction of an object—based on causal relation and thus, in itself, an indexical sign—that enables the embedding of an index within an icon.

48. This is why theories of imitation cannot be cleanly distinguished from theories of expression (see note 25) and why the former tend to turn into the latter. In fact, the doctrine of mimesis is not annihilated by but, rather, embedded within theories of expression: "when considered historically, expression theories have their origin in mimetic theories" and "concepts of expression are seen to retain features of mimesis" (Paddison 2010: 127).

49. "Soll demnach die Instrumentalmusik . . . bestimmte Gefühle erwecken und unterhalten, so muß sie in solche politische, religiöse oder häusliche Umstände und Handlungen verflochten werden, die für uns von merklichem Interesse sind, und wobey unser Herz für den Ausdruck der Empfindungen, die sie erwecken und unterhalten soll, empfänglich ist" (Koch 1802: cols. 792–93).

50. "Bey der Vocalmusik hingegen bereitet der Text den Zuhörer vor, hilft ihm zu der beabsichtigten Stimmung, und giebt den ausdrückenden Empfindungen Interesse" (Koch 1802: col. 793).

51. Daniel Chua (1999: 123) speculates that the idea of such communication, presented by Chabanon in France and assimilated by Herder in Germany, foreshadows the end of music semiotics proclaimed by Roland Barthes. In an essay about Schumann's *Kreisleriana*, Barthes declares that there should be "no more music semiology" (1986: 307) and takes the step from semiotics to "somatics" of music in which "the body passes into music without any relay but the signifier" (308).

52. The difference between topical signification and affective signification of music can be caught in terms of *ratio facilis* and *ratio difficilis* developed by Umberto Eco. "One could say that in cases of *ratio difficilis* the nature of the expression is motivated by the nature of the content" (Eco 1976: 183). This is the case of affective signification, which is determined by every nuance of each musical parameter. If, by contrast, expression relies on broad stylistic features replicable from one composition to another, as is the case with topical signification, it "can indeed almost take on the function of proper names" (240), which exemplify *ratio facilis*. The concepts of *ratio difficilis* and *ratio facilis* are used by Monelle (2000: 15–16), who observes the slippage from the former to the latter involved in the phenomenon of topics, but Eco himself refers to this phenomenon when he lists "musical types" (such as "march") as examples of *ratio facilis* side by side with "literary and artistic genres" (1976: 239).

53. Topics are described as "thesaurus" or "vocabulary" by Ratner (1980) and Allanbrook (1983, 2014). Their comparison to words is drawn by many authors. Agawu defines the topic as a musical sign that forms "the union of a signifier and a verbally mediated signified" (1991: 128). Monelle describes it as "a kind of musical term or word" (2006: 3). Powers calls topics "terminological tags" (1995: 29), and Rumph describes them as "lexical items" (2012: 95).

54. Eco's discussion makes clear that, rather than by a topic, a sample can be represented by "a musical quotation referring to a whole work (/play me 'ta-ta-ta-taaa'/ may mean «play me Beethoven's *Fifth*»)" (1976: 226).

55. Eco's critique of iconic signs leads him to get rid of them and complicates their status in the account of those who retain icons. The conventional character of icons and indices is recognized by Monelle, who admits that "the topic is essentially a symbol, its iconic or indexical features governed by convention and thus by rule" (Monelle 2000: 17).

56. Rumph adopts Monelle's indexical interpretation of topics and tries to justify it by proposing that iconic and indexical signs refer to different types of objects: "Whereas an icon represents a merely possible object, an index is dictated by a real object. Thus, Haydn's *Creation* depicts an imaginary Chaos (icon), while his symphonies and quartets replicate features of actual dances, marches, and vocal styles (indices)" (2012: 83). Unfortunately, this justification has no basis in Peirce's semiotics. For Peirce an icon is "a sign which refers to the Object that it denotes merely by virtue of characters of its own, and which it possesses, *just the same, whether any such Object actually exists or not*" (Cumming 2000: 87, my italics). In other words, icons may or may not have real objects. What distinguishes an icon from an index is not whether their object is imaginary or real but whether their relation to the object is based on similarity (*icon*) or causality (*index*).

57. Topics and pictorialism are distinguished by Hatten (1994: 75). The distinction is preserved by Powers (1995: 28–29).

58. Surely, waves, clouds, storms, and horses are no less real than dances. The fact that for Monelle their portrayals form "musical icons" further undermines Rumph's distinction between indices and icons discussed in note 56.

59. My summary of Engel's discussion is based on Neubauer (1986: 74–75).

60. The first sentence of this translation is taken from Ratner (1980: 25).

61. The interest in rhetoric, sparked by Buelow (1980), is reflected in Bonds (1991) and Sisman (1993). The scepticism was voiced, among others, by Neubauer (1986) and Hoyt (1994, 2001). Rumph (2012) correlates the opposition between rhetoric and semiotics with that between rationalism of René Descartes and sensualism of John Locke. He suggests that the decline of the rhetorical tradition was caused by the rise of sensualism, but the opposition between rhetoric and sensualism is historically unfounded. Writings of Mattheson and Forkel demonstrate that the tradition of rhetoric and the philosophy of sensualism could be embraced by one and the same author. Even the opposition between the neoclassical and sensualist aesthetics was not absolute, as pointed out by Christensen (Baker and Christensen 1995: 4).

62. For a summary of Mattheson's project of musical rhetoric, see Dreyfus (1996: 5–8).

63. For a discussion of these categories, see Baker and Christensen (1995: 17–20, 119–30).

64. Bonds (1991: 83) suggests that Mattheson's classification might have been inspired by Gottsched's *Ausführliche Redekunst* (1736), but this seems unlikely in light of Mattheson's conflict with Gottsched (Kross 1983).

65. This sentence was quoted or paraphrased by Du Bos (1719, 1: 674), Batteux (Le Huray and Day 1981: 50), Rousseau (1986: 243), Sulzer (1792–94, 3: 422), Forkel (1788: 3), and Koch (1802: col. 994). Some of these quotations are mentioned by Hosler (1981: 45), from whom I take the English translation.

66. Instead, he proposes that they reflect the idiosyncratic use of this concept by Giambattista Vico (2012: 90–94).

67. For a brief summary of Heinichen, Mattheson, and Scheibe on invention, see Bonds (1991: 81–82). Similar opinions were expressed by Sulzer (1792–94, 3: 379) and Kirnberger (1776: 152; 1982: 416).

68. The term *loci topici*, derived from the Greek *topoi* and Latin *loci communes*, occurs in German sources since the seventeenth century (Buelow 1966: 162). The semantic problems of this linguistic amalgamate are criticized by Mattheson (1731: 1).

69. "Was haben wir nicht vor ein noch zur Zeit unergründliches Meer vor uns an der eintzigen Expression der Affecten und Worte in der Music?" (Heinichen 1711: 9).

70. "Über haupt [sic] könte man erstlich auff die *Tendresse* des Affectes fallen, und da möchte sich unter andern in einer *Siciliana*, (welche Art der *Composition* gern etwas *languissantes* bey sich führet) folgende *Invention* angeben" (Heinichen 1728: 62).

71. Mattheson took his list of topics from Erdmann Neumeister, who presented it in a lecture given at the University of Leipzig in 1695. This list differs from Cicero's in a few details, and Mattheson alters it further by substituting *locus descriptionis* for Neumeister's *locus definitionis*. See Tatlow (1991: 117–18) and Allanbrook (2014: 92, 203–4 n. 39–40) for further details.

72. This conclusion, drawn from my discussion of topics throughout this introduction, answers the question raised by Sisman: "But what aspect of rhetoric subsumes topics?" (1993b: 69). She speculates that they may belong to invention (*inventio*), arrangement (*dispositio*), style (*elocutio*), or delivery (*pronuntiatio*). While there seems to be no reason to relate topics to *dispositio*, their relation to *pronuntiatio* is a consequence of their relation to style (*elocutio*).

According to Scheibe (1745: 139–40), "style is a certain manner of musical performance and belongs mainly to execution" (*der Styl ist eine gewisse Manier des musikalischen Vortrags, und gehöret hauptsächlich zur Ausdrückung*).

73. "Es ist schwer, genau zu bestimmen, was in jedem Werk zu den Gedanken oder zur Schreibart gehöre" (Sulzer 1792–94, 4: 328).

74. This is the slippage from *ratio difficilis* to *ratio facilis* mentioned in note 52.

References

Agawu, V. Kofi. 1991. *Playing with Signs: A Semiotic Interpretation of Classic Music.* Princeton: Princeton University Press.

——. 2008. Topic Theory: Achievement, Critique, Prospects. In *Passagen, IMS Kongress Zürich 2007: Fünf Hauptvorträge, Five Key Note Speeches*, ed. Laurenz Lütteken and Hans-Joachim Hinrichsen, 38–69. Kassel: Bärenreiter.

——. 2009. *Music as Discourse: Semiotic Adventures in Romantic Music.* New York: Oxford University Press.

Allanbrook, Wye Jamison. 1983. *Rhythmic Gesture in Mozart:* Le nozze di Figaro *and* Don Giovanni. Chicago: University of Chicago Press.

——. 1988. "Ear-Tickling Nonsense": A New Context for Musical Expression in Mozart's "Haydn" Quartets." *St. John Review* 38: 1–24.

——. 1992. Two Threads through the Labyrinth: Topic and Process in the First Movements of K. 332 and K. 333. In *Convention in Eighteenth- and Nineteenth-Century Music: Essays in Honor of Leonard G. Ratner*, ed. Wye J. Allanbrook, Janet M. Levy, and William P. Mahrt, 125–71. Stuyvesant: Pendragon.

——. 1996. Comic Issues in Mozart's Piano Concertos. In *Mozart's Piano Concertos: Text, Context, Interpretation*, ed. Neal Zaslaw, 75–106. Ann Arbor: University of Michigan Press.

——. 2002. Theorizing the Comic Surface. In *Music in the Mirror: Reflections on the History of Music Theory and Literature for the Twenty-First Century*, ed. Andreas Giger and Thomas J. Mathiesen, 195–216. Lincoln: University of Nebraska Press.

——. 2014. *The Secular Commedia: Comic Mimesis in Late Eighteenth-Century Music*, ed. Mary Ann Smart and Richard Taruskin. Berkeley: University of California Press.

Baker, Nancy Kovaleff and Thomas Christensen. 1995. *Aesthetics and the Art of Musical Composition in the German Enlightenment.* Cambridge: Cambridge University Press.

Barry, Kevin. 1987. *Language, Music and the Sign: A Study in Aesthetics, Poetics and Poetic Practice from Collins to Coleridge.* Cambridge: Cambridge University Press.

Barker-Benfield, Graham J. 1992. *The Culture of Sensibility: Sex and Society in Eighteenth-Century Britain.* Chicago: University of Chicago Press.

Barthes, Roland. 1986. *The Responsibility of Forms.* Trans. R. Howard. Oxford: Blackwell.

Batteux, Charles. 1746. *Les Beaux Arts réduits à un même principe.* Paris: Durand.

Bonds, Mark Evan. 1991. *Wordless Rhetoric: Musical Form and the Metaphor of the Oration.* Cambridge, MA: Harvard University Press.

Brossard, Sébastien de. 1703. *Dictionnaire de musique.* Paris: Ballard.

Buelow, George J. 1966. The *Loci Topici* and Affect in Late Baroque Music: Heinichen's Practical Demonstration. *Music Review* 27: 161–76.

——. 1980. Rhetoric and Music. In *The New Grove Dictionary of Music and Musicians*, ed. Stanley Sadie, vol. 15, 793–803. London: Macmillan.

——. 1983. Johann Mattheson and the Invention of the *Affektenlehre*. In *New Mattheson Studies*, ed. George J. Buelow and Hans Joachim Marx, 393–407. Cambridge: Cambridge University Press.

Bukofzer, Manfred. 1947. *Music in the Baroque Era*. New York: Norton.

Caplin, William. 2005. On the Relation of Musical *Topoi* to Formal Function. *Eighteenth-Century Music* 2/1: 113–24.

Chua, Daniel K. L. 1999. *Absolute Music and the Construction of Meaning*. Cambridge: Cambridge University Press.

Cumming, Naomi. 2000. *The Sonic Self: Musical Subjectivity and Signification*. Bloomington: Indiana University Press.

Curtius, Ernst Robert. 1953. *European Literature and the Latin Middle Ages*. Trans. Willard R. Trask. London: Routledge & Paul.

Descartes, René. 1649. *Les passions de l'âme*. Paris: H. Legras.

Doni, Giovanni Battista. 1635. *Compendio del trattato de'generi e de'modi della musica*. Rome: Fei.

Dreyfus, Laurence. 1996. *Bach and the Patterns of Invention*. Cambridge, MA: Harvard University Press.

DuBos, Jean-Baptiste. 1719. *Réflexions critiques sur la poësie et sur la peinture*. 2 vols. Paris: Jean Mariette.

Eco, Umberto. 1976. *A Theory of Semiotics*. Bloomington: Indiana University Press.

Engel, Johann Jakob. 1780. *Über die musikalische Malerey*. Berlin: Voss.

——. 1998. On Painting in Music. In *Source Readings in Music History*, rev. ed., vol. 5, ed. Wye Jamison Allanbrook, 220–31. New York: Norton.

Forkel, Johann Nikolaus. 1788. *Allgemeine Geschichte der Musik*. Vol. 1. Leipzig: Schwickert.

Geck, Martin. 1995. Humor und Melancholie als kategoriale Bestimmungen der „absoluten" Musik. In *Studien zur Musikgeschichte: Eine Festschrift für Ludwig Finscher*, ed. Annegrit Laubenthal, 309–16. Kassel: Bärenreiter.

Gottsched, Johann Christoph. 1730. *Versuch einer Critischen Dichtkunst vor die Deutschen*. Leipzig: Bernhard Christoph Breitkopf.

——. 1736. *Ausführliche Redekunst*. Leipzig: Bernhard Christoph Breitkopf.

——. 1751. *Versuch einer Critischen Dichtkunst*, new expanded ed. Leipzig: Bernhard Christoph Breitkopf.

Grétry, André-Ernest-Modeste. 1978. *Memoiren oder Essays über die Musik*, ed. Peter Gülke. Trans. Dorothea Gülke. Wilhelmshaven: Heinrichshofen.

Harriss, Ernest C. 1981. *Johann Mattheson's* Der vollkommene Capellmeister: *A Revised Translation with Critical Commentary*. Ann Arbor, MI: UMI Research Press.

Hatten, Robert. 1994. *Musical Meaning in Beethoven: Markedness, Correlation, and Interpretation*. Bloomington: Indiana University Press.

——. 2004. *Interpreting Musical Gestures, Topics, and Tropes: Mozart, Beethoven, Schubert*. Bloomington: Indiana University Press.

Heartz, Daniel. *Haydn, Mozart, and the Viennese School, 1740–1780*. New York: Norton.

Heinichen, Johann David. 1711. *Neu erfundene und gründliche Anweisung zu vollkommener Erlernung des General-Basses*. Hamburg: Benjamin Schiller. Reprint, Kassel: Bärenreiter, 2000.

——. 1728. *Der General-Bass in der Composition*. Dresden: Author. Reprint, Hildesheim: Georg Olms, 1994.

Hosler, Bellamy. 1981. *Changing Aesthetic Views of Instrumental Music in 18th-Century Germany*. Ann Arbor, MI: UMI Research Press.

Hoyt, Peter. 1994. Review of *Wordless Rhetoric: Musical Form and the Metaphor of the Oration* by Mark Evan Bonds. *Journal of Music Theory* 38/1: 123–43.

——. 2001. Rhetoric and Music: §II. After 1750. In *The New Grove Dictionary of Music and Musicians*, 2nd ed., ed. Stanley Sadie and John Tyrrell, vol. 21, 270–73. London: Macmillan.

Irving, John. 1998. *Mozart: The "Haydn" Quartets*. Cambridge: Cambridge University Press.

Katz, Erich. 1926. *Die musikalischen Stilbegriffe des 17. Jahrhunderts*. Ph.D. diss., Albert-Ludwigs-Universität zu Freiburg i. Br.

Kircher, Athanasius. 1650. *Musurgia universalis*. Rome: Francesco Corbelletti. Reprint, Hildesheim: Georg Olms, 1970.

Kirnberger, Johann Philipp. 1771–79. *Die Kunst des reinen Satzes in der Musik*. 2 vols. Vol. 1, Berlin: Rottmann, 1771. Vol. 2, sections 1–3, Berlin and Königsberg: Decker und Hartung, 1776, 1777, and 1779.

——. 1982. *The Art of Strict Musical Composition*. Trans. David Beach and Jurgen Thym. New Haven: Yale University Press.

Koch, Heinrich Christoph. 1782–93. *Versuch einer Anleitung zur Composition*. 3 vols. Vol. 1, Rudolstadt, 1782. Vols. 2 and 3, Leipzig: Adam Friedrich Böhme, 1787 and 1793. Reprint, Hildesheim: Georg Olms, 1969.

——. 1802. *Musikalisches Lexikon*. Frankfurt-am-Main: August Hermann der Jüngere. Reprint, Kassel: Bärenreiter, 2001.

——. 1983. *Introductory Essay on Composition*. Trans. Nancy Kovaleff Baker. New Haven: Yale University Press.

Kross, Siegfried. 1983. Mattheson und Gottsched. In *New Mattheson Studies*, ed. George J. Buelow and Hans Joachim Marx, 327–44. Cambridge: Cambridge University Press.

Le Huray, Peter and James Day. 1981. *Music and Aesthetics in the Eighteenth and Early-Nineteenth Centuries*. Cambridge: Cambridge University Press.

Lidov, David. 1999. *Elements of Semiotics*. New York: St. Martin's Press.

Locke, John. 1690. *An Essay Concerning Human Understanding*. 4 vols. London: Thomas Basset.

Mattheson, Johann. 1713. *Das Neu-Eröffnete Orchestre*. Hamburg: Benjamin Schillers Witwe.

——. 1717. *Das beschützte Orchester*. Hamburg: Schiller. Reprint, Kassel: Bärenreiter, 1981.

——. 1731. *Grosse General-Baß-Schule*. Hamburg: Kißner.

——. 1737. *Kern melodischer Wissenschaft*. Hamburg: Christian Herold. Reprint, Hildesheim: Georg Olms, 1976.

——. 1739. *Der vollkommene Capellmeister*. Hamburg: Christian Herold. Reprint, Kassel: Bärenreiter, 1954.

McClelland, Clive. 2012. *Ombra: Supernatural Music in the Eighteenth Century*. Lanham, UK: Lexington Books.

McKay, Nicholas. 2007. On Topics Today. *Zeitschrift der Gesellschaft für Musiktheorie* 4/1. Available: http://www.gmth.de/zeitschrift/artikel/251.aspx. Accessed 12 April 2012.

McKee, Eric. 2005. Mozart in the Ballroom: Minuet–Trio Contrast and the Aristocracy in Self-Portrait. *Music Analysis* 24/3: 383–436.

——. 2012. *Decorum of the Minuet, Delirium of the Waltz: A Study of Dance–Music Relations in 3/4 Time*. Bloomington: Indiana University Press.

Mirka, Danuta. 2008. Introduction. In *Communication in Eighteenth-Century Music*, ed. Danuta Mirka and Kofi Agawu, 1–10. Cambridge: Cambridge University Press.

——. 2014. Review of *Mozart and Enlightenment Semiotics* by Stephen Rumph. *Journal of Music Theory* 58/1: 67–77.

Momigny, Jérôme-Joseph de. 1806. *Cours complet d'harmonie et de composition*. 2 vols. Paris: Author.

Monelle, Raymond. 2000. *The Sense of Music: Semiotic Essays*. Princeton, NJ: Princeton University Press.

——. 2006. *The Musical Topic: Hunt, Military and Pastoral*. Bloomington: Indiana University Press.

Neubauer, John. 1986. *The Emancipation of Music from Language: Departure from Mimesis in Eighteenth-Century Aesthetics*. New Haven: Yale University Press.

Niedt, Friedrich Erhard. 1721. *Musikalische Handleitung*. Vol. 2, ed. Johann Mattheson. Hamburg: Benjamin Schillers Witwe und Joh. Christoph Kißner.

Otto, Irmgard. 1937. *Deutsche Musikanschauung im siebzehnten Jahrhundert*. Berlin: Hayn.

Paddison, Max. 2010. Mimesis and the Aesthetics of Musical Expression. *Music Analysis* 29/1–3: 126–48.

Palisca, Claude V. 1983. The Genesis of Mattheson's Style Classification. In *New Mattheson Studies*, ed. George J. Buelow and Hans Joachim Marx, 409–23. Cambridge: Cambridge University Press.

Powers, Harold. 1995. Reading Mozart's Music: Text and Topic, Syntax and Sense. *Current Musicology* 57: 5–44.

Pritchard, Matthew. 2012. "The Moral Background of the Work of Art": "Character" in German Musical Aesthetics, 1780–1850. *Eighteenth-Century Music* 9/1: 63–80.

Ratner, Leonard G. 1980. *Classic Music: Expression, Form, and Style*. New York: Schirmer.

——. 1991. Topical Content in Mozart's Keyboard Sonatas. *Early Music* 19/4: 615–19.

[Raupach, Christoph.] 1717. *Veritophili deutliche Beweis-Gründe*, ed. Johann Mattheson. Hamburg: Benjamin Schillers Erben.

Rousseau, Jean-Jacques. 1768. *Dictionnaire de musique*. Paris: Veuve Duchesne.

——. 1986. *The First and Second Discourses Together with the Replies to Critics and Essay on the Origin of Languages*, ed. and trans. Victor Gourevitch. New York: Harper and Row.

Rumph, Stephen. 2012. *Mozart and Enlightenment Semiotics*. Berkeley: University of California Press.

Scacchi, Marco. 1649. *Breve discorso sopra la musica moderna*. Warsaw: Elert.

Scheibe, Johann Adolph. 1745. *Critischer Musikus*, new expanded ed. Leipzig: Breitkopf.

Schmidt, Marlene. 1981. *Zur Theorie des musikalischen Charakters*. Munich and Salzburg: Emil Katzbichler.

Schubart, Christian Friedrich Daniel. 1806. *Ideen zu einer Ästhetik der Tonkunst*, ed. Ludwig Schubart. Vienna: J. V. Degen. Reprint, Darmstadt: Wissenschaftliche Buchgesellschaft, 1969.

Sisman, Elaine. 1993a. *Haydn and the Classical Variation*. Cambridge, MA: Harvard University Press.

——. 1993b. *Mozart: The "Jupiter" Symphony No. 41 in C major, K. 551*. Cambridge: Cambridge University Press.

Sulzer, Johann Georg. 1792–94. *Allgemeine Theorie der schönen Künste*, new expanded 2nd ed. 4 vols. Leipzig: Weidmann. Reprint, Hildesheim: Georg Olms, 1994.

Tatlow, Ruth. 1991. *Bach and the Riddle of the Number Alphabet*. Cambridge: Cambridge University Press.

Thomas, Downing A. 1995. *Music and the Origins of Language: Theories from the French Enlightenment*. Cambridge: Cambridge University Press.

Turino, Thomas. 1999. Signs of Imagination, Identity, and Experience: A Peircian Semiotic Theory for Music. *Ethnomusicology* 43/2: 221–55.

Wellbery, David E. 1984. *Lessing's* Laocoon: *Semiotics and Aesthetics in the Age of Reason*. Cambridge: Cambridge University Press.

SECTION I

ORIGINS AND DISTINCTIONS

CHAPTER 1

··

TOPICS AND OPERA BUFFA

··

MARY HUNTER

OPERA buffa, wildly popular across Europe for the latter half of the eighteenth century, and seedbed for stylistic innovation and its associated debates and *querelles*, is often said to be the source of late eighteenth-century instrumental music's proclivity to topical mixture. Wye Allanbrook states the case most forcefully in *The Secular Commedia: Comic Mimesis in Late Eighteenth-Century Music*:

> All of these new features [of late eighteenth-century style], as I hope I have demonstrated beyond a reasonable doubt, stem from opera, and opera buffa in particular. These comic-opera values, I concluded—an interminably varied, all-inclusive image of a peopled topological space given a strong dramatic impetus by a powerful thrust toward closure—transferred themselves to instrumental music, but without the precise story-bound meanings that a text provides. (Allanbrook 2014: 129)

Richard Taruskin's chapter on "the comic style" in his influential *Oxford History of Western Music* follows Allanbrook closely, asserting that all of late eighteenth-century music is at base a version of (musical) comedy (Taruskin 2005: 437). However, even without Allanbrook and Taruskin, the idea that opera buffa was a seminal influence on late eighteenth-century instrumental music is now more or less tacitly assumed. This is perhaps best illustrated by the following paragraph in the standard music history text, *A History of Western Music* by Peter Burkholder, Donald Jay Grout, and Claude Palisca:

> The periodic phrasing, tuneful melodies, simple harmonies, spare accompaniment, direct expression, *emotional fluidity, strong stylistic contrasts*, and *amusing mixtures of elements* that characterized Italian comic opera became central elements of the international idiom of the later eighteenth century. (Burkholder, Grout, and Palisca 2010: 489; italics mine)[1]

And as *fons et origo* of the current interest in topics, Leonard Ratner is worth quoting:

> Comic-rhetoric—*quick juxtapositions of contrasting ideas*, short and lively figures, *active interplay of dialogue*, light textures, marked articulation, *unexpected turns*—is

found throughout the great instrumental and vocal works of the classic style. (Ratner 1980: 395; italics mine)

It is also not unusual to find opera buffa either listed as a topic among other topics, or as a style to which instrumental music has frequent recourse. For example, Alexander Silbiger invokes both opera buffa and *commedia dell'arte* in his essay on topics in the *locus classicus* of topical discussion, Mozart's Piano Sonata in F major, K. 332 (Silbiger 2000, cited in Agawu 2008: 41 n. 2). And Kofi Agawu includes opera buffa in his listing of the "universe" of topics, at least as covered in his *Playing with Signs* (1991: 31).[2]

Opera, both buffa and not, also shows up among the first examples in descriptions of individual topics, as if to validate the set of cultural memes typically associated with a given musical formula or cliché. Clive McClelland's book on the *ombra* topic in all genres, for example, locates the source of the topic's identity in Hermann Abert's description of an accompanied recitative in Hasse's *Cleofide*, in which the heroine hallucinates a variety of appalling supernatural phenomena (McClelland 2012: 1).

These examples suggest several ways in which opera buffa is thought to relate to the issue of topicality in eighteenth-century music: as origin for topical variety in instrumental music, as a topic within instrumental music, and as a repository of topics with unambiguous referential, or correlative, meaning.[3] Let us take each of these in turn.

ORIGINS

As suggested above, it is generally taken as given that the galant style—the primary basis for the classical style—was operatic in origin. Both opera seria and opera buffa contributed regular periodicity and melody-plus-accompaniment texture to the break from Baroque musical habits, but only opera buffa is said to have contributed the jostling variety of topics—the quicksilver contrasts both between and within clearly defined and palpably cadence-oriented phrases, that are regularly cited as the defining feature of this style. The opening of Mozart's Piano Sonata in F major, K. 332, is the canonical example of this burgeoning topical variety.[4] Rather than relying on this hoary example, however, let us consider the last movement of Haydn's Symphony No. 104, where variously delicate (mm.1–18) and heavy-footed (mm. 19–28) peasant dances rub shoulders with contrapuntal devices both apparently "popular" (mm. 31–34) and obtrusively learned (mm. 84–98), with "Turkish" moments (mm. 44–52 and 108–16), identified by repetitive or awkward rhythms and crude harmonies or by the lack of any harmony at all, with opera-buffa scurrying (mm. 64–72), and performative brilliance (mm. 23–28). Example 1.1 gives the string parts for each of these topics.

Once one has started to identify these musical formulas or clichés with particular cultural commonplaces or stereotypes, or with the music that evokes them, it is almost inevitable that ideas about dialogism and theatricality will creep in and opera will be invoked. Allanbrook (2013) and Ratner (1980), among others, give ample evidence from

EXAMPLE **1.1** Topics in Haydn's Symphony No. 104 in D major, iv: (a) light-footed peasant dance with musette drone (mm. 1–6); (b) heavier-footed peasant dance (mm. 19–22); (c) "popular style" counterpoint (mm. 31–34); (d) learned style counterpoint (mm. 84–89); (e) Turkish style 1 (mm. 45–49); (f) Turkish style 2 (mm. 108–10); (g) opera buffa scurrying (mm. 65–68); (h) brilliant style (mm. 23–26).

(*Continued*)

EXAMPLE **1.1** (Continued)

contemporary sources that the classical instrumental style's mixing of expressive modes was noted by critics at the time, and some evidence that it was thought of (often not for the better) as theatrical: perhaps the classic quote on this topic is from Johann Adam Hiller, who laments the intrusion of Hans Wurst (a slapstick figure from Austrian street theater) into the otherwise noble realm of the symphony:

> Nowadays we hear so many concertos, symphonies, etc. that in their measured and magnificent tones allow us to perceive the dignity of music; but before one suspects it, in springs Hans Wurst, right into the middle of things, and the more serious the emotion that had immediately preceded his arrival, the more he arouses our sympathy with his vulgar antics. (Sisman 1997: 22)

This passage deals with the most potentially troubling kind of mixture, namely the juxtaposition of the "low" style with something more elevated. Daniel Weber, writing in 1800, still faults opera buffa itself for not respecting the boundaries between noble comedy and low farce:

> Only the Italian versifiers, who are not troubled by the content of a theater piece, put a *buffo nobile*, a *buffo di mezzo carattere*, a *buffo caricato*, a pair of girls *di mezzo carattere* and a *buffa caricata* together in the most peculiar manner, and excuse themselves from this rule.

> Nur die *Rimailleurs* der Welschen, die den Inhalt eines Theaterstückes für nichts anschlagen, einen *buffo nobile, buffo di mezzo carattere,* und einen *buffo caricato* und ein paar Frauenzimmerchen *di mezzo carattere* und eine *carricata* immer auf die seltsamste Weise zusammenstellen, setzen sich über diese Regel hinaus. (Weber 1800: cols. 137–38)

On the other hand, Weber uses the operas of "Guglielmi, Piccini, Paisiello, Dazaides, d'Allayrac, Hiller, and Neefe" (col. 140) as examples of the noble- or high-comic vein. He is evasive about the relation between comedy in vocal music, which seems to depend on the juxtaposition of different styles, both in noble comedy and in caricature, and the comedy in instrumental music, where wit is the characteristic he emphasizes. It is worth remembering, however, that his purpose is to parse out the variety of classes of comedy possible in music rather than to trace the history of comic characteristics in different kinds of music. For our purposes the important element of Weber's essay is his discomfort with the mixing of levels and the fact that opera buffa is—still in 1792[5]—the place where he finds it most marked.

As Weber's dismissive remarks about hack comic operas suggest, among the most striking and thus presumably influential characteristics of topical variety in opera buffa were the mixed-rank casts of most full-length works, with characters ranging from servants or peasants to some level of nobility, each of which had distinct musical characteristics. But added to the mixedness of the casts were the deployment of action-ensembles involving the simultaneous or juxtaposed utterances of these different types and the inclusion of actively comic (usually male) arias in which the singer is depicted as in some way confused, incompetent or frenetic, thus necessitating frequent changes of musical mode or address. These elements were to some degree or other characteristic of comic opera throughout the century, and they are often opposed to the more homogeneous nature of opera seria, where the characters are all of comparable rank, where ensembles are few and theatrically static, and where characters operate on a high level of eloquence and topical consistency.

The comic characteristics are all evident in Baldassare Galuppi's 1755 opera *La diavolessa* (libretto by Carlo Goldoni). The characters range from the chambermaid Ghiandina to the Conte and Contessa Nastri, and include a foolish Don (Poppone), a landlord (Falco), and the artisan-class couple (Dorina and Giannino). Like many mid-century Goldonian operas, the cast is focused on the middle ranks of society (even the Conte and Contessa rent their land from Falco), but the plot hinges on the comedy of Don Poppone's mistaking Dorina and Giannino for the Count and Countess, and the nonnoble couple's attempt to profit from this. In the second act finale (finales being the *ne plus ultra* of action ensembles) we see quite frequent topical change as Dorina and Giannino, dressed as spirits, participate in an elaborate plot to con Don Poppone out of his money (Example 1.2). The excerpt starts as a merry gigue as Falco notes that the spirits have to be paid ("Ai spirti dell'oro convien offerir"), but changes to something more clumsy and frantic with loud offbeat ornaments as the terrified Poppone tries to suggest another place the gold might be ("dell'orognor sì più tosto di qui") and Falco tells him to keep digging ("Cavate, battete"). The frenzy and terror rise a notch when Giannino adopts something between *ombra* and *tempesta* mode to impersonate the spirit's stentorian demand ("Monete, monete").[6]

Finally, the impecunious Giannino—he plays the basso buffo role—describes in an aria how, as a "nobleman" (his current disguise), he will treat ladies, gentlemen, and lower-class people; he also offers commentary on the ladies and gentlemen. Topical contrast in the music (Example 1.3) enacts his social "flexibility" as it moves quickly between more galant and more comic idioms, and between march, minuet, and gigue.

Colle dame, di Madame	With the ladies, of mesdames,
servitor di buon cuor	I am a loyal servant
all'onor della beltà.	in honor of beauty.
(Non ci ho grazia in verità.)	(But truthfully, I have no grace.)
Coi Signori, riverisco,	With the gentlemen, I'll bow,
Mi esibisco, mi offerisco	Show myself off, and behave
Colla nostra autorità.	With our authority.
(Oh malissimo anderà.)	(This is going to go very badly.)
Vuò provar con bassa gente	I'll prove insolent with the plebs
insolente, [non dò niente	[I'll give them nothing
pagherò quando vorrò.	and pay when I feel like it.
Ne ho bisogno via di qua.]	I need to get out of here.]

These examples, taken from a single opera to show how different kinds of topical mixture coexisted in the same work, are entirely typical of opera buffa. A quick perusal of any score in this genre will generate many comparable examples. At the same time,

EXAMPLE **1.2** Galuppi, *La diavolessa*, Act 2 Finale, mm. 144–59.

opera buffa's characteristic habit of juxtaposing palpably different musical gestures within the same large musical section, in response either to specific words or to the situation in general, was not absolutely unique to it; indeed it is not unusual to find topical shifts even in opera seria arias, in places other than the juncture between the A and B sections of a da capo form. Take, for example, the first period of the first aria for Megacle in Johann Adolf Hasse's Metastasian opera *L'Olimpiade* of 1756 (Example 1.4), where the melodic motives suggest in turn pride ("superbo di me stesso"), an amoroso sentiment ("quel caro nome"), movement toward a sigh ("come mi stà nel cor"), and a return to a mixture of pride and virtuosity ("andrò portando in fronte"). These changes are

EXAMPLE 1.3 Galuppi, *La diavolessa*, Act 1 Scene 9, "Colle dame, colle dame," mm. 5–29.

not as striking as the buffo Giannino's in describing his different manners of address—for one thing they happen within a constant tempo, meter, and texture—but they are nonetheless sufficiently coordinated with the words to be noticeable, and if the hand gestures and facial expression of the singer changed in synchronization with the shades of meaning in the text, as the acting manuals of the time suggested (Barnett 1987: 149), the topical variety in the music would be amplified. Similarly, it is worth noting that the characters of opera seria, despite being from a relatively narrow stratum of society, always represented a mixture of aesthetic and ethical stereotypes: the innocent beloved, the jealous princess, the heroic but conflicted lover, the faithful confidant, the virtuous ruler, and so on. And although these characters were not as firmly associated with

EXAMPLE 1.4 Hasse, *L'Olimpiade*, Act 1 Scene 2, "Superbo di me stesso" mm. 22–35.

particular musical characteristics as were some buffa characters (see below for a discussion of topics within opera buffa), the music and dramatic *Gestalt* of each character was of course constituted by an amalgamation of recognizable and contrasted topics. Again, it is important to remember that the compositional features associated with opera buffa may be typical of it, and may strongly characterize it, but they also may not be absolutely unique to it.

However, if we do take seriously the notion that opera buffa was an important source for classical-style instrumental music with respect to the mixing of topics then it behooves us to compare the ways topical mixture played out in the two genres. Obviously the juxtaposition of social opposites (most notably high and low, but also public and private and masculine and feminine) is shared by opera buffa and instrumental music. For example, Giannino's aria is structured around high and low, and the Haydn symphony movement noted above juxtaposes peasants with scholars and uncouth barbarians with virtuosi. But the pace and manner of the juxtaposition is quite different. For example, in the Haydn, where the first *alla turca* moment occurs, it begins as an elision with the end of the previous phrase (m. 44) and it is not really until the offbeat *fz* in m. 45 that we realize that we are in the realm of the barbarians (Example 1.5a). Similarly, the buffa-like moment in m. 65 takes on its topical significance by developing the tail end of the counterpoint to the first group.[7] Only the change in dynamic in m. 65 and then the little anacrustic figure in the accompaniment signals the change in topic (Example 1.5b). By contrast (and this is admittedly a crude contrast, but lack of subtlety is characteristic of most opera buffa), Giannino's changes of address are typically preceded by cadences and thus essentially announced in advance, especially given the subject of the text. In the second-act finale (see Example 1.3) the topical changes are both less stiff and more subtle, perhaps because they are

EXAMPLE 1.5 Haydn, Symphony No. 104 in D major, iv: (a) mm. 42–49; (b) mm. 65–72.

signaled most strongly in the accompaniment. Nevertheless, the changes tend to coincide with changes in speaker, which mitigates the delicious momentary sense of topical ambiguity that the Haydn (and so much comparable instrumental music) projects. This co-ordination also gives a sense of a rather crude mechanical process of grinding through the changes in topic. It is, of course, precisely the over-obvious mechanism that makes moments like these in the Galuppi (and so much comparable opera buffa) comic, but that mode of comedy was not exported wholesale to instrumental music.

INSTRUMENTAL MUSIC'S READINESS
FOR THE COMIC MODE

It was an eighteenth-century commonplace—uttered throughout the century—that the *Cammerstyl*—that is, the style of most purely instrumental music—allowed for a more disjunctive (and, by implication, topically or affectively various) melodic progress than could the church and theater styles. As early as 1739, and with composers such as Corelli and Vivaldi rather than Galuppi in mind, Johann Mattheson described the chamber (or instrumental) style as follows:

> Slurs, syncopations, arpeggios, alternations between tutti and solo, between adagio and allegro, etc., are such essential and characteristic things that one for the most part seeks them in vain in churches and on the stage...even if the melody should occasionally suffer a little thereby, it is still embellished, ornamented and effervescent. That is its distinctiveness. (Harriss 1981: 222)

Obviously the relevant features here are the alternations between forces and styles in idiomatically instrumental music, and Mattheson's description of the absence of such alternations in the church and theatrical styles is quite striking.

An even more common comment about the chamber style was that it encouraged much finer distinctions and much closer working than did the theater or church styles. For example, the entry "Cammermusik" in Sulzer's *Allgemeine Theorie der schönen Künste*, first published in 1771, notes that the texture in chamber music can be more complex than is the case in public (that is, church or theater) music:

> Since chamber music is for connoisseurs and amateurs, the pieces can be set in a more learned and artificed way than those destined for public use, where everything has to be simpler and more singable so that everybody can understand....Generally, then, one has to work harder in public music, which has a clear purpose, to make sure that the expression can be grasped in the simplest and surest way; and in chamber music one must use the strictest technique of composition, a more refined expression, and more artful turns of phrase.

> Da die Cammermusik für Kenner und Liebhaber ist, so können die Stüke gelehrter und künstlicher gesetzt seyn, als die zum öffentlichen Gebrauch bestimmt sind, wo alles mehr einfach und cantabel seyn muß, damit jedermann es fasse.... Ueberhaupt also wird in der öffentlichen Musik, wo man allemal einen bestimmten Zwek hat, mehr darauf zu sehen seyn, daß der Ausdruk auf die einfacheste und sicherste Weise erhalten werde, und in der Cammermusik wird man sich des äusserst reinen Satzes, eines feinern Ausdruks und künstlicherer Wendungen bedienen müssen. (Sulzer 1771: 189)

Although this is not superficially about topical variety, the notion of "more artful turns of phrase," when contrasted with the "simpler and more singable" mode of church and theatrical styles, certainly leaves room for subtle but meaningful alterations in topic.

Heinrich Christoph Koch's entry on the chamber style in his *Musikalisches Lexikon* echoes parts of Sulzer's quite closely, but stresses much more explicitly the imaginative effects of affective disjunction, also linking this to closer, more refined listening:

> If music has the purpose of pleasing a few people, or even a whole gathering, by means of the expression of happy, tender, sad, or elevated sentiments arbitrarily following one another, or of representing tone paintings that allow the imagination to freely play with the ideas derived from them, one thus understands the intention of the chamber style. Since works of this sort are primarily intended for connoisseurs, and particular amateurs of the art, this style distinguishes itself particularly by having all parts of the whole more finely imagined than in works that have another purpose.

> Wenn die Musik den Zweck hat, einzelne Personen, oder eine ganze Gesellschaft durch den Ausdruck willkührlich auf einander folgender, froher, zärtlicher, trauriger, oder erhabener Gefühle zu vergnügen, oder auch solche Tongemälde darzustellen, die der Einbildungskraft freyes Spiel der daraus zu schöpfenden Ideen überlässt, so bedient man sich zu dieser Absicht des Kammerstyls, der, weil Tonstücke von der so eben angezeigten Art zunächst für Kenner oder besondere Liebhaber der Kunst bestimmt sind, sich besonders dadurch unterscheidet, dass alle Theile des Ganzen feiner ausgemalt sind, als bey Tonstücken, die eine andere Bestimmung haben. (Koch 1802: col. 1454)

There is no suggestion here that the instrumental style owes anything to comic opera. At the same time, Koch notes later in the entry that the theatrical style is both less nuanced than the chamber style and very hard to distinguish from it. What I am suggesting overall, then, is that instrumental music, with its propensity to variety and expressive subtlety and/or multiplicity, was in a sense by midcentury already discursively primed not only to accommodate the topical mélange of opera buffa, but also to turn it into something more finely wrought. In other words, opera buffa was surely a potent resource for topical variety in instrumental music, but sonatas and symphonies also translated the habits of opera into instrumental music's already well established habits of variety and fluidity.

Opera Buffa as a Topic in
Instrumental Music

As mentioned above, opera buffa is quite commonly cited not only as the source for aspects of late eighteenth-century musical style but also as a topic within instrumental music. In his *Playing with Signs*, Kofi Agawu describes the opening of Mozart's Piano Concerto in C major, K. 467 (Example 1.6), as "theatrical" and "opera buffa like." He adds: "The articulation calls the theatre to mind—especially the short pithy figures of opera buffa. One can almost hear Leporello lurking behind the scenes" (Agawu 1991: 34–35). And indeed, the resemblance to Leporello's "Notte e giorno faticar," the opening solo of the opera, does seem striking at first glance (Example 1.7). But a closer comparison of these two moments is instructive. The concerto's decorous, all-*piano* two-measure motive has neither the repetitiveness of Leporello's figure, nor the "grotesque" intrusion of the loud fanfare figure at the end of the motive. Whereas the Leporello motive is immediately comic by virtue both of its local "poverty" of invention and its grotesque—or at least rude—juxtaposition of loud and soft in, as it were, the wrong order, the opening of the concerto is simply a quiet, staccato march that may in some relatively undefined way remind a listener of opera buffa. Is Agawu's invocation of a topic, then simply a case of an amplified thematic resemblance? If not, how might we distinguish a "regular" staccato march (if such a thing exists) from one that counts as an opera buffa topic, whether or not it is reminiscent of a particular moment in a well-known comic opera? One feels intuitively that the soft dynamic of this opening may have something to do with Agawu's invocation of topicality rather than local resemblance, but that does not narrow the field very much. Are all quiet staccato marches reminiscent of opera buffa?

Similarly, Charles Rosen describes the Presto final section of the last movement of Mozart's Piano Concerto in G major, K. 453 (Example 1.8), as an "opera buffa coda" (Rosen 1971: 226). This is another march—*pianissimo*—in staccato quarters: a sequence starting on the tonic and continuing on the third over thrumming

EXAMPLE **1.6** Mozart, Piano Concerto in C major, K. 467/i, mm. 1–4.

EXAMPLE 1.7 Mozart, *Don Giovanni*, Act 1 Scene 1, "Notte e giorno faticar," mm. 1–5.

repeated eighteenths in the lower voices. This rudimentary melodic and textural device is demonstrably like the opening of many opera buffa overtures and also the beginning of the *stretto* sections of many finales, and thus might easily be understood as an element of opera buffa directly exported to instrumental music. But it seems likely that what prompted (or at least confirmed) Rosen's designation of the passage as opera-buffa-like was at least as much the quiet march gesture as the resemblance to some moments in actual comic operas. If that is the case, then we must ask once again whether all quiet staccato marches evoke opera buffa. Does the opening of the Alla Marcia section of the last movement of Beethoven's Ninth Symphony qualify as both *alla turca* and buffa, for example? How about the opening of Haydn's "Lark" quartet, Op. 64 No. 5 (Example 1.9)?

What the moments identified by Rosen and Agawu have in common beyond their march-like rhythms and melodies is that the normally proud striding motion of a march (often denoted by triadic melodies) is "subverted" by the soft dynamics and the staccato articulation of these passages. Both moments would be entirely plausible as actual marches if played loudly and less staccato: the triadic tune of K. 467, with the triple-sixteenth fanfare at the end of the phrase (m. 2), and the little answering tattoos in the wind parts of K. 453 confirm the military correlation in both. The fact that the "true" march characteristics of these moments are perceptible through the "subversive" veil of quiet dynamics and extremely staccato articulation gives them a slightly off-kilter quality that may evoke the gestural and bodily presence of opera buffa. Both these moments also communicate a sort of doubleness, possibly readable as irony, that resonates with a comment by the eighteenth-century opera theorist Antonio Planelli, who notes that comic roles are the proper vehicles for (male) actors of short stature—the implication

EXAMPLE 1.8 Mozart, Piano Concerto in G major, K. 453/iii, mm. 171–77.

being that short actors will make many of the same gestures as tall ones but they will be comic because they do not make them with the same grace or nobility (Planelli 1772: 85). These "tiptoe" marches, then, have an exactly analogous effect to a conspicuously under-sized actor trying to cover the same ground in the same number of steps as a tall one, and may signify both a generally comic idea, and the more specific, and more or less ridiculous, gestural world of the comic opera stage.

This comparison also clarifies why the Alla Marcia section of Beethoven's Ninth and the opening of Haydn's "Lark" quartet are not—at least not so obviously or com-fortably—examples of an opera buffa topic. The tune in the Haydn is perhaps too per-sistently scalar and continuous to be unambiguously march-like. Thus the staccato articulation and quiet dynamics are not subverting anything. In the Beethoven, the *alla turca* element is what colors the march, and the soft dynamic is easily interpreted

EXAMPLE 1.9 Haydn, String Quartet in D major, Op. 64 No. 5, "The Lark," i, mm. 1–8.

as geographical distance rather than a sort of incongruity of gesture.[8] Rosen's and Agawu's descriptions of their chosen moments as opera-buffa-like are thus entirely justifiable due partly to the exportation of opera buffa musical figures to instrumental music and, more significantly, to an evocation of the *gestural* world of the comic stage.

Rosen also identifies the very end of Mozart's F-major concerto, K. 459, with its cheeky antiphony between piano and orchestra, as buffa-like (Example 1.10). The antiphony may suggest two characters, the spirit of the music is clearly lighthearted, and the excessive repetition is comic, as is the foreshortening of the antiphony and alternation of the dynamics nine measures before the end. The little section from the duet between the Count and Figaro in the first act of Giovanni Paisiello's *Barbiere di Siviglia*, shown in Example 1.11, is similar in the mechanistic alternation of brief question and answer between the two characters, and also in the excessive number of repetitions.

Just as a march may need to have particular characteristics in order to evoke the world of opera buffa, so, of course, may antiphony. In his topical analysis of the first movement of Mozart's String Quartet in B flat major, K. 458, John Irving pursues the idea of the hunt topic through the piece. When he gets to the development section, however, much of which is conspicuously antiphonal, he notes that the hunt topic is attenuated without pointing out that it has morphed into a more buffa-like presentation (Irving 1998: 68–72). Perhaps the more sophisticated writing of this passage

EXAMPLE **1.10** Mozart, Piano Concerto in F major, K. 459/iii, mm. 487–504.

EXAMPLE 1.11 Paisiello, *Il barbiere di Siviglia*, Act 1 Scene 10, "Diamo alla noia il bando," mm. 108–14.

distances it from the stereotype of comic opera; perhaps the fact that it is a quartet whose model is "conversation" rather than a concerto with a "protagonist" prevents the theatrical notion of opera buffa from occurring to Irving. The point here is not that Irving should have identified this moment as buffa-like. Indeed, it is not clear that it is. The reason that Rosen's description of the end of the F-major concerto rings true as an example of an opera buffa topic is partly the antiphony (which suggests more than one interlocutor), partly the fact that it is easy in a concerto to hear piano and orchestra as theatrical protagonists, but largely the extraordinarily rudimentary nature of the material, which both echoes the primitive musical nature of some vocal lines in comic dialogue, and, to reiterate, concentrates the listener's attention on the *gesture* of passing the idea back and forth, as if the two characters were sticking out their tongues (or worse) at each other. Finally, my own description of mm. 65–72 of the finale of Haydn's Symphony No. 104 (see Example 1.6) as buffa-like depends entirely on the light-footed and dialogic quality of the music, which quite viscerally evokes the sense of several characters variously running and gesturing to each other.

Exportation versus Translation

The gestures that scholars have identified as opera-buffa-like are obviously not dissimilar to music one might find in opera buffa but they do not at all represent the music that is most particular to the genre—the opera buffa topics within opera buffa, so to speak. The musical devices within opera buffa that most effectively and unambiguously reference the genre itself are (1) patter, (2) short, neutral, recitative-like vocal fragments within a more highly profiled orchestral "blanket," and (3) highly gestural and illustrative orchestral accompaniments. These are devices that essentially never appear in serious opera and that are routinely used at the most "stereotypical" moments of opera buffa. Could these formulae be added to the comic-gesture repertory as markers of opera buffa?

Let us begin with patter. Patter is a standard feature of basso buffo arias and also (to a lesser extent) of lower-class female arias, and is also used in ensembles. It generally occurs after the beginning of a number, setting words that have already been heard once or twice, or, in finales, setting the same words again and again, and suggests panic, frenzy, or mounting confusion, anger, or inappropriate insistence on a subject. It is completely absent from opera seria, and the serious or more elevated numbers of opera buffa also eschew it entirely. The music of patter sections involves repeated notes, or repeated figures covering a narrow range, and such sections are often immediately comic. Their humorous effect relies on the "impossibly" quick spitting out of syllables and often on a more or less breathless contraction of a text. Is this translated to instrumental music in such a way as relatively unambiguously to indicate opera? One example cannot answer the question, but it can be suggestive. Measures 41–47 of the finale of Haydn's Symphony No. 101 (Example 1.12) could conceivably be thought to replicate patter in the antiphonal use of short eighth-note figures which cover a small pitch range. However, "extroversive semiosis" indicating patter—that is, a suggestion of an operatic analogue outside the frame of the symphony—seems to me not only questionable, in the absence of actual syllables, but also to take a distinctly secondary role to the "introversive semiosis" (loosely, structural significance) of the melodic sequence that conspicuously enacts the all-important modulation to the dominant.[9] In other words, if opera-buffa-like patter is a topic here, it is not all that prominent.[10] And in general, repetitive, fast, narrow-ranged, detached eighth or sixteenth notes in instrumental music are not terribly likely to draw attention to an operatic model. A listener *might* hear patter here, and a performer *might* use the idea of patter to lend a certain spritz to his or her playing, but its presence is anything but unambiguous.

The second very characteristic buffa device within opera buffa is the use of neutral or almost recitative-like vocal interjections carved out from, and set against, a more strongly characterized (and often repetitive) orchestral figure. The effect of this texture is to communicate both seamless musical/dramatic continuity and theatrical life and motion, as in Example 1.13 from Vincente Martín y Soler's *L'arbore di Diana*. This texture is not to

EXAMPLE 1.12 Haydn, Symphony No. 101 in D major, "The Clock," iv, mm. 41–47.

be found in instrumental music, even concertos. Usually, when the solo instrument in a concerto uses recitative-like, or brief and "neutral" phrases, it is more likely to be in alternation with the orchestra than set within a more continuous and highly profiled "blanket" of orchestral music, presumably so that it is heard. The third uniquely buffa topic within comic opera is the highly gestural or depictive orchestral accompaniment to a less neutral vocal line: Mozart's aria "Non più andrai," where Figaro relates Cherubino's future in the army to his pampered life in the Almaviva household, is a famous example. However, in instrumental music, even in concertos, where some relationship between a solo voice and an orchestra is built in, these textures (or persuasive analogues thereof) will not evoke opera buffa because there is nothing explicit to illustrate.

Less conspicuously distinctive musical markers of opera buffa style within the genre itself include the following: the simultaneous use of contrasting topics, especially in ensembles; this often takes the form of a "sincere" cantabile melody undercut by patter grumbling or ridicule (the quintet "Di scrivermi" from Mozart's Così fan tutte is a familiar example); ensemble hocket, where groups of characters toss extremely short (one or two-note) motives back and forth; extremely detached delivery of the text (often written as eighth notes followed by eighth-note rests); highly repetitive but also highly characterized accompaniments;[11] and sudden, apparently nonstructural changes of dynamic or texture. Each of these features can readily be found in late eighteenth-century instrumental music but not one of them unambiguously signifies opera buffa. Leonard Ratner (1980: 394) lists some of the characteristics I have mentioned as part of a more general

EXAMPLE **1.13** Martín y Soler, *L'arbore di Diana*, Act 1, "Dove vado," mm. 46–52.

list of the features of comic-opera *style* but, given his trailblazing enthusiasm for topics, it is quite striking that he does not describe these elements as *topics* per se, nor does he include opera buffa in his earlier listing of common topics in the Classical style (1–30). We are left, then, with the conclusion that the musical features most strongly associated with the buffa mode in opera—that is, the "buffa topics" within opera buffa—are neither exportable nor translatable to instrumental music because they rely on the delivery of text and thus because, once embedded in an instrumental phrase, they do not stand out from their surroundings in such a way as to signify extroversively.

In brief, then, opera buffa as a topic in instrumental music is more a translation of theatrical gesture than an exportation of the genre's most characteristic music. This should not be surprising and may even reflect historical reality. Opera buffa—like all opera—was always a multisensory experience for its audiences; there was no way in performance to detach the visual element from the music "itself" (nor, indeed, any reason or incentive to do so). Thus even when the music may have been topically consistent or univocal, the whole experience may have suggested both a greater variety of associations and more fluid and rapid juxtapositions of topics than we now see on the page. For example, we hear of episodes like the one reported from Milan by Charles Burney where, because the tenor was indisposed and thus not performing the night Burney went to the theater, the basso buffo, playing the scene where the old father berates his son (the absent tenor), turned the ire of the aria on the prompter, delighting the audience and causing an encore (Burney 1773: 106); or theatrical habits like Nancy Storace imitating the castrato Luigi Marchesi (Link 2002: viii–ix); or, more generally, the much-appreciated acting style of Rosa Ungarelli and Antonio Ristorini, early eighteenth-century interpreters of comic intermezzos (Piperno 1982). These kinds of behavior on, and responses to, the stage indicate that there were always multiple layers of reference at play, and that the topical (in all senses) resonances of these works lay only partly—perhaps even minimally—in the notes and words.

TOPICS WITHIN OPERA BUFFA

To propose, as I have, that there are opera buffa topics within opera buffa is somewhat to revise the notion, adopted in this volume, that topics are always formulae marked by being borrowed from a different musical genre or social context. Opera buffa is by no means unique in having certain musical clichés that identify it. One could equally well argue that coloratura passages and accompanied recitative form opera seria topics within that genre, that certain versions of the brilliant style constitute a concerto topic within concertos, that particular iterations of the cantabile style constitute an aria topic within arias, or that specific orchestral textures represent a symphonic topic within symphonies.[12] The function of such topics is presumably to confirm that one is indeed witnessing the genre one has previously identified. A concerto with no brilliant passages, a (mid-century Metastasian) opera seria with no coloratura, an opera buffa with no patter and/or no ensemble chatter wrapped in its orchestral blanket of gestural music, would all be confusing at the very least. The internal musical devices that help to identify these genres could count as topics because they are discrete and identifiable musical formulae that refer to recognizable musical practices with clearly defined nonmusical associations.

But buffa-confirming musical topics such as patter and finale-style vocal/orchestral writing are the minority of characteristic topics within opera buffa, which contains a "universe" of such devices entirely comparable, and often overlapping, with that of instrumental music.[13] Social dance types, pastoral, hunting, *alla turca*, occasional counterpoint, *ombra, tempesta*, and many more, are all very much present, as Wye Allanbrook's (1983) analyses of *Le nozze di Figaro* and *Don Giovanni* attest. Opera buffa also includes a host of not-purely-musical topics;[14] indeed, as I have argued elsewhere, like a lot of comedy, indeed, like much entertainment in general, the genre is essentially about the interplay of conventions, clichés, and formulae that occupy the domains of plot, character, text, and music.[15] Lecherous old men, ingénue lovers, worldly wise serving girls, idiot bumpkins, pretentious social climbers, wily servants, and arrogant nobles populate these works, and all have characteristic musical devices that only take on unambiguous signification when "redundantly" coupled with these characters. In addition, each instance of such a character with his or her associated musical topics evokes many other examples of the type, in very much the same way as a hunting call in an instrumental piece will evoke both actual hunting horns and many other imitations thereof. Thus as soon as, say, a young female singer stepped out on stage wrapping a rich old man around her little finger, or a hopeless wannabe started detailing his spurious lineage, that character was endowed with a kind of depth and resonance contributed by all the other such characters who had entered public consciousness, again in much the same way as, say, the minuet topic in instrumental music could endow the music with intertextual richness based on memories of actual social minuets, minuet movements in larger works, and references to the minuet in other kinds of pieces. Similarly with plot devices. The audience knew, for example, that Figaro would not literally have the power to make the Count dance to his tune, and that in the Galuppi/Goldoni *La diavolessa* the buried treasure in foolish Poppone's cellar would not actually be given to anyone else. And such conventional plot devices are (if the work is competent) endowed with a kind of depth by virtue of sharing resonances with all the other instances of the same thing.

STUDYING TOPICS IN OPERA (BUFFA)

Such examples of genre-, plot-, and character-reinforcing topics could be multiplied infinitely. But the ways opera in general and opera buffa in particular use topics are not simply to "turbo-charge" the mechanisms of signification in instrumental music. For one thing, in opera the accumulation of always already meaningful layers (words, gestures, plot context, character type, etc.) on top of (or around) the music allows for *both* redundancy (turbo-charging, or super-clear signification) *and* various levels of complexity, conflict, irony, or parody. Character types and plot devices were, of course, associated with particular musical configurations but the same musical configurations could be used to complicate or ironize the dramatic or theatrical moment. For example, the false pride of the fool, impostor, or charlatan was typically indicated with seria-like triadic melody and *Trommelbass*, as in the opening of the aria for the cowardly Perrucchetto in Domenico Cimarosa's *L'infedeltà fedele*, or the worldly cynicism of the flirt (often but not always a serving girl) with insouciant galanterie, as in the following example from Stephen Storace's insertion aria in Paisiello and Casti's *Il re Teodoro in Venezia*, where Lisetta (daughter of the deposed King Teodoro) describes both her many admirers and her cleverness in not letting them bamboozle her.

In Perrucchetto's number (Example 1.14), he has just descended from a tree that he had scrambled up in terror, pursued by a boar. Having let others actually dispatch the animal, he claims credit for its demise in this aria, in which he boasts of his sword and his bravery. His social and dramatic status thus could not be clearer. The topic of the opening of the aria is the opera seria version of the "elevated march" (Allanbrook 1983): the long notes in the vocal line over the busy accompaniment providing the clear evocation of opera seria, while the meter and the dotted rhythms remind us of the march. Perrucchetto is no hero, and his use of the heroic mode is clearly parody. In Lisetta's aria (Example 1.15) Storace has used the gavotte topic, but put it in what might be understood as serving-girl register by writing it in 2/4 rather than 2/2.[16] Depending on the performance, this could indicate either that Lisetta cannot help showing her (minimally) royal origins despite her reduced circumstances, or that she lives firmly in the comic register despite her ability to "speak gavotte." The scalar sixteenth-note couplets are typical of the grazioso version of this kind of aria, but the textual sentiment is a bit frank for gentility: "Dear ladies who want to make prey of loving hearts, I have more than I know what to do with." Thus at this moment in the aria the character has a kind of social liminality—she stands somewhere between comedy and grace, and this is achieved largely by the layered deployment of musical and theatrical topics. Later on in the aria, she devolves into patter and sediments her social (and theatrical) status as a comic figure worthy of fellow-feeling but not admiration.

Both Allanbrook and Agawu suggest that topical study of opera is essentially the same as topical study in instrumental music, but with the story "added." Agawu writes: "In opera, drama offers a ready-made *corroborative* framework for the analyst" (Agawu 2008: 44; my italics). Allanbrook suggests: "Opera is the easier case, because in a texted medium the meanings of these gestures can be inferred from or *confirmed by* the words that they set" (Allanbrook: 2014: 111; my italics). But as we have seen, corroboration and confirmation are not by any means the only possibilities: if that were the case, Perrucchetto would be heroic and Lisetta's social status would be clear. It is of course possible for a particular topic to signify a kind of wit or irony in instrumental music: for example, the little ornamented 4–3 suspension in the alto voice of the second phrase of the celebrated K. 332 (m. 8; see Example 18.11) could be taken both as a confirmation that the canonic opening of that phrase is to be taken as "proper" counterpoint, and as a sly dig about the appropriateness of "learned" counterpoint in a galant sonata. But there is an ambiguity or slipperiness—even a quality of special pleading—about this reading

EXAMPLE **1.14** Cimarosa, *L'infedeltà fedele*, Act 2, No. 20 "Di questo audace ferro," mm. 11–16.

EXAMPLE **1.15** Stephen Storace, insertion aria in Paisiello's *Il re Teodoro in Venezia*, Lisetta, "Care donne, che bramate," mm. 8–16.

that is less true of topical readings of opera, where meaning beyond the structure of the music is both more concrete and more insistently necessary, and where the genre's multivalence almost demands the sort of complexity of meaning created by the collision of different systems of signification.[17]

The excitement of topic theory in its early days, and as applied to instrumental music, was that music whose cultural capital depended to a large extent on its so-called purity—its detachment from the groundings of life in society and its apparent eschewal of fixed signification—could be shown, with historical support, to be deliciously and stimulatingly "impure." Another excitement of topic theory was that that "impurity" produced meanings, or at least evocations, that were often readily apprehensible and part of a common stock of associations, thus allowing scholars and performers to describe the expression of a given piece of music without descending into the purely subjective or fanciful, and possibly even gaining a glimmer of historical insight in the process. As applied to opera, the essential contribution of Allanbrook's work on *Le nozze di Figaro* and *Don Giovanni* was, first, to show that the "impurity" of the music itself contributed to the overall meanings of these operas and, second, that, as in instrumental music, the more or less verifiable referents of topics expanded the reach of historically plausible signification. It is, for example, both historically and interpretatively richer and more suggestive to know that Don Alfonso's "Vorrei dir," where he tells the girls in *Così fan tutte* that their lovers have been called to war, is a parody of a specific kind of female panic aria than it is to know that it sounds generally grief-stricken. But because it is opera, we—like contemporary audiences—can apprehend that the invocation of this particular aria type is parodic, and also that Don Alfonso is speaking to the sentimental and as-yet-unenlightened girls in a language they will understand.

The value of topic study for opera buffa is thus the same as the value of the study of conventions in any highly conventionalized genre, namely, to understand the ways they are deployed in relation to other topics or conventions and thus to access deeper or broader layers of meaning. For example, the minuet topic in Figaro's angry "Se vuol ballare" means something rather different from the same topic used at the moment when Susanna emerges from the closet in the second-act finale. In the first case the uprightness and primness of the music stands in comic contrast to the fury that Figaro feels, and that mismatch between feeling and gesture contributes to the rightness of the devolution into the contredanse in the second section of the aria; there is no way for Figaro to sustain the nobility of posture he assumes at the beginning. By contrast, when Susanna emerges from the closet, she really does have the "right" to use the minuet, as she is completely poised and in charge of the situation. There may be some tension between her social station and her evocation of a noble dance, but there is none between the way she feels and the gesture she uses to express it. At the same time, the fact that both Susanna and Figaro use the minuet topic at moments where the power of the Count is crucially at issue reinforces the bond between them and their common interest in establishing an acceptable balance of power in the household. Again, this level not only of specificity, but also complexity, is particular to opera.

Most modern study of topics focuses on instrumental music, as the contents of the present volume attest. It is important, however, to remember that opera buffa was not merely a source for the idea of topical mixture in instrumental music. Its own complex deployment of topics provides a rich and interesting comparison with instrumental music, and is worthy of further study.

Notes

1. Pre-Burkholder editions of this text, which remain largely unchanged on this subject from 1960 until 2001, note that the devices of comic opera entered the mainstream of *operatic* composition but also that in a more general way this genre answered Enlightenment demands for greater naturalism.
2. In *Music as Discourse* the topic of opera buffa becomes the "buffa style" (Agawu 2009: 43).
3. See Monelle (2006: 20–25) for a discussion of the problem of "referentialism."
4. Wye Allanbrook (1983: 7–8) is probably the first occurrence of this analytical topic. She amplifies it in "Two Threads through the Labyrinth: Topic and Process in the First Movements of K. 332 and K.333" (1992: 125–171).
5. The essay was originally written in 1792, then published with additions in the *Allgemeine musikalische Zeitung* in 1800.
6. *Tempesta*, formerly known as *Sturm und Drang*, is discussed elsewhere in this volume by Clive McClelland.
7. The first occurrence of this motive takes place in the second violins in m. 13.

8. The contrabassoon grunts at the beginning of this section have often been heard as inappropriately comic (Cook 1993: 103), but as far as I know, opera buffa has not been the comic world invoked.

9. Agawu (1991) uses these terms, which derive from Roman Jakobson.

10. See William Caplin (2005) on the formal functions of topics. He gives opera buffa as a topic no characteristic formal function; thus, in the absence of the notion that this topic is frequently associated with transitional passages, it seems likely that the transitional nature of this passage in Symphony No. 101 will be perceptually prior to an evocation of opera buffa.

11. By which I mean accompanimental figures more irregular or interesting than repeated eighth notes, Alberti basses, or other accompanimental commonplaces.

12. The last suggestion is, in fact, endorsed in the following chapter by Elaine Sisman.

13. The term is Kofi Agawu's (1991: 30).

14. Danuta Mirka deals with the confusion surrounding the meaning of "topic" in this volume's introduction. The meaning I am discussing in this paragraph corresponds to that inherited by Ratner from Curtius, according to Allanbrook (2014).

15. For a thorough discussion of these opera buffa topics, see Hunter (1999).

16. Allanbrook writes that the gavotte is in 4/4 meter (1983: 49) but shows examples in alla breve (2/2), and this last meter is associated with the gavotte in eighteenth-century sources (Sulzer 1792–94, 2: 309; Koch 1802: col. 630).

17. Although Allanbrook leaves room for the ironic or parodic use of topics in indicating that meanings in vocal music could be "inferred from" the visual or verbal domains, her relegation of opera to the realm of (relatively) easy signification is surprising, as her 1983 study of *Le nozze di Figaro* in particular teases out precisely the hidden and complicated meanings of the opera, identifying a substrate of the pastoral that is evident neither on the surface of the text nor from a purely plot-oriented analysis of the music.

References

Agawu, Kofi V. 1991. *Playing with Signs: A Semiotic Interpretation of Classic Music.* Princeton: Princeton University Press.

——. 2008. Topic Theory: Achievement, Critique, Prospects. In *Passagen, IMS Kongress Zürich 2007: Fünf Hauptvorträge, Five Key Note Speeches,* ed. Laurenz Lütteken and Hans-Joachim Hinrichsen, 38–69. Kassel: Bärenreiter.

Allanbrook, Wye J. 1983. *Rhythmic Gesture in Mozart:* Le nozze di Figaro *and* Don Giovanni. Chicago: University of Chicago Press.

——. 1992. Two Threads through the Labyrinth: Topic and Process in the First Movements of K. 332 and K. 333. In *Convention in Eighteenth- and Nineteenth-Century Music: Essays in Honor of Leonard G. Ratner,* ed. Wye J. Allanbrook, Janet M. Levy, and William P. Mahrt, 125–71. Stuyvesant, NY: Pendragon.

——. 2014. *The Secular Commedia: Comic Mimesis in Late Eighteenth-Century Music,* ed. Mary Ann Smart and Richard Taruskin. Berkeley: University of California Press.

Barnett, Dene, and Jeannette Massey-Westrop. 1987. *The Art of Gesture: Practices and Principles in 18th-Century Acting.* Heidelberg: Carl Winter Universitätsverlag.

Burkholder, Peter, Claude Palisca, and Donald J. Grout. 2010. *A History of Western Music,* 8th ed. New York: Norton.

Burney, Charles. 1773. *The Present State of Music in France and Italy; Or, The Journal of a Tour through Those Countries, Undertaken to Collect Materials for a General History of Music*, 2nd ed. London: Bechet.

Caplin, William. 2005. On the Relation of Musical Topics to Formal Function. *Eighteenth-Century Music* 2/1: 113–24.

Cook, Nicholas. 1993. *Beethoven: Symphony No. 9*. Cambridge: Cambridge University Press.

Harriss, Ernest C. 1981. *Johann Mattheson's* Der vollkommene Capellmeister: *A Revised Translation with Critical Commentary*. Ann Arbor, MI: UMI Research Press.

Hunter, Mary. 1999. *The Culture of Opera Buffa in Mozart's Vienna: A Poetics of Entertainment*. Princeton: Princeton University Press.

Irving, John. 1998. *Mozart: The "Haydn" Quartets*. Cambridge: Cambridge University Press.

Koch, Heinrich Christoph. 1802. *Musikalisches Lexikon*. Frankfurt am Main: August Hermann der Jüngere.

Link, Dorothea. 2002. *Arias for Nancy Storace, Mozart's First Susanna*. Madison, WI: A–R Editions.

McClelland, Clive. 2012. *Ombra: Supernatural Music in the Eighteenth Century*. Lanham, MD: Lexington.

Monelle, Raymond. 2006. *The Musical Topic: Hunt, Military and Pastoral*. Bloomington: Indiana University Press.

Piperno, Franco. 1982. Buffe e buffi (considerazioni sulla professionalità degli interpreti di scene buffe ed intermezzi). *Rivista Italiana di Musicologia* 17/2: 240–84.

Planelli, Antonio. 1772. *Dell'opera in musica*. Naples: Campo.

——. 1981. *Dell'opera in musica*, ed. Francesco Degrada. Fiesole: Discanto.

Ratner, Leonard. 1980. *Classic Music: Expression, Form, Style*. New York: Schirmer.

Rosen, Charles. 1971. *The Classical Style*. London: Faber and Faber.

Sisman, Elaine. 1997. Haydn, Shakespeare, and the Rules of Originality. In *Haydn and His World*, ed. Elaine Sisman, 2–48. Princeton: Princeton University Press.

Sulzer, Johann Georg. 1771. *Allgemeine Theorie der schönen Künste*. Vol. 1. Leipzig: Weidmann.

Taruskin, Richard. 2005. *The Oxford History of Western Music*. Vol. 2: *The Seventeenth and Eighteenth Centuries*. New York: Oxford University Press.

Weber, Daniel. 1800. Über komische Charakteristik und Karrikatur in praktischen Musikwerken. *Allgemeine musikalische Zeitung* 3 (26 November–13 December), cols. 137–43, 157–62.

CHAPTER 2

....

SYMPHONIES AND THE PUBLIC
DISPLAY OF TOPICS

....

ELAINE SISMAN

MOZART'S visit to Prague in January 1787 introduced him to a city awash in *Le nozze di Figaro*: "For here they talk about nothing but Figaro; nothing played, tooted, sung, or piped but Figaro," he exulted on the 15th. To make his concert debut in that city, he brought his new grand symphony in D major, just completed on 6 December, later nick-named the "Prague" (No. 38, K. 504). To an audience familiar with the opera, the sym-phony's finale can only have conjured up Susanna's frantic knocking on the closet door to get Cherubino out (Act 2, No. 14, "Aprite presto aprite!"). Beyond the near-quotation of the opening, however, the resemblance to the opera is heightened by an expressive connotation of *imbroglio*, so characteristic of *Figaro*'s overture: confusion, entangle-ment, a lot of running around. Quick rhythms, syncopations, *piano* dynamics, detached articulation, the initial lack of bass register all conspire to make the listener sense both intrigue and motion, qualities intensified as the motive returns frequently, rescored for winds as the embodiment of huffing and puffing. This distillation of comic opera's active essence lends the aura of buffa to the entire movement, and encourages us to understand other details as part of the imagined theatrical setting: outbreaks of timpani-reinforced string tuttis sound angry or joyous, musical dialogue between phrases and instrumen-tal groups contribute to a sense of argument and activity. In addition, the witty and concentrated wind passages conjure up the more rustic side of the pastoral tradition, another reference to the "green world" of *Figaro*, in Wye J. Allanbrook's lovely phrase (1991: 83–84). The finale's expressive topic, then, is the action-comedy of opera buffa, understood and appreciated by its audience for culturally resonant characteristics of *imbroglio* (a word used by both Count and Countess referring to Cherubino's unwel-come appearance in Acts 2 and 4), the *mercurial* quickly shifting moods (arising from changes in dynamics, orchestration, mode), and the instrumental color of *rusticity*, an inflection of *pastoral*.

Imbroglio was announced as the veritable topic of the entire opera in its first bustling moments, however, in a way that forecasts the conflicts of rusticity and courtliness. The overture begins with a whirling string unison that is counterintuitively quiet and in a middle register; the tutti that bursts out (after an intermediate phrase rising in register and adding winds) is filled with martial fanfares and flourishes. At the return of the unison, a countermelody featuring flutes now locates the imbroglio in a pastoral zone. The level of rhythmic activity, whether with tremolos or running figurations, never lets up, so that the audience understands the comic mode of action that will dominate the next few hours, and the exciting crescendo that introduces the closing theme reveals just how pleasurable that action will be. (Allanbrook, who describes the entire opera as a comic imbroglio, nevertheless refers to the overture only as a "mélange" [1983: 75].) As the *sinfonia avanti l'opera*, the overture was designed for such preparation. In serious opera, the reform of Gluck and Calzabigi and the theater criticism of Lessing and Sonnenfels, all during the 1760s, made clear that the opening sinfonia should be no mere crowd-quieter but rather should have a specific role in the dramatic arc of the performance. (There is still no agreement about the bright C-major overture to Gluck's *Orfeo ed Euridice*: does it forecast the happy ending of the opera even though it in no way leads in to the opening *tombeau* scene at Euridice's grave, or does it simply avoid its obligations and bow to the necessity of celebrating the Emperor's name-day in October 1762?) Operas that begin with or refer to shipwrecks and stormy landings (*tempesta*), like Haydn's *L'isola disabitata*, find those characteristic musical styles in their overtures; operas with a dark or supernatural component (*ombra*) find the slow introduction to a bright Allegro the appropriate place to express the darker side of the opera, as in Salieri's *La grotta di Trofonio* or Mozart's *Don Giovanni*. And the exotic coloration required by a Turkish-themed opera makes its first appearance in the overture as well, with its triangle, cymbals, snare drums, and bright percussive sound, as in Gluck's *La rencontre imprévue* (1764), Haydn's *L'incontro improvviso* (1775), and Mozart's *Die Entführung aus dem Serail* (1782), Mozart's only overture besides *Figaro* to begin quietly, here expressly so that the Turkish instruments can "break out" at the first tutti.

EIGHTEENTH-CENTURY VIEWS
OF THE GENRE

Symphonies were in a variety of senses the inheritors and counterparts to opera overtures: called overtures throughout the eighteenth century, placed first on concert programs as though to introduce the solo-inflected numbers to follow, and maintaining the original multimovement format of the *sinfonia avanti l'opera* even as the opera overture itself turned into a single movement, symphonies were also associated with aspects of drama, character, and affect. Accounting for such a combination in symphonies of the period led a number of writers to imagine that the entire genre was by analogy an instrumental version of works with text. In reviewing a symphony by Friedrich Witt in the *Allgemeine musikalische Zeitung* (17 May 1809), E. T. A. Hoffmann noted that "the symphony, especially following the impetus it received from Haydn and Mozart, has become the ultimate form of instrumental music—the *opera* of instruments as it were—...unit[ing] all the common instruments of the orchestra, voicing their individual characteristics in the performance of one great drama" (Charlton 1989: 223). The Comte de Lacépède suggested that the composer of symphonies should consider its three movements to be "like three grand acts of a play [*une pièce de théâtre*], as though he believes he were working on a tragedy, on a comedy, or on a pastorale, according to the specific goal [*but*] of the symphony" (1785, 2: 331). Indeed, the celebrated French opera composer Grétry wrote in his *Mémoires*, first published in 1797, that Haydn's symphonies should be considered a "vast dictionary" by opera composers to be mined "without scruple" for musical figures to be fitted to the expression of texts: the melodic fecundity of the symphonies reflected the composer's freedom to create "out of nothing" yet were so expressive that their figures could easily accompany texts whose very specificity fettered the imagination. In this way the symphonic composer was "like the botanist who discovered a plant, awaiting the doctor to discover its use" (1829, 1: 200).

Outside such drama-infused language, expressive values were seen to arise from the essential aesthetic goals of variety and contrast. Charles Burney noted in 1804, à propos of Haydn's greatness in the genre, that his symphonies featured "majesty, fire, grace, and pathos *by turns*" (Grant 1983: 216; emphasis added) while Triest in 1801 referred to the way Haydn's instrumental music "sings so beautifully," no matter how complex the passage nor whether it is "in the serious or in the comic style" (1801: col. 406–7; 1997: 372). Read in conjunction with Daube's description of melodic figures as consisting of "the thundering" or "the singing," Burney and Triest's adjectives might be turned into nouns and hence into topics: the majestic, the fiery, the graceful, the pathetic, the thundering, the singing, the serious, the comic. An anonymous series of letters on the "Present State of Music in Paris" in the *Allgemeine musikalische Zeitung* turned to descriptive (*malenden*) symphonies (1800: cols. 748–50) and used both nouns and adjectives to describe the kinds of meanings that could be discovered within a symphony. Only such things as a hunt, a storm, or a battle were self-explanatory; the listener needed a program ("Konzertzettel"), such as was required by Rosetti's (now lost) *Telemachus* symphony, to discern specific events like the shipwreck on Calypso's isle and personified instrumental voices narrating and interacting (1800: cols. 588, 711, 731, 745). The author deplored the prevailing tendency to think of Haydn's symphonies as attempts to tell a specific story and preferred to think of them as revealing the "diversity of their effects, and the styles therein": "now it is serious, or noble, or military, or fiery; now joyous, pleasant, galant; now religious and elevated [*erhaben*]. These are the types which we discover therein" (col. 749). Effects, styles, types: a perfect series of synonyms for the topic theorist.

Triest confirmed and made more specific this approach to symphonic topics when he asserted that "the attraction of this type of composition [the symphony] consists precisely in *variety, in the display of the whole mass of instruments toward the development of the beauty and meaning that lies within the main theme, which is, in itself, intelligible and often seemingly simple*" (1801: col. 400; 1997: 371; his emphasis). One must parse the "meaning" of the main theme, its intelligibility, its (only) apparent simplicity, as well as the means of instrumental deployment that create its "development." In Haydn's Symphony No. 82, "The Bear" (1786), the heading "C-major Symphony" already inclines the audience to expect the bright scoring of trumpets and drums with attendant march rhythms and festive air (Brown 1996). The main theme in fact conjoins three related topics intelligible to the Parisian audience (Example 2.1): the *coups d'archet* of the sweeping unison triadic ascent (accented by tremolo in the violins) assert the grand style (x); the sequel executes a quiet turn to a minuet topic in the strings (y), after which the tutti returns in a stirring martial fanfare (z), extended to a half cadence: "now the noble, now the pleasant, now the military"! The first phrase is repeated immediately, rescored, *piano*, with the string tremolo displaced into a new counter-figure of repeated wind chords; a sequential restatement in *forte* launches the modulation to the dominant.

Perhaps Haydn thought this trifold theme would succeed in Paris because his earlier Symphony No. 56 (1774) was hugely popular there, having been performed by both the *Concert spirituel* and the *Concert des amateurs* and published several times (Harrison 1998: 6). In the first movement of that work, also in triple meter, the opening *coup d'archet*'s unison triad descends, and the quiet sequel, far from being a minuet, is actually a learned-style *soggetto* suggestive of the "Jupiter" finale (Example 2.2). (The suspensions and deceptive cadence on vi remind one irresistibly of the punch line to *Così fan tutte*.) The succeeding fanfare uses a martial pattern with the dotted rhythm on the downbeat. In both movements, it is the vibrant grand-style topic that propels the modulation to the dominant, and that marks the closing passages of the exposition and recapitulation.

A comparison of the playful second themes is also instructive, both having been reached after minor-mode accents. In Symphony No. 82 (Example 2.3), the lightly scored violin tune in singing style is supported by bassoon drones on I and V, turning it "rustic." In Symphony No. 56 (Example 2.4), by contrast, the melodic topic is identical except for the crucial omission of the drone, so the quiet strings functions as a kind of oasis, a songful respite from the grand style without a pastoral location. In both development sections, the x–y contrast forms the basis of modulation and directional and textural manipulation; only in the later work does the second theme come in for developmental treatment, without the drone and as the subject for imitation throughout the registers and colors of the orchestra. Each movement brings back its most stirring fanfare (z) at the end.

The most often-cited description of the symphony is that in Sulzer's *Allgemeine Theorie der schönen Künste*, written by Johann Abraham Peter Schulz in 1774 and later quoted in Koch's *Musikalisches Lexikon* of 1802. Schulz declared that the symphony is like an "instrumental chorus" in that "each voice is making its own contribution to the whole." The genre is "most excellently suited to expression of the grand, the festive, and the sublime," and when not acting as the overture to a dramatic or religious work, is meant to "call up all the splendor of instrumental music":

> The chamber symphony, which constitutes a self-sufficient whole and is dependent on no following music, achieves its goal only by means of a full-toned, brilliant, and

EXAMPLE **2.1** Haydn, Symphony No. 82 in C major, i, mm. 1–10.

EXAMPLE **2.2** Haydn, Symphony No. 56 in C major, i, mm. 1–14.

EXAMPLE 2.3 Haydn, Symphony in C major No. 82, i, mm. 70–74.

EXAMPLE 2.4 Symphony in C major No. 56, i, mm. 53–56.

fiery manner. The allegros of the best chamber symphonies contain grand and bold ideas, free handling of compositional techniques, apparent irregularity in the melody and harmony, strongly-marked rhythms of various sorts, powerful bass melodies and unisons, concerting middle voices, free imitations, often a theme handled fugally, sudden transitions and shifts from one key to another, which are the more striking the weaker the connection is, bold shadings of *forte* and *piano*, and particularly the *crescendo*, which has the greatest effect when used with a rising melody and its climax (Bonds 1997: 133).

Some of these descriptors have been assimilated to musical topics: brilliant and grand styles, fugue as emblem of "learned style" more broadly, the Mannheim crescendo, topics deriving from "strongly-marked rhythms." The sublime as a category of aesthetic experience may or may not be a topic, but Schulz compares the symphonic allegro to the Pindaric ode in that it "elevates and moves the soul of the listener in the same way, and it requires the same spirit, the same sublime imagination, and the same knowledge of art in order to achieve this effect." Bonds explains the relevance of the Pindaric ode through Sulzer's own entries on Pindar and on the ode: it offers the characteristics of high style and sublime, disorder, artifice, textural complexity, and the communal aspect of massed voices, the latter taking into account the celebratory function of the odes after athletic competitions (hence Schulz's term *feyerlich*, "festive" or "celebratory"). Certainly the scoring, *coups d'archet*, fanfares, and sometime harmonic and contrapuntal "disorder" of Symphonies Nos. 56 and 82 emphasize those qualities.

COMPOSERS AND AUDIENCES

For Schulz, the composer whose Allegros serve as a model of the genre is the Belgian virtuoso violinist Pierre van Maldere (1729–68), "whose premature death has robbed art of many more masterpieces of this kind" (*dessen frühzeitiger Tod der Kunst noch viele Meisterstüke dieser Art entrissen hat*; Sulzer 1774: 1122). Maldere's Habsburg connections (his patron was Maria Theresa's brother-in-law, Charles of Lorraine) brought him into the Viennese orbit, where his symphonies became known to Haydn and Mozart; the Esterházy catalogue reveals that Prince Paul Anton had already acquired six of Maldere's symphonies by 1759 (Harich 1975: 75). Also praised in vigorous terms by Hiller and Burney, Maldere is much less known today than he deserves. Maldere's Symphony in D major, Op. 5 No. 1 (Paris, 1768), is especially notable for its thematic use of a crescendo with rising register and corresponding increase in expressive power (beginning and end of exposition and recapitulation, beginning of development), each time leading to a climactic turning figure. The communally celebratory aspect of the crescendo *topic* (thus differentiable from a "mere" crescendo) alternates with an evocation of an Irish folk tune over a drum bass that forms the second theme. (Maldere had spent two years in Dublin, 1751–53; Clercx-Lejeune 2001: 683.) The exciting orchestral gestures and textures "that call up the splendor of instrumental music" in their triadic and turning figures thus give way to a simpler two-part texture revealing the topic of folk-like melody, with its more popular social location and its differently configured sense of community. The grand style descends to popular in a way that reaches out to all listeners.

The appropriation of a folk or folk-like or popular-style song, with its evocation of the world outside the concert hall and its sometimes exotic flavor, reminds us that the increasing breadth of musical life required composers, in choosing musical ideas for their symphonies, to communicate with multiple audiences in multiple locations. Audiences at all levels of musical knowledge attended performances, whether local and known or faraway and imagined, and symphonies formed part of all public concerts and most private ones with a large enough instrumental band. Composers also wrote for, and had to consider as their audience, the patrons and employers who commissioned and supported them, the musicians reading from their stands, the publishers who evaluated what would sell, and the increasing numbers of critics. To appeal expressively to the experiences of connoisseur and amateur, aristocrat and bourgeois, small provincial orchestra and "army of generals" (as Burney [1959: 35] called the crackerjack Mannheim ensemble in his published travel diary), composers found an array of melodic, rhythmic, and textural styles for their symphonies that could evoke expressive metaphors for human dramas, characters, and feelings by drawing on actual communal activities like hunting, dancing, singing songs, making war, going to church or the theater, and experiencing nature. Some of these styles originated in or were associated with the portrayals of such activities in opera buffa and opera seria, others in suites of dances for the ballroom or the countryside (which also had stylized representations in opera or *Tafelmusik*), still others in "characteristic" pieces with titles meant to represent or depict a battle, hunt, riverbank, or storm. "Elevated" styles associated with choral textures of mass, cantata, and oratorio—learned counterpoint and fugue, *alla breve* motet styles, *cantus firmus*, the French overture—found their way into concert symphonies. (As Neal Zaslaw [1982] has shown, the symphonies played during church services were by no means limited to the *sinfonia da chiesa*, with initial slow movement.)

Thus the initial rhetorical act of a composer—to choose the low, middle, or high stylistic level appropriate to the audience—is immediately muddled for the symphonist by the diverse nature, interests, and knowledge of the concert-goers. The symphony may have been innately "grand," per Schulz, but it could move easily among social levels and locations, and could appeal by the very variety of topics at those levels. Indeed, Haydn and Mozart both created downward trajectories from grand style to popular style, over the course of an exposition, in ways that aroused the ire of German critics who disliked such mixtures of serious and comic. Haydn's Symphony No. 80 in D minor (1783–84), from his second set of three written for an English publisher and an as-yet-unknown English audience, begins with a driving *tempesta* topic, like that at the beginning of Gluck's Dance of the Furies concluding his *Don Juan* ballet (1761), discussed (this volume) by Clive McClelland. Haydn draws the listener into the work's frenzied action, then immediately personifies the work with a single *pianto* gesture (Monelle 2000: 17–18), a sighing appoggiatura (m. 7–8), before it drives onward with an even greater degree of tremolo (Example 2.5a). Although the turn to F major seems more *agitato* than *tempesta*, the pace is unrelenting. These terms offer rhythmic and affective designators for what has been formerly known as a *Sturm und Drang* topic, a term taken from literature and drama of the 1770s. Whether these topics invariably connect to the minor mode is an intriguing question (Churgin 2004). At the very end of Symphony No. 80's exposition, however, a sly dance appears (Example 2.5b), with Lombard rhythms in the melody (violin doubled by flute for the first time) and pizzicato oom-pah accompaniment, that hijacks the development section, where it appears in remote keys and is rescored every time. In the words of Johann Hiller (1767) about initially "dignified" concertos and symphonies, "before one suspects it, in springs Hans Wurst, right into the middle of things" (Sisman 1997b: 22).

In the first movement of Mozart's "Jupiter" Symphony, No. 41 in C major (1788), the grand-style *coups d'archet* mark the first theme, singing style the second, and, heralded by pizzicato, popular style for the closing theme, a quotation from Mozart's own aria "Un bacio di mano," K. 541. Charles Rosen has suggested that the presence of popular-style melodies in closing sections puts their regular phrase structure to work grounding the accumulated tension of the exposition's modulatory scheme (Rosen 1971: 334–35). Just as *coups d'archets* are effective curtain-raisers, then, and melodic sweetness and thin texture provide effective contrast in the new key area, a square-cut popular-melody topic

EXAMPLE **2.5** Haydn, Symphony No. 80 in D minor, i: (a) mm. 1–10; (b) mm. 58–64.

(Continued)

EXAMPLE **2.5** (Continued)

finds its most compelling placement as part of the closing group. In the same way, fina-les often featured contredanses, gigues, and other popular-style themes for rondos and their hybrids.

Representation and Affect

Just as an opera overture might refer in its choice of topics to a storm (*tempesta*), a vein of supernatural terror (*ombra*), or a heroic or pastoral tone (fanfare or siciliana, say) the symphony could call on the same musical resources but without the "cover" pro-vided by narrative and drama. In approaching the contested ground of musical mimesis and tone painting, the aesthetic battles engendered by the propriety of these ideas were fought and re-fought over the eighteenth century and into the next. Instrumental com-posers felt they had to deny that they were engaged in mimetic endeavors no matter how explicit their titles, because simple "description" or "representation" was held to be shallow: only the imitation of "passion" and "affect" found philosophical justifica-tion. Yet the strong connection between feelings and tone painting, as between emo-tional and expressive characters and topics, reflects, as Wye J. Allanbrook assures us, the deep mimetic roots of musical expression (1988, 2014). Beethoven's declaration that his *Pastoralsinfonie*, despite its movement titles and scenic trajectory, was "more the expression of sentiments than tone painting" was possibly a defensive move prompted by the articles like the one cited above on the "Present State of Music in Paris" (1800) and particularly by the backlash against depictions of nature in Haydn's late oratorios. Beethoven wanted to draw attention to the affective rather than the descriptive content of his topics. Yet in pastoral, these qualities are so easily conjoined.

Even without titles for the individual movements, Beethoven's listeners would have been able to discern aspects of pastoral topics in the drone passages of the first move-ment, the compound meter and ruffled figuration long associated with gentle waves and breezes in the second (what Daniel Heartz calls *zefiro* in opera [1990: 223–25,

230–31]), the rustic dancing in the third, the thunderstorm (*tempesta*), a tremolo-laced minor-mode outbreak, and the host of topics associated with gentle nature in the finale. His first movement also adapted the rising-crescendo topic in two significant ways: first, it is an important element in both the first theme and the second theme, and second, its twofold appearance in the development expands outward not only in register but also in tonality (B flat to D major, G to E major). And these latter crescendos do not reach a great climax but rather dissociate motivically as soon as they reach the loudest dynamic level, finally revealing the two-note cuckoo-call at the end of the main theme's motive. Thus the repetition of motives in conjunction with the crescendo all work to broaden the topical associations made by "the awakening of happy feelings upon going into the country." As a "characteristic symphony," Beethoven's *Pastoral* takes pastoral to the level of an "umbrella" topic covering a host of interrelated signifiers and specific representations. David Wyn Jones writes of the breadth of pastoral:

> As a metaphor for idealized emotions the pastoral extended from the robustly rustic, even vulgar, to the elevatingly Christian. As well as the generalized musical finger-prints noted above [pedal points (or in a mannered context, drone basses), compound time, piping melodies, repetition, and measured delivery of material], the pastoral often included more specific pictorial images too: birds of all kinds, but especially the cuckoo, hen, nightingale and turtledove; storms on land and on sea, often with the ensuing calm; and waterscapes of all kinds (seas, rivers and brooks). (1995: 14–15)

One may contrast the multiplicity of pastoral topics with the comparably "outdoor" but more one-dimensional topic of the hunt: the latter is invariably quick and vibrant, as well as in major and in a compound meter. Haydn's Symphony No. 73, nicknamed "La chasse," has only a single movement dominated by that topic, the finale that originated as an opera overture where it evokes the goddess Diana (*La fedeltà premiata*). In Dittersdorf's *Metamorphosis* symphony on Acteon's transformation into a stag, the hunt topic sets the scene at the outset in a unison arpeggiated figure that is familiar from such noncharacteristic (and nonsymphonic) pieces as Haydn's String Quartet Op. 1 No. 1 in B flat major and Mozart's "Hunt" Quartet in B flat major, K. 458 (Will 2002: 55–59). The succeeding Adagio, depicting Diana wearying of the hunt and turning to the cool refreshment of bathing, calls on the time-honored *zefiro*, here a "murmuring" figure of sixteenth notes in circular patterns of neighbor-notes for violins in thirds (Example 2.6), familiar from opera (especially the terzetto "Soave sia il vento" from Mozart's *Così fan tutte*) and Beethoven's "Scene by the Brook" (Will 2002: 43–44). The prominent melodic flute over the string figuration also recalls the second Adagio of Haydn's Symphony No. 7, *Le midi*, a restorative pastoral after the panic engendered by Noon's heat (see below).

Karl Spazier's critical translation of Grétry's memoirs noted that Haydn's *Seven Last Words* seemed perfectly to embody Grétry's desideratum that musical expression be made specific (1800: 185). (Even though Grétry found that the symphonies of Haydn and Gossec were the perfect riposte to Fontenelle's supposed quip, "Sonate, que me veux-tu?", they stopped well short of legibility.) Koch called those works "simphonies à programmes," which together with Dittersdorf's *Ovid* symphonies and Rosetti's

EXAMPLE 2.6 Dittersdorf, *Metamorphoses*, Symphony No. 3 in G major, "Acteon Turned into a Stag," ii, mm. 1–4.

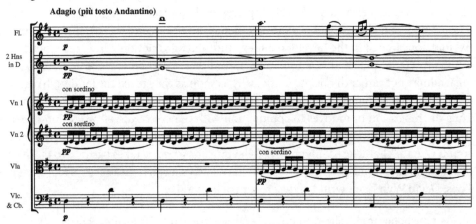

Telemachus symphony constituted a genre not cultivated very extensively (Koch 1802: col. 1384–85). Whether Haydn's seven orchestral Adagios are also *topically* rich, however, has never been explored. Surely instrumental music this expressive must include an array of topics in its armamentarium of meaning. The Introduzione in D minor begins with slow-introduction rhetoric—an announcement of the grand style in the dotted tread of the French overture—yet the entire movement, like each of the *Words*, is slow, and the dotted idea turns out to be the main theme. The movement is also filled with portentous pulsating chords and bass notes, clearly identifying a declamatory strain. Pulsations, whether of chords or single notes (often in the bass), with their clear evocations of high-style accompanied recitative and the fantasia, feature prominently in nearly every one of the *Seven Words*. Incorporating Baron van Swieten's earliest known musical advice to Haydn—that he use the rhythms of the "word" in question to shape the opening melody of each movement—the use of vocally inspired topics in these symphonic movements enhanced their intelligibility and led to their immediate and enduring popularity. But purely instrumental topics also appear at crucial moments. The last Word, "Into Thy Hands I Commend My Spirit," offers a phrase based on the horn fifth as part of the first group in the exposition but as a closing gesture in the recapitulation; as Rosen has demonstrated (1995: 116–24), this topic unites the temporal and spatial meanings of landscape: the echoing horns over distant terrain intersect with the play of memory in recalling past events. (In Haydn's string-quartet arrangement, the passage is played only by the violins.) Topically, the retrospective aspect of the horn fifth underscores Christ's preparation for death with a farewell, later thematized in the first movement of Beethoven's *Les adieux* sonata (Op. 81a, 1809). The *Terremoto* is completely given over to the *tempesta* topic, often in unison, as in Gluck.

A similar appearance of declamatory recitative-inspired pulsating chords, now with the part-writing suggesting learned style, appears in the Capriccio slow movement of the contemporaneous Symphony No. 86 (mm. 41–46, with plaintive flute), after preparation by *accompagnato*-style dotted chords as transition to the development (mm. 30–32). A *fortissimo* eruption doubles the pulsations from eighth to sixteenth notes in a clear *agitato* outbreak. The speed and character of pulsating chords are clearly key to their interpretation as a topic (Example 2.7). The Capriccio's main theme is a sunrise topic like the slow introduction of Symphony No. 6, *Le matin* (Monelle 2006: 3–4; Sisman 2013: 9–18). Perhaps it is these mixtures of topics, as well as the unusual presence of the opening four-measure unit in the same key to begin exposition, development, and recapitulation,

EXAMPLE 2.7 Haydn, Symphony No. 86 in D major, ii, mm. 29–44.

that prompted the Capriccio heading. Haydn's only other slow-movement Capriccio, in the C-major String Quartet, Op. 20 No. 2, similarly combines instrumental and vocal genres, in that a concerto-inspired ritornello acts as introduction to an aria-like concerto section, with declamatory, recitative-like passages to punctuate both sections.

It thus appears that composers could find topics in the rhythms and textures of human activities that reflected the feelings those activities evoked, rather than the activities themselves, and could thereby convey a generalized sense of meaning and intelligibility. Indeed, even without specific references, instrumental music, especially symphonic music, was heard by contemporary audiences as highly characterized. The *Morning Herald* of London reported in March 1783 that Haydn's latest symphony was both original and "*loaded* with *meaning*" (McVeigh 1993: 122–23); Haydn himself commented to Marianne von Genzinger that the Adagio of the E-flat-major sonata he had written for her (Hob. XVI:49) was "very full of meaning" (*sehr vieles zu bedeuten*; Bartha 1965: 240, letter of 20 June 1790). Both of Haydn's biographers, based on widespread sentiment that his symphonies were "about something," as evidenced by the *Allgemeine musikalische Zeitung*'s Parisian correspondent cited above, asked him whether he sought to depict specific character-types like "the coquette or the prude"; needless to say he denied such an intention, claiming only to have depicted "moral characters," like an old Adagio in which God argues with a sinner. Certainly his Symphony No. 60, "Il distratto," incorporating the overture and entr'acte music to Regnard's old play *Le distrait* about an absent-minded man, renders that character vividly in the first movement with a phrase repeated too often as it trails off (marked *perdendosi*), then "coming to" as it recollects itself; in the finale the orchestra distractedly interrupts itself to tune up, having "forgotten" to do so before the movement started. When a comparable phrase peters out without the expressive framing of "distraction," as in the finale of Haydn's Symphony No. 23 (1764), does it "mean" the same thing? That movement's conceit is a motoric rhythmic character whose quiet racing string thirds are frequently interrupted by forte chords (Example 2.8). Yet no chords articulate the ending, and the finale motive repeats several times, at a loss, until the movement, and thus the entire symphony, simply stops. The fingerprint of a recognizable musical character does not necessarily correlate with a recognizable musical topic, but the witty play with endings may intersect with other characterized styles and effects.

Haydn's symphonic style developed in a particular direction during the 1760s as his involvement with theater increased: providing orchestral music for the resident troupes at Eszterháza encouraged his natural proclivity for symphonic discourse leavened by variation and surprise, learned-style intensity, rhythmic disruption, and mixtures of high and low, serious and comic styles. Topical references became inextricably merged or conflated with a heightened sense of theatrical rhetoric. Symphony No. 60 may be his only symphony associated with a specific play, but Haydn, described as "music director" to the theatrical troupe of Carl Wahr and his successors at Eszterháza, surely wrote much of his highly characterized music for multiple uses (Sisman 1990). Symphony No. 56, mentioned above as popular in Paris, features an Adagio movement with poignant concertante winds in constantly changing formulations. Yet it is the muted strings

EXAMPLE 2.8 Haydn, Symphony No. 23 in G major, iv, mm. 80–96.

that frame the whole with a hymn-like opening (a topic emphasized by its immediate restatement by wind choir) and delicate filigree closing, and that emerge as prominent during the artfully placed *ombra* passages. The breakneck finale makes perfect sense as an imbroglio in a theatrical context, as does the finale of Symphony No. 62 (1780). The Allegretto second movement of the latter work is very possibly a barcarole, a topic otherwise unused by Haydn; only A. Peter Brown has recognized and named this topic (Brown 2002: 183–84), while Landon has speculated on theatrical origins for the symphony (Landon 1978: 584). Thus, Haydn's role in the theater at Eszterháza makes plausible the appearance of unique topics in some of the symphonies of these decades.

Perhaps Triest's trilevel view of musical listening offers an ingenious way to transition from expressive metaphors to topics that describe music about music (1801: col. 397; 1997: 369). Texted ("applied") music had to be specific, but instrumental ("pure") music calls forth a freer response. The three levels of experiencing instrumental music first affect the senses (*Sinnenkitzel*), then the understanding (*Verstand*), and finally the imagination (*Einbildungskraft*): such music "has the greatest effect when the listener— even without auxiliary elements like ballets, marches, etc.—believes that he perceives, in the composition that is being performed, the expression of specific ideas or feelings that have simply not been expressed, and easily supplements the text, as it were, with his thoughts." In listening to Haydn's symphonies, then, his contemporaries might well have performed such a "supplementing," a dance of meaning the composer was wise not to specify.

TOPICS OF ORCHESTRAL SONORITY

The many topical uses of the Mannheim crescendo focus attention on topics derived from the capabilities and colors of the orchestra. The special forms of orchestral crescendo associated with Johann Stamitz and the Mannheim orchestra (though used earlier by Italian composers especially in the opera overture)—thus the frequent references to it as the "Mannheim crescendo," comparable to Sulzer's description in that the register rises while instruments are added—became a successful topic in the hands of composers like Maldere (as noted above) and Mozart (e.g., K. 297, "Paris," and K. 318), though sparingly in Haydn's symphonies (e.g., No. 1). Mozart appeared especially keen to incorporate the dynamic effects favored by Paris audiences (Range 2012). The staged rising-register crescendos at the beginnings of movements (most often finales) in Dittersdorf's *Metamorphoses* symphonies ensure that the listener recognizes an emerging course of action: the outraged Diana setting Acteon's hounds on him, the Iron Age's military adventurism, Phaeton's ascent in Apollo's chariot and Jupiter's increasing ire, the sunrise in the second movement of the Rescue of Andromeda by Perseus. The staged crescendo's principal afterlife was in the overtures of Rossini, famously in closing themes like that of *The Barber of Seville*. Yet whereas Haydn's and Mozart's symphonic opening themes usually juxtapose segments in *forte* and *piano*, the opening Allegro of every one of Beethoven's symphonies except No. 8 incorporates a crescendo leading to a climactic and fully scored statement of the first theme. (In Symphonies Nos. 1, 2, 4, and 7 this occurs after the slow introduction.) Of course every musical genre develops ways of creating an effective crescendo, and in a slow tempo may enact the swelling of sunrise or other emergent bodies, in what I have called a sunrise topic, later examples of which are Wagner's Prelude to *Das Rheingold* and Ravel's *Daphnis and Chloe* Suite No. 2. Particular types of Mannheim crescendo are in fact topics from within the symphonic genre per se. Delimiting topical boundaries, a special concern of topic theory as it polices the borders between different kinds of signs, figures, representations, and stylistic borrowings and quotations, should not prevent us from seeing that as sources of meaning, pleasure, and intelligibility, topics may arise from within the genre as well as from the outside. Orchestral effects whose home is in symphonies can be thought of as symphonic topics within the symphonic genre and thus as analogous to buffa topics in opera buffa identified in the previous chapter by Mary Hunter.

The appearance of concertante solo instruments, most often in slow movements, may represent a "borrowing" from the concerto, but the actual expressive valence of a concertante topic changes according to its treatment, making *concertante* another topical "umbrella." Indeed, Lacépède advised the composer of symphonies to assign to different instruments the roles of dialoguing "interlocutors" (1785, 2: 332–33). Paired flutes function as a pastoral signifier in the second Adagio of Haydn's No. 7, *Le midi* (1761), and signal the restorative course of action required by the searing sun at noon; the solo violin's recitative in the first Adagio (a high-style inheritance from the *recitativo accompagnato* of opera seria) suggested the panic, bewilderment, and ennui of that special time of day (Sisman 2013: 57–69). In the Larghetto Siciliana of Gossec's Symphony in B flat major, B. 81 (1783–85), paired flutes sound the cuckoo (or is it mere rustic piping?) in the pastoral location of the movement's heading. Entirely different is the "speaking" oboe in the first movement of Beethoven's Fifth, emerging from the orchestral body's fermata in the recapitulation as a moment of recitative-like fantasia and uttering its repeated *pianto* as the violins restate the first theme during the final cadence.

When actual cadenzas appear, like the beautiful wind cadenzas in the slow movements of Haydn's Nos. 84 and 87, not only do the treatments differ but also their very sound reflects differences in the movements themselves. Solo winds emerge as a complete surprise after the Andante variations of No. 84 because they had not previously been highlighted. But the cadenza's layering of winds and pizzicato strings, together with aspects of imitation and learned-style suspensions, pick up on the instrumental layering and treble-bass imitation of the theme and the *minore* variation. In the key-area structure of No. 87's Adagio, on the other hand, the hymn-like theme is immediately repeated with a solo flute, and the sequel/modulating phrase gives the melody to oboes over noodling strings; the recapitulation conflates the hymn's two statements in a version for winds and then solo flute. The exposition has a hymn-like cadenza for flute and oboes, and while the recapitulation's cadenza begins with comparable music for oboes and violin, it is extended to include faster solo entries for all winds including bassoon, picking up on the style of earlier figurations. It should be noted that "hymn" is a topos, as are "recitative," "fantasia," "cadenza," "siciliana," and "learned style." In fact, although "minore" is not a topic, minor-mode variations (in symphonies as well as other genres) tend to change the topical nature of a variation theme, tending toward "sensibility" (sighing, chromaticism), the "learned" (imitation, "difficulty"), or the stentorian unison.

Thus, "crescendo," "concertante," and "cadenza" are topics that require the resources of the orchestra for their greatest effect, and have an especially good chance of making an impression on an audience keen to experience timbral and dynamic difference. Haydn knew that reaching his audience was key: "As head of an orchestra, I could make experiments, observe what created an impression and what weakened it." Mozart used almost the same language, especially in his letters from Paris: over and over he describes passages that seek to make an effect (e.g., Anderson 1985: 521 and the letters quoted by Range 2012). And some of these effects require a shared understanding of the public nature of the symphonic experience. While the tutti effect of big chords and tremolos could be thought of as "brilliant style" (Ratner 1980), it was also often described by contemporaries as "noisy"; William Jones deplored the popularity of "a noisy vulgar *allegro*, full of impertinence and repetition" (1784: ii). Yet orchestral effects underlie many topics, as suggested by Adena Portowitz's topical "maps" of Sammartini symphonies (Portowitz 2004). The second movement of Dittersdorf's Symphony "in the Taste of Five Nations" (1767) entertainingly parodies the big introductory chords of Italian-style symphonies.

(Of the five nations—German, Italian, English, French, Turkish—that is the only one to be satirized rather than represented.) An imposing orchestral unison, on the other hand, may operate as a *coup d'archet* opening that instantly announces the grand style, or as an interruption that might delimit a passage of solo instruments, or as a return to grandeur in a closing gesture: all of these may suggest what Janet M. Levy refers to as the "single most pervasive quality of a unison passage: its aura of authoritative control" (1982: 507). That controlling "unison topic" may intersect fruitfully with other topics, like the *tempesta* (as at the beginning of Gluck's Dance of the Furies). Instrumentation itself has topical value, as pastoral's flutes or oboe groupings, the "shadowed" bassoon, the martial fanfare of trumpets, drums, and horns, the concertante character of solo "interlocutors" emerging from the group, now singing, now virtuosic. When topics emerge from the tone colors and textures characteristic of symphonies, the resultant melding of expressive idea and genre helps to explain the symphony's enduring popularity, as well as the difficulty of regarding topics only as imported mechanisms of meaning.

The Mannheim crescendo had life as a topic; that's why we recognize it in Rossini. Its opposite, the staged diminuendo, was not a Mannheim trick but rather a Haydn one. Together with a repeated motive, it signified distractedness (Symphony No. 24/iii; Symphony No. 60/i); as a retransitional ploy it signified that the theme is about to return; writ large, it signified "farewell" (Symphony No. 45/iv). Or it could suggest uncertainty, as in Dittersdorf's *Metamorphosis* symphony, in which Actaeon loses his way and hesitates before spying Diana bathing (the Minuet's second reprise). Deployed in ways characteristic of their sonic valences, the sections of the orchestra seemed to signify any of these: strings (lyric "singing," *tempesta*), winds (pastoral, rustic, ethereal), brass (martial, hunting, courtly fanfare, stentorian-supernatural, epic), and timpani (grand, triumphal, sinister). The possibility of textural layering among instrumental groups points to a continuum from contrapuntal subtlety to "disorder," often mixing imitative motives, tremolo, and dissonances with a regularizing tread of sequence; the coda of the "Jupiter" finale is a kind of apotheosis of this technique. Seen through the lens of these genre-based topics, the rather broad terminology so common to the period comes to seem more specific: invention, fire, energy, grandeur, sublimity.

THE SYMPHONIC CYCLE AND OPUS

The opening moments of a symphony, whether slow or fast, soft or loud, clarion or emergent, are never expressively neutral. Here a fruitful interaction with the art of rhetoric again becomes evident. The opening of any public utterance must gain attention, secure goodwill, announce the subject or else prepare the listeners to respond appropriately to it when it arrives. Thus the composer must choose a kind of *exordium*—direct and forceful, to impress the listener (e.g., *coups d'archet* whether fast as in Mozart's "Paris" Symphony No. 31, K. 297, and "Haffner" Symphony No. 35, K. 385, or slow as in the stentorian motto of Haydn's "London" Symphony No. 104) or indirect and quiet, to steal into the mind (e.g. fast *agitato* together with melodic *pianto* as in Mozart's Symphony No. 40 in G minor, K. 550, or the slow "sunrise" topic of Haydn's *Le matin*, Symphony No. 6, or hymn-like chords as in Haydn's "Surprise" Symphony No. 94). The indirect form is vastly rarer in movements beginning Allegro; most symphonies with quiet Allegro main themes count on a slow introduction to do the work of exordium so that the listener is already disposed to hear a *piano* theme. In fact, Haydn tinkered with the ordering of his works in multi-opus prints so that the first work might constitute an exordium for the whole. For example, he originally sent his Paris symphonies along in something like the order of composition: Nos. 83 in G minor, 87 in A major, 85 in B flat major in 1786, then Nos. 82 in C major, 86 in D major, and 84 in E flat major in 1787. (They were published in this order by Imbault in January 1788.) Neither set of three begins with a slow introduction. In August 1787 he hoped that Artaria would publish them in Vienna in the order 87, 85, 83, 84, 86, 82; the following month he sent them to Forster in London as 82, 87, 85, 84, 83, 86. Artaria went ahead with the familiar ordering; Forster inserted 87 right after 82. Finally, both Sieber and Hummel published them in 1788 with the celebrated "La Reine," No. 85 in B flat major, at the beginning (Somfai 1980: 105). Thus, in no ordering connected to Haydn is there a grand-style slow introduction at the beginning, though in the groupings he sent to Artaria and Forster, the second set of three began with No. 84's Adagio.

Haydn's London symphonies, his first effort to appeal to a large paying audience while on the scene outside of his home milieu, afford an opportunity to explore symphonic topics designed to make an effect. Some of the memorable nickname-producing ideas are not themselves topics: there is no "big bang" topic to explain the "surprise" chord in the Andante of No. 94, nor does the "ticking" accompaniment in the Andante of No. 101 do more than thematize the orderly beats that underpin a more rhythmically elaborate melody. However, military topics in Symphony No. 100, in the form of the noisy "Turkish" instrumentation (cymbals, triangle, bass drum) and a trumpet signal in the Allegretto second movement, together with the return of the percussion section in the recapitulation and coda of the finale, brought to contemporary ears a raucous evocation of the sounds of battle that some audience members found terrifying. Here the visual element signifies in the concert hall: one sees the instruments that are not playing during the entire first movement and the two-reprise theme of the second, and one waits, perhaps uneasily, for the outburst. Like the unexpected use of tutti and timpani in the slow movement of Symphony No. 88, the sudden jangling of the percussion makes maximum invasive impact here. And once the first shoe has dropped, one waits until the finale for the second shoe, for the entire symphony to bring the wars of 1794 into thrillingly close focus. The listener would likely reinterpret the timpani rolls in the slow introduction to the first movement, especially the one in its last measure, as forecasting the percussive and military turn later in the symphony. (Indeed, No. 100 has the first slow introduction in the London symphonies to use the timpani roll this way; previously only No. 93 had it and only at the outset. Subsequently it became essential to Haydn's new sonic explorations for the last three symphonies performed in the larger King's Theatre.) The piping main theme (a *Harmonie*) and pizzicato-accompanied popular style of the second theme in the first movement may also be interpreted as topics of a peaceful pre-war kind, not precisely pastoral but certainly signifying a realm of enjoyment before the cataclysm. That contemporaries might have thought in these naturalistic terms is suggested by a descriptive program provided by the French theorist Jérôme-Joseph de Momigny for the first movement of No. 103 ("Drumroll"); he also offered a purely music-analytical reading (1994). The celebrated drum-roll becomes the terrifying thunderstorm that sends a frightened populace to the temple for safety, where the priest intones a chant, no doubt suggested by the similarity of the unison bass notes to the *Dies irae*. Then the dance-like theme of the Allegro, in the pastoral meter 6/8, signifies rejoicing that the storm has passed, as the melody passes from higher to lower "voices."

In considering "the origins of the sinfonia in the opera pit," Neal Zaslaw has plausibly imagined over-arching theatrical topics for the four movements of an eighteenth-century symphony: the heroic first movement charts a conflict between honor and love, the slow movement is pastoral, the dance movement alternates between courtly (minuet) and antic (trio) modes, and a finale draws on rustic or popular dance styles (1989: 417; see also 510–44). Such a context offered considerable scope but also helps to explain why composers might feel it necessary to break out of the mold, to take a pastoral Andante or Adagio and interject topical distortions all the more significant for being so out of place. Yet a slow movement may create a beautiful sound-world, initially removed from the sphere of action in the opening Allegro, that touches only occasionally or not at all on the specific markers of the pastoral topic. In Mozart's last four symphonies, the Andantes are strikingly different from those in his earlier symphonies: each creates an initial reverie (with only No. 38, the "Prague," using the drone bass, treble movement in thirds and sixths in both first and second themes) and then dramatically disrupts it, returning to the idyllic state only in the latter parts of exposition and recapitulation. In every one but No. 40, the disruptions are in minor, in churning *agitato* style, sometimes (Nos. 39 and 41) with syncopations and dissonances. Each of the movements poignantly evokes the learned style with passages of imitation and suspensions, sometimes both at once (No. 39 second theme, No. 40 main theme as well as "disruption" passage in remote flat keys, No. 41 extended *agitato* passage in the development) (Sisman 1993b: 55–59). The main themes of the last three symphonic Andantes are somewhat more elevated than pastoral: No. 39 is a hymn, No. 40 an imitative elaboration of the four-note *soggetto* of the "Jupiter's" finale, No. 41's sarabande a courtly dance far from the meadow. These quite diverse topics remind us of the complexity of pastoral as a genre always implicated in remembrance, loss, and melancholy (Sisman 1997a: 73–80).

Haydn was recognized by his contemporaries as the first to write theme and variations movements in his symphonies, especially in the slow movements (Sisman 1993). Although changing concertante configurations are essential in Haydn's tone-color rich imagination, there are few topical changes in these movements outside of the minore. Perhaps Haydn's development of the alternating variations on a major and a minor theme, were one way to increase topical variety, as in the austere invertible counterpoint of the learned style in the Symphony No. 70's A theme alternating with variations on its lyrically singing B theme. But a few movements do introduce a new topic, and in a

startling way. The beautiful muted hymn theme of No. 75's Poco Adagio second movement (Example 2.9) and its subsequent melodic elaboration in the first variation do not
prepare one for the wind fanfare that erupts in Variation 2. And after the solo cello's concertante in Variation 3, the final rescored ("tutti") variation introduces the *zefiro* topic
in its turning figuration for interior strings. Indeed, this is the movement that evidently
persuaded a minister in London, correctly, that he would meet his Maker that night,
as Haydn noted in his Second London Notebook (Landon 1959: 271–72); did he hear
the trumpet of the Last Judgment or the murmurings of breezes in the Elysian Fields?
Perhaps the powerful C-major fanfare in the variation movement of Beethoven's Fifth
Symphony finds the origin of its topical disparity in this work.

Beethoven's other symphonic slow movements also revel in topical density, disparity, and contrast. In Symphony No. 1, a catchy popular-style melody, initially unaccompanied, is treated to a series of imitative learned-style entries (attractively altered in the
recapitulation). At the beginning of the development, its initial rising fourth expands
in a sunrise topic to stir up remote modulations and evocative concertante winds. By
the end of the exposition of Symphony No. 2, the radiant pastoral hymn, a harbinger of
Mendelssohn's *Midsummer Night's Dream*, has become a dance, while the development
undergoes topical transformations by fanfare. The funeral march topic in the "Eroica"
gives way to a broadly flowing hymn in the relative major, later to a wind-saturated par-
adisal evocation in the parallel major redolent of the "Hodie mecum erat in paradiso"
movement of Haydn's *Seven Last Words*. Even the Ninth Symphony alternates themes
and their variations on two topics, a hymn and a song, until the latter is dispelled by an
oracular fanfare. Viewed topically, development sections and recomposed recapitula-
tions in the slow movement are often topically transformative, with local intensifications
and dramas created by a panoply of expressive hallmarks: *agitato, tempesta, pianto, zefiro,
ombra*, fanfare, concertante, recitative, fantasia, and various forms of the learned style.

The remaining movements of a symphonic cycle similarly evoke topical play but usually
with less density. While a minuet is not a topic per se in the minuet movement, canonic
treatment on the elevated end of the spectrum and rustic drones at the terrestrial end
suggest topical incursions into the dance. Lowe finds that topics intersect with stylistic
levels from "noble" to "common" in symphonic minuet movements (2007: 107–32). The
varieties of pastoral are often called into play, especially in trios. In the Trio of Beethoven's
"Eroica," for example, the wind band echoes over the landscape, while in that of the Ninth
Symphony, the scalar motion and reduced range suggest a foil to the dramatic Scherzo that
is consciously naive. The Trio of Symphony No. 5 enjoys its topical disparity (E. M. Forster's
"Trio of elephants dancing," in *Howard's End*) with a fugato beginning in the double basses.

Finales, as noted above, not infrequently employ a square-cut popular-style
theme as a foil for adventures (some topical) and as a familiar home base for differently prepared returns. In Haydn's Symphony No. 101, for example, the theme might
initially pass for a hymn were it in a slow tempo, but as a Vivace in cut time its opening white notes soon give way to rhythmic and registral play. The central developmental episode, in the movement's complex combination of sonata, rondo, and
variation, is a fully elaborated *tempesta* in tonic minor, after which the theme's final

EXAMPLE 2.9 Haydn, Symphony No. 75 in D major, ii: (a) Theme, mm. 1–4; (b) Variation 2, mm. 37–40; (c) Variation 3, mm. 55–58.

return is fugal, fulfilling the promise of both its white notes and its faster rhythms. Expressive gestures similarly come to the fore in the finale of Symphony No. 102 in precisely the kind of sparkling, ever-changing mimetic surface that Allanbrook identifies as the hallmark of this style. Indeed, the notion of rhythmic gesture is challenged and enriched by comparing this movement (Example 2.10), with its hilariously ubiquitous three-note scalar motives (an anapest, two eighths and a quarter), with the first movement of Mozart's Symphony No. 40, the passionate

EXAMPLE **2.10** Haydn, Symphony No. 102 in B flat major, iv: (a) mm. 1–4; (b) 187–96; (c) 223–32.

three-note *piano* figures of which have the identical rhythm (Example 2.11). The former is a tag—an upbeat when it ascends and a cadence when it descends in the theme—that is extended into longer scale passages in the contrasting areas and is always the source of disconcerting and witty effects. So much is it a launching pad for comedy that the episodes of *tempesta*, learned style, and eerie wind "voices"

EXAMPLE **2.11** Mozart, Symphony No. 40 in G minor, K. 550/i: (a) mm. 1–4; (b) 114–19; (c) 139–45.

seem like mock bluster rather than elevated or dark turns. In No. 40, however, the figure is the substance of the theme itself, where its upbeat character requires its immediate transformation into a four-note version, a double iamb, as well as a pounding cadential version all on the same pitch. The array of *tempesta*, learned style, and eerie winds in the development section here deepen the experience of the opening theme's *agitato* and *pianto* topics.

Classical composers found topics for their symphonies in the expressive worlds of opera and theater, as well as in the realms of human activity in nature, at court, or (less often) in the church. In so doing, they heightened their listeners' range of musical experiences and the possibility of shared interpretations. The variety of orchestral colors and textures encouraged sometimes fanciful but always pleasurable interpretive possibilities, the very kind that Grétry hoped to hammer into specificity with words: the fanfare could suggest calls to attention from the court, town, battlefield, or oracular voice; the rising-register crescendo might mean sunrise, growing excitement, anticipated arrival; in the stately dotted-rhythm passages of the French overture, one heard the tread of the sovereign or the elevated style of the church. The orchestra might "speak" directly, through the plangent voices of solo winds or in a recitative full of drama and pathos, or it might conjure up an imbroglio, bustling with comic intrigue. Poignant laments and sighing intervals might give way to the stormy activity of the *agitato* or *tempesta*, while the pleasant place of pastoral might be tinged with rusticity or melancholy; learned style could be difficult or satirical; courtly dances could be juxtaposed to obscure their original social context; the Turkish topic might mean comedy or war. The very multiplicity of symphonic topics led to the generalities of eighteenth-century reviews and criticism but also to the enduring sense that of the instrumental genres, the symphony was the grandest of all canvases.

References

n.n. 1800. Gegenwärtiger Zustand der Musik in Paris. *Allgemeine musikalische Zeitung* 2: 14 May (cols. 588–91), 21 May (cols. 605–7), 9 July (cols. 711–14), 23 July (cols. 745–51).

Allanbrook, Wye J. 1983. *Rhythmic Gesture in Mozart:* Le nozze di Figaro *and* Don Giovanni. Chicago: University of Chicago Press.

———. 1988. "Ear-Tickling Nonsense": A New Context for Musical Expression in Mozart's "Haydn" Quartets. *The St. John's Review* 38/1: 1–24.

———. 1991. Human Nature in the Unnatural Garden: *Figaro* as Pastoral. *Current Musicology* 51: 82–93.

———. 2002. Theorizing the Comic Surface. In *Music in the Mirror: Reflections on the History of Music Theory and Literature for the 21st Century*, ed. Andreas Giger and Thomas J. Mathiesen, 195–216. Lincoln: University of Nebraska Press.

———. 2014. *The Secular Commedia: Comic Mimesis in Late Eighteenth-Century Music*, ed. Mary Ann Smart and Richard Taruskin. Berkeley: University of California Press.

Anderson, Emily, ed. 1985. *The Letters of Mozart and His Family*, 3rd ed. New York: Norton.

Bartha, Dénes. 1965. *Haydn: Gesammelte Briefe und Aufzeichnungen*. Kassel: Bärenreiter.

Bonds, Mark Evan. 1997. The Symphony as Pindaric Ode. In *Haydn and His World*, ed. Elaine Sisman, 131–53. Princeton: Princeton University Press.

Brown, A. Peter. 1996. The Trumpet Overture and Sinfonia in Vienna (1715–1822): Rise, Decline and Reformulation. In *Music in Eighteenth-Century Austria*, ed. David Wyn Jones, 13–69. Cambridge: Cambridge University Press.

——. 2002. *The Symphonic Repertoire*. Vol. 2: *The First Golden Age of the Viennese Symphony: Haydn, Mozart, Beethoven, and Schubert*. Bloomington: Indiana University Press.

Burney, Charles. 1959. *Dr. Burney's Musical Tours in Europe*. Vol. 2: *An Eighteenth-Century Musical Tour in Central Europe and the Netherlands*, ed. Percy A. Scholes. London: Oxford University Press.

Charlton, David, ed. 1989. *E. T. A. Hoffmann's Musical Writings: Kreisleriana, The Poet and the Composer, Music Criticism*. Trans. Martyn Clarke. Cambridge: Cambridge University Press.

Churgin, Bathia. 2004. Stormy Interlude: Sammartini's Middle Symphonies and Overtures in Minor. In *Giovanni Battista Sammartini and His Musical Environment*, ed. Anna Cantoretti, 37–62. Turnhout: Brepols.

Clercx-Lejeune, Suzanne. 2001. Maldere, Pierre van. In *The New Grove Dictionary of Music and Musicians*, 2nd ed., ed. Stanley Sadie and John Tyrrell, vol. 15, 683–84. London: Macmillan.

Grant, Kerry. 1983. *Dr. Burney as Critic and Historian of Music*. Ann Arbor, MI: UMI Research Press.

Grétry, André-Ernest-Modeste. 1829. *Mémoires, ou Essais sur la musique* [1797], ed. J. H. Mees. Brussels: Academy of Music; Paris: Lyre Moderne.

Harich, Janos. 1975. Inventare der Esterházy-Hofmusikkapelle in Eisenstadt. *Haydn Yearbook* 9: 5–125.

Harrison, Bernard. 1998. *Haydn: "Paris" Symphonies*. Cambridge: Cambridge University Press.

Heartz, Daniel. 1990. *Mozart's Operas*, ed. Thomas Bauman. Berkeley: University of California Press.

Jones, William. 1784. *Treatise on the Art of Music*. Colchester: Printed for the Author by W. Keymer.

Koch, Heinrich Christoph. 1802. *Musikalisches Lexikon*. Frankfurt am Main: August Hermann der Jüngere. Reprint, Hildesheim: Georg Olms, 1964.

Lacépède, Comte de. 1785. *La poétique de la musique*. Paris: Author.

Landon, H. C. Robbins. 1959. *The Collected Correspondence and London Notebooks of Joseph Haydn*. London: Barrie & Rockliff.

——. 1978. *Haydn: Chronicle and Works*. Vol. 2: *Haydn at Eszterháza, 1766–1790*. Bloomington: Indiana University Press.

Levy, Janet M. 1982. Texture as a Sign in Classic and Early Romantic Music. *Journal of the American Musicological Society* 35/3: 482–97.

Lowe, Melanie. 2007. *Pleasure and Meaning in the Classical Symphony*. Bloomington: Indiana University Press.

McVeigh, Simon. 1993. *Concert Life in London from Mozart to Haydn*. Cambridge: Cambridge University Press.

Momigny, Jérôme-Joseph de. 1994. Analysis of Haydn's Symphony [No. 103 in E♭ ("Drumroll")] from *Cours complet d'harmonie et de composition* (1805). In *Music Analysis in the Nineteenth Century*, ed. Ian Bent. Vol. 2: *Hermeneutic Approaches*, 130–40. Cambridge: Cambridge University Press.

Monelle, Raymonde. 2000. *The Sense of Music: Semiotic Essays*. Princeton: Princeton University Press.

——. 2006. *The Musical Topic: Hunt, Military and Pastoral*. Bloomington: Indiana University Press.

Portowitz, Adena. 2004. Links between Structure and Expression in a Selected Group of Sammartini's Middle and Late Symphonies. In *Giovanni Battista Sammartini and His Musical Environment*, ed. Anna Cantoretti, 261–83. Turnhout: Brepols.

Range, Matthias. 2012. The "Effective Passage" in Mozart's "Paris" Symphony. *Eighteenth-Century Music* 9/1: 109–19.

Ratner, Leonard. 1980. *Classic Music: Expression, Form, and Style*. New York: Schirmer.

Rosen, Charles. 1995. *The Romantic Generation*. New York: Norton.

——. 1998. *The Classical Style: Haydn, Mozart, Beethoven*, 2nd ed. New York: Norton.

Sisman, Elaine. 1990. Haydn's Theater Symphonies. *Journal of the American Musicological Society* 43/2, 292–352.

——. 1993a. *Haydn and the Classical Variation*. Cambridge, MA: Harvard University Press.

——. 1993b. *Mozart: The "Jupiter" Symphony: No. 41 in C Major, K. 551*. Cambridge: Cambridge University Press.

——. 1997a. Genre, Gesture, and Meaning in Mozart's "Prague" Symphony. In *Mozart Studies 2*, ed. Cliff Eisen, 27–84. Oxford: Clarendon.

——. 1997b. Haydn, Shakespeare, and the Rules of Originality. In *Haydn and His World*, ed. Elaine Sisman, 3–56. Princeton: Princeton University Press.

——. 2008. Six of One: The Opus Concept in the Eighteenth Century. In *The Century of Bach and Mozart*, ed. Sean Gallagher and Thomas Forrest Kelly, 79–107. Cambridge, MA: Harvard University Press.

——. 2013. Haydn's Solar Poetics: The *Tageszeiten* Symphonies and Enlightenment Knowledge. *Journal of the American Musicological Society* 66/1: 5–102.

Somfai, László. 1980. Opus-Planung und Neuerung bei Haydn. *Studia Musicologica* 22/1: 87–110.

Spazier, Karl. 1800. *Grétry's Versuche über die Musik*. Leipzig: Breitkopf & Härtel.

Sulzer, Johann Georg. 1774. *Allgemeine Theorie der schönen Künste*. Vol. 2. Leipzig: Weidmann.

Triest, Johann Karl Friedrich. 1801. Bemerkungen über die Ausbildung der Tonkunst in Deutschland im achtzehnten Jahrhundert. *Allgemeine musikalische Zeitung* 3: cols. 225–35, 241–49, 257–64, 273–86, 297–308, 321–31, 369–79, 389–401, 405–10, 421–32, 437–45.

——. 1997. Remarks on the Development of the Art of Music in Germany in the Eighteenth Century. Trans. Susan Gillespie. In *Haydn and His World*, ed. Elaine Sisman, 321–94. Princeton: Princeton University Press.

Webster, James. 1991. *Haydn's "Farewell" Symphony and the Idea of Classical Style: Through-Composition and Cyclic Integration in the Instrumental Music*. Cambridge: Cambridge University Press.

Will, Richard. 2002. *The Characteristic Symphony in the Age of Haydn and Beethoven*. Cambridge: Cambridge University Press.

Wyn Jones, David. 1995. *Beethoven: Pastoral Symphony*. Cambridge: Cambridge University Press.

Zaslaw, Neal. 1982. Mozart, Haydn, and the "Sinfonia da chiesa." *The Journal of Musicology* 1/1: 95–124.

——. 1989. *Mozart's Symphonies: Context, Performance Practice, Reception*. Oxford: Oxford University Press.

CHAPTER 3

....

TOPICS IN CHAMBER MUSIC

....

W. DEAN SUTCLIFFE

"Topic theory," first developed by Leonard Ratner in his book *Classic Music* (1980), seeks to account for the stylistic plurality that emerges so strikingly in the music of the eighteenth century: in particular, the possibility that an individual movement may now incorporate disparate materials, leading to abrupt contrasts of style. Such materials typically derive from some original functional context in which their defining musical elements are heard—a social dance, a ceremonial fanfare, or music for worship, for example—and are then lifted out of that context. Thus a keyboard instrument can play a horn call or a string quartet can evoke sacred polyphony. This sense of music being imported from elsewhere is the most characteristic aspect of topical discourse. It implies a world with newly enlarged musical horizons, suggests that music can be found everywhere in a society and readily transferred from one place to another; it also tends to overturn hierarchies that may exist when types of music are confined to their original functional contexts. High, middle, and low styles may now rub shoulders. This is often understood as part of a thoroughgoing theatrical orientation, as if the different topics can be heard as characters interacting on a stage; more broadly, it can be understood as—to put this into a contemporary vernacular—a celebration of difference.

However, given that the field of topical analysis is now well enough established, its proponents have generally shown little curiosity about the origins of topical mixture. While Ratner writes that "music in the early 18th century developed a thesaurus of *characteristic figures*" (1980: 9), the examples and writings cited in support derive almost entirely from the late part of the century. More recently, the work of Raymond Monelle (2006) has shown plenty of curiosity, though this was directed more toward establishing a cultural history of individual topics or topical fields, namely the hunt, military, and pastoral. He did not address the historical emergence of a topically mixed style as such nor the conditions whereby that seems to have become a norm. There is a general consensus that topical mixture emerges from the world of opera, in particular opera buffa, but this has been more assumed than demonstrated in any detail, and in Chapter 1 of this volume Mary Hunter points to the limitations of such a view.

If the field of enquiry has been rather restricted chronologically, this also seems to apply geographically. Both are evident in the fact that the scholarly literature has concentrated on a particular, traditional repertory, Viennese Classicism, and indeed on a single composer, Mozart. In fact, one might argue that topic theory, as a means of accounting for developments in the art music of the later eighteenth century, has been made in the image of Mozart; in other words, what may be a peculiarly suitable way of accounting for some of his compositional procedures has been taken to represent a more widespread practice to which the theory may not entirely apply.[1] One might even argue that it came about from a desire to elevate Mozart in the face of prevailing Beethoven-inspired assumptions about what constitutes the core of Classicism's technique and spirit (above all organicism). Such essentializing may be especially apparent when one considers the "hard end" of the theory, whereby the speed of topical interplay becomes a defining feature. Thus the quickfire juggling of seemingly disparate material is held up as a stylistic norm, and Mozart is then proclaimed, in the words of Ratner, to be "the greatest master at mixing and coordinating topics, often in the shortest space" (1980: 27).

However, one might question whether this is even a fair characterization of Mozartean procedures. Many topical exegeses deal with sonata-form first movements of multimovement instrumental works, which do tend to be highly varied in their types of musical material. Certain showpieces, such as the first movement of Mozart's Sonata in F major K. 332, are undoubtedly remarkable in their rapid changes of texture and topical stance, but may not be that typical of the composer. Other movement types like slow movements, variations, rondo finales, and minuets and trios, which would not seem readily to allow such mercurial shifts of expression, have also been neglected.

If we expand our terrain geographically, the status of topical play as it has been defined is also uncertain. Rather than a European universal, it is closely bound to Italianate composers and compositional traditions—though admittedly that can encompass much of the continent. In particular, connection with the world of opera does seem to have been a stimulus. Carl Philip Emanuel Bach, who never engaged with that world compositionally, is an instructive figure in this regard. His music does not seem to have become part of the canon for topical explication—understandably so, since there is but intermittent evidence that he sought to mix and match material in the quasi-theatrical way that is suggested by the literature.

On the other hand, no creative output could be more marked by quick changes, and a distinct taste for discontinuity, which often amounts to the impulsive pulling-apart of individual phrase units. If we wish to reconcile such features with the notion of topical mutability, we may need to revise our terms of reference. There is little doubt about the increasing cultivation over the course of the eighteenth century of a manner that offers contrast and interaction between types of musical material, within the span of a single movement—but whether topic is the best controlling term for such a syntactical aesthetic is open to debate. More fundamental, perhaps, is simple changeability of discourse, made possible by the rise of periodic phrase structures—which encourage such "short-term" thinking—and underpinned by an attitude of skepticism or relativism about the nature of musical utterance. A relativistic attitude derives from the fact that individual expressive tokens—whether we call these topics or gestures or textures—are potentially worlds unto themselves and may often have "filled the screen" in some original functional or generic context. However, when they are conjoined with other material within a single musical unit, they lose any absolute claims, becoming merely another possible means of musical expression. Within such a style, topics may be symptomatic rather than foundational, the larger development being a sort of creative abdication of discursive authority; a musical utterance marked by variety of stance and gesture no longer seems to compel a particular response or enforce a single "message." Thus greater weight is now placed on the listener, who is invited to make sense of such plurality.[2]

One way of asserting the foundational status of topics has been to widen the terms of engagement, as Ratner attempted to do: in addition to various well-known musical styles, "we can include specific figures—appoggiaturas, tiratas, arpeggios, suspensions, turns, repeated notes etc.—in the theatrical climate generated by the constant presence of topical content. These short figures take on topical character as postures, as gestures that carry affective value. They enter the discourse as subjects that surround the more sharply delineated topics" (1991: 616). Given that such figures can indeed carry particular kinds of affective and gestural character, it seems plausible to suggest that they might not be so different in that respect from topics proper. In her posthumous book *The Secular Commedia: Comic Mimesis in Late Eighteenth-Century Instrumental Music*, Wye J. Allanbrook also considered just how far "topicality" extends in this repertory: "All topical identities are relational. 'Legato' and 'lyrical' are topoi by virtue of being juxtaposed to and hence differentiated from passages that are staccato, or that clearly mimic orchestral rather than vocal idioms. The mercurial gestural shifts of the style delimit one another in a variegated web across the surface, and the absence of a fortunate name for a particular gesture does not mean that it is not differentiated from its neighbor in the topical thread of the piece" (2014: 123). Unlike Ratner, who differentiates phenomena such as repeated notes or arpeggios from topics by dubbing them "figures," Allanbrook states that different types of articulation (legato, staccato), for example, also assume a topical identity. The notion that such contrasting materials are defined relative to each other is hardly controversial,[3] yet the larger assumption made by both writers exposes a tension in the conception of the field. On the one hand, topics are understood as conventions of any kind, including the phenomena proposed by Ratner and Allanbrook (an appoggiatura, legato articulation, and so forth). On the other hand, topics are understood as larger-scale phenomena, as characteristic combinations of such figures, recognizable more or less as styles that are lifted from some original functional context and placed elsewhere. Certainly the latter is the prevalent working assumption for most scholars in the field. One might argue that the more inclusive definition, implying a brand of musical discourse that is always topically saturated, reduces the explanatory power of "topic theory." It becomes just another "theory of everything," an "organic" or holistic world of its own, and there is no ready means to differentiate topical phenomena from other strands that go toward making up such music. From a more style-historical point of view, other types of music are also full of such "figures"; why should they not therefore carry the same theatrical and gestural weight in those circumstances? If they do, then how is topical analysis in any way addressing the particularities of later eighteenth-century style and its social premises?

All these concerns about the purview of topic theory may be particularly applicable to the world of instrumental chamber music, since this seems to be where the greatest changeability can routinely be found. To concentrate on capturing this in standard topical terms, what we now define as chamber music—music for one player per part, music-making that does not demand the presence of listeners—could be lighter on its feet, using a wider spectrum of topics than other media, changing topics more quickly and combining them with greater versatility. Useful here is Michael Broyles's classic distinction between a "sonata style" characterized by smaller-scale phrase syntax, and hence admitting of greater expressive flexibility, and the relatively more continuous "symphony style."[4] The former can to an extent be tied to chamber-musical forms, though Broyles himself pointed out that most of Mozart's instrumental oeuvre, for example, was animated by the broader-brush "symphony style" (1983: 235). Allanbrook writes in *The Secular Commedia* that "the primary trait of the chamber style was its expressive openness" (2014: 125); Ratner states that "it is in…chamber music that the kaleidoscopic variety of the classic style is most vividly manifested," since chamber forms can act as a "clearinghouse for texture and topic" (1980: 142). Hunter glosses this as the "domestic consumption and replication of 'public' music" (1997: 107). The use of scare quotes signals that the distinction between private, or domestic, and public is of course a ticklish one. It may be best drawn for our purposes by noting that nonchamber genres virtually demand listeners and/or participants: these include opera, church music, orchestral music, ceremonial occasions, and social dances.

In fact chamber genres are somewhat parasitic, since their specific contribution to the topical universe of eighteenth-century music seems to have been negligible. Chamber genres did not readily generate topics for other genres to borrow; it was barely conceivable for other media to suggest anything specifically chamber-like, to the extent that such a distinction even arose in the minds of eighteenth-century composers and listeners. (An apparent exception might be a movement like the Largo cantabile of Haydn's Symphony No. 93, which begins with a theme for string quartet, but then this only invokes an unlikely medium rather than suggesting a type of material peculiar to the quartet.) The sense that chamber music absorbs the topics associated with other genres is literally manifested in the case of arrangements, so common at the time, and this includes opera, though rarely, it would seem, sacred music. Haydn's *Seven Last Words*, an admittedly unusual sacred work written for orchestra that quickly appeared in arrangements for keyboard and string quartet, would represent one celebrated exception. In addition, chamber genres seem formally heterogeneous when set against these other elements of musical life. They come in more shapes and sizes: as well as arrangements of all types, self-contained single-movement works are possible, including variations, and multimovement works start at two movements and proceed more or less indefinitely upward. Such factors suggest why chamber music could readily deliver greater variety of topical discourse, even though all musical genres played a part in the process of stylistic miscegenation that accompanied the emergence of a changeable manner.[5]

The presumed author of the entry "Sonate" in Johann Georg Sulzer's *Allgemeine Theorie der schönen Künste*, Johann Abraham Peter Schulz, seems to confirm the relative freedom possible in chamber genres when writing that the sonata—by which he means multimovement instrumental music for one or more players—"can take on every type of character and expression" (*alle Charaktere und jeden Ausdruk annihmt* [*sic*]; Sulzer 1774: 1094). This is compared with the symphony and overture, which have on the other hand a more definite character. However, the sort of freedom Schulz has in mind does not accord sweetly with our topical plurality. He specifically takes to task "the Italians and their imitators" for producing "a great noise of notes following randomly one after another," and this includes sudden transitions between effects like the pathetic and the playful.[6] While framed negatively, this does confirm the perception of a mixed and changeable style. It also tends to confirm that such mixture (while presented in terms of contrasting effects rather than topics) could be understood as a particularly Italianate proclivity.

If I suggested earlier that we need a more expansive historical treatment of this phenomenon, and a reserved attitude to the centrality of "topic" to its development, we might consider the work of one noisy Italian, Domenico Scarlatti. In his keyboard sonatas Scarlatti offers us perhaps the first recognizably topically volatile repertory; and it is no accident this occurs in a chamber genre. The worldly orientation of this output is most obvious in the prominent use of various folk and popular-style materials, but these are just a part of what sounds like an unprecedented openness to the "sounds of the world." Ralph Kirkpatrick's remark, occasioned by the kaleidoscopic Sonata K. 24, that the keyboard "is no longer a solo instrument; it is a crowd" (1953: 160) captures very nicely this spirit of pluralism, and the social implications of such a stance, as composer authority yields to listener invitation (the pluralism of the "crowd"). It is instructive that writers have been trying to identify topics in the Scarlatti sonatas for a long time, well before the advent of topic theory and its application to a home territory of Viennese Classicism. That the sonatas have prompted such curiosity, including an urge to define and label the materials being heard, is itself a sign of their allure for a listener. Giorgio Pestelli wrote of the sonatas' "theatrical vocation" (*vocazione teatrale*) (1967: 195), which of course fits with one assumed explanation for the origins of topical mixture, while Sacheverell Sitwell evoked a composer who "travels at unheard-of speeds, creates an atmosphere in the flash of a second; he populates, as it were, the streets and squares, needing no more than a moment or two to complete his work" (1935: 165–66). This suggests not just a worldly and cosmopolitan mindset but also the taste for instantaneous changes of stance characteristic of the modern "impatient" style, engineered at great speed in Sitwell's futurist-style formulation.

While many Scarlatti sonatas can be accommodated more or less within the prevailing understanding of topical play as found in the later eighteenth century—the well-known K. 96 in D major, for example, with its vertiginous succession of distinct musical images—there are other features that cast doubt, not on the principle of changeability, but on the notion of topic as foundational to this process. For example, many sonatas enact what I have termed a process of "stylistic modulation" (Sutcliffe 2003: 224), a gradual shift in style or topic without there being any marked points of discontinuity in the handling of material. One common scenario is to begin with a contrapuntal gambit and by degrees move toward the realm of the dance-like and popular, sometimes with suggestions of flamenco rhythm. In K. 497, for example, the opening features a chain of 7–6 suspensions between soprano and alto voices. The closing idea from m. 31 onward takes the initial suspensions and reverses them—both texturally, since they are now heard in tenor and bass, and in trend, since they now rise, turning into a 5–6 succession. The pattern is now accompanied not by another mobile contrapuntal strand, as happened at the start, but by rapid repeated-note figuration in the right hand. Upon repetition of the phrase this changes to even more brilliant-sounding alternating octaves high on the instrument. The "worked" style of the opening is now infused with the more open sonority and virtuoso gestures that had been heard in the interim. Such a process operates on the basis of what we would now characterize as monothematicism, or *Fortspinnung*, premised on the constant reuse of various cells or motives and a high level of continuity from one phrase unit to the next. This is a resource that is largely lost later in the century, yet the composer's procedure seems clearly to be animated by the wish to bring together styles and gestures that are not readily compatible. However, it does not seem to depend on the notion of topics as more or less discrete, readily recognizable units of invention.

This is even more apparent when the points of topical reference that seem to flood into the sonatas of Scarlatti are heard in quite different ways. For example, the Sonata K. 477 in G major, in 6/8 and to be played Allegrissimo, has been taken to evoke a Spanish dance, an Italian dance (the tarantella), and hunting horns.[7] These topical connotations do not seem readily compatible, the hunting horns, for example, being distinctly more upmarket than a tarantella or popular Spanish dance form. While the piece offers some distinctive shapes along the way, it is rhythmically continuous, being written throughout in eighth notes that are only interrupted around cadence points. Thus it is nearer to being "monothematic," once again, than embodying the sort of contrasting impulses one expects of a topically mixed style.

Given the relatively uniform motion of the piece, it is hard to imagine a reading that tries to allow for all the topical possibilities mentioned above. This kind of case occurs often in the interpretation of Scarlatti, yet firmly identifying a topical source may not in fact be of great importance. What seems to count for more is a pervading sense of "exteriority," with the listener being invited to imagine and speculate on the source of the sounds; this can create "not just a *successive*, but a *simultaneous* variety of the musical surface" (Sutcliffe 2003: 82). Scarlatti, in other words, seems to specialize in what Robert Hatten describes in his contribution to this book and elsewhere (2004) as topical troping. The notion that no single topic may be plainly in control could seem to contradict a premise of the theory that material should be readily recognizable in order to engage the listener. But arguably such cases simply invite participation in the music on a different level, emphasizing "the power of a listener to construct a framework of understanding" (Sutcliffe 2003: 83). While this leaves things more democratically open for the listener, it may also make for a more demanding type of engagement with the music.

Such openness may be a particular trait of Scarlatti's, but these principles can also be borne in mind for the topical analysis of later repertoire, which generally aims to be taxonomically specific. A style that appeals so markedly to the prior experience of the listener is going to have to allow room for diverging responses.

The challenge to a listener is magnified in the case of those sonatas that feature very dramatic changes of style, sometimes so extreme that rupture seems a better description than simply topical contrast. One recurring pattern involves switching into a very broad pastoral manner, generally involving a change of meter and tempo as well (as in K. 202, 273, and 513). In such cases one has the impression less of interplay than of an entirely new piece of music beginning. Once again, such a handling of disparate materials may not be easy to accommodate within the terms of reference that have emerged for the analysis of topics in later eighteenth-century music. The ethos of mediation—and perhaps reconciliation—between contrasting materials that seems to underpin topic theory is not very evident.

On the other hand, Scarlatti's Sonata in A major K. 181 (Example 3.1) shows more obvious points of contact with our understanding of later eighteenth-century practice. The most striking moment of the first half arrives from the upbeat to m. 16, where an enormous stylistic shift takes place. This is most apparent in the jarring augmented second heard in the melodic line as it moves from C♮ to D♯. The continuation into m. 17, with its brief flurry of sixteenth notes, seems to offer a different way of realizing the same melodic syncopation. Further, the harmonic sense of the whole unit is obscure. If we are moving into the tonic minor after the A major start, then why the D♯s? If we are moving toward E major, why the C♮s? The G♯ heard on the second sixteenth note of m. 17 adds to the confusion. If this were a G♮, one could understand the right hand's rising line as the scale of E harmonic minor, and the harmonic process as a mode switch from the previous E major chord of mm. 14–15. The material is unquestionably exotic in flavor, and it is only with its arrival that we can start to define the opening in topical terms.

The symmetrical phrase syntax found in the first eight measures pronounces that the music is behaving according to galant style. This involves a complex equilibrium between the matching and opposition of material. Thus each phrase unit begins on an eighth-note anacrusis and lasts for exactly two measures, a simple form of symmetrical construction. Three of the four units begin with a large intervallic rise, marked (a), and three of the four units rhyme by closing with a restruck suspension, (b). As against these forms of matching, each pair of phrase units is also complementary, with a rising contour in the first part being answered by a falling one in the next (this is indicated by arrows on the score). On a larger scale, the first four measures are answered by the next four, to form a sectional period. Unusually, it is the first four that reach a firmer close on $\hat{1}$ in m. 4, whereas the second phrase closes on a more open-sounding $\hat{3}$, C♯. The less stable, more dynamic nature of mm. 5–8 is set up in m. 6 by a prolonged syncopated passing note G♯ within a line that rises by step, marked (x). The rise from F♯ to G♯ at the start of the measure parallels the rising steps that are heard at the beginning of mm. 2 and 4, but with a reversal of diminutional values: it is now the second note that is dissonant. This lingering syncopated G♯ all but overrides the neat periodicity of the phrase

EXAMPLE **3.1** Scarlatti, Sonata in A major, K. 181, mm. 1–72.

(Continued)

EXAMPLE **3.1** (Continued)

structure; it resolves to the A heard on the final eighth note of the measure, creating an overlap between phrase units. This feature is picked up in the more animated material that follows from m. 9, also marked (x).

The fact that this opening is succeeded by such a strongly contrasting style relativizes its status, meaning that it is now just part of a wider picture; it no longer speaks with absolute authority. This illustrates Hatten's point (this volume, page 514) that topics are defined oppositionally, that "a familiar style type only becomes topical when it is *imported*, without losing its identity, into different contexts." The difficulty in this case is that trying to capture the topical identity of the first eight measures through any particularizing label seems misguided when what is presented seems simply to be the modern vernacular of the time:[8] is the term "topic" out of scale as a means to describe such contrast?

What seems more certain is that the phrase syntax is a marked parameter in what follows. When the exotic two-measure unit at mm. 16–17 is repeated exactly at mm. 18–19, this means there are none of the complementary contours that we heard in the first four measures of the piece: instead of reciprocity we hear insistence. In fact, the rising contour of the exotic line suggests a kind of parody of the initial two-measure unit. That element of parody is also apparent in the syncopated rhythm and rising line of m. 16, marked (x), because they seem to pick up on what we heard first in m. 6. A compressed form of the same features then follows immediately in m. 17. In the third two-measure unit, at mm. 20–21, we do then hear a complementary falling contour, and the sense of correction is enhanced by the melodic resemblance to the opening motives: over the bar at mm. 19–20 there is a form of (a), then over the bar at mm. 20–21, more weakly felt, a version of (b). Further, the falling sixteenth-note figure in m. 21 clearly reverses the compressed forms of (x) heard at mm. 17 and 19. However, the abrupt end to the phrase after that, together with the unexpected swerve to a C-sharp-major harmony, achieved through an enharmonic reinterpretation of C♮ as B♯, catches us short. The phrase as a whole certainly lacks the discursive clarity with which we were presented at the start.

A further level of insistence is apparent when the entire exotic phrase starts to repeat itself down a third from m. 22, intensifying the sense of harmonic obscurity. The level of dissonance also increases as the harmony starts to accumulate clusters in the left hand from the end of m. 25 (which enharmonically changes the B♯ back to a C♮ once more) through to m. 28. On the other hand, the complementary falling phrase unit is now repeated, which yields the balance of two rising units being answered by two falling ones, and resemblances to the melodic conduct of the first eight measures become stronger: we hear two plain forms of (b), and with the second of the two correcting units a form of (a), with an intervallic jump over the barline. In any case, m. 29 then brings some relief: with the arrival on B we find ourselves on V/V.

What follows in the right hand retains the basic contour of motive (x), with the rhythm and stepwise ascent of that shape, but the melodic augmented second has become a simple rising minor second, set to mellifluous figuration in the left hand as opposed to the repeated chords of the exotic passage. If the previous use of (x) could be described as a parody, here we have a parody of the parody, meaning that stylistically we are back on more normal ground. This phrase too leads to V/V, with B major being prolonged for three whole measures (mm. 34–36): it is as if the passage pointedly shows a more fluent way of reaching the harmonic goal. Note from m. 32 the easy continuation compared with the effortful, tense gestures of the exotic material. But the antagonistic nature of the topical contrast is then affirmed, since in m. 37, instead of the expected move to E major, the exotic material tauntingly returns yet again, and that also means a renewal of harmonic ambiguity. However, this is then turned on its head: the compressed form of (x) featuring two sixteenth notes at the start of the measure is presented in rhythmic diminution in mm. 41–42. This turns it into that characteristically galant rhythm, the Lombard; it domesticates the exotic turn of phrase. A further level of domestication is apparent in the embedding of this new rhythm within an example of Robert Gjerdingen's Fenaroli schema (2007: 225–40). As marked in Example 3.1, this involves a partial exchange of note-pairs between the outer parts, with the $\hat{7}$–$\hat{8}$ D♯–E succession in the right hand of m. 41 being answered by a $\hat{7}$–$\hat{8}$ in the bass in the following measure. In addition, on a larger scale the exotic two-measure unit is embedded within a lucid eight-measure sentence structure (again as marked on the score), composed of a statement and restatement followed by a continuation toward a cadence. The immediate repetition at pitch of the whole eight-measure unit also represents a consolidating move.

At the start of the second half this process of topical alternation is replaced by a sort of fusion. But the result is less comfortable than this sounds. The right hand matches its opening unit from the first half of the sonata, but replacing any form of (b) at the start of m. 58 is a roulade involving a rising third. This recalls the Lombard figures from the first half but seems to return them to stylistic source, the compressed form of motive (x): thus the shape once more sounds exotic. The left hand then offers a sort of nightmare imitation of the right hand's repeated notes, expressed in the form of a cluster. This seems to throw the melody off course, and by the end of the four-measure unit at mm. 59–60 it is playing a diminished third from F♮ to D♯, a clear counterpart to the exotic augmented second we heard so often in the first half. It is as if the opening has been sucked into the vortex of the exotic material, and there is little trace of reciprocal shaping within the four-measure unit. The earlier harmonic obscurity also returns.

A repetition of the four-measure unit is succeeded from m. 65 by a 5–10 linear intervallic pattern, which sounds quite incongruous: it would seem that we have suddenly entered a world of Vivaldian sequences. Yet as a sort of impasse has arguably been reached, maybe this very strong form of patterning represents an appropriate escape, helping to restore some sense of equilibrium to proceedings after a moment of stylistic crisis. Certainly no piece of material could better exemplify the classic notion of a topic, since in this context one has the strong sensation of music being imported from elsewhere, to a place where it might seem not to belong. The pure sequential drive, in one-measure units, is arguably more foreign than the exotic material, since that after all was still built on the basis of two-measure units arranged in various permutations. And this material does not return after its sole appearance. However, it does lead, at mm. 69–70, to another Fenaroli, though this one is heard twice in immediate succession, which is more typical of the schema. The exotic phrase that we first heard from m. 16

finds new ways of making mischief in the remainder of the second half; for instance, it reworks the chain of Lombard rhythms into a form that now spirals downward, with a Phrygian inflection (mm. 82–84), and later gives them a Lydian twist that confuses the tonal sense just when we were expecting a clear cadential approach (mm. 97 and 106).

Scarlatti's K. 181 exemplifies what Ratner described as the "speculative" treatment of topics, one that seems to have flourished especially strongly in the chamber (1980: 142). Yet it also makes us question certain fundamentals. For example, I have implied with my label "exotic" that the relevant material can be understood as a topic, but how can that be possible when so few listeners of the time could ever have encountered such material, would not therefore experience a moment of recognition, would not in other words be "competent" listeners? If this is a topic, the definition has to be broadly conceived; perhaps it is better understood as a topical field, in the manner of the pastoral, rather than a more focused point of reference such as a fanfare or minuet. In fact it may be that the "bum notes" and "untutored" harmony are best understood as part of that subset of pastoral that includes aberrant pitch behavior, alluding to types of music-making that fall outside the norms of art music. However, this material seems to have little innocent about it, given its detailed interaction with a galant lingua franca throughout the sonata. Indeed, perhaps the main thing to note about K. 181 in connection with topic theory is simply the small-scale interaction of material, all the hard edges, all the checks and balances, as materials that originally belonged in different places collide. This has much in common with received ideas about topical play, though the orientation may appear to be less conciliatory than antagonistic, as the sonata essentially alternates between two typologies, though with great versatility in the small print. And, as suggested, it is difficult to feel satisfied with the classifications given to either type of material—both "galant" and "exotic" seem like blunt instruments. But simply to play down the importance of such labels might be to duck the issue. The taxonomic side must carry some weight if the claim underpinning the theory is that materials that count as topics are readily recognizable and evoke specific associations.

If, as K. 181 and many other Scarlatti sonatas attest, music destined for chamber performance tended to be more changeable in its materials and manner, yet lacked its own idiomatic topical vocabulary, how else might we distinguish its topical practice from that found in other areas of eighteenth-century musical life? One answer, implicit in the question, is that chamber genres are able to explore extremes of topical expression more frequently; they can support degrees of "speculation" that would have been less likely in brands of music that would always demand an audience. One characteristic field of more sustained exploration involves the use of old-style material. In his contribution to this handbook Keith Chapin explores the awkward nomenclature of this topical field. What we (but not the eighteenth century) call the learned style embraces a range of materials and circumstances; it cannot just automatically be equated with the techniques characteristic of strict counterpoint. In fact, for all that there are famous examples of strict counterpoint found in chamber forms such as the string quartet (for example, the finales of Mozart's K. 387 and Haydn's Op. 50 No. 4), chamber music may distinguish itself more clearly in the incorporation of other types of "learned" material. All this material "shows its age" in one way or another. At the softer end of the scale would come that style of sequential writing that evokes baroque practice. We have already glimpsed one specimen in Scarlatti's K. 181, where the stylistic context argues for hearing the sequence in mm. 65–69 as a reversion to an older manner, if hardly an exemplar of learned style. Among countless other examples in eighteenth-century chamber music one could cite the Op. 5 string quartets by Peter Hänsel, written in 1797 and dedicated to his teacher Haydn; descending linear intervallic patterns that seem frankly to evoke an earlier style are found, for example, in the finale of No. 3, mm. 104–108. When marked by chains of suspensions, as in the first movement of No. 1, mm. 123–28, or the Andante of No. 2, mm. 65–68 (Example 3.2), the sense of stylistic reversion becomes stronger.

Such a feature belongs at the softer end of the scale because it may not sound that marked in a particular context, for all that sequential construction is potentially at odds with the periodic phrase syntax that underlies all later eighteenth-century style. For example, Roman Ivanovitch (2011) has recently codified a type of Mozartean retransition that is often based on descending sequential writing, including chains of suspensions, over a dominant pedal point, yet traces of an older style seem to be largely absorbed into what is a thoroughly idiomatic feature of the composer's style. But harder-edged appropriations of material that has an "aura of age," to use Chapin's phrase, can quite readily be found in chamber music of the time. Many of the most striking instances occur in slow movements. The second movements of Haydn's Sonata in E major Hob. XVI:31 and the Trio in the same key, Hob. XV:28, for example, are both set in the tonic minor and feature passacaglia-style constant bass movement in eighth notes. The very constancy of the movement already starts to mark the style out as exceptional, precisely because it tends to override the principles of periodic organization; as Hatten comments, "perpetual motion is marked in opposition to the unmarked, stylistically established articulations of texture" found in later eighteenth-century style (2004: 240). Ostinato bass lines are also found, for example, in the Andante of Mozart's Violin Sonata K. 526 and Andante cantabile of Haydn's Piano Trio Hob. XV:20, though in terms of stylistic signals these movements show their age less clearly.

EXAMPLE 3.2 Hänsel, String Quartet in E flat major, Op. 5 No. 2/iii, mm. 63–69.

Other slow movements take matters further, offering material that virtually recreates an older style. A supreme instance is found in Haydn's Sonata in D major Hob. XVI:37, in which brilliantly animated outer movements are separated by a Largo e sostenuto in D minor that sounds like a sarabande written in the grandest, most solemn High Baroque style. Only toward the end, with the climax on a sustained Neapolitan-sixth harmony and the subsequent settling on repeated low-register dominant chords, does the sense of topical fidelity definitively weaken. The two Haydn trio movements cited above also break topical ranks toward their ends, in both cases through a torrent of figuration that sounds incompatible with what went before. Nevertheless, in the case of all these "antique" movements the real topical contrast obtains not internally, but at an inter-movement level. Within the movements themselves there is little overt topical interplay, as one stylistic strand predominates. In a sense such unadulterated presentation stays truer to the premises of the original topic and the musical world of which it formed a part, since materials normally "ran their course" without interruption or sudden inter-nal contrast. As suggested near the outset, this is an aspect of slow movements that topic theory, promoting a norm of quick topical turnover, has yet to come to terms with.

For all the apparent fidelity of Haydn's recreation of a sarabande in the slow movement of Hob. XVI:37, the ornamental flourishes suggest that the topic is being rendered more lavishly than one might expect to hear in the real thing. This aspect is shared by many of the antique recreations of Clementi, one of the great late-century proponents of older styles (often in fact more specifically learned, given the composer's frequent canonic treatment of material). In particular, the second movement of his Sonata Op. 50 No. 1, marked Adagio sostenuto e patetico, more literally recreates an older style, reworking the opening material from the Sarabande from Bach's English Suite No. 2 in A minor (compare Examples 3.3 and 3.4). The texture is richer than Bach's original, dissonances are made stronger, and Clementi adds his own four-note figure to the mix, this often being treated in close imitation to create a form of contrapuntal saturation. An inde-pendent central section, a canon based on this four-note figure at the quicker speed of Andante con moto, and marked *dolce* and *sempre legato*, withdraws from this hyperex-pressive world and presents an elevated, more "objective" lyricism. Another memorable example is the Adagio of the composer's Sonata in G major Op. 37 No. 2, whose heading, "In the solemn style," plainly advertises an antiquity of topic. Written in a freely imita-tive but quite plain dotted style, it seems to aim for a "noble simplicity and quiet gran-deur" that supports at least one aspect of Anselm Gerhard's claim (2002) that Clementi represents the true "Classicist" among composers of his time. The sense of commitment to the topics in such instances, mining them for the utmost expressive potential, once more means that topical interaction operates primarily at the level of the whole work. The more profuse manner of surrounding movements offers not just a more typical modern style, but also a different kind of topical rhythm.

Topical rhythm is also fundamentally affected by mode in the music of the later eigh-teenth century—another respect in which an identikit picture of constant topical inter-play needs reconsidering. Use of the minor mode not only typically brings certain kinds of material to the fore, it also tends to mute topical variety. While this is no peculiarity

EXAMPLE 3.3 Clementi, Sonata in A major, Op. 50 No. 1/ii, mm. 1–16.

EXAMPLE 3.4 J. S. Bach, Sarabande from English Suite in A minor, BWV 807, mm. 1–5.

of chamber works set in minor keys, such works make the point more plainly because of the tendency toward extremes noted earlier. Pleyel's Piano Trio in E minor, Ben. 435, published in 1788, offers an instructive example. Its first movement is dominated by a stentorian motto and features agitated passagework, sigh figures, and falling sequences, often infused with chains of suspensions. The motto figure acts like a kind of disembodied contrapuntal subject; compare the use of motto-like material in the first movement of Mozart's Piano Quartet in G minor, K. 478, or Haydn's own Piano Trio in E minor, Hob. XV:12, published in 1789. Pleyel's finale quickly introduces invertible counterpoint, and near the end treats its own dominating motive in stretto. The rhetorical insistence and process-driven nature of this minor-mode manner means it is less likely to consider matters from an alternative point of view, as it were. Major-key works are much more liable to be generous with material and topical contrast.

Kozeluch's Piano Trio Op. 28 No. 3 in E minor, published around 1786, offers a similar typology of thematic dominance constantly inflected by older stylistic means (Example 3.5). It starts with a motto-type theme played in octaves (though *piano*) that includes a "pathotype" falling diminished seventh (from the C of m. 3 to the D♯ of m. 4) and a falling chromatic tetrachord (moving from the E of m. 3 to the B of m. 5).[9] The consequent phrase from m. 9, played *forte*, is counterpointed by a line in continuous quavers, sounding like a baroque walking bass. The phrase does not cadence in the tonic but veers off to the mediant, G major; however, this tonal twist only brings a transposed version of the same material (m. 14). This soon leads to rapid figuration (m. 18), for which the topical category of "brilliant style" makes sense on a comparative if not an absolute basis (recall our earlier notion of the "oppositional" definition of topics). This material has clearly switched to a contemporary manner, but within a few measures the walking-bass subject enters once more (m. 23), together with a falling suspension chain entwined with another falling chromatic tetrachord. Thus the initial older-style material refuses to give way entirely to a more modern manner, and such alternations accelerate in the development section.

EXAMPLE **3.5** Kozeluch, Piano Trio in E minor, Op. 28 No. 3/i, mm. 1–28 (piano part only).

As these examples suggest, minor-key works and movements from this time tend to be especially tautly argued, using a reduced amount of material and often approaching monothematicism. Indeed, one could even suggest, given the historical predominance of the sociable major mode at this time, that the later eighteenth century never really acquired a minor-mode manner of comparable novelty (Allanbrook has described the prevalence of major keys at this time as a "striking new trope" [1994: 175]). Perhaps the minor mode always tended to function as the dependent pair in a binary opposition, intrinsically more remote from contemporary sensibilities, hence the frequent recourse to gestures from the past.[10] Encapsulating such a distinction is the second movement of Boccherini's String Quintet in A major Op. 10 No. 1, a Largo in 6/8 and in the tonic minor. It is governed by the common slow-movement topic of the siciliana, itself a sign of stylistic age, and the initial falling chromatic tetrachord and fragmentary *lamentoso*-style melodic writing fall into the same category.[11] Significantly, when the music moves to C major, there is a topical modulation to the musette, with a long octave pedal held by the second cello and greater melodic continuity. There is also a change from melodic lines being carried by a single instrument to their being carried by two instruments at a time in parallel intervals (creating together with the pedal a texture that so often signifies pastoral). Thus the major mode replaces tightness with lyrical plenitude, and solitariness with companionship.

Indeed, pastoral idioms represent another topical field that may be encountered especially often in the chamber. This may owe something to the fact that many of the folk styles typically evoked were performed not by massed forces but by small bands of players. Within this field the outright exotic figures from time to time, for instance in the finales of Hummel's Piano Trios No. 2, a *rondo alla turca*, and No. 7, a *rondo alla russa*. Final movements in fact seem to be the favored place for such material, just as full-scale evocations of older styles tend to be found internally within a work. The "Rondo, in the Gypsies' style" of Haydn's Piano Trio Hob. XV:25 in G major is a familiar example, though for sheer audacity one should turn to a passage heard twice in the final movement of Dittersdorf's String Quartet in E flat major, K. 195, in which the lower three instruments hold a C-minor chord *fortissimo* for nearly forty measures while the first violin performs a Gypsy lamentation.[12]

However, when the pastoral or folk style is less marked than in such instances, difficulties of topical exegesis readily arise. In a set like the Piano Trios Op. 41 by Kozeluch, for example, the composer uses the characteristic texture of pedal points and melodic lines moving in parallel motion so frequently as to suggest that it is less relevant to speak of "topic" than of a general orientation of later eighteenth-century style. The Andantino con Variazioni of Op. 41 No. 1, for example, proceeds from a simple tune that sounds like a folk melody together with a simple harmonic style, with pervasive doublings in thirds and sixths. The coda section (Example 3.6) returns to the tune and sets it almost entirely over a tonic pedal, variously expressed by the cello and the keyboard's left hand, thus adding the missing textural ingredient to create a full pastoral "topic." After the tune ends there are several measures of fade-out (marked *mancando* in the cello), featuring pure tonic triadic degrees and marked *aperto* (open) in the keyboard part. While picturesque

EXAMPLE **3.6** Kozeluch, Piano Trio in B flat major, Op. 41 No. 1/ii, mm. 124–41.

enough, and easy to hear as an evocation of pastoral simplicity, there is really nothing especially marked about such musical imagery—rather, the "open," (mock-)innocent, fresh quality is one toward which composers were more generally aspiring.

Indeed, one way of accounting for the momentous changes in European musical style during the eighteenth century is to think in terms of a pastoralization of art music, the movement away from the higher-flown diction of the late Baroque toward something that was, or at least announced itself to be, simpler and more unassuming. Monelle links the musical pastoral in the early eighteenth century more or less specifically with the genre of the siciliana (2006: 215–20), and while I think this is too rigid an equation, the siciliana can usefully symbolize a particular relationship of high art to modest subject matter—one that is formalized and self-contained. The later eighteenth century sheds much of the high pastoral manner represented by the siciliana, with rustic effects, for example, becoming less stylized and more vigorous, and in addition the pastoral spreads itself much more generously. A tone of popular simplicity becomes fundamental to art music; it is no longer an occasional discourse. This can be seen even on a more technical level: the parataxis characteristic of the pastoral mode, the tendency toward short, self-contained statements, comes to dominate compositional practice. Accompanying this is the move toward our more changeable musical style, which may include the free play of musical topics within a single formal frame, which will of course include the pastoral. Thus the generic purity of the older pastoral is compromised; the contrast between low and high styles which animated it, but was not spelt out, may now be directly addressed through juxtaposition.

A remarkable confirmation of how the pastoral style develops along these lines may be found in the six *Pastorelas* written by the Seville-based Manuel Blasco de Nebra (1750–84). Each work consists of an Adagio followed by a movement named Pastorela in its own right, and concludes with a minuet. The initial Adagios offer a civilized, Arcadian version of pastoral simplicity, but the succeeding Pastorelas are much less idyllic. While based on the 6/8 meter and dotted-rhythmic ingredients of the siciliana, they twist these into rhythmically quirky, consistently syncopated forms that constantly fight against the "natural" flow of the meter. And while particular shapes do recur from phrase to phrase, in general there is a conspicuous lack of art in the way individual phrases succeed one another; we tend to hear an untutored profusion of ideas. After this angular, vigorous style, the subsequent minuet movements give a sense of regaining stylistic equilibrium or decorum. This is apparent in the much more polished nature of their diction, with phrases arranged in reciprocal pairings and rhythms more settled after the "disorder" of the Pastorelas.

To write such a stylistic-topical progression into a multimovement keyboard work is not unprecedented. It recalls what Sebastián de Albero (1722–56), a younger colleague of Scarlatti's at the Spanish court, does in his six keyboard triptychs titled *Recercata, fuga y sonata*. As the titles imply, these works proceed from oldest to newest musical styles over the course of their three movements. In both cases, as we have seen in a number of examples already, "topic" does not entail frequent contrasts within individual movements, but rather exists more in how the relations between whole movements are conceived. But Albero's and Blasco de Nebra's triptychs are clearly animated by the same underlying precept—that there are very different types of music out there that can be juxtaposed, whose mutual incongruity can be exploited, or at least held up for inspection. In fact Blasco de Nebra's minuets have their own oddities, and a pervasively cryptic flavor, but these are held in place by a sense of controlled utterance after the frankness of the Pastorelas, together with the minuet's associations of elegance of movement. In thus leaving a question mark over the succession of styles, inviting the listener to try to make sense of the contrasts, the *Pastorelas* embody that attitude of skepticism or relativism that seems to underpin an aesthetic of changeability.

One final feature that is indubitably peculiar to chamber music is its ability to evoke more "public" musical genres (as explained earlier, the reverse process seems barely to exist). A favored topic in first movements is the orchestral overture. This is not just a topic but, one might suggest, also a schema, based on a tonic pedal above which a succession of scale steps rises from $\hat{1}$ to a higher degree of the triad, sometimes, as at the start of Dittersdorf's String Quartet K. 191 in D major, tracing a full octave scale to the upper tonic.[13] A crescendo is either explicitly prescribed or implied by the nature of the writing. Certain favored orchestral keys may prompt the use of this topic. D major is clearly one of these for Mozart, who tends to employ such material not as the very first gambit, as Dittersdorf does in K. 191, but as the second thing we hear. In the Sonata K. 284, the Sonata for Piano Duet K. 381, and the Sonata for Piano Duo K. 448, all in D major, the initial statement is played in unison. Then from m. 9 of the solo sonata, m. 6 of the duet, and m. 5 of the duo, the overture topic unfolds. Over a repeated-note *Trommelbass* on the tonic we hear a two-measure module controlled by $\hat{1}$, elaborated by movement up from and back to that scale degree, followed by two measures controlled by $\hat{3}$, being realized in similar fashion in all three cases. From m. 49 of the first movement of K. 448 we hear a further version of the overture schema, with each successive measure controlled by a higher scale degree of the dominant A major until a complete octave has been traversed. However, another schema is overlaid, the "Corelli"-style suspension chain whereby each successive melodic entry turns the previous pitch into a dissonance, which then resolves down by step and so yields its place at the top of the texture. This fusion of two topics and schemata is realized via brilliant rising figuration that suggests a dialogue between orchestral first and second violins.

An alternative to fusion is transformation of one topic into another. From m. 15 in the first movement of Mozart's Violin Sonata in E flat major K. 302 we hear a lengthy specimen of the overture formula, rising by step in three stages to cover the interval of a twelfth. This allows a real crescendo of excitement to unfold. Yet the climax is no sooner reached than the melodic material out of which the ascent was constructed is transformed into a horn call, to be played *piano* (mm. 27–29). This offers a humorous change of perspective, not just because of the different spatial implications of the two topics (it is as if we have moved from the opera house to the countryside), but also because the horn call contradicts the previous build-up: the overture formula normally leads to a climax of sustained tutti writing, as it does in the three D-major works just discussed. Here it is as if the "horns" are asserting their rights in a key associated with their activities.[14]

Such changes of perspective are especially likely to occur in chamber genres. Because of the typically more intimate circumstances in which these genres were performed, many topics could take on an especially loaded character, owing to the disparity between style and medium. In the finale of Clementi's Piano Trio Op. 27 No. 3 what is being suggested is not the overture topic but rather a broader arsenal of closing devices that are typically used by orchestral forces. From m. 277 of the movement (Example 3.7) the three players are clearly building up for a big orchestral-style close, with rapid alternations of V–I chords and a melodic $\hat{7}$–$\hat{8}$, *forte*, and the chords are then repeated with $\hat{2}$–$\hat{3}$ at the top, *fortissimo*—a common closing schema. But these gestures are not met with the expected two or three final loud repeated tonic chords. Instead the players offer a soft falling arpeggiated figure played in unison (though the keyboard right hand plays

EXAMPLE 3.7 Clementi, Piano Trio in G major, Op. 27 No. 3/iii, mm. 276–84.

a syncopated version starting a quaver later). This completely undercuts the closing rhetoric; it functions as a reminder that this is no orchestra playing in a large space, but three individuals playing in a (presumably) smaller venue. In similar fashion, the three finales of Gyrowetz's Op. 44 string quartets occupy themselves predominantly with comic-operatic topical types and set themselves up for big "orchestral" closes but then finish with understated *pianissimo* material, as if the players are shrinking their medium back to its true size. At this point the ironic realization may dawn that all the material that went before was imported from elsewhere, that it does not naturally belong in the current medium. In other words, the materials functioned as topics. While such a dualism between expansive gestures and gentler material in fact more widely characterizes the style of the time, it can assume a more pointed form in the chamber. Such moments also make clear that chamber genres were almost by definition likely to be especially self-conscious about their use and manipulation of topics, within a generally changeable and self-conscious discursive style.

NOTES

1. This sentence derives from my study of topical manipulation in Boccherini's string quartets Op. 32 (Sutcliffe 2007: 245).
2. How listeners can go about this task can be glimpsed from Melanie Lowe's chapter in this volume.
3. In a recent survey of the literature on topics, Nicholas McKay remarks, "Semioticians know that meaning resides not in the signs themselves but in the relation among signs" (2007: 167).
4. Heinrich Christoph Koch draws the same distinction in his *Versuch einer Anleitung zur Composition*. For him the first allegro of the symphony differs from that of the sonata in that its melodic sections "usually are more attached to each other and flow more forcefully" (1983: 199). Apart from solo sonatas, Koch applies this last concept to other genres of chamber music: duo, trio, and quartet (202).
5. While "chamber music" is hardly the monolith that the term might imply, and while different chamber genres may have different topical capacities and tendencies, for the purposes

of this study I will be treating it mainly as a block. Ratner emphasizes the role of the forte-piano as "a quintessential locale for the play of topic," largely because it "had to compensate with lively action for what it lacked in full body or sound" (1991: 616). He thus suggests that keyboard music will tend to have a quicker rate of topical turnover than other instrumental genres. While this makes sense, other factors might tend to level the comparison, for instance, the fact that the interplay of voices and lines is a less obvious modus operandi in keyboard music than in chamber genres for two or more players.

6. "Freylich haben die wenigsten Tonsezer [sic] bey Verfertigung der Sonaten solche Absichten, und am wenigsten die Italiäner, und die, die sich nach ihnen bilden: ein Geräusch von willkührlich auf einander folgenden Tönen, ohne weitere Absicht, als das Ohr unempfindsamer Liebhaber zu vergnügen, phantastische plözliche [sic] Uebergänge vom Fröhlichen zum Klagenden, vom Pathetischen zum Tändelnden, ohne daß man begreift, was der Tonsezer damit haben will, charakterisiren [sic] die Sonaten der heutigen Italiäner" (Sulzer 1774: 1094–95).

7. One of a number of "sonatas in dance style which show a Spanish influence" (Gillespie 1965: 71); "il ricordo della Tarantella, attivo al massimo nella L 290 [K. 477]" (Pestelli 1967: 243); "une sonnerie de cor" (Chambure 1987: 157); "there are so many horn calls, and they have such a feeling of urgency and expectation, that one's thoughts go flying to the introduction and opening scene of Act II of 'Tristan and Isolde'" (Dale 1941: 120).

8. Note, however, that the opening material does feature its own harmonic ambiguities, at the start of mm. 3 and 7. At these points the V^6_4 chord heard in the left hand seems to be at odds with the diminutional structures suggested in the right hand. In the second half of each measure the left-hand chords feature an acciaccatura note, often thought of as a (mild) harmonic "cluster." But as this is a signature technique of the composer's, it is not clear how stylistically "marked" these dissonances are.

9. The "pathotype" formula was so dubbed by Warren Kirkendale (1979: 91–92) and always involves "awkward" intervals like the falling diminished seventh.

10. The last few sentences are also taken from my study of topical manipulation in Boccherini's string quartets Op. 32 (Sutcliffe 2007: 251).

11. The falling chromatic tetrachord represents the *lamento* bass discussed in Chapter 15 (this volume) by William Caplin. Caplin notes the origins of this structure in baroque music and its conflict with the rising tendency of classical bass lines.

12. Haydn's "Rondo, in the Gipsies' Style" is discussed by Catherine Mayes (this volume), who suggests that eighteenth-century representations of Hungarian-Gypsy music most frequently take place in finales. The Gypsy lamentation in the Dittersdorf finale represents the *hallgató* style discussed by Mayes.

13. Another case of an intimate link between topic and schema is the *lamento*, discussed by Caplin (this volume).

14. E flat major was "the essential German hunting key," according to Monelle (2006: 42).

References

Allanbrook, Wye J. 1994. Mozart's Tunes and the Comedy of Closure. In *On Mozart*, ed. James M. Morris, 169–86. Cambridge: Cambridge University Press, in association with the Woodrow Wilson Center Press.

——. 2014 *The Secular Commedia: Comic Mimesis in Late Eighteenth-Century Music*, ed. Mary Ann Smart and Richard Taruskin. Berkeley: University of California Press.

Broyles, Michael. 1983. The Two Instrumental Styles of Classicism. *Journal of the American Musicological Society* 36/2: 210–42.

Chambure, Alain de. 1987. *Catalogue analytique de l'oeuvre pour clavier de Domenico Scarlatti: Guide de l'intégrale enregistrée par Scott Ross*. Paris: Costallat.

Dale, Kathleen. 1941. Hours with Domenico Scarlatti. *Music and Letters* 22/2: 115–22.

Gerhard, Anselm. 2002. *London und der Klassizismus in der Musik: Die Idee der "absoluten Musik" und Muzio Clementis Klavierwerke*. Stuttgart: Metzler.

Gillespie, John. 1965. *Five Centuries of Keyboard Music: A Historical Survey of Music for Harpsichord and Piano*. New York: Dover.

Gjerdingen, Robert O. 2007. *Music in the Galant Style*. New York: Oxford University Press.

Hatten, Robert S. 2004. *Interpreting Musical Gestures, Topics, and Tropes: Mozart, Beethoven, Schubert*. Bloomington: Indiana University Press.

Hunter, Mary. 1997. Haydn's London Piano Trios and His Salomon String Quartets: Public vs Private? In *Haydn and His World*, ed. Elaine Sisman, 103–30. Princeton: Princeton University Press.

Ivanovitch, Roman. 2011. Mozart's Art of Retransition. *Music Analysis* 30/1: 1–36.

Kirkendale, Warren. 1979. *Fugue and Fugato in Rococo and Classical Chamber Music*. Trans. Margaret Bent and Warren Kirkendale. Durham, NC: Duke University Press.

Kirkpatrick, Ralph. 1953. *Domenico Scarlatti*. Princeton: Princeton University Press.

Koch, Heinrich Christoph. 1983. *Introductory Essay on Composition*. Trans. Nancy Kovaleff Baker. New Haven: Yale University Press.

McKay, Nicholas. 2007. On Topics Today. *Zeitschrift der Gesellschaft für Musiktheorie* 4/1–2: 159–83.

Monelle, Raymond. 2006. *The Musical Topic: Hunt, Military and Pastoral*. Bloomington: Indiana University Press.

Pestelli, Giorgio. 1967. *Le sonate di Domenico Scarlatti: Proposta di un ordinamento cronologico*. Turin: Giappichelli.

Ratner, Leonard G. 1980. *Classic Music: Expression, Form, and Style*. New York: Schirmer.

——. 1991. Topical Content in Mozart's Keyboard Sonatas. *Early Music* 19/4: 615–19.

Sitwell, Sacheverell. 1935. *A Background for Domenico Scarlatti, 1685–1757*. London: Faber.

Sulzer, Johann Georg. 1774. *Allgemeine Theorie der schönen Künste*. Vol. 2. Leipzig: Weidmann.

Sutcliffe, W. Dean. 2007. Archaic Visitations in Boccherini's Op. 32. In *Boccherini Studies*, ed. Christian Speck, 245–76. Bologna: Ut Orpheus.

——. 2003. *The Keyboard Sonatas of Domenico Scarlatti and Eighteenth-Century Musical Style*. Cambridge: Cambridge University Press.

SECTION II

CONTEXTS, HISTORIES, SOURCES

CHAPTER 4

....

MUSIC AND DANCE IN THE
ANCIEN RÉGIME

....

LAWRENCE M. ZBIKOWSKI

In 1777 Johann Philipp Kirnberger paused in the production of his monumental *Die Kunst des reinen Satzes in der Musik* (1771–79) to publish a *Recueil d'airs de danse caractéristiques*. On the one hand, the relationship between the modest dances of Kirnberger's collection and the careful, methodical setting out of the art of strict musical composition is not immediately evident, as the two seem to belong to rather different intellectual registers. On the other hand, there is evidence that, for Kirnberger, the relationship between the two works was quite intimate. As the preface to the *Recueil* makes clear, the twenty-odd dances gathered by Kirnberger were meant to set out for the young musician the characteristic features of different dance types, as he believed familiarity with these was essential to understanding musical organization.

> In order to acquire the necessary qualities for a good performance, the musician can do nothing better than diligently play all sorts of characteristic dances. Each dance has its own rhythm, its passages of the same length, its accents on particular places in each measure; one thus easily recognizes them, and becomes accustomed, through playing them often, to attribute to each its particular rhythm, and to mark its patterns of measures and accents, so that one recognizes easily, in a long piece of music, the rhythms, sections and accents, so different from each other and so mixed up together. One learns, furthermore, to give each piece its special expression, for each type of dance melody has its own characteristic movement and value.

> Um die zum guten Vortrag nothwendigen Eigenschaften zu erlangen, kann der Tonkünstler nicht bessers thun, als fleissig allerhand *charakteristische Tänze* spielen. Jede dieser Tanzmusiken hat ihren eignen Rhythmus, ihre Einschnitte von gleicher Länge, ihre Accente auf einerley Stelle in jedem Saz [*sic*]; man erkennet sie also leicht, und durch das öftere Executiren gewöhnt man sich unvermerkt, den einer jeden eigenen Rythmus zu unterscheiden, und dessen Säze [*sic*] und Accente zu bezeichnen, so dass man endlich leicht in einem lange Musikstücke die noch so verschiedenen und durch einander gemischten Ryhthmen, Einschnitte und Accente erkennet. Man gewöhnt sich ferner jedem Stücke den eigenthümlichen Ausdruck zu

geben, weil jede Art dieser Tanzmelodien eignen charakteristischen Tact und Wehrt der Noten hat. (Kirnberger 1777: 1–2)

It was knowledge of this sort that Kirnberger believed was essential to anyone wishing to learn composition, not least because he understood it to form the basis for musical expression. Thus in the first section of the second volume of *Die Kunst des reinen Satzes*—the section toward which Kirnberger, at the end of the preface to the *Recueil*, directed his reader for a fuller account of the importance of studying dance—it becomes clear that the discussion of tempo, meter, and rhythm taken up there will only make sense if one has studied dances. In noting, for instance, that the aspiring composer must acquire the correct feeling for the natural tempo implied by different meters, he observes: "This is attained by diligent study of all kinds of dance pieces. Every dance has its definite tempo, determined by the meter and the note values that are employed in it" (Kirnberger 1982: 376).

Kirnberger's observations in the *Recueil* were important for the development of topic theory during the late twentieth century, for his remarks provided evidence that musical materials associated with different dances could serve as a compositional resource and that these materials could be combined within longer musical compositions. Within topic theory the dance topic has usually been conceived of in terms of the characteristic rhythmic features and character of dances popular in the eighteenth century. In Kofi Agawu's analysis of the first movement of Mozart's String Quintet in C major, K. 515, for example, the bourrée topic found in mm. 46–54 (and which is shown in Example 4.1a) is a rhythmic figure in duple time that begins with two eighth notes on the last quarter of the measure; by contrast, the gavotte topic found in mm. 57–65 (shown in Example 4.1b) begins with two quarter notes starting in the second half of the measure (Agawu 1991: 87). In her work on the topical organization of Mozart's *Le nozze di Figaro* and *Don Giovanni*, Wye Allanbrook took the idea of a dance topic somewhat further and proposed that the musical materials associated with different dance types could activate knowledge about the movements specific to the dance and the affectual states correlated with such movements. On this view, Mozart's use of a bourrée topic for Figaro's music in the opening duet of *Le nozze di Figaro* (which is shown in Example 4.2a) activates knowledge about the physical movements characteristic of the dance, which includes steps whose central feature is a lift onto the first beat of the measure (Allanbrook 1983: 75–76).[1] Employing a gavotte topic, as Mozart does with Susanna's music in this same duet (and which is shown in Example 4.2b), activates knowledge about a contrasting set of physical movements that begin on the third beat of the measure and then pass through the first beat to conclude on the second. This knowledge then shapes our understanding of the dramatis personae to whom we have been introduced—as Allanbrook observes, "the swaggering, cocksure bridegroom and his pert bride-to-be celebrate their coming marriage right in character, the one surveying for the nuptial bed, the other in innocent vanity admiring her new hat" (Allanbrook 1983: 76).[2]

The fuller understanding of dance topics that follows from Allanbrook's approach points to the importance of understanding the relationship between the steps of a dance and the music for a dance. Indeed, this is much the same point Kirnberger makes in *Die Kunst des reinen Satzes* in his discussion of meter. Having likened the steps of a regular walk to a musical measure and proposed that each step consists of small movements that are like beats, Kirnberger observes, "If a precise uniformity is observed in the steps and small movements, this results in the measured walk which we call dance, and this is precisely analogous to measured melody. In just the same way as dance expresses or portrays various sentiments merely by motion [*Bewegung*], melody does it merely by notes" (1982: 382).[3] A close affinity between the steps of a dance and the music for that dance is part of the legacy of French noble dance of the seventeenth and early eighteenth centuries, which had as its ideal a perfect alignment of choreography and music. Another part of that legacy was an extensive assortment of dances, each with its own character. As one indication of the importance of French dance practice to conceptions of dance music in the later eighteenth century, twelve of the sixteen different dance types set out in Kirnberger's *Recueil* derive from the dance traditions of France's *ancien régime*.

EXAMPLE 4.1 Mozart, String Quintet in C major, K. 515/i: (a) mm. 47–55 (bourrée topic) and (b) mm. 58–65 (gavotte topic).

(*Continued*)

EXAMPLE **4.1** (Continued)

(b) **[Allegro]**

EXAMPLE **4.2** Mozart, *Le nozze di Figaro*, Act 1 Scene 1, Duettino "Cinque…dieci…venti": (a) Figaro's entrance (bourrée topic) and (b) Susanna's entrance (gavotte topic).

(a) *18*

(Continued)

EXAMPLE **4.2** (Continued)

(b) *30*

O - ra si___ ch'io son___ con - ten - ta;   sem - bra fat - to in- ver___ per___ me,

In this chapter I would like to explore the contribution French noble dance made to the topical universe available to composers in the latter half of the eighteenth century. The first section that follows will focus on the dance culture of the *ancien régime* (especially as it was developed during the reign of Louis XIV) and on dance notations of the period that shed light on the relationship between the steps of a dance and its music. The second section will offer a close reading of the steps and music for a bourrée, the choreography for which was published in 1700, with the aim of developing a fuller understanding of the sort of knowledge that dance topics summoned during the eighteenth century. The third section will conclude with a brief overview of the role of dance topics in analyses of the instrumental music of the later eighteenth century.

MUSIC AND DANCE IN THE *ANCIEN RÉGIME*

The French dance master Pierre Rameau, writing in his *Maître à danser* of 1725, made an observation with which few of his contemporaries would argue: "We can say, to the glory of our race, that we have a real gift for beautiful dancing. Foreigners, so far from denying this, have, for nearly a century, come to admire our dances, and to educate themselves at our performances and in our schools. There is hardly a Court in Europe where the dancing master is not French" (Rameau 1970: xii). That this should be so was a consequence of a variety of factors, a full consideration of which would warrant its own study: the young Louis XIV's gift for dancing; the deployment of this gift in entertainments for the court organized by Jules Mazarin, prime minister during the regency of Louis's mother, Anne of Austria (which began in 1643); and Louis's determination, once he assumed absolute power, to exclude other members of the nobility from active roles in the governance of the country and to keep them occupied with courtly entertainments, central to which were a wide range of dances (Hilton 1997: 7–9). The study of dance thus had political as well practical aims, both of which are evident in the decree through which Louis XIV established the Académie Royale de Danse in 1661, the same year he became the absolute ruler of France:

> In that the Art of Dance has always been recognized as one of the most honorable and necessary methods to train the body, and furthermore as the primary and most natural basis for all sorts of Exercises, including that of bearing arms, consequently

it is one of the most advantageous and useful to our Nobility, as well as to others who
have the honor of approaching Us, not only in time of War for our Armies, but even
in Peacetime while we enjoy the diversion of our court Ballets. (Needham 1997: 180,
translation modified)[4]

One of the results of the establishment of the academy was the development of dance
notations, which were aimed at recording choreographies so that they could be preserved and taught to others. By the 1680s there were as many as four kinds of dance
notation in circulation (Harris-Warrick and Marsh 1994: 83–87; Pierce 1998), although
that of Pierre Beauchamps—at that time composer of the royal ballets and private dance
tutor for the king—was by far the most successful. Having developed the notation, however, Beauchamps apparently saw no need to publish it or his choreographies, being
content to allow them to circulate among other dance masters and their students. It was
left to another dance master, Raoul-Auger Feuillet, to realize the broader potential of
Beauchamps's notation through a series of publications in the early eighteenth century,
beginning with his *Chorégraphie, ou l'art de décrire la dance* (1700a).[5] The "art of describing dance," published by Feuillet, involved an exhaustive system of figures and diagrams
that made it possible to represent both the steps of a dance and the paths the dancers
took as they moved across the floor. Using this notation, Feuillet was able to publish
annual collections of ballroom dances; among the first of these was a collection of nine
ballroom dances choreographed by Louis Guillaume Pécour, each of which was for a
man and a woman (Feuillet 1700b).

The first page of Feuillet's notation for Pécour's choreography *La bourrée d'Achille*
is shown in Figure 4.1. At the top of the page are the first eight measures of a bourrée
to which the opening of the choreography is set. (*La bourrée d'Achille* takes its music
from the "Entrée des Genies de Talie" in the prologue to Jean-Baptiste Lully's *Achille et
Polixène* (Lully 2007). (It bears mention that Lully completed only the overture and Act
1 of *Achille et Polixène*; the Prologue and Acts 2–5 were written by Pascal Collasse.[6]) This
part of the entrée consists of a bourrée followed by a minuet, which Pécour arranged
into a short suite by following the minuet with a reprise of the bourrée; all told, the
choreography published by Feuillet runs to eleven pages.) The space below the musical notation represents a bird's-eye view of the performance space for the dance. The
portion of the performance space corresponding to the top of the page was reserved for
what was known as the Presence, and would be occupied by the person, or persons, of
highest rank (Hilton 1997: 85). At the bottom of the page are two symbols that represent
the starting positions for the two dancers: the man on the left (a semicircle joined to a
straight line), the woman on the right (two nested semicircles joined to a single straight
line); showing due deference, they begin by facing toward the Presence. Immediately
above the symbols for the dancers are two small circles to which short lines are connected; these indicate that the dancers start with their feet in fourth position.[7] Two solid
lines extend toward the top of the page; these indicate the track that the dancers will take
across the floor. Midway up the page the track shows each dancer making a right-angle
turn; the man to his left, the woman to her right, such that they briefly proceed in

la Bourée d'Achille.

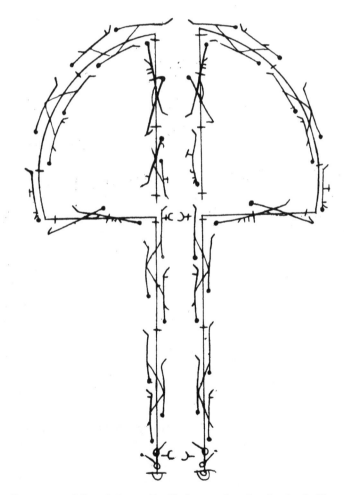

FIGURE **4.1** The first page of Raoul-Auger Feuillet's notation for Louis Guillaume Pécour's choreography *La bourrée d'Achille*, from Feuillet, *Recueil de dances* (1700), 2.

opposite directions. Each dancer then makes another turn (the man to his right, the woman to her left) and then follows an arc toward the top of the room and each other. The dancers then make one more sharp turn (the man to his right, the woman to her left) and, once again side by side, move toward the center of the room. The track itself is crossed by a number of very short perpendicular lines, each of which corresponds to a bar line of the music shown at the top of the page; the first portion of the track (when the dancers move directly toward the Presence) corresponds to two measures of music, their movement in opposite directions from each other after their first turn corresponds to one measure, and so on for the eight measures of the bourrée given on this page. Symbols for the steps each dancer performs are drawn to either side of (and occasionally across) the track; those on the left side of the track are for the left foot, and those on the right side of the track are for the right foot.

In her work on French noble dance (a large portion of which was given over to the interpretation of Feuillet's notation) Wendy Hilton offered helpful distinctions between the step (a passage of the foot forward, backward, or to the side), a step-unit (made up of a number of steps), and a step-sequence (a sequence of step-units that reaches a point of conclusion) (Hilton 1997: 73). In the opening of the choreography shown in Figure 4.1, the male dancer begins with three steps (left–right–left) that together make up the step-unit known as the *pas de bourrée*. (The female dancer also does a *pas de bourrée*, but starting on the right foot, thus creating a mirror image of the movements of the male dancer.) As do many of the step-units within the French noble style, the *pas de bourrée* begins with a *mouvement*—bending the knees down and then up again (a *plié* followed by an *élevé*)—that leads directly to a step, a combination known as a *demi-coupé* (Hilton 1997: 75).

One of the challenges faced by those notating choreographies was the precise coordination of music and movement: in some cases a number of steps were correlated with a single musical event (such as a held note); in other cases a single step was correlated with a number of musical events (such as make up a short scalar passage). A further complication was that most step-units could be used interchangeably in duple and triple time: the *pas de bourrée*, for instance, could be employed equally well to dance a bourrée (in duple time) or a sarabande (in triple time) (Hilton 1997: 186). As a means of clarifying the relationship between music and movement, Feuillet's *Chorégraphie* included a brief section that described in slightly more detail how various aspects of musical rhythm corresponded with different dance movements (Feuillet 1700a: 87–92); most subsequent dance tutors included similar sections, often given the title "Treatise on Cadence." In the "Traité de la cadence" appended to his 1725 *Abbregé de la nouvelle méthode dans l'art d'écrire ou de traçer toutes sortes de danses de ville*, Pierre Rameau made one aspect of the relationship between movement and music particularly clear: in all cases the *plié* of the initial *demi-coupé* in a step-unit occurred on the upbeat to the measure, and the *élevé* on the downbeat (Rameau 1725: 103–11). The *élevé* of the *demi-coupé* was thus associated with an accent, a feature that could, in some instances, be used to create cross rhythms between movement and music (as occurred with the second *demi-coupé* of the typical *pas de menuet* step-unit) (Hilton 1997: 191).

As suggested by this brief overview, the "gift for beautiful dancing" that Rameau attributed to his countrymen was hardly an accident but instead a consequence of the importance accorded to dance within France's *ancien régime*. This, backed by France's political power during the seventeenth and eighteenth centuries, gave rise to a highly influential set of cultural practices in which music and dance were in an intimate relationship with one another. As a way of studying this relationship, I would like to take a closer look at Pécour's choreography for the first bourrée in the choreography of *La bourrée d'Achille* with the aim of developing a fuller sense of the nature of the knowledge that dance topics activated for composers of and listeners to eighteenth-century instrumental music.

Music and Dance in La *bourrée* d'Achille

As with many of Pécour's choreographies for *danses à deux*, that for the initial bourrée from *La bourrée d'Achille* involves a relatively small number of step-units (Witherell 1983: 7–15). In addition to the *pas de bourrée*, these include the *contretemps de chaconne* (which, after the initial *plié*, involves a spring from one foot onto the same foot, followed by two plain steps), the *temps de courante* (a *mouvement* that leads to a single sliding step), the *coupé soutenue* (a *demi-coupé* followed by a sliding step), the *coupé simple* (a *demi-coupé* followed by a single plain step), and the *pas de sissonne* (a hop, or *jeté*, that finishes on two feet, followed by another hop that finishes on one foot).[8] Table 4.1

Table 4.1 Step-Units Used by the Male Dancer and Corresponding Measures for Pécour's Choreography for the Initial Statement of the Bourrée from *La bourrée d'Achille*

Step-Unit	Measure	Step-Unit	Measure
pas de bourrée	1	*pas de bourrée*	5
pas de bourrée	2	*pas de bourrée*	6
contretemps de chaconne	3	*contretemps de chaconne*	7
temps de courante	4	*coupé soutenue*	8
pas de bourrée	9	*pas de bourrée*	17
pas de bourrée	10	*pas de bourrée*	18
pas de bourrée	11	*pas de bourrée*	19
pas de bourrée	12	*pas de bourrée*	20
pas de sissonne	13	*pas de sissonne*	21
pas de sissonne	14	*pas de sissonne*	22
pas de bourrée	15	*pas de bourrée*	23
coupé soutenue	16	*coupé simple*	24

EXAMPLE 4.3 Meredith Little's analytical symbols for the main features of step-units.

provides a list of the various step-units used by the male dancer in Pécour's choreography for the initial statement of the bourrée from *La bourrée d'Achille*, together with the measure that corresponds with each step unit.

A fuller account of Pécour's choreography for *La bourrée d'Achille* would have to include not only a much more thorough description of the various steps and step-units but also the movement of the dancers' arms, the small differences between the step-units used by the male dancer and those used by the female dancer, and the paths the two trace across the floor (including movements forward and backward) as they perform the dance. For the purpose of understanding the relationship between movement and music in the French noble style, however, it will be sufficient to limit consideration to the most distinctive aspects of the step-units given in Table 4.1 and the musical events with which they were correlated. To this end, I would like to introduce an analytical notation developed by Meredith Little for the purposes of studying relationships between music and movement in French noble dance (Little 1975). Little used five symbols for the main features of different step-units, which are shown in Example 4.3: these include symbols for the *plié* and *élevé* of the *mouvement*, as well as for the *jeté*, the plain step, and the *glissé* (the sliding step used in the *temps de courante* and *coupé soutenue*). Example 4.4 provides the score for the whole of the bourrée in a keyboard reduction of the harmonization used in the prologue to *Achille et Polixène* together with the appropriate symbols for the main features of the various step-units. Brackets beneath these symbols show each of the step-units, and the letters above the symbols show whether the right foot (R), left foot (L), or both together (T) are being used.

Both Collasse's music and Pécour's choreography for the bourrée fall into two main parts: Section 1 comprises mm. 1–8, and Section 2 comprises mm. 9–24. Each of these is divided by a reprise: in Section 1, mm. 5–8 restate the material of mm. 1–4 (with the material for the last measure changed as a way to mark the end of the section); and in Section 2 mm. 17–24 restate the material of mm. 9–16 (with the last measure changed to signal an end to the dance). In what follows I shall consider the music and choreography for each section in turn.

Section 1 of the Bourrée

In Section 1 the harmonies alternate in a regular pattern: m. 1 is focused on the dominant, m. 2 on the tonic, m. 3 on the dominant, and so on throughout the section. In

EXAMPLE **4.4** Keyboard reduction of the bourrée from the "Entrée des Genies de Talie" from Pascal Collasse's prologue to Jean-Baptiste Lully's *Achille et Polixène*, with analytical symbols for Pécour's choreography.

general, the dominant is rendered less stable than the tonic, either through a bass line that leads away from the root of the chord (mm. 1 and 5) or with an auxiliary harmony on the second quarter of the measure (as in mm. 3 and 7).

Rhythmically, the compositional strategies used by Collasse are focused on creating a steady succession of quarter notes, with three exceptions: the first halves of mm. 1, 2, 4, 5, and 6 all include a dotted-quarter note leading to an eighth note or two sixteenths; mm. 3 and 7 include eighth notes on the second quarter of the measure, and a dotted-quarter/ eighth figure in the last half of the measure; and mm. 4 and 8 begin with a dotted half note in the upper parts (which, in the case of m. 8, coincides with a dotted half note in the bass). These disruptions to the flow of quarter notes inform the rhythmic design of Section 1 in two ways: first, most measures begin with an agogic accent; second, the two measures that do not begin with an agogic accent (namely, mm. 3 and 7) have an agogic accent on the second main beat of the measure, which is preceded by an auxiliary harmony embellished with eighth-note motion.

This rhythmic design together with the harmonic strategies deployed by Collasse produce a sounding representation of a series of regular movements (mm. 1–2 and 5–6) that are disrupted (mm. 3 and 7) and then pause (equivocally in m. 4, more definitively in m. 8). I should note that my wording here reflects a desire to maintain a distinction between sequences of sound materials and the displacement of objects in the material world: I view the relationship between the two to be analogical, and "musical motion" to be a metaphorical concept.[9] From this perspective, Collasse's music offers a sonic analog for a dynamic process that begins with regular movement, is disrupted, and then comes to a pause.

As I have described it, the dynamic process represented by the music of Section 1 conforms, in most respects, with the dynamic process enacted by Pécour's choreography. Pécour begins with two *pas de bourrée* (which set up something close to a series of regular movements) that are followed by a *contretemps de chaconne* (which introduces a *jeté* and which disrupts the alternation of L–R–L and R–L–R) leading to a *temps de courante* that momentarily halts the progression of steps. This pattern is then repeated almost exactly, save for the introduction of a *coupé soutenue*—a step-unit that typically concludes a step-sequence—in m. 8. One aspect of the dance not as clearly represented by the music is the regular succession of *mouvements*, which provide a physical correlate for the arrival on each strong beat. Although these arrivals are also marked by a change in harmony, the music does not provide a strong analog for the physical tension created on each upbeat as the weight of the dancer's body is taken on flexed knees.

Section 2 of the Bourrée

In comparison with Section 1 the harmonies of Section 2 are rather more varied and participate in a compositional design that unfolds over a longer span of musical time. Collasse opens the section with the submediant in $\frac{5}{3}$ position. This gives way to a succession of $\frac{6}{3}$ harmonies (beginning on the fourth quarter of m. 9 and extending through the first half of m. 11, mediated only by the $\frac{5}{3}$ chord on the last quarter of m. 10) that leads, in the latter half of m. 11, to the dominant of A major, embellished by a 4–3 suspension. (All of the features of mm. 9–16 are, of course, reprised in mm. 17–24.) The subsequent arrival on A major leads, almost immediately, to a return to the tonic. Collasse then repeats the melody of mm. 9–12 but provides it with a new harmonization: m. 13 (which corresponds to m. 9) begins with the tonic in $\frac{5}{3}$ position, and m. 15 (which corresponds to m. 11) is focused on the dominant of D major. Perhaps most important, however, are two details of this reharmonization. First, although the opening of m. 14 is identical to that of m. 10, Collasse harmonizes the last quarter of m. 13 with the leading-tone chord of D major, thus connecting the tonic in $\frac{5}{3}$ position on the third quarter of m. 13 with the tonic in $\frac{6}{3}$ position on the first quarter of m. 14. Second, beginning with the fourth quarter of m. 14 the harmonies set out an orderly circle-of-fifths progression (F♯ minor, B minor, E minor, A major) which culminates in an arrival on tonic in m. 16.

In contrast to the comparatively subtle play of rhythm in Section 1, the rhythmic strategies used by Collasse in Section 2 are both simpler and of more marked effect. The half notes on the second quarter of mm. 10, 12, and 14 create an agogic accent at a moment in the rhythmic cycle that has not, up to this point, received any emphasis at the same time that they preclude the possibility of marking a moment—the third quarter of the measure—that *has* received emphasis. The contrast provided by these measures is mitigated in two ways: first, mm. 9, 11, and 13 each make use of rhythmic patterns established in mm. 1–8; and second, mm. 15 and 16 revisit the basic materials of the rhythmic cadences of mm. 3–4 and 7–8. As a consequence, the displaced accents introduced in Section 2 function as interruptions of the normative rhythmic patterns established in Section 1 rather than as a permanent shift of the pattern of metrical accents.

Within Section 2 Collasse uses the resources offered by harmony and rhythm to craft a succession of musical events that suggest a dynamic process that begins with the upbeat to m. 9 and continues through the downbeat of m. 16 (and which is revisited in mm. 17–24). The midpoint of this temporal span is articulated by the arrival on A major in m. 12—an arrival prepared by giving over the last half of m. 11 to the dominant of A, complete with a 4–3 suspension in the alto voice and an octave skip in the bass— which is rendered contingent by the displaced accent on the second beat of the measure. (Compare, for instance, the effect of mm. 11–12 with that of mm. 3–4.) The fluidity— even uncertainty—associated with successions of $\frac{6}{3}$ harmonies and displaced accents only starts to resolve with the circle-of-fifths sequence and more regular rhythmic structure that commences on the last quarter of m. 14 and that reaches its conclusion with the arrival on the tonic in m. 16. As a whole, the passage provides an analog for a dynamic process that moves away from previously established safe ground, ventures over novel topography, and then slips almost effortlessly back to the place where it began.

In contrast to the clear sense of departure occasioned by the introduction of the submediant at the opening of Section 2 (and affirmed by the displaced accents of mm. 10 and 12), the first portion of Pécour's choreography begins with four successive *pas de bourrée*—that is, an unbroken succession of the same step-unit that served to anchor the choreography of Section 1. With regularity of movement thus having been established,

Pécour then introduces the most animated step-units thus far: two successive *pas de sissonne*, which comprise four successive hops. These are then followed by another *pas de bourrée*, and the step-sequence concludes with either a *coupé soutenue* (in m. 16) or a *coupé simple* (in m. 24). The overall pattern is one of regular movement interrupted by a brief flurry of activity and concluding with a smooth approach to closure. The dynamic process enacted by the dance steps of Section 2 is, in consequence, markedly different from that suggested by the music. Emblematic of this difference is the mismatch between movement and music on the third quarters of mm. 10, 12, and 14 (as well as mm. 18, 20, and 22) when the dancer's step (or hop) onto his left foot is met with no corresponding musical event.

It bears mention that while Collasse's music and Pécour's dance steps both reach a conclusion in m. 16 (and again in m. 24) they do so through different means. The music initiates in a rather precipitate manner the sequence of events that culminate in m. 16; once on its way, however, the music proceeds as though its goal is never in doubt, each two-measure unit leading securely to the next. The dance steps, by contrast, continue with their *pas de bourrée* as though oblivious to the adventurous course of the music but then hurry to catch up, becoming slightly unpredictable at the very moment that the music catches sight of the course it will take to cadence. This sort of playful divergence between music and dance constituted a significant expressive resource within French dance practice: in Nicholas Cook's terms, the independence of music and dance created a true instance of multimedia (Cook 1998: 98–129).

Relationships between Music and Dance in *La bourrée d'Achille* and the *Ancien Régime*

In summary, then, Pécour's choreography for the first statement of the bourrée in *La bourrée d'Achille* demonstrates two slightly different strategies for the correlation of music and dance. In Section 1 music and dance fit closely with one another: the dynamic process summoned by Collasse's music finds a visible and physical representation in the movements of Pécour's dancers. In Section 2 music and dance are more independent of one another, although they ultimately arrive at similar goals.

Although I chose to begin my analysis of relationships between music and dance in *La bourrée d'Achille* with Collasse's music (which, after all, was created long before Pécour's choreography), I could just have easily started with the dance steps and then proceeded to the music. One of the distinctive features of the French noble style of dance was the close coordination of music and dance in both conception and practice: those known chiefly as composers were intimately familiar with choreographic conventions (and were often, as was Lully, dancers themselves), and those known chiefly as choreographers were also performers and composers of dance music (Beaussant 1992: 24–36; La Gorce 2002: 56–102; Hilton 1997: 23–33). For practitioners of dance within the *ancien régime*, the two were likely inseparable: hearing the music summoned the steps of the dance, and seeing the movements of the dance summoned the sound of the music.[10] In terms of the perspective I adopted in my analysis of *La bourrée d'Achille*, and have developed more fully elsewhere (Zbikowski 2008a, 2012), the music for the dance may thus serve as a sonic analog for the dynamic process constituted by the steps of the dance.

Broadly speaking, this approach to the relationship between music and dance is quite similar to that developed by Wye Allanbrook, with two differences. First, my view is shaped by recent research in cognitive science, and especially on processes of analogy: for music to serve as an analog for the steps of a dance there must be clear correlations between the music and the dance. This, then, was part of the reason for my close reading of *La bourrée d'Achille*: I was interested in discovering the features of Collasse's music that correlated with the movements set out by Pécour's choreography. The second difference between my approach and that of Allanbrook follows from the first. Through her close consideration of the history and rhythmic characteristics of different dance types Allanbrook laid the groundwork for understanding how dance topics shaped the way listeners hear music. As my analysis of *La bourrée d'Achille* shows, however, we also need to pay attention to details of harmonic and melodic design if we are to fully understand how a sequence of musical sounds can evoke a sequence of physical movements and all these carry with them.

I should also note, however, that the relationships between music and dance that obtained within French noble dance could be considerably more complicated and more subtle than those demonstrated by a ballroom dance such as *La bourrée d'Achille*. There are, for instance, numerous examples of dance phrasing that runs contrary to musical phrasing and strong evidence that composers and choreographers played with this variability in their compositions (Schwartz 1998; Harris-Warrick 2000). One of the advantages of Feuillet's notation is that it makes it possible to discover such complications, for it was expressly designed to show how dance steps and music related to one another. As do all notations (whether for music or dance), it has its limitations. Since the music is only shown in a single stave, details of harmony or counterpoint can only be inferred—it is quite possible that the version of Collasse's music envisioned by Pécour was somewhat different from that used in the published prologue to *Achille et Polixène* (and there are indeed minor differences between Collasse's melody and that which accompanies Pécour's choreography). Understanding how the steps of the dance were to be performed requires an equal measure of interpretation, although thanks to the work of Hilton and others there is now far less guesswork than there once was. With that in mind, I would again emphasize that my analytical account of Pécour's choreography is radically simplified, having for the most part omitted mention of movements through the performance space, having nothing to say about steps performed backward or with turns, and having ignored the movements of hands and arms. It is also important to recognize that the practice of French noble dance embraced a wide range of dance types, and that choreographers responded to these dances in a variety of ways. And so while the general characterization of a bourrée as a dance expressing "moderate joy" (Allanbrook 1983: 49) conforms with the basic expressive resources offered by the dance it hardly exhausts them. To fully understand the affective character of a given bourrée— or any of the dances of the *ancien régime*—it is necessary to consider carefully how the musical materials for the dance are organized, to explore how these are correlated with dance steps, and to place the whole in the broader context within which it took place.

The Culture of Dance in the *Ancien Régime*

Thanks to a complex coincidence of factors—not the least of which was Louis XIV's talent for dancing—the practice of dance held a central place in the court life of the *ancien régime*. On the one hand, the noble classes viewed dance as a means of refining the physical disposition through which they distinguished themselves from those whom they ruled (Needham 1997: 180; Rameau 1970: xii). On the other hand, dance provided an opportunity for the nobility to give corporeal presence to the aesthetic of *galanterie* (Cowart 2008: 14). Although *galanterie* was hardly a stable construct during the time of the *ancien régime*, to the extent that it was construed as a desirable attribute it was an intensely social one, the essence of which was to gain distinction by bringing pleasure to others (Viala 1997). Accordingly, the ballroom settings that Feuillet and other dance masters had in mind was one in which the dancers performed before an audience of their peers, beginning with the couple of highest rank and proceeding through the rest of those assembled (Rameau 1970: 37–39). Within the *ancien régime*, then, dance was a site for the development and display of a comportment that pleased, something possible only if dance and music were carefully adapted to one another. A sense of the pleasure afforded by such an adaptation is readily apparent in Kellom Tomlinson's early eighteenth-century account of the effect of a close coordination of music and dance:

> every Turn, Step, Spring or Bound seen in one will be at the same Instant observed in the other, in such an exact Symmetry and Harmony of the Parts agreeing with the Notes of the *Music*, as to cause the most agreeable Surprize in the Beholders of the two *Dancers*; or admitting a Dozen or more in Number, by observing them all to move as only one Person. This is the natural Effect of good *Dancing* adorn'd with all its Beauties, in that the *Music* seems to inspire the *Dancing*, and the latter the former; and the Concurrence of both is so requisite to charm those who behold them, that each of them in some Measure suffers by a Separation. (Tomlinson 1735: 150)

The extent to which this ideal persisted over the course of the eighteenth century is an open question. While Allanbrook notes the importance of training in the Kapellmeister tradition—which included developing a thorough knowledge of courtly dance—to composers like Mozart, she also notes that by midcentury styles had changed, and that the bourgeoisie of the later eighteenth century were far more interested in dances that could be easily learned than in those that required specialized training and hours of practice (Allanbrook 1983: 30–31). Indeed, that Kirnberger saw a need to publish his *Recueil* suggests that knowledge about courtly dances was fast waning. And yet the larger lesson of the *Recueil*—and, for that matter, Allanbrook's *Rhythmic Gesture in Mozart*—is that a true knowledge of music must include deep familiarity with the rhythmic and melodic patterns of dance music, patterns that I here suggest serve as sonic analogs for the dynamic process of performing the steps of the dance. This, then, is perhaps the most important contribution dance topics drawn from the traditions of French noble dance make to the discourse of—and about—music of the late eighteenth century, for they foreground the importance of embodied knowledge to the ways that musical materials are organized in order to facilitate musical communication.

DANCE TOPICS IN ANALYSIS

Leonard Ratner began his discussion of musical topics in *Classic Music* with a survey of different forms of dance, which he viewed as making an important contribution to the topical universe available to composers in the latter half of the eighteenth century. Ratner used this opportunity to draw an important distinction between two different ways topics could be employed: as types (by which he meant fully worked-out compositions) and as styles (in which figures or progressions characteristic of a type appeared as part of a longer composition). He noted that the distinction between type and style was flexible: "minuets and marches represent complete types of composition, but they also furnish styles for other pieces" (Ratner 1980: 9).

In that Ratner's focus was more on the expressive resources represented by dance types than on the patterns of movements associated with various dances, he tended to view diverse forms of dance as relatively closely related to one another. Thus the passepied was classified as a rather lively minuet and the sarabande as a slow minuet, despite important differences between the execution of the steps and the musical organization of each dance as well as the social context within which they would have been performed. In this Ratner seems to have been influenced by Johann Mattheson, who, in the chapter of his *Der vollkommene Capellmeister* in which he considered categories of melodies, described different dance types in terms of their broad affective characteristics with no mention whatever of the steps of the dance (Mattheson 1739: 224–32; Harriss 1981: 451–64). Again, Allanbrook's work serves as a healthy corrective to this approach: while retaining Ratner's focus on the affective aspects of each dance, her detailed consideration of the steps, musical organization, and social context of different dance types shows how the interaction of these two expressive media shapes listeners' understanding.

Taking a cue from Allanbrook's work, I would like to propose that composers of the later eighteenth century could deploy dance materials in a number of different ways, and that these can be thought of as occupying places along a continuum organized according to the social and cultural function to be realized by the music they produced.[11] On one end of this continuum is music specifically intended for dancing, whether in social or balletic settings. In such music there was a close relationship between music and dance, not least because the two were conceived as intimately coordinated with one another. Connecting with but conceptually distinct from music for dancing are instrumental dances of the sort found in dance suites of the seventeenth and eighteenth centuries. On the one hand, there is a clear connection between, for instance, bourrées that were danced and those written for instrumental performance (especially within seventeenth-century French practice); on the other hand, inasmuch as the only communicative medium involved in an instrumental dance movement was that of music, the "dance" aspects would have to be imagined by the listener. As I have shown elsewhere, in at least some cases the result was a work that adhered even more closely to the basic rhythmic and melodic figures associated with a given dance than did those works meant to be performed with dancers (Zbikowski 2008a: 295–96). At a further remove from actual dance practice would be the incorporation of portions of dance pieces within longer works (which was the compositional strategy to which Kirnberger alluded in the preface to his *Recueil*): in such cases not only would the relevant dance have to be imagined by the listener, but she would have to decide when the "dance" ended and when another dance—or nondance music—began. I would regard dance topics of the sort identified by Allanbrook in her analysis of Figaro and Susanna's opening duet (and shown in Example 4.2) as exemplifying this sort of compositional strategy. Finally, at the far end of the continuum would be passages that borrow portions of the rhythmic figuration of different dance types but whose meaning is largely dependent on the musical context within which they are embedded. I would include here instances of the sort that Agawu identified in his topical analysis of Mozart's String Quintet in C major, K. 515. Although the entry of the bourrée topic in the second violin on the last beat of m. 46 (shown in Example 4.1a) provides a clear analog for the forward motion of the dance (in which the *plié* and *élevé* of the *pas de bourrée* step-unit carry the dancer across the barline), the repeated f's that conclude the figure seem to stall that motion. This is offset slightly by the entrance of the two violas at the end of m. 47, but the effect is less that of a single dancer (or pair of dancers) moving forward and more that of successive dancers entering and then pausing. With the entry of the first violin at the end of m. 48 and the successive iterations of the bourrée topic that follow the forward momentum picks up, but against the anchoring A♭ of the cello the figures sound more antic than dance-like. The cumulative effect, then, is of music that recalls momentarily some of the characteristic features of a well-known dance but only to use them as a means of enacting the larger harmonic discourse within which they are embedded. (Compare, for instance, the regular pattern of movement built up by the bourrée topic that accompanies Figaro's entrance, and which is shown in Example 4.2a.) The sense that one is dealing more with dance-like music than a topical reference to a specific dance is, if anything, more pronounced in the case of the gavotte topic that Agawu identified in mm. 57–65 of the string quintet (and shown in Example 4.1b). Here only the half-measure upbeat typical of the dance remains; the one time its forward motion is continued (the first violin's version in mm. 58–59) stands out as an exception. The regular repetitions of the figure and the strong sense of movement toward the downbeat that it offers are indeed dance-like, and yet there is little sense that reference here is to any specific dance. At this end of the continuum we are indeed a considerable distance from the exquisite coordination of music and dance described by Tomlinson, but we have also entered a domain in which musical communication, and all that it offers to the imagination, has taken center stage.[12]

These last examples would seem to suggest that labels for different dance topics that some analysts have applied to music of the eighteenth century are less important than offering a careful account of the rhythmic and melodic features of the musical materials that a composer deploys, especially where the compositional strategies behind these materials seem to contrast with each other in marked ways (as do those identified by Agawu in his topical analysis of mm. 47–65 of Mozart's quintet). By means of such analyses we might come to a better understanding of the ways in which musical materials can serve as sonic analogs for dynamic processes, whether the processes are those associated with the dance steps of the *ancien régime*, with patterned movement of a rather different sort, or with psychological and physiological processes associated with the emotions.[13] Through an understanding of this sort—one that fully embraces the importance of embodied knowledge across the range of human experience—we can come to a more complete appreciation of the resources that dance music of the seventeenth and eighteenth centuries provided to composers of the later eighteenth century.

Notes

1. On the steps characteristic of the bourrée see Little and Jenne (2001: 37).
2. A detailed discussion of the interplay between the bourrée and the gavotte in Mozart's Duettino can be found in Stephen Rumph's chapter, this volume (pages 493–96).
3. Note that the term used here for the movement associated with dance—*Bewegung*—is the same frequently used for tempo (and which indeed served as the heading for the section on tempo in *Die Kunst*). For the use of *Bewegung* within a musical context in the early nineteenth century, see Koch (1802: col. 241–42).
4. For a similar perspective on the importance of dance for distinguishing nobility see Rameau (1970: xii).
5. The part played by Beauchamps in the development of the notation broadly attributed to Feuillet has only recently come to light. Although Beauchamps filed a petition against Feuillet in 1704 for infringement of his work, he failed to win the case and it was only with the appearance of two English translations of *Chorégraphie* in 1706 (subsequent to the expiration of the royal privilege granted Feuillet) that Beauchamps's role in the development of the notation became more widely known, for each acknowledged Beauchamps as the inventor of the notation that had been so successfully exploited by Feuillet. For a full discussion see Hilton (1997: 46–49).
6. My thanks to Rebekah Ahrendt for drawing this to my attention.
7. The five canonical positions used in French noble dance (and later adopted for ballet) were first codified by Pierre Beauchamps in the late seventeenth century. See Rameau (1970: 5) and Hilton (1997: 98–99).
8. On the *contretemps de chaconne*, the *temps de courante*, the *coupé soutenue* and the *coupé simple*, and the *pas de sissonne* see Hilton (1997: 214, 201, 177, and 223).
9. For a further discussion of the role of metaphor in conceptualizations of music see (Zbikowski 2008b).
10. Although we can only speculate on the knowledge of dancers of the seventeenth and eighteenth centuries, recent neuroimaging studies of expert dancers supports the close

relationship between movement and music I suggest here. See Calvo-Merino et al. (2005) and Brown, Martinez, and Parsons (2006).

11. The continuum I describe here captures some of the strategies outlined by Ratner in his consideration of how dances were incorporated into classic music; see Ratner (1980: 17–18).

12. For more on this approach to musical communication see Zbikowski (2008a).

13. With respect to sonic analogs for the psychological and physiological processes associated with the emotions see Zbikowski (2011).

References

Agawu, Kofi. 1991. *Playing with Signs: A Semiotic Interpretation of Classical Music*. Princeton: Princeton University Press.

Allanbrook, Wye J. 1983. *Rhythmic Gesture in Mozart:* Le nozze di Figaro *and* Don Giovanni. Chicago: University of Chicago Press.

Beaussant, Philippe. 1992. *Lully, ou, Le musicien du soleil*. Paris: Gallimard / Théâtre des Champs-Elysées.

Brown, Steven, Michael J. Martinez, and Lawrence M. Parsons. 2006. The Neural Basis of Human Dance. *Cerebral Cortex* 16: 1157–67.

Calvo-Merino, Beatriz, Daniel E. Glaser, Julie Grezes, Richard. E. Passingham, and Patrick Haggard. 2005. Action Observation and Acquired Motor Skills: An fMRI Study with Expert Dancers. *Cerebral Cortex* 15: 1243–49.

Cook, Nicholas. 1998. *Analysing Musical Multimedia*. Oxford: Clarendon.

Cowart, Georgia J. 2008. *The Triumph of Pleasure: Louis XIV and the Politics of Spectacle*. Chicago: University of Chicago Press.

Feuillet, Raoul-Auger. 1700a. *Chorégraphie, ou l'art de décrire la dance*. Reprint, New York: Broude, 1968.

——. 1700b. *Recueil de dances composées par M. Pécour*. Reprint, New York: Broude, 1968.

Harriss, Ernest C. 1981. *Johann Mattheson's Der vollkommene Capellmeister: A Revised Translation with Critical Commentary*. Ann Arbor, MI: UMI Research Press.

Harris-Warrick, Rebecca. 2000. The Phrase Structures of Lully's Dance Music. In *Lully Studies*, ed. John Hajdu Heyer, 32–56. Cambridge: Cambridge University Press.

Harris-Warrick, Rebecca, and Carol G. Marsh. 1994. *Musical Theatre at the Court of Louis XIV*: Le mariage de la Grosse Cathos. Cambridge: Cambridge University Press.

Hilton, Wendy. 1997. *Dance and Music of Court and Theater: Selected Writings of Wendy Hilton*. Stuyvesant, NY: Pendragon.

Kirnberger, Johann Philipp. 1771–79. *Die Kunst des reinen Satzes in der Musik*. 2 vols. Vol. 1, Berlin: Rottmann 1771. Vol. 2, sections 1–3, Berlin und Königsberg: Decker und Hartung.

——. 1777. *Recueil d'airs de danse caractéristiques, pour servir de modele aux jeunes compositeurs et d'exercise à ceux qui touchent du clavecin*. Berlin: Jean Julien Hummel.

——. 1982. *The Art of Strict Musical Composition*. Trans. David Beach and Jurgen Thym. New Haven: Yale University Press.

Koch, Heinrich Christoph. 1802. *Musikalisches Lexikon*. Frankfurt am Main: August Hermann der Jüngere.

La Gorce, Jérôme de. 2002. *Jean-Baptiste Lully*. Paris: Fayard.

Little, Meredith Ellis. 1975. The Contribution of Dance Steps to Musical Analysis and Performance: *La Bourgogne. Journal of the American Musicological Society* 28/1: 112–24.

Little, Meredith, and Natalie Jenne. 2001. *Dance and the Music of J. S. Bach*, rev. ed. Bloomington: Indiana University Press.

Lully, Jean-Baptiste. 2007. *Achille et Polixène: Tragédie: Facsimile of the first edition, Paris, 1687.* Preface by Elma Sanders. The Tragédies Lyriques in Facsimile / Jean-Baptiste Lully, vol. 15. Williamstown, MA: Broude.

Mattheson, Johann. 1739. *Der vollkommene Capellmeister.* Hamburg: Christian Herold. Reprint, Kassel: Bärenreiter, 1954

Needham, Maureen. 1997. Louis XIV and the Académie Royale de Danse, 1661: A Commentary and Translation. *Dance Chronicle* 20/2: 173–90.

Pierce, Ken. 1998. Dance Notation Systems in Late 17th-Century France. *Early Music* 26/2: 286–99.

Rameau, Pierre. 1725. *Abbregé de la nouvelle méthode dans l'art d'écrire ou de traçer toutes sortes de danses de ville.* Paris: Author. Reprint, Farnborough: Gregg, 1972.

——. 1970. *The Dancing Master.* Trans. Cyril W. Beaumont. Brooklyn, NY: Dance Horizons.

Ratner, Leonard G. 1980. *Classic Music: Expression, Form, and Style.* New York: Schirmer.

Schwartz, Judith L. 1998. The *Passacaille* in Lully's *Armide*: Phrase Structure in the Choreography and the Music. *Early Music* 26/2: 300–20.

Tomlinson, Kellom. 1735. *The Art of Dancing Explained by Reading and Figures.* London: Author. Reprint. Farnborough: Gregg, 1970.

Viala, Alain. 1997. *Les Signes Galants*: A Historical Reevaluation *of Galanterie.* Trans. Daryl Lee. *Yale French Studies* 92 (= *Exploring the Conversible World: Text and Sociability from the Classical Age to the Enlightenment*, ed. Elena Russo): 11–29.

Witherell, Anne L. 1983. *Louis Pécour's 1700 Receuil de dances.* Ann Arbor, MI: UMI Research Press.

Zbikowski, Lawrence M. 2008a. Dance Topoi, Sonic Analogues, and Musical Grammar: Communicating with Music in the Eighteenth Century. In *Communication in Eighteenth Century Music*, ed. Danuta Mirka and Kofi Agawu, 283–309. Cambridge: Cambridge University Press.

——. 2008b. Metaphor and Music. In *The Cambridge Handbook of Metaphor and Thought*, ed. Ray Gibbs, Jr., 502–24. Cambridge: Cambridge University Press.

——. 2011. Music, Emotion, Analysis. *Music Analysis* 29/1–3: 1–25.

——. 2012. Music, Dance, and Meaning in the Early Nineteenth Century. *Journal of Musicological Research* 31/2–3: 147–65.

CHAPTER 5

··

BALLROOM DANCES OF THE LATE
EIGHTEENTH CENTURY

··

ERIC MCKEE

As long as Carnival goes on, people think here of nothing else but dancing. In every corner there are balls.

Leopold Mozart writing from Vienna during Carnival, 30 January 1768[1]

The people of Vienna were...dancing mad.

Michael Kelley writing from Vienna during Carnival, c. 1785[2]

DANCES provided composers the largest and most pervasive source of late eighteenth-century topics. As Leonard Ratner has observed, "there is hardly a major work in this era that
does not borrow heavily from the dance" (1980: 18). Perhaps this is not surprising given
that social dancing, whether in the ballroom, in the beer hall, or in the home, was by far the
most popular social activity of the time, especially during Carnival season. As such, dance
was a vital and vibrant part of the creative imagination of eighteenth-century listeners,
performers, and composers. Moreover, the choreographies of each dance (and the manner in which one performed them) were associated with particular feelings or "motions
of the soul" (*Gemüthsbewegungen*),[3] characters, and indications of one's social class. And,
according to eighteenth-century writers, the vocabulary of dance gestures encompassed
the entire gamut of the human condition from grave to gay, from noble to vulgar.

Gestures of dance and gestures of music share a conceptual basis in that they both
may be conceived as dynamic processes (either literally or metaphorically) involving
motion, velocity, weight, height, depth, and gravity. To the degree that dance composers are able to render the physical gestures of the dance into correlated musical gestures,
music is able to provide a "sonic analogue" of the dance, thereby evoking its associated
expressive states.[4] All ballroom dance music to some extent provides a sonic analogue of
the dance; but music as a distinct medium will also contain elements that have no corollary to the movements of the dancers (and vice versa). Such noncorrelative elements
may be agents of social, cultural, and/or expressive meanings (as cued by ornamentation, instrumentation, or the overlay of other topics), or they may be a result of music's

tonal syntax and formal conventions (such as cadential types, patterns of thematic repetition, and counterpoint). The dynamic, interactive relationship between the two media is a defining feature of this art form.

A distinction to be made with dance topics in Classic music is that between *current* dances that were part of the ballroom repertoire and *historical* dances that were no longer danced, but known indirectly apart from their original context through their music or by their performances on stage in ballets and operas (Table 5.1). Topical reference to current dances aroused spontaneous mimetic bodily participation[5] and drew on direct associations with familiar environments with all the cultural, social, and expressive entailments of those environments. Historical dances, on the other hand, were disembodied voices of the past whose expressive meanings may have had little connection to their original social settings. Audiences had very little or, more likely, no firsthand knowledge of the dance steps involved in their choreographies.[6] Expressive meaning in historical dances is rooted in the characteristic melodic and rhythmic gestures of the music (which may suggest remnant traces of their original movements and attitudes), as well as in the construction of meanings and associations that accrued with each dance over time. Thus, compared to current dances, historical dances tended to engage listeners on much more fictional levels in their evocations of idealized pasts, locations, and bodily motions.

This essay examines the music, choreography, and habits of current ballroom dancing in Vienna during the last quarter of the eighteenth century. My repertoire is largely drawn from the *Redoutentänze* that Mozart composed for the Imperial court balls held during Carnival season during the last three years of his life (1788–91). This rich and diverse group of works includes the most popular ballroom dances of the Classic period: minuets, contredanses, *Deutsche*, and *Ländler*. Mozart, who was a considerably more accomplished and enthusiastic dancer than Haydn or Beethoven, well understood the practical requirements of ballroom dancers.[7] Yet within the tight confines of

Table 5.1 Partial Listing of Historical and Current Dances in the Time of Mozart

Historical Dances	Current Dances
Allemande	Contredanse
Bourée	*Kehraus*
Chaconne	Minuet
Courante	Polonaise
Gavotte	Spinning Dances
Gigue	*Deutsche*
Loure	*Ländler*
Musette	*Langaus*
Sarabande	
Siciliano	

utilitarian craft music, Mozart found ways to create musical interest, expressive impact, and social commentary.

I have two objectives. The first is to provide an account of the prototypical features of each dance's choreography and music and the correlations found between the two; the second is to briefly introduce some of the cultural, social, and expressive meanings associated with these dances. Over the past thirty years the minuet has received in-depth, sustained critical attention.[8] In this chapter I shift focus to those ballroom dances that have received far less attention—contredanses, *Deutsche*, and *Ländler*.

CONTREDANSES

The Darling or favourite Diversion of all Ranks of People from the Court to the Cottage.

Kellom Tomlinson[9]

The contredanse, a group dance of rural origins, first entered English ballrooms of the upper classes in the mid-seventeenth century, and a century later it had unseated the minuet as the most popular ballroom dance throughout Europe and beyond. Three distinct types of contredanses were practiced in the eighteenth century: the *contredanse anglaise*, the *contredanse française*, and the *contredanse allemande*. All three types employed fast-paced music set in duple meter. While 2/2 and 6/4 were commonly used in the early contredanse repertoire, by Mozart's time 2/4 and 6/8 were the standard meters.

Contredanse Anglaise

The *contredanse anglaise* (also known as country dance, *anglaise*, or *englischer Tanz*) is first given extensive treatment in John Playford's *The English Dancing Master* issued in London, 1651.[10] In contrast to French court dances of Louis XIV, which involved a single couple performing alone while everyone else watched (*danse à deux*), Playford's country dances required multiple couples (at least three), arranged in squares, rounds, or longways, performing a sequence of figures. By far the most common arrangement of couples was longways whereby couples—three, four, or "as many as will"—arranged themselves in a double column of opposing men and women.[11] The lead or top couple then introduces a sequence of figures together with the second couple and thereafter dances it successively with the remaining couples until the lead couple has reached the bottom of the column. The second couple, now at the head of the column, then dances the same figure set down the line and so on until all couples have rotated to the top of the line. The dance ends when the lead couple, after having assumed the bottom position, work their way back to the top. During the course of the dance, all couples thus mix and meet successively with all other couples. Because the repertoire of individual figures was rather large and new figures were invented each season, the possible combinations of figures into figure sets was seemingly endless. Each year publishing houses issued the most fashionable contredanses of the season, including both music and instructions. From 1730 to 1830 27,000 contredanses were published in England alone (Keller 1991: 8).

Contredanse Française

Possibly related to a dance titled "Le Cotillon" (choreographed and published by Raoul-Auger Feuillet in 1705), the *contredanse française* (also known as *cotillon*) gained ascendency in midcentury. According to the Leipzig dancing master Charles Pauli, "the French, having declared themselves in favor of [English] contredanses, soon changed the form, adapting the figures to suit their own tastes.... They made them cotillons such that there are now two types of contredanses: the *anglaise* and the *cotillon*" (1756: 67).

The first choreographies of the *contredanse française* appear in the 1760s, most notably with the publications of Sieur de La Cuisse (1762–65). The dance requires four couples arranged in a square formation to perform a series of nine, ten, or twelve figures called *entrées* (or changes). Entrées alternate in rondo-like fashion with the main figure of the dance called the refrain. The sequence of *entrées* was generally fixed and remained the same from one dance to another. Solely the refrain distinguished one *contredanse française* from another, and dancing manuals devoted their attention to it rather than the *entrées*, which were commonly known (Reichart 1984: 180). Besides a rondo-like design, the *contredanse française* is distinguished by the prevalence of French steps, particularly the rigaudon step and the gavotte step, the latter of which requires a half-measure upbeat (a half-measure upbeat is also a defining feature of the music). The popularity of the *contredanse française* extended into the early nineteenth century and influenced the development of the quadrille and the square dance of America.

Contredanse Allemande

The *contredanse allemande* (also known as *allemande*) swept Paris in the mid-1760s. Like the *contredanse française*, the *contredanse allemande* is performed by four couples arranged in a square and follows the same rondo-like design of a fixed series of *entrées* alternating with a repeating refrain. The difference is that *contredanse allemande* contains at least one German figure that requires partners to turn while interlacing their arms and hands in various manners, some of which were quite intricate. La Cuisse (1765, 3: [1]) believes the introduction of German figures into the Parisian ballrooms was due to the French exposure to German culture that occurred during the Seven Year's War, which ended in 1763. Another likely avenue of Austro-German influence was the arrival of Marie Antoinette from Vienna to marry the Dauphin Louis-Auguste in 1770 (she would later become queen of France in 1774). Both forms of the contredanse—the *contredanse française* and the *contredanse allemande*—were performed in Parisian ball-rooms until the end of the eighteenth century.

The available evidence suggests that out of the three forms of the contredanse, the Viennese, including Mozart, favored the *contredanse anglaise* (Mössmer 1990: 97). In what follows I focus my attention on the *contredanse anglaise*. Unless noted otherwise, the terms "contredanse" and *contredanse anglaise* will be used interchangeably.

Some Expressive and Cultural Associations of the Contredanse

Contemporary sources routinely described the contredanse as fast and energetic, simple and relatively easy to perform (especially in comparison with the minuet and other French court dances), and of a spirited, playful, and gay character. Dance steps often included skipping (especially for tunes in 6/8), hopping, stomping of heels, clapping, and partners turning with arms joined—all physical gestures associated with playfulness and gaiety.

Folk Associations

Commonly cited were its rural English origins. As the dancing master Gennaro Magri (1779) explains, "*Contredanses* emanated from simple Woodland dances.... Therefore the *Contredanses* as still preserved today are no more than an imitation of natural instincts expressed in happiness" (1988: 198). In 1791 Nicolas Framéry expands on both the rustic nature and the spontaneous expression of pleasure through bodily motion:

> The word seems to come from the English *country-dance*, dance of the country; indeed it is in the village above all that people love to gather, and prefer shared pleasure. The slow minuet, which employs only two people and does not allow the spectators any occupation except admiring the dancers, could only be born in the cites, where people dance for the sake of *amour-propre*. In the village people dance for the sole pleasure of dancing, to move limbs accustomed to violent exercise; they dance to breathe out a feeling of joy which grows constantly in proportion to the number of dancers, and has no need for spectators. (Allanbrook 1983: 62)

Thus the two primary dances of European ballrooms in the second half of the eighteenth century—the minuet and the contredanse—in execution and in expression occupied opposite ends of the spectrum. The minuet, the "queen of all dances" (Feldtenstein 1767: 37), was designed and performed as a spectator dance to showcase all the accruements of aristocratic behavior. Artfully simple yet fiendishly difficult to master, the minuet not only was the choreographic ideal of natural(ized) grace and noble simplicity but also represented the collective historical weight and power of the *ancien régime*. Thus the minuet was both a current dance and a historical dance. The contredanse, on the other hand, was little more than a divertissement designed not for the pleasure of the viewing audience, as Framéry observes, but rather for the dancers themselves—as a communal social activity that required a minimum of technique and hence a minimum of practice.

While the minuet was also commonly believed to have folk origins (Framéry is an exception), those origins were of a constructed past viewed from afar through the lens of aristocratic sensibilities. According to the myth told by dancing masters such as Magri and others, the peasant minuet was "rescued" by high culture whereby its *artless* simplicity was sublimated into the *artful* simplicity of the aristocratic minuet.[12] The rustic nature of the contredanse, on the other hand, was more direct, unprocessed, and spontaneous than that of historical dances commonly associated with images of folk life, such as the musette, gigue, and siciliano. As Wye J. Allanbrook (1983: 63) observes, these historical pastoral dances "are only secondhand rustic; they have been refined from mere rustic dances into vehicles for expressing qualities of character which are considered to accompany the rustic way of life."

Comic Associations

The participation of the upper classes in a simple and spirited dance of such strong rural associations lent it not only a sense of gaiety, but also, according to Daniel Gottlob Türk, an air "bordering on the moderately comic" (1982: 393). Johann Georg Sulzer in his *Allgemeine Theorie der schönen Künste* likewise observes that "[contredanses] are very lively, and for the most part have something comical about them in the way they unite pleasure and gallantry."[13] Later in his lexicon under his general discussion of "Tanz," Sulzer divides theatrical dance into four categories (grotesque, comic, *halbe Charaktere*, and noble). The *contredanse anglaise* was regularly used on stage in comic pantomime ballets as finales, often involving the entire cast performing a series of intricate figures (Harris-Warrick 2001a: 573). In its class associations, quality of motion, and expression, the contredanse—both on the stage and on the ballroom dance floor—falls most comfortably within Sulzer's category of "comic dances." Such dances "portray customs, amusements, and love intrigues of the common people. Movements and leaps are a little less abandoned, but still lively, rather mischievous, and very striking. They must always be amusing and merry. The main thing in them is agility, a quick, artful movement, and a mischievous affect" (Allanbrook 1983: 68).

While the choreography of the minuet is unified by the consistent use of a single step (*pas de menuet*), the contredanse suffered from a lack of such consistency. The German dancing master Carl Joseph von Feldtenstein complains that the contredanse "just looks bad when a man jumps around according to his own fancy" (1767: 88). As a corrective he recommends "five comical steps," which include a running step forward and sideways, a tap and hop step, and circling steps. Here the comical nature of the steps stems from their sprightly manner executed at a quick tempo.

Music and Dance–Music Relations

The music for contredanses is described in similar terms as the choreography: upbeat, merry, playful, and gay. Among its most important characteristics, says Gerhard Vieth, a Viennese pioneer in the field of physical education, is "music with a *lift*, that is, music that has a marked rhythm and a cheerful melody" (1794: 437). According to Magri, the combination of dance and music arouses "jubilation" and "moves our hearts to happiness" (1988: 198). Indeed, such is the evocative power of the music alone that to bring herself out of the doldrums, Johann Wolfgang von Goethe's character Lotte from the novel *The Sorrows of Young Werther* needs only "drum out a contredanse on my out-of-tune clavier, then everything is fine again" (Goethe 2005: 25).

In the repertoire, musical markers of gaiety abound: lively tempo, major mode, clear and uncomplicated melodic organization, and simple rhythms with a swinging gait (triplet figures are common). As previously mentioned, contredanse tunes are set in duple meter, either simple (2/4) or compound (6/8).[14] In their ballroom contredanses, though, Mozart, Haydn, and Beethoven much preferred 2/4. To illustrate the characteristic melodic qualities of Mozart's contredanses, Example 5.1 provides a selection of eight melodies drawn from his Viennese contredanses.

EXAMPLE 5.1 A selection of eight melodies drawn from Mozart's Viennese contredanses.

(a) K. 462 No. 3, mm. 1–8 (January 1784)

(b) K. 462 No. 3, mm. 9–16 (January 1784)

(c) K. 462 No. 5, mm. 9–16 (January 1784)

(d) K. 603 No. 1, mm. 9–16 (February 1791)

(e) K. 603 No. 2, mm. 1–8 (February 1791)

(f) K. 609 No. 3, mm. 1–8 (c. 1787–88)

(g) K. 609 No. 5, mm. 1–8 (c. 1787–88)

(h) K. 609 No. 5, mm. 17–24 (c. 1787–88)

Often cited is the song-like quality of contredanse melodies, and especially those of the *contredanse anglaise*. Sulzer comments that "it is pleasing that most [contredanse] melodies are modeled after popular English songs, so that the English dance unites poetry, song, and dance into one, and the songs cannot only be sung, but also danced, so that the melodies naturally have far greater impact."[15] Some twenty years earlier Pauli observes that the contredanse is danced "to small gay and merry airs, such as simple songs and light comedies."[16] As Pauli's quote suggests, contredanse music was influenced not only by popular songs but also by stage music, such as the vaudeville repertory used in *opéras comiques* (Harris-Warrick 2001b: 900) and opera buffa. In the opening contredanse of K. 609 (1791), for example, Mozart borrows from his own aria "Non più andrai" from *Le nozze di Figaro*, premiered four years earlier (Example 5.2).[17]

Closely tethered to the image of the contredanse as a rural dance of the common people was the view that contredanse melodies should be artless in nature. Sulzer observes that the music "is usually very lively because of its great simplicity, with especially clearly marked divisions."[18] In their lexicons both Jean-Jacques Rousseau (1768: 122) and Charles Compan (1787: 101) also cite simplicity and clear melodic punctuation as core characteristics of contredanse melodies. Heinrich Christoph Koch in his 1802 *Musikalisches Lexikon* expands on the notion of simplicity: "the melody has a consistently even number of rhythmic sections that are sharply differentiated from one another by clearly marked breaks; also, they must be entirely artless, and have the character of gladness and good humor."[19]

EXAMPLE **5.2** Mozart, *Fünf Kontretänze*, K. 609, No. 1, mm. 1–16 (c. 1787–88).

Thus simplicity of musical materials, including an overly determined melodic organization, is a marker of the contredanse. This attribute suits its fast tempo, in which melodies are "stripped down for action" (Allanbrook 1983: 57), its low style, and its rustic associations.

Dance–music relations offer another viewpoint as to the prominence of a clearly marked melodic organization. Whether at formal balls or informal balls, balls of the upper class, lower class, or mixed classes, contredanse dancers and musicians sought to coordinate the music and dance in such a way that the beginnings and ends of the dancers' figures synchronized with the beginnings and ends of the melodies. Dance manuals throughout the eighteenth century offer advice to both dancers and musicians on how best to achieve such lockstep coordination between the dance and the music.

La Cuisse (1762, 1: 10) instructs dancers to make adjustments to their steps—speeding them up or slowing down—in order to avoid ending before or after the tune ends. Giovanni Battista Gherardi (1768: 380) recommends that dancers should "always hear the tune played once over" so that, "noticing where the figure of the first part ends, and where the figure of the second part...begins, they would...arrive together at the end of the figure of the first part; and, consequently, would return to their places in the just time of the tune, to commence the figure of the second." In order to better hear the music and communicate with the orchestra leader, Magri (1988: 192–93) insists on arranging the dancers so that the lead couple is closest to the musicians. Turning to the musicians, Gherardi (1768: 380) recommends that "the first violin ought to know the air by heart," so that he can watch the dancers and "keep pace with their movements," and, if need be, lengthen or shorten the melody so that they arrive together at the end of their figure. Giovanni Gallini (1766, appendix: 4) likewise instructs musicians to coordinate the tunes with the figures of the dancers. And for Gerhard Ulrich Anton Vieth, writing from Vienna in 1794, among the chief characteristics of a good contredanse anglaise are "figures that are properly suited to the music, not too short or too long," so "that they properly enmesh with one another."[20]

In comparison, ballroom minuet dancers generally did not concern themselves with coordinating the beginnings and ends of their figures to the beginnings and ends of the melodies.[21] Rather, the required level of dance–music congruence was the coordination of the dancers' six-beat pas de menuet step to the music's two-measure hypermeter. To assist dancers, composers throughout the eighteenth century turned to sentence form (2 + 2 + 4) as one means of supporting a consistently maintained two-measure hypermeter. As shown in Table 5.2, an inventory of theme types in Mozart's Viennese ballroom minuets, the composer follows standard practice: by a wide margin, sentence form is his preferred theme type.[22]

As for the contredanse, because of the faster tempo and the utter lack of consistency in the dancers' choice of steps, the basic choreographic unit was the figure—typically four or eight measures in length—rather than the step.[23] Since, as we have seen, dancers were required to coordinate their figures to the music's melodic organization, for the music to be "danceable" the beginnings and ends of the melodies needed to be clearly articulated and the measure lengths of the melodies in some multiple of four. Thus, for dance

Table 5.2 Mozart's Viennese Ballroom Minuets: Theme
Types of First Strains from K. 461, K. 568, K. 585, K. 599,
K. 601, and K. 604

4 + 4 periods	16/42	38.0%
parallel periods	9	21.4%
hybrid periods	7	16.6%
eight-measure themes	26/42	61.9%
sentence forms (2 + 2 + 4)	22	52.3%
nonsentential eight-measure themes	4	9.5%

Table 5.3 Mozart's Viennese Ballroom
Contredanses: Theme Types from K. 462, K. 463,
K. 603, K. 609, and K. 610

4 + 4 periods	47/53	88.6%
parallel periods	34	64.1%
hybrid periods	13	24.5%
eight-measure themes	6/53	11.3%
sentence forms (2 + 2 + 4)	6	11.3%

composers, the contredanse presented very different types of compositional constraints than those of the minuet.

Not surprisingly, the repertoire shows that dance composers responded to the needs of the dancers. In a statistical study of phrase types found in published collections of eighteenth-century contredanses, David Neumeyer (2006) observes that not only was contredanse music "firmly rooted in … 'quadratic syntax,'" but that 4 + 4 periods "gain ascendancy … early in the eighteenth century and hold that status to the end." Whereas sentence form is the ideal means of supporting a two-measure hypermeter needed by minuet dancers, for the contredanse period organization is the ideal means of musically cuing the beginnings and ends of the dancers' predominantly four-measure and eight-measure dance figures. The melodic organization thus provides a "helping hand" by reflecting the higher-level proportions of the dance figures.

Mozart well understood the generic requirements for the contredanse both in terms of its character and in terms of what dancers needed. A breakdown of theme types found in Mozart's Viennese contredanses is provided in Table 5.3. Nearly nine out of ten of Mozart's contredanse strains are organized as 4 + 4 periods, and the majority of those are parallel periods. To make the quadratic syntax even clearer, the four-measure segmentation of over half of Mozart's contredanse tunes (twenty-five out of fifty-three) are overly determined by terrace dynamics and/or changes in orchestration, as shown in Example 5.3.

EXAMPLE **5.3** Mozart, *Sechs Kontretänze*, K. 462, No. 1, mm. 1–8 (January 1784).

Spinning Dances: *Deutscher–Walzer* and *Ländler*

Walzer: An oft and loudly denounced, and therefore increasingly popular, dance that originated on German soil.

Gerhard Ulrich Anton Vieth[24]

Deutscher–Walzer

The early history of German spinning dances remains an impregnable tangle. While it is clear that in the 1760s a family of dances emerged that required couples to rotate using some sort of embrace in synchronization with a lead couple, detailed choreographies of spinning dances do not appear until the beginning of the nineteenth century (Aldrich 1997: 134).[25] Further complicating matters, spinning dances during this time appear under a dizzying array of names that were often applied inconsistently.[26] Moreover, the fashions and practices of the dance hall changed from season to season, with marked differences between geographic regions.

A somewhat clearer picture begins to emerge in Vienna during the 1780s. While the term *deutscher Tanz* was often used to refer to any spinning dance of German origin, after 1780 it was increasingly used, along with the term *Walzer*, to refer to a specific type of spinning dance in which embraced couples executed large circles around the perimeter of the dancing space while simultaneously performing smaller loops (Landon 1976, 3: 208–11; Reichart 1984: 346–51; Aldrich 1997: 132–33). After 1800 *Walzer* (or the English translation "waltz") became the preferred term for what is widely considered the direct predecessor of the nineteenth-century Viennese waltz. In the remainder of this study, I use the conflated terms *Deutscher–Walzer* to refer to the early form of the waltz. My sources, however, use the terms *Deutscher, Walzer,* and "waltz" interchangeably. I use the term "Viennese waltz" to refer to the waltz form of the nineteenth century.

An important distinction between the *Deutscher–Walzer* of the late eighteenth century and the Viennese waltz of the early nineteenth century involves the coordination of the couples, or lack thereof. With the Viennese waltz, couples, aside from a general counterclockwise movement around the room, did not attempt to coordinate their movement with other couples. By extending or limiting the length of their strides while keeping to the beat of the music, dancers were free to choose how fast or slowly they moved around the room; they were also free to circumscribe smaller perimeters on the inside of the dancing space or larger ones on the outside. With the *Deutscher–Walzer,* as well as other early spinning dances, it appears that couples in some fashion coordinated their movements with each other as a type of group dance.

Gallini provides an early account in his 1762 treatise: "The Germans have a dance … in which the men and women form a ring. Each man holding his partner round the waist, makes her whirl round with almost inconceivable rapidity; they dance in a grand circle seeming to pursue one another; in the course of which they execute several leaps, and some particularly pleasing steps" (192–93). Writing in 1767, Feldtenstein observes that "each gentleman may lead his lady as he pleases, through circling turns, and setting revolutions in motion; he must only take care to keep his place in line."[27] Vieth's description, published in Vienna in 1794, reaffirms this practice: "Many couples may waltz behind one another, which looks good as long as everyone correctly remains on the perimeter of the circle, and everyone follows the lead of the first couple."[28]

These accounts refer not only to an intimate physical bond between the man and woman but also to a bond between all the couples on the dance floor, who move in synchronization behind a lead couple. According to Reingard Witzmann (1976: 59, 61), only during the opening decade of the nineteenth century did dancers begin favoring a less regimented approach to waltzing, giving greater independence to each couple. However, in some regions an ordered arrangement of dancers continued to be practiced. As late as 1816 in a dance hall in Innsbruck, upon his second warning a man could be reported to the police commissioner for passing ahead of another waltzing couple on the ballroom dance floor (Fink 1990: 39).

The following list summarizes the choreographic features of the *Deutscher–Walzer* as found on the Viennese dance floors prior to 1800:

- The *Deutscher–Walzer* was a group dance;
- Couples, using some sort of embrace, followed a lead couple in a large circular path around the perimeter of the dancing space while performing smaller loops;
- Couples stayed in order and may have coordinated their steps and arm positions to a lead couple;
- The *Deutscher–Walzer* required continuous movement (the only ballroom dance of the time to require this);
- Early versions of the *Deutscher–Walzer* drew on a variety of steps, including hopping and skipping. By the end of the century the range of steps narrowed when

a smoother gliding step was introduced (Kattfuss 1800: 154; Gstrein 1990: 120; Witzmann 1976: 58, 63);[29]

- The *Deutscher–Walzer* was faster than the *Ländler* and other spinning dances.[30] And compared to other urban centers, Viennese dancers were the fastest;
- The *Deutscher–Walzer* was the direct predecessor of the Viennese waltz.

Ländler

While it had already gained popularity as a folk dance in rural regions of Austria, southern Germany, and German Switzerland, the *Ländler* was first introduced into the upper-class Viennese ballroom during the 1780s. Among the first publications are two sets of *Ländler* by Johann Baptist Vanhal included in the 1785–87 Breitkopf thematic catalogue (Reichart 1984: 326–27). However, only the incipits of the Vanhal dances survive. Written in February 1791, Mozart's six *Ländler*, K. 606, are the first, extant published set and the only set of *Ländler* he composed.

In contrast to the *Deutscher–Walzer*, the *Ländler* involved a variety of steps and body motions (including hand clapping and foot stamping), and a wider range of embraces, all much more varied than those found in the waltz. As Sarah Reichart (1984: 324) notes, the intricacies of the figures and the nature of the dance, which was casual and relaxed, demanded a slower tempo than the *Deutscher–Walzer*.[31] Additionally, while continuous movement characterizes the *Deutscher–Walzer*, the figures of the *Ländler* often required dancers to stop while they clapped or stamped their feet. Typical figures included the woman revolving under the man's raised arm or couples revolving around each other back-to-back (Scott 2008: 118). While some of the *Ländler* figures do require couples to rotate, most of the movements used in the *Ländler* are not found in accounts of the *Deutscher–Walzer* and appear to be associated with rural dress and rural dancing spaces (heeled, hobnailed shoes and boots rather than soft-soled shoes without heels; dirt or rough hewn wood floors rather than polished wood floors).

Physical, Expressive, and Cultural Associations of the Spinning Dances

In looking at a variety of primary sources, four themes or associations are evident: vertigo, romance, immorality, and Austrian folk music.

Vertigo

The revolutionary nature of the *Deutscher–Walzer* was not so much that it involved a "dangerously" close physical embrace between a man and a woman, but that couples *maintained* their embrace throughout the entire dance while continuously turning in circles. Using the term *ilinx* (the Greek word for whirlpool), the social theorist Roger Caillois classifies the waltz as a type of "game" based on the "pursuit of vertigo" in which dancers "attempt to momentarily destroy the stability of perception and inflict a kind of voluptuous panic upon an otherwise lucid mind" (1961: 23). This description aligns well with Vieth's 1794 assessment of the waltz's rotary effects: "In this dance everything is circle-shaped and whirling movement, everything designed to provoke giddiness and seduce the senses....In order to avoid getting dizzy," Vieth continues, "those who are susceptible to it find it helpful always to look their partner in the face, and not at things in their vicinity, which all seem to spin around in a circle."[32]

The dancing master Johann Kattfuss in 1800 was one of the first in a long line of commentators to recognize the importance of making sure waltzing women stayed on their feet. "Yet another unrecognized error that gentlemen dancers frequently are guilty of is suddenly releasing their lady's hands when she steps into the forward path after turning. Many ladies are inclined to get dizzy and are put in danger of falling at the end of the turn....The gentlemen should never overlook such precautions, because he still cannot know whether his lady is susceptible to dizziness or not" (1800: 153).[33] Indeed, "only [women] with iron characters, are indifferent to its entrancing swing," writes an anonymous German reporter in 1797 (Reeser 1949: 19).

The constant spinning motion visually blurred the couple's perception of the world around them—the only objects they could see clearly were each other's bodies. Thus waltzing couples were able to construct an intimate and private world within an often-crowded public space. It was up to the gentlemen to keep their place in line behind the other couples in front of them. The lady was thereby free to abandon herself, within the bounds of proper decorum, to the waltz's dizzying effects.

While spinning dances were a source of physical and psychological pleasure, they could also lead to loss of control, complete disorientation, and physical collapse, especially, it was often reported, among women. The heating and ventilation of the dance hall, the physical and mental condition of the dancers (including how much alcohol they had consumed), the tightness of the women's corsets, and the speed at which they performed were all factors that could lead to physical or mental breakdown. The *Langaus*, in particular, an extremely vigorous dance in which couples raced, while spinning, from one end of the hall to the other with the greatest possible speed, was responsible for the demise of many dancers, both women and men, to the extent that it was banned in Vienna in 1791. The ban was reaffirmed in 1794, 1803, and again in 1804 (Hanson 1985: 164).

Romance

"I imagine two enraptured creatures, drunk with love, gliding away in their joyous ecstasy," waxes an anonymous writer in 1801 (Reeser 1949: 18). Largely as a result of the sustained, close embrace and the harmonious rhythms of two bodies in motion, the *Deutscher-Walzer* became the choreographic emblem of romance and—for many worried mothers and fathers—a thinly veiled sexual act.

For the upper classes, the ball was one of the very few occasions where the young and unmarried could openly meet and talk, and the *Deutscher-Walzer* offered the ideal opportunity for them to continue their conversations in a much more intimate and physically stimulating manner. In stage works and in literature the *Deutscher-Walzer* was quickly appropriated as a vehicle for validating the romantic status of a couple. In one of the earliest literary examples—and one of the best—again in Goethe's *The Sorrows of Young Werther*, Werther, in a letter to his friend Wilhelm, recounts his experience at a ball in a small country village. Much to his delight, he finds himself dancing with a beautiful woman with whom he has tragically fallen in love.

> Now it began! We were delighted for a while with all the diverse interweaving of arms. How charmingly, how fleetingly she moved! And when it came to waltzing and the couples circled around each other, things got, at the beginning, pretty muddled, because only a few people could do it. We were clever and let them have their fling, and after the clumsiest left the floor, we jumped in and valiantly kept it up with another couple....Never have I got started so easily. I was no longer a person. To have the most charming creature in my arms and fly around with her like lightening, so that everything around us vanished....I swore an oath to myself that a girl that I loved, and on whom I had a claim, should never waltz with anyone but me, even if it cost me my life! (Goethe 2005: 26–27)

His having been smitten with this beautiful dancing partner certainly played some role in Werther's flight of imagination, but more practically speaking, the extinction of the external world also resulted from the couple's constant rotary motions. Werther's admonition to himself that a woman he love should never waltz with another man underscores the physical and emotional intensity of the waltzers' intimate embrace. The constant circling motion creates a physical bond uniting the two dancers as one self-enclosed body of motion—as a spinning orb.[34]

Immorality

In Goethe's novel, Werther reveals his uneasy awareness of the erotic powers of the waltz. Because of the implicit sexual nature of this embrace, many critics of the time, quite unsuccessfully, urged that, if the *Deutscher-Walzer* was danced at all, only married couples should be allowed to do so. Writing in 1782 one such critic, Karl Zangen, firmly stakes out his position on the matter: "We shall not consent that our wives, daughters or beloveds should be embraced by other men's arms, chest to chest with them in a full reckless abandon of themselves, being tossed around to wild music" (Witzmann 1976: 61). Even the slower and calmer *Ländler* was considered off-limits by mothers who wanted to protect the reputations of their daughters. In a diary entry written during Carnival in 1786, a young handmaiden in a palace in Vienna records the following incident:

> Countess Wallerburg walked in while Marie and Maria were trying out the new dance. It's called *Ländler*, and gets into your feet immediately. I tried it, too. Heavenly! Nobody had heard Wallerburg coming...she then scolded us for a quarter of an hour. She complained about the indecent dance, done in pairs, and generally about the girls of today. She will tell the Duke. (Stainer 1978: 8)

Moralists not only believed that a woman's honor and reputation would be sullied by waltzing, but also that spinning dances were responsible for the decline in morality of all mankind. A tract decrying the moral dangers of the waltzing, published in 1797, was titled *Discussions of the Most Important Causes of the Weakness of Our Generation in Regard to the Waltz*. After quickly selling out, it was republished two years later with the new title, *Proof That the Waltz Is the Main Source of the Weakness of Body and Mind of Our Generations, Most Urgently Recommended to the Sons and Daughters of Germany*.[35] Surprisingly, perhaps, religious authorities penned some of the most sexually charged literary descriptions of waltzing women. The stated purpose of their publications was to warn readers about the dangers of what could, should, and would happen to unmarried women who dared to waltz. The authority of the church rendered dance criticism a literary forum where describing and reading about "improper" sexual conduct was socially permissible. Thus the majority of these publications contain extended lyrical descriptions of sexual behavior, often voyeuristic in nature. Their widespread popularity suggests they were not so much read for their moral message, as for their sexual content; in other words, they represent a form of literary erotica.

Austrian Folk Music

During the last decade of the eighteenth century the *Deutscher–Walzer* shed much of its image as a lower class, rustic dance. Due to the enticing opportunity of embracing

EXAMPLE **5.4** Two *Ländler* melodies from Mozart's *Sechs Ländlerische Tänze*, K. 606, No. 1 and No. 4 (December 1789).

EXAMPLE **5.5** Two *Ländler* melodies from an anonymous manuscript tunebook (c. 1810).

someone of the opposite sex in a game of vertigo and the critical outcry by parents and moralists, the *Deutscher–Walzer* quickly became the most fashionable urban dance of the young in Paris, Berlin, Warsaw, Vienna, and, eventually, London. The *Ländler*, however, continued to maintain strong rural associations. An 1801 Viennese customs report makes the class distinction between the *Walzer* and the *Ländler* quite clear, especially in terms of the music: the ballroom "provides a truly pleasing spectacle, especially when the music of the Galant *Walzer* suddenly degenerates into a rustic *Ländler*" (Witzmann 1976: 57–58). And, according to Litschauer and Deutsche (1997: 51), at Viennese house balls dancers often wore peasant costumes when performing the *Ländler*.

The music of Mozart's *Ländler* is characterized by a slow harmonic rhythm, an extremely limited harmonic vocabulary (only tonic and dominant chords), and arpeggiating melodies often in constant eighth notes. As Rainer Gstrein suggests, the melodic style of Mozart's *Ländler* was likely influenced by and closely associated with Linz violinists who entered Vienna via the Danube on ships from Northern Austria (1990: 117, 125).[36] The similarities of melodic style are readily apparent from comparison of Examples 5.4 and 5.5, which present, respectively, two Mozart *Ländler* melodies and two other *Ländler* melodies taken from an anonymous manuscript tunebook entitled "Linzer Tänze" compiled sometime during the first decade of the nineteenth century.[37]

Mozart's *Deutsche*

All of Mozart's *Deutsche* were written in Vienna during the winter dancing seasons between the years 1787 and 1791. Without exception, they are organized as symmetrically balanced, small binary forms: 8 :||: 8. As with Mozart's minuets, each *Deutscher* is paired with a second *Deutscher*, titled as a "trio," within a ternary da capo layout. Mozart assembles these dances into sets ranging from six to thirteen *Deutsche*.

Three features of Mozart's *Deutsche* define his approach to the genre, and all of them became signature features of the nineteenth-century Viennese waltz.

- Artless simplicity
- Codas
- Irregular 1 + 3 melodic groupings

Artless Simplicity

As in the contredanse, a simpler approach to the musical materials of the *Deutscher* may have been motivated by its lower-class associations. And to the extent that the *Deutscher* was considered a low-brow dance, in a class-conscious society a simpler style would have been important since it rubbed shoulder-to-shoulder on the dance floor with the queen of the ballroom, the aristocratic minuet. Nonetheless, while a simpler approach to rhythm and melody is evident in Mozart's *Deutsche*, many of those he composed before 1789 draw on stylistic traits found in his minuets. Perhaps this cross-fertilization is not so surprising given that both are triple-meter dances, both were written for Vienna's Imperial ballrooms—large and often crowded acoustical spaces that required certain tried-and-true orchestral effects in order for the music to be heard—and, as only recently introduced into the Viennese ballroom, the *Deutscher* lacked a well-defined set of distinguishing musical features. Certainly the oom-pah-pah accompaniment had not yet been established as a defining feature and would not become so until the second decade of the nineteenth century (McKee 2012: 67–73). Only with K. 586, written in December of 1789, does Mozart begin to develop an approach to the *Deutscher* that is consistently distinct from the minuet.

But a simpler approach to the musical materials of the *Deutscher* was also necessitated by its faster tempo, whereby the primary beat shifts from the quarter note to the measure. The faster tempo did not allow for rhythmic or melodic nuance within the measure as was possible with the slower, nobler tempo of the minuet. Constant, flowing eighth-note patterns are quite common, providing the music with a strong sense of motion and exuberance, which at times resulted in a "damned see-saw up and down sort of tune," according to Lord Byron (1907: 156).

Other elements of simplicity include:

- slow harmonic rhythm (typically one harmony per measure)
- narrow range of rhythmic values
- simple outer-voice counterpoint
- prominent use of pedal tones
- prominent use of repeated one-measure motives
- little or no motivic development

Rarely does Mozart's artless simplicity apply to all aspects of his music; it will typically be apparent in two or three musical elements. The last *Deutscher* (No. 12) of Mozart's K. 586 (Example 5.6) provides a good example in which simplicity prevails in rhythm, harmony, and melody. Musical interest in this dance in large part stems from the tension created by the incessant and unvaried repetition of the opening one-measure gesture, which effectively correlates to the patterns of exertion required of the dancers (where the man and the woman twirl on alternating measures).[38] In both eight-measure phrases Mozart increases the sense of spinning and its associated effect of vertigo by a composed-out rhythmic acceleration and, in the first phrase, a gradual crescendo. This is wild, unbridled music of the sort Zangen harshly criticized (previously cited on page 178).

Codas

Mozart's *Deutscher* sets follow a medley format that exhibits no large-scale pattern of thematic repetition. Major keys prevail within a range of up to three sharps and three flats. While fifth and third key relations are common between individual *Deutsche*, and sets typically begin and end in the same key, there are no overarching tonal trajectories that provide unity or a sense of structural momentum. It is noteworthy, however,

EXAMPLE 5.6 Mozart, *Zwölf deutsche Tänze*, K. 586, No. 12, mm. 1–16 (December 1789).

that all of Mozart's *Deutscher* sets are anchored by substantial codas, which provide a strong sense of rhetorical closure. He does not employ codas in either his minuets or his contredanses. The format of Mozart's codas is consistent: they begin with a noisy and theatrical move to an extended half cadence. The half cadence concludes with a fermata followed by a grand pause, which effectively terminates the meter—and with it the dance. After the silence, the tune of the previous *Deutscher* is reintroduced. There follows an extended closing passage often punctuated by a series of hypermetrically accented perfect authentic cadences.

It is likely that the beginning section of the coda was aurally marked with a grand pause so that dancers would know that global closure was imminent. Unlike the contredanse and the minuet, *Deutscher* dancers, as we saw in the Goethe excerpt, were free to enter or leave the dancing space at their own discretion.[39] Thus the official end of the dance is not determined by the choreography of the *Deutscher*, but rather by the termination of the music. If dancers wished to remain on the dance floor for the entire duration of the *Deutscher*, they needed to be cued when musical closure was close at hand in order not to be taken by surprise. The announcement of the coda thus signaled the beginning of a time period during which the gentlemen could carefully escort their dancing partners, who might be suffering from the effects of vertigo, safely back to their seats before the beginning of the next dance.

1 + 3 Melodic Groupings and Hypermetrical Disruptions

As previously discussed, Mozart's contredanse melodies, as well as those of his contemporaries, strictly observe a quadratic syntax yielding symmetrical proportions on all levels of melodic organization. Moreover, the four-measure phrases are invariably in phase with a duple hypermeter. Dancing masters implored dancers to coordinate the beginnings and ends of their figures to the beginnings and ends of the contredanse dance tunes. Conversely, they also instructed dance musicians to keep an eye on the dancers in order to align their melodies to the dancers' figures. Thus, in order to aid the dancers, the grouping organization of contredanse melodies should be quadratic, symmetrical, in phase with the hypermeter, and overly determined. And in the vast majority of cases, it is. Mozart's minuets are also characterized by a quadratic grouping organization aligned with the hypermeter, although, as the research of Tilden Russell (1992, 1999) reveals, earlier repertoires were a bit more varied in their use of irregular phrase rhythms.

A rather remarkable feature of Mozart's *Deutsche*, distinguishing them from other dance types, are irregular 1 + 3 melodic groupings (or 2 + 3 if the groups overlap), which occasionally result in hypermetrical disruptions. In Mozart's K. 586, which can be considered his first *Deutscher* set to shed the stylistic influence of the minuet, nine of the twenty-four *Deutsche* (or 38%) begin with a 1 + 3 or 2 + 3 grouping. I am not able to determine whether this technique was Mozart's own contribution to the genre or one already associated with *Deutscher* music. It is, however, a technique that continued to play an important role in waltz music of the nineteenth century, especially in the waltz music of Lanner, Strauss Sr., Chopin, and Strauss Jr., among others.

There are two possible ways a 1 + 3 or 2 + 3 melodic grouping may be aligned with a two-measure hypermeter: Type A and Type B (Figure 5.1). As we will see, these two types are not self-contained categories, but rather represent two poles on a continuum of possibilities.

In Type A, the beginning of the melody is coordinated with both the beginning of the accompaniment and a hyperdownbeat. While the four-measure melody as a whole is in phase with the hypermeter, its internal segmentation is not and, to some degree, conflicts with the hypermeter. The beginnings of the three-measure groups, because of their greater lengths, garner a stronger beginning accent than the one-measure groups, especially on the repetition of the eight-measure strain.[40] It is the textural, tonal, and rhythmic stability of the accompaniment pattern that prevents the hypermeter from shifting to an even-numbered metrical scheme.

Type 1: Four-measure melody in phase with the hypermeter and the accompaniment.

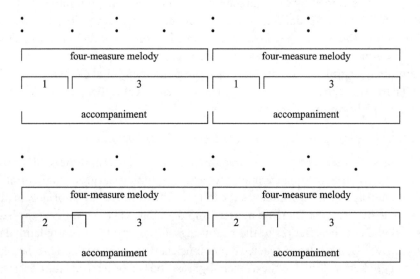

Type 2: Four-measure melody out of phase with the hypermeter and the accompaniment.

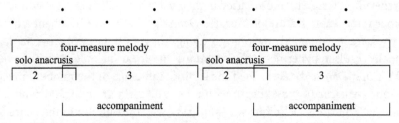

FIGURE 5.1 Irregular groupings in Mozart's *Deutsche.*

The opening strain of the trio from the fifth *Deutsche* of K. 586 (Example 5.7) begins with a one-measure ascent to a three-measure segment consisting of a repeated one-measure motive. While the opening one-measure segment linearly "leads to" the beginning of the three-measure segment, several factors prevent us from reading it as anacrustic. First, the odd-numbered hypermeter of the previous *Deutscher* (not shown) provides a perceptual momentum that continues into the trio. That is, based on the previous music we expect the first measure of the trio to be a hyperdownbeat. Second, the opening one-measure segment is coordinated with the beginning of a rhythmically and tonally stable accompaniment pattern. It opens not only with a tonic but also with an octave on $\hat{1}$. And finally, while the stepwise ascent provides linear motion into m. 2, there is little rhythmic momentum. The sudden crash of the Spanish tambourine and *forte* tutti entrance of the winds and brass in m. 5 puts to rest any notion of an even-numbered

EXAMPLE 5.7 Mozart, *Zwölf deutsche Tänze*, K. 586, No. 5, Trio, mm. 1–8 (December 1789).

metrical scheme. But even so, we notice how changes to the three-measure segment in the second half (mm. 6–8)—particularly the melodic hemiola, heightens the metrical dissonance without calling into question the dominance of an odd-numbered hyper-metrical scheme.

With its steady stream of eighth notes and dissonance appoggiaturas, the opening segment from the first *Deutscher* of K. 586 (Example 5.8) engenders a greater sense of forward motion than the previous example.[41] While the low pedal bass of the accompaniment enters on the downbeat of m. 1, its accentual presence is undercut by the delayed entrance of the second violins, which on beat two double the first violins' eighth notes in tenths, thereby lending more support for hearing the opening eighth notes as anacrustic. At the downbeat of m. 2, the second violins switch roles from melodic support to an upper-voice accompaniment pattern. The overall effect is that the accompaniment proper does not begin until the second measure. Apart from the pedal bass, all other factors suggest hearing m. 2 as a hyperdownbeat.

The varied repetition of the 2 + 3 phrase heightens the beginning accent of the three-measure segment. The ascending anacrustic eighth notes are now doubled at the onset by the second violins and oboe. At the expected entrance of the three-measure segment, the staccato articulation returns but, upon leaping to a high C, the violins play a new melody descending in eighth notes. Somewhat hidden in the texture, the oboes play a variant of the three-measure melody. Notice that the "delayed" entrance of the bass and cellos also highlights the beginning of the three-measure segment. Rubbing against the 2 + 3 phrase rhythm of the melody is the resumption of the pedal C in m. 5 by the timpani, clarinets, and bassoons, now filled out to a full C-major triad. The conflict between an odd-numbered metrical scheme (Type A) and an

EXAMPLE 5.8 Mozart, *Zwölf deutsche Tänze*, K. 586, No. 1, mm. 1–8 (December 1789).

even-numbered metrical scheme (Type B) is thus not decisively settled one way or another.

In the phrase rhythm represented by Type B, the opening one-measure segment enters as a one-measure solo anacrusis leading to the initiation of the accompaniment pattern in m. 2, the beginning of the three-measure segment, and a hyperdownbeat. While the four-measure melodic phrases and the hypermeter are out of phase with each other, the beginnings of the three-measure segments are aligned with a hyperdownbeat.

The trio from *Deutscher* No. 8 of the same set (Example 5.9) presents a clear case of Type B, very similar in design to the previous example. An opening melodic gesture in flowing eighth notes, doubled in quarter notes by a bassoon and clarinet, gently winds its way down from $\hat{6}$ to $\hat{1}$, at which point a new three-measure segment commences. The primary difference between this example and the previous one is that here both voices of the accompaniment enter in m. 2. All aspects of the texture, phrase rhythm, and harmony support an even-numbered metrical scheme.

Why would Mozart introduce phrase rhythms that appear antithetical to the dance? One would think unambiguous grouping segmentation and hypermetrical regularity would be a *sine qua non* of ballroom dance music. Perhaps Mozart's use of these phrase rhythms may be read as social commentary whereby the risqué embrace of the *Deutscher–Walzer*, which itself violated social convention, is matched by transgressions in the music. Or perhaps metrical disruptions and irregular groupings may be read as markers of lower-class dance music.

Johann Knaffl in 1813 recognized the violation of musical convention as a potent source of expression in peasant spinning dances of Styria:

> The various twists and connections of notes rising and falling down one after the other without any regard to the rules of voice leading, should, judged individually, sound bad, but in the context of the overall rhythmic context, are surprisingly are not offensive, but rather a source of enthusiasm amongst the dancers. (Knaffl 1928: 109–10)[42]

EXAMPLE 5.9 Mozart, *Zwölf deutsche Tänze*, K. 586, No. 8, Trio, mm. 1–8 (December 1789).

Joseph Riepel makes a similar observation some sixty years earlier. His imaginary student observes that in the local beer halls, when musicians played a German dance with an irregular phrase, all the dancers would "begin to jump around as if they were crazy" (Russell 1992: 119). So perhaps, on musical grounds, the final motivation for these techniques is that it adds for listeners—on and off the dance floor—musical interest and excitement. Unlike Haydn and Beethoven, Mozart was passionate about the dance, and the autograph manuscripts show that he took great care in providing music that was beautifully fit for dancing, but also rubbed against it in interesting ways.

But what about the dancers? Apparently the choreographical requirements of the *Deutscher–Walzer* were such that breaches of musical conduct of this sort did not disturb or confuse the dancers. A key distinction of the *Deutscher–Walzer* from other ballroom dances is that it lacks a set sequence of figures whose boundary points must coordinate with the music. If dancers did not require anything beyond an appropriate tempo and meter, then the composer was not obligated to provide clear grouping boundaries. This lack of constraint between the dance and the music allowed Mozart greater creative license to explore new rhythmic relationships on the Viennese ballroom dance floor.

NOTES

1. Cited in Bauer and Deutsch (1962–71, 1: 255).
2. Kelley (1968, 1: 201–2).
3. Concerning the meaning of *Gemüthsbewegungen* and its relationship to the eighteenth-century notion of mimesis, see Allanbrook (1983: 8; 2014: 64–70) and this volume's introduction.
4. "Sonic analogue" is a term used by Lawrence Zbikowski (2008).
5. For studies on various ways listeners may embody music, see Zbikowski (2012) and Cox (2006, 2011).
6. The status of dance music as current or historical has other consequences for its signification to listeners. For example, upon hearing a lively tune in simple duple meter with a half-measure anacrusis, the likely default interpretation of a listener from the second

half of the eighteenth century would be to hear it as a *contredanse française* rather than a gavotte. Musically, both dances are characterized by a half-measure anacrusis and simple duple meter and, choreographically, both employ the gavotte step. After midcentury, however, the gavotte as a French court dance was no longer part of the active repertoire of ballroom dancers.

7. For a detailed discussion of Mozart's activities as a dancer, see Busch-Salmen (1990: 65–81).

8. For in-depth studies of the minuet, see Russell (1983, 1992, 1999), Wheelock (1992), Lowe (1998, 2002), Ferraguto (2010), and McKee (2012).

9. Tomlinson (1735: 157).

10. *The English Dancing Master* (retitled in subsequent editions as *The Dancing Master*) was widely popular and was reissued by Playford and his successors in seventeen subsequent editions. The first edition contains 105 dances; the last edition, published in 1728 in three volumes, contains 918 dances.

11. The number of dancers varied according to the size and accommodations of the dancing space and the availability of dancers. In the first edition of Playford's treatise thirty-nine out of 105 dances are listed as "longways for as many as will." In subsequent editions added dances were almost entirely in longways formation, while omitted dances were most often in round and square formations. By the fourteenth edition, issued in 1709, 345 out of 348 dances are listed as "longways for as many as will."

12. See McKee (2012: 55–58) for a discussion of the folk associations of the minuet in the treatises of eighteenth-century dancing masters.

13. "Alle kommen darin überein, daß sie sehr lebhaft sind, und größtentheils etwas mäßig comisches haben, dadurch sie Vergnügen und Artigkeit miteinander vereinigen" (Sulzer 1773–75, 1: 427). I am grateful to Laura Hedden for her assistance in translating the original German passages found in this chapter.

14. I use these terms in their modern senses, which differ from those adopted in the eighteenth century. For the eighteenth-century distinction between simple and compound meters, see Danuta Mirka's chapter in this volume.

15. "Artig ist haben, das die meisten Melodien zu bekannten englische Liedern gemacht sind, so das man bey den englischen Tänzen Poetie, Gesang und Tanz mit einander vereinigen, und Lieder nicht blos fingen. sondern auch tanzen kann, wodurch sie naturlicher Weise weit mehr Eindruk machen" (Sulzer 1773–75, 1: 427).

16. "C'est une danse de plusieurs personnes qui dansent l'une contre l'autre par de petites figures qui sont toujours reprises; faite sur de petits airs gais & gaillards, comme font les chansonnettes & les Vaudevilles" (Pauli 1756: 66).

17. Another transfer from the comic stage to the dancehall is reported by Mozart in a letter written from Prague in January of 1787: "I watched with great pleasure how all these people danced with joy and vivacity to the music of my Figaro arranged as contredanses and German dances" (Bauer and Deutsche 1962–75, 4: 9).

18. "Die Musik zu den englischen Tänzen, die man in Deutschland insgemein Angloisen nennt, ist insgemein bey einer grossen Einfalt sehr lebhast, mit ungemein deutlich bemerkten Einschnitten, und hat vierfältig das besondere, dass die Cadenzen in den Aufschlag fallen" (Sulzer 1773–75, 1: 427).

19. "Die Melodie hat beständig geradzahlige rhythmische Theile, die sich von einander durch stark markirte Einschnitte unterscheiden; das bey muss sie ganz ungekünstelt seyn, und das Gepräge der Fröhlichkeit und des artigen Scherzes haben" (Koch 1802: 535).

20. "2. dass die Touren der Musik gehörig angepasst, nicht zu lang und nicht zu kurz seyn, 3. dass sie gehörig in einander greifen, und die vorhergehende gleichsam die folgende vorbereite" (Vieth 1794: 438).

21. For discussion of dance–music relations in eighteenth-century ballroom minuets, see Russell (1992, 1999) and McKee (2012: 15–45).

22. My approach to theme types, including sentence form, is based on Caplin (1998).

23. Allanbrook makes a similar observation (1983: 61).

24. Vieth (1794: 440).

25. It is possible that spinning dances were neglected in the dance literature not only because of their lower-class status, but also because their steps were so well known that there was no reason to devote space to them in publication. Dancing masters concentrated their efforts on dances that required a higher level of mastery, such as contredanses and minuets. E. C. Mädel's treatise *Die Tanzkunst für die Elegante Welt* (1805) is one of the earliest dance treatises that describes a six-count, six-step spinning step.

26. As Andrew Lamb (2001: 72) observes, names of spinning dances typically indicate the motion found in the dance (*Walzer, Dreher, Hopfer, Weller, Spinner, Schleifer*) or to a national or geographic region (*Deutscher, Allemande, Tedesco, Schwäbischer, Steirer, Ländler*).

27. "Jeder Tänzer kann seine Tänzerin nach eigenen Gefallen, durch Cirkelwendungen, und Touren in Bewegung setzen, nur muss er die Reihe in obacht nehmen" (Feldtenstein 1767: 100).

28. "Es können viele Paare hinter einander herumwalzen, welches sich gut ausnimmt, wenn Alle richtig in der Peripherie des Kreises bleiben, und Alle sich nach dem ersten Paare richten, und zugleich *führen* oder *walzen*" (Vieth 1794: 441).

29. Already by 1772 Carl Joseph von Feldtenstein observes that for the *Deutscher* "there is only one basic step necessary (if the opportunity is lacking for the student to learn more from a teacher)" (100).

30. According to an anonymous writer in the *Journal des Luxus und der Moden*, the waltz "surpassed everything in headlong speed" (Reeser 1949: 19).

31. While the dancing master Johann Heinrich Kattfuss provides no detailed choreographic information and is certainly guilty of oversimplification, he does note the importance of tempo as distinguishing feature of spinning dances: "Waltzes, *Dreher* or *Ländler* have no difference in their steps, except that Waltzes are danced swiftly, and *Ländler* slowly" (*Walzen, Drehen, Ländern hat in dem Pas keinen Unterschied, außer daß Walzen geschwind, das Ländern aber langsam getanzet wird*; 1800: 149).

32. "Bey diesem Tanze ist alles kreisförmig-wirbelnde Bewegung, alles dazu geschickt, Taumel zu erregen und die Sinne zu verführen. . . .Um sich vor dem Schwindel zu bewahren, finden solche, die demselben unterworfen sind, es dienlich, immer der Moitié ins Gesicht, und nicht auf die umliegenden Gegenstände zu sehen, welche sich alle im Kreise herum zu drehen scheinen" (Vieth 1794: 441).

33. "Noch ein anderer unerkannter Fehler, den die Tänzer häufig zu verschulden pflegen, ist, dass sie ihre Tänzerinnen plötzlich aus den Händen lassen, wenn sie zum Wiedererholen vom Drehen, in den geraden Gang eintreten. Viele Personen sind zum Schwindel geneigt und gerathen in Gefahr des Niederfallens am Ende des Drehens. . . . Es ist solches eine Vorsicht, die sich ein Tänzer nie erlassen sollte, da er doch nicht missen kann, ob seine Tänzerin zum Schwindel geneigt ist, oder nicht" (Kattfuss 1800: 153).

34. As a side note, in classic Hollywood cinema the waltz, either as an on-screen dance or as nondiegetic music, is a staple of romantic love scenes. Max Steiner's 1933 score to *King Kong*,

the first movie to make extensive use of nondiegetic music, underscores the love scene with waltz music. Perhaps the most well known diegetic example is found in the Disney princess movie *Cinderella* (1950). Upon seeing his son, Prince Charming, take interest in Cinderella at the royal court ball, the King shouts to the orchestra conductor: "The waltz! Quick! The waltz!" Once the Prince and Cinderella begin to dance, the King yawns and retires to his bedchamber, confident in the waltz's power to bring Cinderella and the prince together in matrimony. "When the boy proposes," he orders the Grand Duke on his way to bed, "notify me immediately!"

35. These publications are cited in Sachs (1952: 431–32).
36. Schaller and Kühner (1956: 159) and Gstrein (1990: 125) note strong similarities between the melodies of Mozart's *Ländler*, K. 606, and the repertoire of North-Austrian folk violinists.
37. A page from the manuscript is reproduced in Gstrein (1990: 118).
38. Concerning how composers provided sonic analogues for the patterns of exertion required of waltzes, see Zbikowski (2008: 286–89) and McKee (2012: 146–63).
39. Vieth also observes that couples may remain in the dancing space for "as long as one likes" (*so lange man Lust hat*; 1794: 441).
40. Concerning the concept of agogic (or durational) accents, see Lerdahl and Jackendoff (1983: 80–87, 348) and Mirka (2009: 42–46).
41. The soft, unassertive opening of the first *Deutscher* of the set is curious (the openings from K. 536, K. 571, and K. 600 have similar understated openings). Performed in the crowded and noisy *Redoutensaal* during Carnival, one wonders how well dancers could hear that a new dance had begun? One possible explanation is that musicians played some sort of generic fanfare or march introduction as an announcement to the dancers to assemble themselves for the beginning of a new dance. Since the same introduction (or set of introductions) could be used over and over again (with appropriate transposition), there was no need to notate it since it was so well known by the dance musicians. Many of the early waltzes of Lanner and Strauss Sr. of the late 1820s open with short fanfare or march introductions. In the 1830s these introductions became longer and much more highly stylized.
42. This source is also cited in Russell (1992: 119).

References

Aldrich, Elizabeth. 1997. *Social Dancing in Schubert's World*. In *Schubert's Vienna*, ed. Raymond Erickson, 119–40. New Haven, CT: Yale University Press.

Allanbrook, Wye Jamison. 1983. *Rhythmic Gesture in Mozart:* Le nozze di Figaro *and* Don Giovanni. Chicago: University of Chicago Press.

———. 2014. *The Secular Commedia: Comic Mimesis in Late Eighteenth-Century Music*, ed. Mary Ann Smart and Richard Taruskin. Berkeley: University of California Press.

Bauer, Wilhelm A., and Otto Erich Deutsch, eds. 1962–75. *Mozart: Briefe und Aufzeichnungen. Gesamtausgabe.* 7 vols. Kassel: Bärenreiter.

Busch-Salmen, Gabriele. 1990. Der Tanz im Leben Mozarts. In *Mozart in der Tanzkultur seiner Zeit*, ed. Walter Salmen, 65–81. Innsbruck: Helbling.

Byron, George Gordon. 1907. The Waltz: An Apostrophic Hymn. In *The Complete Poetical Works of Lord Byron*, ed. Sir Leslie Stephens, 156–64. New York: Macmillan.

Caillois, Roger. 1961. *Man, Play, and Games*. Trans. Meyer Barash. New York: The Free Press of Glencoe.

Caplin, William E. 1998. *Classical Form: A Theory of Formal Functions for the Instrumental Music of Haydn, Mozart, and Beethoven*. New York: Oxford University Press.

Compan, Charles. 1787. *Dictionnaire de danse, contenant l'histoire, les règles et les principes de cet art, avec des réflexions critiques, et des anecdotes curieuses concernant la dance ancienne et moderne*. Paris: Cailleau.

Cox, Arnie. 2006. Hearing, Feeling, Grasping Gestures. In *Music and Gesture*, ed. Anthony Gritten and Elaine King, 45–60. Aldershot, UK: Ashgate.

——. 2011. Embodying Music: Principles of the Mimetic Hypothesis. *Music Theory Online* 17/2. Available: http://www.mtosmt.org/issues/mto.11.17.2/mto.11.17.2.cox.html. Accessed 21 May 2012.

Feldtenstein, Carl Josef von. 1767. *Die Kunst nach der Choreographie zu tanzen und Tänze zu schreiben*. Brunswick: Schröder.

——. 1772. *Erweiterung der Kunst nach der Chorographie zu tanzen, Tänze zu erfinden, und aufzusetzen; wie auch Anweisung zu verschiedenen National-Tänzen; Als zu Englischen, Deutschen, Schwäbischen, Pohlnischen, Hannak- Masur- Kosak- und Hungarischen; mit Kupfern; nebst einer Anzahl Englischer Tänze*, 2nd ed. Braunschweig.

Ferraguto, Mark. 2010. Haydn as "Minimalist": Rethinking Exoticism in the Trios of the 1760s and 1770s. *Studia Musicologica* 51/1–2: 61–77.

Feuillet, Raoul Auger. 1705. *4e Recueil de dances de bal pour l'année 1706*. Paris: Chez le Sr Feuillet.

Fink, Monika. 1990. Tanzveranstaltungen und Bälle. In *Mozart in der Tanzkultur seiner Zeit*, ed. Walter Salmen, 33–46. Innsbruck: Helbling.

——. 1996. *Der Ball: Eine Kulturgeschichte des Gesellschaftstanzes im 18. und 19. Jahrhundert*. Innsbruck: Studien Verlag.

Framéry, Nicolas-Étienne. 1791. Contre-Danse. In *Encyclopédie méthodique: Musique*, ed. Nicolas-Étienne Framéry and Pierre Louis Ginguené, vol. 1, 316. Paris: Chez Pankoucke.

Gallini, Giovanni Andrea Battista. 1762. *A Treatise on the Art of Dancing*. London: Author.

——. 1766. *Critical Observations on the Art of Dancing*. London: Author.

Gherardi, Battista Giovanni. 1768. Instructions for the More Ready and Perfect Attainment of the Cotillons or French Country Dances. *The London Magazine, or Gentleman's Monthly Intelligencer* 37 (July): 380.

Goethe, Johann Wolfgang von. 2005. *The Sorrows of Young Werther*. Trans. Burton Pike. New York: The Modern Library.

Gstrein, Rainer. 1990. Deutsche Tänze. In *Mozart in der Tanzkultur seiner Zeit*, ed. Walter Salmen, 117–26. Innsbruck: Helbling.

Hanson, Alice. 1985. *Musical Life in Biedermeier Vienna*. Cambridge: Cambridge University Press.

Harris-Warrick, Rebecca. 2001a. Ballet, §1 (iii): The 18th Century. In *The New Grove Dictionary of Music and Musicians*, 2nd ed., ed. Stanley Sadie and John Tyrrell, vol. 2, 570–78. London: Macmillan.

——. 2001b. Dance, §5: 1730–1800. In *The New Grove Dictionary of Music and Musicians*, 2nd ed., ed. Stanley Sadie and John Tyrrell, vol. 6, 899–901. London: Macmillan.

Kattfuss, Johann Heinrich. 1800. *Choreographie oder vollständige und leicht fassliche Anweisung zu den Verschiedenen Arten der heut zu Tage beliebtesten gesellschaftlichen Tänze*. Leipzig: Heinrich Gräff.

Keller, Kate Van Winkle. 1991. *If the Company Can Do It! Technique in Eighteenth-Century American Social Dance*. Sandy Hook, CT: Hendrickson.

Kelley, Michael. 1968. *Reminiscences of Michael Kelley*. New York: Da Capo.

Knaffl, Johann Nepomuk Felix. 1928. *Die Knaffl-Handschrift, eine obersteirische Volkskunde aus dem Jahre 1813*, ed. Viktor von Geramb. Berlin und Leipzig: Walter de Gruyter.

Koch, Heinrich Christoph. 1802. *Musikalisches Lexikon*. Frankfurt-am-Main: August Hermann der Jüngere.

La Cuisse, Sieur de. 1762–65. *Le répertoire des bals*. 5 vols. Paris: Cailleau.

Lamb, Andrew. 2001. Waltz. In *The New Grove Dictionary of Music and Musicians*, 2nd ed., ed. Stanley Sadie and John Tyrrell, vol. 27, 72–78. London: Macmillan.

Landon, H. C. Robbins. 1976–80. *Haydn: Chronicle and Works*. 5 vols. Bloomington: Indiana University Press.

Lerdahl, Fred, and Ray Jackendoff. 1983. *A Generative Theory of Tonal Music*. Cambridge, MA: MIT Press.

Litschauer, Walburga, and Walter Deutsch. 1997. *Schubert und das Tanzvergnügen*. Vienna: Holzhausen.

Lowe, Melanie. 1998. Expressive Paradigms in the Symphonies of Joseph Haydn. Ph.D. diss., Princeton University.

——. 2002. Falling from Grace: Irony and Expressive Enrichment in Haydn's Symphonic Minuets. *Journal of Musicology* 19/1: 171–221.

Mädel, E. C. 1805. *Die Tanzkunst für die Elegante Welt*. Erfurt: Henning.

Magri, Gennaro. 1779. *Trattato teorico-prattico di ballo*. Naples: Orsino.

——. 1988. *Theoretical and Practical Treatise on Dancing*, ed. Irmgard E. Berry and Annalisa Fox. Trans. Mary Skeaping. London: Dance Books.

McKee, Eric. 2012. *Decorum of the Minuet, Delirium of the Waltz: A Study of Dance–Music Relations in 3/4 Time*. Bloomington: Indiana University Press.

Mirka, Danuta. 2009. *Metric Manipulations in Haydn and Mozart: Chamber Music for Strings, 1787–1791*. New York: Oxford University Press.

Mössmer, Günther. 1990. Kontretänze. In *Mozart in der Tanzkultur seiner Zeit*, ed. Walter Salmen, 97–116. Innsbruck: Helbling.

Neumeyer, David. 2006. The Contredanse, Classical Finales, and Caplin's Formal Functions. *Music Theory Online* 12/4. Available: http://www.mtosmt.org/issues/mto.06.12.4/ mto.06.12.4.neumeyer.html. Accessed 17 April 2012.

Pauli, Charles 1756. *Elemens de la danse*. Leipzig: Saalbach.

Playford, John. 1651. *The English Dancing Master*. London: Thomas Harper.

Ratner, Leonard. 1980. *Classic Music: Expression, Form, and Style*. New York: Schirmer.

Reeser, Eduard. 1949. *The History of the Waltz*. Stockholm: Continental.

Reichart, Sarah. 1984. The Influence of Eighteenth-Century Social Dance on the Viennese Classical Style. Ph.D. diss., City University of New York.

Richter, Joseph. 1917–18. *Eipeldauer Briefe*, ed. Eugen Paunel. 2 vols. Munich: Müller.

Riepel, Joseph. 1754. *Anfangsgründe zur musikalischen Setzkunst*. Vol. 1: *De Rhythmopoeïa oder von der Tactordnung*, 2nd ed. Regensburg: Johann Leopold Montag.

Rousseau, Jean-Jacques. 1751–72. Menuet. In *Encyclopédie*, ed. Denis Diderot and Jean d'Alembert, vol. 10, 346. Paris: Briasson.

Russell, Tilden A. 1983. Minuet, Scherzando, and Scherzo: The Dance Movement in Transition, 1781–1825. Ph.D. diss., University of North Carolina.

——. 1992. The Unconventional Dance Minuet: Choreographies of the Menuet d'Exaudet. *Acta Musicologica 64*: 118–38.

——. 1999. Minuet Form and Phraseology in *Recueils* and Manuscript Tunebooks. *Journal of Musicology 17/3*: 386–419.

Sachs, Curt. 1952. *World History of the Dance*. Trans. Bessie Schönberg. New York: Seven Arts–Publishers.

Schaller, Paul, and Hans Kühner. 1956. *Mozart: Aspekte*. Olten and Freiburg: Otto Walter.

Scott, Derek B. 2008. *Sounds of the Metropolis: The Nineteenth-Century Popular Music Revolution in London, New York, Paris, and Vienna*. New York: Oxford University Press.

Stainer, Anna Maria. 1978. Das Kochbuch der Anna Maria Stainer: 1789. Vienna: Ueberreuter.

Sulzer, Johann Georg. 1773–75. *Allgemeine Theorie der schönen Künste*. 2 vols. Leipzig: Weidmann.

Tomlinson, Kellom. 1735. *The Art of Dancing Explained by Reading and Figures*. London: Author. Reprint, Farnborough: Gregg, 1970.

Türk, Daniel Gottlob. 1982. *School of Clavier Playing for Clavier Teachers and Students*. Trans. Raymond H. Haggh. Lincoln: University of Nebraska Press.

Vieth, Gerhard Ulrich Anton. 1794. *Versuch einer Encyklopädie der Leibesübungen*. Berlin: Hartmann.

Wheelock, Gretchen A. 1992. *Haydn's Ingenious Jesting with Art: Contexts of Musical Wit and Humor*. New York: Schirmer.

Witzmann, Reingard. 1976. *Der Ländler in Wien: Ein Beitrag zur Entwicklungsgeschichte des Wiener Walzers bis in die Zeit des Wiener Kongresses*. Vienna: Arbeitsstelle für die Volkskundeatlas in Österreich.

Zangen, Carl Georg von. 1782. *Etwas über das Walzen, nebst einigen Gedichten und Anhang einiger Oden*. Wetzlar: Winkler.

Zbikowski, Lawrence. 2008. Dance Topoi, Sonic Analogues and Musical Grammar: Communicating with Music in the Eighteenth Century. In *Communication in Eighteenth-Century Music*, ed. Danuta Mirka and Kofi Agawu, 283–309. Cambridge: Cambridge University Press.

——. 2012. Music, Dance, and Meaning in the Early Nineteenth Century. *Journal of Musicological Research 31/2-3*: 147–65.

CHAPTER **6**

....

HUNT, MILITARY, AND PASTORAL TOPICS

....

ANDREW HARINGER

Introduction

....

It is likely that the late Raymond Monelle's 2006 *The Musical Topic: Hunt, Military and Pastoral* will endure as one of the foundational texts of the field for many years to come. In his in-depth study of three of the most ubiquitous musical topics, Monelle draws on an impressively diverse array of sources, ranging from anthologies of horn and bugle calls to pastoral iconography and poetry. The result is a rich, multifaceted understanding of these topics that provides solid grounding for both signifier (whether a horn call, march, or siciliana) and signified (whether manly heroism or bucolic innocence).

However, while Monelle's research for *The Musical Topic* was commendably thorough, it was not comprehensive. Most conspicuously, he devotes but scant attention to the writings of eighteenth-century music theorists and critics, who frequently reference these topics in one way or another. When such figures do appear in *The Musical Topic*, it is frequently via secondary sources, as in the case of Monelle's discussion of the siciliana (2006a: 219). This is curious, since Monelle shows great interest in contemporary writings outside the realm of music, particularly in literature and poetry.[1]

The explanation for this omission is to be found in Monelle's previous book, *The Sense of Music* (2000), where he takes Leonard Ratner to task for questionable citations of Koch, Heinichen, and others in his seminal *Classic Music* (1980). According to Monelle, Ratner erred in attempting to demonstrate that such writers conceived of topics in ways analogous to our own. In opposition to this, Monelle argues, "if theoretical ideas have any real interpretative force, it is unlikely that they will be proclaimed by contemporaries, for contemporaries are engaged in the justification of their music and thus in concealing vital features" (2000: 24). Singling out the pastoral topic in particular, he writes:

> The few words written by Ratner, or for that matter Heinichen, Mattheson, Koch, Rousseau, and the rest, do not begin to elaborate the complexities of this topic, which

embraces the musette and siciliana among eighteenth-century dance measures, and is reflected throughout the libretti of *opera seria*. Its roots lie deep in the literary traditions of Italy and France as well as the ancients. (Monelle 2000: 29)

Monelle was undoubtedly correct both in drawing a distinction between eighteenth-century and modern understandings of topics, and in calling for a broader examination of the cultural roots of these musical phenomena. Nevertheless, we should not be so hasty to discount the importance of eighteenth-century music writers, especially since study of them can aid in both of these endeavors. As Kofi Agawu puts it, "'semiotic awareness'—if that is taken to mean the awareness of music as a sign system or a system of signification—was very much in the minds of eighteenth-century music theorists such as Johann Mattheson, Francesco Galeazzi, Heinrich Koch, and Johann Friedrich Daube" (1991: 11). These authors display an obvious awareness of the connotations of such gestures as march rhythms and rustic drones, even if they rarely identify such features outside of pieces bearing programmatic or generic titles. Still, one does encounter instances of writers calling for the importation of features from one genre into another, such as the cultivation of a singing style in keyboard music advocated by both C. P. E. Bach and Daniel Gottlob Türk, among others (Bach 1949: 85; Türk 1982: 318). Extrapolating from these examples, it is reasonable to assume that eighteenth-century theorists and critics were aware of the use of hunt, military, and pastoral signifiers in a variety of genres, even if they do not explicitly address this phenomena.

Contemporary writings about music also enhance Monelle's rich picture of the signified gleaned from other primary sources, with the added advantage of a greater emphasis on art music. Eighteenth-century theorists and critics offer some of the most direct references to the power of the hunting horn, the warlike nature of marches, and the natural simplicity of shepherd songs. As we will see, the colorful writings of such figures as Friedrich Wilhelm Marpurg and Christian Friedrich Daniel Schubart complement the choice quotes Monelle assembles from other contemporary writers, offering instances of both self-mythologizing and self-awareness. Most importantly, eighteenth-century authors provide thorough descriptions of musical characteristics that help us to draw important distinctions between closely related topics. Monelle himself acknowledges the value of these sources in the aforementioned discussion of the siciliana. Such subtleties can help us identify a range of different inflections and connotations, resulting in a more sophisticated awareness of the manifold ways in which eighteenth-century composers employ topics.

The purpose of this chapter, then, is to supplement Monelle's research with these overlooked sources. The varied perspectives of eighteenth-century authors both underscore the complexity of hunt, military, and pastoral topics and provide helpful interpretative insights for scholars and performers alike. I will proceed in the same order as Monelle, from relatively sparse and straightforward references to the hunt, to frequent and varied mention of the military and pastoral topical fields. I will conclude with some thoughts on Raymond Monelle's unique contribution to the field of music semiotics, and offer some suggestions on how best to carry on his legacy.

HUNT

Of the three topics in question, the hunt is referenced the least by eighteenth-century theorists, and typically only within the context of actual hunting. In his musical dictionary, first published in 1703, Sébastien de Brossard defines the horn as "a sort of musical instrument of the wind kind, chiefly used in hunting, to animate the hunters and the dogs, and to call the latter together" (1769: 106). But Johann Mattheson, writing a decade later, notes the migration of the instrument out of the field and into the three main styles of eighteenth-century music: "The delightfully pompous horns…have become very en vogue in music for the church as well as the theater and chamber. This is partly because they are not by nature as *rude* as the trumpet, and partly because they can be handled with greater ease."[2] Koch provides some technical characteristics of the topic, identifying *bicinia* horn fanfares in 6/8 (1802: 554). Some eighteenth-century writers were also aware of hornlike passages in pieces written for other instruments. For example, Friedrich Wilhelm Marpurg notes the prevalence of trumpet and horn effects in Giuseppe Stefani's harpsichord music (1760–63, 2: 143–44).

One of the most compelling descriptions of the effects that can be achieved by playing the horn appears in the poet Christian Friedrich Daniel Schubart's *Ideen zu einer Ästhetik der Tonkunst* (1806).[3] Schubart praises the sweet sound of this "heavenly instrument" (*himmlische Instrument*) and traces its German names *Waldhorn* (forest horn) and *Jagdhorn* (hunting horn) to its use in hunting. Like many eighteenth-century writers, Schubart endeavors to draw connections between modern practice and distant past: "Even as early as the heathen times, the name *Jagdhorn* appears so often in writings that we can be sure the Germans knew of the instrument before the time of Charlemagne."[4] Most memorable is Schubart's rhapsodizing on the bewitching qualities of the horn:

> The entire forest stops and heeds when the sonorous horn is sounded. Deer lie at the spring and listen; even the frogs slip out of the water; and sows lie nearby in sweet slumber, while their piglets suckle in 3/8 time. All across Europe, hunting melodies have the uncanny ability to arouse venatic feelings in man and beast alike. How great is the soul of Man! A horn call summons the dogs, that they might brave the frightful forest and pit themselves against the jaws of the boar, the piercing antlers of the deer, and the cunning of the fox. But the same all-powerful horn, ringing out in gentle tones from forest hills, compels the deer lying by the mossy spring to raise up its antlers and, as it were, to soak up the sound.

> Ein Wald voll Thiere stutzt und horcht, wenn das volltönende Horn angeblasen wird. Die Hirsche legen sich an den Quell und lauschen; die Frösche selber schlüpfen an die Luft; und die Schweinemutter legt sich dabey in süssen Schlaf, und lässt sich von ihren Ferkeln unter dreyachtels Tact die Zitzsen aussaugen. Die Jagdmelodien, die durch ganz Europa erfunden worden, haben daher die unaussprechliche Wirkung, dass sie nicht nur jedem Menschengefühle zur Jagdzeit, sondern sogar auch den Thiernaturen in allen Scenen der Jagd angemessen sind.

Wie gross ist die Seele des Menschen! Ein Hornstoss befehligt die Hunde, dass sie in dem schaurigen Forst stürzen; dem Zahn des Ebers, dem bohrenden Geweih des Hirsches, und der List des Fuchses trotzen. Aber eben diese allgebietende Horn, in sanftern Tönen vom Waldhügel herabschallend, macht auch, dass sich der Hirsch an Moosquell lagert, und mit hoch aufgerichtetem Geweih die Töne gleichsam zu verschlingen scheint. (Schubart 1806: 313–14)

Written without a trace of discernible irony, Schubart's idealized image of the hunt echoes quotes compiled by Monelle about what was a decidedly unheroic enterprise. What is particularly interesting is the claim that the horn transcends the human realm and that, as Schubart writes a few sentences later, "the horn is an instrument of primary importance, since it is heeded by man and beast alike."[5] Schubart's anthropomorphizing lifts his description out of reality and firmly roots it in the myth of the signified.

While further research may uncover more pertinent information about hunting signifiers in art music, the hunting manuals cited by Monelle remain the most reliable source for particulars on actual horn calls. The primary value of writings left by eighteenth-century theorists and critics is in better understanding contemporary perceptions of hunting as a manly enterprise with an almost mystical aura. Of particular interest is the role accorded to the horn in achieving this effect, especially since both Mattheson and Schubart ascribe to it a more pleasing sound than the shriller tone that Monelle seems to consider more likely in actual practice (Monelle 2006a: 53). This suggests that eighteenth-century writers were already conceiving of the instrument in more stylized terms. This trend is even more pronounced in the case of military and pastoral topics.

MILITARY

Eighteenth-century theorists define trumpets and drums as military instruments first and foremost, a function they trace to ancient times. Brossard identifies the use of trumpets and related brass instruments in classical (especially Roman) and biblical military practice (1769: 306). Among other examples, he cites Moses's use of the instrument described in the Book of Numbers (10:1–10), a connection emphasized even more by Johann Adolph Scheibe, who baldly states: "Moses was the discoverer of the trumpet."[6] Schubart notes the use of timpani by the Phoenicians, Egyptians, and Jews, and offers the following grisly origin story for the instrument: "Terrible and true is the idea that revenge was the impetus behind the invention of the drum. 'My enemy is dead!' was perhaps the thought of a barbarian; 'and yet I would still beat upon his hide.'"[7]

Initially, eighteenth-century descriptions of trumpets and drums place them squarely in the world of warfare. Brossard details many of the calls mentioned in Monelle's *The Musical Topic*, from *cavalquet* ("when an army approaches a city") to *boute selle* ("the call to decamp"), and correctly identifies the trumpet as chiefly a cavalry instrument (1769: 306–7). Brossard also defines the drum as "a military musical instrument of the pulsatile kind," noting that "there are divers beats of drum, as the march, double march, *assemblée,* charge, retreat, *chamade,* etc." (67). For Schubart, "the character of the trumpet, as everyone knows, is entirely heroic, as a result of its blaring, stirring sound; bellicose and shouting."[8] He later declares that "a warlike tone is the sole character" of the drum.[9]

Despite both instruments' martial origins, eighteenth-century writers attribute a broader ceremonial role to them dating back to ancient times. In his *Historisch-Kritische Beyträge zur Aufnahme der Musik,* Marpurg writes of the trumpet's role in classical festivities:

> Dictators, consuls, praetors and other military leaders all ostentatiously celebrated their victories with the peal of trumpets. Trumpeters marched in celebratory parades and filled the air with a great din, which the joyful shouts of the people doubled. Incidentally, the trumpet was not so exclusively associated with wars as to preclude its use in other, totally unrelated contexts. Both the Romans and the Greeks used them for their sacred festivals and fertility games.

> Unter dem Schalle eben dieser Trompeten, hielten auch die Dictatores, Consuls, Prätores und andere Heerführer, ihr Siegesgepränge. Sie giengen vor diesen feyerlichen Aufzügen her, und erfülleten die Luft mit einem Geklirre, welches die Freude des Volks verdoppelte. Uebrigens war die gerade Trompete dem Kriege doch nicht so gar vorbehalten, daß man sie nicht auch noch zu andern Dingen gebraucht hätte, die gar keine Verbindung damit hatten. Die Römer bedienten sich derselben, so wie die Griechen thaten, bey der Feyer einiger ihrer heiligen Spiele, und unter andern auch, bey den floralischen Spielen. (1756–78: 42)

A number of writers note the continuation of such practices in the eighteenth century. Brossard identifies in contemporary trumpet music "various flourishes, voluntaries, etc. used in rejoicings" (1769: 307), Johann Gottfried Walther defines the *Abblasen* as the concluding call of the town bugler (1732: 3),[10] and Johann Altenburg details an array of non-military calls and drumbeats in his *Versuch einer Anleitung zur heroisch-musikalischen Trompeter- und Pauker-Kunst* (1795).

The ceremonial and militaristic come together in the use of both instruments in the three main styles of eighteenth-century music. Brossard states that tympani are "often used in operas, oratorios, tragedies, and concerts" (1769: 67), while Mattheson notes that "heroic drums" are used not only "in the field by the cavalry," but also "in the church, in operas, and in solemnities."[11] Significantly, Schubart maintains that the trumpet must always retain heroic connotations: "If this instrument does not adhere to its nature, if it is run aground through excessive virtuosity, then it loses its true character. Therefore, the trumpet should only be used by composers for grand, festive, and majestic occasions."[12]

The military topic is notably the first to be identified by eighteenth-century writers, as indicated by several passages. Even before Marpurg criticizes excessive use of horn and trumpet effects by Stefani, Mattheson praises Reinhard Kaiser for imitating trumpets and kettledrums, which he describes as "warlike instruments" (*kriegerischen Instrumente*), in a piece written for strings (1739: 86; see Example 6.1). In at least two

EXAMPLE **6.1** Mattheson, *Der vollkommene Capellmeister* (1739), 85.

instances, Scheibe references the same instruments used in sacred music, with unintended martial connotations:

> When for example Stax applies trumpets and kettledrums elsewhere in his church music, as when the dying Simeon[13] says in his aria, "my fading eyes should break, and gently and blessedly close," these proud instruments make such a resounding noise that the listener is completely deafened by these warlike sounds, and the words of the singer can no longer be understood; this amounts to a characteristic example of the author's simplemindedness.

> Wenn zum Exempel Stax bey andern Stelle seines Kirchenstücks Trompeten und Pauken anbringt, als nur wenn der sterbende Simeon in seiner Arie saget: die verfallenen Augen sollten brechen, und sich sanft und selig zuschließen; dabey aber ein solches tönendes Geräusche dieser muntern Instrumenten machet, daß die Zuhörer durch ein so kriegerisches Lärmen ganz übertäubet werden, und die Worte des Sängers nicht einmal zu verstehen sind: so ist solches ein gewisses Merkmaal von der Einfalt des Verfassers. (Scheibe 1745: 84)

In the second instance, Scheibe once again shows a keen awareness of the military connotations of these instruments:

> The glory of courts, the merriment of feast days, joyful occasions of which one wishes to sing, or the renown and creditable commemoration of saints and high persons, whom one wishes to revere: all these compel composers to write joyful, glorious, and martial Kyries…. Therefore, I certainly do not insist that funeral odes, funeral music, or memorial music… be written without the requisite trumpets and drums. Far from it; but some precautions must be taken given the circumstances. Namely, one must muffle these warlike instruments, in order to eliminate their attendant harshness.

> Die Pracht der Höfe, die Fröhlichkeit der Festtage, die freudigen Begebenheiten, welche man besingen will, oder auch das Ansehen und rühmliche Gedächtniß des Heiligen, oder auch der hohen Person, welsches man verehren will,

zwingen den Componisten, auch das Erbarmen freudig, prächtig und kriegerisch auszudrücken....Ich verlange deswegen gar nicht, daß man die Traueroden,
Trauermessen, oder auch Gedächtnißmusiken...ohne Trompeten und Pauken zu
gebrauchen, abfassen soll. Keinesweges; es müssen aber dabey einige Umstände
genau in Acht genommen werden. Man muß nämlich diese kriegerische
Instrumente dämpfen, und ihnen folglich das ihnen sonst beywohnende Prasseln
entziehen. (Scheibe 1745: 172)

A similar trajectory from battlefield to beyond defines eighteenth-century conceptions of the march. In his *Allgemeine Theorie der schönen Künste*, Johann Sulzer defines
the march as "a short piece, played by wind instruments, that accompanies festive processions, especially those of soldiers. Its goal is doubtless to liven up those who take
part in the procession and to alleviate their discomfort." He goes on to note the primal
power of rhythm in motivating human action: "Already before the invention of music,
mankind probably observed that measured tones, by the mere fact that they make
noise, have the ability to support the body's strength in physical ordeals, and to stave
off exhaustion."[14] Schubart expresses similar sentiments, tracing the German propensity for marches to the land's tragic history as the principal battleground for the Thirty
Years' War (1806: 73). He has high praise for "the old German march" that "greatly sur-
passes most newer marches in its high bellicose manner; for nothing is more laughable
than cooing and singing in a march, which one tends to hear so frequently these days."[15]
Like Sulzer, Schubart stipulates: "The movement of foot soldiers is slow, that of the cavalry quick. The march is an invaluable discovery for war; even horses sense its omnipo-
tence, and move to the beat of the march."[16] Just as he did in his discussion of the horn,
Schubart betrays a fondness for anthropomorphizing, contributing to the myth of the
topic.

As with trumpets and drums, eighteenth-century writers identify other march
traditions in the theater and in public ceremonies. In 1713 Mattheson writes in *Das
Neu-Eröffnete Orchester* that "the march is essentially a serious yet brisk, rousing melody,
the true place for which is before the troops on the parade ground. However, one also
encounters them in theatrical processions and in suites."[17] Writing in *Der vollkommene
Capellmeister* (1739), he allows that marches may also be playful, as when they accompany a "group of harlequins" (*einen Hauffen Arlequins*) (227), but stresses that they are
most properly for "warriors" (*Kriegesleuten*) (226; Harriss 1981: 456). They can even be in
triple meter, if only they preserve their pride and warlike nature.[18] Later writers increasingly widen the gulf between military and nonmilitary marches. According to Sulzer,
"there are other, nonmilitary marches, that occur in festive processions for such groups
as trade societies, where such rules need not be so strictly obeyed. They may be written in all manner of meters; they must merely always be lively and cheerful."[19] In his
Klavierschule of 1789, Daniel Gottlob Türk makes concessions similar to Sulzer's: "Since
the character of the true march is brave, bold, and rousing, the performance of it must be
forceful. The dotted notes especially call for full and emphatic playing." In contrast to his
strict guidelines for military marches, "an exception can be made here for marches written for certain processions which are not martial" (1982: 395). Likewise, Koch observes

that "the march, which properly pertains to martial music, has the aim of facilitating a complete equality of steps. This category has also been taken up in larger works of the art, particularly in the opera, where it is used for processions; in this case, the march always contains the character of the sublime and the splendid." However, he goes on to note the more permissive stipulations of the operatic march: "It requires a grave tempo in duple time and a very clear and uninterrupted meter. Reprises are as unnecessary in it as are a definite number of measures. Even the rhythmic ratio of sections need not necessarily be even-numbered. The usual overhang of the caesuras of phrases and cadences in the march, which consists of repeatedly striking the caesura note, is not really essential in this category" (1983: 82).

Such broad definitions of nonmilitary marches help to explain Monelle's reluctance to grant them separate topical status (2006a: 127) and yet, he concedes, "it may be that we should identify another topic, that of the *processional march*, with references to ceremony, solemnity, or high occasions" (2006a: 127). The widespread acknowledgement among eighteenth-century theorists of a ceremonial march tradition merits our attention. In particular, these writers note a kinship between the march and the French overture and its variants. This connection should not surprise us, given the dual status of eighteenth-century nobles as both military leaders and courtiers, and the theatricality of both realms, especially in France. As William McNeill writes:

> Nearly all of the officers in Louis' [XIV] new standing army were French noblemen, usually of lower rank than the courtiers. Military march-pasts and maneuvers were very much part of the rituals of the court; and their effect, like that of courtly dances and levées, was to make the aristocracy more peaceful at home and far more obedient to the royal will than ever before. (McNeill 1995: 134)

We find similar heroic qualities imputed to the march and the overture, with a greater emphasis on grandeur in the latter case. Mattheson writes of the "noble courage" (*Edelmuth*) of overtures "which deserves more praise than words have space here" (1739: 234; Harriss 1981: 467). Scheibe discusses the overture in considerable detail, and traces its development to "lively France" (*das lebhafte Frankreich*):

> The fieriness of this nation, her brightest ways, her ingenious yet frivolous jests, and above all her natural liveliness all account for the creation of so beautiful and lively a musical genre...no other nation has devised so beautiful a genre, if we discount the symphonies and concertos of the Italians.

> Das Feuer dieser Nation, ihr aufgewecktes Wesen, ihr sinnreicher, doch oftmals auch leichtsinniger Scherz, und überhaupt ihre natürliche Munterkeit waren allein vermögend, ein so schönes und lebhaftes musikalisches Stück zu erfinden...keine andere Nation ein so schönes Musikstück erfinden hat, wenn wir nämlich die Symphonie der Italiener und das Concert ausnehmen. (Scheibe 1745: 667–68)

Scheibe writes that the overture is defined by "a noble liveliness, a serious, manly, and splendid manner, and overall by a steadfast fieriness,"[20] and lists rich chords, strong cadences, and clear, well-ordered melodies as the defining characteristics of the genre.

He details the use of reprises and fugues in the overture genre, and suggests that the character of such pieces ought to correspond to the drama that is to follow, whether serious or lighthearted (1745: 673). After lamenting the decline in popularity of the genre, he posits: "The great similarities that the beginnings of all overtures share with one another may account in large part for their not being as beloved as they once were."[21]

Like Scheibe, Sulzer faults the homogeneity of the genre for its decline in popularity, though he also notes the unfashionable learnedness of its fugal sections (1792–94, 3: 389). Koch comments on these critiques:

> Nowadays the overture has been almost entirely supplanted by the symphony. It may be, as *Sulzer* thinks, because its composition and manner of performance are so difficult. Or it may be because the strict fugue is too austere nourishment for the fashionable taste of our time, which likes fugal composition and double counterpoint in an instrumental work only when it is combined with comic ornaments in one and the same movement to provoke laughter.... Whether this or that is the reason for the decline of the overture will be set forth in its place. (Koch 1983: 197)

These statements confirm the markedness (to use Hatten's term) that invariably accompanies late eighteenth-century instances of the overture topic, a relic of a more formal, regimented age. The late eighteenth-century need for novelty compels Sulzer to praise the surprising shifts in dynamics and texture (from loud and homophonic to soft and polyphonic) that frequently occur in overtures, while Türk instructs that "an overture must have splendor, greatness, and variety" (1982: 385).

Several theorists draw a direct link between processional marches (*entrées*) and overtures, on the one hand, and between *entrées* and marches, on the other, suggesting a shared lineage. As Mattheson notes, "marches and *entrées* bear many similarities, except that the former category includes more varied examples than the latter."[22] Mattheson also considers the *entrée* to be similar to the overture: "The *entrée* is a serious, harmonious aria with two reprises, purely for instruments; it is not dissimilar from the first part of an overture, excepting that the final reprise is the same as the first."[23] Using the equivalent term *Aufzug*, Sulzer places the *entrée* as the opening of a theatrical work, analogous to the overture: "The character of the *Aufzug* is one of ceremonial grandeur that should be appropriate to the circumstances in which it occurs. It is marked by powerful orchestration in all voices, richness of harmony, and a solemn, strongly defined meter."[24] Koch broadens the realm of the *entrée* to include a number of ceremonial functions, including processions for trade societies and religious festivals. However, he considers military and civil *entrées* (*militärischen und bürgerlichen Aufzügen*) to be essentially marches and, like Sulzer, mostly associates the *entrée* with the stage. Notably, though, he sees as their primary function the introduction of important characters and their retinues, rather than the drama itself. The social status of those characters and their importance for the dramatic plot should inform the character of the marches:

> This is why the festive character, which every *Aufzug* should generally display, in an opera receives various modifications to suit its function; it will be different at the entrance of the hero after defeating the enemies of the Fatherland than at the

procession of a group of priests dedicated to wisdom and goodness, of which type Mozart has provided us with a splendid example in *Die Zauberflöte*.

Eben daher bekommt der Charakter des Feyerlichen, den jeder Aufzug überhaupt behaupten muss, in der Oper so verschiedene Modificationen; so zeigt er sich z.B. anders bey dem Einzuge des Helden nach der Ueberwindung der Feinde des Vaterlandes, anders in dem Aufzuge einer Gesellschaft Priester, die sich der Weisheit und Tugend widmen, von welcher Gattung uns Mozart in der Zauberflöte ein fürtrefliches Beyspiel gegeben hat. (1802: col. 178)

Finally, Türk refers to the *entrée* as a "march-like composition" that "requires a rather slow tempo and a powerful delivery suitable to its serious character" (1982: 394). The *entrée*, then, is typically a slower, more serene piece than its counterparts.

The Italian *intrada* (or *intrata*) is another related genre that draws comparisons to both the *entrée* and the overture. In the second volume of his *Musikalische Handleitung*, published by Mattheson in 1721, Friedrich Erhard Niedt describes the overture as the French counterpart to the Italian and German *intrata* and *sinfonia*, respectively, and especially contrasts the *entrée*—described as a dance in an even duple meter—with the *intrata*, examples of which may be slow or fast, joyful or somber (Niedt 1989: 138). Mattheson observes in *Das Neu-Eröffnete Orchester* that "the Italians likewise use intradas instead of overtures in secular settings.... [Intradas] generally have two reprises in the same meter, such as 6/8 or 3/8; a pathetic opening theme that merits attention; and dense polyphonic texture without fugues. Also, they are shorter than symphonies."[25] In *Der vollkommene Capellmeister* he adds that the *intrata* should instill a feeling of "longing for more" (1739: 233; Harriss 1981: 466).

These and other sources suggest a continuum of genres ranging from the French overture, to the slightly less severe *entrée*, to the still more relaxed Italian *intrata*. According to Mattheson and Koch, overtures invariably include fugues, but Mattheson's words on the *entrée*'s resemblance to "the first part of an overture" (1713: 188) suggests that here fugues do not appear. More tellingly, Johann Joachim Quantz calls for the *entrée* to be played "majestically" and very detached but states that—unlike the overture—it may or may not feature dotted rhythms (1966: 291). Finally, the *intrata* marks the furthest departure from the realm of the march, since it may possess a wholly different character and meter.

While in most cases the differences between an overture and a march are self-evident, there is a sufficient degree of overlap between both signifier and signified in these instances to merit further scrutiny. All four genres—march, overture, *entrée*, and *intrada*—call for the composer to imbue the music with serious, heroic, resolute characteristics. Together these constitute a topical field providing a direct link from military to courtly and theatrical pomp, though specific examples may bear little relation to the original military topic. For example, the Mozart processional from *Die Zauberflöte*, cited by Koch, contains ecclesiastical and theatrical signifiers—choral textures and rising scales in dotted rhythms, respectively—but bears little resemblance to military marches.[26] Eighteenth-century sources, then, are of great value in determining which of these similar yet distinct topics a composer may be invoking in a given piece.

PASTORAL

As Monelle argues in *The Musical Topic*, the pastoral is one of the most complex of all topics.[27] This is reflected in its many manifestations in eighteenth-century music and in the high number of comments formulated by eighteenth-century writers. Several contemporary music critics and theorists discuss not only pastorals, musettes, and sicilianas, but also pastoral plays, poems, and related genres in detail, and their insights illuminate some of the complexities of the topic.

Descriptions of the pastorale—a dance melody not to be confused with the same term for shepherd plays—invariably relate the genre to the musette and siciliana. According to Sulzer, the pastorale is "a small piece designed for dancing and similar to the musette, which we have already described. It has two beats per measure but the tempo is slower than in the musette. The Italians write pastorals in a 6/8 meter, which are no different from the musette."[28] Koch defines the pastorale as a simple, rustic piece "in which the singing of the idealized world of shepherds is expressed. It is generally in a fairly slow 6/8 meter ... [and] is very similar to the musette and the siciliano, except that it is played more slowly than the former, and has fewer dotted eighths than the latter" (Monelle 2006a: 229).

Monelle's overview of contemporary descriptions of the siciliana in *The Musical Topic* establishes the basic parameters—12/8 or 6/8 meter, slow tempo, dotted rhythms, tender, noble, and simple qualities (219)—but leaves out some important considerations. Walther writes that the siciliana should contain a reprise, which speaks to its simple, dance-like qualities (Walther 1732: 139). Quantz offers detailed instructions for adopting a suitably leisurely character for the dance, by stressing the first and third beats in each dotted quarter, being careful not to linger on the latter (Jung 1980: 149). Türk warns: "The dotted notes which appear frequently should not be played in a detached manner" (1982: 396). Elaborating on the differentiation expressed above, Koch distinguishes the siciliana from the pastorale by a slower tempo, "and in particular because (1) usually the first of the three first eighth notes in the first half of the measure is lengthened by a dot and the following shortened note is slurred with the longer, and (2) in the second half of the measure there rarely appear eighth notes, but more often quarter notes with two following sixteenths" (Allanbrook 1983: 44)

Several authors note the similarities between the siciliana and the musette, but what exactly differentiates them can be difficult to ascertain. Quantz writes that the musette should be "executed in a very flattering manner" in 3/4 or 3/8, with each eighth note receiving a beat, continuing: "Sometimes, however, in accordance with the whim of the dancer, it is performed so quickly that a pulse beat falls only on each bar" (Quantz 1966: 291). Sulzer offers a detailed definition of the genre:

> Musette. This small piece of music, which received its name from an instrument (the
> bagpipe), is usually set in 6/8 meter and can start either with the downbeat or in the

middle of the measure. Its character is naïve simplicity with a soft and delicate melody. It distinguishes itself from the gigue and other peasant dances in the same meter through a slower and more dragged tempo. For instance, in the gigue the eighth notes should be somewhat struck but in the musette they should be slurred [Example 6.2]. Very frequently the piece is set over the sustained bass note; therefore the composer must know how to vary the harmony over the same bass. The dance under this name is designed for naïve rustic entertainments but it can portray noble shepherd characters as well as lowly peasants. In either case, the music must closely follow the character.

Musette. Das kleine Tonstück, welches von dem Instrumente dieses Namens (dem Dudelsack) seinen Namen bekommen hat, wird gemeiniglich in 6/8 Takt gesetzt, und kann so wohl mit dem Niederschlag, als in der Hälfte des Takts anfangen. Sein Charakter ist naïve Einfalt mit einem sanften, schmeichelnden Gesang. Durch eine etwas langsamere und schmeichelnde Bewegung unterscheidet es sich so wohl von den Giguen, als von den Baurentänzen, die diese Taktart haben. In der Gigue, z.B. werden die Achtel etwas gestossen, in der Musette müssen sie geschleift werden [Example 6.2]. Gar oft wird das Stück über einen anhaltenden Basston gesetzt; deswegen der Tonsetzer verstehen muss, die Harmonie auf demselben Basston hinlänglich abzuwechseln. Der Tanz, der diesen Namen führet, ist allemal für naïve ländliche Lustbarkeiten bestimmt, kann aber so wohl zu edlen Schäfercharakteren, als zu niedrigen bäuerischen gebraucht werden. Aber die Musik muss in beyden Fällen sich genau nach dem Charakter richten. (1792–94, 2: 421)

Koch defines the musette as "a dance of merry, but at the same time naïve and cajoling character … clothed in a 6/8 meter, and performed at a moderately brisk tempo; and a short piece very similar to the gigue, but played at a slower tempo, and in which the 6/8 meter is more dragged out than pushed along."[29]

What truly separates the musette from the siciliana is the former's obligatory use of a drone, as befits its roots as a stylized bagpipe for the French nobility (see Monelle 2006a: 210). As Rameau writes in his *Traité de l'harmonie*, "airs called *Vielle* and *Musette* are in a sense derived from the organ point" (1971: 437) and, as seen above, Sulzer notes the presence of a persistent *Basston*, while later in his definition Koch calls for the imitation of a bagpipe with a drone on the tonic or dominant (1802: col. 992). Monelle acknowledges this crucial point in *The Sense of Music*, after quoting Koch's comparison of the musette, siciliana, and pastorale (2000: 25).

To summarize these points, the musette topic necessarily possesses a drone, and is typically in a 6/8 meter.[30] Compared with the siciliana, it possesses a more self-conscious air of simplicity, as one would expect in so studied an emulation of Arcadian ideals. Whereas numerous examples exist of more melancholy, minor-key sicilianas, musettes

EXAMPLE **6.2** Sulzer, *Allgemeine Theorie der schönen Künste* (1792–94), vol. 2, 421.

are typically in major.[31] Such distinctions raise the question of the high and low pastoral, as hinted at in some of the above statements, especially the extended quote by Sulzer. A striking example can be seen in two very different assessments from Mattheson's *Das Neu-Eröffnete Orchestre* (1713). First is his scathing critique of the Neapolitan and Sicilian styles:

> The Neapolitan and Sicilian styles chiefly appear in a very particular and regrettable manner of singing. The most common type is either a slow English jig or a simple meter,[32] which has an unflattering tenderness. The latter type, though, in an Allegro or lively meter, usually consists of a barcarole-like song, which in these countries baser men sing, usually with guitar, to their acquiescence. And since much depends here upon the approbation of the amateurs, this manner of composition always bears traces of the popular taste.

> Der Neapolitanische und Sicilianische Stylus kommt hauptsächlich auf eine ganz particuliere und negligente Art zu singen. Ihre vornehmste Species ist entweder ein langsamer Englischer *Giquen* oder ein schlechter Tact, da eine ungeschminckte Tendresse statt hat; die andere Species aber, vom Allegro oder lustigen Tact, enthält meistentheils einen Gesang à la barquerole, den weil sich in diesen ländern der gemeine Mann beym Singen meistens der Guitarre zu seiner Ergebung bedienet, und weil zugleich daselbst von der Approbation des Vulgi viel dependiret, so bleibet auch immer bey derselben Art zu componiren von dem gemeinen Gusto etwas kleben. (1713: 204)

In contrast, Mattheson holds pastorals (here meaning shepherd plays) in high esteem:

> At the opera one also encounters Pastorals (Shepherd Plays), operettas and ballets, which are so praised for their brevity and humor, that one almost wonders why six to seven hour long operas are still being written, since these little pieces (the Leipzig Fair notwithstanding)[33] bring more delight, and require less time, hassle, learning, and expense to produce. They are invariably comedies, and consist of many dances, processions and other diversions, so that the play remains engaging almost without pause.

> Auff die *Opern* folgen die Pastorals (Schäfer-Spiele), Operetchen und Ballets, welche jederzeit so wol ihrer Kürze als Lustigkeit wegen solche *Approbation* gefunden, daß einen fast wundern möchte, warum man noch fortfähret 6. bis 7. Stunden-lange Opern zu machen, da man doch mit den kleinen *Pieçen* (die Leipziger Messe will ich ausnehmen) mehr Ergetzlichkeit zuwege bringen kann, und hergegen weniger Mühe, weniger Lernens, weniger Zeit, und weniger Unkosten anzuwenden hat. Es sind sonst allezeit *Comœdien*, und bestehen in vielen Täntzen, Auffzügen und Füllungen, die das *Theatrum* fast ohne Unterlaß occupiren müssen. (1713: 169–70)

More than two decades later, Mattheson writes that a shepherd play may be either tragic or comic, but "finds its truest, most important characteristic not in jubilation, rejoicing, nor grand parades; but in a pure, modest love, in an unadorned, innate and pleasant simplicity (*naïveté*), according to which all types and sections must be constructed: The melodies especially" (1739: 218; Harriss 1981: 443). He stresses the importance of "innocence" (*Unschuld*) and "goodheartedness" (*Gutherzigkeit*) in all shepherd plays, whether high or low in style (1739: 219).

Sulzer devotes an entire section of his *Allgemeine Theorie der schönen Künste* to shepherd plays, in which he calls for a transference of the "innocence, naturalness, and placid tenderness" (*Unschuld, die Natur, und eine sanfte Zärtlichkeit*) of shepherd poems to music (1792–94, 2: 279). Later, he laments the scarcity of musical pastorals in terms analogous to Mattheson's:

> However, the composer must seek to cultivate an expression of simplemindedness and naïve innocence. This rarely happens, though, and it is perhaps easier to find composers more willing to write grand operas than pastorals. One wishes that the latter were more in demand, so that the noble innocence of music might not continue to fade from the lyric stage.

> Der Tonsetzer aber muß sich einer großen Einfalt, und eines naiven unschuldigen Ausdrucks befleißen. Sie kommen doch nicht sehr ofte vor, und es ist vielleicht auch leichter, einen Tonsetzer zu finden, der mit Muth an die Verfertigung einer großen Oper geht, als einen, der sich in dem Pastoral mit Vortheil zu zeigen hoffet. Es wäre aber zu wünschen, dass sie mehr im Gebrauch wären, damit die edle Einfalt der Musik nicht nach und nach ganz von der lyrischen Schaubühne verdrängt werde. (1792–94, 2: 660)

Paradoxically, Sulzer calls on the composer to assiduously cultivate a supposedly naïve style in order to preserve the "noble innocence of music," a statement that simultaneously debunks and affirms the pastoral myth.

As Monelle argues, the eighteenth-century aristocracy was largely aware of the artificial nature of the pastoral (2006a: 228), and yet these and other passages suggest a degree of ambiguity, or perhaps ambivalence, toward this question. On the one hand, the writers seem to believe in the pastoral myth. Marpurg traces the siciliana to a nonexistent antecedent, writing that it "has the rhythm and style of a Sicilian shepherd dance."[34] Likewise, Quantz describes the "alla Siciliana" as an "imitation of a Sicilian shepherd's dance" (1966: 168). Sulzer claims that pastoral poetry was originally an authentic art form that later became stylized (1792–94, 2: 581–82), while he traces the musical pastoral back to Theocritus and the "fabled golden age" (*die fabelhafte goldene Zeit*; 1792–94, 2: 660). He argues that stylized shepherd songs should emulate actual shepherd music: "One must have an ear accustomed to lovely sounds, so as to know how to emulate the light and gentle sounds of a shepherd flute in one's songs."[35]

On the other hand, these writers betray a certain amount of skepticism toward authentic provenances for pastoral genres. Brossard describes the pastorale as "an air composed after a very sweet, easy, gentle manner, in imitation of those airs the shepherds are *supposed* to play" (1769: 175; my emphasis). This view is shared by Scheibe, that great lover of the natural in art, who equates pastoral genres with a "low style" (*niedrige Schreibart*), a humble, unschooled style of music: "[shepherd songs] are uniform, and possess only a few chords used sparingly. They tend to have short phrases, and require very little by way of structure. They display almost no fiery qualities, but rather are marked by a uniform, placid, comfortable, and peaceful style."[36] Despite their simplicity,

Scheibe emphasizes that such pieces should possess "a certain beauty" (*eine gewisse Schönheit*; Scheibe 1745: 129).

Sulzer cautions against too literal a cultivation of rusticity: "Let us not be misled by poets who sometimes present their shepherds as coarse and boorish. Just because a poet has abandoned his characters, it does not follow that composers must make the same mistake."[37] In general, Sulzer equates pastoralism with a studied nonchalance that should shun all extravagance, and represents a mixture of middle and low compositional styles (1792–94, 2: 279). These quotations reflect a spectrum of approaches to the pastoral that spans different degrees of refinement. Sulzer acknowledges this range of possibilities in pastoral genres: "In their verse and music, their general character is meant to coincide with that of happy shepherd folk. Their manner may take on many forms, though, including epic, dramatic, and lyric."[38]

In all these cases, what is most interesting is the awareness by theorists of a range of options afforded the composer in evoking the high or low pastoral. The more harmonic, rhythmic, and melodic richness in the pastoral topic, the more cultivated and farther removed it is from its putative earthy origins. These authors, then, furnish us with a rich body of knowledge about the musical pastoral. Their insights provide important guidelines for both analysts and performers of eighteenth-century music.

Conclusion

In the preface to *The Musical Topic*, Monelle describes himself as more of a "storage room" than an "arrow" (2006a: ix), but in truth he was an excellent example of both types of scholar. Given the power of his musical insights, we should not mind that he did not give every source its due. On the contrary, we should be grateful to him for leaving a solid foundation on which future scholars may build. Still, his hesitancy to fully consider the sources discussed above merits some discussion.

As a twentieth-century concept, it should come as no surprise that topics have, at best, shaky footing in eighteenth-century theory. Contemporary descriptions of dances, marches, and other signifiers typically refer to styles or genres, not discrete topics found within a given piece. While we do see instances in which authors note the migration of functional music into ceremonial or concert settings, we are hard pressed to find copious examples where they identify multiple topics occurring within the same piece.[39] Monelle's misgivings about the efficacy of eighteenth-century theoretical writings as justification for topics theory, then, were well founded (2000: 24–33).

However, Monelle's desire to avoid the same pitfalls as Ratner—an author he otherwise greatly admired (see Monelle 2006a: x)—results in the omission of essential sources. Far from contradicting Monelle's arguments, eighteenth-century writings enhance his basic claims while providing helpful musical and cultural nuances. Their authors show the close connections between military and nonmilitary marches, and provide many specifically musical details about such closely related genres as the overture, *entrée*, and *intrata*, suggesting that there are more conventions governing such music than Monelle may have realized. Finally, eighteenth-century theorists express a range of views about the appropriate levels of sophistication in the pastoral topic, and bring both clarity and complication to its musical characteristics.

To conclude, I would like to reflect on Monelle's contribution to the field of topic theory, and to suggest some ways to build on his scholarship.[40] As noted in *The Musical Topic*, Monelle's work draws on the best traditions of German and Anglo-Saxon musical scholarship (2006a: 16). On the one hand, his research was both deep and broad, spanning a wide variety of sources and disciplines, from poetry and literature, the plastic and visual arts, to musicology, semiotics, and literary theory. While this chapter may suggest otherwise, Monelle's scholarship is far more notable for its thoroughness than for its gaps. Not content with merely cataloguing these findings, though, Monelle was a shrewd interpreter, taking nothing at face value. This inquisitive nature is behind some of his most penetrating observations, from the noncontemporaneous and fictitious nature of many topics (a view derived from literary theory and Saussure, among others) to his view that "topics are at their most powerful when the reflection of an item of contemporary life is least in evidence, and the musical gesture refers most directly, even unconsciously, to the mythic world of cultural signification" (Monelle 2006b: 94). Monelle's natural skepticism—while healthy overall—may, ironically, have led him to discount some of the most obvious sources for studying eighteenth-century musical practices. Admittedly, the utility of such sources is limited; a compositional treatise can no more explain a great musical work than can a grammar guide explain a great work of literature. However, this does not mean that such sources should be neglected. As some of the leading musical thinkers of their time, eighteenth-century theorists and critics demand our attention, both as firsthand witnesses of their culture, and as authorities on technical matters that are central to musical signification. Monelle's inclination to treat such biased observers with caution is wise, but they remain essential resources for those seeking to better understand the ways in which music of the era held meaning for its listeners, and can hold meaning for us today.

NOTES

1. See, for example, Monelle's charting of the course of chivalry throughout poetic history (Monelle 2006a: 152–57).
2. "Die lieblich-pompeusen Waldhörner…sind bey itziger zeit sehr en vogue kommen, so wol was Kirchen als Theatral und Cammer-Music anlanget, weil sie theils nicht so *rude* von Natur sind, als die Trompeten, theils auch, weil sie mit mehr *Facilité* tönnen tractirt werden" (Mattheson 1713: 267).
3. Though it was not published until 1806, Schubart dictated his treatise from Hohenasperg prison near Stuttgart in 1784.
4. "Schon zu den heidnischen Zeiten kommt in den Schriften der Nahme *Jagdhorn* so oft vor, dass man nicht zweifeln darf, die Deutschen haben das Horn schon vor Carl des Grossen Zeiten gekannt" (Schubart 1806: 311–12).

5. "Das Horn ist also ein Instrument von erster Bedeutung, weil ihm Menschen und Thiere horchen" (Schubart 1806: 314).

6. "Moses war der Erfinder der Trompete" (Scheibe 1745: 14). In the relevant passage of the Old Testament, the Lord commands Moses to fashion two silver trumpets to summon the tribes of Israel, to call on the Lord in battle, and to aid in religious celebrations.

7. "Schrecklich und wahr ist der Gedanke, dass *Rache* den ersten Stoff zur Erfindung der Trommel hergab. Mein Feind ist todt! dachte ungefähr ein Barbar; aber auf seinem Felle will ich mich noch tummeln" (Schubart 1806: 329).

8. "Der Charakter der Trompete ist, wie jedermann weiss, wegen ihres schmetternden herzerschütternden Tons, ganz heroisch; schlachteinladend, und aufjauchzend" (Schubart 1806: 309).

9. "Kriegerischer Ton ist der einzige Charakter dieses Instruments" (Schubart 1806: 329).

10. Koch singles out the *Abblasen* for criticism, owing to its lack of musical qualities (1802: 3).

11. "Die heroischen Paucken…im Felde bey der *Cavallerie*, in der Kirchen in Opern und sonsten bey Solennitaeten offte gebrauchet" (Mattheson 1713: 272).

12. "Wenn dieses instrument nicht in seiner Natur bleibt, wenn man es durch Virtuosenkünste aus seinen Ufern zwingt; so hört auch sein Hauptcharakter auf. Die Trompete kann mithin vom Componisten, nur bey grossen, festlichen, und majestätischen Anlässen gebraucht werden" (Schubart 1806: 310).

13. Possibly a reference to the New Testament figure who blesses the infant Jesus in the temple of Jerusalem (Luke 2:25–36).

14. "Ein kleines Tonstück, das unter festlichen Aufzügen, vornehmlich unter den Zügen der Kriegsvölker, auf Blasinstrumenten gespielt wird. Der Zweck desselben ist ohne Zweifel, diejenigen, die den Zug machen, aufzumuntern, und ihnen auch die Beschwerlichkeit desselben zu erleichtern. Man hat, vermuthlich schon vor der Erfindung der Musik, bemerkt, daß abgemessene Töne, auch in sofern sie ein bloßes Geräusch ausmachen, viel Kraft haben, die Kräfte des Körpers bey beschwerlichen Arbeiten zu unterstüzen und die Ermüdung aufzuhalten" (Sulzer 1792–94, 3: 363).

15. "Der alte deutsche Marsch übertrifft die meisten neuern Märsche weit an hohem kriegerischen Sinn; denn nichts ist lächerlicher, als welsche Girren und Seufzen in einen Marsch aufzunehmen, wie man jetzt so häufig zu thun pflegt" (Schubart 1806: 361).

16. "Die Bewegung ist beym Fussvolk pathetisch, bey der Reiterey *schnell*. Der Marsch ist eine unschätzbare Erfindung für den Krieg; sogar die Pferde fühlen dessen Allgewalt, und bewegen sich nach dem Tacte des Marsches" (Schubart 1806: 361).

17. "*Marche* ist eigentlich eine *serieuse*, doch dabey frische ermunternde Melodie, welche ihren eigentlichen Sitz vor den *Troup* auff der Parade hat, doch findet die auch in Theatralischen Auffzügen und in Suiten statt" (Mattheson 1713: 192–93).

18. "Also the seriousness of such a melody is not hindered, as many believe, even when it has an uneven meter. Lully has set very many marches in the uneven meter; however he always paid the greatest attention thereby to expressing very clearly pride and the warlike nature" (Mattheson 1739: 227; Harriss 1981: 456).

19. "Es giebt auch andre, nicht kriegerische Märsche, die bey festlichen Aufzügen, dergleichen die verschiedenen Handwerksgesellschaften, bisweilen anstellen, gebraucht werden, wobey es nicht nothig ist, die gegebenen Regeln so genau zu beobachten. Sie können in allerley Taktarten gesezt werden; nur muß der Ausdruck immer lebhaft und munter seyn" (Sulzer 1792–94, 3: 365).

20. "Eine edle Lebhaftigkeit, ein ernsthaftes, männliches und prächtiges Wesen, und überhaupt ein beständiges Feuer" (Scheibe 1745: 669). Given Scheibe's censure of Bach, it is

surprising to see him write so favorably about a genre that "many connoisseurs" (*viele Kenner*) deride as "old-fashioned and ridiculous" (*veraltete und lächerliche*). I suspect that Scheibe responded favorably to the simple, direct nature of its form and rhythm.

21. "Vielleicht dass auch diese sehr grosse Aehnlichkeit, die alle Ouverturen im Anfange mit einander haben, ein grosses dazu beytragen hat, dass sie nicht mehr so beliebt sind, als sie sonst waren" (Scheibe 1745: 670).

22. "Eine *Marche* hat mit einer *Entrée* grosse Gemeinschaft, nur daß jene mehr Passagen als diese admittiret" (Mattheson 1713: 193).

23. "Entrée ist ebenmäßig eine *serieuse Arie* mit zwei *Reprisen*, aber bloß vor Instrumente; sie siehet dem ersten Theil einer *Ouverture* nicht unähnlich, nur daß die letzte Reprise eben der Art ist wie die erste" (Mattheson 1713: 188).

24. "Das Wesen des Aufzuges ist eine feyerliche Pracht, die dem Charakter des Aufzuges und der Gelegenheit, bey welcher er geschieht, angemessen sey. Dazu gehört eine starke Besetzung aller Stimmen, grosse Vollständigkeit der Harmonien, und ein feyerlicher stark abgemessener Takt" (Sulzer 1792–94, 1: 124).

25. "*Intraden* brauchen die Italiäner gleichfalls an statt der *Ouverturen* in weltlichen Sachen.…Sie haben gemeiniglich zwey *Reprisen*, von einerley *Tacte*, als 6/8 3/8 &c. ein pathetisches, zur *Attention* bequemendes, intonirendes *Thema*, und vollstimmiges Wesen, ohne *Fugen*, auch sind sie dabey kürzer zu fassen, als die *Symphonien*" (Mattheson 1713: 172–73).

26. The opening of this march—found at the beginning of Act 2 of *Die Zauberflöte*—inspired the Canadian national anthem, "O Canada."

27. In so doing, he echoes Robert Hatten, who labels the pastoral an "expressive genre" containing many discrete topics (1994: 91).

28. "Ein kleines zum Tanzen gemachtes Tonstück, das mit der Musette, die wir beschrieben haben, übereinkommt. Es ist von zwey Zeiten, aber die Bewegung ist gemässigter, als in jenem. Die Italiäner machen Pastorale von 6/8 Takt, die völlig mit der Musette übereinkommen" (Sulzer 1792–94, 2: 884).

29. "Musette bezeichnet … 2) einen Tanz von lustigem, aber dabey naivem und schmeichelndem Charakter … in den 6/8 Takt eingekleidet, und in mässig geschwinder Bewegung vorgetragen wurde; und 3) ein kleines Tonstück, welches viel Aehnlichkeit mit der Gigue hat, aber in einem langsamern Zeitmaasse gespielt wird, und in welchem die Achtel des 6/8 Taktes mehr geschleift als abgestossen werden" (Koch 1802: col. 992).

30. Like her mentor Ratner, Wye Allanbrook is seemingly unaware of this convention: "[The musette] could be composed in any meter, duple or triple" (Allanbrook 1983: 52). In fairness, musette–gavottes are a notable exception, and Allanbrook considers these to be the most common.

31. It is worth noting that Jacques Hotteterre's *Méthode pour la musette* (1738) features a number of pieces in minor.

32. The term "simple meter" (*schlechter Tact*) denotes common time or alla breve (Niedt 1989: 31).

33. Mattheson is presumably alluding to the bankruptcy of the Leipzig opera house in 1720, resulting in sporadic, unorthodox performances held during the fair until the construction of a new house in 1764.

34. "Siciliana, alla Siciliana, in der Bewegung und Art eines Sicilianischen Schäfertanzes" (Marpurg 1765: 17).

35. "Man muß an liebliche Töne gewöhntes Ohr haben, das in den Liedern den leichten und sanften Ton der Schäferflöte zu treffen wisse" (Sulzer 1792–94, 2: 585).

36. "Sie ist gleich, sie duldet wenig und nur mäßige Harmonie. Ihre Sätze sind allemal kurz, und erfordern fast gar keine Ausführung. Sie zeiget fast gar kein Feuer, sondern sie schleichet nur gleichsam in einer sanften, bequemen, und sich selbt ähnlichen und ruhigen Stille fort" (Scheibe 1745: 129).

37. "Man lasse sich also auch nicht den Dichter verführen, der etwa seine Schäfer einmal grob und bäurisch reden laesst. Es ist nicht die Folge, dass wenn der Poet die Charactere verlassen hat, denen er nachkommen sollen, der Componist eben diesen Abweg betreten müsse" (Sulzer 1792–94, 2: 280).

38. "Ihr allgemeiner Charakter ist darin zu suchen, dass der Inhalt und der Vortrag mit den Sitten und dem Charakter eines glücklichen Hirtenvolks übereinstimme. Die Arten aber können vielfältig seyn, episch, dramatisch und lyrisch" (Sulzer 1792–94, 2: 585).

39. Danuta Mirka identifies some examples in her introduction to this volume. Agawu's argument for a precedent based on the mention of "mixed style" in some sources is not entirely convincing, since in these cases the authors refer to principles of thematic variation and contrast, not the invoking of different topics (Agawu 1991: 26).

40. I offer a more thorough assessment of Monelle's work in my review of *The Musical Topic* (Haringer 2010).

References

Agawu, V. Kofi. 1991. *Playing with Signs: A Semiotic Interpretation of Classic Music.* Princeton: Princeton University Press.

Allanbrook, Wye Jamison. 1983. *Rhythmic Gesture in Mozart:* Le nozze di Figaro *and* Don Giovanni. Chicago: University of Chicago Press.

——. 2008. Mozart's k331, First Movement: Once More, with Feeling. In *Communication in Eighteenth-Century Music*, ed. Danuta Mirka and Kofi Agawu, 254–82. Cambridge: Cambridge University Press.

Altenburg, Johann. 1795. *Versuch einer Anleitung zur heroisch-musikalischen Trompeter- und Pauker-Kunst.* 2 vols. Halle: Hendel.

——. 1974. *Essay on an Introduction to the Heroic and Musical Trumpeter's and Kettledrummer's Art, for the Sake of a Wider Acceptance of the Same, Described Historically, Theoretically, and Practically and Illustrated with Examples.* Trans. Edward H. Tarr. Nashville: Brass.

Bach, Carl Philipp Emanuel. 1949. *Essay on the True Art of Playing Keyboard Instruments.* Trans. William J. Mitchell. New York: Norton.

Brossard, Sébastien de. 1769. *A Musical Dictionary: Containing a Full Explanation of all the Terms Made Use of in the Historical, Theoretical, and Practical Aspects of music.* Trans. James Grassineau. London: Robson.

Haringer, Andrew. 2010. Review of The Musical Topic: Hunt, Military and Pastoral by Raymond Monelle. *Current Musicology* 89: 121–37.

Harriss, Ernest C. 1981. *Johann Mattheson's* Der vollkommene Capellmeister: *A Revised Translation with Critical Commentary.* Ann Arbor, MI: UMI Research Press.

Hatten, Robert. 1994. *Musical Meaning in Beethoven: Markedness, Correlation, and Interpretation.* Bloomington: Indiana University Press.

——. 2004. *Interpreting Musical Gestures, Topics, and Tropes.* Bloomington: Indiana University Press.

Heinichen, Johann David. 1728. *Der Generalbass in der Komposition*. Dresden: Author. Reprint, Hildesheim: Georg Olms, 1969.

Hotteterre, Jacques. 1738. *Méthode pour la musette*. Paris: Ballard.

Jung, Hermann. 1980. *Die Pastorale*. Bern: Francke.

Koch, Heinrich Christoph. 1782–93. *Versuch einer Anleitung zur Composition*. 3 vols. Reprint, Hildesheim: Georg Olms, 2000.

——. 1802. *Musikalisches Lexikon*. Frankfurt am Main: August Hermann der Jüngere. Reprint, Hildesheim: Georg Olms, 1964.

——. 1807. *Kurzgefasstes Handwörterbuch der Musik für praktische Tonkünstler und für Dilettanten*. Reprint, Hildesheim: Georg Olms, 1981.

——. 1983. *Introductory Essay on Composition*. Trans. Nancy Kovaleff Baker. New Haven: Yale University Press.

Marpurg, Friedrich Wilhelm. 1754–78. *Historisch-Kritische Beyträge zur Aufnahme der Musik*. Berlin: Lange. Reprint, Hildesheim: Georg Olms, 1970.

——. 1760–63. *Kritische Briefe über die Tonkunst*. 2 vols. Berlin: Friedrich Wilhelm Birnstiel. Reprint, Hildesheim: Georg Olms, 1974.

——. 1765. *Anleitung zum Clavierspielen*, 2nd improved ed. Berlin: Haude und Spener. Reprint, Hildesheim: Georg Olms, 1970.

Mattheson, Johann. 1713. *Das Neu-Eröffnete Orchestre*. Hamburg: Benjamin Schillers Witwe.

——. 1739. *Der vollkommene Capellmeister*. Hamburg: Christian Herold. Reprint, Kassel: Bärenreiter, 1954.

McNeill, William. 1995. *Keeping Together in Time: Dance and Drill in Human History*. Cambridge, MA: Harvard University Press.

Monelle, Raymond. 2000. *The Sense of Music*. Princeton: Princeton University Press.

——. 2006a. *The Musical Topic: Hunt, Military and Pastoral*. Bloomington: Indiana University Press.

——. 2006b. Mahler's Military Gesture: Quotation as Proto-Topic. In *Music and Gesture: New Perspectives on Theory and Contemporary Practice*, ed. Anthony Gritten and Elaine King, 91–103. Aldershot, UK: Ashgate.

Niedt, Friedrich Erhard. 1989. *The Musical Guide: Parts 1 (1700/10), 2 (1721), and 3 (1717)*. Trans. Pamela L. Poulin and Irmgard C. Taylor. Oxford: Clarendon.

Quantz, Johann Joachim 1966. *On Playing the Flute*. Trans. Edward R. Reilly. Boston: Northeastern University Press.

Rameau, Jean-Philippe. 1971. *Treatise on Harmony*. Trans. Philip Gossett. New York: Dover.

Scheibe, Johann Adolph. 1745. *Critischer Musikus*. Reprint, Hildesheim: Georg Olms, 1970.

Schubart, Christian Friedrich Daniel. 1806. *Ideen zu einer Ästhetik der Tonkunst*. Reprint, Darmstadt: Wissenschaftliche Buchgesellschaft, 1969.

Sulzer, Johann Georg. 1792–94. *Allgemeine Theorie der schönen Künste*, new expanded 2nd ed. 4 vols. Leipzig: Weidmann.

Türk, Daniel Gottlob. 1982. *School of Clavier Playing*. Trans. Raymond H. Haggh. Lincoln: University of Nebraska Press.

Walther, Johann Gottfried. 1732. *Musikalisches Lexikon*. Leipzig: Deer. Reprint, Kassel: Bärenreiter, 1953.

CHAPTER 7

....

TURKISH AND HUNGARIAN-GYPSY STYLES

....

CATHERINE MAYES

IN a comment from 1859 on Haydn's "Rondo, in the Gipsies' style," the third movement of the Piano Trio in G major, Hob. XV:25, István Bartalus noted that "Joseph Haydn also has an *Alla Ongarese* (the finale of one of the G-major trios, the opus number of which I can't remember) that sounds quite Hungarian, but is in places rather Turkish."[1] In what Ervin Major (1928–29) has identified as the first known Hungarian assessment of the movement, Bartalus made two observations that are applicable to innumerable late eighteenth-century representations of Hungarian-Gypsy music: first, the implicit equivalence of "in the Gipsies' style" and *alla ongarese*—the movement was subtitled "Rondo, in the Gipsies' style" in the original 1795 Longman & Broderip edition as well as in the 1796 Artaria edition but became the "Rondo all'Ongarese" in later editions (Hoboken 1957: 707–10)—and, second, the explicit stylistic overlap between such representations and music *alla turca*. Bartalus did not provide further details on the latter point, but one can easily imagine how the pervasive alternating thirds of the rondo's refrain would immediately conjure the *alla turca* style (Example 7.1). To mention only one other analogous case among many, despite the specificity of its title, Beethoven's short keyboard piece *Alla ingharese, quasi un Capriccio*, Op. 129 (1795), incorporates gestures that could just as well suggest music *alla turca*: a repetitive and percussive accompaniment, and triadic figures as well as jangling ornamentation in the melody (Example 7.2).[2] It is hardly surprising, therefore, that the unlabeled exotic interlude in the final movement of Mozart's Violin Concerto in A major, K. 219, has been interpreted as an evocation of Turkish music and/or of Hungarian-Gypsy music.[3]

Ralph P. Locke (2009: 118–21) lists in his recent thorough tabulation of the gestures of the *alla turca* style

> keys with few sharps or flats; simple harmonic vocabulary with little harmonic change; sudden shifting from one tonal area to another; duple meter; repeated notes (or thirds) in melodies and repeated brief rhythmic figures; specific repeated

rhythmic patterns; unison textures and parallel part-writing; melodies decorated by neighbor notes or escape notes; long note-values at the beginning of a phrase; quick melodic decorations; melodic motion that moves rapidly stepwise up and down or "hops" back and forth between two notes; loud playing and full instrumentation; percussion instruments; modal touches in the melodic line; phraseological inanity or impulsivity; simplicity of phrase structure and form; and other features that somehow "characterize" the area and its inhabitants.

EXAMPLE 7.1 Haydn, Piano Trio in G major, Hob. XV:25/iii, "Rondo, in the Gipsies' Style," mm. 1–8.

EXAMPLE 7.2 Beethoven, *Alla ingharese, quasi un Capriccio*, Op. 129, mm. 1–8.

Of these seventeen features, only four (two of which are closely related) do not clearly also map onto Western European representations of Hungarian-Gypsy music in the late eighteenth century: phrases beginning with longer note values followed by shorter ones, loudness and percussion instruments, and extensive use of *échapées*.[4] Only in the 1820s, coinciding with the gradual disappearance of the *alla turca* style, did a unique Hungarian-Gypsy topic begin to emerge, eventually resulting in Liszt's highly impassioned and virtuosic representations later in the century.[5] Very few works from the late eighteenth century anticipate this later style; a notable exception is the second movement of Haydn's String Quartet in C major, Op. 54 No. 2. Although it bears no national label, the improvisatory quality of the first violin's line, winding its way through chromatic runs, repeated notes, and augmented seconds performed in fluid and varied rhythm, resonates strongly with contemporary descriptions of the performance style of Hungarian-Gypsy musicians, with which Haydn was undoubtedly more familiar than most composers due to his extended residence at Eszterháza (Example 7.3).[6]

Several hypotheses have been put forward to explain why Western European representations of Hungarian-Gypsy and of Turkish musics were often stylistically indistinguishable from one another in the late eighteenth century. Writing from an ethnomusicological perspective, several scholars have supplied evidence suggesting that various Central and Eastern European and Turkish musics are in fact closely related stylistically.[7] Perhaps most interestingly, Bence Szabolcsi (1956) has traced the rebounding thirds typical of much music *alla turca* to the Hungarian *törökös*, a parodic dance

EXAMPLE 7.3 Haydn, String Quartet in C major, Op. 54 No. 2/ii, mm. 9–12.

performed in Turkish costume at weddings in central Hungary that originated during
the period of the Ottoman occupation, rather than to the music of the Janissary bands
on which the *alla turca* style was ostensibly originally based. According to Szabolcsi,
the first notated *törökös* to be preserved appears in a manuscript dating from 1786.
Examples 7.4 and 7.5 reproduce the melody of this manuscript and a 1937 transcription
of a twentieth-century version of the dance, respectively.[8]

That music *alla turca* and early representations of Hungarian-Gypsy music cannot,
for the most part, be considered discrete topics from a stylistic point of view is due,
furthermore, to the fact that they were largely constructed by the same culture. Larry
Wolff (1994) has argued that Eastern Europe was first conceived as a geographically and
culturally cohesive entity during the Enlightenment, at which time Hungary joined the
company of the Turks, long since established as Western Europe's foremost barbaric
Other.[9] The stylistic conflation of a wide variety of foreign musics in Western representations may be understood in part as a manifestation of this broader outlook.[10] Indeed,
Mary Hunter (1998: 48) has convincingly argued that the *alla turca* style is better understood not as an imitation of Turkish music, but as a translation of the Western European
perception of its "deficiency and incoherence or irrationality." Moreover, as Hunter suggests, repetitive rhythms and melodic figures, and simplified or unison harmonies, for
instance, hint not only at the Western European perception of the primitive stage of
development of Turkish music, but also at the perceived rudimentary state of Turkish
culture and society more generally. Certainly, Hungary—and, as Wolff has argued,
Eastern Europe as a whole—was considered to be similarly underdeveloped. Writing
from the Habsburg capital in 1793, for example, the British traveler Robert Townson
(1797: 32–33) noted: "I impatiently waited at Vienna for fine weather; and only in fine
weather could it be prudent to travel in a country which, according to the accounts

EXAMPLE 7.4 Szabolcsi, "Exoticisms in Mozart" (1956), 330, ex. 11.

EXAMPLE 7.5 Szabolcsi, "Exoticisms in Mozart" (1956), 330, ex. 12.

* (completed from variants)

current at Vienna, was little better than in a state of nature, and its inhabitants half savage ... If I came back alive I was told I ought to think myself fortunate."

Although the Ottoman Empire and Hungary clearly belonged, in Western eyes, to the same realm of the un(der)civilized, and although their musics were largely represented through very similar stylistic means by Western European composers, in this chapter I explore how Turkish and Hungarian-Gypsy topics nonetheless carried rather different associations and meanings for late eighteenth-century composers, performers, and audiences. As Lawrence Zbikowski (2012: 153) has recently observed, topics are "not limited to ... configurations of pitches and rhythms ... but exten[d] to the network of cultural associations activated by each topic," and it is mainly because of such associations that Turkish and Hungarian-Gypsy topics may be considered distinct in the late eighteenth century. I suggest that although these topics share, in the broadest sense, the same "subject for musical discourse"—the Other—a closer examination of contemporary evidence reveals that Hungarian-Gypsy music was primarily associated with dancing, while Turkish music was closely tied to the military tradition of the Janissaries, and these associations, in turn, carried generic and syntactical implications.

"The Hungarian," wrote an anonymous correspondent from Pest in the winter of 1810, "dances much and often: his national music is therefore in the first instance dance music."[11] Indeed, the earliest known account of Hungarian-Gypsy music performed in Vienna, which appeared in the 1 December 1781 issue of the then newly founded Hungarian-language newspaper *Magyar Hírmondó* (Hungarian News), published in Pozsony (or Pressburg in German; now Bratislava, the capital of Slovakia), details a court occasion at the palace of Schönbrunn during which six pairs of dancers performed in Hungarian national costume, accompanied by what were presumably Gypsy musicians, who, for social and historical reasons, had long been Hungary's professional musicians.[12] Titled "Lively Celebrations in Vienna," the article further specifies that "the dances of the Hungarian recruiting soldiers ('Verbungus') were demonstrated as well. It was even danced by the Royal Imperial Guard officers, who followed the music" (Papp 1986: 25; see also Domokos 1985).

We know from contemporary documents that Gypsy musicians played a wide range of music.[13] "Verbungus" or *verbunk*, as it is now commonly called, was only one of the types of music they performed. The word itself is a Magyarized rendering of the German *Werbung*, and refers in the most specific sense to the dance music used by the Habsburg army in military recruiting in Hungary, especially during the eighteenth and nineteenth centuries.[14] It developed from both Hungarian and Gypsy influences, including folk music and dances, *Tafelmusik* such as the *ungaresca* and *saltus hungaricus*, and the performance practices of Gypsy musicians (Bartók 1981: xv; Istvánffy 1982: 18–23; Papp 1986: 27–28). At least in its more urbanized versions, *verbunk* may have reflected influences from Western European art music as well, including homophony (melody and accompaniment texture), major–minor tonality, and the typical instrumentation of two violins, cello or bass, and cimbalom (dulcimer) instead of a keyboard instrument.[15]

Verbunk was an effective aid to military recruiting in large part because it drew on familiar, established, and popular elements of Hungarian music and dance; Townson (1797: 367), for example, described dancing at a wedding in the town of Nehre as being "in the Hungarian style, like the recruiting parties at Pest." *Verbunk* was therefore synonymous with Hungarianness, not only in the minds of the supporters of the Hungarian national movement, which was bolstered in the 1780s by a variety of unpopular reforms instituted by Emperor Joseph II, ranging from administrative centralization to the abolishment of serfdom and the institution of German as the official language, but also in the popular consciousness of Western Europeans, who wrote about *verbunk*, represented it in their own compositions, and used these representations for their own enjoyment as *Hausmusik* and as an accompaniment to social dancing.[16] In a society for which social dancing was one of the primary forms of entertainment, it is perhaps unsurprising that *verbunk*, a dance genre, rather than Hungarian or Gypsy vocal music or the *hallgató* style of instrumental music, was the basis for the vast majority of Western European representations of Hungarian-Gypsy music in the late eighteenth century. (*Hallgató*, meaning "to be listened to" rather than danced to, is the style potentially evoked by the second movement of Haydn's String Quartet in C major, Op. 54 No. 2.)

Descriptions of how to perform Hungarian dances in contemporary dance treatises offer insight into the Western European perception of their affect and confirm that they were deemed appropriate to social dancing outside Hungary. In his 1825 treatise, for instance, Carlo Blasis favorably compared "the Hungarian dance," along with several other national dances, to those of Spain, which he considered too wild for general enjoyment:

> Dancing, among most nations, is a delightful and innocent amusement, but with the Spaniards it becomes a kind of dangerous excitement. Compare the Spanish dances with those of other countries, and it will be found that the *Chica*, the *Fandango*, the *Sarao*, and some others, bear the stamp of the strongest, deepest, and most immoderate passion; while the *Tarantella*, the *Fourlane*, the *Montferine*, the *Contre-danse*, the *Provençale*, the *Mazurka*, (usually called *la Russe*,) *l'Ecossaise*, *l'Allemande*, *la Hongroise*, the *Polonaise*, the *Anglaise*, &c., all well known popular dances, are kept within such limits as to render them acceptable to all classes of society. (Blasis 1847: 32)[17]

A much more specific description of *la Hongroise* had appeared decades earlier in Carl Joseph von Feldtenstein's 1772 treatise *Erweiterung der Kunst nach der Chorographie zu tanzen*. Along with more general instruction on social dancing, Feldtenstein devoted roughly half of his lessons to the performance of national dances, including a Hungarian dance, about which he wrote at length:

> The Hungarian dance has the same affects as the three previously introduced, namely the *Hannakischer, Masurischer,* and *Kosakischer,* and these go so well together that those who dance them (even when they must dance them on command—these are always the dullest dances) dance them nonetheless with feeling because they are

carried away by the composition of the charming and comical music. The affects expressed through this dance are, as it were, divided, and each sex is allocated its role, so that the flirtatious affect is given to the female dancer, and the free, comical wildness is given to the male dancer. I would still need to have various copper engravings made of choreographic symbols if I wanted to work with the steps and figures of this dance, but because I am writing mostly for my own pupils so that they can remember the information they received, I will make do with a demonstration. I mention as a caveat that the female dancers must avail themselves of flirtatious manners and the steps associated with these [manners], as well as *solid* turns, just like the male dancers, higher, and with confused positions, whereby regular and irregular [false positions] are mixed together… so that every trained dancer must adopt a comfortable wildness (if I may say so). However, he must also spin his female partner in a certain, *solid* manner, and at the same time, unite himself with her in the flirtatious affect, revealing the apparent wildness as a boisterous and somewhat exaggerated joy only when each partner dances figures alone. Thus will the beautiful be granted also to this nation in its dance.

Der Ungarische Tanz hat von den vorherangeführten dreyen, als den Hannakischen, Masurischen, und Kosakischen Tänzen die Affekten zugleich, und diese sind so angenehm zusammen geseßet, daß die, so ihn tanzen (und wann sie auch auf Befehl tanzen müßten, welches allemal der matteste Tanz ist,) wegen der Einrichtung der reizenden und komischen Musik hingerissen werden, daß sie dennoch aus Affektion tanzen würden. Dann die Affekten in der Declamation dieses Tanzes sind gleichsam getheilet, und jeden Geschlecht seine Rolle angewiesen, so daß der tändelnde Affekt der Tänzerin, und der Freye, und in das komische Wilde fallende dem Tänzer zugeeignet ist. Ich würde, wann ich nach chorographischen Zeichen von denen Schritten und Touren dieses Tanzes handeln wollte, noch verschiedene Kupfer müssen stechen lassen, und da ich großtentheils für meine Lernenden schreibe, damit sie sich an die erhaltene Information erinnern können: so will ich es diesmal bey einer Demonstration bewenden lassen. Ich sage also zur Nachricht, daß die Tänzerinnen sich in ihrem Tanz eines tändelnden Anstandes, und damit verknüpften Schritts, wie auch *solider* Umdrehung oder *Tournées* bedienen müssen, so wie die Tänzer höher, und mit verwechselnden Positionen, wobey sie regulaire, und irregulaire zusammen mischen… wobey ein jeder gebildeter Tänzer doch ein angenehmes Wildes (wann ich so sagen kann und darf) anzunehmen hat, doch muß er auch seine Tänzerin im drehen mit einen gewissen *soliden* Anstand führen, und gleichsam sich mit ihr in dem tändelnden Affekt vereinigen, das anscheinende Wilde aber als eine ausgelassene, und in etwas übertriebene Freude nur zeigen, wann jedes allein figuriret. Dadurch wird auch dieser Nation in ihren Tanze das Schöne bestimmt. (Feldtenstein 1772: 103–4)

Although Feldtenstein's description provides little explicit instruction as to how one would perform such a dance, it nonetheless captures what he felt to be its essence, namely trifling flirtatiousness and comical wildness. Feldtenstein's description of the *Hannakischer*, which he specified was comparable in its affect to the Hungarian dance, may provide a clue as to how one might perform this latter dance with so few details at hand. The *Hannakischer*, according to Feldtenstein, "possesses the ease of the *Schwäbischer*, that each couple can dance according to their own expression, without it being necessary to follow [what] others [do]."[18] In this sense, the Hungarian dance, like other national dances according to Feldtenstein, was similar to the contredanse, which Wye Allanbrook (1983: 60–66) has described as the "danceless dance" of the eighteenth century. Unlike the elaborately choreographed dances of the French court, which required extensive training to perform, the contredanse was simple, "essentially a walk or alternation of steps" in which groups of couples trace a series of figures with what Adolf Bernhard Marx termed a "dancelike movement" (61).[19] The collection of twelve *Contredanses hongroises*, which appeared in manuscript copy in Vienna in 1788, for instance, may well have accompanied a decorous display of flirtatious and comically wild dancing, lending a touch of exoticism to an evening's entertainment.[20]

Eva Campianu (1982: 174) has suggested that some national dances became popular social dances only after first having been presented in the theater, and this may have been the case with the Hungarian dance. Christian Friedrich Daniel Schubart includes a discussion of the Hungarian dance in the section headed "Pantomimic Style" (*Pantominischer [sic] Styl*) in his treatise *Ideen zu einer Ästhetik der Tonkunst*, written during his imprisonment in the 1780s and published in 1806. The "pantomimic style," as he explains it, is "partly dramatic and partly social," and "where national dances are concerned, it may be divided into different branches according to differences in national tastes."[21] He proceeds to describe the minuet, also known as the French dance, followed by the English, Dutch, Polish, Hungarian, and German dances. Schubart observes that the Hungarian dance is quite similar to that of the Gypsies, and notes that it is always in duple meter, is more often slow than fast, and contains bizarre modulations. He concludes by affirming that "this dance is very much worthy of being used in the theater."[22]

Schubart addresses Turkish music (*Die türkische Musik*), in contrast, in the section of his *Ideen* on wind instruments. He writes: "The character of this music is so warlike that it emboldens even cowardly souls. Whoever has had the pleasure of hearing the Janissaries themselves play music, in their typical bands of eighty to one hundred persons, must smile pityingly at the imitations through which Turkish music is most often deformed by us.... In short, Turkish music is the first and the most valuable of all warlike musics when it is as perfect as its nature and its heroic purpose demand that it should be."[23] Writing during the same decade as Schubart, Franz Joseph Sulzer began his own description of *türkische Musik* in his *Geschichte des transalpinischen Daciens* by imploring the reader "to distinguish Turkish chamber music from the so-called *Tambulchana* (not *Tubulchanu*, as some have written)—in Wallachian: *Kindia*—that is, the military or Janissary music." He takes for granted that the reader would implicitly equate Turkish music with the military music of the Janissaries, and must be reminded that other kinds of Turkish music exist. He also agrees with Schubart that "what is more, one must beware of mistaking for genuine Turkish military music that Janissary music which has for some time been introduced in most regiments of the imperial Roman army, and for which new pieces appear daily from German pens. The difference between the two is endlessly great. Our German-Turkish military music cannot even boast the same instruments, much less the same taste, which one will exert himself in vain to imitate with European meters and German ear" (Whaples 1959: 320).[24] Sulzer himself does include brief descriptions of the instruments used in Turkish chamber music and of Turkish dancing.

Perhaps the most extensive eighteenth-century account of a variety of Turkish musics may be found, however, in the famous *Turkish Embassy Letters*, penned by Lady Mary Wortley Montagu, the wife of the British ambassador to Turkey from 1716–17, and first published in 1763. In a letter to the poet Alexander Pope, she writes of slaves singing or playing music while their masters drink coffee in the shade of gardens, of "the ancient fistula, being composed of unequal reeds with a simple but agreeable softness of the sound," and of tunes "gay and lively, yet with something in them wonderfull soft" (Montagu 1993: 73–75). Her lengthiest description of Turkish music appears in a letter to her sister, in which she relates a visit to the "Kabya's lady," the wife of the second highest ranking officer in the empire:

> Her fair maids were ranged below the sofa, to the number of twenty, and put me in mind of the pictures of the ancient nymphs. I did not think all nature could have furnished such a scene of beauty. She made them a sign to play and dance. Four of them immediately begun [*sic*] to play some soft airs on instruments, between a lute and a guitar, which they accompanied with their voices, while the others danced by turns. This dance was very different from what I had seen before. [She is referring here to the entertainment she had experienced while visiting the Grand Vizier's wife, described earlier in the same letter.] Nothing could be more artful or more proper to raise certain ideas; the tunes so soft, the motions so languishing, accompanied with pauses and dying eyes, half falling back and then recovering themselves in so artful a manner that I am very positive the coldest and most rigid prude upon earth could not have looked upon them without thinking of something not to be spoke of. I suppose you may have read that the Turks have no music but what is shocking to the ears, but this account is from those who never heard any but what is played in the streets, and is just as reasonable as if a foreigner should take his ideas of English music from the bladder and string or the marrow-bones and cleavers. (Montagu 1993: 90–91)

The seductive femininity of the music Lady Mary experienced in Turkey is strikingly at odds with Schubart's overt declaration of the masculinity of Janissary music: "no other genre of music requires such a firm, decided and overpoweringly predominant beat. The first beat of each measure is so strongly marked with a new and manly accent that it is virtually impossible to get out of step."[25]

Hunter (1998) has questioned why Western European representations of Turkish music in the eighteenth century were restricted only to the hypermasculine *alla turca* style, and she notes, as I have here, that the Janissary music from which it originally took its cue represents only one version of Turkishness among many, a version that tells us more about Europeans and their experience of the Ottoman Empire than it does about Turks themselves; the same is true of representations of Hungarian-Gypsy music and their putative indebtedness to *verbunk*.[26] Hunter's focus is primarily on operatic depictions of Turks and their intersection with power and gender, and she posits that "it was exactly the need for multivalent representations of captive womanhood that prevented the development of a feminine *alla turca* style in late eighteenth-century opera" (72). Instrumental music also relied on the same limited vocabulary, undoubtedly because it encoded the primary Western European experience of the Ottoman Empire as a military rival through the saber-rattling *alla turca* style. Although the 1683 Ottoman siege of Vienna was a distant memory by the late eighteenth century, Austria and Turkey were again embroiled in a costly and unpopular war as late as 1788–91. The fashionability of the *alla turca* style, especially in Vienna, reflects at once a fascination with the Turks as well as a lingering, and perhaps still unsettling, memory of their military power. As Locke (2009: 110) has summarized, a craze for paintings that depicted "splendid but fiercely guarded Ottoman palaces" or "Turkish emissaries in turbans and voluminous robes" also bears witness to this complicated relationship, as do Janissary musicians and instruments sent by Constantinople to European courts, which Head (2000: 35) characterizes as "perhaps at once a reminder of fabled Ottoman military might and a sign of peaceful accord." Yet Head notes that the Western European appropriation of Janissary music through the *alla turca* style signals, ultimately, "a response to a historical shift of power ... turn[ing] the tables, appropriating the formerly fearful sounds of the Janissary band, absorbing their strength" (33). By the late eighteenth century, the music of the Turkish military was ripe for parody and fit for the purpose of entertainment.

Head notes, however, that Schubart's description of the decisiveness, forcefulness, and manliness of the Janissaries' music reveals yet another aspect of the Western European perception of the Ottoman Empire: admiration. He explains that "this admiration focused on the manly-warrior mentality that came through for European listeners in [the] regimented downbeats and awe-inspiring sense of purpose [of the Janissaries' music]. Ottoman military discipline was the stuff of lore in Europe and it was to this discipline that the earlier expansionist success of the empire was attributed" (84). In the article "Janitscharenmusik" in his *Musikalisches Lexikon* of 1802, Heinrich Christoph Koch makes clear, however, that he interprets the very same features described by Schubart as evidence of the Turks' crudeness: "Janissary music betrays the distinguishing marks of the music of a still barbarous people, namely noisiness and the most tangible display of the rhythm on monotonous percussion instruments."[27] No other type of Turkish music could embody the simultaneous attraction and repulsion Western Europeans felt for the Ottoman Empire as a military foe, and the *alla turca* style consequently translates this particular, if limited, experience of Turks and their music.

Similarly, representations of Hungarian-Gypsy music reveal more about the interests of Western Europeans than they do about the actual state of music-making in Hungary in the late eighteenth century: the primary association of Hungarian-Gypsy music with dancing was an extremely marketable one. From the 1780s through the 1820s, hundreds of representations of Hungarian-Gypsy dances appeared in Vienna alone, and they were explicitly identified as such through titles such as *Danses hongroises, Zingaresi,* and *Ungarische Nationaltänze*; although this is by far the largest repertoire evoking Hungarian-Gypsy music, it is the least studied.[28] Most of the dances were published in collections containing from six to twenty-eight dances, and the appearance of individual dances in multiple collections suggests their popularity, as does the reissuance of entire collections.[29] Example 7.6, which reproduces the third dance from Stanislaw Ossowski's collection *VI Danses hongroises pour le fortepiano ou clavecin*, published in Vienna as early as 1791 and reissued by Hoffmeister in 1804, gives a taste of the style of these dances and of their distribution. A version of Ossowski's dances for two violins and bass was also advertised in the *Wiener Zeitung* in 1791, and three of Ossowski's six dances had appeared in the anonymous collection of *Contredanses hongroises* of 1788.[30] Several stylistic features of this dance are typical of the hundreds of others like it: duple meter; regular four-measure phrases; major mode, in this case with a brief excursion to the relative minor; exclusive or nearly exclusive use of tonic and dominant harmony; a simple and repetitive accompaniment pattern; and a melody composed of short motives or cells, themselves often constructed of chordal leaps or circling figures, which favor repetition over development.[31]

The collections of dances I have examined generally contain very few performance markings beyond intermittent tempo and dynamic indications. The marking *dolce*, as in Example 7.6, occurs only very occasionally in these collections, perhaps reminding the keyboardist to embrace the same joviality and flirtatiousness that Feldtenstein recommended dancers should adopt when performing a Hungarian dance. This indication alone, even without knowledge of the title of the collection, provides strong evidence

EXAMPLE 7.6 Ossowski, *VI Danses hongroises pour le fortepiano ou clavecin*, No. 3.

that the prominent rebounding thirds in the melody of the opening period were not meant as an evocation of the military music of the Janissaries or of the military function of *verbunk* in Hungary. The beginning of the second half of the dance, from mm. 9–12, however, seems to depart from this character, with a sudden shift to G minor and *forte* dynamic. Perhaps this passage reflects the assertion of the *Allgemeine musikalische Zeitung*'s correspondent in Pest that Hungarian national music is not only dance music, but that "it is gloomy, plaintive, passionate, but then also raging and inspiring to war.... [It is] proud and warlike."[32] The indication *maestoso*, which also appears on occasion in representations of Hungarian-Gypsy music, may acknowledge this same understanding of *verbunk* not only as dance music, but as dance music that served, at least in part, as an aid to military recruiting in Hungary. That the primary character of most Western European representations of Hungarian-Gypsy dances, like that in Example 7.6, is one of jovial or trifling simplicity rather than of "warlike rage" reflects the desire of Western Europeans to translate an impression of Hungarian-Gypsy music that served their own needs and tastes.

Although the principal and earliest association of Hungarian-Gypsy music for Western Europeans was to dance music, representations gradually appeared in smaller numbers in other genres as well: sets of variations, rondos, and marches. Some of these works draw directly on the dance repertoire, such as Josepha Barbara von Auernhammer's *Six variations sur un thême hongrois* for solo keyboard, published by the Chemische Druckerey and advertised in 1810. The theme of the set is a very slightly altered quotation of the first sixteen measures of a dance that appeared in at least three Viennese collections of Hungarian-Gypsy dances during the first decade of the nineteenth century.[33] Similarly, several scholars have commented on the resemblance of Haydn's "Rondo, in the Gipsies' Style" to Hungarian dances published in the early nineteenth century; although the direction of influence is impossible to ascertain in this case, and although there is no direct quotation as in Auernhammer's work, the "Rondo" highlights the stylistic continuity between the dance repertoire and works in other genres.[34] This is true even of marches such as Friedrich Starke's *Neuer millitairischer* [*sic*] *Marsch* for keyboard published in Vienna in the *Musikalisches Wochenblatt* in 1807, the first trio of which is marked *alla Ungarese* (Example 7.7). Staccato markings lend brilliance to a passage that is otherwise indistinguishable from representations of Hungarian-Gypsy dances; a Hungarian evocation within a military march may perhaps be interpreted as analogous to the occasional *maestoso* markings in collections of such dances.

A characteristic of virtually all representations of Hungarian-Gypsy music, and one that distinguishes them strongly, moreover, from music *alla turca*, is that they are restricted almost exclusively to private genres suitable for domestic performance. Alexander Weinmann's two lists of Hungarian music published in Vienna between 1770 and 1880, which may be considered representative even though they are far from comprehensive, confirm as much (Weinmann 1969, 1973).[35] In analyzing his lists, I have only considered works published until 1820 and whose titles identify them incontrovertibly as representations of Hungarian-Gypsy music, although Weinmann also includes works that he considers Hungarian "by dint of the nationality of their composer" (Weinmann

EXAMPLE 7.7 Domokos, "Kiegészítések a verbunkos zene és tánc bécsi adataihoz" (1985), 108, ex. 7.

1969: 407).[36] Of the twenty-four works that fulfill both criteria, eighteen, or three quarters, are for keyboard. The remaining six compositions call for varying chamber instrumentation: violin duet; two or three violins and bass; guitar; and flute (or violin) and guitar. The same conclusion is borne out also by the volume of Hungarian dances edited by Géza Papp, which includes seventeen collections of dances (238 dances in total) that appeared between 1784 and 1810, all of which were intended for performance by soloists or small chamber ensembles. Representations of *verbunk* thus largely maintained at least one aspect of its original performance practice: its execution by a small ensemble of musicians. *Verbunk* was rooted in the tradition of Hungarian *Tafelmusik*, and its representation outside Hungary rarely exceeded this context, in which it provided private, domestic entertainment now spiced by a suggestion of exoticism. Orchestral depictions of Hungarian-Gypsy music were very rare in the eighteenth century; Haydn's "Rondo all'ungarese," the last movement of his Piano Concerto in D major, Hob. XVIII:11 (1784), is unusual in this respect. Indeed, the only orchestral works included in Weinmann's lists are Beethoven's incidental music for *König Stephan* (1811) and two much later, little-known compositions, both dating from the mid-1820s: Franz Pechatschek's *Variations sur un thême hongrois*, Op. 17, for violin and orchestra (1825) and Johann Peter Pixis's *Introduction et grand rondeau hongrois*, Op. 64, for piano and orchestra (1825).[37]

In contrast, music *alla turca* thrived in public genres that called for large performing forces: operas and symphonies. Examples of the *alla turca* style in eighteenth-century operas are among the best known and include numerous passages in Gluck's *La rencontre imprévue* (1764), Haydn's *L'incontro improvviso* (1775), and Mozart's *Die Entführung aus dem Serail* (1782). Hunter (1998: 56–57) has also identified several lesser-known operas that involve Turkish themes and musical representations, including most notably Mozart's unfinished *Zaide* (1779–80) and Grétry's *La caravane du Caire* (1783). Symphonic representations of Janissary music from the eighteenth century are considerably less familiar and have received significantly less scholarly attention, although they are also relatively abundant; they include the *Turco* trio in the fourth movement and the *Turco* episode in the rondo finale of Carl Ditters von Dittersdorf's *Sinfonia nazionale nel gusto di cinque nazioni* (c. 1766), Georg Druschetzky's *Sinfonia turcia* (c. 1775), Franz Xaver Süssmayr's *Sinfonia turchesa* (c. 1790), Andreas Romberg's *Sinfonia alla turca* (1798), and Friedrich Witt's *Sinfonie turque* (1st ed. 1808), among others.[38]

The representations of Turkish music in many of these works depend heavily on evocations of the characteristic instrumentation and volume of Janissary music—through the use of bass drum, cymbals, triangle, piccolo, and tambourine—performed, as Schubart noted, by large bands of musicians in order to rouse soldiers during battle. The *alla turca* style was thus particularly apt in large-scale works destined primarily for public performance, much in contrast to representations of Hungarian-Gypsy music. In fact, according to Schubart, the Germans were eager to augment the instrumentation of their representations of Janissary music even further. He writes: "The Germans have amplified this music with bassoons, through which [its] effect is greatly heightened. Punctuating trumpet calls also work well."[39] Even when the *alla turca* style was deployed in solo keyboard works intended for domestic enjoyment, such as the famous *alla turca* movement concluding Mozart's Piano Sonata in A major, K. 331, the performer could have imitated the boisterous, militaristic character of Janissary music through the application of a Turkish stop or pedal, which activated cymbals or bells and a drumstick striking the soundboard of the instrument. Eva Badura-Skoda (2001: 897) has noted that in some cases, bass drums were actually fixed to the underside of fortepianos.

Although the melodic, harmonic, and rhythmic gestures evident in representations of both Turkish and Hungarian-Gypsy music overlapped, the timbres and affects of these representations, intimately tied to their respective associations with military and dance music, often differed markedly. This distinction is reflected not only through the different genres in which each type of representation was customary, but also through the positioning of these representations within multimovement works. As Melanie Lowe (2007: 54) has explored, the use of topics and styles in specific movements contributes to what she calls the "syntactic logic of multimovement works." She notes that virtually all public entertainments in the late eighteenth century began with the performance of the first movement of a symphony or an opera overture; in both cases, the role of this opening music was therefore not only to commence a given work, but to attract the audience's attention to the beginning of an event more generally. To succeed as a "noise killer," such music, according to Abbé Vogler, must display "fire and splendor. It must enthrall the listener by virtue of the force of its harmonious organization" (Sisman 1993: 6). The *alla turca* style was certainly equal to this task, as evidenced by its deployment in the overtures to *La rencontre imprévue* and *Die Entführung aus dem Serail* as well as the first movements of Druschetzky's *Sinfonia turcia* and Süssmayr's *Sinfonia turchesa*. The imitation of Janissary instrumentation at a *forte* dynamic level in these passages is crucial in coding the music as Turkish and in fulfilling its function within the larger context of the performance.

The final movement of a multimovement work (in any genre) in the eighteenth century, in contrast, was typically the lightest and liveliest, often evoking rustic music-making and popular dances. Unsurprisingly, when representations of Hungarian-Gypsy music were incorporated into multimovement works, they almost invariably appeared in the final movement; examples include the aforementioned finale of Haydn's Piano Concerto in D major as well as his "Rondo, in the Gipsies' style" concluding the Piano Trio in G major. The rondo, furthermore, one of the most typical forms of eighteenth-century finales, was the most common large-scale form in which Hungarian-Gypsy music was evoked (in both independent compositions and multimovement works), undoubtedly because of its own affective associations. As Koch declared in the article on the rondo in his *Musikalisches Lexikon*, "the rondo must be performed with an artless and naïve execution,"[40] a characterization that is consonant with Feldtenstein's depiction of the Hungarian dance as trifling, flirtatious, and comical. Yet music *alla turca*, more syntactically versatile than representations of Hungarian-Gypsy music, also appears in rondo finales, including those of Mozart's Piano Sonata in A major and Süssmayr's *Sinfonia turchesa*. Its forceful, military character resonated with the function of first movements, but its perceived barbarity rendered it equally appropriate to the "low" style of finales and especially of rondos.

Neither representations of Janissary music nor of *verbunk* were particularly suited to the "middle" style of slow movements of multimovement works, which generally evoked the lyrical, sentimental, and pastoral.[41] The nobility of the minuet, however, was sometimes compromised by the timbral characteristics of music *alla turca*, as may be observed in Süssmayr's *Sinfonia turchesa* and Druschetzky's *Sinfonia turcia*. In both movements, what is even more striking is that the Turkish percussion instruments that are so prominent in the minuets are all but absent in the trios, seemingly reversing the common noble–rustic dichotomy of the minuet and trio pairing.[42] The *Turco* designation of Dittersdorf's trio from the analogous movement of his *Sinfonia nazionale nel gusto di cinque nazioni* does not depend on colorful instrumentation but on a largely scalar and directionless melody that repeatedly turns back on itself, drone harmonies, and constantly alternating *forte* and *piano* dynamics, resulting in a thoroughly comical and parodic passage (Example 7.8). Neither Süssmayr's nor Druschetzky's minuets, in contrast, include the typical melodic, harmonic, and rhythmic features shared by eighteenth-century representations of both Turkish and Hungarian-Gypsy music; in triple-meter movements, strikingly at odds with the pervasive duple meter of such representations, perhaps these composers judged timbre to be the most effective means of evocation.

Indeed, the subversive rusticity that results from accommodating a representation of duple-meter *verbunk* within the triple meter of the minuet is highlighted by the "Menuet alla Zingarese" from Haydn's String Quartet in D major, Op. 20 No. 4; it is the only minuet of which I am aware that refers to Gypsy music-making. In an attempt to reconcile the conflicting meters of the two styles—noble minuet and exotic Hungarian-Gypsy—Haydn made extensive use of durational accents reinforced by *fz* markings on weak beats, resulting in pervasive hemiola that thoroughly destabilizes the triple meter indicated by the time signature (Example 7.9). It is noteworthy, however, that no other markers of the Hungarian-Gypsy style inform this minuet, potentially suggesting that the descriptor "alla Zingarese" in the movement's title is best interpreted not as a compositional style but as a performance indication: "Play this minuet like Gypsies would," Haydn tells the performers, helping them in their interpretation by notating the hemiola that would result from performing the music in the duple-meter style of *verbunk*.[43]

Although we will never know with certainty what Haydn's intentions were when he gave this minuet its title, the possibility that designations such as *alla zingarese, all'ongarese,* or *alla turca* may have been meant and/or understood at least in part as performance indications highlights a potential practical application of this exploration of the cultural associations of Turkish and Hungarian-Gypsy styles in the late eighteenth century. By bringing to light the connotations of military and dance music, respectively, that were identified with these styles by composers, performers, and listeners alike, I hope that these meanings and their attendant characters might not only come to bear on historical and analytical scholarship, but might also become an integral facet of historically informed performance.

EXAMPLE 7.8 Dittersdorf, *Sinfonia nazionale nel gusto di cinque nazioni*, iv, mm. 1–8.

EXAMPLE 7.9 Haydn, String Quartet in D major, Op. 20 No. 4/iii, "Menuet alla Zingarese," mm. 1–20.

ACKNOWLEDGMENT

I thank Ralph P. Locke for suggesting perspicacious clarifications to this chapter.

NOTES

1. Major is quoting a footnote in István Bartalus, "Zenészetünk hajdan és most," *Budapesti Hírlap* 148 (22 June 1859) in German translation: "Auch Josef Haydn hat ein *Alla Ongarese*

(das Finale eines der G dur Trios, die Opusnummer ist mir nicht erinnerlich), das ziemlich ungarisch klingt, stellenweise aber eher türkisch ist" (Major 1928–29: 601). The sentence preceding this one refers to the *alla turca* finale of Mozart's Piano Sonata in A major, K. 331. I thank Balázs Mikusi for providing me with excerpts from Bartalus's article.

2. For further discussion of the *Capriccio*, see Bellman (1993: 59–61) and Pethő (2000: 226). Kinsky (1955: 390) indicates that the title *Alla ingharese, quasi un Capriccio* appears in Beethoven's hand on the autograph of the piece.

3. See, for instance, the discussions of this passage in Szabolcsi (1956: esp. 325–28), Bellman (1993: 55–57), and Rice (1999: 69). Rice asserts erroneously that this passage bears the label *alla turca*.

4. Compare Locke's list to Mayes (2009: 168–73).

5. Loya (2011: 77) dates this emergence slightly earlier, to c. 1810. He writes, "Composers' obligations to the discourse of authenticity were flexible, and in the first three decades of representation (ca. 1784–1810), Hungarian-Gypsy markers were often mixed with Turkish ones."

6. For a selection of such descriptions, see Mayes (2009).

7. See, for example, Županovic (1986) and Kos (1993).

8. The manuscript is the subject of Falvy (1971). The dance in question, labeled "Turciee," is reproduced on page 39 of Falvy's article. Several scholars have referenced the observation originally made by Szabolcsi; see, for instance, Bartha (1958: 173–75), Bellman (1993: 36–38), Rice (1999: 68–69), and Head (2000: 67–70; 2005: 78–79).

9. See also Head (2000: 72–73).

10. I explore this issue in greater detail in Mayes (2014). More generously, Head (2005: 85–86) has interpreted Haydn's compositions in which Hungarian-Gypsy evocations are mixed with other "national and ethnic references" as "experiments…[that] could effortlessly suggest that national boundaries are unnatural, in the sense of man-made and culturally specific," reading these works in light of Enlightenment ideals of universality.

11. "Der Ungar tanzt sehr viel und sehr gern: seine Nationalmusik ist also zunächst Tanzmusik" (n.n. 1810: col. 369). Some of the earliest representations of Hungarian music were dances; Giovanni Picchi's *Intavolatura di balli d'arpicordo* (1621), for example, includes a "Ballo ongaro" and a "Padoana ditta la Ongara."

12. The *Magyar Hírmondó*, founded in 1780, was the first Hungarian-language newspaper, a reflection of contemporary nationalist sentiment. See Szlatky (1991: 235) and Head (2005: 274 n. 30). On the role of Gypsies as the professional musicians of Hungary, see Mayes (2008: 12–47).

13. See, for example, Krüchten (1826).

14. The use of music, dance, alcohol, and monetary incentives in military recruiting has a long history, but became especially important in the Habsburg Empire from the establishment of a permanent army in 1715 until the introduction of general military service in 1868. See Sárosi, (1978: 86; 1990: 94) and Istvánffy (1982: 16). In this chapter, I use the term *verbunk* in only one of its possible senses, that which relates more closely to its etymological origin. As Loya (2011: 60–61) has recently summarized, the terms *verbunk* (a noun) and *verbunkos* (an adjective) historically have had a variety of meanings, from dance music in various tempos to music that was primarily intended to be listened to, and from a tempo indication to a style in general to an entire repertoire.

15. Dobszay (1993: 126) has hypothesized that the cimbalom acted as a substitute for a key-board continuo instrument, and Sárosi finds a parallel between the importance of string

instruments in Gypsy ensembles and in Viennese music of the late eighteenth century. Sárosi (1970: 26; 1986: 222; 1999: 59) notes, however, that *verbunk* retained stronger ties to traditional music in rural settings than it did in urban ones.

16. For more information on Joseph II's reforms, see Braunbehrens (1990: 310–12).

17. Blasis was influential throughout Europe as a choreographer and teacher, and his students spread his ideas about dance throughout the world. See Testa (1998: 440–41).

18. He interpolated in this sentence, however, that "if one wishes to dance in an educated manner, then training is necessary": "Er hat das bequeme von Schwäbischen an sich, daß jedes Paar nach ihren eigenen erfindenden Wendungen (es sey dann daß man in etwas gelehrt Tanzen will, so sind gelernte Führungen nöthig,) tanzen kann, ohne genöthiget zu seyn, sich nach andern zu richten" (Feldtenstein 1772: 101). In his afterword to the facsimile edition of Feldtenstein's treatise, Kurt Petermann (1984: xix–xx) notes that exhortations to such improvisatory execution are frequent throughout Feldtenstein's descriptions of national dances, in which the taste and skill of the dancers are more important than a pre-determined form.

19. For further discussion of the contredanse, see Eric McKee's chapter in this volume.

20. See Papp (1986: esp. 352–53) for more information on this collection.

21. "Er ist theils dramatisch, theils aber auch gesellschaftlich.... Was den gesellschaftlichen Tanz betrifft, so vertheilt es sich, nach der Verschiedenheit des Nationalgeschmacks, in verschiedene Zweige" (Schubart 1806: 350–51).

22. "Dieser Tanz verdient sehr auf das Theater gebracht zu werden" (Schubart 1806: 352).

23. "Der Charakter dieser Musik ist so kriegerisch, dass er auch feigen Seelen den Busen hebt. Wer aber das Glück gehabt hat, die Janitscharen selber musiciren zu hören, deren Musikchöre gemeiniglich achtzig bis hundert Personen stark sind; der muss mitleidig über die Nachäffungen lächeln, womit man unter uns meist die türkische Musik ver-unstaltet.... Kurz, die türkische Musik ist unter allen kriegerischen Musiken die erste, aber auch die kostbarste, wenn sie so vollkommen seyn soll, als es ihre Natur, und ihr heroischer Zweck erheischt" (Schubart 1806: 330–31).

24. "Vor allem muss ich also den Leser mit den türkischen Instrumenten bekannt machen, und ihn ersuchen, die türkische Kammermusik von der sogenannten *Tambulchana* (nicht *Tubulchanu*, wie einige geschrieben haben) auf wallachisch *Kindia*, d. i. der Feld- oder Janitscharenmusik wohl zu unterscheiden; ja man hüte sich sogar, diejenige Janitscharenmusik, die man bey den meisten Regimentern der römisch-kaiserlichen Armee seit einiger Zeit eingeführt hat, und wozu täglich neue Stücke aus teutschen Federn zum Vorschein, für ächte türkische Feldmusik zu halten. Der Unterschied zwischen bey-den ist unendlich gross. Nicht einmal kann unsere teutschtürkische Feldmusik derselben Instrumente sich rühmen, um wieviel weniger ebendesselben Geschmackes, den man mit europäischen Taktarten, und mit dem teutschen Ohre nachzuahmen sich vergebens bemühen wird" (Sulzer 1781: 431). My translation is largely based on Whaples's (1959: 320).

    Heinrich Christoph Koch echoes much the same sentiment in the article "Janitscharenmusik" in his *Musikalisches Lexikon*: "Es ist bekannt, daß man diese Art der Musik bey uns nicht allein bey militärischen Aufzügen, sondern auch außerdem nachahmt; man würde sich aber irren, wenn man glauben wollte, daß die mehresten Nachahmungen derselben den innern Charakter der türkischen Musik darstellen, weil sie eben so wie jene mit der Trommel, mit Becken u. d. gl. begleitet werden" (1802: col. 775).

25. "Indessen erfordert keine andere Gattung von Musik einen so festen, bestimmten und allgewaltig durchschlagenden Tact. Jeder Tactstrich wird durch einen neuen männlichen

234   CATHERINE MAYES

Schlag, so stark conturirt, dass es beynahe unmöglich ist, aus dem Tacte zu kommen" (Schubart 1806: 332). The translation in the main text is from Bauman (1987: 62).

26. For a discussion of the myriad differences between *verbunk* and Western European representations of it, see Mayes (2009).

27. "Die Janitscharenmusik verräth die Hauptkennzeichen der Musik eines noch rohen Volkes, nemlich das Lärmende, und die aüßerst fühlbare Darstellung des Rhythmus durch eintönige Schlaginstrumente" (Koch 1802: col. 776).

28. A selection of these dances is reproduced in Papp (1986).

29. See Papp (1986: 346–62) for detailed information on specific dances and collections.

30. The *VI Danses hongroises* and the *Contredanses hongroises*, among others, are included in Papp (1986).

31. Mayes (2009) includes a more extensive discussion of the stylistic features of Hungarian-Gypsy dances published in the late eighteenth and early nineteenth centuries.

32. "Der Ungar tanzt sehr viel und sehr gern: seine Nationalmusik ist also zunächst Tanzmusik. Diese ist finster, klagend, schwärmerisch, aber dann auch stürmend und zum Kriege begeisternd.... Ihr langsamer, oder Werbungs-Tanz (Verbunkos) wie man ihn gewöhnlich nennt, ist stolz und kriegerisch" (n.n. 1810: cols. 369–70).

33. For further details, see Mayes (2008: 116–18).

34. For a lengthier discussion of this movement, see Mayes (2008: 117–25).

35. The title of the supplementary article mistakenly identifies 1850 instead of 1880 as the end of the period under consideration.

36. This quotation comes from the English summary of the article at the end of the volume.

37. Joseph Starzer composed several ballets with titles referencing Hungary and Hungarians, including *Les Hussards au marché aux chevaux* (1754), *L'Hongrois* (1754–55), *Les Polonois à la foire hongroise* (1755–56), and *Les Bohémiens* (1756–57), yet as Bellman (2012: 73) has noted, "this music is unavailable, if it survives at all, so its relative 'Hungarianness' or 'Gypsiness' is impossible to gauge. Nevertheless, we can assume [its] characteristic flavor was probably largely a product of the costumes and choreography, since the ballets appeared some years before the first glimmerings of the *style hongrois* in Vienna and elsewhere."

38. Head (2000: 62) discusses Witt's and Süssmayr's symphonies briefly.

39. "Die Deutschen haben diese Musik noch mit Fagotten verstärkt, wodurch die Wirkung noch um ein Großes vermehrt wird. Auch Trompetenstöße lassen sich dazwischen gut anbringen" (Schubart 1806: 331).

40. "Aus dem Vorhergehenden versteht sich übrigens von selbst, daß das Rondo mit einem ungekünstelten und dem Naiven eigenem Vortrage ausgeführet warden muß" (Koch 1802: col. 1274).

41. For a discussion of "middle" style, including contemporary commentary, see Lowe (2007: 60–66). As the second movement of Haydn's String Quartet in C major, Op. 54 No. 2, demonstrates, however, the *hallgató* style of Hungarian-Gypsy music could be used to good effect.

42. This dichotomy is discussed by McKee (2005).

43. Salmen (1986: 245) has suggested that markings such as *all'ongarese* could be interpreted as performance indications, and Locke (2009: 70) concurs that "a title or other verbal indication...can easily suggest not just a composed style but also a way of playing." I applied this insight to this minuet in Mayes (2008: 160–61), and it is also explored in Bellman (2012: 79).

References

n.n. 1810. Nachrichten: Pest in Ungarn, d. 6ten Febr. *Allgemeine musikalische Zeitung* 24 (14 March): cols. 369–78.

Allanbrook, Wye Jamison. 1983. *Rhythmic Gesture in Mozart*: Le nozze di Figaro *and* Don Giovanni. Chicago: University of Chicago Press.

Badura-Skoda, Eva. 2001. Turca, alla. In *The New Grove Dictionary of Music and Musicians*, 2nd ed., ed. Stanley Sadie and John Tyrrell, vol. 25, 897–98. London: Macmillan.

Bartha, Dénes. 1958. Mozart et le folklore musical de l'Europe centrale. In *Les influences étrangères dans l'oeuvre de W. A. Mozart, Paris, 10–13 octobre 1956*, ed. André Verchaly, 157–81. Paris: Centre National de la Recherche Scientifique.

Bartók, Béla. 1981. *The Hungarian Folk Song*, ed. Benjamin Suchoff. Trans. M. D. Calvocoressi, with annotations by Zoltán Kodály. Albany: State University of New York Press.

Bauman, Thomas. 1987. *W. A. Mozart: Die Entführung aus dem Serail*. Cambridge: Cambridge University Press.

Bellman, Jonathan. 1993. *The Style Hongrois in the Music of Western Europe*. Boston: Northeastern University Press.

——. 2012. *Ongherese*, Fandango, and Polonaise: National Dance as Classical-Era Topic. *Journal of Musicological Research* 31/2–3: 70–96.

Blasis, C. 1825. *Traité élémentaire, théorique et pratique de l'art de la danse, contenant toutes les démonstrations et tous les principes généraux et particuliers qui doivent guider le danseur*. Milan.

——. 1847. *Notes upon Dancing, Historical and Practical*. Trans. R. Barton. London: Delaporte.

Braunbehrens, Volkmar. 1990. *Mozart in Vienna 1781–1791*. Trans. Timothy Bell. New York: Grove Weidenfeld.

Campianu, Eva. 1982. Langaus, Quadrille, Zingarese: Joseph Haydn und der Tanz. *Morgen* 6/23: 171–77.

Dobszay, László. 1993. *A History of Hungarian Music*. Trans. Mária Steiner. Budapest: Corvina.

Domokos, Mária. 1985. Kiegészítések a verbunkos zene és tánc bécsi adataihoz. *Zenetudományi dolgozatok*: 95–111.

Falvy, Zoltán. 1971. Danses du XVIIIe siècle en Hongrie dans la collection "Linus." *Studia Musicologica Academiae Scientiarum Hungaricae* 13/1–4: 15–59.

Feldtenstein, Carl Joseph von. 1772. *Erweiterung der Kunst nach der Chorographie zu tanzen, Tänze zu erfinden, und aufzusetzen; wie auch Anweisung zu verschiedenen National-Tänzen; Als zu Englischen, Deutschen, Schwäbischen, Pohlnischen, Hannak- Masur- Kosak- und Hungarischen; mit Kupfern; nebst einer Anzahl Englischer Tänze*, 2nd ed. Braunschweig. Reprint, ed. Kurt Petermann, Leipzig: Zentralantiquariat der Deutschen Demokratischen Republik, 1984.

Head, Matthew. 2000. *Orientalism, Masquerade and Mozart's Turkish Music*. London: Royal Musical Association.

——. 2005. Haydn's Exoticisms: "Difference" and the Enlightenment. In *The Cambridge Companion to Haydn*, ed. Caryl Clark, 77–92. Cambridge: Cambridge University Press.

Hoboken, Anthony. 1957. *Joseph Haydn: Thematisches-bibliographisches Werkverzeichnis*. Vol. 1: *Instrumentalwerke*. Mainz: B. Schott's Söhne.

Hunter, Mary. 1998. The *Alla Turca* Style in the Late Eighteenth Century: Race and Gender in the Symphony and the Seraglio. In *The Exotic in Western Music*, ed. Jonathan Bellman, 43–73. Boston: Northeastern University Press.

Istvánffy, Tibor. 1982. All'Ongarese: Studien zur Rezeption ungarischer Musik bei Haydn, Mozart und Beethoven. Ph.D. diss., Ruprecht-Karls-Universität Heidelberg.

Kinsky, Georg. 1955. *Das Werk Beethovens: Thematisch-bibliographisches Verzeichnis seiner sämtlichen vollendeten Kompositionen.* Completed by Hans Halm. Munich: Henle.

Koch, Heinrich Christoph. 1802. *Musikalisches Lexikon.* Frankfurt am Main: August Hermann der Jüngere. Reprint, Kassel: Bärenreiter, 2001.

Kos, Koraljka. 1993. Die angeblichen Zitate von Volksmusik in Werken der Wiener Klassiker. In *Internationaler musikwissenschaftlicher Kongreß zum Mozartjahr 1991 Baden–Wien.* Vol. 1, ed. Ingrid Fuchs, 225–40. Tutzing: Hans Schneider.

Krüchten, J. 1826. Über das Musikwesen in Ungarn. *Cäcilia: eine Zeitschrift für die musikalische Welt* 5/20: 299–304.

Locke, Ralph P. 2009. *Musical Exoticism: Images and Reflections.* Cambridge: Cambridge University Press.

Lowe, Melanie. 2007. *Pleasure and Meaning in the Classical Symphony.* Bloomington: Indiana University Press.

Loya, Shay. 2011. *Liszt's Transcultural Modernism and the Hungarian-Gypsy Tradition.* Rochester: University of Rochester Press.

Major, Ervin. 1928–29. Miszellen: Ungarische Tanzmelodien in Haydns Bearbeitung. *Zeitschrift für Musikwissenschaft* 11: 601–4.

Mayes, Catherine. 2008. Domesticating the Foreign: Hungarian-Gypsy Music in Vienna at the Turn of the Nineteenth Century. Ph.D. diss., Cornell University.

——. 2009. Reconsidering an Early Exoticism: Viennese Adaptations of Hungarian-Gypsy Music around 1800. *Eighteenth-Century Music* 6/2: 161–81.

——. 2014. Eastern European National Music as Concept and Commodity at the Turn of the Nineteenth Century. *Music and Letters* 95/1: 70–91.

McKee, Eric. 2005. Mozart in the Ballroom: Minuet–Trio Contrast and the Aristocracy in Self-Portrait. *Music Analysis* 24/3: 383–434.

Montagu, Lady Mary Wortley. 1993. *Turkish Embassy Letters*, ed. Malcolm Jack. Athens: University of Georgia Press.

Papp, Géza, ed. 1986. *Hungarian Dances 1784–1810.* Budapest: Magyar Tudományos Akadémia, Zenetudományi Intézet.

Pethő, Csilla. 2000. *Style Hongrois*: Hungarian Elements in the Works of Haydn, Beethoven, Weber and Schubert. *Studia Musicologica Academiae Scientiarum Hungaricae* 41/1–3: 199–284.

Rice, Eric. 1999. Representations of Janissary Music (*Mehter*) as Musical Exoticism in Western Compositions, 1670–1824. *Journal of Musicological Research* 19/1: 41–88.

Salmen, Walter. 1986. Diskussionsrunde 1. In *Bericht über den internationalen Joseph Haydn Kongress Wien 1982*, ed. Eva Badura-Skoda, 242–47. Munich: Henle.

Sárosi, Bálint. 1970. Gypsy Musicians and Hungarian Peasant Music. *Yearbook of the International Folk Music Council* 2: 8–27.

——. 1978. *Gypsy Music.* Trans. Fred Macnicol. Budapest: Corvina.

——. 1986. Parallelen aus der ungarischen Volksmusik zum "Rondo all'Ongarese"-Satz in Haydns D-dur Klavierkonzert Hob. XVIII:11. In *Bericht über den internationalen Joseph Haydn Kongress Wien 1982*, ed. Eva Badura-Skoda, 222–26. Munich: Henle.

——. 1990. *Volksmusik: Das ungarische Erbe.* Trans. Jürgen Gaser. Budapest: Corvina.

——. 1999. *Sackpfeifer, Zigeunermusikanten ... Die instrumentale ungarische Volksmusik.* Trans. Ruth Futaky. Budapest: Corvina.

Schubart, Christian Daniel Friedrich. 1806. *Ideen zu einer Ästhetik der Tonkunst.* Reprint, Hildesheim: Georg Olms, 1969.

Sisman, Elaine. 1993. *Mozart: The "Jupiter" Symphony, No. 41 in C major, K. 551.* Cambridge: Cambridge University Press.

Sulzer, Franz Joseph. 1781. *Geschichte des transalpinischen Daciens, das ist: der Malachey, Moldau, und Bessarabiens.* Vol. 2. Vienna: Gräffer.

Szabolcsi, Bence. 1956. Exoticisms in Mozart. *Music and Letters* 37/4: 323–32.

Szlatky, Maria. 1991. Hungary. In *The Blackwell Companion to the Enlightenment*, ed. John W. Yolton, 235. Oxford: Blackwell.

Testa, Alberto. 1998. Blasis, Carlo. In *International Encyclopedia of Dance*, ed. Selma Jeanne Cohen, vol. 1, 440–41. Oxford: Oxford University Press.

Townson, Robert. 1797. *Travels in Hungary, with a Short Account of Vienna in the Year 1793.* London: Robinson.

Weinmann, Alexander. 1969. Magyar muzsika a bécsi zeneműpiacon: Bibliográfiai kísérlet. In *Magyar zenetörténeti tanulmányok: Szabolcsi Bence 70. születésnapjára*, ed. Ferenc Bónis, 131–77. Budapest: Zeneműkiadó Vállalat.

——. 1973. Magyar muzsika a bécsi zenemű-piacon (1770–1850): Kiegészítő közlemény. In *Magyar zenetörténeti tanulmányok: Mosonyi Mihály és Bartók Béla emlékére*, ed. Ferenc Bónis, 13–28. Budapest: Zeneműkiadó Vállalat.

Whaples, Miriam Karpilow. 1959. Exoticism in Dramatic Music, 1600–1800. Ph.D. diss., Indiana University.

Wolff, Larry. 1994. *Inventing Eastern Europe: The Map of Civilization on the Mind of the Enlightenment.* Stanford: Stanford University Press.

Zbikowski, Lawrence. 2012. Music, Dance, and Meaning in the Early Nineteenth Century. *Journal of Musicological Research* 31/2–3: 147–65.

Županovic, Lovro. 1986. L'influence du chant populaire des Croates, spécialement de Burgenland, sur la création de Joseph Haydn. In *Bericht über den internationalen Joseph Haydn Kongress Wien 1982*, ed. Eva Badura-Skoda, 209–17. Munich: Henle.

CHAPTER 8

THE SINGING STYLE

SARAH DAY-O'CONNELL

OF all the topic descriptions presented by Leonard Ratner in *Classic Music*, that of the singing style is, at four lines, certainly the shortest—and arguably the least clear (1980: 19). Ratner lists four characteristics (three if we omit the tautologous first one), but tersely: a lyric vein, a moderate tempo, slow note values, and a narrow range. He includes two examples, but confusingly: neither actually illustrates all four qualities. He cites two historical sources, Koch (1802) and Daube (1797), but plumbs neither for insight into the term's meaning or context. Whether because of a "significant omission" (Monelle 2000: 26) or on account of his general style of "deceptive informality" (Agawu 2008: 40), Ratner leaves the singing style little explained. Its low profile notwithstanding, however, the singing style has been prominent in the thinking that grew out of Ratner's work. It is a familiar concept to students and performers—not least because it is spotlighted in analyses of Mozart's Sonata in F major K. 332, the topic theorists' "demonstration piece par excellence" (Agawu 2008: 40)—and it is broadly deployed in scholarship, where it indicates many things: sung melodies, unsung melodies one can imagine being sung; melodies for amateur singers, melodies for professional singers; folksong melodies, salon melodies; melodies with square or symmetrical phrases, melodies unencumbered by strong phrase structure or meter; melodies with an emotional high point, undramatic melodies; melodies in general. The "singing style" seems to mean so many things that it risks meaning nothing.

Or, if not nothing, perhaps nothing more than a generic catch-all for everything that is not passagework. Raymond Monelle describes an alternation of "progressive" and "lyrical" temporalities as the fundamental building blocks of eighteenth-century music, and he equates that lyrical component with the singing style, calling it

> an essential aspect of classical construction as well as a particular instrumental manner, because singing style alternates with "flowing" or "brilliant" styles to form the temporal amalgam of the classical movement, which is extended in time by the interposition of passages of progressive temporality or *Gänge*, which tend to contrast stylistically with lyric evocations. (Monelle 2006: 5)

Monelle thus apparently demotes the singing style to one half of a binary opposition, and from topic to stylistic trait. And yet, as other scholars' frequent usage demonstrates, many find the singing-style topic to be real, useful, and even (to some degree) distinct. If this frequent usage has been based, in the absence of detailed grounding by Ratner, in intuition, what might we do to transform that intuition into knowledge? To start, we might be so bold as to subject the singing style to the skeptic Monelle's own test, asking whether the musical sign has "passed from literal imitation" or "stylistic reference" into "signification by association" (2000: 80). In other words, might we reasonably describe the first four measures of K. 332 in terms of the singing-style topic, not because it imitates singing or refers to a song, but because it evokes a network of associations that are found in the wider culture or practice of singing? Next, we must ask whether there is a "level of conventionality in the sign" (80). That is to say, given that topics are obviously not *unique* instances of musical signification, does the composer write in a way that essentially follows mutually agreed-on rules—rules that other contemporary composers follow, or alternatively, rules that he himself follows elsewhere within his oeuvre? As we consider whether we might answer these questions in the affirmative, we might even take further implicit direction from within Monelle's apparent dismissal. After all, Monelle himself chooses the term "lyric evocations" to contrast with the *Gänge*, passagework, progressive temporality, and whatever else the singing style supposedly is not. Further, he posits that there exist "great topical worlds" where "signifiers may be multifarious, and the signified complex and elusive" (2006: 5). The pastoral, the hunt, and the military are examples of topical worlds that Monelle pursues; they "represent major cultural themes" (2006: ix). "A full elucidation of a topic, both as signifier and signified," he writes, "must depend on investigations of social history, literature, popular culture, and ideology as well as music" (2006: ix). The position I shall advance in this chapter is that indeed, the lyric *is* evocative, and "evocations" have much to do with "signification by association." Singing, with its many genres and contexts of performance, *is* complicated, multifaceted, and elusive. What is more, it is integral to the realms of social history, literature, popular culture, and ideology. Singing is indeed a cultural theme.

So, without disputing that the singing style can sometimes be understood simply as the opposite of the brilliant style, I will focus here on the singing style as topic, namely, the conception at which Ratner hints and that Monelle dismisses. My goal is to begin the necessary "elaborate case study" (Monelle 2000: 80) that will clarify the origins, history, and meaning of the singing style as topic, and to recover its implications for performance. In order to do so I will first examine the signifier: features of vocal composition and vocal performance. Next, I will sketch out an investigation of the signified: the culture of singing, the network of associations around the act of singing. These are what eighteenth-century instrumental music may participate in when it incorporates the singing-style topic.

Before turning to the signifier, I set the stage by way of an extended, close look at the passage from Heinrich Christoph Koch's *Musikalisches Lexikon* that Ratner cites (and, incidentally, that Monelle uses as grounds to call the singing style into question). Koch outlines multiple meanings of the singing style:

"Singing" is generally the quality of a melody that makes it able to be performed with ease by the human voice. In particular it is understood, however, to indicate a comprehensible and smooth melody, as opposed to the uneven, angular, or so-called Baroque. The singing style has much in common with the Flowing, because these qualities seem to differ only in that the Flowing, for the most part, is made up of small intervals that in performance are more smooth than detached. However the "singing style" must also apply to those melodies that contain a lot of leaping intervals and detached notes, as well as to melodies in which the notes flow continuously, because even in the expression of stormy passions or in a tumult of sounds, all harshnesses that are avoidable or unnecessary to the expression, and all unsingable sequences of tones, must still be avoided in the melody.

In this sense, the "singing style" is the basis whereby a melody becomes the language of emotion, which is comprehensible to every person. If a musical piece lacks this property, it becomes incomprehensible, and it lacks that which should capture one's attention.

In a limited sense one uses the word "singing" or *cantabile* also (1) in order to distinguish the gentler portions of a piece from the very active, so one says, for example, the singer performed the passagework better than the *cantabile* or singing phrases; (2) one indicates with *cantabile* or "singing" a phrase of slower motion, the melody of which is to such a great extent singable, that no acquisition of training and the like is required. See *Cantabile*.

Singend, ist überhaupt genommen diejenige Eigenschaft einer jeden Melodie, wodurch sie geschickt wird von der menschlichen Stimme mit Leichtigkeit vorgetragen zu werden. Insbesondere verstehet man aber darunter das Faßliche und Zusammenhängende der Melodie, welches man dem Holperichten und dem, was man barock nennet, entgegensetzt. Das Singende hat vieles mit dem fließenden gemein, denn beyde Charaktere scheinen sich bloß dadurch zu unterscheiden, daß das Fließende größtentheils aus nahe an einander liegenden Intervallen bestehet, die bey dem Vortrage mehr zusammengezogen, als abgestoßen werden. Das Singende hingegen muß sich auch in solchen Melodien behaupten, die viel springende Intervallen und viel abgestoßene Noten enthalten, und in welchen die Töne gleichsam fortströmen; denn auch bey dem Ausdrucke stürmender Leidenschaften oder im Getümmel der Töne, müssen dennoch in der Melodie alle, zum Ausdrucke nicht unumgänglich nothwendige Härten und unsangbare Tonfolgen vermieden werden.

In diesem Sinne ist das Singende die Grundlage, wodurch die Melodie zu derjenigen Sprache der Empfindung wird, die jedem Menschen faßlich ist. Mangelt einem Tonstücke diese Eigenschaft, so wird es unverständlich, und es fehlt ihm dasjenige, was die Aufmerksamkeit fesseln sollte.

In einem eingeschränktem Sinne braucht man das Wort singend oder *cantabile* auch noch, 1) um die sanftern Stellen eines Tonstückes von den mehr rauschenden zu unterscheiden; so sagt man z. B. der Sänger habe in seiner Arie die Passagen besser vorgetragen, als die cantabeln order singenden Sätze; 2) bezeichnet man mit *cantabile* oder singend einen Satz von langsamer Bewegung, dessen Melodie in einem so hohen Grade singend ist, dass sie keiner Anhäufung von Spielmanieren u. d. gl. bedarf. S. *Cantabile*. (Koch 1802: cols. 1390–91)[1]

First Koch presents what we might consider a casual or straightforwardly literal meaning: *singend* applies to that which could easily be performed by the human voice. Then he offers another, distinct meaning: music in the singing style is "comprehensible." At this point he appears to move on to a new style, which he terms the "flowing." But the flowing style turns out to be a subset of the singing style: it applies to passages of small intervals played smoothly. The singing style encompasses the flowing style *as well as* music that is "leaping and detached," two qualities that relate to the expression of stormy passions. *Singend* applies as long as stormy passions are properly expressed, that is, when unnecessary harshness is avoided. Koch pairs that avoidance of unnecessary harshness with the avoidance of what he calls unsingable sequences of tones. Next, with a paragraph break that bestows emphasis, Koch continues to expound on the "comprehensibility" of the singing style: it is the basis whereby music becomes a "language of emotion" understood by "every person." Without the singing style, music is neither comprehensible nor captures the attention. Finally, in the third paragraph, Koch changes tone, as if shifting from philosopher back to lexicographer. He states that there is also a "limited" sense of *singend*, which he three times equates with *cantabile*. Here, *singend* is simply that which is not passagework. It may also indicate music easily sung, as per the first sentence in the passage, but here more specifically, it is easily sung even without training.

Koch's repeated equation of *singend* and *cantabile* will prove relevant. In fact, neither he nor (Ratner's other source) Daube (1797: 10) actually refers to a *singender Styl*, though there is no apparent reason why they could not have done so. Rather, their terms are *das Singende* and *das Singbare*, respectively. The term "singing style" was newly coined by Ratner, presumably for rhetorical reasons: "the singing" sounds awkward and confusing in English because it can be understood as a noun referring to the act of singing (of course, this is also the case in German) and "singable" does not convey meanings of *singend* that go beyond "able to be sung." Moreover, it should be noted that outside Koch and Daube, *singbar* and *singend* are themselves uncommon. It will be very reasonable, indeed necessary, to follow Koch's concluding direction and "see *Cantabile*"—that is, to consider the history of the term *cantabile* as part of the history of the term *singend*.[2]

But what is especially important to note is that Koch's first definition of *singend*, "performed with ease by the human voice," occupies him only briefly. He opens with it, not in order to indicate its primacy, but to get it out of the way: it is what *singend* is "generally taken" to mean. Already in the second sentence, and flagged with the metadiscursive marker "however," Koch turns to the other definition, one that will occupy the rest of that paragraph as well as the next: music that is *singend* is music that is comprehensible. When he does this, he moves away from a sense of *singend* that has directly to do with the act of singing. Therefore, even the reference to *unsangbar* should be understood as "unsingable" only with attention to the surrounding context: here, *unsangbar* implies incomprehensible. This is clear because the next paragraph, which is about comprehensibility, begins with the transition "in this sense." But the equation of *unsangbar* and incomprehensible was also suggested by the prefix *un-*, for if Koch were returning his discussion to the *degree* of singability, the notion with which he began, he would likely have said "difficult" to sing, not impossible to sing, or unsingable. Indeed, it could even be argued that the connection between *unsangbar* and incomprehensible was suggested from the start: when Koch opens by referring to a melody performed "with ease" (*mit Leichtigkeit*), instead of saying "easily sung" (*leicht gesungen*), he chooses a noun form that suggests more than the opposite of difficult: lightness, gentleness, mildness, even flimsiness.[3] If he had had "easy," in the sense of "the opposite of difficult," exclusively in mind, Koch would likely have clarified his use of *leicht*, for example by referring to a narrow range, an avoidance of many subdivisions within the beat, or any other familiar marker of "easy" or accessible. In fact, this sense of "easy" is not what Koch intends to convey. He refers to "leaping intervals and detached notes," which are difficult, or at least not easy, to sing. *Singend* is generally taken to mean singable, yes, but more importantly, *singend* is comprehensible. What Koch provides, then, is something like a concentrated summary of a process, a microcosm of semiotic "unfolding": his description begins with a sense of *singend* that is directly connected to singing, but moves quickly to, and ultimately emphasizes, a sense of *singend* that has to do with something other than a direct association with actual singing. As we shall see, this understanding of the "singing style" as rooted in comprehensibility—as a "language of emotion" understood by "every person"—had a diffuse lineage. We can speculate that Koch's explicit point of departure was Jean-Jacques Rousseau by way of Johann Georg Sulzer, specifically, Sulzer's articles "Gesang" and "Singen" in the *Allgemeine Theorie der schönen Künste* (see Danuta Mirka's Introduction, which emphasizes the importance of singing within Rousseau's aesthetics, as well as Rousseau's influence on Sulzer). But what interests me here is not so much tracing a direct line of influence as exploring the way comprehensibility impinged on, and sometimes even permeated, a variety of discourses concerning the singing style in the eighteenth century. The claim of comprehensibility would in fact have depended on a reliance on language and codes shared by the society in which the songs were sung, but comprehensibility was nevertheless a quality that could and would trump tempo, articulation, range, level of training, role of the accompaniment, and even the connection of "singing" with the voice.

SIGNIFIER

Signifiers of the singing-style topic include vocal melodies themselves (musical elements chosen by the composer, such as a narrow range or regular rhythm) and aspects of vocal performance practice (choices made by a singer to render a passage through certain means—for example, legato articulation).[4]

Melodies

The nature of vocal melodies, and specifically their differences from instrumental melodies, is a subject taken up by Johann Mattheson in an entire chapter of *Der vollkommene Capellmeister*. Mattheson writes:

The first difference, of seventeen, between vocal and instrumental melodies is that *the former is, so to speak, the mother and the other is her daughter.* Such a comparison shows not only the degree of difference, but also the nature of the relationship. For just as a mother must necessarily be older than her natural daughter, so also vocal melody doubtless existed earlier in this world than did instrumental music. The former therefore not only holds rank and priority, but also inspires the daughter to follow her maternal instructions as best she can, making everything perfectly singable and flowing, so that one can well hear whose child she is.

Based on these observations we can easily discern which instrumental melodies are true daughters and which are, so to speak, begotten out of wedlock, by considering how they either resemble their mother or reject her style.

Der erste Unterschied, deren es seibzehn gibt, zwischen einer Vocal- und Instrumental-Melodie, bestehet demnach darin, *dass jene, so zu redden, die Mutter, diese aber ihre Tochter ist.* Eine solche Vergleichung weiset nicht nur den Grad des Unterschiedes, sondern auch die Art der Verwandtschafft an. Denn wie eine Mutter nothwendig älter seyn muss als ihre natürliche Tochter; so ist auch die Vocal-Melodie sonder Zweifel eher in dieser Unter-Welt gewesen, als die Instrumental-Music. Iene hat dannenhero nicht nur den Rang und Vorzug, sondern besielet auch der Tochter, sich nach ihren mütterlichen Vorschrifften bestmöglichst zu richten, alles fein singbar und fliessend zu machen, damit man hören möge, wessen Kind sie sey.

Aus dieser Anmerkung können wir leicht abnehmen, welche unter den Instrumental-Melodien ächte Töchter, und welche hergegen gleichsam ausser der Ehe gezeuget sind, nachdem sie nehmlich der Mutter nacharten, oder aber aus der Art schlagen. (Mattheson 1739: 204)

When he describes playing as emulating singing, Mattheson appears to fall in step with an old tradition. Sébastien de Brossard, for example, wrote under *"Voce"* in his *Dictionnaire* (1703) that instruments were artificial imitations of human voices, meant to substitute for, accompany, or sustain them. Yet Mattheson's account is especially forceful: not only does vocal melody, as the "mother," come before instrumental melody, the "daughter," but this mother–daughter relationship is conceived in strong terms of subordination. The instrumental is a compliant daughter, eager to please and disinclined to stand apart. Other, less obedient daughters exist, but they—instrumental melodies that insufficiently resemble their superior vocal matriarchs—are not just prodigals but bastards. Never mind the faulty representation of genetics here (for children born out of wedlock resemble their mothers as much as their half-sisters with married parents): Mattheson's point is that instrumental melodies can be illegitimate, that is, freighted with associations of impropriety and disrespectability, ostracization and shame.

And yet, even in the wake of this striking analogy, Mattheson continues with an about-face. "On the other hand," he writes, mothers and daughters are naturally different, and should not pretend to be otherwise:

On the other hand, the maternal character calls for demureness and restraint, whereas the child's character is more lively and youthful. From this it can be concluded how indecent it would be, if the mother decked herself out in the finery of the daughter, while the daughter chose the covering [i.e., veiling] of the mother. Each in its own place is the best way.

Andern theils da die mütterliche Eigenschafft viel sittsames und eingezogenes erfordert, so wie bey der kindlichen hergegen mehr muntres und jugendliches statt findet, kan auch hieraus geschlossen werden, wie unanständig es sey, wenn sich die Mutter etwa mit dem Putz der Tochter behängen; diese aber die Verhüllung einer Matrone wehlen will. Ein jedes an seinem Ort hat die beste Art. (Mattheson 1739: 204)

Mattheson admits that he is changing his tune here, but even so, the move is abrupt. Suddenly, the imitative daughter is the faulty one; it is the mother who is "called on," "required," "demanded" to be the way she is. Instrumental melodies have their place. As the chapter progresses, in fact, instrumental melodies find ever-greater favor, as vocal melodies are consistently described in terms of their limitations. Vocal melody allows none of the kind of melodic leaps that instrumental melody does; exemplary vocal melodies are "restrained" (*sittsam*; 205). Composers of vocal melody must consider the nature of breathing, lest they make life difficult for the singer (205). Vocal melody does not permit impetuous rhythms, and its range is narrower (206). Quick notes and arpeggios require "caution" (*Behutsamkeit*; 207). Vocal melody is more dependent on meter (209). There is only one exception to vocal melody being "so very restricted" (*so sehr Eingeschränkte*): vocal melody is at home in any key (206).

Like many of his contemporaries, Mattheson may have been ambivalent about the relative merits of vocal and instrumental music. But the passage cited seems blatantly self-contradictory, and therefore demands explication. Elsewhere, when Mattheson writes that all playing is imitation of singing, he adds that while sung music has words to express meaning, the composer of instrumental music must express meaning by working harder (82). More specifically, he must "know how, without resorting to words, to truly express the inclinations of the heart through the skillful combination of sounds, so that the listener completely and clearly understands the impetus, the meaning, the perspective, and the emphasis in all the pertinent sections as if it were his actual speech. It is then a pleasure! It takes much more art and a stronger imagination to bring this about without, rather than with, words."[5] It may be more demanding to write instrumental music, but it can be done successfully. The measure of that success is when the auditor completely grasps the "impetus, the meaning, the perspective, and the emphasis." It is then that instrumental music succeeds as well as vocal music does. Because composers of vocal music work with words, they necessarily know what it is to write music that has clear meaning, and they therefore have an advantage when writing instrumental music: a clear sense of what it is like to write something intelligible and clear. Mattheson inserts another colorful anecdote to drive home his point: "as the old Germans used to say, one always knows when a sow has rubbed up against the school wall."[6]

In fact, this is a point on which Mattheson is remarkably consistent. A quarter century prior, he wrote in *Das Neu-Eröffnete Orchestre* that the "first and foremost" (*erste und vornehmste*) rule of composition was that one compose *cantable*—that is, whatever one writes, be it vocal or instrumental, it must be "singable" (1713: 105). This does not mean singable as in avoiding leaps, incorporating breaths, and adhering to the compass of the voice, but singable in the sense of comprehensible. Mattheson, joining the "old Germans," might have put it this way: one always knows when an instrumental composer has background in writing vocal music—not because he writes instrumental lines that sound like vocal lines, but because he writes music so clearly comprehensible it might as well have had words. As was the case with Koch, if Mattheson seems to contradict himself, it is because we interpret too narrowly what he means by "singable." The qualities of vocal music may be signifiers of the singing style, but when it comes to understanding the meaning of *singend*, they can also be a red herring. *Singend* encompasses comprehensible, and the "mother" inspires the "daughter" to make everything thus.

Performance

While both the inherent qualities and accrued meanings of vocal melody could act as signifiers, so too could aspects of vocal performance. How were vocal melodies sung? And, just as important for our purposes, how were vocal-performance choices described, advocated, and justified? With what analogies, emphases, and assumptions? We need sources that tell a singer how to sing, but in order to thoroughly sleuth out the way vocal performance operated as signifier, we also do well to consider even subtle differences between the sources, for it is there that implicit values come to the surface. In this respect, the *Opinioni de' cantori antichi e moderni*, written by Pier Francesco Tosi in 1723, is exceptionally useful. This is, first, because Tosi's focus is on expressive singing rather than quasi-instrumental, brilliant, virtuosic display,[7] and, second, because Tosi's treatise had multiple lives throughout the eighteenth century through translations— into English as *Observations on the Florid Song* in 1742 by John Ernest Galliard, and into German as *Anleitung zur Singkunst* with the addition of extensive commentaries in 1757 by Johann Friedrich Agricola. Later, in 1810, Domenico Corri, despite writing in a new century and being exposed to a very different aesthetic, quotes Tosi, whom he calls his "countryman," at length in *The Singer's Preceptor*. These sources offer explicit directions on vocal performance and they also bear traces of the meanings, priorities, and associations that accrued to vocal performance in the eighteenth century; in short, they provide evidence of the signifying powers of singing.

In the words of Tosi's English translator Galliard, expressive singing "does not consist in a continual Velocity of the Voice which goes thus rambling on, without a Guide, and without Foundation; but rather, in *Cantabile*" (Tosi 1743: 129). This *cantabile* consists of several qualities. The singer should hold notes without "trembling" (vibrato), practicing long, steady tones to avoid "Flutt'ring in the Manner of all those that sing in a very bad Taste" (27). Long notes can also be conveyed *messa di voce*, swelling from soft to loud and back again on a single pitch; if this technique is used sparingly and only on open vowels, it can "never fail of having an exquisite Effect" (28). Galliard emphasizes

sparing usage in his accompanying note. Similarly, the dragg, a slow descending glis-
sando, is an exceptionally effective aspect of *cantabile*, but not to be overused: "there
is no Invention superior or Execution more apt to touch the Heart than this, provided
however it be done with Judgement" (179). Finally, Tosi's conception of *cantabile* singing
includes *rubato*: subtly pushing and pulling the tempo of the melody while maintaining
regular time in the bass (129).[8] *Rubato* is conceived as a litmus test for singers, for "whoever does not know how to steal the Time in Singing knows not how to Compose, nor to
Accompany himself, and is destitute of the best Taste and greatest Knowledge" (156). The
test determines whether the singer is a complete musician—is he broadly competent,
or is he a one-trick (singing) pony? The overall impression left by Tosi via Galliard of an
ideal singer is steady but unspoken confidence—a confidence that is well earned due to
his breadth of expertise, and a confidence that empowers him to deploy his alchemical
techniques of *messa di voce*, dragg, and *rubato* sparingly; he need not rely on even them
to prove his worth or ensure his acclaim.

German translator Agricola maintained (in Julianne C. Baird's words), "an apprecia-
tive and respectful attitude" toward Tosi, "almost always translating him as faithfully
as possible" (1995: 2). But even "faithful" translations require choices on the part of the
translator, choices that derive from his subjective understanding of the source text.
Moreover, Agricola not only translated his source text, he also added voluminous commentary. Comparing Agricola to Tosi and Galliard, we can discern connotative meanings of nonbrilliant vocal performance. For example, readers of Agricola's translation
are led to be wary of vibrato lest it convey an uncertainty (*hin und her wanke*; 1757: 47),
and yet they are advised, *pace* Tosi, not to avoid it, for it is effective on sustained notes,
especially when applied toward the end (121–22).[9] And while Agricola closely translates Tosi's warnings about sparing use of *messa di voce*, he makes clear in a note that
his taste is for liberal application of the effect. He posits as a "principle of good taste"
(*Grundregel des guten Geschmackes*) that every note, no matter how long, should be sung
with increasing and decreasing strength (that is, with *crescendo* and *decrescendo*) and he
compares these undulating dynamic swells to Hogarth's "line of beauty" (48). William
Hogarth's brief, accessible essay *The Analysis of Beauty* (1753) presented six tenets, of
which Agricola must have had "variety" particularly in mind: "all the senses delight in
it, and equally are averse to sameness. The ear is as much offended with one even continued note, as the eye is with being fix'd to a point, or to the view of a dead wall" (1753: 16).
Agricola's interpolation of Hogarth has the effect of imparting a didactic yet aspirational
tone: just as Hogarth sought to make the domain of the artist or connoisseur accessible
to the common reader, breaking down beauty into discrete principles, so also Agricola
wrenches Tosi's text from a privileged audience of (castrato) insiders and presents it
instead to students of varied abilities and both sexes. In this light, his warning about
uncertain-sounding vibrato takes on the tone of a forthright admission: confidence is
acquired and sometimes pretended.

Agricola continues his democratizing efforts when turning to the subjects of *rubato*,
articulation, and ornamentation. Regarding *rubato*, he adds two notated examples
with precise instructions: add or subtract some duration from one note (in the first

example a quarter note is made an eighth note) and compensate this adjustment by adding or subtracting that same duration to or from another note (1757: 219). Whereas in Galliard's translation this compensation must be made with "ingenuity" (Tosi 1743: 156), in Agricola's it is with "insight" (*Einsicht*; 1757: 219). As a result, Galliard's *rubato* suggests spontaneity and creativity whereas Agricola's *rubato* is more calculated and requires correctness. This difference is reinforced by the discussion of how to learn *rubato*: Galliard's position is that personal "Experience and Taste" must teach *rubato* (Tosi 1743: 156) whereas for Agricola learning depends on the external observation of skilled and wise performers (1757: 220). Moreover, Agricola also translates *rubato* in different ways depending on subtle differences in type, thereby demonstrating, as Baird points out, a desire to "solidify and crystallize the free and subtle fashion of the Italian practice into a regular, precise, and predictable one" (1995: 33). Regarding the dragg, Agricola is elusive and twice changes the subject, first to an extensive original commentary on the need for legato. Unless the composer writes rests or staccato signs, or unless a breath is needed, legato is the default articulation. If novice singers are allowed to leave space between notes, a "bad habit" (*üble Gewohnheit*) can result, which "must be avoided in time" (*bey Zeiten vorgebauet*); instead, a foundation must be laid for legato singing (1757: 50–51). Agricola's second commentary on the dragg turns quickly toward ornamentation (234–35). He and Galliard differ on the key question of whether the composer should dictate ornaments or the performer should invent his own. In Galliard's translation, advance planning would "always be wanting that Spirit which accompanies extempore Performance and is preferable to all servile Imitations" (Tosi 1743: 92).[10] Tosi, a castrato writing with castratos in mind, becomes quite vehement on the subject, exhorting singers to extemporize all manner of ornaments, from appoggiaturas to elaborate cadenzas. "Poor Italy!" he bemoans,

> pray tell me: do not the singers nowadays know where the appoggiaturas are to be made, unless they are pointed at with a finger? In my time their own knowledge showed it them. Eternal shame to him who first introduced these foreign puerilities into our nation, renowned for teaching others the greater part of the polite arts, particularly that of singing! Oh, how great a weakness in those that follow the example! Oh, injurious insult to your modern singers, who submit to instructions fit for children!" (39–40).

But Agricola intends to advocate for any who wish to be "guided" by the composer. He retorts that, despite what Tosi says, writing out appoggiaturas is the custom, and then he embarks on a lengthy discourse of his own to examine "exactly and comprehensively" (*genauer und vollständiger*) the nature and use of appoggiaturas (1757: 59). And, as for more extended, improvised variations of melodies, he refers the reader to Quantz's list of suggestions in his *Versuch einer Anweisung die Flöte traversiere zu spielen* (1752), an "excellent service" (*vortreffliche Dienste*) from which any singer can benefit (1757: 235).[11]

Tosi may make gestures toward equipping would-be singers with abilities they do not already possess, but for the most part his treatise is directed to those in the know; his true purpose is to launch a vociferous defense of the expressive style of singing.[12] (This becomes especially apparent when near the conclusion he launches into an exaggerated diatribe in the format of an imagined dialogue between himself and a hot-headed junior colleague.[13]) By midcentury in London, Galliard, though downplaying the by-then dated debate between "ancient" and "modern," nevertheless frames Tosi's text as a historical document, describing the author as "a zealous well-wisher to all who distinguished themselves in music, but rigorous to those who abused and degraded the profession" (1743: ix). But roughly two decades later in Berlin, where familiarity with vocal performance was attained through the filter provided by Agricola, singing was discussed through a vocabulary of learning and accessibility. The language is of students, learning, good habits, and foundations; the motivation is to take vocal performance practice and break it down, make it regular, make it predictable—and thereby make it teachable.[14] Agricola plays the role of teaching assistant, translating the inspired but arcane lectures of the erudite professor into language students can understand and make practical use of. One text, three versions: the transformation is signaled by the titles, where "opinions" become "observations" and finally a "guide."

Aspects of vocal performance that could serve as signifiers of the singing style, then, include vibrato, *messa di voce*, legato, dragg, and *rubato*, none of which, incidentally, is mentioned by Ratner. Corri names the same techniques (though he places a significantly stronger emphasis on legato).[15] As was the case in the discourse of Mattheson et alia surrounding vocal composition, vocal performance is articulated as a form of comprehensibility, and to a certain extent, this notion of comprehensibility is equivalent. For example, Tosi (via Galliard) insists that singers must "make the words understood" (1743: 180); if the words are not understood, "the singer deprives the hearer of the greatest part of that delight which vocal music conveys" (59). Agricola goes further: if the words are not heard, the singer "shuts the truth out of art" (*schließt...die Wahrheit von der Kunst aus*; 136). Agricola, likewise, makes his case for correct *rubato* by appealing to the need to be understood: he cautions the singer not to distort the rhythm to the extent that the melody becomes "unclear or unintelligible" (*undeutlich und unverständlich*), that is, incomprehensible (1757: 220). Corri not only includes comprehensibility in his list of requisites ("deliver your words with energy and emphasis, articulate them distinctly, let the countenance be adapted to the subject, and fear not your success") but he also uses the analogy of text-based communication to describe good vocal technique, which "may justly be compared to the highest degree of refinement in elegant pronunciation in speaking" (1810: 4). But to a greater extent, sung performance as signifier increasingly draws on a different notion of comprehensibility, one that connects singing with learning. Singing can be taught. It is at home in the amateur, domestic domain. Concluding his own treatise, Corri steals from Tosi the rhetorical technique of scripted dialogue, but gone are the larger-than-life interlocutors with no common ground; his speakers are a reasonable and respectful "master" and "scholar" with whom the reader can identify.

Finally, this notion of singing introduces an association with the beautiful. While Agricola quotes Hogarth on beauty, Corri quotes lines by Milton prominently highlighted by Edmund Burke in his commentary on "the beautiful in sounds" in the

Philosophical Enquiry: the singing style evokes "notes of linked sweetness long drawn out" (1990: 111). Beauty, as we shall see, will prove to be one of the links between signifier, signified, and topic.

SIGNIFIED

In the *Village Curate* (1788), poet James Hurdis describes how music takes on many shapes, shifting according to context:

> And oft we feel the soul-subduing power
> Of vocal harmony, breath'd softly forth
> And gently swell'd accordant, without aid
> Of quaint embellishment, save only such
> As Nature dictates, and without design
> Lets fall with ease in her impassion'd mood.
> Then serious glee and elegy delight,
> Or pious anthem, such as Croft inspires,
> Or graver Purcel [sic] or endearing Clark.
> The noble harmonies of Brewer, Este,
> Webbe, Baildon, Ravenscroft, we hear
> With ever new delight. Brisk canzonet
> Then pleases, gay duet, or Highland air
> Divinely warbled, and with cadence sweet
> And tender pause prolong'd by one we love,
> Spontaneous and unask'd . . .
> But who shall tell in simple strain like mine
> The many shapes that Music, Proteus-like,
> Puts on, with grateful change of subject, time,
> Contrivance, mood, soothing the captive ear,
> And filling the rapt soul with fare so sweet
> That still it feeds and hungers. (lines 2230–45, 2252–57)

Music's various genres carry specific associations, and Hurdis points in particular to genres of vocal music: the glee and elegy are "serious," the anthem is "pious," and the canzonet "pleases." Yet music is changeable in response to the forces of "subject, time, contrivance [instrument], [and] mood." In a few short lines, then, Hurdis establishes the starting point for—and the challenge involved in—our effort to reveal the home of the singing style. The singing style has a home, that is, a home filled with "rooms" or different genres of song; and yet, music's "Proteus-like" nature necessitates that we understand these rooms as at once unique and fluid. They are rightly categorized, yet when contexts change, they defy neat categorization. To continue the metaphor, the home is in a constant state of remodel: walls between rooms are built up and torn down; passages between rooms are wide and open. With this in mind, we can start excavating the home through the rooms it contains.

We begin with the lied. James Parsons (2004) has done much to clarify the early history of German song, termed "lied" or "ode," especially its genesis in the writings of critic Johann Christoph Gottsched and his followers starting in the 1730s. According to Gottsched in *Versuch einer critischen Dichtkunst für die Deutschen* (1730), setting a poem to music requires a "clear reading" of the "content" of the words (Parsons 2004: 38). This is the by-now familiar definition of song, based on comprehensibility: songs bear meanings that are to be perceived and grasped. But Gottsched has a particular take on what that meaning should be: the "exact observation of nature" (38). Nature is the stuff of which the text should be made. For Gottsched's pupil Scheibe, writing in *Critischer Musikus* later in the same decade, nature (together with order or reason) is the ideal to which the writer should aspire—a manner of composing. Natural melodies stay close to the tonic, adhere to a moderate range, and have a free, flowing manner; a natural melody fits every verse even though the words change (39). Another criterion of Gottsched is simplicity: "everything you write must be modest and simple," he begins his treatise, quoting Horace (38). Scheibe's reiteration of this point prefigures Koch: a natural melody is one that can be "sung at once and without particular effort by anyone inexperienced in music" (39). And in 1749 the poet Johann Peter Uz followed Gottsched by calling for "the likeness of nature, the noble simplicity of unadorned expressions, or the beautiful essence of long ago antiquity" (38). Uz's simplicity is noble simplicity—an oxymoronic and counterintuitive juxtaposition, and yet a highly suggestive one. As Parsons points out, Johann Joachim Winckelmann would famously write in 1755 of the "noble simplicity and quiet grandeur" of Greco-Roman sculpture (35). This is a pairing of oxymorons that—through Uz—we can view as an opposition, for if noble simplicity accords with beauty, then quiet grandeur might be seen as according with the sublime. It is significant, then, that when "noble simplicity" (*edle Einfalt des Gesanges*) is applied to song again, this time by C. P. E. Bach when describing his goals as a composer in an autobiographical sketch (Burney 1773: 209), it is without the quiet grandeur. Viewed through the lens of the lied, the home of the singing style is the realm of nature, simplicity, and beauty.

We do well to start with discourses surrounding the lied, for C. P. E. Bach, Mozart, Haydn, and Beethoven—composers we describe as making use of the singing-style topic in instrumental music—themselves all wrote lieder. But while experience might well incline a composer to incorporate the topic within his instrumental music, so also might general exposure. As the above-quoted passage from James Hurdis indicates, many types of songs were heard alongside one another; Johann Georg Sulzer, likewise, advised that singers "practice all types of songs": they are to them "what dance pieces are to instrumentalists."[16] There is in fact a vast array of types of songs to consider: work songs, evening songs, morning songs, sacred songs, bawdy songs, elegies, lullabies, *Volkslieder, Gassenlieder, Wiegenlieder*, canzonets, ballads, airs, ariettas, cavatinas, pastorals, and the list goes on—just as there are many settings for singing. A "cultural study" (to borrow Monelle's phrase again) refines our understanding of the singing style by both delineating subsets and identifying characteristics in common.

To that end, I turn to a character from Mary Hays's novel *The Victim of Prejudice* (1799): the wholesome Mrs. Neville who sings canzonets, airs, and ballads. The "amiable" Nevilles,

> upon an annual income of sixty pounds, contrived to preserve even an air of liberality. It is true, the product of a well-planted garden, and the profits of a few acres of land, cultivated by the labour of the worthy curate, added something to their yearly store. The morning, lengthened by early rising, was devoted to business, in which equal skill and perseverance were displayed. In the after-part of the day, literature, music, the instruction of their children, a ramble among the neighbouring hamlets, (to the sick and infirm of which they were benevolent friends) a walk on the sea-beach, through the meadows, or on the downs, divided their time. Not an hour passed unimproved or vacant: when confined by inclement seasons to their tranquil home, Mrs. Neville employed herself with her needle in preparing simple vestments for her household, while her husband read aloud selected passages from a small collection of books, which was annually increased by an appropriated sum. Music frequently concluded the evening: Mrs. Neville touched the piano-forte with more feeling than skill, and accompanied by her voice (sweet, but without compass) simple canzonets, impassioned airs, or plaintive ballads. (Hays 1799: 109–11)

Music and measured labor make up the book-ends of the Nevilles' day; both activities, as well as the instruction and exercise that fill the intervening hours, participate in the day's dedication to enrichment, for "not an hour passed unimproved or vacant." While labor is conducted with equal parts skill and effort, and singing is undertaken with more feeling than skill, both are equally undertaken in an atmosphere of enjoyment. Hays sums up: "Through this happy family, perfect harmony and tenderness reigned" (1799: 111) and the metaphor of harmony is reinforced by the presence of actual harmony in keyboard and voice. The contrast to the world outside is stark:

> Happiness, coy and fair fugitive, who shunnest the gaudy pageants of courts and cities, the crowded haunts of vanity, the restless cares of ambition, the insatiable pursuits of avarice, the revels of voluptuousness, and the riot of giddy mirth, who turnest alike from fastidious refinement and brutal ignorance, if, indeed, thou art not a phantom that mockest our research, thou art only to be found in the real solid pleasures of nature and social affection. (112)

Happiness is a "fugitive" or "phantom" only insofar as it is hard to find. It will not be found in vices (vanity, ambition, avarice), of course, nor within excessiveness (the gaudy, crowded, restless, or insatiable). Happiness lies in the "real solid pleasures of nature and social affection."

Singing relates to both. Mrs. Neville's canzonets, airs, and ballads are among the "pleasures of nature" in both Gottsched and Scheibe's sense, for she not only sings after rambling along beaches, meadows, or downs, but she also sings sweetly, not due to practice (which would be tantamount to artifice), but only due to innate, natural ability.[17] As for "social affection," Hays is loosely referring to the Greek *storge*, which indicates what we might today call a kind of involved sociability—a love and sympathy for others developed through familiarity. Happiness is sought but not found in the superficial and abundant interactions of "courts and cities," or "crowded haunts." The Nevilles' happiness derives from repeated, shared experience with one another and with the less fortunate (the "sick and infirm") whom they frequently visit. When Mrs. Neville sings, she brings the family together, engages in a familiar and repeated act (she probably has a repertoire of favorites), and (especially when she sings "plaintive ballads") cultivates those social affections toward pity, sympathy, and charity.

Seven decades later another fictional female plays a variety of types of song at home. When George Eliot's *Middlemarch* character Rosamond makes music, she seems to invert every one of the values exhibited and upheld by Mary Hays's Mrs. Neville:

> Rosamond played admirably. Her master at Mrs. Lemon's school (close to a county town with a memorable history that had its relics in church and castle) was one of those excellent musicians here and there to be found in our provinces, worthy to compare with many a noted Kapellmeister in a country which offers more plentiful conditions of musical celebrity. Rosamond, with the executant's instinct, had seized his manner of playing, and gave forth his large rendering of noble music with the precision of an echo. It was almost startling, heard for the first time . . .
>
> Her singing was less remarkable, but also well trained, and sweet to hear as a chime perfectly in tune. It is true she sang "Meet me by moonlight," and "I've been roaming"; for mortals must share the fashions of their time, and none but the ancients can be always classical. But Rosamond could also sing "Black-eyed Susan" with effect, or Haydn's canzonets, or "Voi che sapete," or "Batti, batti"—she only wanted to know what her audience liked. (Eliot 1874: 117)

Eliot uses music to say a great deal about Rosamond, for it turns out that her musical ability reflects something fundamental about her personality. Not only her singing but her appearance, manners, and actions are "perfectly in tune" with a certain ideal for a young, moneyed woman of marriageable age. She even converses with the "precision of an echo":

> Certainly, small feet and perfectly turned shoulders aid the impression of refined manners, and the right thing said seems quite astonishingly right when it is accompanied with exquisite curves of lip and eyelid. And Rosamond could say the right things; for she was clever with that sort of cleverness which catches every tone except the humorous. Happily she never attempted to joke, and this perhaps was the most decisive mark of her cleverness. (115)

Rosamond's qualities are not innocent and naïve. Hers are shrewd capabilities, deployed strategically within the context of a complicated situation. Upon being asked to describe to her future suitor, Lydgate, what she saw on a recent trip to London, she responds,

> "Very little." (A more naïve girl would have said, "Oh, everything!" But Rosamond knew better.) "A few of the ordinary sights, such as raw country girls are always taken to."
>
> "Do you call yourself a raw country girl?" said Lydgate, looking at her with an involuntary emphasis of admiration, which made Rosamond blush with pleasure. But she remained simply serious, turned her long neck a little, and put up her hand to

touch her wondrous hair-plaits—an habitual gesture with her as pretty as any movements of a kitten's paw. Not that Rosamond was in the least like a kitten: she was sylph caught young and educated at Mrs. Lemon's. (116)

Mrs. Neville and Rosamond differ point for point. Whereas Mrs. Neville is untrained and natural, Rosamond is highly trained (by a master of Kapellmeister quality, no less) and studied, putting her training in service to precisely the "fastidious refinement" and vices (vanity, ambition, and avarice) to which happiness, according to Hays, is opposed. Mrs. Neville sings familiar songs for family; Rosamond sings for an "audience," changing her repertoire according to "what they liked." The nature and social affections with which Mrs. Neville is allied are described as "real" and "solid"; Rosamond is a "sylph"—a mythical figure who is changeable and inconstant. But this is not to say that the signification of singing in *Middlemarch* is new; rather, it is exactly the same, its precise inversion a testament to the clarity, salience, and tenacity of the original. Ultimately Rosamond's sylph-like ability to adapt to—and indeed perfectly fit—circumstances allows her to manipulate her way into a marriage with Lydgate, which she believes, incorrectly, will assure her an affluent lifestyle, and for which both parties are ill-suited. Each spouse is ultimately disappointed by the union, a mismatch based on pretense and false understandings. Rosamond's singing serves as an early clue to its inauthenticity.

Toward Topic

I conclude by way of a review of *Evan's Old Ballads* published in 1810. Its author, Sir Walter Scott, laments the shoddy poetry that has made its way into contemporary song repertoire. To "those who admire music" the collection he is reviewing offers "a means of escaping from the too general pollution":

> But where taste and feeling for poetry happen to be united with a sweet and flexible voice, it is scarcely possible to mention a higher power of imparting and heightening social pleasure. We have heard Dr. Aikin's simple ballad, "It was a winter's evening, and fast came down the snow," set by Dr. Clarke, sung with such beautiful simplicity as to draw tears even from the eyes of reviewers. But the consideration of modern song opens to the critic a stronger ground of complaint, from the degeneracy of the compositions which have been popular under that name. Surely it is time to make some stand against the deluge of nonsense and indecency which as of late supplanted, in the higher circles, the songs of our best poets. We say nothing of the "Nancies of the hills and vales." Peace to all such!—let the miller and apprentice have their ballad, and have it such as they can understand. Let the seaman have his "tight main-decker," and the countess her tinseled canzonet. But when we hear words which convey to every man, and we fear to most of the women in society, a sense beyond what effrontery itself would venture to avow; when we hear such flowing from the lips, or addressed to the ears of unsuspecting innocence, we can barely suppress our execration. This elegant collection presents, to those who admire music, a

means of escaping from the too general pollution, and of indulging a pleasure which we are taught to regard as equally advantageous to the heart, taste, and understanding. (Scott 1835: 135–36)

The present chapter obviously cannot constitute the full-blown "elaborate case study" that the singing style requires (Monelle 2000: 80, cited above), but it sets that study aloft. First, it shows that singing is indeed a cultural theme. It is striking how consistent Scott's account is with that of Hays and Eliot, but the points he raises are the established tropes: beauty and simplicity; the amateur, feminine, private domain; the service to "social pleasure" that, in turn, plays an elevating role "advantageous to the heart, taste, and understanding." Singing may be a cultural theme of many facets and significant breadth, but it is coherent, so when Hays and Eliot's singers sing, we learn—without being explicitly told—a great deal about who they are and how their stories will unfold. Second, we can see that singing is evocative even to the extent that its original signifier can be nearly dispensable. Just as Koch's definition of *singend* dispensed quickly with literal singing by the voice and focused instead on comprehensibility, there is in Scott's review no trace of the actual sound of singing, and just a little trace of the act of singing—the "sweet and flexible voice." Third, we see the free movement of that semiotic unit, performance, shifting between signifier (as in Tosi and his translators) and signified (Hays, Eliot, and Scott). Finally, and most importantly, we are in a position to contest Monelle's dismissal of the singing style on the account of what he calls its "simple signifier" and "less focused signified." On the one hand, the signifier is hardly straightforward, encompassing (as Koch puts it) both the smooth *and* the leaping and the detached. On the other hand, the reason the singing style can encompass such disparate musical attributes and still mean anything specific at all is because its meaning is in fact not limited to musical attributes; it is extramusical. As we have repeatedly seen, from Koch through Mattheson and Tosi's translators, the core of the singing style is comprehensibility. That is to say, perhaps the signifier *is* simple—not in the way Monelle suggests, but in that it always boils down essentially to comprehensibility. The same holds true of the signified, which, given that it covers territory from nature to simplicity, from beauty to sociability—is in fact surprisingly focused, and that focus, again, is on comprehensibility. Hays's and Eliot's notion of comprehensible was the "real" and "solid"; Scott's pivots on the quality of the text. He is not a snob, for he takes pains to clarify that he is not opposed to popular songs per se; he allows the miller and apprentice their ballad, the seaman his sea-song, and the countess her canzonet. What he objects to is "nonsense"—the insensible, the incomprehensible.

Singing is indeed a cultural theme, and the singing style is indeed a topic. It may roam away from the voice to the domains of the feminine, the amateur, domestic space, nature, simplicity, beauty, and sociability—all of which, in turn, are available to migrate in some guise to instrumental music. Further research will trace further associations. But in a succinct yet useful description, it is possible to be even more brief than the deceptively informal, pithy Leonard Ratner was, and point simply to the centrality of comprehensibility to the singing style.

NOTES

1. Unless otherwise noted, all translations are my own. I am grateful to Neil Blackadder for his suggestions regarding the translation of this passage and the block quote from Mattheson, below.

2. Türk (1789: 115) defines *cantabile* as *singend*.

3. For example, Quantz uses the terms "light" (*leicht*) and "calm" (*gelassen*) to describe the bow stroke in a *cantabile* (1752: 200). Reilly translates *leicht* as quiet, which is colloquial among string players; one should prevent the mechanism of the bow from being audible (1966: 231).

4. A third signifier would be the voice itself, particularly its timbre. I focus on vocal melodies and vocal performance practice here and leave the fascinating area of timbral semiotics to future research.

5. "Wird er aber auf eine edlere Art gerühret, und will auch andre mit der Harmonie rühren, so muß er wahrhafftig alle Neigungen des Herzens, durch blosse ausgesuchte Klänge und deren geschickte Zusammenfügung, ohne Worte dergestalt auszudrucken wissen, dass der Zuhörer daraus, als ob es seine wirckliche Rede wäre, den Trieb, den Sinn, die Meinung und den Nachdruck, mit allen dazu gehörigen Ein- und Abschnitten, völlig begreiffen und deutlich verstehen möge. Alsdenn ist es eine Lust! Dazu gehöret viel mehr Kunst und eine stärckere Einbildungs-krafft, wenns einer ohne Worte, als mit derselben hülffe, zu Wege bringen soll" (Mattheson 1739: 207–8).

6. "Die alten Teutschen pflegten zu sagen, man könne es einer Sau gleich anmercken, wenn sie sich einmahl an eine Schulwand gerieben hat" (Mattheson 1739: 105).

7. For the most part, Tosi terms expressive singing "pathetic," but when he uses *cantabile* it is clear that he considers the terms interchangeable. Galliard typically keeps *cantabile*, but Agricola substitutes more colloquial terms such as "tender" (*zärtlich*), "a singing style" (*singendes Wesen*), and "pleasing and flattering arias" (*gefälligen und schmeichelnden Arien*; 1757: 183, 196, 200). Agricola explains that

> in a general sense, pathetic means everything that is filled with strong passion. So even fast, even furioso arias can, in a certain sense, be termed pathetic. There is also a convention introduced in Italy, of specially identifying as pathetic arias those slow arias that express a high degree of tender, sad, or otherwise lofty serious emotions: the performer can typically recognize this style in only a glance when the descriptions adagio, largo, lento, mesto, grave, etc., are given.

> Pathetisch heißt zwar, in seinem allgemeinen Verstande, alles was voll starker Leidenschaften ist. Also könnte auch eine geschwinde, ja gar furiose Arie in gewisser Art pathetisch genennet werden. Der Gebrauch hat aber, zumal in Wälschland, eingeführet, daß man, in besonderm Verstande, die langsamen Arien, welche gemeiniglich Ausdrück in hohem Grade zärtlicher oder trauriger, oder sonst sehr erhaben ernsthafter Empfindungen sind, und mehrentheils durch die Beiwörter adagio, largo, lento, mesto, grave, u.d.g. den Ausführern ihren Charakter beim ersten Anblicke zu erkennen geben, mit dem Namen pathetischer Arien beleget. (Agricola 1757: 183)

8. The standard and most comprehensive study of *tempo rubato* is Hudson (1994).

9. This interjection appears as part of a lengthy commentary on trills, implying that Agricola understood vibrato as an ornament. It is also significant that Agricola defines vocal vibrato

by comparing it to vibrato on a string instrument; if string vibrato is essentially a reference to a human voice, Agricola is using a *topic* to explain its own signifier.

10. Tosi is in fact ambivalent on this point. In Galliard's translation: "let a Scholar provide himself with a Variety of Graces and Embellishments and then let him make use of them with Judgment; for, if he observes, he will find that the most celebrated Singers never make a Parade of their Talent in a few songs, well knowing that if Singers expose to the Publick all they have in their Shops they are near becoming Bankrupts" (1743: 95–96).

11. While Tosi favors spontaneous ornamentation, he also urges the singer to avoid excessive ornamentation and thereby preserve music in its "chastity" (1743: 98) and its "established and chaste" (*gesetztes und züchtiges*) nature (Agricola 1757: 176). The connection of expressive singing and purity/chastity is one that Corri will perpetuate when he accuses audiences of having been "seduced" by the "decorated style" of "excessive and improper ornamentation" (1810: 2). While the call for unadorned simplicity in expressive singing may have been for Tosi mostly rhetoric, theory did in fact become practice in the nineteenth century: Clive Brown (1999: 374) points out that in Charles Dibdin's first edition of his *Music Epitomized*, cantabile indicated the "introduction of extempore ideas gracefully" (1808: 67); by the ninth edition *cantabile* indicated "in a singing style" (1820: 41).

12. The vehemence of Tosi's defense of *cantabile* obscures his apparently more balanced view. He asserts that "the Ancients' taste was in fact for a mixture of the lively and the tender" (1743: 183); "if the Moderns would only attend a little more to the expressive and a little less to passagework, they could congratulate themselves for having brought singing to the highest degree of perfection" (184). Tosi also advocated practicing the rapid runs and divisions of the modern style, since the benefit of such exercise would be an agile and therefore "obedient" (*gehorsam*) voice in the pathetic; the singer should strive to be "more master than slave" (*mehr Gebieter als Sclave*) of his voice "if he wishes to be called a pathetic-style singer" (166).

13. The firestorm is ignited inconspicuously enough by an apparently civil question: in what tonality (i.e., major or minor) is your composition? But the hot-headed modern responds:

What tonality? What tonality?...The modern school, in case you do not know it, does not concern itself with tonality...In your time the world slept, and you should not be offended if our exceptionally singular style has reawakened it through mirth that pleases the heart and makes the foot want to dance...It is true that we have an irrefutable law among us to ban the pathetic forever, since we hate sadness...If a singer does not hold with our guild, he will surely find no protector to even look at him or pay the slightest bit of attention to him. But tell me (since we are speaking in confidence with sincerity on our lips), who can sing or compose well without having had our approval beforehand? No matter how much merit he has (as you know), we do not lack the means to bring him down. Yes, only a few syllables are necessary to bring down all of his merits: he is old fashioned...Oh, how beautiful is our style of composing! It forces none of us to the tedious learning of the rules; it does not trouble the soul with thinking; and it does not give us the illusion that makes us want to put into practice everything that we might have discovered through much racking of the brain...and it finds enough admirers who treasure it and are willing to pay richly for it. (Baird 1995: 201–3)

14. Presumably because he associates the pathetic with the singing style, Agricola objects to Tosi's claim that the pathetic is lost (1757: 184).

15. Corri developed a unique notation to indicate where singers should breathe, implying that phrases should always be connected between breaths.

16. "Dem angehenden Sänger rathen wir, sich unabläßig in dem guten Vortrag aller Arten von Liedern zu üben: sie sind in allen Absichten für ihn eben das, was die Tanzstücke den Spielern sind, und bedürfen daher keiner weitern Anpreisung" (Sulzer 1792–94, 4: 712).

17. Mrs. Neville's natural style of playing recalls Hurdis's description of the canzonet, duet, and air, for these genres are "warbled" (1788: line 2243) as if by birds of nature, and their cadences are prolonged, as Tosi would have advocated, with ornaments apparently "spontaneous and unasked" (line 2245).

REFERENCES

Agawu, Kofi. 2008. Topic Theory: Achievement, Critique, Prospects. In *Passagen, IMS Kongress Zürich 2007: Fünf Hauptvorträge, Five Key Note Speeches,* ed. Laurenz Lütteken and Hans-Joachim Hinrichsen, 38–69. Kassel: Bärenreiter.

Agricola, Johann Friedrich. 1757. *Anleitung zur Singkunst.* Berlin: George Ludewig Winter.

Baird, Julianne C. 1995. *Introduction to the Art of Singing by Johann Friedrich Agricola.* Cambridge: Cambridge University Press.

Brossard, Sébastien de. 1703. *Dictionnaire de musique.* Paris: Christophe Ballard.

Brown, Clive. 1999. *Classical and Romantic Performing Practice 1750–1900.* Oxford: Oxford University Press.

Burke, Edmund. 1990. *A Philosophical Enquiry into the Origin of Our Ideas of the Sublime and Beautiful,* ed. Adam Phillips. Oxford: Oxford University Press.

Burney, Charles. 1773. *Tagebuch einer musikalischen Reise.* Berlin: Bode.

Corri, Domenico. 1810. *The Singer's Preceptor.* London: Chappell.

Daube, Johann F. 1797. *Anleitung zur Erfindung der Melodie und ihrer Fortsetzung.* Vienna: Täubel.

Dibdin, Charles. 1808. *Music Epitomized: A School Book in Which the Whole Science of Music Is Completely Explained.* London: Author.

———. 1820. *Music Epitomized: A School Book in Which the Whole Science of Music Is Completely Explained,* 6th ed. revised and corrected by Jean Jousse. London: Goulding.

Eliot, George. 1874. *Middlemarch: A Study in Provincial Life.* New one volume ed. Edinburgh and London: William Blackwood.

Gottsched, Johann Christoph. 1730. *Versuch einer critischen Dichtkunst für die Deutschen,* 4th ed. Leipzig: Bernhard Christoph Breitkopf.

Hays, Mary. 1799. *The Victim of Prejudice.* London: Johnson.

Hogarth, William. 1753. *The Analysis of Beauty.* London: Reeves.

Hudson, Richard. 1994. *Stolen Time: A History of Tempo Rubato.* Oxford: Clarendon.

Hurdis, James. 1788. *The Village Curate.* London: Johnson.

Koch, Heinrich Christoph. 1802. *Musikalisches Lexikon.* Frankfurt am Main: August Hermann der Jüngere.

Mattheson, Johann. 1713. *Das Neu-Eröffnete Orchestre.* Hamburg: Benjamin Schillers Witwe.

———. 1739. *Der vollkommene Capellmeister.* Hamburg: Christian Herold.

Monelle, Raymond. 2000. *The Sense of Music.* Princeton: Princeton University Press.

———. 2006. *The Musical Topic: Hunt, Military and Pastoral.* Bloomington: Indiana University Press.

Parsons, James. 2004. The Eighteenth-Century Lied. In *The Cambridge Companion to the Lied*, ed. James Parsons, 35–62. Cambridge: Cambridge University Press.

Quantz, Johann Joachim. 1752. *Versuch einer Anweisung die Flöte traversiere zu spielen*. Berlin: Johann Friedrich Voss.

——. 1966. *On Playing the Flute*. Trans. Edward R. Reilly. London: Faber and Faber.

Ratner, Leonard G. 1980. *Classic Music: Expression, Form, and Style*. New York: Schirmer.

Scheibe, Johann Adolph. 1745. *Critischer Musikus*. Leipzig: Bernhard Christoph Breitkopf.

Scott, Sir Walter. 1835. Article 6: Evans's Old Ballads. In *The Prose Works of Sir Walter Scott*, vol. 17, 119–36. Edinburgh: Robert Cadell; London: Whittaker.

Sulzer, Johann Georg. 1792–94. *Allgemeine Theorie der schönen Künste*, new expanded 2nd ed. 4 vols. Leipzig: Weidmann.

Tosi, Pier Francesco. 1723. *Opinioni de' cantori antichi e moderni*. Bologna: L. della Volpe.

——. 1743. *Observations on the Florid Song; or, Sentiments on the Ancient and Modern Singers, Written in Italian by Pier Francesco Tosi*. Trans. John Ernest Galliard, 2nd ed. London: Wilcox.

Türk, Daniel Gottlob. 1789. *Klavierschule, oder Anweisung zum Klavierspielen für Lehrer und Lernende*. Leipzig: Schwickert und Hemmerde.

CHAPTER 9

....

FANTASIA AND SENSIBILITY

....

MATTHEW HEAD

Fantasia

....

RATNER (1980) introduced the "fantasia style" as if, like a dance, it were a type of material specific to the fantasia and recognizable in other genres as a metamusical allusion.
However, Ratner's gloss on and use of this putative topic contradicts that premise. In
detailing the "fantasia style" he lists elements of style (some imprecisely defined) that
self-evidently belong to several genres, vocal and instrumental: "The *fantasia* style is
recognized by one or more of the following features—elaborate figuration, shifting harmonies, chromatic conjunct bass lines, sudden contrasts, full textures or disembodied
melodic figures." As the definition continues, Ratner shifts the focus away from stylistic elements to an aesthetic illusion of improvisation and narrative wandering, specifically "a sense of improvisation and loose structural links between figures and phrases"
(Ratner 1980: 24).

The vagueness of Ratner's discussion has inspired attempts to crystallize a fantasia
topic, as if the challenge were to wrest musical concreteness from a hasty or provisional
starting point. Although not fruitless, these attempts create new problems by tidying
away ambiguity and imposing artificial boundaries. Moyer (1992) rightly objected to
Ratner's sweeping statement that "the *fantasia* style is used to evoke the supernatural" in
opera (1980: 24). Productively, she distinguished in principle between the fantasia as an
improvised or improvisatory piece and operatic supernaturalism that sought to evoke
"man's terror and awe of hell" through elevated and majestic orchestral texture and
rhythm (Moyer 1992: 283). But the distinction proves too categorical, and Moyer's discussion (inadvertently) marks affinities between the fantasia and *ombra*. For example,
she describes the fourth movement ("La Malinconia") of Beethoven's String Quartet in B
flat major, Op. 18 No. 4, as "a fantasia in spirit if not in name," while also highlighting its
"otherworldly *pianissimos*" in mm. 12–20, as if the fantasia and the otherworldly discovered their affinity in strangeness of dynamic level. Subsequently she refers to dynamic
contrasts in this nine-measure passage as "a good example of the improvisatory style"

(304), the same passage thus described in terms of both fantasia and *ombra*. Similarly, in asserting the *ombra* style of Mozart's Piano Concerto in D minor, K. 466/i, Moyer provides an analytical diagram that takes the form of a figured-bass skeleton reminiscent of those in C. P. E. Bach's discussion of the free fantasia in the last chapter of the *Versuch über die wahre Art das Clavier zu spielen* (Bach 1762: 325–41).

There are music-historical reasons for these and other ambiguities about the boundaries and topical makeup of Ratner's "fantasia style." Opera, accompanied recitative and (what has become known as) *ombra* were models for the emerging genre of the free fantasia, a genre defined by C. P. E. Bach in the first part of his *Versuch* (1753). Here Bach advocated "the declamatory style," a potently emotional but also erudite keyboard idiom that emulated the melodic accents, metrical freedom and wide-ranging modulations of "accompanied recitative" (Bach 1974: 153). His earliest surviving free fantasia, H. 339 in E flat major (composed by 1749), contains extended passages modeled literally on accompanied recitative, a texture the composer later refined into a supple, soliloquizing idiom. In opera seria, accompanied recitative was associated with moments of emotional turmoil and with the internalized supernaturalism of hallucination. Indeed, the term *ombra* was coined in 1908 by Hermann Abert in a study of accompanied recitatives in Jommelli's operas in which deranged characters "see" ghosts of departed or absent loved ones (see Clive McClelland, Chapter 10, this volume). It is no surprise that when the poet Gerstenberg sought texts for C. P. E. Bach's Free Fantasia in C minor, H. 75 (1753), he turned to the genre of the suicide soliloquy, adapting Hamlet's "To be, or not to be" and inventing for Socrates a philosophical rumination on life, death, and hemlock. These texts, though not literally supernaturalizing the music, located the free fantasia at the boundary of life and death. Gerstenberg's choice of subjects reveals sensitivity to the monologic, theatrical, and death-haunted aspects of the free fantasia that (in Bach's hands) drew on the Baroque tradition of *tombeau* (Wiemer 1988, with reference to *Free Fantasia* in C minor, H. 75) and *memento mori* (Poos 1988, with reference to *Free Fantasia* in F sharp minor, H. 300).

The haunting gloom of H. 75 and H. 300 notwithstanding, Bach's fantasias encompass diverse styles and generic motives. Head (1995) argued that the fantasia was not a topic so much as a *locus classicus* of C. P. E. Bach's aesthetic and technical practice as a musician. This assertion drew on several types of evidence, chiefly the comments of contemporary theorists and the range of pieces that Bach titled fantasia. Kirnberger (a coauthor of music articles in the *Allgemeine Theorie der schönen Künste*) observed in the article "Fantasiren; Fantasie" that "several fantasias wander from one genre to another" (*einige Fantasien schweiffen von einer Gattung in die andre aus*; Sulzer 1771: 368). Kollmann, who deemed this license to roam a paradoxical rule of fantasias, admonished that "it would be as improper to pay no regard to any style at all, as to confine the fancy to one fixed style. For the former would betray a want of consideration, and the latter render the fancy limited" (1796: 272). As for Bach's fantasias, many are miniatures, not extended rhapsodies. They include solfeggio-like finger-studies (H. 195, H. 223, and H. 224, all from 1766); whimsical dances (H. 141 from 1759 with its minuet and sarabande topics); a rococo march encrusted with ornaments and dotted rhythms (H. 146 also from 1759);

and free fantasias in miniature (H. 148 from 1759, and H. 234 from 1767). Some of the late "free" fantasias from the six volumes of *Clavier-Sonaten und freye Fantasien nebst einigen Rondos...für Kenner und Liebhaber* (1779–87) employ clear themes, are almost entirely measured, contain little recitative-like texture, and employ both rondo and sonata forms in a seemingly conscious effort to hybridize the different genres included in the collections. Nonetheless it is reasonable to posit a fantasia topic in the more limited sense of a distinctive type of material at home in improvisatory keyboard works and recognizable in other contexts. Following Bach's *Versuch*, fantasias were distinctive in their use of passages of generic figuration (arpeggiations, scales, broken chords) elaborating harmonic progressions that can be expressed as figured bass. These progressions typically involve abrupt, remote, and evaded modulations, achieved through chromaticism, enharmony, and the diminished seventh chord. This restricted definition is far removed from Ratner's proposal that the fantasia style is present throughout Classic music as a pervasive "sense of improvisation" (1980: 24). For Ratner, this sense of improvisation consisted in "freedom of action," and, as his example from the end of the second movement of Haydn's String Quartet in D minor Op. 76 No. 2 implies, "freedom of action" involves narrative effects of digression, interruption, and wandering. The way in which uncertainty and apparent spontaneity in thematic and harmonic action are contained within conventional patterns is strongly implied by the larger context of Ratner's argument. Wollenberg (2007), returning to Bach's *Versuch*, emphasizes how a sense of improvisation arises from the composer's erudite and orderly harmonic technique. Resisting the metaphors of disorder and freedom endemic to modern thinking about the fantasia, she stresses how Bach's fantasias generate and frustrate expectation through underlying figured-bass progressions enriched with "rational deceptions." Wollenberg wisely avoids speaking of the influence of the fantasia on other genres, even as she suggests that the narrative thread of Bach's esoteric harmonic art offered a path through the less charted territory of the emerging solo keyboard sonata. Webster (2007), building on Ratner (1980) and Head (1995), proposes a typology of what he calls "improvisatory rhetoric" in Haydn's music, rhetoric that he also proposes as "the topos of improvising." Not all examples of this improvisatory topos are related to the fantasia specifically: Webster includes notated passages that would otherwise be improvised by the performer, such as the varied reprise in sonata movements, embellished returns of rondo refrains, cadenzas, and modulatory transitions between movements. Resemblance to (some version of) the fantasia, involving, for example, continuous, contrastive forms, is posited as a subtype of the improvisatory topos. The link to rhetoric, though inevitably a part of topic as an intellectual construct, comes to the fore in Webster's third variant of the "improvisatory topos" in which Haydn is said to create "the impression of excessive freedom, unmotivated contrast, or insufficient coherence" in the musical narrative (2007: 175–76). This interpretation follows not only the detail of Ratner's "fantasia style" but also its broader import. Just as, for Ratner, the "fantasia...[is] sensed...in unexpected, even eccentric turns," and "colored and placed a personal stamp upon the individual styles of classic composers, giving a fresh twist and new vitality to the familiar clichés of the eighteenth-century musical vocabulary" (Ratner

1980: 314), so Webster ultimately declares the improvisatory topic a source of Haydn's individuality and a pervasive feature of his music (Webster 2007: 210).

Though framed in quasi-empirical terms, and seemingly grounded in the analysis of genre and style, such comments belong to the domain of hermeneutics. In other words, to describe much of Haydn's music (or that of C. P. E. Bach) as improvisatory is a highly interpretive move. Topic theory, though not narrowly historicist, does seek substantiation in terms of the eighteenth-century critical landscape, and so it is appropriate to ask whether contemporaries concurred with the views expressed (but not restricted to) Ratner and Webster. (I say "not restricted to" because notions that a piece of music is *quasi una fantasia* and, correspondingly, should be played as if created afresh are deeply embedded in the culture of Western art music to this day). Curiously, these ideas have almost no currency in the second half of the eighteenth century: I have failed to spot a single instance in which a reviewer or composer employed the idea of the improvisatory (specifically), or of the influence of the fantasia, to explain features that are now, almost self-evidently, regarded by musicians as "fantasia-like" or improvisatory. Only at the end of the century did the German-born theorist Kollmann redeploy the term "fancy" (through which he designated fantasias to his English readership) to describe a digressive phrase—the "fancy period"—in which "the composer seems to lose himself in the modulation [i.e., the harmonic progression], for the purpose of making the ear more attentive to the resolution of the period" (1796: 171).

As a concept, Kollmann's "fancy period" anticipated an explosion in analogies between the fantasia and other types of piece in German criticism of the early nineteenth century. Beethoven famously employed the analogy *quasi una fantasia* for the sonatas Op. 27 (1801). After the Viennese premiere of the "Eroica" Symphony, an anonymous reviewer described the piece in 1804 as "a very far-fetched, bold and wild fantasia." By 1817 the critic Gerber complained of a crisis of genre in contemporary music in which sonatas, overtures, and symphonies—"at least those by Beethoven and his crowd"—resemble fantasias (Head 1995: 76). Thus the idea of art music in the grip of the fantasia is an early nineteenth-century refrain and served, in that historical moment, to signal departures from customary limits, decorum, and generic norms. There is an irony in Ratner's recourse to this idea given his broader project of deromanticizing later eighteenth-century music. I say "irony" not only because of the romantic provenance of the idea but also because, insofar as it lends agency to a musical genre that is felt to seize control of other pieces "like a despot" (in Gerber's formulation), it belongs to an idealist metaphysics of music that Ratner's *Classic Music* seeks to dispel. It is idealist because it grants agency to music as if it were a living thing, mediated but not authored by human actors. In both positive and negative uses of the fantasia metaphor in the early nineteenth century, "music" is said to transcend worldly boundaries, the decorum of genre, the formalities of composition with pen and paper. The epithet *quasi una fantasia* hinted that the music was not consciously composed so much as self-generated in the composer's imagination.

Music criticism of the later eighteenth century reveals a different order of thought. Genres were not rigid or unchanging but they were essential contexts for music to be meaningful in the sense of possessing any social and artistic value. Critics and composers did not speak of one musical genre influencing another (even if, to more modern ears, that is what seems to be happening in the music). This is remarkable, given that critics were rich in metaphors: in music reviewing and pedagogy, culinary, sartorial, and travel analogies abounded, alongside comparisons between music and the arts of landscape, literature, and painting (see Morrow 1997 and Richards 2001). The path of interpretation led not from one musical genre to another but from music to other (nonmusical) domains of human activity and experience. Music criticism was alive to features that would subsequently be understood in terms of the fantasia—features such as Ratner's "unexpected, even eccentric turns" of theme and harmony—but explained those features in terms of the composer. Viewed negatively, such features were deemed signs of incompetence or of striving after absent originality. Viewed positively, they testified to the composer's individual personality.

Thus Ratner's "fantasia," which he ultimately enshrines as *Classic Music*'s expressive, animating force "thrusting against rhythmic and harmonic controls with digressions and melodic elaborations" (1980: 233), is an anachronistic name for what the late eighteenth century called original genius or, in North-German reviews, identified simply as "Haydn" and "C. P. E. Bach" (on the reviews, see Morrow 1997). Not improvisation, nor the fantasia, but the composer's individuality explained those departures from "the familiar clichés of the eighteenth-century musical vocabulary" that Ratner attributes to the pervasive influence of the fantasia (Ratner 1980: 233). One of the reasons Ratner does not define his fantasia topic precisely (even as he introduces it under the heading of topic) is that he uses it as a broad and redemptive presence: it resembles the Dionysian force of Romantic musical aesthetics and, as a source of originality, it enables Ratner to preserve some possibility of compositional originality within a critical framework otherwise poorly equipped to explain the greatness of the great composers. At times, as when the fantasia topic is said "to impart warmth and expressive color to the style" (233), it resembles something approaching music as a whole, at least within the ruling ideas of expressiveness with which Ratner begins—and to which this essay now turns.

Sensibility

While affirming the centrality of expression to the Classical style in his opening chapter, and noting the emotional character of several of the musical topics presented in chapter two, Ratner's concern with the expressive ambitions of late eighteenth-century music flickers off and on through *Classic Music*. The first sentence of the book announces music's aspiration to stir feelings—"expression was an ever-present concern in 18th-century musical thought and practice" (1980: 1)—but the expressive characteristics of forms, harmonic tours, styles, and topics do not form a consistent focus, and it is unclear whether they are always part of music's "expressive concerns" or (to follow Koch's *Versuch*) a "mechanical" aspect.

In this context, where expression both is and is not the central issue of the Classical style, Ratner offers two topics devoted to the cause of expression: sensibility (or *Empfindsamkeit*) and *Sturm und Drang*. These form a pair (they are neighbors in chapter 2), enshrining two modes of feeling. The "sensibility" topic, Ratner advises, is an "intimate personal style," involving "rapid changes of mood…directly opposed to the statuesque unity of baroque music" (1980: 22). Mercurial, he implies, but not violent or blustering: his example from Mozart's Fantasia in D minor, K. 397 (1782), displays "a plaintive melody, broken by sighing figures" (Ratner 1980: 22). In other words, Ratner's sensibility topic is distinguished by tearful, trembling fragility. *Sturm und Drang* is a more turbulent, even thrusting complement, marked by storminess, "driving rhythms…sharp dissonances, and an impassioned style of declamation" (Ratner 1980: 21). It is central to the music of "Beethoven [and] Cherubini"—a cipher, perhaps, for revolutionary and heroic verve. Perhaps Ratner found it useful to make a clear distinction: musicology has often equated these categories. But whether they are deemed discrete or overlapping is hardly the point: neither label was used to describe musical style in the eighteenth century, though even as authoritative a source as *New Grove 2* claims in error that *empfindsamer Styl* was a period designation (Heartz and Brown 2001). Ratner's sensibility topic makes an error of categorization by attributing to musical material that sensitivity to feeling that belonged to contemporary conceptions of the human.

"Sensibility" (the term explored in this essay) referred to human disposition, not to musical materials. It identified a capacity to respond with pleasure or pain, with feeling, and with self-awareness to the impressions made on the body and mind by the senses. Consciousness, subjectivity, and reflexivity are key terms in conceptualizing sensibility, which referred not simply to a capacity to be moved but also to an awareness of that capacity and its moral obligations. In natural philosophy and medicine it referred to "the psychoperceptual scheme explained and systematized by Newton and Locke…[specifically] the operation of the nervous system, the material basis of consciousness" (Barker-Benfield 1992: xvii). As such, sensibility referred to all perception and sensation, but in the course of the eighteenth century the term came to describe feelings and emotions specifically (Goehring 1997: 119). In parallel developments, the nervous system replaced an older model of the humors in the physiology of sensibility, a vocabulary of "sentiment," "feeling," and "emotion" gradually superseded that of "affect" and "passion," and emotions were understood not as fixed and relatively stable but as subject to constant fluctuations in intensity, rapid change, and paradoxical combination. These related changes are evident in the compositional titles of C. P. E. Bach. The Trio Sonata in C minor, H. 579, composed in 1749, was published two years later with a clunky humoral subtitle, "Sanguineus und Melancholicus," and a program that personified the upper parts as (initially stubbornly opposed) affects. Almost forty years later, in 1787, when Bach arranged his Free Fantasia in F sharp minor, H. 300 for publication by adding a ghostly accompaniment for violin (H. 536), he subtitled the piece *C. P. E. Bachs Empfindungen*, a locution (literally meaning "C. P. E. Bach's Sentiments") apt to evoke the restless, ruminative, and sometimes bafflingly incongruous emotions revealed in and fueling improvisatory confessions. Another way of describing the change is to speak of a movement from a manifestly distanced representational apparatus that treats the passions as rationalized, even impersonal states, to (at least an illusion of) first-person immediacy and autobiography.

Sensibility, though often treated as a literary fashion beginning with Samuel Richardson's epistolary novel *Pamela*, was more broadly the subject matter of the fine arts and their theoretical branch, aesthetics. Against the backdrop of a stigmatization of the passions in natural philosophy of the late seventeenth and early eighteenth centuries—in Germany, the rationalist philosopher Christian Wolff (1720) influentially figured the passions as enslaving and irrational—the arts were charged with understanding the realm of sensibility, refining it, and directing it to moral ends. In an archaeology of the term sensibility, Cowart (1984) highlights a (then controversial) recourse to instinct, or *sentiment intérieur*, in French debates of the late seventeenth and early eighteenth century over the basis of aesthetic judgment. Against a neoclassical doctrine that attributed beauty in the arts to rules derived from antiquity—a doctrine expounded by Boileau and Batteaux in France and by Gottsched and Scheibe in Germany—subjectivists such as the Chevalier de Méré attributed taste (*bon goût*) to a sensation or feeling for the beautiful that bypassed rational appraisal (Cowart 1984: 252–53; Baker and Christensen 1995: 1–2). The productive tension between a "rational" and rule-based knowledge of the arts, on the one hand, and an understanding based on sensibility (on how art is felt, experienced, and accorded subjective significance), on the other, was captured in the discipline of aesthetics (so named by Baumgarten in 1750), which sought (as Sulzer put it in 1771) "the theory of indistinct knowledge and feelings" (Baker and Christensen 1995: 25). Sensibility, in this broad sense, was not a musical topic, a style, or a period but the capacity to experience sensations and feelings and thus a foundational concern of art.

Throughout the eighteenth century, music was often accorded a special power to awaken sensibility, a fact that complicates recent attempts to define a "period" or "movement" of sensibility between roughly 1760 and 1780 (as proposed in Webster 2004). Initially, this "marvelous power to move us" was explained through the vocabulary of mimesis: "The musician imitates the tones, accents, sighs, [and] inflections of the voice" (DuBos 1994: 324–35). To modern eyes, the notion of imitation seems to render music's expressiveness secondhand and thus different in kind from the immediacy associated today with music and sensibility (in German, variously, *Empfindlichkeit* and *Empfindsamkeit*). But, as Hosler (1981) advised, the distinction between imitative and expressive paradigms, derived from literary history (especially Abrams 1953), is a misleading framework for eighteenth-century musical aesthetics. As DuBos influentially argued, the "signs of the passions" employed by musicians are "those [same] sounds with which nature [the human voice] itself expresses its sentiments and passions" (DuBos 1994: 324). In other words, music is not a man-made language involving arbitrary signs (words) that must be decoded, but a natural language of feeling. Music is mimetic only in the sense that the original cry of passion is mimetic, too—a gesture communicating what is being felt. It is evident from Jean-Jacques Rousseau's article "Expression" in his *Dictionnaire de musique* that music could be conceptualized as mimetic—indeed Rousseau sends musicians off to the theater to listen to actors declaim—and also so powerful in its effects that it transports and intoxicates (Rousseau 1775: 333–43).

Later writers found additional ways of explaining the reported immediacy and naturalness of music's effects. While not abandoning mimetic terminology completely, they understood music to operate directly on the nervous fibers of the body. In this mechanistic, sensual view, music, like emotion, is movement. Sulzer spelled this out to his readers: "Every passion is actually a series of moving impressions. This is already revealed by the phrase we use to express passion: the movement of the emotions [*Gemüthsbewegung*]" (Baker and Christensen 1995: 52). Sulzer and his coauthors sometimes employed this mechanistic, nerve-based explanation of why "hearing is the most effective sense for awakening the emotions" (Baker and Christensen 1995: 81). In the article "Musik" they asserted that "nature has established a direct connection between the ear and heart...the material that affects the aural nerves—air—is much coarser and more physical than ethereal light, which affects the eye. The aural nerves consequently transmit to the entire body the impact of the shock they receive" (Baker and Christensen 1995: 81–82). At other times, however, they explained music's expressive effects through the vocabulary of mimesis: "The composer [must be] sufficiently accomplished and possess enough knowledge to imitate these movements [of the emotions] in harmony and melody" (Baker and Christensen 1995: 52). Such remarks were offered without any sense that a composer's consciously mimetic authorship jeopardized the immediacy and power of musical expression. In the pages of Sulzer's encyclopedia, rational theories of musical composition exist alongside fantasies of music as operating directly on the body, and even an ontological fantasy of music *as* emotion. In the article "Sonate," in which readers learn of sonatas' suitability to rousing a variety of sentiments because the genre possesses no fixed character, Schulz praised C. P. E. Bach's Trio Sonata in C minor, H. 579, "Melancholicus and Sanguineus," as a model of "passionate conversations in tones," even though (as noted above) the piece is framed by the composer in terms of a theory of humors.

Thus the idea that music was particularly suited to rousing what were variously termed affects, passions, sentiments, feelings, and emotions was a central aesthetic precept that cannot be contained within a specific phase of eighteenth-century musical history or a particular musical genre or style. Musicians and theorists even had a term for this basic aspect of music: pathetics. Musical pathetics concerned moving the audience. The term (which has escaped musicological attention) derived from Classical rhetoric, where the art of persuasion included two classes of argument: those appealing to logic and those appealing to emotion. The latter were pathetic arguments, and, insofar as they were effective, they resulted in intense feelings that elicited sympathetic identification. A standard reference work for the English-speaking eighteenth century—Ephraim Chambers's *Cyclopaedia* (1728)—defined "pathetic" as "something that relates to the passions; and particularly that is proper to awake or excite them" (Chambers 1728, 2: 764). In this sense, music was in essence a pathetic art. Indeed, the next entry in the *Cyclopaedia* essentially equates music and pathetics, while acknowledging that composers also have ways of intensifying expressive impact (in this case through chromaticism and dissonance):

> PATHETIC, in music, something very moving, expressive, or passionate; capable of exciting pity, compassion, anger or the like. In this sense we say the *pathetic* style, a *pathetic* fugue, *pathetic* song, etc. The chromatic genus, with its greater and lesser semi-tones, either ascending or descending, is very proper for the *pathetic;* as is also an artful management of discords; with a variety of motions, now brisk, now languishing, now swift, now slow. Nieuwentyt tells us of a musician at Venice, who excelled in the *pathetic* to that degree, that he was able to play any of his auditors into distraction: he adds, that the great means he made use of, was the variety of motions, etc. (Chambers 1728, 2: 764)

In his *Dictionnaire de musique*, Rousseau employed the term "pathetic" in two overlapping senses to mean both the expressive accents of melody in general and a tenderness, even sadness, in particular. Throughout the century, the idea that music became meaningful through its pathetic power served as an evaluative standard in arguments over music's origins and history, the merits of national styles and genres, and the achievements of individual composers and performers. The "discovery" that music moves authorized critiques of mathematical rationalizations of music (the Pythagorean tradition), of compositional artifice (such as learned counterpoint and the modern system of harmony), and of "mechanical" virtuosity in performance. In sociological terms, the emphasis on music's capacity to move tended to valorize amateur and bourgeois musical practice, privilege performance and listening over composing, validate relatively untutored musical response over professional and technical appraisal, and lend music sensual, even erotic, power.

Confusion potentially arises, however, in multidisciplinary times because (following Northrop Frye 1956) the term "sensibility" is used in studies of English literature to denote a phase between c. 1740–1789: a phase that used to be called "pre-Romanticism." Emphasizing emotional responsiveness, particularly to the suffering of others, sensibility, in this context, fostered fellow feeling and officially acted as a moral guide, a source of sympathetic tears, and a spur to good deeds. A wide range of literary genres thematized and sought to stimulate sensibility: the epistolary novel featuring female virtue distressed, undone, and triumphant; odes and other poetic apostrophes to fear and melancholy; the rough, passionate verse and poetic prose of Ossian, a counterfeit bard "translated" from ancient Gaelic; and the pleasures of terror roused by gothic novels, supernatural tales, and ghostly ballads (in which contexts sensibility merges with the Burkean sublime). Not all were easily reconciled with the notion of sympathetic feeling as a moral guide, and literary culture was alive with parody of sensibility's excesses, on the one hand, and moral panic, on the other. Indeed, the culture of sensibility was racked with guilt over its vicarious pleasure in suffering once removed. An anonymous British author sought to assuage the national conscience in a parable published in *The Times* (1 July 1786). Readers of "The Birth of Sensibility" were treated to a tale of the author, wandering in a twilight grove, his heart in turmoil at the pleasure he derived from reading "tragical stories.—Can the human heart delight in the misfortunes of another" he mused? Enter the spirit of Sensibility, "born at the foot of *Parnassus*," and raised on "plaintive songs, and melancholy music." She informs the now dozing author that she is the source of that "pleasing pain" that "agitates his breast." Fear not, the "delightful sensations of pity" and the reader's "sweet anxieties," the inverse of apathy, are elevated pleasures, authorized by the muses.

Scholars of other European literatures, and music, order their histories differently. In Italy, for example, the idea of sensibility has had little purchase on literary and musical history. The persistence throughout the eighteenth century of mimesis in Italian aesthetic writings is generally understood, in modern scholarship, to preclude an expressive paradigm based on sensitivity of response. This situation looks set to change, as musicologists, in particular, discover themes of expressive immediacy, absorption, realism, and embodiment in (to date) Italian ballet and pantomime (Lockhart 2011), opera buffa (Hunter 1985, 1997; Castelvecchi 1996; Goehring 1997), and—in Elizabeth Le Guin's study of performativity (2002)—Boccherini's chamber music. In France, *sensibilité* is an established component of the literary culture of what is styled "first-romanticism," but Rousseau's diagnosis of French music as a dead and monotonous product of neoclassical regulation leaves a long musicological shadow. Lockhart (2011) is an important contribution in this context, documenting how French theories of sensation (Condillac's *Traité des sensations* of 1754 specifically) were thematized in Italian stage works on the subject of the animated statue, and, through the travels and collaborations of the Florentine choreographer Gasparo Angiolini, were also known in Vienna. (As Lockhart observes, Angiolini is remembered today as the choreographer for Gluck's *Don Juan* [1761]).

In German literary and musical history, sensibility's cognate *Empfindsamkeit* has long served as a period designation for c. 1760–1790, and *empfindsamer Styl* a rubric for the solo keyboard music of C. P. E. Bach, involving fluctuating emotional intensity and rapid changes of affect. Not surprisingly, German-language scholarship has also investigated the historical basis for these terms. Berg (1997) concluded that there was little evidence for *empfindsamer Styl* in musical writing of the period but discovered in Johann Friedrich Reichardt's description of songs possessing "sentimental tune[s]" (*empfindsame Weise[n]*) an association of *Empfindsamkeit* with (as she extrapolates from context) the musically "introverted, gentle, pensive, somewhat melancholy" and with private performance (Berg 1997: 95). That conclusion is based in part on the distinction Reichardt drew between an *empfindsame Weise* and songs expressing "joy" (*Freude*). Though largely content to define the musically *empfindsam* in these terms, as a matter of affect and of social context, Berg also suggests that "sighs within phrases" (*Binnenseufzern*) are a specific stylistic feature of such music in Bach's context. Her musical examples from *Gellerts geistliche Oden und Lieder* (1758), *Cramers übersetzte Psalmen* (1774), *Oden mit Melodien* (1775), and *Sturms geistliche Gesänge* (1780) illustrate Bach's endlessly inventive deployment of the sighing figure, unadorned, ornamented, as appoggiatura (approached by step or leap), tied suspension, and suspended note restruck. The sigh was naturalized by the prevailing theory of melody as an imitation of the natural accents of passionate speech. It was frequently coupled with other Baroque conventions of lament—the descending chromatic tetrachord in the bass (evoking death), brief scalar figures in imitation (suggesting the flow of tears), and a dotted "farewell" motive (involving a sobbing repeated note)—that lent an antique character to melancholy (as in the opening of Beethoven's Sonata Op. 81a, *Les adieux*; Mme. Herz's "Da schlägt des Abschieds Stunde" from Mozart's *Der Schauspieldirektor* K. 486; or the gloomy, preludial arpeggiations of the first movement of the Sonata Op. 27 No. 2, "Moonlight," that appear like revenants of the arpeggiation preludes of J. S. Bach's *Das Wohltemperierte Clavier*).

These pathetic conventions, though not equivalent to sensibility in a broader sense, amount to a flexible topic of sensibility in late eighteenth-century music, one grounded in vocal music. The topic is recognized in melodies that thematize or stage vocally inspired and first-person expression. At midcentury, two operatic idioms were particularly prized in those terms: accompanied recitative, on the model of opera seria, and the relatively simple melodies of opera buffa arias. For C. P. E. Bach, writing of improvisation, *accompagnati* were the model for "mastering the feelings of [the] audience" (Bach 1974: 152). Though drawn from a courtly, elevated genre, this "declamatory style" corresponded to DuBos's "natural signs of the passions." As Bach emphasized, accompanied recitative at the keyboard also released the improviser from constraining regularity of key and meter, allowing him or her "[to] move audaciously from one affect to another" (Bach 1974: 153). In the four and a half decades between the first part of the *Versuch* (1753) and his death in 1788, Bach developed a supple, declamatory idiom from the initially raw *accompagnato* texture of his first free fantasia (H. 339, composed by 1749; see Example 9.1). Bach's nuanced and lyrical transformation of recitative, enriched with other pathetic gestures of vocal melody, may have prompted Schulz's description of the composer's keyboard sonatas in Sulzer's *Allgemeine Theorie*:

> The possibility of endowing sonatas with character and expression is shown in a number of easy and challenging harpsichord sonatas written by our Hamburg Bach. The majority of these are so eloquent that one almost believes [oneself] to be hearing not a series of musical tones, but a comprehensible speech that moves and engages our imagination and emotions. (Baker and Christensen 1995: 104)

A late example of this investment in recitative as particularly moving is met in the first movement of Beethoven's Sonata Op. 31 No. 2, "Tempest," in which a solo, declamatory passage (mm. 143–58), suspending time, signals a moment of intense inwardness at the boundary of the development and recapitulation (see Example 9.2). Arguably, this passage is ushered in by the sixth chord that opens the sonata—a hallmark of recitative.

Songful melody—enshrined in a region's popular tunes or in the unadorned strains of opera buffa airs in moderate tempos—was another zone of heightened expression throughout the century. Ideas of untutored simplicity, of the natural beauty of the female singing voice, of flowing movement, and (again) of melody as a natural language of the passions informed the celebration—and sometimes sentimental idealization—of songfulness. Already in the pamphlet war over musical canon in the 1720s between

EXAMPLE **9.1** C. P. E. Bach, Free Fantasia in E flat major, H. 339 (no measure numbers).

EXAMPLE **9.2** Beethoven, Piano Sonata in D minor, Op. 31 No. 2/i, "Tempest," mm. 143–58.

Bokemeyer and Mattheson, the latter affirmed the greater value of touching the heart over display of compositional technique and, with that dichotomy, elevated melody over harmony and the performer over the composer: "A simple, moving melody, sung by a pretty voice, coupled with a very simple accompaniment, has more power over the heart than all artificial harmonies" (Mattheson 1722–23: 244; cited in Hirschmann 1995: 1768). As with recitative, songful melody created the aesthetic illusion of music as human utterance and presence and invited sympathetic identification. As Sulzer expressed the point in the article "Gesang" from the *Allgemeine Theorie*, "melody alone possesses the irresistible power of animated tones [that] one recognizes as the utterance of a sensitive soul" (Baker and Christensen 1995: 94). As Sulzer acknowledged, that remark was inspired by the writings of Rousseau. Needless to say, songfulness, as an occasion for feeling, is a fuzzy category, easier to exemplify than delimit.

Several pointed examples appear in recent discussions of the influence of English sentimental literature on opera buffa (Castelvecchi 1996; Goehring 1997). These discussions were inspired by Mary Hunter's study (1985) of Carlo Goldoni's adaptation of Samuel Richardson's epistolary novel *Pamela* (1740) as the libretto for Niccolò Piccinni's *La buona figliuola* (1760). Though Hunter and followers are primarily concerned with literary and theatrical issues, their music examples perhaps inadvertently testify to the privileged position of (a kind of) *singing* (or, more abstractly, music) in the culture of sensibility. Hunter's comments on the opening aria for Cecchina (the Pamela figure in *La buona figliuola*) are suggestive of that special status. In "Che piacer, che bel diletto," Goldoni and Piccinni achieve an effect of immediacy, an "illusion of… 'slipping invisible' into the privacy of [the heroine's] thoughts"; the aria begins immediately after the overture, without introduction, and resembles a soliloquy (see Example 9.3). Hunter—making a comparison with "Che farò senza Euridice" from Act 2 of Gluck's *Orfeo ed Euridice* (1762)—notes the "extraordinary sweetness" of this melody, which is marked by a certain noble simplicity and restrained pathos. Arguably (and Hunter does not suggest this) the technique is one of thematizing song through the idiom of bel canto, such that the aria can be imagined as one Cecchina is actually singing. That aside, the melody downplays the composer's art and sets the heroine's plaintive, natural voice center stage.

This "pared down," lyrical melodic style emerges as a hallmark of sentimental heroines of opera buffa as they sing to themselves in dramatic soliloquy and is met in another

EXAMPLE **9.3** Piccinni, *La buona figliuola*, Act 1 Scene 1, "Che piacer, che bel diletto," mm. 1–8.

of Hunter's examples: Nina's "Il mio ben, quando verrà" from Giovanni Paisiello's *Nina, o sia La pazza per amore* (*Nina, or the Girl Stricken Mad by Love*) of 1789, the libretto translated from the *opéra comique* by Benoît-Joseph Marsollier. *Nina* also includes a stage song for its virtuous, suffering heroine that explicitly thematizes the power of song: "Lontana da te," discussed by Castelvecchi (1996). The dramatic conceit is that Nina invented this song but, because she has forgotten it in her temporary grief-born insanity, a female chorus sings it to her to jog her memory. (The chorus comprises loving and compassionate social inferiors who take care of Nina during her pastoral retreat, a scene of harmonious all-female community, structured hierarchically but sustained by affection that is as much a hallmark of the feminized culture of sensibility as the more extreme distress experienced by Nina.) The subtly sacred and lamenting style of this G-minor song is particularly pronounced in the initial presentation by the chorus ("choir" might be a better description of the sound). Taking a didactic turn, Nina sings it back to them with "more expression" (*più d'espressione*). To this end, she presents the word "Lontana" in single syllables broken up with eighth-note rests ("Lonta...na...da te"), introduces a tritone appoggiatura or sighing figure, interrupts the short tune with a fermata, and employs a flattened (Neapolitan) second scale degree that winds mournfully around the tonic in a chromatic neighbor note figure (A♭, G, F♯, G). As she continues, her already heightened sensibility intensifies into a stylized musical delirium, her song (in Castelvecchi's description) "dissolving into recitative" (1996: 105). As Castelvecchi states, the idea here is that sensibility enriches musical language but in more extreme versions shatters syntax and formal closure. What Castelvecchi does not suggest is that, within the discourse of sensibility, music, or at least pathetic vocal melody, occupied a special place; if language fragments under the pressure of feeling (as in the "breathless" arias discussed by both Castelvecchi 1996 and Goehring 1997), it also opens out on to the domain of music, even, in stage songs most explicitly, "music" as a topic, represented as expressive vocal accent and songfulness.

Another metamusical trope, met in pathetic scenes concerned with loss, was music's evanescence as sound—its vanishing. The sentimental aesthetic of music as a sign of human presence—as the voice of a sensitive soul—was elaborated, paradoxically, in poignant representations of loved ones departing, absent, or deceased. Dispatching his precious Silbermann clavichord instrument to a former student, the nobleman Dietrich Ewald von Grotthuß, C. P. E. Bach mingled his receipts and tears, evoking the *empfindsamer Styl* of farewell in both a letter and, accompanying it, a "plaintive" rondo (as he described it), the *Abschied von meinem Silbermannischen Claviere in einem Rondo*, H. 272 (1781). The *Abschied* rondo itself returns to gestures of lament, lending its grief an antique dignity and suggesting the internalization of the theatrical as one compositional response to the cult of sensibility. The refrain is a slightly expanded version of the lament bass (a descending tetrachord, from tonic to dominant) projecting a series of sighs in the upper voice (mm. 1–4; see Example 9.4). These sorrowing suspensions are minutely elaborated, as if the music set sentiment under the microscope. Most conspicuous is the vibrato applied to the note of resolution (the sixth), suggestive of trembling and, more abstractly, of farewell, because (like the parting instrument) the note sounds, reverberates, and dies

EXAMPLE **9.4** C. P. E. Bach, *Abschied von meinem Silbermannischen Claviere in einem Rondo*, H. 272, mm. 1–8.

away. Bach can be understood here to thematize music *as* farewell, making a sentimental issue of its transience as sound, just as, at the larger scale, the returns of the refrain freeze the moment of departure in a moving tableau, whose theatricality (like an aria of taking leave) only intensified the immediacy and realism of its effect.

The lavish use of vibrato in Bach's *Abschied*—a poignant effect given the instrument's lack of sustaining power—highlights the importance of the human voice as a model for expressive nuance in the musical culture of sensibility. Of course, vibrato at the keyboard was only possible on the touch-sensitive clavichord, an instrument that enjoyed celebrity status in what Annette Richards describes as the North German cult of "inwardness, melancholy and solitude" (Richards 2001: 148–49). Contemporary eulogies of the clavichord spoke of "the sensitivity of its action." In the language of Klopstock's *Odes*, Ossian's fragmentary verse, and Goethe's *Werther*, Christian Friedrich Daniel Schubart (1806) evoked intimate nocturnal performances of melancholy and joyful celebrations of spring: "Sweet melancholy, languishing love, parting grief, the soul's communing with God, uneasy forebodings, glimpses of Paradise through suddenly rent clouds, sweetly purling tears…Behold player, all this lies in your clavichord" (Richards 2001: 151). The violin playing of Franz Benda was also a touchstone (or even "proof") of music's expressive power, at least in the eulogies of Charles Burney and Johann Friedrich Reichardt. Burney, describing the vocal inspiration of Benda's compositions in which "scarce a passage can be found…not in the power of the human voice to sing," assured his readers that Benda "is so affecting a player, so truly pathetic in an Adagio, that [even] several able professors have assured me that he has frequently drawn tears from them in performing one" (Lee 2001: 226).

The efforts of C. P. E. Bach and his German contemporaries to install music in the culture of feeling could draw on native traditions of sentimentalism and weeping that predated the English novel of sentiment and its influence in Germany. Lutheran and pietistic cultivation of "divine sadness," an "anxious heart," and penitential tears shed in private primed German musicians and audiences to weep publically over sacred cantatas and national oratorios by Telemann, Graun, Handel, and C. P. E. Bach (Van Elferen 2007: 80). Such a public display of private feeling fostered a bourgeois public sphere as a community bound by shared affective experience and expressive codes (Le Guin 2002: 210; Van Elferen 2007: 84). Reichardt, a prolific critic who promoted a feeling-oriented mode of musical response, was a champion of Carl Heinrich Graun's *Der Tod Jesu* and of Handel's *Judas Maccabeus* in its Berlin revival of 1777. Reviewing the former, he dwelt particularly on the recitative "Nun klingen Waffen," praising both the setting and performance of the concluding words ("where it says about Peter: [']he weeps bitterly[']"). Notably, Reichardt praised not only the pathetic melodic accents that paint Peter's tears and the performer's use of *rubato* to produce "truly frightened sobbing" but also the harmonic chromaticism: "the beautiful expressive harmony" (Van Elferen 2007: 90). If the *Abschied* topos in keyboard music deployed antique and operatic figures of grief, so in listening to Graun there was a sense of the Christian past, as if the German burghers of the later eighteenth century did not simply weep so much as weep again.

Nonetheless, the efforts of a C. P. E. Bach, a Benda, or a Reichardt to lend music significance within the culture of sensibility sometimes met with resistance from musicians accustomed to explaining (and perhaps even experiencing) music in more technical and abstract ways. The contemporary reception of C. P. E. Bach's keyboard music highlighted problems with the composer's expressed purpose "to touch the heart" (Newman 1965: 371). The esoteric harmonic resources and rhapsodic freedom that Bach invited readers of the *Versuch* to understand as potently moving sometimes failed to move emotionally. In an oft-cited review of 1783, Carl Friedrich Cramer distanced Bach's improvisations from the whole project of rousing the passions, discovering in the music a more abstract, nonrepresentational discourse that testified to Bach's inventive genius and technical knowledge (Ottenberg 1988: 170–71). Perhaps Cramer felt that a primarily *empfindsam* response was insufficiently distinctive, and distinguished, for a writer seeking a position of leadership in musical criticism. Speculations aside, Cramer's resolutely unsentimental response highlights a fundamental contradiction in contemporary discussions of music in relation to the cult of sensibility. Even Bach appeared to vacillate on whether or not free fantasias roused the passions. Having announced this in volume 1 of the *Versuch* (1753), he all but omitted reference to the passions in his detailed discussion of improvisation in the last chapter of part 2 (1762), focusing instead on what Koch (1782–93) called the mechanical elements of music.

Koch's locution, while highlighting aspects of music outside the domain of sensibility, nonetheless maintained the possibility that, however fascinating and significant music's internal procedures and rules might be, they are subordinate to the higher goal of (as he put it, following Sulzer) "awakening noble feelings in us" (Baker and Christensen 1995: 144). In the first part of the second volume of his *Versuch einer Anleitung zur Composition* (1787), Koch went some way to show how composers might set about achieving this goal in technical (mechanical) terms. He addressed listeners' differing degrees "of receptiveness for the particular feeling which music is endeavoring to awaken" and described an ideal listener who attends a concert "merely with the intention of abandoning themselves to the pleasure which music affords them…their heart, open to every beautiful sentiment, is receptive to all those feelings which the music will arouse" (Baker and Christensen 1995: 146). Acknowledging that many listeners are already preoccupied with their own feelings, he recommended ways of drawing them in to the music and suggested that surprise and the unexpected can shake them from their current state (147). Koch described not a neutral, formalistic attentiveness but a sympathetic mingling with tones as signs of human presence: "With beautiful melodies," composers can "coax the hearts of their listeners" (Baker and Christensen 1995: 153), Koch advised, as if listening were like falling in love. Indeed, in the case of texted and dramatic music, Koch is explicit about suspension of disbelief and the shedding of real tears: "We see Alceste between anguish and hope; we see her form her noble resolution having heard the utterance of the oracle. She becomes dear to us, we love her. In brief, after the most tender parting from her husband and her children, we see her finally die. We shed many tears over her" (Baker and Christensen 1995: 149–50).

In bringing music into the domain of sensibility, Koch recommended many reforms: performers need to stop seeking applause for mechanical dexterity, they must be true to the higher goal of rousing feelings; composers should not seek to be witty or entertain the intellect with pictorial music that represents eccentric and comic characters or that imitates other types of sound (such as music boxes, post horns, and cuckoos). In offering "vulgar" imitations, the composer resembles a jester, Koch chided; such clowning is beneath music's sentimental calling. Koch's gripes against mechanical dexterity and the low comic are conventional in themselves but reveal how sensibility dignified not only its bourgeois practitioners (Castelvecchi 1996) but also the art of music itself. The point is worth making because of the subsequent reversal of fortune exemplified by Eduard Hanslick's derisive references to aesthetics of feeling and the ascendency of formalist convictions that still play a part in musicians' professionalization as performers and academics (Hanslick 1954).

More striking than Koch's complaints against virtuosity and pictorialism is his questioning of formal conventions on the grounds of their truthfulness to the passions. Admittedly, his comments on this are brief and tinged with north German disdain for affective variety in instrumental music. But his point shows an awareness of the implications of an aesthetic paradigm that granted the heart such authority:

> Consider the form of our usual compositions. Does not custom show herself a tyrant?...In the performance of a symphony, for example, the first Allegro will lift us to a noble emotion. Hardly has this feeling taken possession of us, than in the Adagio it gives way to sadness; in order, as it were, to compensate for this sad feeling, which came suddenly and without apparent reason, we jump just as quickly thence to even greater joy in the last Allegro. Does this treatment correspond to the nature of our souls, is it appropriate to the nature of the succession of feelings? (Baker and Christensen 1995: 156–57)

In this moment of theoretical reflection, sensibility, as an aspiration to emotional truth and realism in art, authorized the critique of tradition and potentially legitimated change, innovation even, in the Enlightenment rhetoric, progress.

However, some ambivalence and uncertainty are evident in Koch's *Versuch* about the new reign of sensibility. Was it adequate as a framework for understanding and teaching music? Like Ratner, Koch affirmed music's purpose to rouse noble feelings only to proceed with a largely technical discussion that made little reference to emotion. In the preface to the second volume, he confided that he had initially planned to pass over the whole matter of expression in favor of a purely technical explanation aimed at beginners. But, on reflection, he had determined to relate some of these technical features to music's aesthetic purpose. The results (briefly summarized above) are striking, but why this indecision over the inclusion of what was ostensibly music's purpose? A seasoned pedagogue, Koch was surely aware of potential problems in a program of instruction that did not relate musical rules and techniques to the purpose of the art. It can appear that Koch struggled to reconcile his own technical and professionalized relationship to music with aesthetic precepts of relatively recent and not specifically musical origin. Inadvertently, perhaps, Koch's treatise resisted the appropriation of music for sensibility even as it paid prefatory, and intermittent, homage to that ideal. In affirming that expression was and was not central to the Classical style, Koch was among the first to capture the paradoxes and uncertainties of musical meaning in bourgeois culture. To Ratner's credit, *Classic Music* captures them too.

References

n.n. 1786. The Birth of Sensibility. *The Times* 476 (1 July): 2.

Abert, Hermann. 1908. *Niccolò Jommelli als Opernkomponist*. Halle: Niemeyer.

Abrams, Meyer Howard. 1953. *The Mirror and the Lamp: Romantic Theory and the Critical Tradition*. New York: Oxford University Press.

Bach, Carl Philipp Emanuel. 1753–62. *Versuch über die wahre Art das Clavier zu spielen*. 2 vols. Vol. 1, Berlin: Christian Friedrich Henning. Vol. 2, Berlin: Georg Ludewig Winter.

——. 1974. *Essay on the True Art of Playing Keyboard Instruments*. Trans. William J. Mitchell. London: Eulenberg.

Baker, Nancy Kovaleff, and Thomas Christensen, eds. 1995. *Aesthetics and the Art of Musical Composition in the German Enlightenment: Selected Writings of Johann Georg Sulzer and Heinrich Christoph Koch*. Cambridge: Cambridge University Press.

Barker-Benfield, Graham J. 1992. *The Culture of Sensibility: Sex and Society in Eighteenth-Century Britain*. Chicago: University of Chicago Press.

Berg, Darrell. 1997. Carl Philipp Emanuel Bach und die "empfindsame Weise." In *Carl Philipp Emanuel Bach und die europäische Musikkultur des mittleren 18. Jahrhunderts*, ed. Hans Joachim Marx, 93–105. Göttingen: Vandenhoeck & Ruprecht.

Castelvecchi, Stefano. 1996. From "Nina" to "Nina": Psychodrama, Absorption and Sentiment in the 1780s. *Cambridge Opera Journal* 8/2: 91–112.

Chambers, Ephraim. 1728. *Cyclopaedia: or, An Universal Dictionary of Arts and Sciences*. 2 vols. London: Chambers.

Cowart, Georgia J. 1984. Sense and Sensibility in Eighteenth-Century Musical Thought. *Acta Musicologica* 56/2: 251–66.

Cramer, Carl Friedrich, ed. 1783–86. *Magazin der Musik*. 4 vols. Hamburg: Musikalische Niederlage.

——. 1994. Critical Reflections on Poetry, Painting, and Music. In *Music and Culture in Eighteenth-Century Europe: A Source Book*, ed. Enrico Fubini, trans. Wolfgang Freis, Lisa Gasbarrone, and Michael Leone, 324–33. Chicago: University of Chicago Press.

Frye, Northrop. 1956. Towards Defining an Age of Sensibility. *English Literary History* 23/2: 144–52.

Goehring, Edmund J. 1997. The Sentimental Muse of *Opera Buffa*. In *Opera Buffa in Mozart's Vienna*, ed. James Webster, 115–45. Cambridge: Cambridge University Press.

Hanslick, Eduard. 1854. *Vom Musikalisch-Schönen*. Leipzig: Weigel.

Head, Matthew W. 1995. Fantasy in the Instrumental Music of C. P. E. Bach. Ph.D. diss., Yale University.

Heartz, Daniel, and Bruce Alan Brown. 2001. Empfindsamkeit. In *The New Grove Dictionary of Music and Musicians*, 2nd ed., ed. Stanley Sadie and John Tyrrell, vol. 8, 190–92. London: Macmillan.

Hirschmann, Wolfgang. 1995. Empfindsamkeit. In *Die Musik in Geschichte und Gegenwart*, ed. Ludwig Finscher, Sachteil, vol. 2, 1765–71. Kassel: Bärenreiter.

Hosler, Bellamy. 1981. *Changing Aesthetic Views of Instrumental Music in 18th-Century Germany*. Ann Arbor, MI: UMI Research Press.

Hunter, Mary. 1985. "Pamela": The Offspring of Richardson's Heroine in Eighteenth-Century Opera. *Mosaic* 18: 61–76.

——. 1997. Rousseau, the Countess, and the Female Domain. In *Mozart Studies* 2, ed. Cliff Eisen, 1–26. New York: Oxford University Press.

Koch, Heinrich Christoph. 1782–93. *Versuch einer Anleitung zur Composition*. 3 vols. Vol. 1, Rudolstadt: 1782. Vols. 2 and 3, Leipzig: Adam F. Böhme, 1787 and 1793.

Lee, Douglas A. 2001. Franz Benda. In *The New Grove Dictionary of Music and Musicians*, 2nd ed., ed. Stanley Sadie and John Tyrrell, vol. 3, 225–27. London: Macmillan.

Le Guin, Elizabeth. 2002. "One Says That One Weeps, but One Does Not Weep": Sensible, Grotesque, and Mechanical Embodiments in Boccherini's Chamber Music. *Journal of the American Musicological Society* 55/2: 207–54.

Lockhart, Ellen. 2011. Alignment, Absorption, Animation: Pantomime Ballet in the Lombard Illuminismo. *Eighteenth-Century Music* 8/2: 231–51.

Matheson, Johann. 1722–23. *Critica Musica*. Vol. 1. Hamburg: Author.

Morrow, Mary Sue. 1997. *German Music Criticism in the Late Eighteenth Century: Aesthetic Issues in Instrumental Music*. Cambridge: Cambridge University Press.

Moyer, Birgitte. 1992. *Ombra* and Fantasia in Late Eighteenth-Century Theory and Practice. In *Convention in Eighteenth- and Nineteenth-Century Music: Essays in Honor of Leonard G. Ratner*, ed. Wye J. Allanbrook, Janet M. Levy, and William P. Mahrt, 283–306. Stuyvesant: Pendragon.

Newman, William S. 1965. Emanuel Bach's Autobiography. *The Musical Quarterly* 51/2: 363–72.

Ottenberg, Hans-Günther. 1988. *Carl Philipp Emanuel Bach*. Trans. Philip J. Whitmore. New York: Oxford University Press.

Poos, Heinrich. 1988. "Nexus vero est poeticus: Zur fis-Moll-Fantasie Carl Philipp Emanuel Bachs." In *Studien zur Instrumentalmusik, Lothar Hoffmann-Erbrecht zum 60. Geburtstag*, ed. Anke Bingmann, Klaus Hortschansky, and Winfried Kirsch, 189–220. Tutzing: Hans Schneider.

Ratner, Leonard G. 1980. *Classic Music: Expression, Form, and Style*. New York: Schirmer.

Richards, Annette. 2001. *The Free Fantasia and the Musical Picturesque*. Cambridge: Cambridge University Press.

Rousseau, Jean-Jacques. 1775. *Dictionnaire de musique*, 4th ed. 2 vols. Paris: Duchesne.

Schubart, Christian Friedrich Daniel. 1806. *Ideen zu einer Ästhetik der Tonkunst*, ed. Ludwig Schubart. Vienna: Degen. Reprint, ed. Jürgen Mainka. Leipzig: Reclam, 1977.

Sulzer, Johann Georg. 1771. *Allgemeine Theorie der schönen Künste*. Vol. 1. Leipzig: Weidmann.

Van Elferen, Isabella. 2007. "Ihr Augen weint!" Intersubjective Tears in the Sentimental Concert Hall. *Understanding Bach* 2: 77–94.

Webster, James. 2004. The Eighteenth Century as a Music-Historical Period? *Eighteenth Century Music* 1: 47–60.

——. 2007. The Rhetoric of Improvisation in Haydn's Keyboard Music. In *Haydn and the Performance of Rhetoric*, ed. Tom Beghin and Sander M. Goldberg, 172–212. Chicago: University of Chicago Press.

Wiemer, Wolfgang. 1988. Carl Philipp Emanuel Bachs Fantasie in c-Moll—ein Lamento auf den Tod des Vaters? *Bach-Jahrbuch* 74: 163–77.

Wolff, Christian. 1720. *Vernünftige Gedanken von Gott, der Welt und der Seele des Menschen*. Frankfurt and Leipzig: Andrea.

Wollenberg, Susan. 2007. "Es lebe die Ordnung und Betriebsamkeit! Was Hilft das beste Herz ohne jene!": A New Look at Fantasia Elements in the Keyboard Sonatas of C. P. E. Bach. *Eighteenth Century Music* 4: 119–28.

CHAPTER 10

··

OMBRA AND *TEMPESTA*

··

CLIVE MCCLELLAND

When Horror ombers o'er the Scene,
And Terror with distorted Mien,
Erects the Hair, and chills the Blood,
Whose Painting must be understood
To strike such Feelings to the Soul?
              SHAKESPEARE alone.

THIS passage is taken from William Havard's *An Ode to the Memory of Shakespeare*, and was set to music by William Boyce in 1756. The verb "ombers" employed here implies a sense of shadowiness and approaching fear.[1] Boyce sets these lines as an accompanied recitative for solo bass (see Example 10.1). The tempo is Adagio, and it opens with strings and continuo presenting an unaccompanied melodic line remarkable for its lack of conjunct motion. Most of the notes make up a G-flat-major triad, which is to be heard in this context as the submediant in the remote key of B flat minor. The outline of a diminished seventh chord is traced in mm. 2–3, just before the word "horror" appears, and another one occurs, suddenly fortissimo, under the word "terror" in m. 5. The shifting tonalities, contrasting dynamics, and portentous dotted rhythms convey a mysterious, even threatening, mood, and it is clearly Boyce's intention to unsettle his audience by introducing discontinuous elements into his music:

The style of music that Boyce employs has been known as *ombra* since Hermann Abert (1908) first used the term to refer to the ghost scenes in Jommelli's operas, although it is doubtful if he was aware of Boyce's example.[2] There are numerous instances of the style to represent the supernatural in opera and sacred music from the Renaissance onward, most notably by Handel, Gluck, and Mozart. The appearances of oracles, demons, witches, and ghosts were a commonplace in Classical mythology and therefore in much seventeenth- and eighteenth-century serious opera, and they proved popular with audiences because of the opportunities provided for spectacular stage effects as well as the special musical language employed. The numerous settings of the myths concerning Orpheus, Iphigenia, and Alceste, and their underworld adventures are sufficient evidence on their own. Similarly awe-inspiring moments are

EXAMPLE **10.1** Boyce, *Titles and ermines fall behind*, No. 3, Recitative, mm. 1–7.

found in the biblical narratives used in oratorios, and even in parts of the liturgy. In such circumstances, where stage effects could not be employed, it was necessary for the music alone to convey the horror of the subject matter. *Ombra* is also found as a topical reference in instrumental music from the second half of the eighteenth century, which explains the strong musical similarity between the supper scene in Mozart's *Don Giovanni* and the slow introduction to his "Prague" Symphony. Whether such music literally "erects the hair and chills the blood" is open to debate, but by introducing discontinuous elements into the music composers were aiming not only to depict horror but actually to convey an unsettling feeling to the audience, and the use of *ombra* was therefore highly effective as a rhetorical gesture in symphonies.

Another style of music designed to unsettle eighteenth-century audiences was the so-called *Sturm und Drang*, a label that has persisted despite its misleading implications. The original attempt by Théodore de Wyzewa (1909) to draw parallels between certain movements of Haydn's middle-period symphonies and the trend in German Romantic literature was misguided, and there is no credible evidence that Haydn was suffering any kind of personal crisis in the years around 1770. What is clear is that there are several examples of a similar character in Haydn's output that date from other periods in his life, not to mention those by other composers, including symphonies by Sammartini, J. C. Bach, Dittersdorf, Vanhal, Ordonez, and Mozart among others.

Scholars have been uncomfortable with the label for some time. Jack Westrup (1967) refers to the "popular legend that Haydn had a *Sturm und Drang* period," and Brook (1970), Landon (1978), and Todd (1980) began to pick up on this. Landon preferred to think of an "Austrian musical crisis" rather than one that was personal to Haydn, but again without any real evidence, especially as he also acknowledged that the style was used in other countries. Yet the *Sturm und Drang* myth persisted, so powerful was the appeal of linking figures as prominent as Haydn and Goethe. Ratner (1980) does little to dispel the myth. One example of *Sturm und Drang* he gives is Haydn's String Quartet in F minor, Op. 20 No. 5 (1772). Much of the first movement can be described as unsettled, even restless, but certainly not stormy. This is true also of many passages in Haydn's *Sturm und Drang* symphonies. Ratner is scarcely any clearer on *ombra*, which he sees as a kind of subset of *fantasia* (itself problematic as a topic), but this cannot be true, not least because *fantasia* requires quasi-improvisatory figurations that are absent from *ombra* (see Moyer 1992 and the chapter by Matthew Head in this volume).

In writing about Mozart's early Symphony in G minor, K. 183, Neal Zaslaw (1989) is uncompromising in his dismissal of the "adjectival excesses" commonly applied to minor-key music of the 1770s, and suggests that the work and others like it can best be understood by "looking forward from the first two-thirds of the eighteenth century, rather than backwards from the nineteenth." In particular he draws attention to the origins of the musical language in the theatrical tradition: "These tempestuous effects had been invented in the opera houses to portray nature's storms as well as storms of human emotion." Elaine Sisman (1990) and Mark Evan Bonds (1998) also mention theater music as being important in this respect. Bonds concludes that Haydn's *Sturm und Drang* period should be seen as "a period of unusually intense and quasi-systematic exploration" (176). It is worth adding that Haydn was not alone in such experimentation. Abigail Chantler (2003: 18) observes that, "since the application of *Sturm und Drang* as an historical construct to the study of music is implicitly reliant on the notion of *Zeitgeist*…it does little to facilitate an historical understanding of the music it purports to describe." Importantly, she associates the aesthetic context not just with the German literary *Sturm und Drang*, but with Burke's ideas about the sublime, a point that will be addressed below.

When Raymond Monelle (2010: 110) commented that "it is probably no longer OK to speak of a 'Sturm und Drang' topic," he was returning to a point that he had made earlier (2000: 28), when he suggested that *Sturm und Drang* "has become a modern myth to associate the Haydn symphonies of this period [i.e., the late 1760s and early 1770s] with the literary movement thus named." The use of *Sturm und Drang* in relation to music is certainly problematic, it must now be recognized that it is no longer fit for purpose in the discipline of topic theory. In order to establish specific topical references more clearly, the *Sturm* really needs to be separated from the *Drang*. The *Sturm* characteristics are relatively easy to identify, deriving as they do from essentially pictorial representations of storms, whereas *Drang* is rather more difficult to pin down. The usual translation of "stress" is not very accurate. "Passion" is closer (Heckscher 1966–67: 102), and even "inner voice" (Landon 1978: 268). As far as music is concerned, the qualities of restlessness and yearning have much more to do with an extreme kind of *empfindsamer Styl* (Todd 1980 and Head in this volume).

My proposal is to adopt the term *tempesta* for all storm-related references. It acknowledges the origins of *Sturm* not in Haydn's symphonies, but in early opera, since the musical language clearly derives from depictions of storms and other devastations in the theater. Disorder in the elements in Classical mythology (and therefore in much of

Figure 10.1 A comparison of *ombra* and *tempesta* characteristics.

	Ombra	*Tempesta*
General	high style, sombre, sustained	agitated, declamatory, stormy
Tempo	slow or moderate	fast
Tonality	flat keys (especially minor keys) occasionally remote, shifting, unusual modulations	mainly minor keys, especially D minor, shifting, unusual modulations
Harmony	"surprise" progressions, bold, chromatic, especially diminished sevenths	"surprise" progressions, bold, chromatic, frequently on the dominant
Melody	exclamatory, often fragmented, sometimes augmented/diminished leaps, occasionally narrow intervals contrasting with wide leaps, monotones/triadic lines for oracles and invocations	disjunct motion, often fragmented, with very wide leaps, sometimes augmented or diminished leaps
Bass	chromatic stepwise movement, descending tetrachord, sometimes augmented or diminished leaps, repeated notes, pedals, ostinato	occasionally chromatic, sometimes augmented or diminished leaps, repeated notes, pedals, ostinato
Figuration	motivic repetition (including "sigh" motives), tremolo effects, sometimes rising and falling scales	rapid scale passages, tremolo effects, repeated notes
Rhythm	restless motion, syncopation, majestic or ponderous dotted rhythms, sometimes dactyls/*versi sdruccioli*, pauses	restless motion, driving forward, syncopation, irregular rhythms, sometimes pauses
Texture	sudden contrasts, often dense, sometimes lines doubled in octaves, rarely imitative	full textures, but often lines doubled in octaves, sometimes imitative or sequential
Dynamics	strong contrasts, sudden outbursts, *crescendo* effects, unexpected silence	mostly loud, strong accents, *crescendo* effects
Instrumentation	unusual, low tessitura, dark timbre, especially trombones	prominent string writing, full scoring often involving brass and timpani

opera seria) is almost invariably instigated by irate deities, and frequently quelled by benevolent ones, so the supernatural associations are clear. Scenes involving storms, floods, earthquakes, and conflagrations had appropriately wild music, and the musical style is often reflected in scenes involving flight or pursuit, and even metaphorically in depicting rage and madness. In choosing this term I also aim to provide an Italian counterpart to *ombra*, since the two styles are evidently complementary.[3] A comparison of their musical characteristics reveals a considerable degree of overlap, as shown in Figure 10.1.

Any one of these features taken in isolation would not in itself constitute an *ombra* or *tempesta* reference, but when several occur together the effect is unsettling because of the variety of discontinuous elements introduced. Such effects provided the eighteenth-century composer with a rich palette from which to choose in order to arouse feelings of awe and terror in audiences. For *ombra*, tempos are invariably on the slow side, allowing a portentous or mysterious atmosphere to be established. In some cases the tempo is changed several times in one scene. The lack of a regular pulse and a constant shifting of speed (including short bursts of fast *tempesta* music) contribute to the audience's sense of disquiet. The *ombra* scenes of Handel, Hasse, and Jommelli were written as accompanied recitatives, where the lack of a rigid rhythmic framework allowed for such flexibility. Typically, they incorporated at least two changes of tempo. Later composers continued to vary the tempo even when the meter was more regular. Melodramas on supernatural subjects, such as those by Georg Benda and Fomin, invite a similarly unstructured musical approach, allowing greater freedom in tempo, as well as tonality and texture. Other styles that overlap with *ombra* (e.g., lament, church style, fantasia, and *Empfindsamkeit*) are normally at a slow or moderate tempo, and it is clear that a slow tempo is the most appropriate way to convey a sense of awe and mystery. Only when the composer wishes to convey a sense of panic is the fast tempo of *tempesta* employed.

Certain keys are used more frequently than others, suggesting a clear understanding of a tonal convention. Rita Steblin has demonstrated the importance of the "Sharp–Flat principle" in understanding the characteristics of various keys, where flat keys have psychological associations with "weakness and somberness" (Steblin 1983: 103).[4] Purcell was especially fond of C minor and F minor for supernatural scenes, and Handel's operas contain several instances involving the use of flat keys, especially in the minor. Jommelli showed a preference for E flat major in his numerous *ombra* scenes, although Gluck and Mozart favored D minor and C minor. Because minor keys afford greater opportunity for chromaticism, augmented and diminished intervals, and other aspects of instability, it follows that flat minor keys would be especially suitable for *ombra*. When combined with the unequal temperaments used in the seventeenth and early eighteenth centuries, such keys would certainly have had an unsettling effect on audiences. By the end of the century, even as equal temperament was beginning to become more firmly established, the old associations still held sway. For *tempesta* the more remote keys are used less frequently. The simple explanation for this may well be the difficulty for instrumentalists in executing rapid passages in awkward keys. C minor and D minor are relatively unproblematic, and are certainly the most popular choices.

Another important feature of both styles is tonal instability. There is a strong psychological factor at work here, namely the unsettling effect of moving the keynote around, sometimes to unexpected places. In the accompanied recitatives used for *ombra* scenes by composers like Handel, Hasse, and Jommelli, rapid modulation was easily achievable. Tonal instability is often seen to go hand in hand with harmonic instability. As might be expected, therefore, harmonic dissonance can be an important ingredient of both styles, since it serves to add to the psychological effect of unsettling the audience. Where minor keys are involved, there are more opportunities for a composer to exploit the harmonic dissonances created by augmented and diminished intervals, and sometimes this is achieved by minor inflections in major-key passages. Chromaticism is employed chiefly as a disruptive element, whether to add color to a particular key, or as a means of modulation. Chromatic chords (particularly diminished sevenths, but also augmented sixths and Neapolitan sixths) are commonly used in supernatural scenes in the eighteenth century.

Unstable elements in the harmony can sometimes be reflected by discontinuity in the melodic and bass lines. The absence of "normal" linear progressions such as diatonic stepwise motion or triadic outlines can be considered as disruptive in eighteenth-century musical language. Such disturbance may be achieved by angular progressions, wide leaps, and dissonant melodic intervals, and also by the use of chromaticism. In *tempesta* passages these effects are strongly representational. One aspect of the *ombra* style that has little to do with instability is the use of repeated notes and pedals. It might be thought that such devices would represent a highly stable force, since both involve a focus on a single note. In practice, however, their appearance in a supernatural context provides a firm foundation against which other features are heard as disruptive. At the same time, they have their own expressive value. Repeated notes figure very prominently in eighteenth-century *ombra* scenes, and are highly suitable for conveying a sense of imminent danger. At a psychological level there may well be associations with a heartbeat or footsteps, both of which are linked to a fear response. The insistent repetition of lower frequency sounds certainly relates to heartbeats because of the sympathetic vibrations produced in the chest cavity. A regular rhythm imitating footsteps can indicate some approaching menace, but may also be associated with solemn processions such as funerals or quasi-religious ceremonials. At a faster tempo, repeated notes are stimulating and exciting, as are rapidly executed rising and falling scales.

Pauses were another method by which composers could break up the flow of the music by interrupting the regular pulse, either by lengthening a note or a rest. It is difficult to know how long such pauses might have been held, if indeed there was any consistency from one performance to the next, but they were a valuable device for creating the dramatic effect of expectancy. One way of doing this was to pause on an unstable chord that needed to be resolved, such as a dominant seventh or chromatic chord. Another was to interrupt a stable harmonic progression with an extended rest. A sudden silence after a lengthy (and perhaps noisy) passage is as surprising as an unexpected loud chord in a quiet one.[5]

Certain musical motives appear with some frequency in *ombra* scenes. The *Seufzer* or "sigh" motive sometimes appears, its momentary dissonance used to express not longing but fear or pain. The use of an uneven dotted rhythm is a means by which to express fear and agitation, and there may even be an underlying suggestion of an irregular heartbeat. But when combined with other march-like characteristics, such as triadic melodic lines (associated with fanfares), the effect is one of awe and majesty. There is a direct link here with the French overture, which has its origins in ceremonial music for Louis XIV. It is therefore entirely appropriate as a gesture to show the power of supernatural forces such as oracles, ghosts, and walking statues. The link between dotted rhythms in overtures and *ombra* scenes can sometimes be difficult to disentangle. Audiences came to expect dotted rhythms in overtures as a ceremonial topical reference, so they have little impact in an overture where a composer might wish to express something more sinister, unless they appear in combination with other *ombra* characteristics. However, their appearance in *ombra* music is a reminder of this majestic association to the listener. There is therefore a complex meld of agitation and awe wrapped up in the use of dotted rhythms as part of an *ombra* reference. Dactylic rhythm patterns (i.e., a stressed beat followed by two weaker ones) are another frequent occurrence in *ombra* scenes. The association between dactylic rhythms and the supernatural lies in Italian verse meters, and in *quinari sdruccioli* in particular. In most Italian poetry, *versi piani* are the norm, with the stress on the penultimate syllable.[6] In *versi sdruccioli*, however, the stress is followed by two weak beats (*sdrucciolo* translates as "sliding"). A *quinario* is a line of five syllables, but in *quinari sdruccioli* the result is six syllables with the last two unstressed. The effect is to disrupt the meter, and the association of this verse form with the subject of death in Italian poetry may well have led to a conscious use of the meter by composers.

Syncopation in both *ombra* and *tempesta* is even more effective than dotted rhythms and dactyls as a destabilizing influence, because the regular beat is undermined further. The throbbing effect of a strong syncopated pattern is another way by which a possible allusion to a pulsating heartbeat can be made. Most commonly syncopation is used as an accompanying figure, providing a rhythmic counterpoint to the melody and bass. It is ubiquitous in the so-called *Sturm und Drang* symphonies of Haydn's middle period. Perhaps the most commonly used device is the tremolando, easily associated with fear and agitation. The analogy with physical shaking of the body is obvious, and there are also opportunities for comic allusions (knocking knees, chattering teeth, etc.). As a convention, tremolando was well established as a pictorial device by the eighteenth century, although not solely to express fear. As a weapon in the expressive armory of composers of *ombra* scenes it is widely used, and also conveys great agitation and excitement in the faster *tempesta* passages.

The juxtaposition of full and reduced textures, rapid alternations between loud and soft, sudden accents, and the introduction of special instrumental colors are all methods that are employed in both styles to introduce further discontinuities in the music. Low textures, dark timbres, and the use of trombones in association with Hell go right back to Monteverdi's *Orfeo* (1607), although Jommelli was the first operatic composer regularly to exploit the special coloring of wind instruments for accompanied recitative passages in *ombra* scenes, sometimes in combination with the darker sonorities of divided violas.[7] He would frequently introduce oboes, horns, and bassoons either separately or in various combinations at the first reference to anything supernatural. Gluck reintroduced trombones for infernal scenes, and Mozart famously exploits their unique timbre in the oracle scene of *Idomeneo* and in the damnation scene of *Don Giovanni*.

It is worth reemphasizing that the principal difference between *ombra* and *tempesta* involves tempo. The creeping terror of *ombra* at a slow or moderate pace elicits a quite different emotional response in the audience than the fast frenzy of *tempesta*. They can therefore be viewed as representing different sides of the same coin. It can even be inferred that *ombra* equates to horror and *tempesta* to terror.[8] In general, it can be said that *ombra* is reserved for darkly ceremonial or ominous references, while *tempesta*

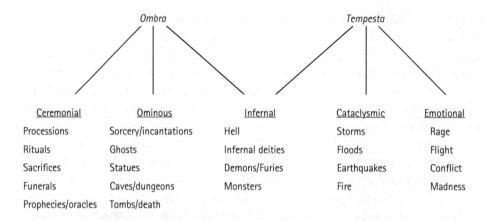

Ombra			Tempesta	
Ceremonial	Ominous	Infernal	Cataclysmic	Emotional
Processions	Sorcery/incantations	Hell	Storms	Rage
Rituals	Ghosts	Infernal deities	Floods	Flight
Sacrifices	Statues	Demons/Furies	Earthquakes	Conflict
Funerals	Caves/dungeons	Monsters	Fire	Madness
Prophecies/oracles	Tombs/death			

FIGURE 10.2 Dramatic contexts for *ombra* and *tempesta* references.

applies to cataclysmic events or emotional outbursts. Both will be found in infernal scenes, depending on the context. These contexts are summarized in Figure 10.2.

Where there is a need to create a sense of awe and horror, then *ombra* music is employed. Strictly speaking, the term *ombra* should apply to scenes involving ghosts, but the musical style was appropriate to a wider set of circumstances, and not just those I have listed under "ominous." Ceremonial music in a supernatural context derives from two sources: the martial (such as the French overture and the funeral march) and the ecclesiastical (including *stile antico* ideas such as *alla breve*, monophonic textures, and chanting). The solemnity and mystery surrounding ritual practices and sacrifices, and the quasi-religious utterances (always by bass voices) of oracles on monotones or with triadic outlines certainly derive from such ecclesiastical origins. Oracle scenes in general seem to have their own specific language within the *ombra* style, to the extent that they can be regarded as a subcategory. Often with a simple homophonic accompaniment and dark timbres, such references work well for incantations and statues as well. *Ombra* characteristics can also be employed in dungeon or night scenes to portray the fear of the protagonist even if there is no supernatural occurrence.

By contrast, scenes of devastation involve *tempesta* characteristics.[9] The style was originally used to depict storms and other natural disasters (even if instigated or quelled by a supernatural entity). *Tempesta* was also employed metaphorically to show stormy emotions, as in the archetypal rage aria, or to accompany scenes involving flight or pursuit, and would also apply to mad scenes. Mozart certainly made good use of such features in the opening scene of *Die Zauberflöte*, where Tamino is fleeing from the serpent, and in the Queen of the Night's bravura aria "Der Hölle rache." Infernal scenes are particularly fertile territory for both *ombra* and *tempesta*. Spectacular set designs showing the Underworld were quite literally awesome, and utterances of the Infernal Deity had to be suitably portentous, so *ombra* came into play. However, when depictions of anger, pursuit or flames were needed, perhaps involving vengeful Furies or tormenting demons, then *tempesta* was required, as it would be for appearances of dragons and monsters.

Sometimes these references are juxtaposed, and an excellent example to illustrate this is Gluck's music for the ballet *Don Juan* (1761), which is discussed in the case study below.[10]

A rather different kind of supernatural music might be termed *celestial*, for references to benevolent deities, heaven, paradise, or the Elysian fields. Such references typically draw on the pastoral tradition of soothing, tranquil music, often in the galant style, and employ devices including a gentle tempo, smooth major keys like G and F, conjunct motion in thirds, lilting melodic lines, regular phrasing, and soft instrumentation including flutes and harps. These elements also appear in enchantment and sleep scenes, and are even appropriate in ghost scenes when the spirit is benevolent or beloved.[11] When placed in close proximity to an *ombra* or *tempesta* passage, the contrast in style can be a particularly striking dramatic device. When Gluck recycled *Don Juan* No. 31 in his Paris production of *Orphée et Eurydice* (1774) Act 2 Scene 1, he could not have created a greater contrast than by following it immediately with the "Dance of the Blessed Spirits." The audience, having been stimulated by the lively *tempesta* music, is then invited to relax and recover.

In all of these cases, the music is directly representational, that is, the composer is trying to depict nonmusical ideas through the music. The presence of a plot, scenery, characters, and text make such references unmistakable. There is also the added dimension of emotivity, the composer deliberately aiming to unsettle the audience by introducing unexpected or disturbing elements. The relationship between music and emotional response is a complex one, but in one recent study (Huron 2006) the reactions associated with "awe" and "frisson" are shown to derive from innate "surprise" responses. "Awe" is related to the "freeze" response, a momentary suspension of activity (including the holding of one's breath) in the face of unexpected danger, while "frisson" derives from the more aggressive "fight" reaction, involving the hair standing on end, which results in "shivers" and "goose flesh."[12] From this, it is not difficult to equate "awe" with *ombra* and "frisson" with *tempesta*. In the case study that follows, both the representational and emotive aspects of the music are clearly demonstrated.

Case Study: Gluck, *Don Juan* (1761), Nos. 30 and 31

At first the confrontation between Don Juan and the statue of the Commander is portrayed at a slow tempo (Larghetto), followed by a fast demonic dance as the unrepentant villain is dragged into hell. Fortunately we have two contemporary descriptions that illustrate the effectiveness of this music. The first is an account in Count Zinzendorf's diary (17 October 1761) of the premiere in Vienna:

> Don Juan mocks [the Statue] and imitates all the ghost's movements, [then] he mounts a sandstone horse on the stage. Don Juan continues to mock him, the ghost

Figure 10.3 *Ombra* in Gluck's *Don Juan*, No. 30.

Measure	Action	Key	Ombra features
1	Don Juan stands in a state of fear before the Commander's tomb	d	No melody, restless motion, repeated notes, tremolandi in viola, angular bass and sudden *f* (4)
9	Appearance of the Statue	→ g → c	Inverted pedal in oboe, rising chromatic line, diminished seventh, sudden *f* for cadential figuration in octaves, with trombone (13–16)
17	The Statue speaks; Don Juan is scornful	→ f	Tremolandi in oboe and violin 1, sudden *f* for cadential figuration in octaves (21–22)
23	The Statue tries again; the heavens are revealed; Don Juan remains unmoved	→ g	Repeated notes *p*, sudden *f* on diminished seventh, with trombone (25), irregular five-measure phrase
28	The Statue is enraged, and takes Don Juan by the arm	→ a	Sequence, tone higher, with added glissando and angular melodic line (31)
33	The Statue stamps its foot; the ground opens; Don Juan is hurled down	→ d	Three repeated notes *f* on trombone, fierce dotted figurations, chromatic descent, diminished sevenths in descending sequence

leaves and all of a sudden hell is shown, the furies dance with torches of fire and torment Don Juan, at the back one sees beautiful fireworks which represent the fires of hell, one sees the devils flying about, the ballet lasts too long, finally the devils carry off Don Juan and throw themselves with him into a sea of fire. All this was very well done, the music most beautiful. (Landon 1993: 6)[13]

The second is an anonymous handwritten program for the Paris production, and as well as giving a lengthy description of the scenario, specific moments in the action are directly linked to the score.[14] A summary is given in Figure 10.3.

The tonal plan is interesting, revealing progressively flatter minor keys to begin with, then a return by way of a rising stepwise sequence. The entry of the Statue at m. 9 is given a particularly striking ascending chromatic sequence against a tonic pedal, a device that Mozart was to employ in *Don Giovanni* (see Example 10.2).[15]

The use of the trombone is also important, as Gluck has reserved it until this number. The loud and emphatic repeated notes are like pronouncements from an oracle, deliberate and authoritative, an idea that is continued in the next number. The expected cadential resolution at the end is not quite achieved, interrupted by a suddenly faster passage. The *tempesta* characteristics of No. 31 are established in the first three sections (identified in Figure 10.4), and the rest of the number is essentially a working-out of these ideas.

There is not a wide range of keys employed, as only the dominant and relative major are established. There are several places where the tonal center is far from clear and a good deal of dominant prolongation and chromatic writing appears. Significantly, the

EXAMPLE **10.2** Gluck, *Don Juan*, No. 30, mm. 9–16.

Figure 10.4 *Tempesta* in Gluck's *Don Juan*, No. 31, mm. 1–40.

Measure	Action	Key	Tempesta features
1	Don Juan tears his hair in despair	d	Angular melody in octaves, no harmony, with tremolando effect in violins, starting *p* but growing louder
11	The demons enter	d	Sudden *ff*, tutti, descending sixteenth-note scales, repeated notes in bass, syncopation in oboes, chromaticism, emphatic trombones
23	The demons torment Don Juan	→ aV	Angular melodic line with syncopated accompaniment alternating with dactyl figure in octaves, *p*/*f* contrasts, diminished seventh over dominant pedal

more remote flat keys are avoided, perhaps because of the difficulties that would arise in execution. The strongest *tempesta* references occur at the first appearance of the demons (see Example 10.3). At m. 171, following a diminished seventh chord, there is a silent pause creating a strong sense of expectation. There follows a coda in D minor, during which Don Juan "is hurled into the deepest region of hell." It is built on rushing semi-quavers, starting loud but gradually dying away, ending on a *tierce de Picardie* as the demons disappear. This is manifestly a metaphorical storm rather than a literal one, but the avenging demons are fulfilling essentially the same dramatic function, and the hapless Don is the one who is caught in its fury. Importantly, the piece is structured in the same way as most other musical storm depictions, with an opening that suggests an approaching storm, a long, raging central section with musical figures that suggest wind and lightning flashes, and a closing section in which the storm subsides. The juxtaposition of *ombra* and *tempesta* here is effective, because although many of the musical devices deployed in both numbers are the same, the contrast between the horror of the approaching statue and the terror of the avenging demons is successfully portrayed. Furthermore, the audience is provided with the opportunity to experience Don Juan's feelings of horror and terror through the music.

EXAMPLE **10.3** Gluck, *Don Juan*, No. 31, mm. 11–22.

AESTHETIC CONTEXT: THE "SUBLIME OF TERROR"

Between the years of Boyce's Shakespeare ode (1756) and Gluck's *Don Juan* ballet (1761), there appeared Edmund Burke's hugely influential treatise *A Philosophical Enquiry into the Sublime and the Beautiful* (1758), which introduced the idea of the "sublime of terror." Burke observed:

> Whatever is fitted in any sort to excite the ideas of pain, and danger, that is to say, whatever is in any sort terrible, or is conversant about terrible objects, or operates in a manner analogous to terror, is a source of the *sublime*; that is, it is productive of the strongest emotion which the mind is capable of feeling. (Burke 1958: 39)[16]

He adds: "Indeed terror is in all cases whatsoever, either more openly or latently the ruling principle of the sublime" (1958: 58).

Burke's ideas were not entirely new. Dionysius Longinus, writing in the first century AD, was the first to consider the possible sources of the sublime, and he was a strong influence on the writing of poet and critic John Dennis (1704), whose six "enthusiastic passions" include terror and horror:

> First, ideas producing terror, contribute extremely to the sublime. All the examples that Longinus brings of the loftiness of the thought, consist of terrible ideas. And they are principally such ideas that work the effects...that ravish and transport the reader, and produce a certain admiration, mingled with astonishment and with surprise. (Ashfield and de Bolla 1996: 35)

Dennis goes on to specify several sources of terror:

> Gods, daemons, hell, spirits and souls of men, miracles, prodigies, enchantments, witchcrafts, thunder, tempests, raging seas, inundations, torrents, earthquakes, volcanoes, monsters, serpents, lions, tigers, fire, war, pestilence, famine &c. (Ashfield and de Bolla 1996: 35)

Such images were appealing not just to the reader. They helped to pull in the crowds at opera houses too, and provided challenges for both set designers and composers. But no one was yet drawing any parallels between these acknowledged sources of the sublime and music. Hildebrand Jacob (1735) had at least identified the powerful emotional effects produced by loud sounds such as:

> the fall of waters in cataracts, or heavy showers; the roaring of the sea; the noise of tempests among lofty trees; thunder; the clash of arms, and voice of war. (Ashfield and de Bolla 1996: 53–54).

Burke takes up this idea, and goes on to relate it to music, although he is evidently not much impressed by its artistic merits:

> Excessive loudness alone is sufficient to overpower the soul, to suspend its action, and to fill it with terror. The noise of vast cataracts, raging storms, thunder, or artillery, awakes a great and aweful [sic] sensation in the mind, though we can observe no nicety or artifice in those sorts of music. (Burke 1958: 82)

Yet earlier, in his discussion on "obscurity," he admits that music on its own is capable of eliciting a strong emotional response:

> So far is a clearness of imagery from being absolutely necessary to an influence upon the passions, that they may be considerably operated upon without presenting any image at all, by certain sounds adapted to that purpose; of which we have a sufficient proof in the acknowledged and powerful effects of instrumental music. (Burke 1958: 60)

Most of Burke's examples deal with poetry and painting, with only oblique references to music, but the wide reception of his work throughout Europe meant that the concepts were generally understood. Before too long, music was being specifically identified as a rich source of sublime emotions associated with awe and terror, firstly in England by Daniel Webb (1769), James Beattie (1783), Archibald Alison (1790), and William Crotch (1806), but also on the Continent by theorists including Christian Friedrich Michaelis (1805). Webb observes that

> in music we are transported by sudden transitions, by an impetuous reiteration of impressions … [A] growth or climax in sounds exalts and dilates the spirits and is therefore a constant source of the sublime. (Le Huray and Day 1981: 118–19)

Beattie is able to be a little more explicit, by making specific reference to horror and terror in relation to sublime music:

> Musick is sublime when it inspires devotion, courage or other elevated affections: or when by its mellow and sonorous harmonies it overwhelms the mind with sweet astonishment: or when it infuses that pleasing horrour [sic] … which, when joined to words descriptive of terrible ideas, it sometimes does very effectually. (Beattie 1783: 187)

Alison's approach is rather more analytical, in that he identifies four pairs of musical features (called "great divisions") which are (1) loud and "low" (by which he means "soft"), (2) grave and acute, (3) long and short, and (4) increasing and diminishing, concluding that:

> The most sublime of these sounds appears to me to be a loud, grave, lengthened and increasing sound. (Alison 1790: 250)

While this is hardly an adequate description of *ombra* or *tempesta*, familiar characteristics are at least present. Crotch was able to improve on this, at least as far as *ombra* is concerned. He invokes Burke in identifying various sources of the sublime, before going on to give examples of different ways it is manifested musically. One such is when the harmony and modulation are learned and mysterious, when the ear is unable to anticipate the transitions from chord to chord and from key to key, if the melody and measure are grave, the effect will be sublime. (1806: unpaginated preface)

This represents one of the best contemporaneous descriptions we have of *ombra* because, as a musician, Crotch is able to identify specific musical features that, in combination, produce the desired emotional effect. Michaelis elaborated on this. He aimed to address Kant's thinking on the sublime by applying it specifically to music. His observations are revealing:

Music can *either* seek to arouse the feeling of sublimity through an inner structure that is independent of any emotional expression, *or* portray the state of mind aroused by such a feeling. In the first case the music can objectively be called *sublime*, like untamed nature, which arouses sublime emotions; in the second case, the music portrays what is pathetically sublime.[17]

References here to "untamed nature" suggest *tempesta*, while the "pathetically sublime" is perhaps more related to *ombra*. But here he is talking in only general terms. He is more explicit further on, and it is worth quoting these passages at length:

The composer also expresses sublimity through the use of the marvellous. This is achieved by the use of unconventional, surprising, powerfully startling, or striking harmonic progressions or rhythmic patterns. Supposing, let us say, the established tonality suddenly veers in an unexpected direction, supposing a chord is resolved in a quite unconventional manner, supposing longed-for calm is delayed by a series of stormy passages, then astonishment and awe result and in this mood the spirit is profoundly moved and sublime ideas are stimulated and sustained....

But when the sounds impinge on the ear at great length, or with complete uniformity, or with frequent interruptions, or with shattering intensity, or where the part-writing is very complex, so that the listener's imagination is severely taxed in an effort to grasp the whole, so that it feels in fact as if it is poised over a bottomless chasm, then the sublime manifests itself....

The objectification, the shaping of a coherent whole, is hampered in music in two principal ways. Firstly, by uniformity so great that it almost excludes variety: by the constant repetition of the same note or chord, for instance; by long, majestic, weighty or solemn notes, and hence by very slow movement; by long pauses holding up the progress of the melodic line, or which impede the shaping of the melody. Secondly, by too much diversity, as when innumerable impressions succeed one another too rapidly and the mind being too rapidly hurled into the thundering torrent of sounds....

Sublime notes, figuration and harmonies stimulate the imagination, which must exert itself and expand beyond its normal bounds to grasp, integrate and recall them. They offer it, not flowing melodies with gentle cadences, but something that appears intractable to rhythmic laws; they have no immediately pleasant effect on the personality and the imagination, but an almost violent one of frightful and terrifying aspect. To the extent that music can depict greatness exceeding the normal capacity of the imagination, thrilling the listener with horror and rapture, it can express the sublime.

There may be less use of musical terminology here than in Crotch, but for the first time we can see a detailed catalogue of musical characteristics that clearly belong to *ombra* and *tempesta*, with references to tonalities that "veer," "unconventional" harmonies and rhythms, "weighty or solemn notes," a lack of "flowing melodies and gentle cadences," repetitions, pauses, frequent interruptions, and sounds of "shattering intensity." In all the extracts quoted above, the distinction between the two styles is not explicit, but there can be little doubt that by linking these musical features with words like "violent," "frightful," "terrifying," "thrilling," and "horror," the idea of the "sublime of terror" is being invoked.

The question "Is the sublime a musical topic?" is raised in an article by Wye J. Allanbrook (2010). Since the sublime encompasses a variety of topics including French overture, fanfare, *empfindsamer Styl*, and learned style, as well as *ombra* and *tempesta*, the answer has to be "No." The "sublime of terror" cannot be regarded as a topic either, but should be viewed as an aesthetic subcategory within the sublime, principally characterized by its two special topics, *ombra* and *tempesta*.

Ombra and *Tempesta* beyond the Theater

While it is evident that the origins of *ombra* and *tempesta* lie in theatrical entertainments, their use in other contexts became more widespread during the eighteenth century. Oratorios (often performed in theaters during Advent and Lent), cantatas, passions, and even parts of the liturgy, provided opportunities for composers to explore the musical language of horror and terror, although perhaps in a slightly more restrained manner than in opera. *Ombra* is appropriate whenever a composer wishes to convey a sense of awe or mystery, or if there is a direct reference in the text to death. Less obviously, but with a degree of consistency, some of the more mysterious or penitential parts of the Mass, such as the "Qui tollis" or "Crucifixus," give rise to similar treatment (McClelland 2012: 163–202). *Tempesta* is rather less common in sacred music, but there are a few famous examples, such as the double chorus "Sind blitze, sind donner" in J. S. Bach's *St. Matthew Passion* (1727) and the chorus "He Gave Them Hailstones" in Handel's *Israel in Egypt* (1738).[18] Requiems are a particularly rich source of both *ombra* and *tempesta* passages, because of the references to death, hell, and the Last Judgment. The familiar tonalities of C minor, D minor, and E flat major tend to predominate in eighteenth-century Requiem settings (McClelland 2012: 192). By the time that Mozart and Haydn were writing sacred music, the practice of referring to the musical supernatural was well established. Mozart's Mass and litany settings contain several examples of *ombra*, and his *Requiem* has both *ombra* and *tempesta* passages in the "Dies irae" and "Confutatis" (McClelland 2012: 177–200). As for Haydn, "The Representation of Chaos" in *The Creation* and the introduction to "Winter" in *The Seasons* draw heavily on *ombra* characteristics, while *tempesta* is represented in *The Creation* in the bass aria "Rolling in foaming billows," and in *The Seasons* there is the vivid storm chorus "Hark! How the deep tremendous voice of thunder roars!" There are also several *ombra* passages in the late Masses (McClelland 2012: 221). As with theater music, these passages are essentially representational, yet still retain the power to elicit a strong emotional reaction from audiences.

Of greater interest for the purposes of this study is the use of *ombra* and *tempesta* as topics in instrumental music, where an apparently supernatural reference in a piece of absolute music might be regarded as out of place. *Ombra* references are most frequently made in slow introductions, where their rhetorical purpose is to gain the attention of the listener with an unexpected gesture. The tension created is invariably dissipated by the main theme of the ensuing faster section, the sort of humorous touch much beloved by Haydn (and, indeed, his audiences).[19] The slow introductions to the Symphony in C minor by Joseph Kraus (written in the 1780s) and to Mozart's Symphonies No. 36 ("Linz") and No. 38 ("Prague") contain substantial *ombra* passages, but the mood quickly evaporates (McClelland 2012: 207–9). Where *ombra* references occur in slow movements, they can seem even more threatening. In the slow movement of Haydn's Symphony No. 99, after a good five minutes of placidly serene music, there is a short but highly disturbing passage in the minor (mm. 35–53), and then all is calm once more. In No. 100, which later acquired the nickname "Military," the use of Turkish instruments in long crescendos, again in the minor, suggests the ominous approach of an attacking army (mm. 61–91 and again at mm. 159–67). Although the reference is not intended to be a supernatural one, the effect is equally menacing. Topical references to *tempesta* generally occur in development sections of first movements or finales, where they are well suited to the working out of thematic material in fast modulatory passages. Often the contrast with the generally light-hearted character of the rest of the movement can prove effective. Stylistically there is little to distinguish between such passages and the instrumental storm depictions popular with audiences since Vivaldi.[20] Haydn's instrumental storms in the openings of operas like *Philemon und Baucis* (1773), *La vera costanza* (1779) or *L'isola disabitata* (1779) sound no different in style from the various Allegro passages in his *Sturm und Drang* symphonies. Moreover, there are numerous examples of *tempesta* writing in Haydn's later symphonies, demonstrating an ongoing fascination with the expressive possibilities it had to offer. Mozart, too, had some recourse to *tempesta*, such as in the first movement of the Piano Concerto in D minor, K. 466, where the restless opening leads to a stormier tutti passage in much the same manner as Gluck's *Don Juan* No. 31, followed by further tempestuous displays in the central section of the second movement and in the finale.

The supernatural continued to be a source of inspiration for composers in the nineteenth century, particularly the German Romantic opera composers like Spohr, Weber, and Marschner. The most obvious illustration is the Wolf's Glen scene in Weber's *Der Freischütz* (1821).[21] Although Beethoven displayed little interest in the supernatural, much of his music draws on the stylistic features associated with it. The slow introductions to Symphonies No. 2 (1802) and No. 4 (1806) both contain *ombra* elements, as does the opening of *Christus am Ölberge* (1803) in the remote key of E flat minor. *Tempesta* is certainly ubiquitous in Beethoven's music, and in the storm movement of the "Pastoral" Symphony (1808) it is directly representational. But there is more to this than mere tone-painting, as Berlioz's reaction to it indicates:

> The hurricane approaches and grows in force; an immense chromatic feature, starting from the heights of the instrumentation, pursues its course until it gropes its way to the lowest orchestral depths. There it secures the basses, dragging them with it upwards; the whole shuddering like a whirlwind sweeping everything before it. Then, the trombones burst forth, the thunder of the kettledrums becomes redoubled in violence, it is no longer merely rain and wind, but an awful cataclysm, the universal deluge—the end of the world. This literally produces giddiness; and many people, when they hear this storm, can scarcely tell whether their emotion is one of pleasure or pain. (Jones 1995: 83)[22]

This recalls something else that Burke had said:

> No passion so effectually robs the mind of all its powers of acting and reasoning as fear. For fear being an apprehension of pain or death, it operates in a manner that resembles actual pain. (Burke 1958: 57).

For the Romantics, the power of music to move the emotions was central, but the idea was hardly a new one in the nineteenth century. While twentieth-century music scholars tried to explain its origins by establishing a link between literature and music, encapsulated in the concept of *Sturm und Drang*, this is demonstrably a false association. The origins of awe and terror in music lie further back. The ability of both *ombra* and *tempesta*, as Havard put it, "to strike such feelings to the soul" must be seen as vital to our understanding of expressivity in music.

ACKNOWLEDGMENT

I am grateful to Charlie Gower-Smith for preparing the music examples.

NOTES

1. The Ode can be found at Birmingham University, Barber Music MS5008, and a partly autograph set of parts is at the Bodleian Library, Oxford, MS Mus.C.114. I am grateful to Fiona Smith for bringing this passage to my attention.
2. In Italian, *ombra* means "shade," as in "shadow" but also as in "spirit of the dead."
3. *Ombra* is examined in detail in my book *Ombra: Supernatural Music in the Eighteenth Century* (2012), and its characteristics are summarized in Appendix A. The purpose of the present chapter is to extend the discussion to encompass *tempesta* and to compare the characteristics of these two topics. For more on the "problem" of *Sturm und Drang*, see

Lütteken (2006). Studies of supernatural scenes in opera can be found in Garda (1994), Hammerstein (1998), and Buch (2008).

4. For a fuller discussion with examples, see McClelland (2012: 23–45).

5. For the surprising effect of general pauses, see Danuta Mirka (2009: 101–16) and the experimental work of Elisabeth Hellmuth Margulis (2007) as well as her chapter in this volume.

6. For a clear explanation of Italian verse meters, see the preface to Rice (1998: xvii). An important early example of dactylic rhythm in a supernatural context is Medea's incantation in Cavalli's *Giasone* (1684), Act 1 Scene 14. See McClelland (2012: 113–15).

7. For more on texture, dynamics, and instrumentation in *ombra*, see McClelland (2012: 123–41).

8. Janice Dickensheets (2003) refers to "demonic" and "tempest style" but she does not distinguish clearly between *ombra* and "demonic," and some of her "demonic" features belong more properly to the "tempest style," as she later acknowledges. David Buch (2008) uses the blanket term "marvelous" for all supernatural references, which recognizes the importance of Baroque spectacle (especially the French *merveilleux*) without really understanding the need for separate categorization, and his assertion (154 n. 7) that *ombra* applies only to ghost scenes is inaccurate.

9. Storm scenes in operas were especially popular in France in the generation after Lully, with notable examples by Marais in *Alcyone* (1706) and *Semelé* (1709) and by Campra in *Hésione* (1700), *Tancrède* (1702), *Hippodamie* (1708), *Les fêtes vénitiennes* (1710), and *Idoménée* (1712). This popularity evidently continued as far as Rameau, with examples in *Hippolyte et Aricie* (1733), *Les Indes galantes* (1736), *Platée* (1745), and *Les Boréades* (1763). Grétry's *Zemir et Azor* (1771) has an overture with several stormy interjections. See Wood (1981–82).

10. Gluck later recycled this music in *Orphée et Euridice* (1774), and it is the dance paraphrased by Boccherini in the finale to his Sinfonia in D minor *La casa del Diavolo* (1771). See Ratner (1980: 381–86). For Mozart's use of D minor, see Chusid (1965–66).

11. Dickensheets (2003) acknowledges this tradition in her category of "fairy music."

12. See Huron (2006: 31–35). "Frisson" is explored further on pages 281–83 and "awe" on pages 288–90.

13. The fireworks proved to be a great hazard, as they caused the Kärntnerthortheater to burn down on 2 November.

14. The details are given by the editors in the preface to the relevant volume of Gluck's complete works (Gluck 2010: xiv–xv). In this version the movements under discussion are numbered 14 and 15 (30–50), where the description of the scene and the correspondences with the score are shown in full.

15. Compare with Mozart's overture to *Don Giovanni* (mm. 23–26) and the corresponding passage in Act 2 Scene 15 (mm. 479–82). For more on *ombra* in *Don Giovanni*, see Allanbrook (1983).

16. The discussion that follows is a distillation of McClelland (2012: 10–17) but revised to include references applicable to *tempesta* as well. For more on the sublime in relation to music, see Garda (1995).

17. This and the following quotations are taken from the translation in Le Huray and Day (1981: 289–90). The original appeared in the *Berlinische musikalische Zeitung* (1805).

18. Earlier examples include the chorus "Et proeliabantur venti" in Carissimi's *Jonas* (written in the 1640s), and the vivid portrayals of a downpour, lightning, thunder, and an earthquake in Funcke's *Danck- und Denck-Mahl* (1666). The French, as with their operas, provide several examples of stormy writing in sacred music, including passages in Rameau's

Deus noster refugium (c. 1714), Campra's *Lauda Jerusalem* (1727), settings of *Dominus regnavit* by Mondonville (c. 1735) and Giroust (1764), and Giroust's *Diligam te, Domine* (1772).

19. *Ombra* passages occur in the slow introductions to Haydn's symphonies Nos. 98, 100, 102, and 104.

20. See his Op. 8 concertos (1725), No. 2 *L'estate* and No. 5 *La tempesta di mare*. Eighteenth-century symphonic storm depictions include two by Ruge, subtitled *La tempesta* (1756) and *La nova tempesta* (1761); the finale of Haydn's Symphony No. 8 *Le soir et la tempête* (c. 1761); Holzbauer's Symphony Op. 4 No. 1 *La tempesta* (1769); Knecht's *Le portrait musical de la nature* (1784), which includes a storm and thanksgiving (foreshadowing Beethoven's "Pastoral" Symphony); and the first movement of Massoneau's Symphony No. 3 *La tempête et le calme* (1794).

21. For an account of *ombra* in the early nineteenth century, see McClelland (2012: 215–23). A table of German supernatural operas is given on page 216. For Schubert's use of *ombra* in lieder, see McClelland (2003).

22. Table 3 (Jones 1995: 75) gives a tonal plan of the movement, in which flat minor keys feature prominently.

References

Abert, Hermann. 1908. *Niccolò Jommelli als Opernkomponist*. Halle: Niemeyer.

Alison, Archibald. 1790. *Essays on the Nature and Principles of Taste*. London and Edinburgh. Reprint, Hildesheim: Georg Olms, 1968.

Allanbrook, Wye J. 1983. *Rhythmic Gesture in Mozart:* Le nozze di Figaro and Don Giovanni. Chicago: University of Chicago Press.

——. 2010. Is the Sublime a Musical Topos? *Eighteenth-Century Music* 7/2: 263–79.

Ashfield, Andrew, and Peter de Bolla, eds. 1996. *The Sublime: A Reader in British Eighteenth-Century Aesthetic Theory*. Cambridge: Cambridge University Press.

Beattie, James. 1783. *Dissertations Moral and Critical*. 2 vols. Dublin: Printed for Mess. Exshaw, Walker, Beatty, White, Byrne, Cash, and MᶜKenzie.

Bonds, Mark Evan. 1998. Haydn's "Cours complet de la composition" and *the Sturm und Drang*. In *Haydn Studies*, ed. W. Dean Sutcliffe, 152–76. Cambridge: Cambridge University Press.

Brook, Barry S. 1970. "Sturm und Drang" and the Romantic Period in Music. *Studies in Romanticism* 9: 269–84.

Buch, David. 2008. *Magic Flutes and Enchanted Forests: The Supernatural in Eighteenth-Century Musical Theater*. Chicago: University of Chicago Press.

Burke, Edmund. 1757. *A Philosophical Enquiry into the Origins of Our Ideas of the Sublime and Beautiful*. London: Dodsley.

——. 1958. *A Philosophical Enquiry into the Origins of Our Ideas of the Sublime and Beautiful*, ed. James T. Boulton. London: Routledge and Kegan Paul.

Chantler, Abigail. 2003. The *Sturm und Drang* Style Revisited. *International Review of the Aesthetics and Sociology of Music* 34/1: 17–31.

Chusid, Martin. 1965–66. The Significance of D Minor in Mozart's Dramatic Music. *Mozart Jahrbuch* 14: 87–93.

Crotch, William. [1806]. *Specimens of Various Styles of Music Referred to in a Course of Lectures Read at Oxford and London*. 3 vols. London: Birchall.

Dennis, John. 1704. *The Grounds of Criticism in Poetry*. London: Printed for George Strahan and Bernard Lintott.

Dickensheets, Janice. 2003. Nineteenth-Century Topical Analysis: A Lexicon of Romantic *Topoi*. *The Pendragon Review* 2/1: 5–19.

Garda, Michela. 1994. Da *Alceste a Idomeneo*: Le scene "terribili" nell'opera seria. *Il saggiatore musicale* 1/2: 335–60.

——. 1995. *Musica sublima: Metamorfosi di un' idea nel settecento musicale*. Milan: Ricordi.

Gluck, Christoph Willibald. 2010. *Sämtliche Werke*. Series II, vol. 2, ed. Sibylle Dahms and Irene Brandenburg. Kassel: Bärenreiter.

Hammerstein, Reinhold. 1998. *Die Stimme aus der anderen Welt: Über die Darstellung des Numinosen in der Oper von Monteverdi bis Mozart*. Tutzing: Hans Schneider.

Heckscher, William S. 1966–67. Sturm und Drang: Conjectures on the Origin of a Phrase. *Simiolus: Netherlands Quarterly for the History of Art* 1/2: 94–105.

Huron, David. 2006. *Sweet Anticipation: Music and the Psychology of Expectation*. Cambridge, MA: MIT Press.

Jacob, Hildebrand. 1735. *The Works*. London: Printed for W. Lewis.

Jones, David Wyn. 1995. *Beethoven: Pastoral Symphony*. Cambridge: Cambridge University Press.

Landon, H. C. Robbins. 1978. *Haydn: Chronicle and Works*. Vol. 2: *Haydn at Eszterháza 1766–1790*. London: Thames and Hudson.

——. 1993. Gluck Ballets. In CD booklet for *Gluck: Don Juan / Semiramis*. Tafelmusik, Bruno Weil. Vivarte SK 53119.

Le Huray, Peter, and James Day, eds. 1981. *Music and Aesthetics in the Eighteenth and Early Nineteenth Centuries*. Cambridge: Cambridge University Press.

Lütteken, Laurenz. 2006. Sturm und Drang in der Musik? Mozarts Sinfonien 1773–1775 und die Probleme einer musik-historischen Konstruktion. In *Mozart Handbuch 1: Mozarts Orchesterwerke und Konzerte*, ed. Joachim Brügge and Claudia Maria Knispel, 44–57. Laaber: Laaber.

Margulis, Elizabeth Hellmuth. 2007. Silences in Music are Musically Not Silent: An Exploratory Study of Context Effects on the Experience of Musical Pauses. *Music Perception* 24/5: 485–606.

McClelland, Clive. 2003. Death and the Composer: The Context of Schubert's Supernatural Lieder. In *Schubert the Progressive: History, Performance Practice, Analysis*, ed. Brian Newbould, 21–35. Aldershot, UK: Ashgate.

——. 2012. *Ombra: Supernatural Music in the Eighteenth Century*. Lanham, MD: Lexington.

Mirka, Danuta. 2009. *Metric Manipulations in Haydn and Mozart: Chamber Music for Strings 1787–1791*. New York: Oxford University Press.

——. 2012. Absent Cadences. *Eighteenth-Century Music* 9/2: 213–36.

Monelle, Raymond. 2000. *The Sense of Music: Semiotic Essays*. Princeton: Princeton University Press.

——. 2010. Review of *Music as Discourse: Semiotic Adventures in Romantic Music* by V. Kofi Agawu. *Music and Letters* 91/1: 110–11.

Moyer, Birgitte. 1992. *Ombra* and Fantasia in Late Eighteenth-Century Theory and Practice. In *Convention in Eighteenth- and Nineteenth- Century Music: Essays in Honor of Leonard G. Ratner*, ed. Wye J. Allanbrook, Janet M. Levy, and William P. Mahrt, 283–306. New York: Pendragon.

Ratner, Leonard G. 1980. *Classic Music: Expression, Form and Style*. New York: Schirmer.

Rice, John A. 1998. *Antonio Salieri and Viennese Opera*. Chicago: University of Chicago Press.

Sisman, Elaine. 1990. Haydn's Theater Symphonies. *Journal of the American Musicological Society* 43/2: 292–352.

——. 1997. Genre, Gesture, and Meaning in Mozart's "Prague" Symphony. In *Mozart Studies 2*, ed. Cliff Eisen, 27–84. New York: Oxford University Press.

Steblin, Rita. 1983. *A History of Key Characteristics in the Eighteenth and Early Nineteenth Centuries*. Ann Arbor, MI: UMI Research Press.

Todd, R. Larry. 1980. Joseph Haydn and the *Sturm und Drang*: A Revaluation. *Music Review* 41/3: 172–96.

Westrup, Jack A. 1967. Editorial. *Music and Letters* 47: 1–2.

Wood, Caroline. 1981–82. Orchestra and Spectacle in the Tragédie en musique 1673–1715: Oracle, *Sommeil* and *Tempête*. *Proceedings of the Royal Musical Association* 108: 25–46.

Wyzewa, Théodore de. 1909. A propos du centenaire de la mort de Joseph Haydn. *Revue des deux mondes* 79: 935–46.

Zaslaw, Neal. 1989. *Mozart's Symphonies*. Oxford: Oxford University Press.

CHAPTER 11

....

LEARNED STYLE AND LEARNED STYLES

....

KEITH CHAPIN

THE TERMS OF LEARNED STYLE

As applied to late eighteenth-century music in the Italo-Austrian-German tradition, "the learned style," in the singular, is a twentieth-century neologism that is as anachronistic as it is useful. It was popularized as a label for a topic by Leonard Ratner (1980: 23–24), though it circulated in discussions of musical style before then as well (e.g., Einstein 1945: 145). The modern term refers to a number of styles that had endured into the late eighteenth century linked by common theoretical issues and cultural resonances.

As an umbrella term, "the learned style" can be defined narrowly or broadly. In its narrow definition, it draws on prestigious techniques of imitative and invertible counterpoint, especially fugue and canon. Moving outward in ever greater concentric circles, it can be inspired by other high styles: species counterpoint and *a cappella* polyphony, the chorale, and the harmonic complexities of the fantasy. As it moves outward, it becomes ever less a discrete style and ever more the musical manifestation of an ethos. This ethos of learnedness and poise was often opposed to that of sensibility and sentiment, described by Matthew Head in this volume, despite the many overlaps between them in both social background and compositional technique.

Because of the variety of its forms of manifestation, the learned style is often recognized as much through its marked opposition to various more common, low, or galant styles as it is by set musical techniques (Hatten 1994: 29–66). A paradigmatic example of both markers of learned technique (fugato, equal polyphony, suspensions, long note values set against rhythmically regularized accompaniment patterns) and the opposition to the galant style (with unprepared dominant seventh chords, homophonic separation of melody and accompaniment, and clarity and concision of melody) is Mozart's

String Quartet in G major, K. 387/iv (Example 11.1; see Ratner 1980: 260; Allanbrook 1983: 19–22).

The clarity of such examples, however, can blind one to the complexities of eighteenth-century practice. The term "learned style" (*gelehrte Schreibart*) itself was not used by eighteenth-century German-speaking musicians. Rather, they used a panoply of adjectives to denote various inherited styles: strict, church, a cappella, bound, antique, grave, fugal, elaborate, artful/artificial, and so forth. Each of these terms referred to a different issue, such as compositional technique, social function, place of performance,

EXAMPLE **11.1** Mozart, String Quartet in G major, K. 387/iv, mm. 1–31.

(*Continued*)

EXAMPLE **11.1** (Continued)

historicity, and affective register. In some cases the exact meaning of the adjective shifted from theorist to theorist. Each term points to an aspect of learned compositional practice, yet each term also poses problems of definition and interpretation. The survey of this terminological field serves here to circumscribe and illuminate the many concepts and styles that inform the topic of the learned style.

Strict Style

The term "strict" (Ger. *streng*, Fr. *strict* or *rigoreux*, It. *ligato*) was perhaps the most general of the terms in circulation (Koch 1802: cols. 1447–48; Cherubini 1835: 1), but even around this general term writers differed in their definitions. The term depended on its marked opposition with the unmarked "free" styles that had become the lingua franca of late eighteenth-century composition. In its origin, the term described an approach to dissonance treatment and part writing. Dissonances had to be placed in metrically weak positions (or appropriately prepared as suspensions) and required resolution downward by step. Parts needed to move with maximal smoothness and had to treat perfect fifths and octaves gingerly when they swung in parallel or similar motion. In free styles, by contrast, these conditions were relaxed in various ways. For example, according to the article on the seventh chord for the *Allgemeine Theorie der schönen Künste* (1771–74), whose articles on music were collaboratively written by the man of letters Johann Georg Sulzer and the musicians Johann Philipp Kirnberger and, in later volumes, Johann Abraham Peter Schulz, the dominant seventh chord requires the actual sounding of the third in the strict style. It can be merely implied in the free style (1792–94, 4: 366).

Dissonance treatment and part writing, however, were but indices of general considerations of compositional technique, such as texture, harmony, and phrasing. In his definition of the "strict style" in the *Musikalisches Lexikon* (1802) Heinrich Christoph Koch established a basic opposition between strict and galant styles along lines common to many musicians of the late eighteenth century.

> Strict style. This is the name for the style in which, on account of its serious character, one must not only minutely observe the mechanical rules of composition and not concatenate phrases so loosely as one does in the galant style, but it is also the style in which a melodic theme is developed through the means of various transpositions and imitations.

> Strenge Schreibart. So nennet man denjenigen Styl, bey welchem nicht allein wegen seines ernsten Charakters die mechanischen Regeln des Satzes auf das genaueste beobachtet werden müssen, und die melodischen Theile nicht so locker an einander gereihet werden dürfen, wie in der galanten Schreibart, sondern bey welchem ein melodischer Satz vermittelst mancherley Versetzungen und Nachahmungen durchgeführt wird. (cols. 1447–48; cf. Marpurg 1753: unpaginated dedication [v]; Türk 1789: 405)

In outlining the opposition, Koch defined the strict style not only positively, in terms of strict dissonance control, techniques of imitation, and a serious affective character, but also negatively. It is the style that does not lend itself to the reigning compositional techniques of the late eighteenth century, that is, periodic phrasing, a slow harmonic rhythm, a hypotactic system of cadential articulation, and a homophonic texture of melodic treble and harmonic bass. With respect to the distinction between strict and free, Hatten's insistence on markedness—on the oppositional definitions of styles—is thus rooted firmly in eighteenth-century theoretical perspectives.

While pedagogues generally agreed on the negative definition of the strict style—it was opposed to free styles—they disagreed on the positive definition. Although the strict style took on varied hues in the various writings on musical performance and composition of the time, one can describe a general divergence between North-German writers, who were acutely aware of local Protestant traditions of figural counterpoint, and Austrian ones, who retained an allegiance to Italian compositional and theoretical traditions of vocal polyphony. Thus, in the quotation above, Koch, a Thuringian, located imitation and inversion close to the heart of counterpoint. By contrast, in the *Gründliche Anweisung zur Composition* (1790), Johann Georg Albrechtsberger, an Austrian, aimed at a plainer style. "By 'strict style,'" he wrote, "I mean that style that is written only for voices without any accompaniment of an instrument. It has more rules than the free style. The reason for this is that a singer does not hit tones as easily as an instrumentalist."[1] Like Koch, Albrechtsberger construed a binary opposition between strict and free styles. Like Koch, he drew attention to issues of dissonance treatment and part writing, though he grounded them in pragmatic rather than essentialist terms. But Koch and Albrechtsberger differed dramatically on what stylistic features constituted the strict style. In one case, the development of motives was essential, an obvious bow to the fugue. In the other, the voice leading and dissonance treatment of vocal polyphony were paramount.

Bound Style

Closely linked with the "strict" in its technical orientation is the term "bound" (*gebundene Schreibart*). Like "strict," "bound" suggests limitation and adherence to a law. And like "strict," the term could be given substance in various ways. To what was one bound in the bound style? Koch saw the suspension as the heart of the "bound" style. A note was bound over by a slur (*Bindung*) into the next measure. However, the term had a rich history (Chapin 2006: 96–97). For Gioseffo Zarlino, an imitative voice could be "bound" to another, that is, imitate the first voice throughout a passage, as in a canon, rather than break off before its end. For Athanasius Kircher, a secondary contrapuntal voice was "bound" to a plainchant *cantus firmus*; that is, it was not freely composed. When Johann Mattheson spoke of the "bound, single-voiced, and properly named church style" (*gebundener, einstimmiger, und eigentlich-sogenannten Kirchen-Styl*), by contrast, he had the ties of ligatures in mind. To trace such terminological meandering is to glimpse how learned styles (in the plural) could coalesce into a single field. Terms like "strict" and "bound" circumscribed musical style more than they defined it. Through their recurrence in the writings of musicians, they gave a sense of common identity and coherence to techniques and materials that were of diverse provenance.

Fugal Style

"Fugal style" (*fugierte Schreibart*), more technically precise than "strict" and "bound," points toward the opposite, more elaborate end of the spectrum of learned styles. Where "strict" refers to basic issues of dissonance treatment and part writing, and thus motivated a wide variety of learned styles, "fugal" refers to procedures of imitation and canon (which, as a "perpetual fugue," was often considered a subcategory of fugue; Walther 1732: 132; Koch 1802: col. 284). On first glance, the term seems to be proper to a genre, and thus not transmissible to the issue of topics. However, when theorists discussed fugues, they devoted the greatest attention and space to the initial entries of a fugue and to the niceties of invertible counterpoint. The theory of fugue tended to focus on parts, rather than wholes, in other words, and late eighteenth-century composers such as Haydn were drawn to it primarily because they hoped to learn lessons in invertible counterpoint and motivic imitation (Grier 2010). As a result, the "fugal style" easily lost its genre specificity, sliding easily toward fugato or motivic exchanges more generally.

Church Style

When one turns to the term "church style," one turns from issues of technique to those of place and function. Since the sixteenth century, the church had been the refuge of ornate and highly developed musical styles, in particular those animated by relatively equal polyphony or imitative counterpoint. Again, however, the term masks diversity, capturing styles within a culturally resonant but ultimately wide and porous common net. As Sulzer and Kirnberger noted in the article on church music in the *Allgemeine Theorie*, "figured church music has taken various forms according to the variety of circumstances."[2] The variety would certainly include North-German figural counterpoint and Italo-Austrian vocal polyphony, but it would also include genres and styles that have little to do with the learned style per se. Arias, for example, were examples of figured church music. They could also be treated as examples of high style, especially when they set noble or religious sentiments (Scheibe 1745: 126–27). Yet learned style they were not, though particular examples might well venture in that direction.

To be sure, Sulzer and Kirnberger spoke of church music, not of church style. Yet discussions of place and function regularly gave way to discussions of appropriate musical style, and these did not point unilaterally toward the learned style. In their encyclopedia article, Sulzer and Kirnberger listed various genres of church music, including plainchant, four-part chorale settings, and the oratorio chorus. This list rides over a rift between ideas of church music, one oriented technically toward monophony and modal organization and aesthetically around simplicity, the other oriented technically toward polyphony and imitative procedures and aesthetically around sophistication. Thus, the article sympathetically quotes Jean-Jacques Rousseau's *Dictionnaire de musique* (1768) at length, including his comments on the contrast between the simplicity of plainchant and the degenerate artificiality of modern harmony. Yet despite this critique of artifice, the *Allgemeine Theorie* article concludes with a nod toward the learned tradition. Church music required "a strong harmonist, as well as a man of circumspection and proper feeling."[3] The tension in the *Allgemeine Theorie* article between the two technical and aesthetic ideals of church music is due perhaps to the joint authorship of the article by a learned man of letters and a learned musician, each following his own aesthetic criteria, but it certainly highlights the considerable disparity between concepts of church style and learned style.

The tension also says something about the nature of any definition of style based on criteria of place and function. While it may be possible to find technical commonalities (such as imitative counterpoint in church music) that run through many works written for a particular place, definitions of style will ultimately be based primarily on issues of affect and meaning. The technical parameters of the style, so defined, will be highly malleable. Even as they recognized distinctions between church and theater music, musicians had long recognized that the expressive use of dissonance and the direct forms of address characteristic of recitative and aria were effective ways to move the hearts of their congregations, that is, to put them in the proper frame of mind to participate in the rituals of the church. The theater donated its styles and genres to the church, if with a parsimonious respect for religious propriety. One generation's impermissible mixture of sacred and secular styles could become the next generation's true church style, so long as the affects communicated by the music seemed appropriate to the church. As early as 1732, Johann Walther simply described the *stilo ecclesiastico* as "full of majesty, upright and serious, able to instill in the soul a spirit of devotion and to raise the soul to God."[4]

There were many who resisted the importation of theatrical styles into the church, of course. For them "learned style" had a signifying function that could turn it into an emblem of church music. Yet the signification was difficult to reconcile with compositional practice. Charles Burney, for example, excluded most oratorios, masses, and motets from his notion of church music: "by *Musica di Chiesa*, properly so called, I mean grave and scientific compositions for voices only, of which the excellence consists more in good harmony, learned modulation, and fugues upon ingenious and sober subjects, than in light airs and turbulent accompaniments" (1775: 1:334). Yet this description does not harmonize easily with his enthusiasm in 1772 for a "recently composed" Salve Regina sung to him by Hasse's daughters (a soprano and a contralto) at the composer's Viennese lodgings. "It is an exquisite composition, full of grace, taste, and propriety," Burney wrote (1:317–18). Although Burney did not specify the work more precisely, Hasse's known works include only one Salve Regina with two female soloists (soprano and alto), the *Salve Regina* in E flat major. Date and place of composition (Vienna, 1766) also make it the likely candidate. Though this work met Burney's approval, it does not answer to his restrictive definition of church music. Not only is it occasionally "turbulent" in its instrumental accompaniments, but it is bereft of "fugues on ingenious and sober subjects." Learned style was hardly synonymous with church style or church music.

Stile Antico

Stile antico is a term that is often used today to discuss either various seventeenth- and eighteenth-century versions of Italian *a cappella* polyphony or the seventeenth-century North-German motet style (Fellerer 1929; Wolff 1968). As with the term "learned style," late eighteenth-century musicians rarely used the term as such. It circulated in the seventeenth century, for example in Christoph Bernhard's style categories (Müller-Blattau 1999: 42; Miller 2001), as well as in the early eighteenth century (Heinichen 1728: 586), but it seems to have dropped out of circulation as precise technical terms for styles were absorbed into more general and more fluid categories. However, musicians were highly aware of the historicity of certain styles, as well as of the sea change in compositional technique that occurred in the early decades of the century as Neapolitan operatic styles and French galant aesthetics progressively dominated the musical scene. During his journeys through Northern Europe in 1772, Charles Burney sought out the historical origins of counterpoint through research in the archive, noted when musicians played in superannuated styles, and recorded the opinions of musicians who declared themselves above and beyond the old style, so filled with fugues or luxuriant in their inner voices (1775, 1: 2, 19, 28, 38–40, 306, 351). As a historian, Burney may have been particularly sensitive to issues of historicity, but he was a true representative of his time's confidence in its own taste, achievements, and progress.

However, this historical awareness did not necessarily map neatly onto the distinction between strict and free styles or between fugal and galant writing. Georg Philipp Telemann constructed his Overture–Suite in G major *Les nations anciennes et modernes*, TWV 55:G4 (1721), around three pairs of movements representing "ancient" and "modern" Germans, Swedes, and Danes respectively. As Steven Zohn notes (2008: 77), the "ancient" and "modern" refer in the work to French and Italian stylistic tendencies respectively. Telemann's distinction between ancient and modern can be read as a comment on the shift in German taste from French to Italian models in the early eighteenth century, but not in terms commonly associated with the learned style. Much later, in *An Essay on Practical Musical Composition* (1799), Augustus Frederic Christopher Kollmann noted that church, chamber, and theater styles could each be subdivided into ancient and modern varieties (102). It is thus difficult to reduce the idea of an old style to precise technical criteria. Not only was the reference to antiquity often part of a rhetorical strategy in which a composer preened himself between the pedantry of yesteryear and the modishness of the day (Chapin 2011), but what constituted an old style differed from place to place and time to time. To deal with the range of different historical styles in circulation in the eighteenth century, Michael Heinemann has proposed a useful distinction between those styles cultivated out of respect for reigning compositional norms (and through which musicians show their moral responsibility vis-à-vis tradition) and ones that have been subjected to a loss of awareness of the historical foundations of composition. Heinemann (2001: 226) argues that it is only in the latter case that the *stile antico* is aesthetically motivated, which in turn allows it to infuse church music with the aura of timelessness. It is clear that learned styles fall on both sides of this distinction.

Despite such variations and challenges of definition, however, one can identify principal strands of *stile antico* traditions. In Austria, the equal polyphony of the Catholic mass and motet anchored notions of antiquity. Palestrina provided practitioners with inspiration; Fux offered them a theoretical description. The "Palestrina style," it should be noted, was not Palestrina's style, but was rather one that had been adapted to thoroughbass harmony and that had hidden its original melodic orientation (Jeppesen 1925; Fellerer 1929; Heinemann 1994: 79–100). In Northern Germany, musicians also saw in Palestrina an embodiment of musical procedures set out by Zarlino and Sweelinck. However, the seventeenth-century Lutheran motet, strongly influenced by the expressive counterpoint of Orlando di Lasso, gave a distinct cast to the North-German *stile antico*, as did traditions of complex canonic and imitative procedures (Wolff 2001). This North-German tradition was transmitted to later decades through specialized genres, such as that of funerary counterpoint (Yearsley 1999: 197–200; 2002: 1–41), and through epistolary and musical exchanges within the professional sphere (Snyder 1980). It was further refracted through the exemplary works and practices of J. S. Bach, who offered the opportunity for late-century musicians both to look back nostalgically to a past culture and to indulge in their own time's cult of genius. Yet the contrapuntal procedures of Palestrina and Bach stood next to other genre-bound techniques that had attained the aura of age: prominent examples include the trio sonata texture, the oratorio chorus, and the French overture. These too were learned, historical styles, even when they did not exhibit the imitative exchanges or species organization now associated with the learned style.

Grave style

Another term that had a precise meaning in the seventeenth century but that entered into a more loosely defined conceptual field by the end of the eighteenth century was Christoph Bernhard's *contrapunctus gravis*, that is, the style marked by gravity (Müller-Blattau 1999: 42). For Bernhard, the term had a precise technical meaning. It referred to the style of vocal polyphony practiced by Palestrina and other sixteenth-century composers, and was opposed to the "luxuriant style," in which respectable counterpoint flowered luxuriantly through the many dissonant "figures." (With the stylistic shift of the early eighteenth century, these figures would eventually become essential parts of the learned style.) By the end of the eighteenth century, however, the term "grave" had dissipated into a field of adjectives that circumscribed the affective qualities of learned styles: ceremonial (*feierlich*), serious (*ernst*), grand, and so forth. Such characterizations depended on an aesthetic of feeling that presupposed that, as Heinrich Christoph Koch wrote in 1782, "among the fine arts, music is *the one that expresses sentiments by connecting tones*."[5]

But affective designations of learned styles were not uncontested. Alongside the aesthetic of affects that underpins Koch's writings and that indeed dominated the century, there was an aesthetic of effects that distinguished between moving the heart, on the one hand, and charming the ear or astonishing the mind, on the other. If all music had affective power according to an aesthetic of affects, only those styles that moved the heart did according to an aesthetic of effects.

This aesthetic of effects could be used both to applaud and to condemn learned styles. On the critical end, many writers designated learned styles as without emotional power, that is, as dry and dusty. According to Jean-Jacques Rousseau, frequently quoted on this matter, "in general fugues make music more noisy than agreeable."[6] Because of the lack of "unity of melody," he argued, the various learned artifices of fugues "serve more to display the art of composers than to flatter the ear of listeners."[7] In other words, he contested the emotional power of fugues. (For Rousseau, a writer who excelled in inverting and reworking traditional aesthetic, social, and political categories, to "flatter the ear" was to move the heart. Any music that failed to do that was not music by his book.)

On the honorific end of the same aesthetic of effects, it was possible to see learned styles as adding elevation over and above the emotional quality of a piece of music. In the article on the symphony in the *Allgemeine Theorie*, for example, Schulz distinguishes between the character (the affective quality), the style, and what one might designate the register of the piece:

> The symphony is admirably appropriate for the expression of grandeur, ceremony, and sublimity....If it is to achieve its end perfectly and be an integral part of the opera or piece of church music that it introduces, then, aside from this expression of grandeur and ceremony, it must have a character that puts the listener in the mood of the piece that follows and that is differentiated through a style appropriate for the church or the theater.

> Die Symphonie ist zu dem Ausdruk des Großen, des Feyerlichen und Erhabenen vorzüglich geschikt....Soll sie diesem Endzwek vollkommen Genüge leisten, und ein mit der Oper oder Kirchenmusik, der sie vorhergeht, verbundener Theil seyn, so muß sie neben dem Ausdruk des Großen und Feyerlichen noch einen Charakter haben, der den Zuhörer in die Gemüthverfassung setzt, die das folgende Stük im Ganzen verlangt, und sich durch die Schreibart, die sich für die Kirche, oder das Theater schikt, unterscheiden. (Sulzer 1792–94, 3: 478–79)

"A theme treated fugally" is one of the technical means by which this elevation can be achieved in the symphony. In this article, Schulz does not deny counterpoint and other complex musical techniques their affective force, as Rousseau does. Rather, he distinguishes between the degree of elevation and the feeling that is expressed. For example, joyous music can be light or distinguished. Although they came to different conclusions about the value of learned styles, Rousseau and Schulz had similar presuppositions about their operation. These writers presented the pomp and circumstance of learned styles not as feelings, but rather as qualities of register of a sui generis nature.

Elaborate Style

With "elaborate" or "wrought style" (*gearbeitete Schreibart*) one moves both to the broadest conception of the learned style and also to the heart of its logic, to the issues that held together the panoply of styles in a loose stylistic and conceptual field. The term can refer to the strict discipline required for dissonance control, to the figural elaboration of simple counterpoint, to the imitative treatment of a theme, or to polyphonic textures. It can also point to highly developed textures in general, including those characteristic of the fantasia and the symphony, or to what was later described as "motivic-thematic working" (*motivische-thematische Arbeit*; Lobe 1844). It thus points well beyond the learned style narrowly defined and toward the ethos of the high style in general.

LEARNED STYLES: SOURCE GENRES

Just as musicians could conceptualize learned styles in various ways, they could draw on a varied array of sources. As mentioned above, Palestrina served as an inspiration (if not a direct model) for composers throughout German-speaking lands, while in Northern Germany Johann Sebastian Bach provided a second model of high quality and high sophistication, especially among his sons, students, and musicians in close correspondence with them.

But genre models were perhaps more important than individual composers in the transmission of learned styles. Insofar as genre involves a social contract with the audience, particular genres have sociological implications and communicative power (Kallberg 1996: 5). Thus, when composers used a particular style outside of its original genre context, they could be using it because of associations suggested by the terms surveyed above, but they could also bring into play associations of the source genres. When Mozart drew on the style of chorale fantasy in the scene with the two armed men in the *Zauberflöte* (Example 11.2), he drew on a genre foreign to his Viennese audience (Hammerstein 1956). The alterity of the style thus supported the austerity of the two armed men and the rigors of the law they intone. It also contrasts with the homophonic humanity with which the two armed men and Tamino celebrate the latter's reunification with Pamina (Chapin 2006: 105–6).

Yet even the reference to genre brings up issues of approach. One can define genres of counterpoint in at least two senses, and accordingly there are at least two different types of audience with which a composer might communicate. Most traditionally, genres

EXAMPLE 11.2 Mozart, *Die Zauberflöte*, K. 620, Act 2 Scene 28, "Der, welcher wandert diese Straße," mm. 7–21.

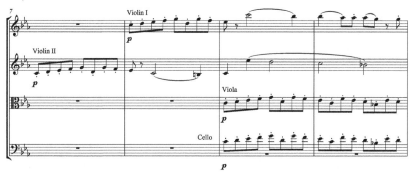

(*Continued*)

EXAMPLE 11.2 (Continued)

involve particular places and functions that put specialized musicians into contact with less specialized audiences. Styles of church music grounded in particular genres might include the fluid equal polyphony of *a cappella* mass and motet, the sober four-part chorale, the densely figured chorale fantasia, and, most generally, the thoroughbass counterpoint of concerted church music. Other prominent genres of counterpoint include the keyboard fugue (including subgenres such as the ricercar or canzona), the trio sonata (with its close polyphony of two upper voices supported by a melodic but functionally distinct bass line), the societal canon (or round), the table-top duet, and the puzzle or visiting-book canon. The list could go on. Each of these genres involves specific performance situations and meanings associated with these situations.

Such was the attention devoted to counterpoint, fugue, and canon in the theoretical literature of the time, however, that musicians could conceive genres of counterpoint from a quite different angle. Lawrence Dreyfus (1996: 135–68) has argued that composers thought about genres of counterpoint in terms of thematic types or technical artifices. From this perspective, genres of counterpoint would include simple fugue, double fugue (with one, two, or three themes), counterfugue, mixed fugue, canon, and cancrizans canon, as well as such thematic curiosities such as *contrapunto alla diritta* (countersubjects that snake in stepwise scales around a subject) or *alla zoppa* (limping countersubjects). Although classicizing theorists tended to caution against canonic artifices and recommend concise, "natural" subjects (Scheibe 1745: 169; Marpurg 1753: 27–30; Mattheson 1739: 387), lexicographers and theorists of baroque sensibility (Walther 1732: 182–83) or pragmatic eclecticism (Albrechtsberger 1790: 189–95) generously enumerated these various genres of counterpoint. Practicing musicians could find inspiration in this multiplicity. Warren Kirkendale (1979: 257–69) has persuasively argued that Beethoven's various thematic procedures in the Grand Fugue, Op. 133 (1826), were inspired by an enumeration of thematic artifices in Albrechtsberger's *Gründliche Anweisung zur Composition* (1790). The audience that eighteenth- and early nineteenth-century musicians courted was diverse and ran the gamut from the specialized musician to the amateur to the indifferent attendee of religious, civic, and social events. Counterpoint could simultaneously invoke quite different types of generic contract, some based on technical procedures, some based on associations of place and function.

Due to its home in genres both serious and societal, canon takes a singular place among learned techniques. While eighteenth-century musicians frequently cited (but rarely practiced) the canonic arts of melodic inversion, retrograde, and canzicrans as the *non plus ultra* of artifice, they could also use simple canons to attain elegance without pedantry. In 1723 Georg Philipp Telemann noted the value of canon to "melodic" modes of composition (Mattheson 1722–25, 1: 358–60), and during his voyage to Paris in 1737–38 he thought it appropriate to establish his position and his fame with the *18 canons mélodieux*, TWV 40:118–23.

The tradition of sophisticated *galanterie* would later flow into the canonic minuet, which had achieved the status of a subgenre by the end of the eighteenth century (see the list and discussion in Russell [1983: 76–97]). When E. T. A. Hoffmann composed his Symphony in E flat major in 1806, he showed off his learning and his modernity with just such a movement. Yet the distance between the simplicity of the minuet and the learnedness of the canon may also have provided musicians with the opportunity to stake positions on high and low stylistic spheres. Modern commentators (for instance, Lowe 2007: 115; see also 123) have entertained the possibility of critical intent or interpretation of such works as Haydn's String Quartet in D minor, Op. 76 No. 2/iii (Example 11.3), and there is no doubt that composers worked within a field that included champions of stylistic purity and critics of contrapuntal artifice, especially in Northern Germany. Joseph

EXAMPLE **11.3** Haydn, String Quartet in D minor, Op. 76 No. 2/iii, mm. 1–11.

Riepel spoke critically of the limits imposed by the "crab-minuet [*Krebsen-Menuet*] and other such paperwork."[8] For the most part, however, Austro-Italian musicians and listeners seem to have relished the collision of stylistic levels. Mozart noted the fun he had in mixing counterpoint and *galanterie*. When he visited a monastery in Augsburg in 1777, Mozart began a fugue, then contrasted it with "something jocular" (*ganz was scherzhaftes*) which was subsequently played "ass backwards" (*arschling*) and finally concluded the session by treating the jocular theme fugally. The dean of the institution was "beyond himself" (*ganz ausser sich*) with admiration, not indignation (Mozart 2005, 2: 82).

LEARNED STYLE: STYLISTIC ACCOMMODATIONS

From this review of terminology and genres of counterpoint, it is evident that eighteenth-century musicians had a sophisticated but unsystematic field of concepts and styles available to them. But if their terminology and their stylistic practice varied, the field that circumscribed it had a logical coherence. Although these various terms referred to different issues, they all pointed to music considered old, uncommon, or difficult. If eighteenth-century musicians did not have a concept of a unitary "learned style" per se, they most certainly did describe certain of their peers as learned, and they often recognized them through their mastery of this range of difficult and uncommon styles.

Moreover, the various learned styles that flowed into the learned style were all reformulated within the stylistic norms of the late eighteenth century (Dahlhaus 2001: 564–65). If the "strict style" originated in a logic of polyphony in which the careful control of intervallic successions maintained the linear integrity of parts and thus musical coherence, by the late eighteenth century coherence depended on the harmonic articulation of hierarchies of cadences at gauged intervals. The "strict style" survived as a term long after the compositional logic it served to support had acceded to a new one.

The strict style could be accommodated with galant norms in two basic ways, either through the elaboration of basic voice leading patterns such that features associated with the strict style (especially suspensions) were readily apparent to the ear, or through the intensification of motivic exchanges into fugatos. In the first case, as Stephen Rumph has argued (2012: 149–54), counterpoint functioned as a "universal grammar" that might suffuse styles both strict and free. Recent scholarship on schemata offers good examples of this procedure. As Robert Gjerdingen (2007: 439–47) has noted, certain contrapuntal passages in modern instrumental works owe much to one of the most common schemata of the eighteenth-century, the Prinner in Gjerdingen's terminology. In its basic form, it involves a descent from the sixth to the fourth scale degree in the upper voice, accompanied in parallel thirds or tenths in a lower voice (normally the bass). In its contrapuntal version, the parallel thirds are splayed through suspensions, ornamented with a tenor harmonization, and fitted out with a dominant pedal. Galant simplicity becomes an elaborate contrapuntal texture. Both versions appear in the concluding Amen to the "Quando Corpus" of Pergolesi's *Stabat Mater* (Example 11.4a–b). Gjerdingen suggests that the "Stabat Mater Prinner" became a fixed variant of the schema, an easy way to produce a texture of amplitude or an aura of antiquity. One example can be seen in the two contrapuntal Prinners (without dominant pedal this time) that conclude the exposition of the Larghetto to Mozart's Quintet for Clarinet and Strings in A major, K. 581/ii (Example 11.5a–b). While much of the Larghetto features either clarinet or first violin, these "learned" passages appear as the culmination of a progressive intensification of texture leading up to the recapitulation (and a return to a homophonic texture). Mozart achieves a replete texture and a character of crystalline quiescence through the use of one of the most typical galant schemata of the eighteenth century, and indeed by using a variant of it that had itself become a stereotype. As Roman Ivanovitch (2011: 3–30) has shown, Mozart called on this strategy time and again in his retransitions.

The passage also exemplifies the tendency of the learned style to merge seamlessly into an elegant high style. While the contrapuntal Prinners contrast markedly with the homophonic vocal style of the recapitulation, the "learning" of the passage is carried lightly. It lies less in the style or in the texture than in the way Mozart uses it to return to

EXAMPLE 11.4 Pergolesi, *Stabat Mater*, "Quando Corpus," Amen: (a) mm. 30–36; (b) mm. 74–80.

the recapitulation. The schema appears first in the dominant key area (Example 11.5a), as one would expect at the end of an exposition. When it reappears a few measures later (Example 11.5b), it is heard in the tonic but concludes on the dominant. The tonal return of the recapitulation is thus prefigured in the second contrapuntal Prinner. Because tonal and thematic return are mildly out of synch, the recapitulation comes with a harmonic gentleness that tallies well with the *dolce* melody and tranquility in dynamics.

If learned textures can be achieved through the elaboration of simple melodic-harmonic formulas, they can also be achieved through the intensification of the imitative exchanges of motives between instruments that are typical of late eighteenth-century instrumental genres. Stefan Kunze (1988: 119–28) emphasized the fundamental difference between early eighteenth-century contrapuntal textures, in which thoroughbass harmony maintains the ideal continuity of polyphonic lines and in which motivic figuration occurs as an elaboration of these lines, and, on the other hand, later textures in which motives are freely developed within a harmonic field ruled by metric organization, cadences, and a slow harmonic rhythm. A Schenkerian might reasonably respond that the relationship between motive and contrapuntal line is loosened rather than lost, but Kunze's distinction is valid if taken as based on a difference in degree rather than in kind.

Mozart's String Quintet in E flat major, K. 614/iv provides a case in point (Example 11.6). A sonata rondo, though one handled less as a form than as play on the conventions of rondo and sonata organization, the movement begins the development section with the first part of the rondo theme. Fragments of this theme are then passed back and forth, a gentle imitation that would hardly pass as an example of strict style. This leads into a fugato with two discrete themes in a self-consciously strict style. For the most part, harmonies change only once per measure, such that the figuration within a measure occurs less as the development of a particular contrapuntal voice than it does as an elaboration of the harmony.

EXAMPLE 11.5 Mozart, Quintet for Clarinet and Strings in A major, K. 581/ii: (a) mm. 33–38; (b) mm. 45–51.

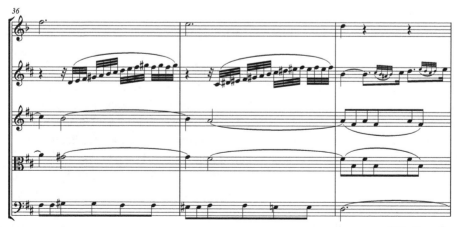

(Continued)

EXAMPLE 11.5 (Continued)

These two examples demonstrate the degree to which "learned style" is a particular formation of standard instrumental styles. This proximity of learned and standard practice was acknowledged by eighteenth-century musicians, even as they also cited the position that strict and free represented opposed styles. For instance, musicians often recognized that imitative procedures (or counterpoints) could be productively used at certain places in a sonata, symphony, quartet, or other such instrumental genre. Sulzer and Kirnberger, in their article on counterpoint for the *Allgemeine Theorie*, noted that "to say that counterpoints are introduced into a symphony, a concerto, etc. is to say that there are passages in which the voices are exchanged against each other."[9]

If the learned style was accommodated to the galant style and its genres, it was often done so in ways that suited particular formal requirements of modern forms and genres. In instrumental music, composers drew on the learned style to invest certain genres with distinction or with the aura of tradition, especially the prestigious symphony and

string quartet, but also for formal reasons, notably to add drama to development sections or to build toward climactic perorations. In both formal roles, composers built
on the opposition between strict and free styles. If musicians celebrated the grace and
elegance of galant or free styles—rooted in the symmetries, simplicities, and stabilities
of periodicity, diatonic harmonic, and homophony—they realized that they could move
toward complication or catharsis by dipping into the stylistic resources of learned styles.
They could do this all the better as learned styles tended to depend on "derivational"
approaches to theme and structure, to use a distinction developed by Adolf Nowak
(1990). Musical material was "derived" or spun forth from the initial theme, which
lent intensity or material gravity to the musical texture. Most late eighteenth-century
instrumental forms, by contrast, depended on "dispositional" treatments of theme and

EXAMPLE 11.6 Mozart, String Quintet in E flat major, K. 614/iv, mm. 102–20.

(*Continued*)

EXAMPLE 11.6 (Continued)

structure in which themes articulated key areas, leaving certain passages, in particular the later portions of theme groups, as motivically faceless if formally fundamental.

One might distinguish between three formal functions assigned the learned style in modern genres and forms: it can provide disruption, emphasis, or variation. Although the disruptive potential of learned styles suited development sections in exemplary fashion—the development fugato would become almost a genre in its own right—it could also be used in bridge sections. Emphasis was exceptionally important to the perorational grandeur of codas and other moments of intensification, such as the double exordiums and bridge sections of Mozart's "Jupiter" Symphony (Sisman 1993: 71–79), but sometimes could be applied to openings or entire movements, as was the case in the tradition of "rococo" chamber music, extensively documented by Warren Kirkendale (1979). Finally, composers could call on learned styles to expand the diversity of textures and characters in their variation movements.

Such uses of counterpoint point toward a different way of understanding the strict dissonance treatment and imitative procedures now associated with the learned style. Eighteenth-century musicians could conceive of them as matters of technique, not of style. As matters of technique, they can be applied to a wide variety of styles. Although Johann David Heinichen distinguished between the "antique style" and the theatrical style, he defined certain aspects of dissonance treatment as fundamental to all composition: "normally, no dissonant passage in the theatrical style can pass as correct if it is not succeeded by a legal resolution of the dissonance."[10]

Imitation could also be treated as technical procedure. Johann Friedrich Daube, for instance, devoted the final chapters of *Der musikalische Dilettante* (1773) to "artificial" or "artistic" compositional procedures (*künstliche Komposition*), including imitation, canon, simple fugue, double counterpoint, and double fugue (151). Yet Daube is at pains to point out the usefulness and even necessity of these techniques, despite their complexity and aura of learnedness. He insisted that they were amenable to all styles, for example devoting several pages to the table top duet, a type of canon that "consists chiefly of singing and brilliant material" (*besonders aus dem Singenden*

EXAMPLE 11.7 Daube, *Der musikalische Dilettante* (1773), 279, double counterpoint applied to brilliant material.

(*Continued*)

EXAMPLE **11.7** (Continued)

und Brillanten besteht; 191). While he associated the technique of double counterpoint most with fugue, he noted that it was generally useful. For instance, it was a way to introduce "the most charming combinations into arias, symphonies, etc." (*die artigsten Vermischungen in Arien, Sinphonien etc. etc.*; 278). "Even in magnificent, brilliant passages, double counterpoint at the octave can be used and produce a good effect."[11] His example demonstrates the difficulty of distinguishing learned style from elevated composition (Example 11.7). Although Daube clearly saw this passage as made possible by one of the most complex compositional techniques, it hardly smacks of antiquity.

Because imitation and procedures of strict dissonance treatment (such as suspensions) could be used to form other styles, they do not by themselves suffice to mark a passage as learned. Elaine Sisman (1993: 68–79) has sensibly argued that a restrictive definition of the learned style is necessary. While elevated composition may frequently draw on techniques associated with learned styles, especially imitative textures and motivic working, it is to be distinguished from the learned style per se—"a consciously artificial mode of display, an ornament" or a "figure" (70).

SIGNIFICATION

The signification of the learned style depends much on context: there is no fixed meaning to the style, but rather its signification needs to be assessed on a case-by-case basis, taking into account the genre origins of the modeled style, presuppositions and prejudices about elaborate or artificial composition, the particular intentions of composers and patrons, venues of performance, the horizon of expectations of performers and listeners, and of course, most importantly, the way the topic is used within a particular musical context. Because of the great diversity of stylistic models and ideas of learned technique, the topic can mean many things. Indeed, it is a serious desideratum of scholarship that greater attention be paid to the types of signification learned styles could have and the ways that such signification could come about. Such examples as the table top duet, the societal canon, or the visiting book puzzle canon, which were undoubtedly associated with artificial modes of composition, show that learned styles did not necessarily gesture toward grandeur and distinction, or, depending on the interpreter's perspective, court pedantry. The aesthetic categories associated with curiosity, ingenuity, and pleasing bizarrerie, materially and prominently displayed in the scientific cabinet of the eighteenth century, remain underresearched in the musical domain.

The process of interpretation can be informed by diverse source types. One can read the signification of learned styles from works of vocal music in which the styles are matched to certain themes in the text, or from the way that learned styles are invoked in works of instrumental music. As for written sources, one can turn to handbooks, treatises, dictionaries, journals, pamphlets, and letters, whether written by specialist musicians or by amateurs. Finally, through studies of manuscript collections and through second-hand accounts, it is possible to document the taste for learned styles among discrete groups or populations: musicians, of course, but also members of the higher nobility, such as the Habsburg Emperor Joseph II or Princess Anna Amalia of Prussia.

Despite the interpretive challenges, there is no doubt that the conceptual field associated with learned styles coalesced around certain nodes. Above all, ties to church music and pedagogical practice made the learned style particularly resonant for dealing with three areas of deep concern and even crisis for eighteenth-century musicians, critics, and listeners: professionalism, religion, and political order. References to the church were obligatory in any dictionary article on counterpoint. By the same token, pedagogues always insisted that it was essential to master fugue and canon if one was to master the art of composition. Religious and professional values could easily intertwine, for laments for the loss of religious values could easily slide into grief at the loss of professional skill and could be further linked to general umbrage taken at any perceived threat to society. Such intersections point toward the fundamental cultural value of counterpoint, as a sign of order and tradition. Other concepts and ideals appear as variations on these themes: God, cosmology, nature, number, law, history, communal collectivity, uncanny alterity, seriousness of purpose, routine and pedantry, the mechanical, and masculinity, among others.

These various significations are motivated by a combination of factors: by the character of the music produced by learned styles, by the social place and function of learned genres, and by the performing forces required by some polyphonic genres. In eighteenth-century oratorios, for example, choruses represent the congregation of the people of Israel, and by implication also latter-day communities, often national in character. The choruses are grand. They use techniques associated with church music and legitimated by their antiquity and sophistication. And the real multitude of performers pointed toward the imagined or represented multitude of a social collective.

If affective, functional, and performance considerations could stand in an easy balance with the cultural significations based on them, the ideas and ideals could also spiral into ideology, particularly when specialized musicians found their values and practices challenged. Anxious to defend counterpoint and fugue against the charge of pedantry and inexpressiveness, expert musicians invested fugue and imitative technique with a cultural significance that often seems forced. In what might be described as an archeology of learned composition, Johann Nikolaus Forkel described the origins of the fugue in social terms:

> Imagine a people that is emotionally captivated by an important event. Now imagine that one member of the community, perhaps overwhelmed by the strength of his sentiment, sings a short and powerful phrase as an expression of his sentiment. Will not this explosion of emotion gradually run through all the members of this people? Will not first one, then many, and finally almost all follow him, each agreeing in general with the main sentiment but also modifying the phrase to fit his individual way of feeling about things?

> Man stelle sich also ein Volk vor, welches durch die Erzählung einer wichtigen Begebenheit in Empfindung gesetzt worden ist, und denke sich nun, daß ein Mitglied desselben, vielleicht durch die Stärke seiner Empfindung zur Aeußerung derselben zuerst hingerissen, einen kurzen, kräftigen Satz als Ausdruck seines Gefühls anstimmt; wird nicht dieser Ausbruch seiner Empfindung nach und nach die sämmtlichen Glieder dieses Volks ergreifen, wird ihm nicht erst eines, dann mehrere, und zuletzt die meisten nachfolgen, und jedes den angestimmten Gesang, zwar nach seiner eigenen individuellen Empfindugsart modificiren, im Ganzen aber dem Hauptgefühl nach mit ihm übereinstimmen? (Forkel 1788: 47–48)

It is clear that the oratorio chorus inspired Forkel's description of the fugue. But it is surprising both that Forkel sought to map the signification of this genre onto the history of the fugue and that he addressed the genesis of the fugue in general, not just the oratorio chorus. To legitimate a genre under attack by men of letters, Forkel drew on the Rousseauvian equation of musical voice with a singing person. The forced argumentation indicates the degree to which the signification of learned styles could outstrip the functional or practical considerations that originally motivated it. In 1802 Heinrich Christoph Koch quoted the passage in his *Musikalisches Lexikon* (cols. 611–14). Forkel's idea of the sentimental fugue clearly struck a chord amongst professional musicians.

In each of field of cultural resonance—professionalism, religion, and political or social order—the positive valuation accorded the style could easily shade into irony or invert into ridicule. While learned styles could be justified as part of a human drive toward sophistication, both critics and composers increasingly criticized them for artificiality and pedantry. (See, for example, Haydn's fugue to *Die Jahreszeiten* No. 20 "O Fleiß, o edler Fleiß!") Such instability was in part due to a shift in musical style from polyphony toward homophony over the course of the eighteenth century, but it also owed much to the mistrust of human artifice that shadowed the Enlightenment, particularly in music, as well as to the interrelated suspicion that the religious and political institutions that were once perceived as natural expressions of a divine order were but the products of human history.

Yet in each field, there was more disagreement than certainty, and that affects how one reads the written sources that suggest the signification of learned styles. They may say as much about the written traditions of speaking about music as they do about the music, though of course the two cannot be disassociated. Take the issue of professionalism, for instance. Men of letters may have professed universal knowledge, but they were often amateurs in musical matters (Lütteken 1999: 214–17). In general, while men of letters tended to value "nature" in music and find fault with artificiality or to restrict it to the church, musicians and critics often had more complex feelings. If they were attuned to the general taste for "nature" and tended to defer to their lettered colleagues when it came to drafting aesthetic manifestos or expounding on their art, they also valued the traditional tools of their trade.

The gap between men of letters and musicians can be seen exemplarily in Sulzer's *Allgemeine Theorie der schönen Künste*. Sulzer was a man of letters; Kirnberger and Schulz musicians. At the end of the highly technical article on fugue, richly illustrated with musical examples, the encyclopedia concludes summarily that "those who consider fugal writing to be superannuated pedantry betray their deficient, flawed understanding of the most essential aspects of art."[12] The article on music in general (Sulzer 1792–94, 3: 421–83), however, draws its examples from Ovid and Jean-Jacques Rousseau—"one of the best minds of our century" (*eines der ersten Köpfe unsers Jahrhunderts*; 432)—and finds the fundamental principles of music embodied in the civic festivals and "folk" songs of the Greeks. While the solidity of strict composition (*reiner Satz*) receives its nod—it is not "unnecesary pedantry" (*unnütze Pedanterey*)—the difference in focus is palpable.

Drawing attention to such differences of audience, Bernard Harrison (1998) argued that learned taste in Paris in the second half of the eighteenth century, represented by Rousseau and the Encyclopedists, favored melody and simplicity. The harmonic extravagances of the symphony, by contrast, were popular with audiences. In other words, the highly self-conscious thought of an intellectual elite could be emblematized in simple musical styles, not just in the complex ones of imitative counterpoint. Because of the wide gap between different takes on learned styles, written documents should be taken as pointing toward poles in a spectrum of opinions on learned styles.

As for religious and political order, musicians and other commentators may have frequently associated learned styles with the church and with the aristocracy, but their reasons for doing so were many. There is no doubt that the church remained a home for music of a conservative stamp and it is also certain that some members of the aristocracy cultivated a taste for counterpoint and fugue. However, musicians had been at pains since the seventeenth century at the latest to apply a rich expressive palette of theatrical and chamber styles in the church. In other words, musicians worked with a range of styles, even as theorists tended to categorize. As Emil Katz pointed out (1926: 39), the seventeenth-century Italian composer and Polish Kapellmeister Marco Scacchi defined church, theater, and chamber styles along technical and aesthetic lines. Only through this turn away from functional and sociological criteria, used by Athanasius Kircher, was he able to represent musical styles in a systematic fashion. Thus, while eighteenth-century musicians may have held fast to elements of the sociological distinction between church, theater, and chamber styles, associating counterpoint with the church, they may have done so in part for apologetic or critical reasons. To mark the style as proper to the church was either to defend it with the institution's prestige and sacred function or, alternatively, to attempt to denigrate the style as slavish to tradition. By the same token, members of the ruling nobility may have had a taste for counterpoint and fugue in part to burnish their own prestige. Musicians, for their part, could claim distinction for their profession by associating their music with royal or imperial tradition. Such associations indicate possible signification, not fixed meanings.

The very difficulty in pinning learned styles to particular places, functions, or populations is responsible for the complex signification of the learned style as a *sign*. While churches and aristocratic chambers resounded with a mixture of styles and stylistic mixtures, musicians and critics clearly *wanted* to associate fugues, fugatos, and other learned procedures with the church and with the nobility. The significations of learned styles outstripped compositional practice by a considerable measure. Learned styles were overdetermined, in other words, perhaps because of their link to the religious and existential concerns of musicians and audiences. To judge from the massive scholarly literature now devoted to counterpoint and the learned style, one that probably outstrips the literature devoted to any other marked style of the eighteenth century, the situation has not changed.

In sum, learned styles were a central concern to musicians throughout the eighteenth and into the nineteenth century and beyond. When adapted to and yet still marked against reigning norms of periodic phrasing, functional harmony, and homophonic texture, they could take on distinct cultural and formal functions as the learned style. The concerns and anxieties of musicians and critics with issues of order—whether professional, religious, or political—allowed both learned styles and the learned style to take on an inordinate importance within the stylistic field of the time and perhaps to interpretations of the repertoire today as well.

Notes

1. "Unter dem strengen Satze verstehe ich den, der für bloße Singstimmen, ohne alle Begleitung eines Instrumentes verfertiget wird. Er hat mehrere Regeln, als der freye. Die

Ursache davon ist: weil ein Sänger die Töne nicht so leicht findet, als ein Instrumentist" (Albrechtsberger 1790: 17).

2. "Der figurirte Kirchengesang hat nach Verschiedenheit der Gelegenheiten mancherley Gestalt angenommen" (Sulzer 1792–94, 3: 19).

3. "Darum erfordert die Kirchenmusik nicht nur einen sehr starken Harmonisten, sondern auch zugleich einen Mann von starker Ueberlegung und einem richtigen Gefühl" (Sulzer 1792–94, 3: 22).

4. "*Stilo Ecclesiastico, gall. Stile pour l'Eglise, lat. Stylus Ecclesiasticus*, der Kirchen-Styl, ist voller Majestät, ehrbar und ernsthafft, kräfftig die Anacht einzuflössen, und die Seele zu Gott zu erheben" (Walther 1732: 584; cf. Albrechtsberger 1790: 378).

5. "Sie ist unter den schönen Künsten *diejenige, die durch Verbindung der Töne Empfindungen ausdrückt*" (Koch 1782–93, 1: 4).

6. "Les *Fugues*, en general, rendent la Musique plus bruyante qu'agréable" (Rousseau 1995: 832).

7. Les artifices de canon et de fugue "servent plus à étaler l'art des Compositeurs qu'à flatter l'oreille des Ecoutans" (Rousseau 1995: 833).

8. "Zu einem Krebsen-Minuet und anderem dergleichen papieren Zeuge hat man sich sonderlich stark an die Regeln zu binden, wodurch zwar der Gesang hinten bleibt" (Riepel 1768: 76).

9. "Man sagt: es seyen in einer Symphonie, in einem Concert u. s. f. Contrapunkte angebracht, wenn man sagen will, es seyen Stellen darin, wo die Stimmen gegen einander verwechselt worden" (Sulzer 1792–94, 1: 580).

10. "Daß ordentlicher Weise kein, in *Dissonanti*en bestehender *Theatrali*scher Satz oder Gang vor richtig *passir*en könne, wo nicht zugleich eine *legale Resolution* der *Dissonanz* darauff erfolget" (Heinichen 1728: 587).

11. "Sogar in prächtigen brillanten Passagen kann der doppelte Kontrepunkt in der Oktave angebracht werden, und eine gute Wirkung verschaffen" (Daube 1773: 279).

12. "Diejenigen, die den Fugensatz für veraltete Pedanterey halten, verrathen sich, daß sie von dem Wesentlichsten der Kunst sehr fehlerhafte und unvollständige Begriffe haben" (Sulzer 1792–94, 2: 277).

REFERENCES

Albrechtsberger, Johann Georg. 1790. *Gründliche Anweisung zur Composition*. Leipzig: Breitkopf.

Allanbrook, Wye Jamison. 1983. *Rhythmic Gesture in Mozart:* Le nozze di Figaro *and* Don Giovanni. Chicago: University of Chicago Press.

Burney, Charles. 1775. *The Present State of Music in Germany, the Netherlands and United Provinces; Or, The Journal of a Tour through Those Countries, Undertaken to Collect Materials for a General History of Music*. 2 vols. London: Becket, Robson, and Robinson.

Chapin, Keith. 2006. Strict and Free Reversed: The Law of Counterpoint in Koch's *Musikalisches Lexikon* and Mozart's *Zauberflöte*. Eighteenth-Century Music 3/1: 91–107.

——. 2011. Counterpoint: From the Bees or for the Birds? Telemann and the *Galant* Quarrel with Tradition. *Music and Letters* 92/3: 377–409.

Cherubini, Luigi. 1835. *Theorie des Contrapunktes und der Fuge / Cours de Contre-point et de Fugue*. Leipzig: Kistner; Paris: Schlesinger.

Dahlhaus, Carl. 2001. Counterpoint: §12–16. In *The New Grove Dictionary of Music and Musicians*, 2nd ed., ed. Stanley Sadie and John Tyrrell, vol. 6, 561–71. London: Macmillan.

Daube, Johann Friedrich. 1773. *Der musikalische Dilettant: Eine Abhandlung der Komposition*. Vienna: Trattner.

Dreyfus, Laurence. 1996. *Bach and the Patterns of Invention*. Cambridge, MA: Harvard University Press.

Einstein, Alfred. 1945. *Mozart: His Character, His Work*. New York: Oxford University Press.

Fellerer, Karl Gustav. 1929. *Der Palestrinastil und seine Bedeutung in der vokalen Kirchenmusik des achtzehnten Jahrhunderts: Ein Beitrag zur Geschichte der Kirchenmusik in Italien und Deutschland*. Augsburg: Filser.

Forkel, Johann Nicolaus. 1788–1801. *Allgemeine Geschichte der Musik*. 2 vols. Leipzig: Schwickert.

Gjerdingen, Robert. 2007. *Music in the Galant Style*. New York: Oxford University Press.

Grier, James. 2010. The Reinstatement of Polyphony in Musical Construction: Fugal Finales in Haydn's Op. 20 String Quartets. *The Journal of Musicology* 27/1: 55–83.

Hammerstein, Reinhold. 1956. Der Gesang der geharnischten Männer: Eine Studie zu Mozarts Bachbild. *Archiv für Musikwissenschaft* 13/1: 1–24.

Harrison, Bernard. 1998. *Haydn: The "Paris" Symphonies*. Cambridge: Cambridge University Press.

Hatten, Robert S. 1994. *Musical Meaning in Beethoven: Markedness, Correlation, and Interpretation*. Bloomington: Indiana University Press.

Heinemann, Michael. 1994. "…alla Palestrina": Zur Etablierung eines satztechnischen Ideals im 17. Jahrhundert. In *Musik-Konzepte No. 86: Palestrina zwischen Démontage und Rettung*, 9–27. Munich: Edition text + kritik.

——. 2001. Carl Philipp Emanuel Bach und der Stile antico. In *Carl Philipp Emanuel Bachs geistliche Musik*, 226–39. Frankfurt an der Oder: Konzerthalle Carl Philipp Emanuel Bach.

Heinichen, Johann David. 1728. *Der General-Bass in der Composition*. Dresden: Author.

Ivanovitch, Roman. 2011. Mozart's Art of Retransition. *Music Analysis* 30/1: 1–36.

Jeppesen, Knud. 1925. *Der Palestrinastil und die Dissonanz*. Leipzig: Breitkopf & Härtel.

Kallberg, Jeffrey. 1996. *Chopin at the Boundaries: Sex, History, and Musical Genre*. Cambridge, MA: Harvard University Press.

Katz, Erich. 1926. Die musikalischen Stilbegriffe des 17. Jahrhunderts. Ph.D. diss., Albert-Ludwigs-Universität zu Freiburg i. Br.

Kirkendale, Warren. 1979. *Fugue and Fugato in Rococo and Classical Chamber Music*. Durham, NC: Duke University Press.

Koch, Heinrich Christoph. 1782–93. *Versuch einer Anleitung zur Composition*. 3 vols. Vol. 1: Rudolstadt, 1782. Vols. 2 and 3, Leipzig: Adam Friedrich Böhme, 1787 and 1793.

——. 1802. *Musikalisches Lexikon*. Frankfurt-am-Main: August Hermann der Jüngere.

Kollmann, Augustus Frederic Christopher. 1799. *An Essay on Practical Musical Composition*. London: Author.

Kunze, Stefan. 1988. *Wolfgang Amadeus Mozart: Sinfonie in C-Dur KV 551, Jupiter-Sinfonie*. Munich: Fink.

Lobe, Johann Christian. 1844. *Compositions-Lehre: Oder umfassende Theorie von der thematischen Arbeit und den modernen Instrumentalformen*. Weimar: Voigt.

Lowe, Melanie. 2007. *Pleasure and Meaning in the Classical Symphony*. Bloomington: Indiana University Press.

Lütteken, Laurenz. 1999. Musik in der Aufklärung—Musikalische Aufklärung? *Musiktheorie* 14/3: 213–29.

Marpurg, Friedrich Wilhelm. 1753. *Abhandlung von der Fuge*. Berlin: Halde und Spener.

Mattheson, Johann. 1722–1725. *Critica Musica*. Hamburg: Author.

———. 1739. *Der vollkommene Capellmeister*. Hamburg: Christian Herold. Reprint, Kassel: Bärenreiter, 1954.

Miller, Stephen R. 2001. Stile antico. In *The New Grove Dictionary of Music and Musicians*, 2nd ed., ed. Stanley Sadie and John Tyrrell, vol. 24, 390. London: Macmillan.

Mozart, Wolfgang Amadeus. 2005. *Briefe und Aufzeichnungen: Gesamtausgabe*. Kassel Bärenreiter; Munich: Deutscher Taschenbücher Verlag.

Müller-Blattau, Joseph, ed. 1999. *Die Kompositionslehre Heinrich Schützens in der Fassung seines Schülers Christoph Bernhard*. Kassel: Bärenreiter.

Nowak, Adolf. 1990. Der Begriff "Musikalisches Denken" in der Musiktheorie der Aufklärung. In *Neue Musik und Tradition: Festschrift Rudolf Stephan*, ed. Josef Kuckertz, Helga de la Motte Haber, Christian Martin Schmidt, and Wilhelm Seidel. 113–22. Laaber: Laaber.

Ratner, Leonard G. 1980. *Classic Music: Expression, Form, and Style*. New York: Schirmer.

Riepel, Joseph. 1768. *Unentbehrliche Anmerkungen zum Contrapunct*. Augsburg: Lotter.

Rousseau, Jean-Jaques. 1995. *Écrits sur la musique, la langue et le théâtre*. Paris: Gallimard.

Rumph, Stephen. 2012. *Mozart and Enlightenment Semiotics*. Berkeley: University of California Press.

Russell, Tilden A. 1983. Minuet, Scherzando, and Scherzo: The Dance Movement in Transition, 1781–1825. Ph.D. diss., University of North Carolina, Chapel Hill.

Scheibe, Johann Adolph. 1745. *Critischer Musikus*. Leipzig: Bernhard Christoph Breitkopf.

Sisman, Elaine. 1993. *Mozart: The "Jupiter" Symphony, No. 41 in C major, K. 551*. Cambridge: Cambridge University Press.

Snyder, Kerala J. 1980. Dietrich Buxtehude's Studies in Learned Counterpoint. *Journal of the American Musicological Society* 33/3: 544–64.

Sulzer, Johann Georg. 1792–94. *Allgemeine Theorie der schönen Künste*, new expanded 2nd ed. 4 vols. Leipzig: Weidmann.

Türk, Daniel Gottlob. 1789. *Clavierschule, oder Anweisung zum Klavierspielen für Lehrer und Lernende, mit kritischen Anmerkungen*. Leipzig: Schwickert; Halle: Hemmerde und Schwetschke.

Walther, Johann Gottfried. 1732. *Musicalisches Lexicon oder Musicalische Bibliothec*. Leipzig: Deer.

Wolff, Christoph. 1968. *Der Stile Antico in der Musik Johann Sebastian Bachs*. Wiesbaden: Steiner.

———. 2001. Motet: §III. Baroque, 3. Germany, (i) The generation of Schütz. In *The New Grove Dictionary of Music and Musicians*, 2nd ed., ed. Stanley Sadie and John Tyrrell, vol. 17, 217–18. London: Macmillan.

Yearsley, David. 1999. Towards an Allegorical Interpretation of Buxtehude's Funerary Counterpoints. *Music and Letters* 80/2: 183–206.

———. 2002. *Bach and the Meanings of Counterpoint*. Cambridge: Cambridge University Press.

Zohn, Steven. 2008. *Music for a Mixed Taste: Style, Genre, and Meaning in Telemann's Instrumental Works*. New York: Oxford University Press.

CHAPTER 12

···

THE BRILLIANT STYLE

···

ROMAN IVANOVITCH

FOUNDATIONS

···

HARDLY anticipating the theoretical edifice to be erected after him, Leonard Ratner sketched out the topic of the "brilliant style" in four deft sentences:

> The term *brilliant*, used by Daube, 1797, Türk, 1789, and Koch, 1802, refers to the use of rapid passages for virtuoso display or intense feeling. Earlier Italian composers—Alessandro Scarlatti, Arcangelo Corelli, and Antonio Vivaldi among them—codified the brilliant style by systematic repetitions and sequences. Ex. 1-1a [a *furioso* aria by Heinichen] illustrates the brilliant style in an aria. Burney, 1789, quotes a number of examples of brilliant passages sung by the great virtuosos of the 18th century. (Ratner 1980: 19)

Three decades (and much ink) later, what strikes one now is how widely Ratner cast his net: lexical support from one end of the century, musical sources from the other, contexts both instrumental and vocal, German and Italian, capped by the fulcrum figure of Charles Burney, whose pancontinental outlook encompassed the broad span of the century, from Handel to Haydn. Slipping easily between the adjective "brilliant" and an implicitly codified "brilliant style," Ratner's description perhaps more surprisingly circumscribes a host of internal dualities, such as feeling and display, expression and mechanism, general character and technical, protosyntactical resource. More concerned with mapping out the topic's operative spaces than with fixing its own potential dualities as oppositions or complements (let alone ironing them out as inconsistencies), his subsequent discussions reveal the brilliant style as a vital presence, available in symphony, sonata, opera, concerto, or quartet. He presses it into service, for instance, for the coruscating elaborations of the learned style in Mozart's "Prague" Symphony (27–28), for the long stretches of virtuosic first violin passagework in the same composer's String Quintet in E flat major, K. 614 (245), or for the "harpsichord-like" flourishes near the beginning of Haydn's first "London" Sonata in E flat major, Hob. XVI:52 (413). It is even distinguished in the concerto from a genuine "bravura style," which Ratner explains as "brilliance for its own sake," and which, unlike the brilliant style, he suggests rarely occurs in Mozart's piano concertos (298). If there is a guiding principle, it is above all that the brilliant style is seen to work in tandem with the singing style to form the basic contrastive mechanism of the lingua franca. As Ratner puts it, "the contrast between the brilliant-vigorous and the gentle-cantabile...permeates classic rhetoric on every scale of magnitude" (219). (For Ratner, of course, it was the smallest scale, that of local events, that was the most salient.)

Subsequent topic theorists, even as they have attempted to shore up the conceptual foundations—variously via Enlightenment thinking (Wye Jamison Allanbrook), semiotics (Raymond Monelle), or indeed Enlightenment semiotics (Stephen Rumph)—have confirmed the indispensability and centrality of the "brilliant style." Allanbrook's study (1992) of Mozart's Piano Sonata in B flat major, K. 333, for example, in one of the cornerstone texts about topical process, places the brilliant style at the heart of a nexus involving virtuoso, concerto, and mechanical styles (yielding such additional compounds as "virtuoso-brilliant" and "mechanical virtuoso"). The brilliant style's counterpole is formed through the singing, intimate, sensitive, *empfindsam*, appoggiatura, and expressive styles. A later analysis of Haydn's String Quartet in B flat major, Op. 50 No. 1, designed in part explicitly to demonstrate the viability of topical analysis beyond the "promiscuous mimesis" of Mozart's piano sonatas (2014: 121), once more reveals the brilliant and singing styles as topical frames. The brilliant style "come[s] to the rescue" of a dangerously enervated main theme, and subsequently "stars in roughly 74 of the movement's 148 measures" (appearing undiluted in "in all but 18 of the 55 measures of the recapitulation" [2014: 123]).

Monelle too recognizes the axiomatic importance of the two styles. His concern is less with their intertextual resonances as such, however, than with the degree to which they project or are "indexical" of two basic types of temporality, the lyric and the progressive. For Monelle, then, the late eighteenth-century "mixed style" is fundamentally a matter of the control of temporality—"passages of progressive temporality" joined with "lyric evocations" to make up "the temporal amalgam of the classical movement" (2006: 65). This shift from the connotative to the functional—that is, away from the meanings called forth by a passage labeled as "brilliant" toward a more purely syntactic understanding of what such passages "do"—injects an important note of caution. For one thing, it calls into question the currency of the label itself: would it have mattered if Ratner had called it the "flowing" or "rushing" style (to select from the many available eighteenth-century synonyms)?[1] Moreover, if the brilliant and singing styles are indeed simply markers of a gross binary opposition that is practically inevitable, assigning a passage to one camp or the other would appear to have accomplished very little. Perhaps, to follow the line of reasoning, this is why analytical invocations of the brilliant style are so frequently shaded and qualified by other topical references: the brilliant style itself is too blunt an instrument.

Even more to the point is Monelle's assertion that the very idea of a "brilliant style" is a "modern perception, weakly supported by contemporary writers" (2000: 26). That is, while the characterization "brilliant" occurs with increasing regularity over the course of the eighteenth century, there is little direct discussion of composing "in the brilliant style." This is another way of addressing the perennial slippage from feature to adjective to topic: is all rapid music by definition "brilliant," and is all brilliant music therefore "in the brilliant style"? Clearly not. With something like rapidity we are dealing with what Rumph calls a figura—a "topical phoneme" or building block from which topics themselves are built. In this way, for example, "the juxtaposition of a rapid melodic line with a slower bass distinguishes both third-species counterpoint and brilliant style" (2012: 96). Importantly, Rumph suggests that, unlike many linguistic phonemes, musical figurae carry an indelible "kinesthetic-emotional" charge, a product of their affinity "with physical and psychic processes" (96). It is in the nature of brilliance to set the pulse racing or to call to mind the visual sensation of sparkle. And it is not purely a verbal sleight of hand to observe that deep within one proposed etymology of the word "brilliant" (the standard French one of *briller*, which derives its Italian source *brillare* from *prillare*, to pirouette) lies an ancient onomatopoeia for turning and jostling (the hypothesized root *pirl-*).[2] The word itself already connects sound and motion.

We should not jettison the term "brilliant," in fact: Ratner's senses were acute. In documentary terms, the eighteenth century was indeed the era in which the word "brilliant" (and its cognates) came to prominence across Europe, retaining just enough semantic shape to hold interest before ubiquity and overuse debased it in the nineteenth century as a cliché.[3] Connected in everyday usage literally to the dazzling effect of light and figuratively to spectacular, excellent actions or personal qualities, the range of musical contexts for the word "brilliant" included a timbral quality that "sticks out,"[4] glinting ornaments,[5] passagework itself,[6] a lively or spirited manner of performance,[7] a general character of magnificence or splendor for public pieces such as overtures and symphonies,[8] the aspect of performance (or "execution") relating to pure technique,[9] and of course a focal point of the mixed style.[10] Such items cannot determine a musical topos—no nominalist approach can—but they add resonance, establishing one type of extended referential field, a repertoire of wider meanings through which we might read the topical play of brilliance even in its narrower music-theoretical sense of virtuosic passagework.

If we reverse the flow to seek a purely musical late-eighteenth-century lens for the topic in this latter sense—a topical "home," in line with the axiomatic definition in this volume—it would surely be the concerto. Brilliance is not the whole story of the concerto, of course, whose virtuoso figurehead was expected theatrically to display equal command over both technical and expressive realms; nor was technical prowess itself foreign to other instrumental genres such as quartets and sonatas (although it is worth noting how often such elements are deemed "concerto-like").[11] Nonetheless, observing where the central aesthetic struggles of the concerto lay—few concertos were criticized for not being ostentatious enough—the lexical and musical trajectories eventually converge, clustering around matters of sheer sound, execution, effect, and attention.

The following sections shall explore these facets of the brilliant style, taking some readings of representative examples chosen from a range of genres. It may well prove fruitful eventually to understand the brilliant style, not through a simple present/

not-present dichotomy, but through a set of core tendencies—a propensity for high registers over low, execution over expression, the instrumental over the vocal, the public over the private, the theatrical over the intimate, the superficial over the substantial, the routine over the characteristic, the difficult over the easy, and so on. The balance between these factors, and their musical referents, would have shifted over the course of the century and from one location to another; our illustrative snapshots can be only that—frozen representations of a dynamic configuration (although, like ice-core samples, their accrued sediment can also be read). *Pace* Monelle, what was "built in" to the brilliant–singing complex was not simply command over matters of temporality, vital as that was, but command over who appeared to be in "control" of the music, where and how the audience should pay attention, and who was "speaking."

A LIMIT CASE: CONCERTO AND ARIA

Such issues come immediately to the fore in Example 12.1, a passage from Mozart's concert aria for soprano with piano obbligato, "Ch'io mi scordi di te...Non temer amato bene," K. 505. Premiered at a farewell concert for Nancy Storace, Mozart's first Susanna, with the composer himself at the keyboard (Mozart's thematic catalogue annotates the work as "für Mlle Storace und mich"), the scena stands at a singular joint of genres, the only such meeting point of the obbligato aria and the piano concerto in Mozart's oeuvre.[12] To a certain extent, this circumstance can help focus one of the obvious questions regarding topical "homes": whether or not under ordinary conditions a topic can be invoked *within* its home. Is it tautological to assert the presence of the brilliant style in the concerto? In part, the issue turns on whether one views topics solely as marked phenomena that emerge against a neutral background, or instead as constituent components of that very background, implicitly ever-present if only occasionally rising to the level of analytical salience. In either case, K. 505 suggests that policing the border may be less important than developing a sensitivity to how the border has been drawn. Adjudicating on the topical credentials of the piano's figuration in Example 12.1, for instance—ruling it in or out as brilliant style according to the degree to which aria or concerto is deemed the dominant context—seems beside the point. The repertoire of figures from which Mozart draws is quite routine, available in any keyboard composition. If there is something of the concerto here, it lies not in the figures themselves but in the particularities of their simultaneous deployment in both hands—with two different patterns in mm. 149–50, and in parallel sixths in mm. 154–55. Such passagework abounds in concertos such as K. 466 in D minor and K. 467 in C major, but is relatively rare outside the genre. (Generally speaking, beyond the concertos, when simultaneous sixteenth notes occur in Mozart's keyboard music, they usually involve right hand runs against an Alberti bass or both hands working in parallel octaves; passages such as the parallel sixths in mm. 154–55—and the same would apply with passages in tenths—are much more commonly found as at the very end of m. 155, with one hand moving in eighth notes.)[13]

EXAMPLE **12.1** Mozart, "Ch'io mi scordi di te...Non temer, amato bene" for soprano and piano, K. 505, mm. 148–57.

(Continued)

EXAMPLE **12.1** (Continued)

More than this, the topical significance of the passage is also shaded by the combination of the passagework with literal singing (not "singing style")—and at the point of a
sob, no less ("ah, perchè?"); by the figuration's subtle shift, moderated via the ascending scale, from outlining harmonic content to tracing the singer's melodic curve, in the
way that a painter might play with figure and ground, or perhaps calling to mind a distinction made a long time earlier by Mattheson between keyboard figuration (*passaggi*)
whose purpose seems to be the demonstration of dexterity alone, and that which originates as elaborations of a melody (*diminutionibus* or *melismis*), and so contains at least a
trace of something inherently "singable" (1981: 858); by the functional shift of the pedal
point, coordinated with the change in figuration, from the extension of a dominant
arrival to a genuine retransition (which itself employs a well-worn Mozartian routine);[14]
by the status of the composition as a reworking of an aria from *Idomeneo*, in which the
obbligato instrument had been a violin (K. 490, itself a later replacement aria within
that opera); and finally by the sense of occasion, with Mozart himself theatrically step-
ping forth after the recitative, fusing together the identity of composer with the roles—at
various points in the rondo—of vocal surrogate, interlocutor, and amorous counterpart,
in a quite brazen display.

Brilliant Style and the Symphony

Such occasions, in which literal person and figurative persona are channeled through specific circumstances for public spectacle, are hardly unusual in late eighteenth-century concert life, and they offer natural opportunities for viewing the brilliant style in action. A glance at the program of one of Mozart's most successful—but not atypical—Viennese "academies," on 23 March 1783, shows the diversity of configurations that brilliance could take: a sliced-up "Haffner" Symphony, K. 385, serves as the frame for performances of piano concertos, arias and scenas, variation sets, an improvised fugue, and extracts from a sinfonia concertante—a dazzling array of contexts and mediums: vocal and instrumental, solo and collaborative, composed and improvised (Zaslaw 1989: 380). If it is easy to imagine how solo vehicles like concertos and arias might incorporate the brilliant style, it is worth investigating how even relatively generic symphonic writing might be described in this way too.

The passage from the "Haffner" Symphony shown in Example 12.2 surely fits the bill; and we can best read the brilliant style in mm. 41–48, even if only as an inflection of a learned topos. There is a residual virtuosity in the tremolo figures in the violins,

EXAMPLE **12.2** Mozart, Symphony in D major, K. 385, "Haffner," i, mm. 35–48.

(*Continued*)

EXAMPLE **12.2** (Continued)

a device that, as John Spitzer and Neal Zaslaw point out (2004: 454), is idiomatically instrumental rather than vocal and string rather than wind instruments. Like other eighteenth-century "orchestral effects," the tremolo had by this point become a general textural resource calling attention to the orchestral apparatus itself, its intrinsic grandeur, as well as to the composer's skill in harnessing it and to the disciplined execution of the performers—the imposing mix of bustle and energy created by "the multiplication of players on the parts" (457). A listener like Johann Friedrich Daube, whose *Musikalische Dilettant* was intended "for the elite circles of Viennese musical amateurs" (Allanbrook 2014: 126), might well have taken note of the correct handling of the wind instruments in the standard "wind-organ" manner. When incorporating winds into a string ensemble, he explains, "sustained tones such as these produce a good effect in large scores. They have been introduced into symphonies in the current taste, where they enliven and strengthen the brilliant passages" (1992: 125).[15] He would have appreciated too the quick shift of gears across the phrase boundary into m. 41; no one was a more astute advocate and elucidator of the Classical style's modular heterogeneity. His discussion of the opening measures of a large-scale symphony movement is typically alert:

> The entrance of the initial theme has a splendid effect, created by the parallel motion of the main voices...The following brilliant passages, the sustaining of the wind instruments, together with the bass melody, provide a very good change from the initial theme. Then, at the commencement of the ninth measure, the full harmony is interrupted by a singing motif. (Daube 1992: 130–32)

Nor is it difficult to imagine Daube—so attuned to the recycling and reworking of material, both for its potential to mediate styles (old and new, bound or unbound) and for its role in ensuring the ultimate aesthetic goal of variety—enjoying the little contrapuntal play between the two roughly invertible phrases of Example 12.2, uphill in outer-voice sixths then downhill in tenths.[16] As Daube notes, "by means of this resource [invertible counterpoint] a composer can introduce a most agreeable variety into arias, symphonies, etc.... Even in magnificent, brilliant passages, double counterpoint at the octave can be introduced, and obtain a good effect"—a claim he tests with the following illustration (Example 12.3).

If the "Haffner" example opens a window onto the conventional handling of a symphonic brilliant style, a more unusual configuration is revealed in the finale of Haydn's Symphony No. 98 in B flat major, which contains one of his most celebrated *coups de théâtre*. In a movement rife with comedic elements—from the limerick-style main theme (Wheelock 1992: 283), through the emergence of the solo violin, the leader of the orchestra Johann Peter Salomon at the first performance, as protagonist of the development section and initiator of the recapitulation, to the coda's slow-fast trick of decreasing the main tempo only to halve the note values a few measures later—Haydn saves his best joke for last. After yet another of the movement's grand build-ups, which have invariably provoked deflating consequences (the comedy of disparity being a mainspring of this movement, as Scott Burnham has observed [2005: 69]), the main theme returns in the most unassuming form possible, softly, with pizzicato accompaniment—and the

EXAMPLE **12.3** Daube, *The Musical Dilettante* (1992), 229, ex. 192.

composer himself, directing from the keyboard that night in London, steps forth for a "cembalo solo," illuminated with a shower of arpeggiated figuration that ticks away like a celestial continuo at the highest reaches of the keyboard (Example 12.4). As Robbins Landon puts it, "one needs only a modicum of imagination to conjure up the cheers of delight and the stamping that greeted this dexterous display on the part of the world's greatest living composer" (1976: 534).

This "take" on the brilliant style is ingenious in complex ways, but initially we can focus on a very simple aspect. The most literal interpretation of the word "brilliant" involves a quality that "sticks out," as in the gloss found in Koch (1802).[17] Türk (1789: 115) had immediately connected this to a type of character or manner of performance—for him "shining, gleaming" (*schimmernd, glänzend*) means "lively, gay" (*lebhaft, munter*)—but we might pause on the basic phenomenal aspect. If there is an obvious correspondence to the visual arts—an association made explicit by Francesco Algarotti, who likened music's natural delight in exploiting "acute notes" (*acuti*) to the use of "striking lights" (*lumi ardenti*) in painting (1763: 34; Strunk 1998: 919)[18]—there is also a tendency in musical literature to associate this quality particularly with the keyboard. Heinichen had noted how broken chord figuration (*harparpeggiaturen*) in thirds or sixths can provide "no little lustre" (*nicht geringen Lustre*) to the harpsichord (1728: 565), and in *L'art de toucher le clavecin*, François Couperin observed the special properties of the harpsichord, in an important comparison with both the sound and idiomatic figuration of the violin:

> Regarding broken chords (*bateries*) or arpeggios…whose origin comes from the
> [Italian] Sonatas [*Sonades*], my opinion would be that the number of them played on

EXAMPLE 12.4 Haydn, Symphony No. 98 in B flat major, iv, mm. 364–76.

the harpsichord should be a little restricted. This instrument has its own properties as the violin has its own. If the harpsichord cannot increase its sounds, if the repeated notes on one key are not extremely suitable, it has other advantages, which are precision, clearness, brilliance (*le brillant*) and range. (Couperin 1974: 46)

Haydn's "cembalo solo," albeit most likely played on a fortepiano rather than a harpsichord, reflects an intrinsic property of brilliance on the keyboard. Yet, if it is hard to imagine how else Haydn might have signaled his presence, the moment here can be read more deeply. The material requires dexterity but it is hardly virtuosic; the broken chords fit neatly under the hand (and to that extent also implicate an antique harpsichord style). At once theatrical, the solo is also modest. Yet this "modesty" is self-effacing in another more literal way, for the blankness of the material, its mechanical impersonality, complicates our sense of compositional responsibility. The shock of seeing the composer at all in this way—the sudden revelation of a controlling hand, which has been pulling the levers all along—is magnified by the incongruity between the persona we imagine responsible for the intricacy of musical thought throughout the symphony and its literal manifestation via the banal medium of conventional arpeggios. It registers perhaps as the sound of glittering intelligence, mischievously impassive. (It should not be forgotten either that the other unexpected solo turn in the movement, from the leader of the orchestra, while similar in its amusing lack of bravura has on the other hand been stamped with the rustic, tuneful, and melodious—the naively vocal, in short.) And as the audience's attention shifts suddenly to the spotlighted soloist (bringing to mind those eighteenth-century descriptions of the faculty of attention that liken it to a cognitive shaft of light, a beam focused as if through a lens),[19] there is—certainly for us now—an inevitably refractive element that scatters the persona: the unrepeatable circumstances of the original performance require an additional layer of impersonation.

VIRTUOSITY AND THE QUARTET

Haydn's tact and restraint in his keyboard solo gains force, of course, in comparison with the antics (the "paroxysms," as Leopold Mozart [1985: 224] put it) of the stereotypical virtuoso, at least in the worst form of that figure.[20] No-one had caricatured the type more richly, and with more irony, than Diderot in *Rameau's Nephew*: at one point, the "nephew" grotesquely (but with what is reported as unnerving fidelity) mimes first a violinist, such as "Ferrari or Chiabrano or some other *virtuoso*," whose "gyrations" are a form of torture for the observer ("for is it not painful to watch the agonies suffered by someone trying to portray pleasure?"), and then a harpsichordist, whose "fingers flew over the keys," while his "features revealed the play of successive emotions: tenderness, fury, pleasure, pain" (2006: 21–22). Another rich seam of invective focused not on the histrionics per se but on empty feats of athleticism, the one too expressive, the other not expressive enough: an excess in either case. Sulzer, for instance, warned that those "employing technical tricks in their music (involving melodic leaps, arpeggios, harmonies) end up saying nothing at all, however virtuosic it all may be. They are as artificial as a circus performer dancing or singing on a tightrope" (Baker and Christensen 1995: 84–85). Similar illustrations could be multiplied innumerably; the important thing is not merely that performative excess was viewed with suspicion but that the figure of the virtuoso functioned as a barometer of the age, a measure both of its aesthetic ideals and, in their breach, of its greatest fears.

There is no better forum to observe such tensions than the quartet. The ideals of the Viennese quartet may have been the height of seriousness, the most "composed" of genres providing sophisticated models of good behavior (especially in comparison with the virtuosic Parisian *quatuor brillant*—the type, as Daube put it, "in which the first part alone shines" [*worinn die erste Stimme allein brilliret*; 1773: 104]). Yet, as many recent studies have shown, it is quite clear that these ideals did not induce a stoic abnegation of performative display, but rather provided the framework for the imaginative exploration of—precisely—the ways in which such display could be harnessed as a topic for discourse.[21] Issues of performativity, that is, far from being marginalized, were built into the very idea of the genre, which at the same time increasingly became "about" its own generic and topical inclusivity (Hunter 2005a: 117). Indeed, Floyd Grave (2001) has shown the many ways in which from the very beginning Haydn's quartets had been entwined with the genre of the concerto, via aria-like slow movements in the early quartets, "concerto style" passagework in fast movements (later tied to the adaptation of the quartet to an overtly public mode), and even elements of ritornello-solo layouts.

Thus the brilliant style of even relatively routine passages can repay close attention. Consider the following passage from Haydn's String Quartet in B flat major, Op. 71 No. 1/i, a public-oriented set associated with the London concerts of Salomon (Example 12.5). The striking passagework of mm. 103–6 is a moment of beautiful craftsmanship. From a formal perspective, it articulates the highpoint of the development section, the culmination of an area of intense motion that began in m. 84 (not shown), moving around the circle of fifths from F minor in carefully constructed waves. For the first two stages, figuration units of 3 + 1 + 2 measures are coordinated with a compressed then

EXAMPLE 12.5 Haydn, String Quartet in B flat major, Op. 71 No. 1/i, mm. 100–13

stretched harmonic rhythm of two, four, then one harmony per measure. Then, at the arrival on G minor (m. 96), as the cello and viola are included in the interchanges of figuration, an overall textural scheme emerges across mm. 96–106 that magnifies and exaggerates the established six-measure pattern of figuration-interchange followed by first violin passagework. This region of activity is itself the complement of the development's first zone (mm. 70–83), which explored the singing-style opening theme. And widening the perspective still further, the development's cycle of "singing" then "rushing" is itself but the latest installment of the movement's basic textural strategy, interpreted by Grave as a concerto-like alternation of "thematic composure" and "solo exuberance" (2001: 93), whose contours cut across—more accurately, reshape—any pre-formatted sonata layout.[22]

Such are the formal niceties; but it is the material component that captivates—the change of figuration for each measure of the octave ascent, for instance, a simple token of Haydn's distinctive resourcefulness in the realm of passagework (a feature noted by Hunter 2012: 296). Although mm. 103 and 105 look similar on the page, the evaporation of the compound melody in m. 103 into octaves in m. 105 brings with it not only the largest intervallic adjacencies of the passage but also the sense of pure, "gratuitous" exertion. Most eye-catching of all, perhaps, are the widening sweeps of arpeggio in m. 104, that most violinistic of figures, crossing three strings here while moving beyond the natural range of the keyboard.[23] The autograph manuscript shows that Haydn's first thoughts for these measures in fact hewed more closely to the materials found in mm. 58–59, at the end of the secondary theme (see Example 12.6).

This initial scheme makes more evident a large-scale rotational structure to the development, and it is interesting to observe Haydn sacrifice some literalness in this domain for the sake of performative display in the elaborated and intensified final version. Nonetheless, performers apparently found ways to make the passage yet more showy, as evidenced in the flashy "syncopated" bowing pattern incorporated in Wilhelm Altmann's Eulenburg edition from the early twentieth century (Example 12.7), the musical justification of which is presumably to bring out the rising melodic line. Such efforts bring to mind Czerny's explanation of the early nineteenth-century "brilliant style of playing" for the keyboard, a finely etched manner adapted especially to performance in public spaces, resembling "a piece of writing which is meant to be read at a distance" (1839, 3: 82).[24] Comparing two ways of performing Example 12.8, Czerny observes that the second, in the brilliant style, will "not only appear more difficult, but it will in reality be so." The resulting demonstration of technical mastery will "command greater attention" from the audience, who "will become anxious to hear more of [the pianist's] performance" (81).

Although it is tempting to read the passage from Op. 71 No. 1 as a battle for supremacy between the composer and performer, the latter straining at the leash in a bid to escape the control of the former, in truth the performer simply takes full advantage of a space already opened up for display by Haydn. There is no reason to think that the composer would be dismayed at a little extravagance here. A final example from the same set, Op. 71 No. 2 in D major, likewise displays the collaborative spirit. The passage

EXAMPLE **12.6** Haydn, String Quartet in B flat major, Op. 71 No. 1/i, mm. 103–8, first version from autograph manuscript.

EXAMPLE **12.7** Haydn, String Quartet in B flat major, Op. 71 No. 1/i, mm. 103–6, first violin part, Eulenburg edition, ed. Wilhelm Altmann.

EXAMPLE **12.8** Czerny, *Complete Theoretical and Practical Piano Forte School*, vol. 3 (1839), 80.

shown in Example 12.9 bursts out as an extraordinary apotheosis in the recapitulation of the first movement. There are two phases of action. First, a pair of learned treatments of a figure in sequence, one (mm. 93–94) with a chain of 7–6 suspensions on a descending bass line, the next (mm. 94–97) made in *stretto* on a dominant pedal point (this is a metrically displaced cousin of the common Mozartian pedal-point pattern seen above in Example 12.1). Then, as the sequential work dissipates, pure solo figuration emerges, the first violin taking wing like a concerto virtuoso all the way to a death-defying vault into the registral stratosphere—without a textural safety net—followed by an exit trill. The collective effort of producing the cadence in m. 103, complete with an inner-voice "response" from the viola to the violin's ascending scale of m. 102, could be read as a restoration and affirmation of the norms of chamber music behavior after a critical breach of etiquette on the part of the first violin. One might just as well observe the rest of the quartet eager to join in the fun, however.

EXAMPLE **12.9** Haydn, String Quartet in D major, Op. 71 No. 2/i, mm. 91–105.

In any case, the important aspect here is the foregrounding of learned and brilliant styles. Although potentially oppositional terms, markers of mind and body, what they share on this occasion is the element of display: the explicit demonstration of technical proficiency, the one belonging to the realm of the composer, the other to that of the performer. The switch from one style to the other in Example 12.9 can be read therefore as a shift of control—a transfer of exuberance—from one domain to the other: each protagonist has their moment in the sun. And to the same extent that the violin's figuration is strikingly virtuosic, so is it important to note that the melodic scrap at the heart of Haydn's contrapuntal play was introduced in the quartet as an unassuming closing theme (m. 39), of a "popular squareness" that, as Charles Rosen notes (1997: 335), itself represents a type of intellectual relaxation. It is quite to the point that Haydn uses this modest material as the object of his compositional dexterity. (The development had hinted at such a treatment of this material, beginning at m. 58; we shall return to this aspect below.)

In the light of such conspicuous, memorable display, it is a surprise to discover that the whole passage is actually a large parenthesis. According to the plan of the exposition, which the recapitulation had only recently rejoined after some drastic recomposition, m. 92 can connect directly with m. 104, corresponding with mm. 38–39.[25] Normal service is indeed resumed in m. 104; the jolly closing theme appears in its original guise and the section unspools as before. What are we to make of this spontaneous extravagance? If it has a cadenza-like quality both in its gratuity and in its provision of a separate space for demonstration, it is certainly more surprising than a normal cadenza, unexpected and unprepared. Functionally, the passage corresponds closely to the "display episode" of a concerto (the virtuosic solo passage designed to produce a rousing cadential arrival [Ivanovitch 2008]), although on that front there is some lingering doubt about whether the start of the ensuing closing theme interrupts the cadential process or elides with it. Haydn's predilection for the peculiar tensions of the memorable parenthesis, its combination of rhetorical power and apparent syntactical surplus, is well known. Some of the examples of outlandish performative play discussed by Grave (2009) involve interpolations in this manner (for example, in the finales of Op. 50 No. 2 and Op. 77 No. 2); and William Rothstein has pointed out how frequently Haydn's "purple patches" (flatward expansions within a phrase) appear likewise as literal parentheses, with voice leading

EXAMPLE 12.10 Hypothetical continuation of sequence implied in mm. 58–59 of Haydn's String Quartet in D major, Op. 71 No. 2/i.

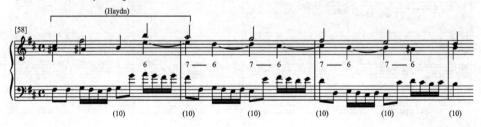

on either side of the patch that can be stitched together (1989: 91). If the prototypical Mozartian parenthesis explores the quality of inwardness, Haydn's parentheses explore the nature of boundaries themselves, what it means to have an inside and an outside. Such situations can often be read humorously or ironically—the disparity between means and ends provides the necessary logical structure—but each must be taken in its own way. In Op. 71 No. 2, one consequence involves the very nature of large-scale listening strategies: the local attentiveness always presupposed by the topical mindset is rewarded here so spectacularly—through learned and brilliant dazzle—that one wonders if attending to the wider picture is even necessary. In fact, all of the ways in which the recapitulation reshapes the exposition (including the earlier fantasia-like intrusion) involve gestures of such immediate force and persuasiveness that an appropriate response might be to relinquish any anxiety over a larger sense of coherence and simply enjoy the ride.[26]

The idea that the composer and quartet are colluding in the genuine demise of a coherent argument is an illusion, of course, but the dizzying sense of a force in such consummate command that inside and outside can be inverted, that its attendant virtuosity can not only unravel an argument but replace it with something even more satisfying, gives rise to the liberating notion that it is the unexpected places in the quartet that count. Accordingly, the final measures of the movement resonate in a special way. Twice already, in the development (mm. 58–62) and in the apotheosis, Haydn has

EXAMPLE **12.11** Haydn, String Quartet in D major, Op. 71 No. 2/i, mm. 119–25.

embarked on a simple sequential treatment of his closing tune—descending 7–6 suspensions with parallel tenths between the outer voices—only to get sidetracked into more intricate shows of learned prowess. (With a less imaginative composer, the trio of sequential treatments squeezed into mm. 58–62 might have been forestalled by taking up the first implication, in the manner shown in Example 12.10.) In the movement's last shadows, however, after all the showmanship Haydn finally unfolds the promised item (Example 12.11, m. 120), a gratifying nod to the patient listener, who now, we might say, shines.

Conclusions

The analytical sketches presented in this chapter can offer only glimpses of how the brilliant style might be approached. Even among this small selection, however, certain arrangements—contrasts and affiliations—are suggestive: the brilliant style "imposition" discussed in Haydn's Symphony No. 98, for instance, elucidates an established space (the coda), whereas the dazzling apotheosis of Op. 71 No. 2 serves to crack open the structure (at the point of parenthesis). Yet both instances share the exploitation of the brilliant style at apparently "gratuitous" points in the discourse, and both do so, as we have seen, in the service of illuminating the role of a controlling agency or persona (whether composer, performer, or some more complex amalgam requiring layers of quotation marks). At the same time, by foregrounding these elements, such moments reveal the malleability and contingency of the discourse: what might often be taken for granted—a certain continuity of authorial tone or structural thought—must be considered afresh, simultaneously distanced and personalized. Such a "double perspective" in fact emerges in many accounts that focus on performativity in the eighteenth century: Elisabeth Le Guin's exploration of virtuosity in Boccherini, for example, argues that inherent in virtuosity itself is a type of "alienation," which arises variously from the gap between what is seen (by the audience) and what is felt (by the performer), or from the "gulf of difference" between the performer's astonishing powers and the humdrum abilities of the observer (2006: 138); Sutcliffe has noted how the observer of Haydn's quartets, tracing through the exchanges, reciprocities, and jokes of the sociable medium, is on occasion "caught in the act of listening" (2009: 118); and in the context of opera buffa, Hunter has written insightfully of the many ways in which the genre thematizes performance itself, inducing a sophisticated "layering" of the audience's attention—an awareness both of the larger narrative and of the performer's skill in carrying out his or her role (1999: 45). The music of the late eighteenth century is a music of cracks, gaps, and frames, of utterances staged at multiple removes, a practice in which styles become "styles," the natural made artificial and the artificial natural. And at root, the study of topics entails a study of such doubleness: after all, any example of a topic is intrinsically both a "thing" and a "type of thing." The brilliant style can be both virtuosic music and music about virtuosity, the protagonist simultaneously a virtuoso and someone playing the role of a virtuoso. The same music that engages viscerally and forcefully, seeming to bypass the intellectual faculties, may nonetheless be apprehended critically through layers of cultural accretion, through the multiple frames that make up the topic's historical antecedents and referents.

In the normal course of things, the status of the brilliant style as a basic stylistic resource and its deployment via routine, "superficial" building blocks of figuration can render it transparent to the analytical filter. When unusually arresting or dazzling events thrust it to the fore, as in Op. 71 No. 2 or Symphony No. 98, of course we take notice. But it is hoped that this chapter also indicates how the topical mindset can be productive even in more run-of-the-mill situations. The figuration-highpoint in the development section of Op. 71 No.1; the typical "halo" of keyboard passagework in Mozart's *aria concertante*; the conventional brilliance of the "Haffner" Symphony, whose shimmer, despite the attenuated virtuosity of its performing challenges, is the bristling, energetic sign of the virtuoso-composer himself, helping to reflect back on his audience the prestige of the orchestral apparatus and the institutions that support it: all such instances can yield insights if we but shine a light in their direction.

NOTES

1. Allanbrook herself notes that the label "brilliant" in connection with the pervasive triplet figure of Haydn's Op. 50 No. 1 is somewhat arbitrary (2014: 123).
2. My discussion of the etymology of the French "briller" follows *Dictionnaire historique de la langue française* (Rey 1992: 291). Most other modern dictionaries, however, while acknowledging some obscurity in the matter, derive "brilliant" from the Latin *beryllus* (the mineral beryl, hence the frequent identification of brilliant, semantically if not geologically, with diamonds). The *Dictionnaire historique* suggests that the more common sense of *briller* as connected to phenomena of light derives from the twinkling activity of the stars.
3. The word traveled from Italian in the fifteenth century (*brillare/brillante*) to French in the sixteenth (*briller/brillant*), whence it entered English in the late seventeenth century and German near the beginning of the eighteenth century (the noun and adjective forms supplemented in German, but not in English, by the verb *brilliren* or *brillieren*, around 1720). Some bookends can illustrate the rise and fall. Its early special aura is captured by Mattheson in *Der vollkommene Capellmeister*. Describing his crowning example of double fugue technique, a complete four-voice fugue with orchestra, which sets the text "Die Finsterniss ist vergangen; und das wahre Licht scheinet itzt" (the darkness is past, and the true light now shineth), he writes: "Whoever performs it right will produce a good effect. It must *briller* [*Brilliren muss es*]. This cannot be said in German with shine [*gläntzen*] and sparkle [*funckeln*], even if I were chairman of all German societies" (1739: 457; Harriss 1981: 824). (The final reference is to newly established societies such as the Deutsche Gesellschaft, designed on the model of the Académie Française to protect the German language from foreign influences). A century after Mattheson, however, the German writer Ludwig Börne, in his *Schilderungen aus Paris* of 1823, would complain of the French attachment to "the insufferable word 'brilliant,' which they use so frequently that it makes your eyes water. Everything that they praise is brilliant: a society, a theatre production, Napoleon's reign, an

academy meeting, a picture, bravery, beauty, every virtue." (*So haben sie das unausstehli-che Wort: »brillant«, das sie so häufig anwenden, daß einem die Augen überlaufen. Alles, was sie loben, ist brillant; eine Gesellschaft, eine Theatervorstellung, Napoleons Regierung, eine Sitzung der Akademie, ein Gemälde, die Tapferkeit, die Schönheit, jede Tugend* [Börne 1964: 10]). A writer in England in the same year observed that "the epithet *brilliant*, is one of very common application in musical criticism" (n.n. 1823: 426), a situation confirmed by a glance at Czerny's commentaries on Beethoven's piano works (1970), wherein the word "brilliant" indeed appears on practically every page.

4. "*Brillante*, schimmernd oder hervorstechend" (Koch 1802: col. 272).

5. See, for instance, Bach (1753: 58; 1949: 83) and Quantz (1752: 87; 1985: 105).

6. For instance, the contemporaneous English translation of Algarotti renders *passaggi* (1763: 34) as "shining passages" or "brilliant passages" (Strunk 1998: 919).

7. See, for instance, Türk (1789: 115) and Clementi (1801: 14). Bailey's entry "Brillante" (1726) marks the early cachet of the Italian term: "brillante (in Musick Books) signifies to play in a brisk lively manner."

8. See, for instance, Galeazzi, for whom the overture to a comic opera should be "brilliant, spirited, and playful" (1796: 289; 2012: 359).

9. Burney uses the description prodigiously for performers of all kinds, usually with appro-bation. Thus, Couperin was "brilliant in execution" (1773: 41); the singer Faustina's "execu-tion was articulate and brilliant" (1775: 189); of Frederick the Great's flute playing, he claims "his finger is brilliant" (1775: 153); the orchestra in Mannheim is famous for its "neat and brilliant execution" (1775: 343), and so on.

10. For instance, Quantz emphasizes that the second allegro of the concerto "must be neither purely cantabile nor purely spirited from beginning to end. And just as each movement must be very different from any other, the individual movements must be in themselves good mixtures of pleasing and brilliant ideas" (1753: 304; 1985: 319). Similar statements can be found as a commonplace throughout the second half of the eighteenth century, in writers such as Bach, Daube, Burney, and Galeazzi, often in connection with genres associated with instrumental display. See also Allanbrook (2014: 118–19, 126–27, 213 n. 133).

11. Along such lines, the term was invoked by Mozart in his well-known letter about his first set of Viennese piano concertos, K. 413–415 ("very brilliant, pleasing to the ear" [Anderson 1985: 833]), and decisively revoked by Beethoven as the subtitle of his "Kreutzer" Violin Sonata in A minor, Op. 47, the autograph manuscript of which shows that the striking phrase *sonata scritto in uno stilo molto concertante quasi come d'un concerto* had originally used *brillante* in place of *molto concertante*. (On the alterations to the "Kreutzer" inscrip-tion and their significance, see Ahn 1997.)

12. See Libin (2006) for a useful discussion of the aria's context.

13. It is not simply a matter of the piano being released here from the obligations of provid-ing the bass voice, for figuration in the manner of K. 505 is rarely seen in the piano trios or quartets either. Conspicuous exceptions include the first movement of the Quintet in B flat major for Piano and Winds, K. 452, and (especially) the end of the first movement of the Piano Quartet in G minor, K. 478—both of which compositions are coded as emphatically *concertante* and virtuosic. For a valuable treatment of the development of Mozart's idiom-atic keyboard figuration see in particular Libin (1998).

14. Ivanovitch (2011) provides further elaboration of this retransitional idiom.

15. Daube's own illustration shows an imitative sequence for two violins with sustained 2–3 suspensions between a pair of flutes. Spitzer and Zaslaw (2004: 464–67) and Snook-Luther (in Daube 1992: 125) provide additional historical context for the wind-organ technique.

16. Through its guise of variation technique, the principle of reworking was close to the center of musical craft for Daube. The most succinct encapsulation is the following: "It is certainly true that all the music which has been brought into the world until now, and which will ever be composed in the future, is inseparable from the art of variation" (1992: 143).

17. Koch (1802), as cited in note 4.

18. Explicit analogies between painting and musical brilliance are in fact relatively rare in the eighteenth century, although it is not surprising that the connection should have occurred to Algarotti. He wrote a much-valued treatise on painting, and was closely connected with the Venetian school of painters (Tiepolo, above all) celebrated, now as then, for their handling of light-effects. As Svetlana Alpers has observed, "one of the most general reactions to Tiepolo, surely, is that his pictures are full of a pure white light" (Alpers and Baxandall 1994: 72).

19. See Riley (2004: 12).

20. The aesthetic plight of the stereotypical virtuoso during the eighteenth century has been well captured in Eisen (2005). Hunter (2005b) traces the story across the divide of the centuries, and from among the voluminous literature on the other side, it is well continued in particular by Gooley (2006) and Samson (2003).

21. A representative sample includes Hunter (2012) on the subtle power-plays encoded in Haydn's fingering indications, Mirka (2009: 298–301) on the potential for poking fun at inept performers, Grave (2009) on moral lessons for performer and listener about the dangers of being seduced by sheer performance, and Sutcliffe (2009) on the ways that the very fabric of the Classical quartet—its resources of texture, style, and tonality—modeled modes of social behavior. A further development of Sutcliffe, offering a useful framework for investigating the play of persona and agency within the quartet, can be found Klorman 2013.

22. The central iteration of the three exposition cycles (mm. 1–20, 21–38, 39–66) takes in both the unexpected return of the opening theme (oddly rerouted back from an apparent transitional dominant in m. 16) and the transition proper (beginning in m. 30). The recapitulation, which begins in m. 113, is shaped into a single singing-brilliant cycle.

23. Galeazzi likens the illusion of multivoice simultaneity in such arpeggios to the way "the eye is deceived by children when they rapidly twirl a glowing coal, which, although it passes through all the points of the circumference of a circle, appears to the eye to make a continuous, uninterrupted movement" (Stowell 1985: 154).

24. The engaging effect of such a style is made through detail and clarity rather than through overwhelming force or volume: "a well arranged illumination, produced by many thousand lamps, and not the confused glare of a flight of rockets in a piece of fire-works" (1839, 3: 82)

25. The recomposition in the recapitulation begins as early as the main theme's consequent phrase. The equivalent of mm. 9–27, which includes both the consequent and a transition section, is deleted and replaced with a fantasia-style incursion, easing back into a bar-for-bar correspondence with the exposition at m. 82 (equivalent to m. 28).

26. At the start of the parenthesis, the appearance of the "expected" material—the closing theme—in its now-transformed guise only serves to heighten the sense of an earlier element being swept aside by sheer exuberance.

References

n.n. 1823. Vauxhall. *The Literary Chronicle and Weekly Review* 216 (5 July): 425–27.

Ahn, Suhnne. 1997. Genre, Style, and Compositional Procedure in Beethoven's "Kreutzer" Sonata, Opus 47. Ph.D. diss., Harvard University.

Algarotti, Francesco. 1763. *Saggio sopra l'opera in musica*. Livorno: Coltellini.

Allanbrook, Wye Jamison. 1992. Two Threads through the Labyrinth: Topic and Process in the First Movements of K. 332 and K. 333. In *Convention in Eighteenth- and Nineteenth-Century Music: Essays in Honor of Leonard G. Ratner*, ed. Wye Allanbrook, Janet Levy, and William Mahrt, 125–71. Stuyvesant, NY: Pendragon.

———. 2014. *The Secular Commedia: Comic Mimesis in Late Eighteenth-Century Music*, ed. Mary Ann Smart and Richard Taruskin. Berkeley: University of California Press.

Alpers, Svetlana, and Michael Baxandall. 1994. *Tiepolo and the Pictorial Intelligence*. New Haven: Yale University Press.

Anderson, Emily, ed. 1985. *The Letters of Mozart and His Family*, 3rd ed., rev. by Stanley Sadie and Fiona Smart. London: Macmillan.

Bach, Carl Philip Emanuel. 1753. *Versuch über die wahre Art, das Clavier zu spielen*. Berlin: Christian Friedrich Henning.

———. 1949. *Essay on the True Art of Playing Keyboard Instruments*. Trans. and ed. William J. Mitchell. New York: Norton.

Bailey, Nathan. 1726. *An Universal Etymological English Dictionary*. 3rd ed. London: printed for J. Darby, A. Bettesworth, F. Fayram, J. Pemberton, J. Hooke, and others.

Baker, Nancy Kovaleff, and Thomas Christensen, ed. 1995. *Aesthetics and the Art of Musical Composition in the German Enlightenment*. Cambridge: Cambridge University Press.

Börne, Ludwig. 1964. *Sämtliche Schriften*, ed. Inge and Peter Rippman. Vol. 2. Düsseldorf: J. Melzer.

Burney, Charles. 1773. *The Present State of Music in Germany, The Netherlands, and United Provinces*, 2nd ed. Vol. 2. London: Becket, Robson, and Robinson.

———. 1775. *The Present State of Music in France and Italy*, 2nd ed. London: Becket, Robson, and Robinson.

Clementi, Muzio. 1801. *Introduction to the Art of Playing on the Piano Forte*. London: Clementi, Banger, Hyde, Collard, and Davis.

Couperin, François. 1974. *L'art de toucher le clavecin*. Trans. Margery Halford. New York: Alfred.

Czerny, Carl. 1839. *Complete Theoretical and Practical Piano Forte School, Op. 500*. 3 vols. London: Cocks.

———. 1970. *On the Proper Performance of All Beethoven's Works for the Piano*, ed. Paul Badura-Skoda. Vienna: Universal Edition.

Daube, Johann Friedrich. 1773. *Der Musikalische Dilettant*. Vienna: Trattner.

———. 1992. *The Musical Dilettante: A Treatise on Composition by J. F. Daube*. Trans. Susan Snook-Luther. Cambridge: Cambridge University Press.

Diderot, Denis. 2006. *Rameau's Nephew and First Satire*. Trans. Margaret Mauldon. New York: Oxford University Press.

Eisen, Cliff. 2005. The Rise (and Fall) of the Concerto Virtuoso in the Late Eighteenth and Nineteenth Centuries. In *The Cambridge Companion to the Concerto*, ed. Simon Keefe, 177–91. Cambridge: Cambridge University Press.

Galeazzi, Francesco. 1796. *Elementi teorico-pratici di musica*. Vol. 2. Rome: Puccinelli.

——. 2012. *Theoretical-Practical Elements of Music, Parts III and IV*. Trans. Deborah Burton and Gregory W. Harwood. Urbana: University of Illinois Press.

Gooley, Dana. 2006. The Battle against Instrumental Virtuosity in the Early Nineteenth Century. In *Franz Liszt and His World*, ed. Christopher H. Gibbs and Dana Gooley, 75–111. Princeton: Princeton University Press.

Grave, Floyd K. 2001. Concerto Style in Haydn's String Quartets. *The Journal of Musicology* 18/1: 76–97.

——. 2009. Freakish Variations on a "Grand Cadence" Prototype in Haydn's String Quartets. *Journal of Musicological Research* 28/2–3: 119–45.

Harriss, Ernest C. 1981. *Johann Mattheson's* Der vollkommene Capellmeister: *A Revised Translation with Critical Commentary*. Ann Arbor, MI: UMI Research Press.

Heinichen, Johann David. 1728. *Der General-Bass in der Composition*. Dresden: Author.

Hunter, Mary. 1999. *The Culture of Opera Buffa in Mozart's Vienna: A Poetics of Entertainment*. Princeton: Princeton University Press.

——. 2005a. The Quartets. In *The Cambridge Companion to Haydn*, ed. Caryl Clark, 112–25. Cambridge: Cambridge University Press.

——. 2005b. "To Play as if from the Soul of the Composer": The Idea of the Performer in Early Romantic Aesthetics. *Journal of the American Musicological Society* 58/2: 357–98.

——. 2012. Haydn's String Quartet Fingerings: Communications to Performer and Audience. In *Engaging Haydn: Culture, Context, and Criticism*, ed. Mary Hunter and Richard Will, 281–301. Cambridge: Cambridge University Press.

Ivanovitch, Roman. 2008. Showing Off: Variation in the "Display Episodes" of Mozart's Piano Concertos. *Journal of Music Theory* 52/2: 181–218.

——. 2011. Mozart's Art of Retransition. *Music Analysis* 30/1: 1–36.

Klorman, Edward. 2013. Multiple Agency in Mozart's Music. Ph.D. diss., City University of New York.

Koch, Heinrich Christoph. 1802. *Musikalisches Lexikon*. Frankfurt-am-Main: August Hermann der Jüngere.

Landon, H. C. Robbins. 1976. *Haydn: Chronicle and Works*. Vol. 3: *Haydn in England, 1791–1795*. Bloomington: Indiana University Press.

Le Guin, Elisabeth. 2006. *Boccherini's Body: An Essay in Carnal Musicology*. Berkeley and Los Angeles: University of California Press.

Libin, Kathryn. 1998. The Emergence of an Idiomatic Fortepiano Style in the Keyboard Concertos of Mozart. Ph.D. diss., New York University.

——. 2006. Mozart's Piano and Dramatic Expression in the Concert Aria: 'Ch'io mi scordi di te...Non temer, amato bene,' K.505. *Early Keyboard Journal* 24: 69–93.

Mattheson, Johann. 1739. *Der vollkommene Capellmeister*. Hamburg: Christian Herold.

Mirka, Danuta. 2009. *Metric Manipulations in Haydn and Mozart*. New York: Oxford University Press.

Monelle, Raymond. 2000. *The Sense of Music: Semiotic Essays*. Princeton: Princeton University Press.

——. 2006. *The Musical Topic: Hunt, Military and Pastoral*. Bloomington: Indiana University Press.

Mozart, Leopold. 1985. *A Treatise on the Fundamental Principles of Violin Playing*, 2nd ed. Trans. Editha Knocker. New York: Oxford University Press.

Quantz, Johann Joachim. 1752. *Versuch einer Anweisung die Flöte traversiere zu spielen*. Berlin: Johann Friedrich Voß.

——. 1985. *On Playing the Flute*, 2nd ed. Trans. Edward R. Reilly. London: Faber & Faber.

Ratner, Leonard. 1980. *Classic Music: Expression, Form, and Style*. New York: Schirmer.

Rey, Alain, ed. 1992. *Dictionnaire historique de la langue française: Contenant les mots français en usage et quelques autres délaissés*. Paris: Dictionnaires Le Robert.

Riley, Matthew. 2004. *Musical Listening in the German Enlightenment: Attention, Wonder and Astonishment*. Aldershot, UK: Ashgate.

Rosen, Charles. 1997. *The Classical Style: Haydn, Mozart, Beethoven*, expanded ed. New York: Norton.

Rumph, Stephen. 2012. *Mozart and Enlightenment Semiotics*. Berkeley: University of California Press.

Samson, Jim. 2003. *Virtuosity and the Musical Work: The Transcendental Studies of Liszt*. Cambridge: Cambridge University Press.

Spitzer, John, and Neal Zaslaw. 2004. *The Birth of the Orchestra: History of an Institution, 1650–1815*. New York: Oxford University Press.

Stowell, Robin. 1985. *Violin Technique and Performance Practice in the Late Eighteenth and Early Nineteenth Centuries*. Cambridge: Cambridge University Press.

Strunk, Oliver, ed. 1998. *Source Readings in Music History*, rev. ed. Leo Treitler, general editor. New York: Norton.

Sutcliffe, W. Dean. 2009. Before the Joke: Texture and Sociability in the Largo of Haydn's Op. 33, No. 2. *Journal of Musicological Research* 28/2–3: 92–118.

Türk, Daniel Gottlob. 1789. *Klavierschule, oder Anweisung zum Klavierspielen für Lehrer und Lernende*. Leipzig: Schwickert und Hemmerde.

Wheelock, Gretchen. 1992. *Haydn's Ingenious Jesting with Art*. New York: Schirmer.

Zaslaw, Neal. 1989. *Mozart's Symphonies: Context, Performance Practice, Reception*. Oxford: Oxford University Press.

SECTION III

ANALYZING TOPICS

CHAPTER 13

....

TOPICS AND METER

....

DANUTA MIRKA

THE connection between topics and meter was established by Wye Allanbrook. In her seminal book *Rhythmic Gesture in Mozart* (1983) Allanbrook observed that in the eighteenth century individual meters carried affects associated with specific styles and genres. She supported this observation with references to eighteenth-century authors representing the tradition of metric notation descending from the mensural system of Baroque music. But, as noted by Allanbrook, the compositional practice underwent an important change between the Baroque and Classic eras. Whereas Baroque composers used one affect for an entire movement, Classic composers began to shape each move-ment around several affects, which necessitated the choice of a time signature suitable for several meters. This practice was related to another tradition of metric notation, not discussed by Allanbrook, in which time signatures had no affective significance and no stylistic implications.

In this chapter I retrace both traditions of metric notation reflected in the practice of Classic composers. I show their origins, respectively, in French and Italian theory and practice that came to bear on German music theory in the course of the eighteenth century. The old tradition, discussed in the first section, was inextricably linked with North-German music aesthetics. The connection between affects and genres, estab-lished by Mattheson, Sulzer, and Kirnberger, extended to meters which, in turn, were linked to tempos of specific genres, especially dances. The new tradition of metric notation, discussed in the second section, severed its ties with aesthetics, uncoupled meter from tempo, and developed notational devices that allowed eighteenth-century composers to change meter without changing the time signature. While these devices enabled composers to include several topics in one piece, they complicate the task of the analyst by making identification of topics contingent on identification of the composed meter and, in some cases, on analysis of phrase structure. I demonstrate this in the third section in relation to the opening theme of Mozart's Symphony in G minor, K. 550. What I show through my analysis is that topic theory cannot dispense with historical music theory, which—among other things—includes the theory of meter.

THE TRADITION OF *TEMPO GIUSTO*

The old tradition of metric notation, which informs Allanbrook's discussion of the connection between topics and meters, forms an integral part of the doctrine of affections (*Affektenlehre*), which dominated German music theory in the eighteenth century. According to this doctrine, affective power of music rested on the analogy between musical motion (*Bewegung*) and emotion (*Gemüthsbewegung*). As explained in the introduction, different qualities of motion could be represented by different musical parameters, but the concept of motion especially pertained to the organization of musical time. Since this organization included absolute values of notes and their values relative to each other, in the early eighteenth century the sense of this term embraced both tempo and meter. This sense is reflected in *Dictionnaire de musique* (1705) by Sébastien de Brossard, for whom the term *mouvement* "sometimes signifies the slowness or quickness of notes" but "it often signifies as well an equality, regularity, and clear articulation of all the beats in the measure (*mesure*)."[1] The French usage was adopted in Germany. In *Das Neu-Eröffnete Orchestre* (1713) Johann Mattheson explains that meter (*Tact*) deals with "the slowness or quickness, which means, the measure (*Zeitmass*)."[2] During his discussion of individual meters he calls some of them *mouvements* and suggests a standard tempo for each of them, based on affects they convey and genres in which they occur. If he refines his view of meter by the time of writing *Der vollkommene Capellmeister* (1739), this happens under the influence of Jean Rousseau's *Méthode claire, certaine et facil, pour apprendre à chanter la musique* (1683). Rousseau's work could have been brought to Mattheson's attention by Johann Gottfried Walther, whose *Musicalisches Lexicon* (1732) takes note of Rousseau's distinction between *mouvement* and *mesure*. Mattheson quotes Rousseau and draws the equivalent distinction between tempo (*Bewegung*) and measure (*Maas*) but he discusses them in the same chapter and treats them as complementary aspects of meter (*Tact*).[3] In other chapters he relates meter to the doctrine of affections and demonstrates its affective qualities in the experiment described in the introduction in connection with Example 0.1. The practical implication of the view of meter exposed by Mattheson was that tempo depends on the rhythmical values of beats indicated by the denominator of time signature. This link between tempo and meter brought about a high number of time signatures with rhythmical values of beats ranging from whole notes to sixteenths. The authority of Mattheson and the popularity of his writings determined that this tradition of metric notation was adopted by other German music theorists, such as Joseph F. B. L. Maier, Franz Anton Maichelbeck, J. Philipp Eisel, Joseph Joachim Benedikt Münster, and Jacob Adlung.[4]

In the late eighteenth century this tradition was continued by Johann Philipp Kirnberger. Kirnberger devotes separate chapters to tempo (*Bewegung*) and meter (*Takt*) in the second volume of his composition handbook *Die Kunst des reinen*

Satzes in der Musik (1776) but he relates them closely to each other in that he postulates standard or "natural" tempo for each meter: the so-called *tempo giusto*. If Matthesons's view of meter was influenced by Brossard and Jean Rousseau, the idea of *tempo giusto* and its corroboration by Kirnberger betray the influence of another French author, Jean-Philippe Rameau, whose works inspired Kirnberger's theory of harmony. In *Traité de l'harmonie* (1722) Rameau proposes a reform of metric notation, according to which the number of beats in the measure should be specified by numerals but their rhythmical values could be indicated by a note that, at the same time, would indicate the tonic pitch through its position on the stave. The same rhythmical values could also indicate the tempo and stand for Italian tempo markings: whole notes for *Adagio* or *Largo*; half notes for *Andante* or *Grazioso*; quarter notes for *Vivace* or *Allegro*; eighth notes for *Presto*; and sixteenth notes for *Prestissimo*.

> Once he knew that the movement of the whole note is slower than that of the half, and similarly, the half slower than the quarter, the quarter than the eighth, and the eighth than the sixteenth, who would not immediately understand that a meter in which the whole note is worth only one beat will be slower than a meter in which the half note is worth one beat, and similarly the half-note meter slower than the quarter-note meter, etc.? (Rameau 1722: 151–52; 1971: 166)

Although Kirnberger prefers to indicate rhythmical values of beats with numerals, he echoes Rameau's view on their relation to tempo and extends it to dynamics:[5]

> From what we have stated already in the preceding section of this chapter about *tempo giusto* and the natural motion of longer and shorter note values, it becomes clear, for example, that a measure of two quarter notes and another of two half notes, and likewise a measure of three quarter notes and another of three eight notes, indicate a different tempo, even though they have the same number of beats. In addition, longer note values are always performed with more weight and emphasis than shorter ones. (Kirnberger 1776: 116; 1982: 384–85)

He illustrates this point with a phrase written in two different meters (Example 13.1). As he observes, "if this phrase is performed correctly, everyone will notice that it is much more serious and emphatic in *alla breve* [Example 13.1a] than in 2/4 [Example 13.1b] meter, where it comes close to being playful" (Kirnberger 1776: 119; 1982: 387). Thus, for Kirnberger the differences of tempo and performance nuance justify the existence of different meters with the same number of beats. Like other authors before him, Kirnberger relates affects of such meters to their use in specific styles and genres. Archaic meters with whole-note beats are no longer in use, he explains, but meters with half-note beats are suitable for church pieces, fugues, and choruses; those with quarter-note beats are used in great variety of styles and genres; and meters with shorter beats occur in amusing dance pieces. While Kirnberger's idea of *tempo giusto* was conservative in his days, it remained influential due to the successful reception of his theory of harmony and the exposition in Johann Georg Sulzer's *Allgemeine Theorie der schönen Künste* (1771–74).

EXAMPLE **13.1** Kirnberger, *Die Kunst des reinen Satzes in der Musik*, vol. 2, section 1 (1776), 118–19.

(a) Tempo giufto.

(b) Tempo giufto.

In the article "Tact" written by Kirnberger's pupil, Johann Abraham Peter Schulz, the author expands on the argument of his teacher regarding time signatures and summarizes Kirnberger's discussion of affects carried by individual meters. Some other music theorists continued the tradition of *tempo giusto* until the end of the eighteenth century. One of them was Augustus Frederic Christopher Kollmann, whose *Essay on Musical Harmony* (1796) brought Kirnberger's theory of harmony to England. Kirnberger's Italian followers included Francesco Galeazzi (1791–96) and Carlo Gervasoni (1800).

The works of Kirnberger and his followers form the historical basis of the affective spectrum of meters reconstructed by Allanbrook. As she demonstrates, this spectrum displays a double order. Regarding denominators of time signatures, meters are organized around the quarter note as the rhythmical value of beats (Figure 13.1).

> The quarter note, measuring the motion of a normal human stride, occupies the center of the spectrum. Meters in half notes (2) or whole notes (1, although rare, is mentioned in some treatises) fall to the left of center, requiring a slower tempo and more solemn style of execution. To the right fall 8 and 16 (and, at the beginning of the century, 32) in ascending degrees of rapidity, lightness, and gaiety. Thus a geometric series of numbers from one to thirty-two corresponds to an ordered range of human strides from the slowest (and gravest) to the fastest (and gayest). (Allanbrook 1983: 15)[6]

Regarding numerators of time signatures, meters are divided into duple and triple. In the early eighteenth century numerators and denominators could be freely combined with each other, but Allanbrook speculates that in the later part of the century the decline of dances in slow triple meters and the prominence of duple meters in church music led to the alliance of triple meters with smaller and duple meters with larger rhythmical values

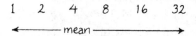

FIGURE **13.1** Allanbrook, *Rhythmic Gesture in Mozart* (1983), 15.

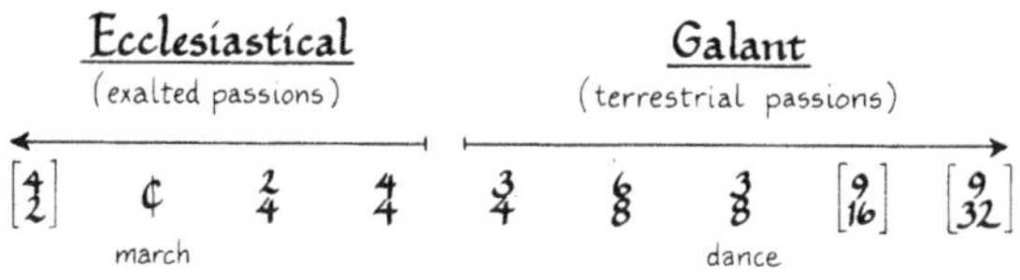

FIGURE 13.2 Allanbrook, *Rhythmic Gesture in Mozart* (1983), 22.

of beats. "The result was a polarization of duple and triple meters—a topical confrontation between the two metrical types which could be characterized as an opposition of divine and mundane subject matters" (17–18). The spectrum of eighteenth-century meters, shown in Figure 13.2, thus mirrors the full range of affects from the most elevated to the most humble and covers the full range of human experience from sacred to profane.

BEYOND *TEMPO GIUSTO*

The new tradition of metric notation, which led to the dissolution of *tempo giusto* in the late eighteenth century, dissociated tempo and affect from meter. Rather than by denominators of time signatures, tempo and affect were indicated by verbal designations.[7] The Italian words for tempo and affect make clear that this tradition originated with Italian composers, but it was adopted by some French theorists. In *Projet concernant de nouveau signes pour la musique*, presented to Académie Royale des Sciences in 1742, Jean-Jacques Rousseau claimed:

> It is a considerable fault in music to represent notes as having an absolute value when their value is only relative, and to make wrong applications of their relations, as it is certain that the duration of whole notes, half notes, quarters and eighths is determined not by the quality of the notes but by the measures in which they are found. It follows from this that a quarter note in one measure may be made faster than an eight in another. (Houle 1987: 53)

Rousseau turned this argument against Rameau's reform of metric notation and used it in favor of his own reform proposed in *Dissertation sur la musique moderne* (1743). Although this reform did not take hold, Rousseau reaffirmed the independence of meter from tempo and criticized the excessive number of time signatures in *Dictionnaire de musique* (1768):

> If all these signatures are instituted in order to mark as many different kinds of measures (*mesures*), they are too numerous; and if they are to express various degrees of tempo (*mouvement*), they are not numerous enough; because, apart from the kind of measure and division of beats, one is almost always constrained to add a word at the beginning of a piece in order to determine the beat.[8]

Understandably enough, his criticism provoked vigorous reactions of the advocates of *tempo giusto*. Schulz quotes Rousseau, only to insinuate that he "must be no good prac-titioner,"[9] and adds offense to injury by suggesting that "others, who with Rousseau take the diversity of meters for an arbitrary invention and are outraged about it, have either no sense of the special performance of each meter or deny it, and hence are in danger of writing things which—because they are not set in the right meter which corresponds to the character of the piece—will be performed in a different way than they have been conceived."[10]

By the time Schulz wrote these words, the "others" had come to include German theo-rists. In *De Rhythmopoeia* (1752), the first volume of *Anfangsgründe zur musicalischen Setzkunst*, Joseph Riepel declared that every piece of music composed "from Jubal's time" could be transcribed in either 2/4 or 3/4 meter.[11] While other authors were not quite as radical as Riepel, they agreed that the choice of meter should be guided by neither tempo nor affect but by convenience. This pragmatic attitude was exposed by Friedrich Wilhelm Marpurg in *Kritische Briefe über die Tonkunst* (1760–63). In a letter addressed to Leopold Mozart, Marpurg writes that "it is good to pay attention to the fastest notes that occur in each piece so as not to take such rhythmical values for the main beats which would compel one to write these fastest notes with sixty-fourth- or hundred-twenty-eighth-notes."[12] He recommends quarter notes and half notes for the rhythmical values of beats, which leads him to accept time signatures 2/4 and 2/2 for duple meters and 3/2 and 3/4 for triple meters. By way of exception he also accepts 3/8 meter. "All other representations of even meters, such as 2/1, 2/8, 2/16, 2/32 etc., and odd meters, such as 3/1, 3/16, 3/32 etc., are inconvenient and should be rejected."[13]

Heinrich Christoph Koch follows in Marpurg's footsteps in the second volume of *Versuch einer Anleitung zur Composition* (1787). His discussion of time signatures is limited to those mentioned by Marpurg and he states as a matter of course that no dif-ference exists between meters whose time signatures have same numerators yet differ-ent denominators. As Marpurg, Koch emphasizes that the choice of meter should be informed by pragmatic considerations:

> As long as one considers the nature of things alone, it does not matter which rhyth-mical values one takes for the main beats of the simple even meter. But, since one must also take into consideration other circumstances, for instance, the subdivision of the main beats into smaller rhythmical values, the convenience of the performer etc., not all rhythmical values have the right to become the main beats of the measure. For instance, if one would like to build a 2/8 meter out of two eighth notes, this would not be against the nature of meter because two eighth notes have the same inner and outer relation to each other as two quarters or two half notes. But, if the eighth notes occur as the main beats, one would be compelled to avail oneself with thirty-second- and sixty-fourth-notes, and in Adagio even with hundred-twenty-eighth-notes, in order to set the fastest notes of the melody, and thus to unnecessarily overload the eye of the performer with too many hooks and beams attached to notes. For this reason one has rightly considered 2/8 meter as superfluous and useless because everything that can be set in this meter can be set with much more convenience in 2/2 or 2/4.

So lange man blos die Natur der Sache betrachtet, so lange ist es gleichviel, welcher Gattung der Noten man sich zu der einfachen geraden Tactart bedient; weil aber auch hierbey auf zufällige Umstände Absicht genommen werden muß, z. B. auf die zergliederung der Haupttheile des Tactes in Theile von geringerem äusserlichem Werthe, auf die Bequemlichkeit des Ausführers u.s.w., so haben aus diesem Grunde nicht alle Notengattungen das Recht erhalten, Haupttheile des Tactes abgeben zu können. Wollte man z.B. aus zwey Achtelnoten einen Zweyachteltact bilden, so wäre dieses zwar nicht wider die Natur des Tactes selbst, denn zwey Achtel haben unter sich eben das innere und äussere Verhältniß, welches zwey Viertel oder zwey Zweytel haben. Weil man aber, im Falle die Achtel als Tacttheile erschienen, genöthigt seyn würde, sich der Zweyunddreißig- und der Vierundsechzigtheile, und bey Adagiosätzen wohl gar der Hundertarchtunzwanzigtheile zu bedienen, um die geschwindesten Töne der Melodie zu bezeichnen, und also ohne Noth das Auge des Ausführers mit zu viel an die Noten gehängten Abtheilungsstrichen zu überhäufen, so hat man mit Recht einen solchen Zweyachteltact als überflüßig und zugleich als unbrauchbar angesehen, weil alles, was in diesen Tact eingekleidet werden könnte, mit weit mehr Bequemlichkeit in den Zweyzweytel- oder Zweyvierteltact eingekleidet werden kann. (Koch 1787: 290)

Convenience should also guide the choice between 2/2 and 2/4 meters. Not only is it irrelevant for affect and style, the choice has no implications for performance. Koch illustrates this with Example 13.2, which is equivalent to Kirnberger's Example 13.1 in that it presents one phrase in two different meters. Koch starts from retracing Kirnberger's argument but rejects it in the further course of his discussion. His remarks demonstrate that he was clearly aware of the idea of *tempo giusto* and granted it in theory. Yet, as he emphasizes, this idea is no longer alive in practice:

A phrase in slow tempo should be set in 2/2 meter and a phrase in fast tempo in 2/4 meter in order that tones in slow tempo be designated with corresponding rhythmical values and so the sign and the signified brought into closer relation. If this rule were accepted, then the following phrase, if dressed in 2/2 [Example 13.2a], would thus necessarily have to be executed slowly and in the following example [Example 13.2b], dressed in 2/4, always fast. The rhythmical values would thus, even if not quite precisely, still to some extent determine the tempo of a phrase, and all the more precisely determined would be the expressions which one used to attach to each phrase in order to designate its tempo. Only that one does not follow the hint offered us by the nature of things. If it sometimes happens, then more by chance than on purpose because the use of both meters regarding tempo is treated completely at will. In most cases one proceeds the other way around and, availing himself with a simple even meter, uses 2/4 for phrases in slow tempo and 2/2 for those which should be performed in fast tempo.

Ein Saz [*sic*] von langsamer Bewegung [sollte] in den Zweyzweyteltact, ein Saz aber von geschwinder Bewegung in den Zweyvierteltact gesetzt [*sic*] werden, damit Töne von langsamer Bewegung auch mit einer ihrer Bewegung entsprechenden Notengattung bezeichnet, und also das Zeichen und die zu bezeichnende Sache in ein engeres Verhältniß gebracht würden. Wäre dieses als Regel angenommen, so müßte alsdenn nothwendig folgender Saz, wenn er in den Zweyzweyteltact eingekleidet wäre, z. E. [Example 13.2a] jederzeit in einer langsamen Bewegung, in folgender Einkleidung in den Zweyvierteltact hingegen [Example 13.2b] jederzeit in einer geschwindern Bewegung vorgetragen werden; und alsdenn würde die gebrauchte Notengattung, obschon nicht auf das genaueste, dennoch einigermaßen die Bewegung des Satzes bestimmen, und um desto bestimmter würden alsdenn die Ausdrücke seyn, die man, um die Bewegung zu bezeichnen, jedem Satze beyzufügen gewohnt ist. Allein man folgt in diesem Stücke dem Winke nicht, den uns die Natur der Sache giebt; geschieht es ja zuweilen, so ist es mehr Zufall als Vorsaz [sic], weil der Gebrauch dieser beyden Tactgattungen in Absicht auf die Geschwindigkeit der Bewegung als ganz willkührlich angenommen ist. Im Gegentheil verfährt man in den mehresten Fällen ganz umgekehrt, und braucht zu Sätzen von langsamer Bewegung den Zweyvierteltact, und zu Sätzen, die in geschwinder Bewegung vorgetragen werden sollen, den Zweyzweyteltact, im Falle man sich der einfachen geraden Tactart bedient. (Koch 1787: 291–93)

From Koch's remarks one can infer how the new tradition of metric notation contributed to the possibility of including several topics in one piece. If it was possible to write the same melody with different rhythmical values in different meters, as demonstrated in Example 13.2, then a melody whose topic requires slow tempo could be notated with larger rhythmical values in a fast piece and a melody whose topic requires fast tempo could be notated with smaller rhythmical values in a slow piece. Further devices that facilitated topical mixtures were *compound meters* and *double measures*.

The criterion used by Koch to distinguish compound from simple meters, in which notated bars correspond to composed measures, is the location of caesuras. This criterion is based on the rule that caesuras of melodic sections must fall on downbeats.[14] Because simple meters have only one downbeat located at the beginning of the notated bar, it is only on this position that caesuras can fall. Instead, every notated bar of a compound meter comprises two composed measures and contains two downbeats. Consequently, caesuras can fall both at the beginning and in the middle of notated bars and the latter position is a clear indicator of a compound meter. Koch demonstrates this in Example 13.3.[15] In mm. 1–6 caesuras of phrases, marked by him with squares, fall

EXAMPLE **13.2** Koch, *Versuch einer Anleitung zur Composition*, vol. 2 (1787), 292.

in the middle of bars but in the passage starting at m. 7 caesuras of phrases (squares) and incises (triangles) occur at the beginnings of mm. 8, 10, and 12, with their caesura notes apparently shifted to weak positions by appoggiaturas. In m. 14 the cadence, falling similarly on the first beat, is elided with the beginning of the subsequent phrase. As Koch explains, the example contains a change from compound 4/4 meter, which could be indicated by the time signature c, to simple 2/2 (alla breve) meter which, under normal circumstances, would have been indicated by ¢. Interestingly, this change coincides with the change of affect, which is emphasized by the dynamic change from *forte* to *piano*. Whereas the first six bars represent the orchestral brilliant style, the passage from m. 7 displays a lyrical affect of the singing style.[16] According to the convention described by Koch and illustrated in Example 13.2b, this passage could have been notated with halved rhythmical values in 2/4 meter. The notation in 2/2 is used to introduce a slow tempo into a fast piece by slowing down the pace of beats from quarter notes to half notes. The change of meter from compound to simple thus fakes a change of tempo.

If in compound meters one notated bar comprises two composed measures, in double measures one composed measure splits into two notated bars. Koch accepts the former notation but criticizes the latter because it misrepresents the relationship of strong and weak beats. What can be seen between two bar lines of Example 13.4a is not a measure of 2/4 but a beat of the composed 2/2 meter.[17] Yet, when all beats are downbeats, the concept of meter as alternation of strong and weak beats is contradicted and the difference between them compromised in metric notation. As a further consequence, double measures misrepresent the phrase structure. This follows from the rule concerning the metrical position of caesuras. Since caesuras fall on downbeats and indicate the last measures of phrases, a regular four-measure phrase appears irregular in double measures, its length being expressed in an uneven number of bars. Koch illustrates this in Example 13.4b. In order to complement the phrase to four composed measures, it is necessary to notate the weak beat of the fourth measure as an eighth bar following the caesura. While not to be counted in the preceding phrase, this bar does not yet start a new phrase. In the melody it is thus either empty or, as in Example 13.4a, filled with an overhang (*Überhang*).[18]

While compound meters and double measures facilitate topical mixtures, these devices complicate topical identification because they imply that the composed meter may differ from the notated meter. From Koch's discussion it follows that identification of composed meter requires careful analysis of phrase structure regarding the location of caesuras and the length of melodic sections. Identification of topics based on the connection between topics and meters is further complicated by the fact that in the new tradition of metric notation the composed meter may not correspond to the meter that would have been associated with the affect and genre of a given passage in the old tradition of *tempo giusto*. Rather than by tempo and performance nuance, the choice of the rhythmical values of beats may be dictated by other considerations, such as to avoid excessively small rhythmical values of fastest notes. In pieces including changes of composed meter, this choice in one passage must be coordinated with other passages and

EXAMPLE **13.3** Koch, *Versuch einer Anleitung zur Composition*, vol. 3 (1793), 224–25.

such changes may be used to fake changes of tempo. All these factors determine that, in order to identify a topic, it does not suffice to look at the time signature. Rather, topical identification is a challenging analytical task that, at times, requires a considerable theoretical knowledge. I will demonstrate the challenge of topical identification in relation to the main theme of the first movement of Mozart's Symphony in G minor, K. 550. Along the way I will show how historical music theory can help us resolve controversies

EXAMPLE **13.4** Koch, *Versuch einer Anleitung zur Composition*, vol. 2 (1787), 398, fig. 13 (a) and fig. 14 (b).

(a) **fig. *13.***

(falſch.)

(b) **fig. *14.*** (falſch.)

1. *2.* *3.* *4.* *5.* *6.* *7.*

between modern authors and how the topical identification reconciles different hermeneutic interpretations of Mozart's theme.

AN EXAMPLE

The celebrated theme of K. 550 (Example 13.5) has been frequently discussed and its phrase structure became the subject of a long-standing controversy.[19] While most authors agree that the theme starts with a structural upbeat, they disagree about the length of the upbeat and the location of the structural downbeat. Some authors constrain the upbeat to the first bar. For Rudolf Réti this bar lies "outside the symmetry" of the phrase structure. As he points out, Mozart could have extended the "introductory accompaniment of the first bar to produce a more symmetric group of two bars" (1951: 120). Glen Carruthers (1998) describes the first bar as a "cushion" and compares it with examples of the same phenomenon in Classic and Romantic music. Channan Willner calls it "bar 0" and takes for a composed-out "pedal call" typical of the Baroque. He states that the first theme starts at the following measure and emphasizes that "*there is no extended upbeat occupying this measure* (the notated bar 2)" (2007: 18).

If Willner feels compelled to reject the hypothesis of a two-bar upbeat with so much emphasis, this is because it has found eminent supporters. The first of them was the great Mozart biographer, Hermann Abert.[20] While he observes that the symphony starts with "a one-measure anticipation of the accompaniment," he adds that "it extends the upbeats...by tripling them, without depriving them of their character as upbeats— for the main accent remains on the third and seventh measures of the theme" (Broder

EXAMPLE **13.5** Mozart, Symphony No. 40 in G minor, K. 550/i, mm. 1–9.

1976: 70). The same opinion is expressed by Heinrich Schenker, who describes the first two bars as an anacrusis.[21] Both hypotheses are weighted against each other by Leonard Bernstein. At first, Bernstein entertains the one-bar upbeat hypothesis and suggests, like Réti, that in order to satisfy the "symmetrical principle" the introductory "vamp-accompaniment" should be "eight bars long, or at least four, or at the very least two" (1976: 93) but he rejects this suggestion when he turns to the discussion of hypermeter. As he observes, "in this Mozart symphony, the tempo is fast enough so that it *approaches* the feeling of one beat per bar" (101).[22] Given that strong and weak beats fall, respectively, in odd- and even-numbered bars, the first bar of the melody is weak and "works as an upbeat bar to the second" (101). In order to substantiate this reading, Bernstein refers to the bass notes alternating between lower and higher octaves and to the restatement of the principal theme, when the accompaniment enters in bar 22, marking the structural downbeat equivalent to bar 3 (107). A similar reading is elaborated by David Epstein. Like Bernstein, Epstein posits a two-measure hypermeter with one beat per bar. "The two-measure hypermeasure pattern is established from the outset since the first two measures act as an upbeat. Thus the first downbeat, structurally, falls upon the third measure" (1979: 70).[23] He justifies this position of the structural downbeat on the basis of the restatements of the theme in mm. 20, 103, 114, 164, 183 and 285 but, rather than to the entrance of the accompaniment, he points to the content of the harmonic progressions: "In all these cases the opening section of the motive ♪♩♪♩♪ is harmonized on the dominant, the following ♪♪ falling on the tonic and thereby receiving a downbeat accent" (70). The hypermetrical readings of the theme by Bernstein and Epstein inspired the analysis of K. 550 by Fred Lerdahl and Ray Jackendoff. One more factor invoked by Lerdahl and Jackendoff in their discussion of the two-bar hypermeter is harmonic rhythm. Although they find the four-bar hypermeter "open to interpretation" (1983: 22), they are inclined to hear strong beats in mm. 3 and 7 rather than 5 and 9 and their hypermetrical reading of the restatement of the theme posits a strong beat in m. 22 (25).[24]

The complex picture emerging from these analyses becomes simpler if one realizes that what Bernstein, Epstein, Lerdahl and Jackendoff take for hypermeter is the composed meter of Mozart's theme. The theme is written in double measures, with bars of the notated meter representing beats of the composed meter (Example 13.6).[25]

EXAMPLE **13.6** Composed meter in Mozart, Symphony No. 40 in G minor, K. 550/i, mm. 1–9.

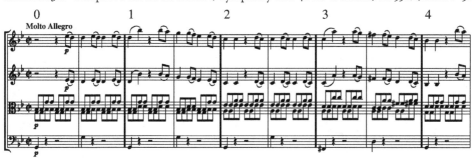

EXAMPLE **13.7** Mozart, *Le nozze di Figaro*, Act 1 Scene 8, "Non più andrai," mm. 1–5.

The caesura of the first melodic section in bar 5 falls on the strong beat of the third composed measure. The weak beat of this measure is represented by bar 6. This bar is structurally "empty" but, instead of an overhang, it is filled with an upbeat to the next composed measure. A similar upbeat fills in bar 2. Although it extends back to bar 1, the upbeat is not extended because its length does not exceed one composed measure.[26] Due to its upbeat function, the first composed measure forms "bar 0" of the principal theme. Willner is right that "bar 0" is only one but he does not realize that it comprises two notated bars.[27] While its connection with the "pedal call" is not precluded, early entrance of the accompaniment setting the stage for the melody is typical of eighteenth-century songs and arias.[28] An example occurs in *Le nozze di Figaro* (Example 13.7). Note that the layout of the first five measures of "Non piú andrai" is identical to the first five double measures of the symphony.[29] As there, so also here the continuation of the accompaniment and its tonic harmony from "bar 0" obliterates the structural beginning of the melody at the downbeat of "bar 1."[30] The harmonic continuation is conditioned by the eighteenth-century rule that every piece should start with the tonic and the assumption that this harmony should also underlie the first downbeat.[31] Each subsequent downbeat of the symphony is marked by a new harmony, which results in the two-bar harmonic rhythm observed by Lerdahl and Jackendoff.[32] The harmonic progressions in both examples support the changing-note melody

EXAMPLE **13.8** "The Pastorella" schema (a) in Mozart's Symphony No. 40 in G minor, K. 550/i, mm. 1–9 and (b) in "Non più andrai," mm. 1–5.

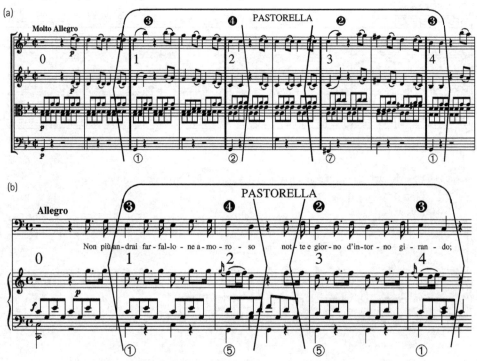

3–4–2–3, whose inversion was labeled by Robert Gjerdingen (2007: 117–22) "The Pastorella" (Example 13.8).

If bars of the notated meter represent beats of the composed meter, the composed meter of Mozart's theme is 2/1. In the tradition of *tempo giusto* this was an archaic meter with ecclesiastical associations but, clearly, the theme does not evoke the church style. Rather, 2/1 meter serves to introduce slower tempo into a fast movement. Instead of Molto Allegro, Mozart could have written the theme with halved rhythmical values in tempo Moderato (Example 13.9). The composed meter would have corresponded to the notated meter, but this notation would have forced him to spill lots of ink and resulted in "overloading the eye of the performer" with many sixteenth-notes in the accompaniment and some thirty-second-notes further in the movement. Mozart's choice of double measures for the principal theme could have been informed by two further considerations. First, between bars 10–21 he changes the phase of the composed meter.[33] If the theme had been notated in ¢ meter with halved rhythmical values, its return would have been shifted by half a bar relative to the notated meter.[34] Second, the notated meter corresponds to the composed meter of the secondary theme (m. 44).

This discussion leads us to the *topic* of the theme. For Meredith Ellis Little (2001a: 120) the theme is related to the bourrée. This topical identification is clearly provoked by what looks like a quarter-note upbeat in a quick 4/4 meter but it does not hold in the composed meter. In the eighteenth century the ¢ meter in a moderate tempo was commonly associated with the gavotte.[35] The slow pace of half-note beats goes hand in hand with the slow harmonic rhythm of this dance, a feature also observable in Mozart's theme. Another and by far the most important feature of the gavotte was its half-measure upbeat. In many examples of this topic from Mozart's music, this upbeat takes an especially characteristic form of two equal notes repeating the same pitch.[36] On the face of it this feature is missing from K. 550. Instead of two equal notes taking up half a measure of the composed meter, the upbeat consists of three smaller upbeat motives, but time-span reduction reveals that these motives form decorations of structural notes by means of "sighs" which could be notated with grace notes. One more written-out grace note is the skip of the sixth, which resembles a *portamento*. Stripped out of these decorations, the double upbeat of the gavotte comes to the surface (Example 13.10a).[37]

EXAMPLE **13.9** Metric reduction of Mozart, Symphony No. 40 in G minor, K. 550/i, mm. 1–9.

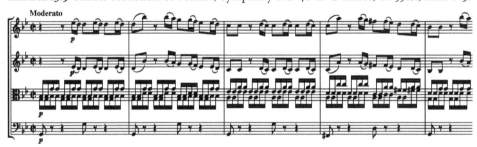

EXAMPLE **13.10** Time-span reduction of the melody (a) and simplification of the accompaniment (b) from Mozart, Symphony No. 40 in G minor, K. 550/i, mm. 1–9.

EXAMPLE 13.11 Hermann Abert's melodic reduction of Mozart, Symphony No. 40 in G minor, K. 550/i, mm. 1–9, shown in Broder, *Mozart: Symphony in G Minor, K. 550* (1967), 70.

EXAMPLE 13.12 "The Pastorella" schema in Mozart, *Die Zauberflöte*, "Dies Bildnis ist bezaubernd schön," mm. 1–6.

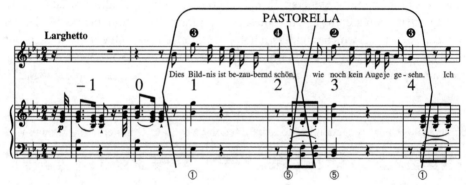

According to Allanbrook, the gavotte was "a courtship dance, and also had from its origin persistent associations with the pastoral, which were still very much alive in the late eighteenth century" (1983: 50–51).[38] The combination of courtly and pastoral characteristics explains why it was associated with the Arcadian world inhabited by "courtly shepherds and rustic nobles" (52) and casts an unexpected light on Robert Schumann's characterization of K. 550 as a work "of Grecian lightness and grace."[39] Although Schumann's words have often been criticized for their supposed insensitivity to the depths of Mozart's music,[40] topical associations of the gavotte could have been familiar to him and its characteristic gestures palpable under the surface of Mozart's theme. For those who described this work as "melancholic," "pathetic," and "tragic" these gestures and their associations with Greek antiquity were apparently not available.[41] Melancholy is suggested by the "sigh" motives while the pathetic or tragic feel of Mozart's theme is conveyed by the accompaniment,[42] but both features operate on the surface of the theme and their affective inflections are closely related to the gavotte topic under the surface. The affect of melancholy was not uncommon in the gavotte.[43] In fact, melancholic nostalgia is the reverse side of its pastoral associations: it expresses eighteenth-century longing for Arcadia—the Paradise lost of ancient Greece and the French Enlightenment. What may seem less characteristic of this dance is the stormy accompaniment, but it derives from the Alberti bass typical of the gavotte (Allanbrook 1983: 50).[44] To restore the Alberti bass, it suffices to take away the tremolos (Example 13.10b). Alberti bass also relates to the singing style. Indeed, gavottes abound in French vocal music, especially in brunettes and other airs (Little 2001b: 593). This association of the gavotte is grasped by those authors who point to a "songful" character of the theme and ask: "Perchè questo tema è cantabile?"[45] Apart from the accompaniment, its vocal characteristics are the "sigh" motives and the quasi-*portamento* but, even without them, the structural melodic line uncovered by time-span reduction has an eminently vocal flair. In fact, it is strikingly similar to the structural melody posited for this theme by Abert (Example 13.11) and compared by him to the contour of Tamino's aria "Dies Bildniss ist bezaubernd schön" from *Die Zauberflöte* (Example 13.12), also based on the inverted "Pastorella."[46]

From my discussion it follows that the topical content of Mozart's theme forms a complex topical trope in the sense attached to this concept by Robert Hatten (this volume). Since different authors attend to different structural levels, they associate the theme with different topics and ascribe it different affects, but all these associations can be derived from or absorbed to the topic of the gavotte. This topic operates on a deeper level, which has been erased from our musical experience by the passage of historical time but can be uncovered by topical analysis.

Conclusion

In this chapter I retraced two traditions of metric notation that informed the practice of Classic composers and showed that the new tradition has implications for identification of musical topics. In conclusion I would like to add a few remarks about the interconnection between metric notation, aesthetic theory, and compositional practice.

The old tradition of metric notation came to Germany from France along with the neoclassical aesthetics. The fact that this tradition was embraced by Rameau, whose *tragédies* form the last highlights of this genre inspired by Corneille and Racine, supports the link with neoclassicism and suggests that the constancy of meter, which remained the fundamental principle of metric notation for two centuries, originated in the aesthetic principle of unity in variety. By contrast, the new tradition of metric notation emerged from the practice of Italian composers in which variety of affects was unconstrained by any claims of unity. It is not by chance that this tradition was defended by Rousseau, an advocate of Italian opera buffa and the main opponent of Rameau in the pamphlet war known as the *querelle des bouffons*. The reforms of metric notation proposed by these French authors were inspired by their aesthetics. In Germany, criticism of the new tradition of metric notation, voiced by Schulz on behalf of Sulzer and Kirnberger, parallels the criticism of South-German composers by North-German critics. But aesthetic positions taken by German authors do not always match their views on metric notation. While the view represented by Mattheson and Kirnberger is consistent with their doctrine of affections, Marpurg, who received this doctrine from Mattheson and, like Kirnberger, adopted Rameau's theory of harmony, does not subscribe to their view of meter. Even more complicated is the case of Koch, who adopts Sulzer's aesthetics but advocates the new practice of metric notation and who criticizes the notation in double measures, although it was an integral part of this practice. His rejection of *tempo giusto* and opposition toward Kirnberger in the field of metric notation is all the more remarkable as, at the same time, Koch develops Kirnberger's theory of meter (Mirka 2009: 3–12). Inconsistencies grow exponentially with composers. Though we cannot reconstruct their aesthetic positions with any certainty, the eighteenth-century practice of metric notation explains what I mean when I write in the introduction that South-German composers were committed to premises of North-German aesthetics, even if they used them *a rebours*. The premise, in this case, was the association of meters with affects and genres. Using it *a rebours* meant to play with meter for the sake of stylistic cross-references. These complementary facets of compositional practice were incorporated in the two traditions of metric notation retraced in this chapter. Without the old tradition associations of meters with styles and genres would have been erased from collective memory. Without the new tradition stylistic cross-references would have been constrained by meter.

An unconcerned juggling with affects and genres, which results from such cross-references, has been compared to *commedia dell'arte*.[47] This comparison hints at the comic impulse behind eighteenth-century instrumental music drawing on a gallery of stock characters who, like Hans Wurst, are always ready to poke their heads and spring into the middle of things without waiting to be invited, but it has a special meaning in reference to meter. In the new tradition of metric notation the constancy of notated meter is not a mark of affective unity but a mask of stylistic variety. Changes of composed meter, hidden behind this mask, form a parade of meters in disguise.

NOTES

1. "Quelques fois il signifie la *Lenteur*, ou la *Vitesse* des Nottes & de la mesure, ainsi on dit, mouvement *gay*, mouvement *lent*, mouvement *vif*, ou *animé*, etc. & dans ce sens il signifie aussi souvent une *égalité*, *reglée* & bien *marquée* de tous les temps de la mesure" (Brossard 1705: 56).

2. "Hier will man nur das langsame und hurtige, ich meyne, die *Mensuram*, oder *Zeitmasse*, (*Italis*, Battuta) welche man den *Tact* nennet (à *Tactu*) examiniren, und derselben verschiedene Arten kurz anführen" (Mattheson 1713: 76–77).

3. In *Der vollkommene Capellmeister* Mattheson does not discuss individual meters but sends the reader back to his discussion in *Das Neu-Eröffnete Orchestre* and *Kleine General-Baß-Schule* (1735).

4. For more information about these theorists and eighteenth-century time signatures, see Houle (1987: 35–61). My discussion in this section benefits from Houle's.

5. Rameau's influence on Kirnberger is also manifest from the fact that Kirnberger admits of simple meters with two, three, or four beats. This sets him apart from Mattheson and most other German authors, who accept simple meters with only two or three beats. For Rameau the number of beats is the proof that meter originates with harmony: "We may derive meter from the source of harmony, for meter consists only of the numbers 2, 3, and 4, numbers which also give us the octave divided arithmetically and harmonically" (1722: 150; 1971: 164).

6. Allanbrook calls the moderate tempo of meters with quarter-note beats *tempo giusto* (1983: 15). As she admits (331–32 n. 10), her usage differs from the sense of *tempo giusto* adopted by Kirnberger, which denotes the natural tempo of any given meter, and follows another tradition reflected in the definition of this term in *Encyclopédie méthodique* published in 1791.

7. Verbal designations are also used by representatives of *tempo giusto* but they serve to modify the natural tempo indicated by time signature (Kirnberger 1776: 107; 1982: 377; Schulz 1774: 1133).

8. "Si tous ces signes sont institués pour marquer autant de différentes sortes de *Mesures*, il y en a beaucoup trop; & s'ils le sont pour exprimer les divers degrés de Mouvement, il n'y en a pas assez; puisque, indépendamment de l'espèce de *Mesure* & de la division des Tems, on est presque toujours contraint d'ajoûter un mot au commencement de l'Air pour déterminer le Tems" (Rousseau 1768: 284).

9. "Hieraus ist zu vermuthen, daß Rousseau kein sonderlicher Praktiker seyn müsse, sonst würde seinem scharfen Beobachtungsgeiste die Verschiedenheit des Vortrages und der Bewegung, der verschiedenen geraden oder ungeraden Takte, nicht unbemerkt geblieben seyn" (Schulz 1774: 1133).

10. "Andere, die mit Rousseau die Vielheiten der Takte für blos willkührliche Erfindung halten, und darüber ungehalten sind, haben entweder kein Gefühl von dem besondern Vortrag eines jeden Taktes, oder verläugnen es, und laufen daher Gefahr, Sachen zu sezen [*sic*], die, weil sie nicht in dem rechten, dem Charakter des Stücks angemessenen Takte gesezt sind, ganz anders vorgetragen werden, als sie gedacht worden" (Schulz 1774: 1133).

11. "Ich getrauete mir alle Musikalien, welche von des Jubals Zeiten her componiret sind worden, theils in einem 3/4, und theils in einen gemeinen oder 2/4 Tacten zu übersetzen" (Riepel 1752: 68).

12. "Weil diese Hauptnoten allezeit in kleinere Noten getheilet werden müssen: so ist es gut, auf die in jedem Gesange vorkommende geschwindeste Noten Acht zu haben, um nicht solche Figuren zur Vorstellung der Hauptnoten zu nehmen, daß man diese geschwindesten Noten mit Vierundsechzig- oder Hundertachtunzwanzigtheilen u.s.w. zu schreiben verbunden sey" (Marpurg 1760: 99–100).

13. "Alle übrige Vorstellungen der geraden Tactart, als 2/1, 2/8, 2/16, 2/32 u.s.w., und der ungeraden Tactart, als 3/1, 3/16, 3/32 u.s.w. sind unbequem und verwerflich" (Marpurg 1760: 100).

14. The rule concerning the metrical placement of caesuras on downbeats is ubiquitous in eighteenth-century music theory, but its application as the criterion of distinguishing compound from simple meters is complicated by decorations of caesura notes. For detailed discussion, see Mirka (2009: 74–82).

15. This example and my summary of Koch's analysis occur in Mirka (2009: 210–12).

16. According to Ratner (1980: 219), the contrast between "the brilliant-vigorous" and "the gentle-cantabile" styles was the basic mechanism of eighteenth-century music. For the brilliant style in orchestral music, see Roman Ivanovitch's chapter in this volume.

17. My discussion in this paragraph draws on Mirka (2009: 218–19).

18. Note that the length of seven bars, which results from an incorrect notation in Example 13.4b, corresponds to the length that can be incorrectly ascribed to the four-measure phrase in mm. 7–10 of Example 13.3, if one overlooks the change from 4/4 to 2/2 meter. Because each notated bar of 4/4 comprises two composed measures of 2/4 meter, bars must be counted twice in order to determine the length of phrases in the first six bars of the example but this

procedure must change at m. 7: "if every measure is counted twice as before, then…the entire phrase until its ending would be regarded as a seven-measure phrase and thus as a melodic section of an uneven number of measures" (Koch 1983: 162–63). Koch's discussion makes clear that the phenomena of compound meter and double measures are closely interrelated. Accordingly, empty bars that serve as indicators of double measures are related to the criterion of caesura used by Koch to recognize compound meters because they arise as a result of the location of the caesura note in the preceding notated bar.

19. The first movement of K. 550 competes for the title of the most overanalyzed piece in the history of music theory with the theme of the first-movement variations from the Piano Sonata in A major, K. 331. The latter piece is discussed by Allanbrook (2008). My discussion is inspired by hers but goes in the opposite direction: if she shows how topical identification explains complexities of structural analysis, I demonstrate how structural analysis aids topical identification.

20. Abert's biography of Mozart (1919–21) was published as "the fifth, completely revised and extended" edition of Otto Jahn's classical work. His analysis of K. 550 occurs in the second volume and has been translated into English by Nathan Broder (1976: 69–83).

21. Schenker's analysis of K. 550 is contained in the second volume of *Das Meisterwerk in der Musik* (1926). English translation in Schenker (1996: 59–96).

22. Bernstein's observation makes sense in conjunction with the metronome tempo markings suggested by Mozart's pupil, Johann Nepomuk Hummel, and adopted by Carl Czerny. Both authors suggest MM 108 for a half note (Zaslaw 1989: 499).

23. Although Epstein writes about two-measure hypermeasures and marks them on the musical example (1979: 68–69 ex. 10), his remark that "the first two measures act as an upbeat" and the assumption that accentual weight "must be different between the downbeats of measures 1 and 3" (70) seem to imply four-measure hypermeasures. In reality, Epstein does not posit such hypermeasures. In the further course of his commentary he explains that different accentual weight of the downbeats of mm. 1 and 3 are due to the fact that the downbeat of m. 1 carries only a metrical accent while the downbeat of m. 3 "needs the emphasis of a structural downbeat" (70). The concept of "structural downbeat" is related to Fred Lerdahl and Ray Jackendoff's "structural beginning" (see note 30). This reveals that the contradictions of Epstein's analysis have their origin in confusion between grouping and meter, which Lerdahl and Jackendoff deserve the credit for clarifying.

24. Lerdahl and Jackendoff's analysis is criticized by Jonathan Kramer, who accuses the authors of "a confusion between rhythmic and metric accents" (1988: 114), that is to say, between grouping and meter. For him "the downbeats of mm. 3 and 7 of the Mozart symphony are indeed accented, but as rhythmic pulses, not metric beats. The metric strong points occur at the downbeats of mm. 1 and 5" (115). Kramer forgets, though, that grouping is a preference factor of metric perception. Given the importance of phrase structure for the perception of hypermeter, grouping and meter are unlikely to be out of phase when metrical accents are derived from phenomenal accents at the beginning of a piece. It is only in the further course of a piece, after hypermeter has been entrained by the listener, that these accents can pull against each other in the way described by Kramer. Another critique of Lerdahl and Jackendoff's analysis was formulated by William Benjamin (1984). Benjamin assumes metrical spans in mm. 2–5 and 6–10 (406 fig. 25) but hears "stronger accents on the downbeats of the second and fourth measures of these spans than on their first and third measures" (407). This betrays a genuine confusion of grouping and meter.

25. Several examples of double measures mistaken for hypermeter are analyzed by Claudia Maurer Zenck (2001). Although this author discusses the opening of K. 550 (303–4), she does not realize that it illustrates the same phenomenon and limits herself to critical remarks about Benjamin's analysis mentioned in note 24.

26. The concept of extended upbeat, adumbrated by Abert and exposed by Ryan McClelland (2006), is equivalent to Rothstein's concept of elongated upbeat: "an upbeat that precedes the first bar of a hypermeasure, and that itself lasts at least one full bar" (1989: 56). Eric McKee (2004: 2) shows the beginning of K. 550 as an example of "extended anacrusis."

27. Interestingly enough, Willner suggests that "bar 0" with a suppressed downbeat is a generic feature of the gavotte (2007: 9–11). As we will see, the gavotte is the topic of Mozart's theme.

28. See Maurer Zenck (2001: 254, 266). Such entrances are frequently responsible for metrical conflicts between metrical patterns in accompaniment and melody described by Roger Kamien (1993).

29. "Non più andrai," too, can occur in double measures. Mozart notates it in 2/4 meter when he uses its tune in a contredanse shown by Eric McKee (this volume, page 171) in Example 5.2. The empty bars 4 and 8 of this example, filled with overhangs, and the location of caesuras at the beginnings of mm. 3 and 5 in Example 13.7 indicate that the composed meter of the aria is simple 2/2 (¢) and not compound 4/4 (c). In fact, Mozart adopts the ¢ time signature when he quotes "Non più andrai" in the second finale of *Don Giovanni*. This and other inconsistencies of Mozart's choice between 2/2 and 4/4 meter are discussed by Maurer Zenck (2001: 86–88).

30. "Structural beginning" is one type of structural accent proposed by Lerdahl and Jackendoff (1983), the other being "structural ending." While structural endings (cadences) influence metric perception, structural beginnings are for their part influenced by meter because, to be a structural beginning, an event must fall on a metrical downbeat. This downbeat can be called a "structural downbeat."

31. The rule is exposed by Kirnberger (1776: 32; 1982: 307). The assumption follows from its comparison with the rule quoted in the next note.

32. As Kirnberger points out, "except at the beginning of a piece, one must never use the same chord on an accented beat that was just used on the preceding unaccented beat, because the progression to a different chord, which the ear expects, is thereby obscured, and a faulty monotony is produced" (1776: 32; 1982: 307). The exception for the beginning of a piece implies that the tonic harmony introduced on the upbeat should be repeated on the following downbeat. Such repetitions should be avoided in the further course of a piece, which explains the harmonic changes between "bar 0" and "bar 1" in the restatements of the theme.

33. This change has been discussed in terms of hypermetrical irregularity by Lerdahl and Jackendoff (1983: 22–25), Benjamin (1984: 407–8), and Kramer (1988: 116).

34. Shifts of composed meter are among the most important reasons for the notation in double measures. For detailed discussion and further examples, see Mirka (2009: 222–24).

35. Allanbrook (1983: 49) suggests that the gavotte meter is 4/4 but historical sources relate this dance to alla breve (Marpurg 1763: 19–20; Sulzer 1771: 424; Koch 1802: col. 630).

36. Such is the case in the Romance from *Eine kleine Nachtmusik*, K. 525, and the slow movement of String Quintet in E flat major, K. 614. Further examples include the finales of the Sonata for Violin and Piano in B flat major, K. 454, and the Quintet for Piano and Winds in E flat major, K. 452, discussed by John Irving in Chapter 20.

37. My time-span reduction of the theme is based on Lerdahl and Jackendoff's figure 6.5 (1983: 127) but does not correspond to their reduction in figure 10.8 (259).

38. The pastoral associations of the gavotte come to the fore in the hybrid genre of the musette–gavotte. Allanbrook notes that "gavotte rhythms are an appropriate gesture for a courtly pastoral musette because they themselves evoke the Arcadian world" (1983: 54).

39. "Diese griechisch schwebende, wenn auch etwas blaße Grazie." These words occur in an article about key characteristics published by Schumann in *Damen Conversations Lexikon* (1834) and reprinted in *Die Neue Zeitschrift für Musik* (1835).

40. Alfred Einstein quotes them without mentioning Schumann's name: "It is strange how easily the world has accepted such a work and has even been able to think of it as a document of 'Grecian lightness and grace'—a characterization that could apply at best only to the divine tranquillity of the Andante or to the trio of the Minuet, otherwise so heroically tragic" (1945: 235).

41. These affective qualities are mentioned, among others, by François-Joseph Fétis, Alexandre Oulibicheff, Sir George Grove, and Donald Francis Tovey (see Broder 1967). The most important contributions to the analysis and criticism of K. 550 are listed by Zaslaw (1989: 437 n.167).

42. Deryck Cooke takes it for granted that the symphony "*is* a melancholy work" (1959: 236). He compares the "sigh" motives to "stabs of anguish" (241) and writes about the accompaniment "in a mood of suppressed agitation" (239). Elaine Sisman (this volume, page 115) writes about "the opening theme's *agitato* and *pianto* topics."

43. Marpurg, quoted by Allanbrook (1983: 50), writes that the gavotte "can be used for various types of expression, happy and sad in various degrees, and can thus be performed in tempos which are more or less quick and more or less slow."

44. Alberti bass occurs, among others, in the gavotte from the ballet music for *Idomeneo*, shown by Allanbrook (1983: 51 ex. 2–26), and in the Romance from *Eine kleine Nachtmusik*, K. 525.

45. The "songful" (*liederisch*) character is observed by Leo Schrade (1964). The question is posed by Gino Stefani (1976). Both authors are quoted by Nattiez (1998: 6–7).

46. Although schemata can be combined with different topics and the three instances of "Pastorella," shown in this chapter, occur in different topical guises, the affective character of this schema, exemplified in its early instantiations and reflected in its name (Gjerdingen 2007: 117–18), concords with the pastoral associations of the gavotte in Mozart's theme.

47. This comparison was used by Allanbrook (1992) and Alexander Silbiger (2000) in reference to the first movement of Mozart's Piano Sonata in F major, K. 332, but it applies to many other pieces of eighteenth-century music.

REFERENCES

Abert, Hermann. 1919–21. *W. A. Mozart*. Leipzig: Breitkopf und Härtel.

Allanbrook, Wye Jamison. 1983. *Rhythmic Gesture in Mozart:* Le nozze di Figaro *and* Don Giovanni. Chicago: University of Chicago Press.

——. 1992. Two Threads through the Labyrinth: Topic and Process in the First Movements of K. 332 and K. 333. In *Convention in Eighteenth- and Nineteenth-Century Music: Essays in Honor of Leonard G. Ratner*, ed. Wye J. Allanbrook, Janet M. Levy, and William P. Mahrt, 125–71. Stuyvesant, NY: Pendragon.

——. 2008. Mozart's K331, First Movement: Once More, with Feeling. In *Communication in Eighteenth-Century Music*, ed. Danuta Mirka and Kofi Agawu, 254–82. Cambridge: Cambridge University Press.

Benjamin, William. 1984. A Theory of Musical Meter. *Music Perception* 1/4: 355–413.

Bernstein, Leonard. 1976. *The Unanswered Question: Six Talks at Harvard*. Cambridge, MA: Harvard University Press.

Broder, Nathan, ed. 1967. *Mozart: Symphony in G Minor, K. 550*. New York: Norton.

Brossard, Sébastien de. 1705. *Dictionnaire de musique*, 2nd ed. Paris: Ballard.

Carruthers, Glen. 1998. Strangeness and Beauty: The Opening Measure of Mozart's Symphony in G minor, K. 550. *Journal of Musicology* 16/2: 283–99.

Cooke, Deryck. 1959. *The Language of Music*. London: Oxford University Press.

Einstein, Alfred. 1945. *Mozart, His Character, His Work*. Trans. Arthur Mendel and Nathan Broder. New York: Oxford University Press.

Epstein, David. 1979. *Beyond Orpheus: Studies in Musical Structure*. Cambridge, MA: The MIT Press.

Galeazzi, Francesco. 1791–96. *Elementi teoretico-pratici di musica*. 3 vols. Rome: Pilucchi Cracas.

Gervasoni, Carlo. 1800. *La scuola della musica*. 2 vols. Piacenza: Niccoló Orcesi.

Houle, George. 1987. *Meter in Music, 1600–1800: Performance, Perception, and Notation*. Bloomington: Indiana University Press.

Kamien, Roger. 1993. Conflicting Metrical Patterns in Accompaniment and Melody in Works by Mozart and Beethoven: A Preliminary Study. *Journal of Music Theory* 37/2: 311–48.

Kirnberger, Johann Philipp. 1776. *Die Kunst des reinen Satzes in der Musik*. Vol. 2, section 1. Berlin and Königsberg: Decker und Hartung.

——. 1982. *The Art of Strict Musical Composition*. Trans. David Beach and Jurgen Thym. New Haven: Yale University Press.

Koch, Heinrich Christoph. 1787–93. *Versuch einer Anleitung zur Composition*. Vols. 2 and 3. Leipzig: Adam Friedrich Böhme. Reprint, Hildesheim: Georg Olms, 1969.

——. 1802. *Musikalisches Lexikon*. Frankfurt-am-Main: August Hermann der Jüngere. Reprint, Kassel: Bärenreiter, 2001.

——. 1983. *Introductory Essay on Composition*. Trans. Nancy Kovaleff Baker. New Haven: Yale University Press.

Kramer, Jonathan. 1988. *The Time of Music: New Meanings, New Temporalities, New Listening Strategies*. New York: Schirmer.

Lerdahl, Fred and Ray Jackendoff. 1983. *A Generative Theory of Tonal Music*. Cambridge, MA: The MIT Press.

Little, Meredith Ellis. 2001a. Bourrée. In *The New Grove Dictionary of Music and Musicians*. 2nd ed., ed. Stanley Sadie and John Tyrell, vol. 4, 119–20. London: Macmillan.

——. 2001b. Gavotte. In *The New Grove Dictionary of Music and Musicians*. 2nd ed., ed. Stanley Sadie and John Tyrell, vol. 9, 591–93. London: Macmillan.

Marpurg, Friedrich Wilhelm. 1760–63. *Kritische Briefe über die Tonkunst*. 2 vols. Berlin: Birnstiel. Reprint, Hildesheim: Georg Olms, 1974.

Mattheson, Johann. 1713. *Das Neu-Eröffnete Orchestre*. Hamburg: Benjamin Schillers Wittwe. Reprint, Hildesheim: Georg Olms, 1993.

——. 1735. *Kleine General-Baß-Schule*. Hamburg: Johann Christoph Kißner. Reprint, Laaber: Laaber, 2003.

——. 1739. *Der vollkommene Capellmeister*. Hamburg: Christian Herold. Reprint, Kassel: Bärenreiter, 1991.

Maurer Zenck, Claudia. 2001. *Vom Takt: Untersuchungen zur Theorie und kompositorischen Praxis im ausgehenden 18. und beginnenden 19. Jahrhundert*. Vienna: Böhlau.

McClelland, Ryan. 2006. Extended Upbeats in the Classical Minuet: Interactions with Hypermeter and Phrase Structure. *Music Theory Spectrum* 28/1: 23–56.

McKee, Eric. 2004. Extended Anacruses in Mozart's Instrumental Music. *Theory and Practice* 29: 1–37.

Mirka, Danuta. *Metric Manipulations in Haydn and Mozart: Chamber Music for Strings, 1787–1791*. New York: Oxford University Press.

Nattiez, Jean-Jacques. 1998. A Comparison of Analyses from the Semiological Point of View (the Theme of Mozart's Symphony in G minor, K550). *Contemporary Music Review* 17/1: 1–38.

Rameau, Jean-Philippe. 1722. *Traité de l'harmonie*. Paris: Ballard.

——. 1971. *Treatise on Harmony*. Trans. Philip Gossett. New York: Dover.

Ratner, Leonard G. 1980. *Classic Music: Expression, Form, and Style*. New York: Schirmer.

Réti, Rudolf. 1951. *The Thematic Process in Music*. New York: Macmillan.

Riepel, Joseph. 1752. *Anfangsgründe zur musicalischen Setzkunst*. Vol. 1: *De Rhythmopoeia oder von der Tactordnung*. Augsburg: Emerich Felix Bader.

Rousseau, Jean. 1683. *Méthode claire, certaine et facil, pour apprendre à chanter la musique*. Paris: Author.

Rousseau, Jean-Jacques. 1743. *Dissertation sur la musique moderne*. Paris: G.-F. Quillau père.

——. 1768. *Dictionnaire de musique*. Paris: Veuve Duchesne.

Rothstein, William N. 1989. *Phrase Rhythm in Tonal Music*. New York: Schirmer.

Schenker, Heinrich. 1926. *Das Meisterwerk in der Musik*. Vol. 2. Munich: Drei Masken Verlag.

——. 1996. *The Masterwork in Music: A Yearbook*, ed. William Drabkin. Vol. 2. Cambridge: Cambridge University Press.

Schrade, Leo. 1964. *W. A. Mozart*. Bern and Munich: Francke.

Schulz, Johann Abraham Peter. 1774. Takt. In Johann Georg Sulzer, *Allgemeine Theorie der schönen Künste*. Vol. 2, 1130–38. Leipzig: Weidmann.

[Schumann, Robert]. 1834. Charakteristik der Tonleitern und Tonarten. In *Damen Conversations Lexikon*, ed. Carl Herloßsohn. Vol. 2, 333–34. Leipzig: Volckmar.

——. 1835. Charakteristik der Tonleitern und Tonarten. *Die Neue Zeitschrift für Musik* 2/11: 43–44.

Silbiger, Alexander. 2000. Il chitarrino le suonerò. *Commedia dell'arte* in Mozart's Piano Sonata K. 332. Paper read at the Southeast Chapter Meeting of the American Musicological Society, Greensboro.

Stefani, Gino. 1976. *Introduzione alla semiotica della musica*. Palermo: Sellerio.

Sulzer, Johann Georg. 1771–74. *Allgemeine Theorie der schönen Künste*. Leipzig: Weidmann.

Walther, Johann Gottfried. 1732. *Musicalisches Lexicon oder musicalische Bibliothec*. Leipzig: Deer.

Willner, Channan. 2007. Bar 0 and the Suppressed Hyperdownbeat. Online. Available: http://www.channanwillner.com/pdf/bar_0.pdf. Accessed 12 April 2012.

Zaslaw, Neal. 1989. *Mozart's Symphonies: Context, Performance Practice, Reception*. Oxford: Clarendon.

CHAPTER 14

....

TOPICS AND HARMONIC SCHEMATA

A Case from Beethoven

....

VASILI BYROS

EXAMPLE 14.1 displays three different realizations of the harmonic and scale-degree schema that Leonard Meyer (1973; 1980; 1989) termed the 1–7, 2–1. The pattern is one among several types of "changing-note schemata," which are united by a shared, underlying harmonic statement–response parallelism of I–V, V–I, and a rhyming scale-degree progression in the top-voice: 1–7, 2–1; 1–7, 4–3; 3–2, 4–3; and so forth. Frequently used as the presentation phrase of a "sentence" (Caplin 1998), the 1–7, 2–1 is treated identically in these three excerpts from Meyer's *Style and Music* (1989), with respect to syntax, structure, and formal function. And yet, their expression could not be more disparate. The Haydn symphony example is a siciliano with an overall pastoral sentiment; the Mozart quartet a bourrée, with march and fantasia characteristics, and *Sturm und Drang* in affect; and the Beethoven trio a sarabande in the *Romanza* style. In none of these cases is the affective reference necessary for an understanding of the 1–7, 2–1 syntax on its own terms: *as* grammar. Nor, the other way round, is the stylistic and generic expression or affect of each theme contingent on the underlying harmonic syntax in any way. Much like the relations between topics and formal functions (Caplin 2005; this volume), topics and harmonic schemata do not significantly correlate in absolute terms, insofar as a given schema does not require a particular topical realization and vice versa. Examples of this topical variability of schemata (and the schematic variability of topics) are readily available in music of the later eighteenth century.

The relative autonomy of the two domains is reflective of a broader conceptual independence of musical syntax from musical semantics. Kofi Agawu (1991) articulated this distinction between music's intrareferential and extrareferential stylistic symbols—following the linguistic and literary theorist Roman Jakobson (1971)—in terms of "introversive" versus "extroversive semiosis."[1] This relative autonomy notwithstanding, neither schemata nor topics remain ends unto themselves, insofar as both domains equally figure in the late eighteenth-century communicative channel (Mirka 2008). Topics and harmonic schemata are assemblies of musical style symbols that interact in

EXAMPLE 14.1 Three topically differentiated versions of the 1–7, 2–1 schema from Meyer, *Style and Music* (1989), 3 (ex. 1.1a), 4 (ex. 1.1b), and 53 (ex. 2.2f): (a) Haydn, Symphony No. 46 in B major, ii, mm. 1–4; (b) Mozart, Piano Quartet in G minor, K. 478/i, mm. 1–8; (c) Beethoven, Trio for Clarinet, Cello, and Piano in B flat major, Op. 11/ii, mm. 1–8.

both syntactic (sequentially structured) and semantic (referentially structured) dimensions to some communicative and expressive end.[2] There exist no sharp boundaries between them, either in categorial or pragmatic terms. That is, in respect to both categorization and language use, syntax and semantics interface in what cognitive linguists call a *syntax-lexicon continuum*—"a continuum of symbolic structures" (Langacker 1987: 1991; see also Zbikowski 2002: 138).

My contribution in this chapter illustrates that, in the case of Beethoven, the musical equivalent of this continuum enables the communication of a powerful philosophical message in the "Eroica" Symphony, Op. 55 (1803–4), one that involves the spiritual consequences of suffering, self-sacrifice, and death. "Dies ist Symphonik als Drama," says Roger Norrington, in a *Konzerteinführung* for a series of performances with the Radio-Symphonieorchester Stuttgart (2002). A specific interfacing of topics and harmonic schemata provides the structural and expressive basis for communicating a cultural unit of "abnegation," with its connotations of "religious drama" (Hatten 1994). The nature of this interfacing involves, on the one hand, the musical equivalent of *form–meaning pairs*: in cognitive linguistics all grammatical constructions are conceived as amalgams of form and content that vary in terms of their lexical specificity (Stefanowitsch and Gries 2003; Langacker 1998). The musical equivalents of form–meaning pairs are *schema–topic amalgams*: as instances of music-grammatical constructions, harmonic schemata also contain lexical significance in both "symbolic" and "indexical" capacities (Monelle 2000: 14–19; after Peirce 1931–58). The *expressive genre* (Hatten 1994) of the "Eroica" emerges from Beethoven's use of a particular schema–topic amalgam, which pivots on the *le–sol–fi–sol* schema (Byros 2012, 2009). The *le–sol–fi–sol* is an instance of harmonic grammar that intersects the semantic world of the *ombra* topic (Ratner 1980; McClelland 2012), with its mortal, funereal, and sacrificial connotations. Its extramusical references are not inherent, however, but rather emerge under specific contextual and deictic conditions. The compositional strategies that produce these conditions involve musical realizations of the principle of "markedness" first outlined in Michael Shapiro's *The Sense of Grammar* (1983) and adapted in Robert Hatten's *Musical Meaning in Beethoven* (1994). The extroversive semiosis of musical grammar is affordant, emerging from its marked use in compositional context. In this way, the syntactic and semantic characteristics of schemata and topics not only interface within hybrid structures that shade into both categories (categorial), but through their relative independence they also powerfully interact in the communicative channel (pragmatic) to produce numerous "correlations," both positive and negative, between structure/form and expression/content (Hatten 1994; adapted from Eco 1976). In the "Eroica," the correlations produced by the schema–topic interface are the basis for communicating what Hatten (1994) calls a "tragic-to-transcendent" *expressive genre* characteristic of music-spiritual drama.

———————

The drama begins with a modulation to G minor that transpires in mm. 6–9 of the opening theme. This modulation was the centerpiece of an earlier case study on the historical perception of tonality, which drew on certain aspects of the symphony's abstract structure and their reception history (Byros 2012; 2009). The *le–sol–fi–sol* is the cause of the modulation. This pattern features a distinctive chromatic turn of phrase in the bass oriented around the dominant, ♭6–5–♯4–5, with reiterations of scale degrees 1 and 3 in the upper voices. Example 14.2 shows an abstract representation of its most common form: as seen, the first three stages result in a chromatic expansion of predominant harmony, with a composing-out of an augmented sixth as a diminished third in the bass, ♭6–5–♯4, which resolves inwardly onto the dominant. The diminished third in the bass renders the schema a chromaticized variant of what Italian musicians in the eighteenth century called a *cadenza lunga* ("long cadence"), whose bass often traverses a 6–4–5 scale-degree progression as part a perfect authentic or half cadence (Sanguinetti 2012: 107–10). As a closing device, the *le–sol–fi–sol* figures among what Heinrich Christoph Koch described as "punctuation formulas" (*interpunctischen Formeln*), "punctuation figures" (*interpunctische Figuren*), or "punctuation marks" (*interpunctische Zeichen*) for realizing one of several "principal resting points of the mind" (*Hauptruhepuncte des Geistes*).[3] In a sonata- or concerto-form context this often

EXAMPLE **14.2** *Le–sol–fi–sol* schema: abstract representation.

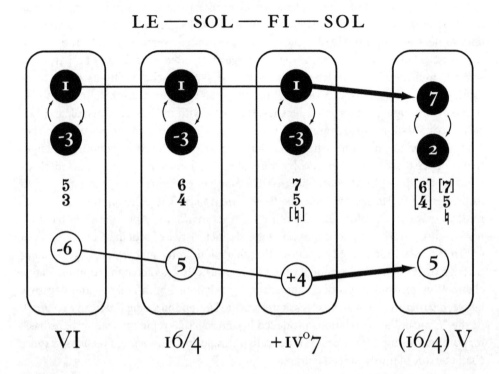

involves what Koch detailed as the *Halbcadenz* and *Cadenz*.[4] These are structurally weighted caesuras that respectively correspond to what James Hepokoski and Warren Darcy (2006) call the "medial caesura" half cadence of a transition, and the perfect authentic cadence that closes the second theme: the cadence of "essential expositional closure" (EEC) in the exposition, and the cadence of "essential structural closure" (ESC) in the recapitulation. Example 14.3a represents a typical *Halbcadenz* usage of the *le–sol–fi–sol* in the first movement of Haydn's "Clock" Symphony (1793–94), specifically at the medial caesura of its recapitulation. Example 14.3b illustrates its *Cadenz* usage in Haydn's String Quartet in D major, Op. 50 No. 6 (1787). This quartet passage also exemplifies a central harmonic and tonal feature of the schema, namely its frequent use to effect a modulation up a major third. Haydn's *Cadenz* in D major is preceded by a brief episode in B flat at mm. 140–44, which issues from an earlier deceptive cadence onto ♭VI at m. 139. Following several exchanges with its own dominant, B flat is reinterpreted from a tonic to a submediant where the *le–sol–fi–sol* begins its semitonal descent. Because of its ability to efficiently produce such a modulation, the schema often appears in structurally and expressively significant modulating contexts, both in sonata- and concerto-form environments (see Byros 2012: 301–5; Byros 2009: 166–69, 292–96).

Analysis of the *le–sol–fi–sol* in a musical corpus of roughly three thousand musical works composed between 1720–1840 revealed a population of 550 instances that

EXAMPLE 14.3 Usage of the *le–sol–fi–sol* schema: (a) *Halbcadenz* usage in Haydn, Symphony No. 101 in D major, "Clock," i, mm. 240–46; (b) *Cadenz* and modulating usage in Haydn, String Quartet in D major, Op. 50 No. 6, "The Frog," mm. 138–49.

(a)

(TRANSITION)   (i: HC MC)

240

[*Halbcadenz*]

(b)
(SECOND THEME)   (i: DC)

138

[*Cadenz*]

(I: PAC)

144

[*Cadenz*]

historically peaks in the 1790s, the decade immediately preceding Beethoven's composition of the "Eroica" Symphony (Byros 2012: 311–13).[5] These details suggest that a contemporary listener would be prompted to hear a G-minor modulation in mm. 6–9 of the opening theme on account of perceiving these bars as yet another instance of the harmonic schema (Example 14.4a). The *le–sol–fi–sol* is evidently the generic stylistic context and grammatical symbol in the communicative channel that caused Friedrich Rochlitz, the editor of the Leipzig *Allgemeine musikalische Zeitung*, to momentarily hear the "Eroica" as a G-minor symphony that begins *in medias res*. In a review of the symphony from

1807, Rochlitz casually describes mm. 7–9 of its opening theme as having "formally" modulated to G minor.

> The symphony begins with an Allegro con brio in three-quarter time in E♭ major . . . Already in m. 7, where the diminished seventh appears over C♯ in the bass, and in m. 9, where the ♭ chord appears over D, the composer prepares the listener to be often agreeably deceived in the succession of harmonies. And even this preludizing deviation, where one expects to be led formally to G minor but, in place of the resolution of the ♭, finds the fourth led upward to a fifth, and so, by means of the ♭ chord, finds oneself unexpectedly back at home in E♭ major—even this is interesting and pleasing.

> Der Anfang dieser Symphonie macht ein Allegro con brio im Dreyvierteltakt aus Es-Dur. . . . Schon im 7ten Takte, wo über cis im Basse der verminderte 7men, und im 9ten Takte, wo über D der ♭ten-Accord vorkommt, bereitet der Verf.[asser] den Zuhörer vor, oft in der Harmonieenfolge angenehm getäuscht zu werden; und schon diese, gleichsam präludirende Abweichung—wo man förmlich nach g moll glaubt geleitet zu werden, aber statt der Auflösung des ♭-ten Accords, die Quarte aufwärts in die Quinte geführt bekommt, und so sich, vermittelst des ♭-ten Accords unvermuthet wieder zu Hause in Es Dur befindet—schon diese ist interessant und angenehm. (Rochlitz 1807: col. 321)[6]

Rochlitz's expectation from m. 9 is realized in Example 14.4b, which gives a hypothetical continuation of the symphony's opening theme that completes the *le–sol–fi–sol* in G minor. The ♭ chord resolves normatively to a dominant seventh in G minor at m. 10, which continues to a full close with a PAC at m. 13. This cadence is suggested by Rochlitz's use of the qualifying adverb *förmlich*, likely an implicit or explicit reference to Koch's *förmliche Ausweichung*, or "formal modulation," which specifies a modulation by way of a cadence and formal phrase ending (Koch 1787: 188). A digital sampling of the recomposition for four-hand piano is realized in Web Example 14.1 ▶.

In the context of the symphony's opening theme, G minor of course never fully materializes by way of a formal cadential close. But the key returns in several dramatic and strategically located G-minor episodes throughout the symphony (Byros 2012: 305–7; 2009: 18–22). Among them is a grand perfect authentic cadence in G minor as the goal of the fugal episode (mm. 114–54) in the Funeral March (Example 14.5). An augmented-sixth variant of the *le–sol–fi–sol* returns in this episode to realize the implications it first laid down in the symphony's opening theme with a PAC in G minor at m. 154. This cadence is preceded by a lengthy dominant expansion, what Robert Gjerdingen would call a "Stabat Mater Prinner" (2007: 442–48): a dominant pedal with braided 2–3 suspensions beginning on scale degrees 5 and 6 in the upper voices, and a 1–2, 7–1, 6–7, 1 countermelody. This schema occupies a unique place in Gjerdingen's typology, as it is the only phrase-level type whose name implicates a distinct genre, named after Giovanni Pergolesi's *Stabat Mater* (1736), which features the schema prominently in its closing fugal Amen (Example 14.6). On the whole, Gjerdingen's galant schemata are abstract forms of scale degree syntax and voice leading with no generic affiliations—"a particular repertory of stock musical phrases" that transcends semantic

EXAMPLE **14.4** Beethoven, Symphony No. 3 in E flat major, Op. 55, "Eroica," i: (a) mm. 1–11 with the *le-sol-fi-sol* schema; (b) hypothetical recomposition in G minor from mm. 6–9.

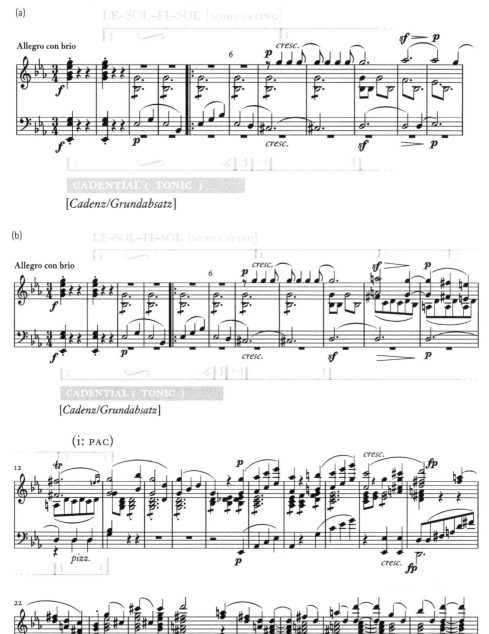

EXAMPLE **14.5** Beethoven, Symphony No. 3 in E flat major, Op. 55, "Eroica," ii, Marcia funebre, mm. 143–52.

EXAMPLE **14.6** "Stabat Mater Prinner," Pergolesi, *Stabat Mater*, Presto assai, mm. 45–51, from Gjerdingen, *Music in the Galant Style* (2007), 442, ex. 30.5.

distinctions such as "light/heavy, comic/serious, sensitive/bravura" (2007: 6). And still, both Gjerdingen (2007: 439) and Roman Ivanovitch (2011: 20), who traced Mozart's usage of the schema as a retransitional device, hear associations of "high church music" in this grammatical structure. To that end, Ivanovitch cites another prominent sacred-music example in the Credo of Mozart's Great Mass in C minor, K. 427, specifically the "Et incarnatus est" (Ivanovitch 2011: 22–24). The implication is that the Stabat Mater Prinner is a cross between schema and topic, or that its grammar is imbued with residues of church music, and therefore affords lexical and/or indexical significance.

Indeed Pergolesi's example is a token of a more general sacred music style type: what Gjerdingen calls a Stabat Mater Prinner is a voice-leading detail of a larger harmonic schema and syntactic process discussed in eighteenth-century *Satzlehre*, treatises, and dictionaries as an *Orgelpunkt* or *point d'orgue*, used to suspend the final close of a fugue or fugato in the church style. In his *Handwörterbuch* of 1807, Koch describes the *Orgelpunkt* as a "sustained cadence," which "is really a delaying of the final *Cadenz* in fugues or fugal compositions."[7] Johann Georg Sulzer's earlier entry in the *Allgemeine Theorie der schönen Künste* similarly describes it "as a delaying of the conclusion" of "polyphonic churchmusic," which in general involves the "final cadence" of fugues, "but it can be used for other church matters."[8] And Friedrich Wilhelm Marpurg, in the *Abhandlung von der Fugue* of 1753, also defines the *Orgelpunkt* as the "fourth and last part of the fugue" (*vierte und letzte Theil der Fuge*; 1753: 152). In terms of its structure, the pedal point is defined as a sustained bass, normally the dominant (but can also be the tonic) scale degree, with various contrapuntal processes in the upper voices. In *Der General-Bass in der Composition* of 1728, Johann David Heinichen discusses these contrapuntal procedures in terms of numerous "variations and foreign syncopations" (*Variationes und frembde Syncopationes*) in the organ manuals (1728: 948), such as the upper-voice 2–3 suspensions of the Stabat Mater Prinner. The entire process is aptly summarized in Daniel Gottlob Türk's *Anweisung zum Generalbaßspielen* from 1800: the "bass…holds the dominant while many sorts of contrapuntal arts begin in the upper voices" (1800: 321). The harmonic schema is illustrated via several examples from Eberlin, Emanuel Bach, and of Türk's own composition, numbered 1 to 3 in Example 14.7, respectively. The last of these, his own contribution, features the same voice leading of the Stabat Mater Prinner (the last two stages of the schema are implied by the figures in Türk's example, and have been realized here in Web Example 14.2) ▶.

Türk's grouping of the Stabat Mater Prinner's voice leading within the larger category of *Orgelpunkte* explicitly identifies the pattern as a token of this more general church-style type. Descending 2–3 (or 7–6) suspensions over a dominant pedal are in fact distinctive features of the *Orgelpunkt* style. Koch's own example in the *Handwörterbuch* pairs only the 2–3 suspensions with a more complex imitative texture, where imitated 7–1–2 trichords take the place of the Stabat Mater Prinner's inner-voice countermelody (Example 14.8a; Web Example 14.3) ▶. In the "Coronation" Mass in C major, K. 317 (1779), Mozart uses this *Orgelpunkt* on three occasions, once again in the Credo, and in each case the suspensions seen in the Stabat Mater Prinner, now realized as 7–6, are but part of a larger *fauxbourdon* process over a dominant pedal (mm. 18–22,

EXAMPLE 14.7 *Orgelpunkt* from Türk, *Anweisung zum Generalbaßspielen* (1800), 322–23.

"Et in unum Dominum"; mm. 85–89, "cum gloria judicare"; mm. 122–28, "Et exspecto resurrectionem mortuorum"). The *fauxbourdon* voice leading in the third of these, shown in Example 14.8b, traverses a complete octave descent in the upper voices (F–F♯, A♮–A♭), creating a nested predominant expansion (within the dominant prolongation) that concludes with a *le–sol–fi–sol* in the upper voice. The same *Orgelpunkt* variant, without the countermelody, appears in the *Stabat Mater* of Girolamo Abos (1750) and that of Giovanni Gualberto Brunetti (1764). The concluding *Orgelpunkt* in Antonio Caldara's *Stabat Mater* (c. 1725) makes imitative use of the 2–3 suspensions themselves. And the same fugal usage of the pattern seen in Pergolesi, Abos, Brunetti, and Caldara, finally, is replicated in the closing Amen of Haydn's own *Stabat Mater* from 1767 (Example 14.9). Here again, the voice-leading and scale-degree content of the Stabat Mater Prinner are part of a larger *Orgelpunkt* and a complete octave descent in the top voice. The Stabat Mater Prinner is thus not a harmonic schema as such, but a topical voice-leading characteristic of the church style within a broader network or chain of indexical significations, hence the "high church music" designations in Gjerdingen and Ivanovitch. As both Monelle and Hatten have maintained, "certain topics represent whole genres" (Monelle 2006: 23; Hatten 1994). The representation here involves a chain of significations: 2–3 (or 7–6) suspensions over a dominant pedal are a *signifier* of the *Orgelpunkt*, which signifies a fugue/fugato, which signifies a *Stabat Mater* (or even a "Credo"), which itself is a *signifier* of the church/sacred style.

Beethoven would certainly have been familiar with the *Orgelpunkt* style type and its various contexts. The treatises of Johann Georg Albrechtsberger, Beethoven's teacher in Vienna, display copious examples of sacred music from Allegri, Bach, Caldara, Carissimi, Fux, Handel, Kirnberger, Lassus, Palestrina, and Peri (Wyn Jones 1998: 36). The second page of the *Kurzgefasste Methode den Generalbass zu erlernen* from 1791 even contains an example of the same *Orgelpunkt* harmonic schema that Beethoven uses in the Funeral March of the "Eroica" Symphony (1791: 2). Perhaps more importantly, Beethoven's own *Materialen zum Generalbass* (Nottebohm 1872) include paraphrased and copied passages from the treatises of C. P. E. Bach, Albrechtsberger, and Türk, including a citation of Bach's discussion of the *Orgelpunkt*, specifically paragraphs 1, 3, 4, and 6 from Chapter 24 of Part Two of the *Versuch über die wahre Art das Clavier zu spielen* (1762), which also describes the pattern as "appear[ing] generally in learned things, especially fugues, near the end over the dominant" (Bach 1949: 319). Among the examples Bach provides is the *Orgelpunkt* in Example 14.10, which once again shows the 2–3 suspensions of the Stabat Mater Prinner as part of a larger dominant pedal, and here also with a chromatic version of uppermost line: ♭6–5–♯4–4–♯3–3–2. And so, Beethoven's use of this church-style type in the context of a symphonic slow movement (Example 14.5), one designated Funeral March at that, becomes a question of "topic" in the deeper sense of the term: as Hatten (this volume, page 514) puts it, "a familiar style type only becomes topical when it is *imported*" into a larger or foreign context or, as Mirka has it in the introduction (page 2), topics are "*musical styles and genres taken out of their proper context and used in another one.*" The funereal and mortal significations of the *Orgelpunkt* in the Funeral March are thus not inherent, but emergent, arising from the pattern's migration

EXAMPLE **14.8** *Orgelpunkte* from: (a) Koch, *Kurzgefaßtes Handwörterbuch der Musik* (1807), xiii–xiv, fig. 93 and (b) Mozart, "Coronation" Mass in C major, K. 317, "Credo," mm. 122–28.

EXAMPLE 14.9 *Orgelpunkt* from Haydn, *Stabat Mater*, "Paradisi Gloria," mm. 143–51.

from the sacred style into a symphonic context. The intended meaning of the importation is to semantically charge the key of G minor with connotations of the mortal and funereal specifically in a sacred context. By staging the *Orgelpunkt* as the conclusion of a fugato (double fugue) in a Funeral March, this pedal point, as a form–meaning pair or schema–topic amalgam, functions as a signifier that brings the mortal, the funereal, the sacred/spiritual, and the key of G minor into a constellated semantic orbit.

This signification is further highlighted by a merging or "troping of topics" in Hatten's terms (1994, 2004, and this volume). The *Orgelpunkt* combines a motive-form derived from the fugue (eighth-and-two-sixteenths pattern), as is common practice, with triplet sixteenths and tremolandi in the first violins that derive from the movement's opening funeral march material (Example 14.5). In a minor-mode and flat-key context, tremolandi and triplet rhythms are common characteristics of the *ombra* style, which Clive McClelland (2012), following the work of Leonard Ratner (1980) and Wye J. Allanbrook (1983), has recently surveyed in a large-scale study dedicated to the subject and further discusses in this volume. Both in theatrical- and sacred-style genres, *ombra* music is used to depict mortal and funereal scenes, or more generally involves death, burial, the afterlife, the supernatural, ghosts, spirits, furies, and so forth. Indeed the texture of Beethoven's passage (Example 14.5) resembles Gluck's setting of Alceste's arrival to the Underworld, cited in McClelland (2012: 125), which features tremolandi sextuplet sixteenths, and in the same key of G minor. Beethoven's example also introduces the more plaintive, lowered form of the supertonic scale degree at mm. 144 (A♭), Neapolitan harmony (here over a dominant pedal) being another characteristic of the *ombra* style. As the tonal and harmonic goal of the fugato, the *Orgelpunkt* and its *ombra* features render G minor a representation of the mortal and funereal in a spiritual context. But these connotations do not begin here.

The sacred-music and funereal resonances of G minor are already intimated by the symphony's opening theme: in the Funeral March, the actual G minor cadence is articulated not by the *Orgelpunkt* but by the *le–sol–fi–sol*. This harmonic schema is not only a grammatical structure and punctuation formula but also a characteristic of the *ombra* style. The *le–sol–fi–sol* articulates the very first cadence in the opening tenor solo of Haydn's *Stabat Mater*: a half cadence in D minor on "lacrymosa," shown in Example 14.11. In the Funeral March, the schema continues the *ombra* texture of the preceding

EXAMPLE **14.10** *Orgelpunkt* from C. P. E. Bach, *Versuch über die wahre Art das Clavier zu spielen*, vol. 2 (1762), 184.

EXAMPLE **14.11** *Le-sol-fi-sol* in Haydn, *Stabat Mater*, "Stabat Mater dolorosa," mm. 20–23.

[*Quintabsatz*]

Orgelpunkt, with its diminished seventh harmony and angular chromaticism in the bass. In the symphony's opening, it serves to introduce mortal and funereal themes in a G minor context with the very first harmonic motion of the movement (Byros 2012: 305). In texted compositions, the *le-sol-fi-sol* is consistently used to represent mortal, funereal, and supernatural qualities and scenes, both in theatrical and sacred music environments. Mozart employs the schema in such a way as early as 1767, in the *Grabmusik*, K. 42 to depict "roaring thunder, lightning, and flames" ("Brüllt, ihr Donner, Blitz und Flammen," mm. 141–51; Byros 2009: 464, ex. 3.51). And the pattern's *ombra* characteristics are treated thematically later in *Don Giovanni* (1787). For example, the *le-sol-fi-sol* stages the very moment that the Commendatore is fatally wounded by Don Giovanni ("Il commendatore mortalmente ferito," Act 1, No. 1, mm. 174–76), and again later in the "O statua gentilissima" Duet of Act 2, where the Commendatore returns to life in ghost form, Mozart uses several variants of the schema (mm. 30–32, 44–46; see also the Finale, mm. 502–3).[9] In the later *Requiem*, K. 626 (1791), the *le-sol-fi-sol* is used to represent eternal life: "Et lux perpetua luceat eis" (And let eternal light shine upon them, mm. 43–46; Byros 2012: 292, ex. 4a). These powerful examples from early and late Mozart are representative of the schema's general *ombra* usage in the theatrical and sacred-style examples outlined in my corpus study of the pattern (Byros 2009,

Appendix B). But the *le–sol–fi–sol* also appears to have had a more specific and circum-scribed use in church music. Namely, it is regularly encountered in the Credo of a Mass, notably in the "Et incarnatus est." The schema is frequently set to the text "et homo factus est" (and he became man), "Crucifixus etiam pro nobis" (crucified for us), and "passus et sepultus est" (suffered and was buried). Example 14.12 shows the "passus et sepultus est" from Mozart's *Missa solemnis* in C minor, K. 139 (1769). McClelland's own illustrations of *ombra* in a sacred-music context show the same usage of the *le–sol–fi–sol* in the "Et incarnatus est" of (the younger) Georg Reutter's *Missa Sancti Caroli* from 1734 (McClelland 2012: 176, ex. 7.7, mm. 17–19). And Jasmin Cameron's analytic study of the *Crucifixion in Music* (2006: 90–91, fig. 5.7, mm. 6–7) cites a "Crucifixus" setting of the schema in a Mass for four voices by Caldara (c. 1720).

The *le–sol–fi–sol* was something of a trope of the Credo of a Mass that expresses the theme of sacrificial death. Table 14.1 profiles a selection of examples from the long eighteenth century (c. 1720–1823): the list includes several variants of the *le–sol–fi–sol* in the Credo of a Mass, and other related sacred music contexts expressing sacrificial death. As a recurrent theme or motive in the "Et incarnatus est," the *le–sol–fi–sol* is a musical equivalent of what cognitive linguists term a "collostruction." As seen above, all grammar is said to consist of form–meaning pairs, but the pairing varies by specificity and level of abstraction. A "collostruction" refers to a frequent co-occurrence of certain lexical and syntactic symbols, or to a consistent and specific form–meaning pair (e.g. Stefanowitsch and Gries 2003). This is one means by which grammatical structure acquires semantic meaning, and an aspect of the syntax–lexicon continuum that

EXAMPLE 14.12 Mozart, Mass in C minor, K. 139, "Credo," mm. 126–27: *le–sol–fi–sol* as *ombra* topic.

[*Quintabsatz*]

Table 14.1 *Ombra* Usage of the *le–sol–fi–sol* Schema in Sacred Music, c. 1700–1823.

	Bach, Johann Sebastian (1685–1750)	
1749	Mass in B minor, BWV 232, "Credo"	"descendit de coelis"
1749	Mass in B minor, BWV 232, "Agnus Dei," m. 39	"peccata," "miserere"
	Beethoven, Ludwig van (1770–1827)	
1807	Mass in C major, Op. 86, "Agnus Dei"	"peccata mundi"
1819–23	*Missa solemnis*, "Credo," Adagio espressivo, mm. 166–68	"sub Pontio Pilato passus"
	Caldara, Antonio (1670–1736)	
c. 1720	Mass for Four Voices (London, Royal College of Music, Gb–Lcm Ms. 105; Cameron 2006), "Credo"	"Crucifixus etiam pro nobis"
c. 1720	Mass in F (London, Royal College of Music, Gb–Lcm Ms. 789; Cameron 2006), "Credo"	"et homo factus est"
	Cherubini, Luigi (1760–1842)	
1816	Mass in C major, "Credo"	"Crucifixus"
	Gassmann, Florian Leopold (1729–1774)	
n.d.	*Requiem* in C minor, "Requiem aeternam" (McClelland 2012)	"et lux perpetua luceat eis"
	Hasse, Johann Adolph (1699–1783)	
1751	Mass in D minor, "Credo" (MacIntyre 1986)	"etiam pro nobis"
	Haydn, Joseph (1732–1809)	
1802	"Harmony" Mass in B flat major, Hob. XXII: 14, "Credo"	"Deo vero"
	Heinichen, Johann David (1683–1729)	
1724	Mass in D major, "Credo"	"homo factus est"
	Lotti, Antonio (1667–1740)	
c. 1700–40	*Crucifixus a 10* (Münster, Santini Sammlung der Bischöflichen Bibliothek D-MÜs SANT Hs 2342; Cameron 2006)	"Crucifixus etiam pro nobis"
c. 1700–40	*Missa I* (Cameron 2006, No. 61), "Credo"	"mortuos"
	Mozart, Wolfgang Amadeus (1756–1791)	
1769	Mass in C minor, K. 139, "Credo"	"et sepultus est"
1769	Mass in C minor, K. 139, "Credo"	"remissionem peccatorum"
1774	*Missa brevis* in F major, K. 192, "Gloria"	"peccata mundi"
1779	"Coronation" Mass in C, K. 317, "Credo"	"et sepultus est"
1791	*Requiem* in D minor, K. 626, "Requiem aeternam"	"et lux perpetua luceat eis"
	Reutter, Georg (1708–1772)	
1734	*Missa Sancta Caroli*, "Credo" (McClelland 2012)	"passus et sepultus est"

is perhaps all the more consequential for musical symbols: a grammatical construction may retain the significance of its collostructural lexical pairs even in their absence. The *le–sol–fi–sol*, specifically, affords the connotations of sacrificial death expressed by the text of the "Et incarnatus est" in its absence. A second means by which grammar inherits meaning is via image schemata: syntax relies on "prelinguistic" structures such as "source–path–goal," "center–periphery," "attraction," and many others (Johnson 1987;

EXAMPLE **14.13** Axial melodies as symbolic representations of the cross in the "Crucifixus" of the Mass, from Cameron, *The Crucifixion in Music* (2006), 57 (a), compared with *le–sol–fi–sol* as symbolic representation of the cross (b).

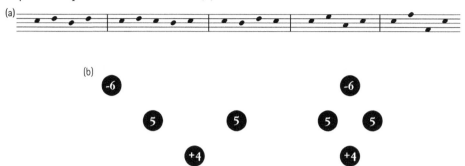

see also Lakoff 1987). These image schemas relate to embodied experiences that inform the structure of language and consequently charge grammar with signification. "Axis balance" is one such image schema, and it underlies the radial structure of the *le–sol–fi–sol*. Cameron discusses several representations of the cross in terms of musical symbolism: among these symbols is a "zig-zag arrangement of notes" (2006: 57) shown in Example 14.13a. They display melodic profiles very similar in concept to what Leonard Meyer called "axial" melodies (Meyer 1973; 1989). The *le–sol–fi–sol* is precisely such a pattern, with its axial symmetry around scale degree 5 (Example 14.13b). The "image schema" of "axis balance," as a characteristic feature of the schema–topic amalgam, further affords semantic meaning in the absence of a specific lexical designation through its musical symbolism—the cross as symbol of sacrificial death.

These sacred-music contexts would likewise have been quite familiar to Beethoven—a Roman Catholic who not only studied a good deal of sacred music with Albrechtsberger (Wyn Jones 1998: 36), but at Bonn was also appointed deputy organist by the elector Maximilian Franz in 1784, and filled in for his teacher and court organist Christian Gottlob Neefe. Beethoven's importation of the schema into a symphonic context, and specifically one that prompts a modulation in its opening theme, once more becomes a question of topic in the deeper sense of the term. But the topical use of the *le–sol–fi–sol* differs from that of the *Orgelpunkt* in terms of the immediacy of its lexical specification—that is, whereas the *Orgelpunkt* is firmly associated with fugal composition and, by extension, with the church style, the *le–sol–fi–sol* is a much more transgeneric instance of musical grammar. Its lexical specifications are consequently even less inherent, and therefore require deictic cues to be realized. To that end, the schema is multiply marked in the symphony's opening through a number of oppositions involving formal function, syntax, tonality, and style types. Hatten (1994: 121) cites the opening of the "Eroica" as an example of a "'developmental' unstable theme" type of "strategic markedness" that results from "cross-matching material and locational functions." This results from Beethoven's having "fronted" a process-orientated, modulatory and cadential schema—that is, positioned it as the opening gesture of a symphony. Meyer called this compositional strategy "positional migration," defined as the (re)positioning of process- and closure-oriented schemata—"punctuation formulas" in Koch's terms—at the beginning of a work (1989:124). As seen above, the *le–sol–fi–sol* was both a common way of producing a modulation up a third and a structurally important cadence—often a *Cadenz* or *Halbcadenz*.

The markedness produced by this fronting strategy is augmented by the *le–sol–fi–sol*'s syntactic disruption at m. 10: after being formally displaced to the opening of a symphony that prompts a modulation to G minor, the dominant of E flat major disrupts the schema's completion with, as Rochlitz put it, an "unexpected" return to E flat major (compare Examples 14.4a and 14.4b). These oppositions in the formal, tonal, and syntactic domains are combined with another level of asymmetry in the form of topical differentiation. The *le–sol–fi–sol* introduces textural characteristics of the *ombra* style: tempestuous syncopations in the first violins (mm. 7–8), along with the tremolandi strings (McClelland 2012: 123–30). Indeed the first violins appear to be lifted straight from Mozart's first G-minor symphony, perhaps as an intertextual referencing of this tonality. These textural characteristics and the angular chromaticism and diminished-seventh harmony of the *le–sol–fi–sol* grammar blend into a larger *ombra*-style topical unit that contrasts with the E-flat major fanfare style of the opening triads and hammer blows in mm. 1–2, and the horn call in the triadic arpeggiations of the cellos in mm. 3–6, which becomes a literal horn call in later restatements and reworkings of the theme. More importantly, the G-minor *ombra* music of mm. 6–9 occurs against the larger stylistic context of the *Ländler*: a rural dance widespread in Austria and Germany in the later eighteenth and nineteenth century (see McKee, this volume). Daniel Heartz (2009: 517, 643) has identified this topic and its close relative, the German dance (*deutsche Tanz* or *Deutscher*), for example, in several works of Haydn and Mozart, including the finale of the Piano Trio in E flat major, Hob. XV: 29, "In the German Style," the Trio from Mozart's Symphony No. 39 in E flat major, and the "Drinking Chorus" that ends the "Fall" of Haydn's *Seasons* (see also McKee 2012). The opening theme of the "Eroica" is also broadly cast in the *Ländler* style, with its characteristic oom-pah | oom-pah | oom-pah-pah | pah rhythmic pattern in mm. 3–6 and 10–15. This is a common feature of the *Ländler* and German dances of Mozart and Beethoven, and often in combination with tonic pedals and arpeggiation.[10] The Trio of Beethoven's "German Dance," WoO 8 No. 3, similarly features a *Ländler* with a literal horn call. But the most famous use of this *Deutscher/Ländler* style may be the Intrada to Mozart's early pastoral Singspiel, *Bastien und Bastienne* (1768), whose main theme is commonly identified as an anticipation of Beethoven's opening in the "Eroica" (Example 14.14).

In his *Late Beethoven* of 2003, Maynard Solomon attributed the affective dissonance of the opening theme to the disruption of a pastoral sentiment caused by the chromatic descent in mm. 6–7. He further highlighted the pastoral tone as a relatively unique instance of this topic in middle-period Beethoven:

> On one conspicuous occasion [Beethoven] unveiled a pastoral moment at the very instant of its fracture by disruptive forces. The two crashing chords that open the *Eroica* Symphony introduce a flowing pastoral negotiation of the common chord [presumably the tonic triad], a shepherd's yodel or an alphorn call that lasts less than

EXAMPLE 14.14 Mozart, *Bastien und Bastienne*, K. 50, Intrada, mm. 38–45: *Deutscher* pastoral topic.

two measures (it may be no accident that it echoes the yodeling figure at the opening of Mozart's *Bastien und Bastienne*…), until it is tipped into disequilibrium by a decisive descent through D to C-sharp at measures 6–7. In a half step, Arcadia has been lost, thus launching a prolonged heroic narrative that will revert to the pastoral mode only in its contredanse finale (Solomon 2003: 75).

The vague "disruptive forces" of which Solomon speaks are the *ombra* style communicated by the *le–sol–fi–sol*, which is synactically, tonally, formally, and topically marked, and "marked entities have a greater (relative) specificity of meaning than do unmarked entities" (Hatten 1994: 291). The *le–sol–fi–sol* and G minor thus only acquire mortal and funereal connotations by virtue of their opposition to the preceding E-flat major fanfare, triadic arpeggiation, and the underlying pastoral landscape of the *Ländler* dance. Their lexical significance arises precisely in their being "disruptive forces."

As in the Funeral March, Beethoven's topical use of *le–sol–fi–sol* is specifically to charge the key of G minor with mortal and funereal connotations in a sacred context, which becomes the symphony's first lexical reference communicated in strictly musical terms. This strategic positioning of the G-minor *ombra* music in the opening theme is the means of a larger expressive end. Through their expressive correlates, G minor and the *le–sol–fi–sol* are structural necessities for communicating a powerful philosophical message that involves the spiritual consequences of death, suffering, and self-sacrifice that is only alluded to in the heroic and memorial themes of the symphony's quasi programmatic title *Sinfonia eroica … composta per festeggiare il sovvenire di un grand Uomo* ("Heroic symphony, composed to celebrate the memory of a great man"), but is more explicit in the intertextual contexts that surround the symphony's composition. The same themes of sacrificial death coded in the *le–sol–fi–sol* and implied in the symphony's heroic and memorial epithets are found in Beethoven's contemporary musical and literary texts. The "Eroica" was composed during a period when Beethoven was "forced to become a philosopher," as confessed in what Solomon has called the symphony's "literary prototype": the Heiligenstadt Testament of 6 and 10 October 1802. The theme of sacrificial death metaphorically runs throughout the testament, particularly in Beethoven's overt submission to and acceptance of his affliction and fate, which were prompted by the benefits of virtue, and oriented toward the achievement of a higher state of existence, in which music would play an integral part:

> I would have ended my life—it was only *my art* that held me back. Ah, it seemed to me impossible to leave the world until I had brought forth all that I felt was

within me. So I endured this wretched existence—truly wretched for so suscep-tible a body which can be thrown by a sudden change from the best condition to the very worst.—*Patience*, they say, is what I must now choose for my guide, and I have done so—I hope my determination will remain firm to endure until it pleases the inexorable Parcae to break the thread....I am ready.—Forced to become a phi-losopher....Divine One, thou seest into my inmost soul, thou knowest that therein dwells the love of mankind and the desire to do good....[*V*]*irtue*...upheld me in time of misery. Thanks to it and to my art I did not end my life by suicide....With joy I hasten to meet death—If it comes before I have had the chance to develop all my artistic capacities, it will still be coming too soon despite my harsh fate and I should probably wish it later—yet even so I should be happy....Come *when* thou wilt, I shall meet thee bravely. (Forbes 1967, 1: 305)

Solomon has interpreted the Heiligenstadt Testament as a "funeral work" in which Beethoven "metaphorically enacted his own death in order that he might live again" (1998: 157). As a "literary prototype of the *Eroica* Symphony," the Testament is a pro-found statement of "heroism, death, and rebirth" (1998: 157–58). John W. N. Sullivan, a literary journalist who wrote a spiritual biography of Beethoven in the early twentieth century, similarly described Beethoven's concept of "hero" as a "synthesis" of "assertion and submission" (1927: 95).

Both the "Eroica" and the Heiligenstadt Testament are but part of a larger "death of the hero" repertoire from Beethoven's output in the first decade of the nineteenth century, which explored death, suffering, and self-sacrifice as correlates of life, joy, and jubilation. This includes, among others, the slow movement marked "Marcia funebre sulla morte d'un Eroe" (Funeral March on the Death of a Hero) in the Piano Sonata in A flat major, Op. 26; the oratorio *Christus am Ölberge* (*Christ on the Mount of Olives*), Op. 85; the opera *Fidelio*; and the Incidental Music to Goethe's *Egmont*, Op. 84 (see also Solomon 1998: 68–73). The most important among these for understanding the expressive signifi-cance of Beethoven's use of the *le–sol–fi–sol* schema–topic in the "Eroica" is the oratorio, which, despite the later opus number, precedes the symphony, written in March of 1803, and performed on 5 April of the same year.[11] *Christus am Ölberge* is the first large-scale work Beethoven composed since writing the Heiligenstadt Testament, and was done by his own volition—it was not commissioned. The oratorio's libretto, penned by Franz Xaver Huber, portrays Christ's prayer in the Garden of Gesthemane. Unlike the Passions of the elder Bach, it focuses primarily on Christ's agony, submission to and acceptance of his fate, and an understanding of his sacrifice as purposive, for the salvation of human-ity. The details of the oratorio's compositional history and subject matter indicate that Beethoven saw in Christ a model, as he was struggling with the pragmatic, moral, and philosophical implications of his own suffering and deafness. He said as much in a later conversation book from January 1820: "*Socrates* and *Jesus* were exemplars for me."[12] From his *Nachlassverzeichnis*, we also know that Beethoven owned and studied several theological and Christian-philosophical works. Among the volumes in his library are, in addition to French and Latin copies of the Bible, the fifteenth-century monastic treatise *The Imitation of Christ* (c. 1427) by Thomas à Kempis, and Christoph Christian Sturm's

Reflections on the Works of God in the Realm of Nature (1772), which Beethoven allegedly advised clergy to read from the pulpit.[13]

The themes of self-sacrifice, death, and rebirth that run through the Heiligenstadt Testament, though likely not derived from the pages of these philosophical and theological works, strongly identify with their dominant messages. In Chapter 23 of à Kempis' treatise, titled "Thoughts on Death," we read the following: "Be wary and mindful of death. Try to live now in such a manner that at the moment of death you may be glad, rather than fearful. *Learn to die to the world now, that then you may begin to live with Christ*" (Kempis 2004: 27). That such passages and messages were meaningful to Beethoven is evident not only from the similar themes expressed in the Heiligenstadt Testament ("With joy I hasten to meet death"), but also from the many annotations and underscorings that survive in his copy of Sturm's *Betrachtungen*. Beethoven's biographer Ludwig Nohl produced a (partially inaccurate) transcription of marked passages in several volumes from Beethoven's library (Nohl 1870), which also includes works by Shakespeare, Homer, Goethe, Herder, Schiller, and others. Critical English translations of the marked passages in Beethoven's copy of the *Betrachtungen* have been produced by Charles Witcombe and collaborators (Witcombe 1998, 2003; Witcombe and Portillo 2003; Witcombe et al. 2003). Many of Beethoven's markings display a man struggling to find meaning and purpose in his affliction. Some of these marked passages reflect the themes of suffering and rebirth directly: "To live eternally one day, to be eternally blessed, to be eternally joyful... [N]ow I have this hope! How insignificant are all the sufferings that I have to endure here. As rough and as long as the winter of my life may be, confidently I wait for spring and the renewal and improvement of my situation in that world" (Witcombe and Portillo 2003: 22). Others reveal Beethoven's attempts to reconcile his suffering as a means of attaining a higher state of being, or as a necessary resource or path to a higher state of existence and joy: "In order to bring people closer to the feeling of their final purpose, the abhorrence of sin, and the practice of goodness, God turns sometimes to violent and sometimes to gentle means. Occasionally he finds it best to arouse the sinner out of his slumber through powerful jolts, through severe punishments, and through continuous judgment.... Illness and other accidents you imposed on me in order to bring me to contemplate my digressions.... I only ask one thing of you, my God: *do not stop working on my improvement*" (Witcombe et al. 2003: 93, Beethoven's emphasis). The title of the following passage in Beethoven's copy was "marked with three emphatic consecutive lines in [the] margin" (Witcombe et al. 2003: 94), and may well be the most illustrative example of Beethoven's attempts to reconcile and submit to his affliction and fate, by understanding his suffering as part of a larger plan overseen by Divine Providence: "If I know that I remain connected with God and my Savior, then I can also be certain that all future destinies, be they sad or pleasant, will serve me for the best. Is it not my reconciling God who orders all events and reigns over the future? ... *What God has chosen for me, That shall and must take place;... I have surrendered myself unto him. To die and to live*" (Witcombe et al. 2003: 94, my italics).

It is precisely at the moment that depicts this surrender in the *Mount of Olives* oratorio that Beethoven employs a dramatic use of the *le–sol–fi–sol*—that is, precisely at the

EXAMPLE **14.15** Beethoven, *Christus am Ölberge* Op. 85, No. 5, Recitativo, mm. 18–30: *le–sol–fi~ti–do* variant as representation of Christ's agony.

moment that Christ submits to his own fate (Example 14.15), and sacrifices himself to die and to live by God's will. Measures 18–24 present the same *ombra* textural features as the "Eroica," syncopated and tremolandi strings, with a variant of the *le–sol–fi–sol* in mm. 20–24 that modulates up a fifth, here from E minor to B minor, via a reinterpretation of ♯4 in the bass to a leading tone in B minor (Example 14.15), which I have described as a *le–sol–fi~ti–do* variant: ♯4 (*fi*) becomes 7 (*ti*) by resolving the chord it carries to a minor (and therefore *tonic*) triad, as opposed to a major (and therefore *dominant*) triad (Byros, 2009: 305, ex. 5.19, Appendix B). The theme of sacrificial death coded in the *le–sol–fi–sol* is thus identified with Christ's own submission. The schema represents the emotional turmoil involved in the very act of surrender, as it is only at its completion in m. 26 that Christ sings to his Father: "Doch nicht mein Wille, nein, dein Wille nur geschehe" (But let not my will, no, Thy will only be done). The *le–sol–fi–sol* is thus coextensive with Christ's agony, his submission to God, and acceptance of his fate, for the purpose of a greater good—in this case, for the salvation of humanity itself.

This powerful example from the *Mount of Olives* suggests that Beethoven conceived of the *le–sol–fi–sol* as a syntactic and semantic musical symbol capable of communicating the submissive and mortal dimensions of his developing hero philosophy or, in Sullivan's terms, of his "spiritual development." The oratorio was one of several such philosophical-spiritual exercises that he revisited persistently throughout his compositional output. The "Eroica" is yet another, early and untexted chapter in what became a life-long narrative, a "long journey" and a "*via dolorosa*" (Solomon 2003: 164). As a philosophical testament, or treatise, similar in ethos to those of à Kempis and Sturm, the symphony portrays a heroism not of a revolutionary (public) order but, written on the heels of the Heiligenstadt Testament and the *Mount of Olives* oratorio, of a spiritual (private) order.[14] Sullivan heard the "Eroica" as the "first piece of music [Beethoven] composed that has a really profound and spiritual content." He continues:

> Indeed, the difference from the earlier [presumably instrumental] music is so startling that it points to an almost catastrophic change, or extremely rapid acceleration, in his spiritual development. We have found that such a change is witnessed to by the Heiligenstadt Testament, and we shall see that the Eroica symphony is an amazingly realized and co-ordinated expression of the spiritual experience that underlay that document. The ostensible occasion of the symphony appears to have been the career of Napoleon Bonaparte, but no amount of brooding over Napoleon's career could have given Beethoven his realization of what we may call the life-history of heroic achievement as exemplified in the Eroica. This is obviously a transcription of personal experience... Heroism, for him, was not merely a name descriptive of a quality of certain acts, but a sort of principle manifesting itself in life. (Sullivan 1927: 90, 95)

Much of Beethoven's so-called "heroic period" has been characterized by a "tragic-to-triumphant schema" of expression exemplified in the Fifth Symphony (Hatten 1994: 79), in which Beethoven externalized and defeated his menace: Fate, personified in C minor, and overcome by C major (Sullivan 1927: 95). And much of the music of the period certainly falls into this generic expressive category. But the "Eroica" is more characteristic of what Hatten identified as the "cultural unit" of "abnegation[, which] is related to Christian notions of sacrifice and spiritual surrender" (Hatten 1994: 281): the "willed resignation and spiritual acceptance of a (tragic) situation that leads to a positive inner state" (1994: 298). The hero philosophy that persists throughout Beethoven's lifetime is not overcoming suffering, but its endurance.

In the very opening entry of his *Tagebuch* (1812), Beethoven inscribes the following article of faith: "Submission, deepest submission to your fate, only this can give you the sacrifices.... You must not be a *human being, not for yourself, but only for others*: for you there is no longer any happiness except within yourself, in your art. O God! give me strength to conquer myself, nothing at all must fetter me to life" (Solomon 2003: 164). And again, in a sketchbook from 1816: "Submission—submission! Thus may we win something even in the deepest misery, and make ourselves worthy to have God forgive our shortcomings. Fate, show your force! We are not lords over ourselves. What is determined must be, and so let it be!" (Schauffler 1929: 358). Submission was the basis for the Christian-philosophical tenet that, in Beethoven's words, one achieves joy through suffering: in a letter to the Countess Anna Marie Erdödy from Vienna, dated 19 October 1815, he writes: "We finite beings, who are the embodiment of an infinite spirit, are born to suffer both pain and joy; and one might almost say that the best of us obtain *joy through suffering*" (Anderson 1961: 527, Letter No. 563).

Not only joy, but endurance through suffering leads to a higher state of being; again to the Countess, in a letter dated 15 May 1816, Beethoven writes: "Man cannot avoid suffering; and *in this respect his strength must stand the test*, that is to say, he must *endure without complaining and feel his worthlessness* and *then again* achieve *his perfection*, that perfection which the Almighty will then bestow upon him" (Anderson 1961: 578, Letter No. 633). The first explicit documentation of this spiritual conversion is the literary prototype of the "Eroica," the Heiligenstadt Testament: what Beethoven realized, in Sullivan's words, was that a "rigid strained defiance was no longer necessary. What he came to see as his most urgent task, for his future spiritual development, was *submission*. He had to accept his suffering as in some mysterious way necessary" (Sullivan 1927: 78).

The *le–sol–fi–sol* is a schema–topic amalgam that semantically charges G minor in the "Eroica" as the musical representation of this necessity. The communicative significance of G minor lies in its structural and expressive opposition to E flat major, as a musical representation of the spiritual transcendence enabled by suffering and sacrifice. G minor and the *le–sol–fi–sol* are a means of musically realizing this philosophical concept of abnegation through what Hatten termed a "tragic-to-transcendent" expressive genre (1994: 28, 281–86), which is akin to religious drama: "tragedy that is transcended through sacrifice at a spiritual level. The pathos of the tragic may be understood as stemming from a kind of Passion music, depicting a personal, spiritual struggle; and the 'triumph' is no longer a publicly heroic 'victory' but a transcendence or acceptance" (79). The *le–sol–fi–sol* is the musical impetus for realizing this expressive genre, as it initiates a number of "correlations of oppositions" (Hatten 1994: 292) in the structural and expressive domains that semantically charge E flat major and G minor as respective representations of life, joy, and perfection, on the one hand, and death, suffering, and self-sacrifice on the other. The major and minor modes are of course among the most readily available oppositions in the classical style, which Hatten aligns with the generic cultural oppositions of "non-tragic" and "tragic." In sacred music the specific relationship between G minor and E flat major in the "Eroica"—down a major third—is explicitly associated with death and resurrection. In his monumental study of the concerted Viennese Mass, Bruce MacIntyre illustrates that the "tonic of the Mass opens the Credo and almost always returns for the 'Et resurrexit'" (MacIntyre 1986: 322). The contrasting tonality for the intervening "Et incarnatus est" section, which profiles Christ's incarnation, crucifixion, suffering, and death, is often the minor-mode mediant, resulting in precisely the key relationship in the opening theme of the "Eroica." The progression iii–I is among the three most common tonal transitions between the "Et incarnatus est" and the "Et resurrexit" (MacIntyre 1986: 325). For example, Caldara's Mass in G minor pursues the following tonal scheme: "Credo" (G major), "Et incarnatus est"–"Crucifixus" (B major–B minor), "Et resurrexit" (G major).[15] In the context of a Mass, the life-death duality expressed by the tonal relationship is of course explicitly communicated by the text. Sacrifice ("homo factus est. Crucifixus etiam pro nobis"), suffering ("passus"), death ("sepultus"), and resurrection ("resurrexit") are literally inscribed into the musical work. In addition to the specificity of natural language, the correlation between structure and expression is supplied by the Church as a social and pragmatic context for the expression.

In the "Eroica," the correlation rests on the affordant meaning of the *le–sol–fi–sol* grammar, as it is responsible for introducing the symphony's first lexical reference. As a form–meaning pair in the communicative channel, the harmonic schema achieves a syntactic and semantic function in one gesture: it produces a modulation to G minor while introducing a sacred-music reference of sacrificial death, thereby marking the mortal, funereal, sacrificial, and submissive connotations of G minor. The specificity of the schema's meaning enabled by its markedness provides a context for a reciprocal semantic charging of E flat major with its fanfare, horn call, and *Ländler* topics. Through their opposition to the G-minor *ombra* music of mm. 6–9, the pastoral and ceremonial lexical significations of these topics become metaphoric representations of life, joy, and jubilation. Dance becomes a metaphor for life.

The same correlation between structure and expression returns in a magnified and powerful restatement of the G-minor–E-flat-major opposition at the very end of the symphony's finale, where it is once more highlighted by a discrete shift in topical discourse (Example 14.16). The finale's theme and variations effectively ends at m. 398, which immediately leads to a "discursive coda" (Hepokoski and Darcy 2006: 284–88) and developmental episode. This episode closes with an imposing perfect authentic cadence in G minor at m. 422, extended via its own codetta in mm. 422–33, before it gives way to a second, fanfare-based coda in E flat major at m. 437. This G-minor episode literally brings back the music of the Funeral March: mm. 419–22 revisit the same shimmering triplet sixteenths and tremolo violins from the *Orgelpunkt* and G-minor cadence in the Funeral March, before giving way to its march-like, processional rhythms in mm. 422–32 (compare Examples 14.5 and 14.16). This intermovement revisitation "topicalizes" the Funeral March itself: imported into the coda of a theme and variations, it becomes marked by its relocation along with the key of G minor. Its *ombra* connotations are further communicated by an ascending chromatic line in the bass that precedes the cadence, which results from sequential repetitions of a *le–sol–fi–sol* variant: its inverse, *fi–sol–le* (♯4–5–♭6). In the "Crucifixus" of a Mass, ascending chromatic bass lines are typically used to represent Christ's *via dolorosa*, as in the "Crucifixus" of Mozart's "Coronation" Mass and of Haydn's "Harmony" Mass in B flat major. These ascending chromatic basses often include inverted *le–sol–fi* progressions, as in Haydn's "Theresa" Mass from 1799 (Example 14.17). The instrumentation following the G-minor cadence at m. 422—flutes, bassoons, and strings—is also a typical characteristic of *ombra* music (McClelland 2012: 134–36). The E-flat-major music that follows the G-minor codetta of this episode is an elaborate fanfare in the military genre, which, through its "connect[ions] with literature, reflect[s] the classical image of the hero" (Monelle 2006: 5–6). The end-result is a bifocal G-minor–E-flat-major ending that mirrors the symphony's similarly bifocal tonal and topical opening: E-flat *Ländler* and fanfare (mm. 1–6) followed by G-minor *ombra* (mm. 6–9).

The symphony's conclusion thus presents a magnified mirror image of the tonal and topical confrontation between E flat major and G minor from its very opening gestures.

EXAMPLE **14.16** Beethoven, Symphony No. 3 in E flat major, Op. 55, "Eroica," iv, mm. 410–42: G-minor *ombra* versus E-flat-major fanfare.

EXAMPLE **14.17** Haydn, "Theresa" Mass in B flat major, "Crucifixus," mm. 79–82: *fi–sol–le* grammar as topical representation of Christ's *via dolorosa.*

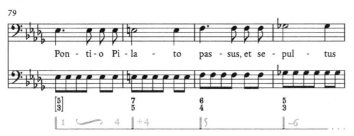

And, as in the opening theme, the competing tonalities are never reconciled to one another. The conclusiveness of the G-minor *ombra* episode creates an impression of two independent tonal endings for the symphony. G minor is not resolved into the follow- ing E-flat-major music so much as merged with or confronted by it: the abrupt changes in tempo (to Presto) and dynamics (to *ff*) enforce a nearly direct modulation in mm. 434–36 that transforms the G octaves of m. 433 from scale degree 1 to scale degree 3 (Example 14.16). There is no *progression* to E flat major as a resolution, but a rupture. The militaristic E-flat-major fanfare from m. 437 to the symphony's conclusion is thus not a representation of a public victory, but, bursting, as it does, from the preceding G-minor *ombra* music, it becomes a metaphor for rebirth, joy, spiritual perfection, and personal victory. The two tonalities are kept in abeyance, or held in suspension. As is character- istic of "religious drama" in general, there is no musical resolution. G minor and E flat major represent inner states only reconciled within the self: the "conflicting elements [of assertion and submission] are . . . both located within the soul itself" (Sullivan 1927: 96). Joy (E flat major) is achieved through suffering (G minor). This synthesis of asser- tion and submission, or abnegation, results in a higher state of existence, which, "for Beethoven, [generally] . . . meant the serene transcendence of a spiritual victory, won not only through heroic striving . . . but through profound abnegation in the face of a tragic reality that cannot be cancelled" (Hatten 1994: 286). Nor is G minor cancelled or over- come. Its "transcendence or acceptance goes beyond the conflicts of the work (after hav- ing fully faced them)" (Hatten 1994: 79).

The earliest sketches for the "Eroica" in the Wielhorsky sketchbook of 1802–3 sug- gest that an opposition between E flat major and G minor was in Beethoven's thinking from the symphony's inception (Byros 2012: 305; 2009: 43–47). Among these sketches are drafts for a third-movement Menuetto serioso in E flat major with a G-minor Trio.[16] In the final version the opposition is not only the central tonal subject of its opening theme, but, as seen, it frames the entire symphony: E flat major (i, mm. 1–6)–G minor (i, mm. 6–9)–G minor (iv, mm. 419–33)–E flat major (iv, mm. 433–end). Web Example 14.4 ▶ provides a summary of this bifocal tonal frame. Through the expressive correlates of these tonalities, brought on by the several correlations of marked opposi- tions in the syntactic and topical domains, the bifocal tonal frame becomes a means of communicating a "tragic-to-transcendent" expressive genre for the entire symphony, and thus expressing a philosophical topic or cultural unit of abnegation. As Nicholas Cook paraphrases Hatten's concept, "expressive genres function rather like the key of a sonata"—not as a continuous expression of the same tonality "in any literal sense, but the overall key coordinates the diverse tonal contents for the music and so provides a means for interpreting them" (Cook 1996: 108). In other words, the expressive genre casts an expressive affect, mood, or theme over the entire drama and its subplots: "once a genre is recognized or provisionally invoked, it guides the listener in the interpretation of particular features...that can help flesh out a dramatic or expressive scenario" (Hatten 1994: 89). The tonal opposition thus becomes the basis for what Hatten termed a "high-level trope": "The opposition may also initiate an ongoing dramatic conflict of characters or agents, perhaps suggesting a dramatic program. In addition, the contrast may lead to tropological interpretation that goes beyond the opposed correlations" (Hatten 1994: 169).

The complexity of the communicative utterances, drawing, as they do, on the syntactic and semantic properties of the *le-sol-fi-sol* as their basis, is conceivably among the characteristics of the "Eroica" Symphony that elicited its contemporary aesthetic judgments as a "serious" and "sublime" composition. In his review of the symphony from 1807, Rochlitz makes clear that he intends to write primarily on technical and less on aesthetic matters. But at the same time, he cautions the readers of the Leipzig *Allgemeine musikalische Zeitung* that, on account of its "elevated, abstract subject matter," the "Eroica" requires a "thoughtful listener," "an audience that at least pays serious attention and can maintain its serious attentiveness" (Senner, Wallace, and Meredith 2001: 30, 24). Beethoven's complex manipulations of both syntactic and semantic symbols in the schema–topic continuum undoubtedly figured among those aspects of the symphony requiring serious attention. An earlier review from 1805 in *Der Freymüthige* attributed its "true originality" to marked oppositions in both syntactic and semantic domains: "strange modulations and violent transitions,...placing together the most heterogeneous things, as when for example a pastorale is played through in the grandest style" (Senner, Wallace, and Meredith 2001: 15). Because of its complexity, audiences had to be prepared in advance. For a performance in Leipzig, reported in the *Allgemeine musikalische Zeitung* on 29 April 1807, "the audience had been made attentive and, as far as possible, prepared to expect exactly what was offered, not only by means of a special announcement on the customary concert program, but also by a short characterization of each movement, particularly in regard to the composer's intended effect upon the feelings. In both regards, the purpose was achieved completely...a truly solemn attentiveness and deathlike silence reigned and was sustained not only throughout the whole...first performance, but also during the second and third, which...followed within a few weeks" (Senner, Wallace, and Meredith 2001: 33). Throughout several reviews by Beethoven's German contemporaries is replicated both the theme of technical and aesthetic difficulty, as well as the requirement of an audience "who listened with heightened attention" (Senner, Wallace, and Meredith 2001: 38). A reviewer of the *Zeitung für die elegante Welt* counted the "Eroica" "among those few symphonies that, with their spirited energy, set the listener's imagination into a sublime flight and sweep his heart away to powerful emotions. But the connoisseur will only enjoy it as a complete work (and a repeated hearing doubles his spiritual enjoyment) the deeper he penetrates into the technical and aesthetic content of the original work" (Senner, Wallace, and Meredith 2001: 35).

Like any philosophical treatise, the symphony requires meditation, study, and time for its message to congeal—presumably owing to the complexity of Beethoven's interactive use of introversive (schemata) and extroversive (topics) musical symbols. For those *Kenner* who devoted their serious attention, the symphony's intended spiritual message was evidently not lost: its overarching theme of death and rebirth is explicitly documented in a later review for the *Allgemeine musikalische Zeitung* from 1814, by one "K. B.," who begins by citing a funereal poem *Das Grab* by Johann Gaudenz von Salis-Seewis (Senner, Wallace, and Meredith 2001: 38–39, my italics):

> 5.
> The grave is deep and still
> and horrible its brink!

> Who has not felt the truth of these words of the poet already in their life? Does not the departure of every citizen from this earth from the "friendly familiarity of being and doing" have in itself something that deeply affects the serious observer? How much more moving is it, then, when an elevated, magnificent spirit departs forever from our midst? In a situation such as this, one should listen to the funeral march from Beethoven's *Eroica* Symphony and sense its effect!—Certainly, a magnificent person is here being led to the gave; *these tones tell us so in the clearest possible way.* All the pain and all the joys of earthly life resound once again in our breast, deep and sweet, but only as the gentle voice of an echo, for already they are gone by, and have now fled irretrievably! Assuredly, *the departed one now walks in the kingdom of clarity and light—refreshingly soothing melodies tell us this in the language of heaven perceptibly enough*—but we remain abandoned at the grave and look up toward that kingdom's nocturnal womb.... [O]nly through resignation can we at last tear ourselves from this place in order to plunge into life's rushing stream and at least to drink forgetfulness from this Lethe!

NOTES

1. The relative independence of the two domains can be further seen in the competing syntactocentric and semantocentric viewpoints that inform several strains of topic theory. The former position is summarized by Caplin's (2005) exploration of the syntax problem in topical analysis, which shows that many efforts to legitimize the enterprise often went hand in hand with attempts to syntacticize topics—to examine what grammatical and structural features they themselves might possess, or how they might otherwise contribute to expressing syntactic, formal, and structural elements. The consequence, as Nicholas McKay (2007) has argued in a broader, disciplinary study, is a serious undervaluing of the expressive significance of topics. Though Caplin numbers them among music's

"significant forces for musical expression," citing recent advances in the topic studies of Raymond Monelle as evidence, their significations operate "quite independently of formal considerations" (Caplin 2005: 124)—so syntax, in a sense, still has the upper hand, whereas topic theory requires a "dialogue" or "balance" between syntax and semantics (McKay 2007; Rumph 2012: 94–95). Monelle (2000) presents a similar cautionary tale from the other, semantocentric side of the platform: we learn from his fictional musicologist, Dr. Strabismus, that attempts to "embrace semantics and syntactics" are destined to fail. "No comprehensive theory was possible for him. Only an overmastering stress on the *sense* of music, rather than its form or its syntax, united his random thoughts" (Monelle 2000: 4). Among the reasons for "Strabismus's failure" is, evidently, the semantic autonomy of the topic. Expressive meaning is self-contained in the topic itself, as the signification of a particular "cultural unit" (Monelle 2000: 13; after Eco 1976: 67, citing Schneider 1968: 2; see also Monelle 2006: 10, 29). For Monelle, topical "meanings are inherent significations, not dependent on the listener; they are *lexical*, or in common language they are 'literal' meanings." The "primary concern of the topic theorist is to give an account of each topic in global terms, showing how it reflects culture and society" (2006: 10).

2. For an earlier analytic investigation of this interaction, specifically as it applies to the communication of wit and humor in Mozart, see Byros (2013).

3. For punctuation formulas, figures, and marks, see the second and third volumes of Koch's *Versuch einer Anleitung zur Composition* (1787: 347–48, 390; 1793: 7, 395) or corresponding passages of its English translation (1983: 2–3, 22, 64, 234). The *Hauptruhepuncte des Geistes* are discussed in the third volume (1793: 342–43; 1983: 213).

4. On the *Cadenz*, see the *Versuch* (1787: 419–20; 1793: 342–43) or the English translation (1983: 38–39, 213). In the *Versuch*, structurally significant half cadences were designated *Quintabsätze* (V-phrases). But later, in the entry "Quintabsatz" from his *Musikalisches Lexikon* (1802: cols. 1211–12), Koch would explicitly fix the structural weight of the medial half cadence (*Quintabsatz*) of the transition relative to the *Cadenz* of the *Schlußsatz* (second theme), by designating it a *Halbcadenz*.

5. Appendix B of my dissertation (Byros 2009) outlines each of these instances, along with several hundred other variants.

6. The review is actually anonymous. The Rochlitz attribution is from Geck and Schleuning (1989). The English translation is based on Senner, Wallace, and Meredith (2001: 21).

7. "*Orgelpunkt* (franz. Point d'orgue), oder *anhaltende Cadenz* ist eigentlich eine Aufhaltung der Finalcadenz in Fugen oder fugenartigen Sätzen" (Koch 1807: 263).

8. "Eine solche Stelle wird ein Orgelpunkt gennent, weil die Orgel, welche dabey im Basse blos den Ton aushält einigermaaßen einen Ruhepunkt hat, da die andern Stimmen fortfahren. Er kommt entweder auf der Tonica oder auf der Dominante vor und ist als eine Verzögerung des Schlusses anzusehen.... Insgemein bringt man in Fugen bey dem Haptschluß einen Orgelpunkt so an, daß die verschiedenen Säze und Gegensäze, die in der Fuge vorgekommen auf einen liegendem Basse so weit es angehet, vereiniget werden. Doch wird er auch bey andern Kirchensachen, die nicht als Fugen behandelt werden, angebracht" (Sulzer 1774: 860–61).

9. All of the examples are referenced in Appendix B of my dissertation (Byros 2009).

10. See, for example, K. 536/i, Trio; K. 571/i, iii; K. 600/vi; K. 602/ii, iii; K. 605/i; WoO 8, 11, 15, and WoO 13/i.

11. The sketches for the oratorio are contained in the Wielhorsky sketchbook of 1802–3 (see Johnson 1985). For more on the circumstances of the oratorio's composition, see also Forbes (1967, 1: 295–96).

12. "*Socrates* u. *Jesus* waren mir Muster" (Köhler, Herre, Beck et al. 1968–2001, 1: 211).

13. According to Anton Schindler's testimony (Schindler 1996: 248).

14. The *Gellert Lieder* Op. 48 (1802), which set six religious and spiritual poems of Christian Fürchtegott Gellert (1715–69), also date from this period.

15. "Mass H" in Walter (1973).

16. See Lockwood (1981) and Byros (2009: 20–24).

References

Agawu, V. Kofi. 1991. *Playing with Signs: A Semiotic Interpretation of Classic Music*. Princeton: Princeton University Press.

Albrechtsberger, Johann Georg. 1791. *Kurzgefasste Methode den Generalbass zu erlernen*. Vienna: Artaria.

Allanbrook, Wye J. 1983. *Rhythmic Gesture in Mozart*: Le nozze di Figaro *and* Don Giovanni. Chicago: University of Chicago Press.

Anderson, Emily, ed. 1961. *The Letters of Beethoven*. Trans. Emily Anderson. 3 vols. London: Macmillan.

Bach, Carl Philipp Emanuel. 1762. *Versuch über die wahre Art das Clavier zu spielen*. Vol. 2. Berlin: Georg Ludewig Winter.

——. 1949. *Essay on the True Art of Playing Keyboard Instruments*. Trans. William J. Mitchell. New York: Norton.

Byros, Vasili. 2009. Foundations of Tonality as Situated Cognition, 1730–1830: An Enquiry into the Culture and Cognition of Eighteenth-Century Tonality, with Beethoven's Eroica Symphony as a Case Study. Ph.D. diss., Yale University.

——. 2012. Meyer's Anvil: Revisiting the Schema Concept. *Music Analysis* 31/3: 273–346.

——. 2013. Trazom's Wit: Communicative Strategies in a "Popular" Yet "Difficult" Sonata. *Eighteenth-Century Music* 10/2: 213–52.

Cameron, Jasmin M. 2006. *The Crucifixion in Music: An Analytical Survey of Settings of the* Crucifixus *between 1680 and 1800*. Lanham, MD: Scarecrow.

Caplin, William E. 1998. *Classical Form: A Theory of Formal Functions for the Instrumental Music of Haydn, Mozart, and Beethoven*. New York: Oxford University Press.

——. 2005. On the Relation of Musical *Topoi* to Formal Function. *Eighteenth-Century Music* 2/1: 113–24.

Cook, Nicholas. 1996. Putting the Meaning Back into Music, or Semiotics Revisited. *Music Theory Spectrum* 18/1: 106–23.

Eco, Umberto. 1976. *A Theory of Semiotics*. Bloomington: Indiana University Press.

Forbes, Elliot. 1967. *Thayer's Life of Beethoven*. 2 vols. Princeton: Princeton University Press.

Geck, Martin, and Peter Schleuning. 1989. *"Geschrieben auf Bonaparte": Beethovens "Eroica": Revolution, Reaktion, Rezeption*. Reinbek bei Hamburg: Rowohlt.

Gjerdingen, Robert O. 2007. *Music in the Galant Style*. New York: Oxford University Press.

Hatten, Robert S. 1994. *Musical Meaning in Beethoven: Markedness, Correlation, and Interpretation*. Bloomington: Indiana University Press.

———. 2004. *Interpreting Musical Gestures, Topics, and Tropes: Mozart, Beethoven, Schubert.* Bloomington: Indiana University Press.

Heartz, Daniel. 2009. *Mozart, Haydn, and Early Beethoven: 1781–1802.* New York: Norton.

Heinichen, Johann David. 1728. *Der Generalbaß in der Composition.* Dresden: Author. Reprint, Hildesheim: Georg Olms, 1994.

Hepokoski, James, and Warren Darcy. 2006. *Elements of Sonata Theory: Norms, Types, and Deformations in the Late-Eighteenth-Century Sonata.* New York: Oxford University Press.

Ivanovitch, Roman. 2011. Mozart's Art of Retransition. *Music Analysis* 30/1: 1–36.

Jakobson, Roman. 1971. Language in Relation to Other Communication Systems. In *Selected Writings*, vol. 2, 570–79. The Hague: Mouton.

Johnson, Mark. 1987. *The Body in Mind: The Bodily Basis of Reason and Imagination.* Chicago: University of Chicago Press.

Johnson, Douglas, ed. 1985. *The Beethoven Sketchbooks: History, Reconstruction, Inventory.* Berkeley: University of California Press.

Kempis, Thomas à. 2004. *The Imitation of Christ.* Trans. Aloysius Croft and Harold Bolton. Peabody, MA: Hendrickson.

Koch, Heinrich Christoph. 1787–93. *Versuch einer Anleitung zur Composition.* Vols. 2 and 3. Leipzig: Adam Friedrich Böhme. Reprint, Hildesheim: Georg Olms, 1969.

———. 1802. *Musikalisches Lexikon.* Frankfurt am Main: August Hermann der Jüngere. Reprint, Kassel: Bärenreiter, 2001.

———. 1807. *Kurzgefaßtes Handwörterbuch der Musik.* Leipzig: Johann Friedrich Hartknoch.

———. 1983. *Introductory Essay on Composition.* Trans. Nancy Kovaleff Baker. New Haven: Yale University Press.

Köhler, Karl-Heinz, Grita Herre, Dagmar Beck et al., eds. 1968–2001. *Ludwig van Beethovens Konversationshefte.* 11 vols. Leipzig: VEB Deutscher Verlag für Musik.

Lakoff, George. 1987. *Women, Fire, and Dangerous Things.* Chicago: University of Chicago Press.

Langacker, Ronald W. 1998. Conceptualization, Symbolization, and Grammar. In *The New Psychology of Language: Cognitive and Functional Approaches to Language Structure*, ed. Michael Tomasello, 1–39. Mahwah, NJ: Erlbaum.

———. 1987–91. *Foundations of Cognitive Grammar.* Vol. 1: *Theoretical Prerequisites.* Vol. 2: *Descriptive Application Prerequisites.* Stanford, CA: Stanford University Press.

Lockwood, Lewis. 1981. Beethoven's Earliest Sketches for the *Eroica* Symphony. *Musical Quarterly* 67/4: 457–78.

MacIntyre, Bruce C. 1986. *The Viennese Concerted Mass of the Early Classic Period.* Ann Arbor, MI: UMI Research Press.

Marpurg, Friedrich Wilhelm. 1753–54. *Abhandlung von der Fuge.* 2 vols. Berlin: Haude und Spener.

McClelland, Clive. 2012. *Ombra: Supernatural Music in the Eighteenth Century.* Lanham, MD: Lexington.

McKay, Nicholas. 2007. On Topics Today. *Zeitschrift der Gesellschaft für Musiktheorie* 4/1–2: 159–83.

McKee, Eric. 2012. *Decorum of the Minuet, Delirium of the Waltz: A Study of Dance–Music Relations in 3/4 Time.* Bloomington: Indiana University Press.

Meyer, Leonard B. 1973. *Explaining Music: Essays and Explorations.* Chicago and London: University of Chicago Press.

———. 1980. Exploiting Limits: Creation, Archetypes, and Style Change. *Daedalus* 109/2: 177–205.

——. 1989. *Style and Music: Theory, History, and Ideology*. Philadelphia, PA: University of Pennsylvania Press.

Mirka, Danuta. 2008. Introduction. In *Communication in Eighteenth-Century Music*, ed. Danuta Mirka and Kofi Agawu, 1–10. Cambridge: Cambridge University Press.

Monelle, Raymond. 2006. *The Musical Topic: Hunt, Military and Pastoral*. Bloomington: Indiana University Press.

——. 2000. *The Sense of Music: Semiotic Essays*. Princeton: Princeton University Press.

Nohl, Ludwig, ed. 1870. *Beethovens Brevier*. Leipzig: Günther.

Norrington, Roger. 2002. Commentary. In CD booklet for *Beethoven: Symphonies Nos. 1–8 (Fragments)*. Radio-Sinfonieorchester Stuttgart, cond. Roger Norrington. Hännsler Classic. CD 093.108.

Nottebohm, Gustav. 1872. *Beethoveniana*. Leipzig: Peters.

Peirce, Charles Sanders. 1931–58. *Collected Papers*. 7 vols. Cambridge, MA: Harvard University Press.

Ratner, Leonard. 1980. *Classic Music: Expression, Form, and Style*. New York: Schirmer.

Rochlitz, Friedrich. 1807. Review. *Allgemeine musikalische Zeitung* 9 (18 February): cols. 319–34.

Rumph, Stephen. 2012. *Mozart and Enlightenment Semiotics*. Berkeley: University of California Press.

Sanguinetti, Giorgio. 2012. *The Art of Partimento: History, Theory, and Practice*. New York: Oxford University Press.

Schauffler, Robert Haven. 1929. *Beethoven: The Man Who Freed Music*. New York: Doubleday, Doran & Company.

Schindler, Anton. 1996. *Beethoven As I Knew Him*, ed. Donald W. MacArdle. Trans. Constance S. Jolly. New York: Dover.

Schneider, David M. 1968. *American Kinship: A Cultural Account*. New York: Prentice-Hall.

Senner, Wayne, Robin Wallace, and William Meredith, eds. 2001. *The Critical Reception of Beethoven's Compositions by His German Contemporaries*. Vol. 2. Lincoln, NE, and London: University of Nebraska Press.

Shapiro, Michael. 1983. *The Sense of Grammar*. Bloomington: Indiana University Press.

Sisman, Elaine. 1993. *Mozart: The "Jupiter" Symphony*. Cambridge: Cambridge University Press.

Solomon, Maynard. 2003. *Late Beethoven: Music, Thought, Imagination*. Berkeley: University of California Press.

——. 1998. *Beethoven*. New York: Schirmer.

Stefanowitsch, Anatol, and Stefan Th. Gries. 2003. Collostructions: Investigating the Interaction of Words and Constructions. *International Journal of Corpus Linguistics* 8/2: 209–43.

Sturm, Christoph Christian. 1772. *Betrachtungen über die Werke Gottes im Reiche der Natur*. Halle: Hemmerde.

Sullivan, John. W. N. 1927. *Beethoven: His Spiritual Development*. London: Jonathan Cape.

Sulzer, Johann Georg. 1774. *Allgemeine Theorie der schönen Künste*, Vol. 2. Leipzig: Weidmann.

Türk, Daniel Gottlob. 1800. *Anweisung zum Generalbaßspielen*. Leipzig: Schwickert; Halle: Hemmerde und Schwetschke.

Walter, Elaine R. 1973. Selected Masses of Antonio Caldara, 1670–1736. Ph.D. diss., The Catholic University of America.

Witcombe, Charles. 1998. *Beethoven's Private God: An Analysis of the Composer's Markings in Sturm's* Betrachtungen. Master's thesis, San Jose State University.

———. 2003. Beethoven's Markings in Christoph Christian Sturm's *Reflections on the Works of God in the Realm of Nature and Providence for Every Day of the Year*. *The Beethoven Journal* 18/1: 10–23.

Witcombe, Charles, and Robert Portillo. 2003. An English Translation of the Passages Beethoven Marked in His 1811 Edition of Sturm's *Betrachtungen über die Werke Gottes im Reiche der Natur und Vorsehung auf alle Tage des Jahres* (Part 1). *The Beethoven Journal* 18/1: 18–23.

Witcombe, Charles, Robert Portillo, Heidi Melas, Hannah Liebmann, and William Meredith. 2003. An English Translation of the Passages Beethoven Marked in His 1811 Edition of Sturm's *Betrachtungen über die Werke Gottes im Reiche der Natur und Vorsehung auf alle Tage des Jahres* (Revised and Complete in One Part). *The Beethoven Journal* 18/2: 87–106.

Wyn Jones, David. 1998. *The Life of Beethoven*. Cambridge: Cambridge University Press.

Zbikowski, Lawrence M. 2002. *Conceptualizing Music: Cognitive Structure, Theory, and Analysis*. New York: Oxford University Press.

CHAPTER 15

TOPICS AND FORMAL FUNCTIONS

The Case of the Lament

WILLIAM E. CAPLIN

IN an earlier essay (Caplin 2005) I examined the conditions under which a relationship between musical topics and formal functionality might be established and evaluated. I discussed the extent to which a given topic has the potential of expressing the general temporal qualities of *beginning, middle,* or *ending* of a formal process, including the framing temporalities of *before-the-beginning* and *after-the-end*. I argued that an association of topic and form must engage a topic's specific musical features—its melodic, harmonic, rhythmic, and textural content—and that a distinct connection between topic and formal function can only arise when such features themselves can be shown to articulate a specific temporal quality. I thus took the "Universe of Topics" (as proposed by Agawu 1991 and supplemented by Monelle 2000) and distinguished individual topics as generating "no formal relation," a "possible formal relation," or a "likely formal relation" (Table 15.1). For each topic that has a likely relation to formal functionality, I discussed which specific musical characteristics—such as its harmonic content, its melodic directionality, or its textural complexities—help establish its ability to express one or more generalized formal functions (Table 15.2).

The present chapter will develop further the relationship of topic to form, but now in connection with a single topic, the *lament*. I have chosen this topic because, unlike the other form-relating topics (see again, Table 15.2), the lament has the potential of expressing the full complement of beginning, middle, and ending functions. The topic is thus suitable for use in a wide variety of compositional contexts. The lament is also interesting because it represents a special case of the relation between topics and contrapuntal-harmonic schemata (Gjerdingen 2007). In principle, topics and schemata are distinct from each other, even if in some cases a given topic can be associated with a specific schema (as discussed in the previous chapter of this book), but the lament topic is inextricably linked with a single schema. This schema, too, is special: whereas most schemata embrace both an upper-voice melody and bass melody, the lament schema is defined essentially by its stepwise descending bass; no one melodic pattern emerges as

416 WILLIAM E. CAPLIN

Table 15.1 "Universe of Topics" from Caplin, "On the Relation of Musical *Topoi* to Formal Function" (2005), 115, table 1

1. No Formal Relation	2. Possible Formal Relation	3. Likely Formal Relation
alla breve	brilliant style	*coup d'archet*
alla zoppa	cadenza	fanfare
amoroso	fantasia	French overture
aria	hunt style	horn call (horn fifths)
bourrée	pastoral	lament
gavotte	sensibility (*Empfindsamkeit*)	learned style
march		Mannheim rocket
military		musette
minuet		*Sturm und Drang*
ombra		
opera buffa		
recitative		
sarabande		
sigh motive (*Seufzer*)		
singing style		
Turkish music		

Table 15.2 Topics and General Temporal Qualities

Topic	Pre-Beg	Beg	Mid	End	Post-end
coup d'archet	✓	✓			
fanfare		✓		✓	
French overture		✓			
horn call (horn fifths)		✓		✓	✓
lament		✓	✓	✓	
learned style		✓	✓		
Mannheim rocket	✓	✓			
musette		✓			✓
Sturm und Drang			✓		

a conventional counterpoint to this bass line. In short, we can say that the lament topic is defined by the lament schema and the lament schema is defined by its bass. Last but not least, the lament's pervasively descending bass is somewhat of a constraining factor, especially in works by classical composers, whose bass melodies typically feature prominent ascending motion. The topic is thus a touchstone for highlighting some important stylistic differences among earlier and later works within the eighteenth century.

The lament schema is characterized by a bass line that descends stepwise from the tonic scale-degree to the dominant, thus spanning an interval of a perfect fourth. This *descending tetrachord* became associated in the early to mid-seventeenth century with

EXAMPLE 15.1 The lament schema: (a) diatonic, minor-mode pattern and (b) chromatic pattern.

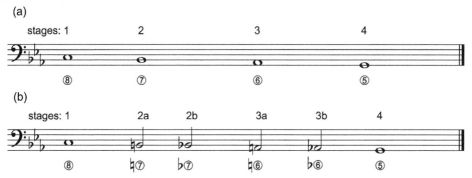

a genre of expressive vocal music containing a mournful text, most especially in works that were titled *lamento* (Rosand 1979). The descending tetrachord was often treated as a ground bass and thus relates as well to the instrumental genres of passacaglia or chaconne. A strictly diatonic, minor-mode version of the lament *schema* is shown in Example 15.1a. Note that, following recent practice (Gjerdingen, 2007; Sanguinetti 2012), I label the scale degrees in the bass by Arabic numerals enclosed in a circle. I further identify four *stages* of the schema (numbered 1 through 4) associated with each bass note. Typically, the expressive quality of lament is made more manifest when the tetrachord is chromaticized, as shown in Example 15.1b. Here, stages 2 and 3 are each subdivided as a or b depending on whether the bass notes ⑦ and ⑤ are natural or flat.[1] This chromatic version, also called *passus duriusculus* (somewhat hard passage) by the seventeenth-century theorist Christoph Bernhard (1648–49; see Williams [1997: 61–62] and Monelle [2000: 73]), could also feature an ascending chromatic line and could appear in upper voices of the musical texture as well as the bass (Williams 1997). For the present purposes, I will deal with the lament topic as confined to the bass voice, for it is there that its form-functional effect is most evident. Moreover, the majority of examples discussed here will feature a chromatic descending motion, with only a small number of purely diatonic examples providing some simpler contexts for comparison. It must be admitted that not all uses of the chromatic tetrachord strongly engage the expressive qualities of mourning and loss; indeed, it is difficult to draw the line between those cases whose nature clearly expresses a lament from those that are more affectively neutral. I will, however, generally restrict my examples to those in which the chromatic tetrachord occurs within minor-mode contexts rather than major-mode ones, where the sense of invoking the lament topic might seem far-fetched.

Let us begin by considering some standard harmonizations associated with the lament bass, for harmonic content normally proves to be the strongest indicator of formal functionality (see Example 15.2). The first passage, Example 15.2a, shows a fully diatonic version of the descending tetrachord so as to reveal the sequential nature of the progression from stages 2 to 3, namely the harmonies v⁶ to iv⁶. A chromatic version,

EXAMPLE **15.2** Standard harmonizations.

(Continued)

EXAMPLE **15.2** (Continued)

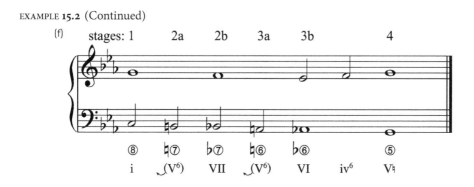

(f)   stages: 1   2a   2b   3a   3b   4

⑧   ♮⑦   ♭⑦   ♮⑥   ♭⑥   ⑤
i   ⌣(V⁶)   VII   ⌣(V⁶)   VI   iv⁶   V♮

shown in Example 15.2b, shows that harmonization remaining the same. Frequently, the descending stepwise motion is elaborated by 7–6 suspensions in the upper voice, as shown in Example 15.2c; in this case, stage 1 can be subdivided and the harmony of stage 1b can initiate the sequential progression with VI⁶. Moreover, the descending sequence can continue into stage 4 when it is supported by a III⁶ harmony (Example 15.2d); the suspension and its resolution can even subdivide this fourth stage into a and b. The sense of sequence can be accentuated if the dominant and subdominant harmonies are preceded by their own dominants, as shown in Example 15.2e. Finally, another sequential pattern can be used if the constituent harmonies of stages 2 and 3 are placed in root position (Example 15.2f).[2] Some variations to these basic harmonic plans can be found, but most can be related to the versions just presented.

Given these various harmonizations, what are their implications for formal functionality? These depend on the particular stages involved, as shown in Example 15.3, which now adds a form-functional analysis to the progressions of Example 15.2. To the extent that the harmonization projects a sequential pattern, a generalized *medial* formal function is expressed: the instability of sequential harmonies naturally associates this progression type with the sense of "being-in-the-middle" of a formal process. The projection of sequence occurs in all of the versions from stage 2 to stage 3; the motions from stage 1 to stage 2 in Examples 15.3e and 15.3f, and from stage 3 to stage 4 in Example 15.3d are sequential as well. When stage 4 consists of a dominant triad, then the motion from stage 3 to stage 4 has the potential of creating a half-cadential progression—pre-dominant to dominant—which clearly articulates an *ending* formal function. If stage 4 is harmonized by a dominant seventh, then this dissonant harmony can be a constituent of an authentic cadential progression, assuming that a root-position tonic follows to complete the progression. Finally, the root-position tonic of stage 1, including its motion to V⁶ in stage 2a, can project a tonic prolongation, whose harmonic stability is suitable for supporting an *initiating* function. We see, therefore, that when the complete schema is used, and when stage 4 brings a cadential dominant of some sort, then the potential for the lament bass to express the complete set of generalized temporal functions can be realized. In many situations, however, the full complement of functions is not present. For example, tonic prolongations also frequently occur in medial formal

EXAMPLE 15.3 Standard harmonizations and formal functionality.

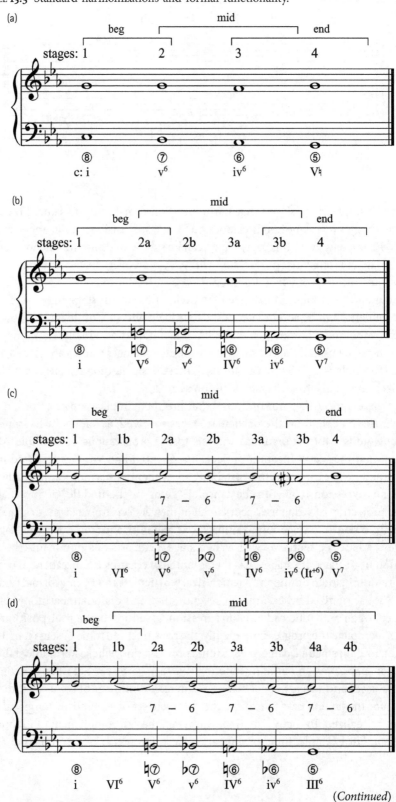

(Continued)

EXAMPLE **15.3** (Continued)

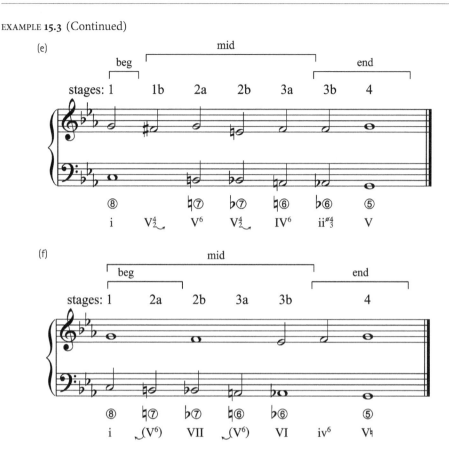

contexts, where other factors besides harmonic content alone can express that function, such as grouping fragmentation, harmonic acceleration, faster surface rhythms. As a result, the tonic prolongation at the beginning of the schema may be entirely associated with medial functionality and not with a formal beginning. The schema may also fail to express a closing function if stage 4 does not create a genuine cadence of some kind.

Up to now, we have been discussing the lament bass schema in the abstract and in isolation of any actual occurrence in the musical repertory. Let us now turn to some specific excerpts in order to investigate the variety of form-functional relationships that the lament bass can enter into. I begin with some relatively simple cases in which the bass remains fully diatonic, turning then to more chromatic bass lines. Example 15.4, from Corelli's "Christmas" Concerto, presents a fairly straightforward situation. The overall formal context represents an early example of what Arnold Schoenberg (1967) first described as the *sentence* theme-type.[3] It begins with a two-measure *basic idea* that is immediately repeated as a dominant response, the two ideas together creating what I term a four-measure *presentation* phrase. Inasmuch as the basic idea is a clear initiating function, its repetition continues to express an even heightened sense of beginning, such that the presentation as a whole sets up strong expectations for a *continuation* that

EXAMPLE 15.4 Corelli, Concerto Grosso in G minor, Op. 6 No. 8, "Christmas," iv, mm. 1–8.

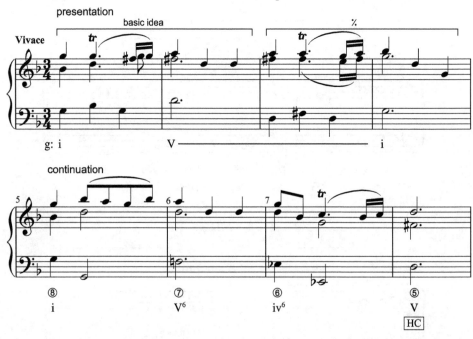

would destabilize the formal context and promote greater mobility, eventually resulting in cadential closure of some kind. Here, the four-bar continuation phrase is supported by the lament bass, which descends diatonically from ⑧ to ⑤, the arrival of the dominant creating a clear half cadence. Following the stability of the presentation phrase, with its firm root-position tonic prolongation, the continuation expresses medial functionality by bringing a minimal sense of harmonic acceleration and by the harmonic sequence expressed in stages 2 and 3 (mm. 6 and 7) of the descending tetrachord. Stage 3 also provides the pre-dominant harmony (iv⁶) needed to articulate the half cadence, which closes the theme. To be sure, the opening tonic harmony of stage 1 (m. 5) continues the prevailing tonic prolongation, thus maintaining a sense of initiating function in that respect; however, we see that Corelli also takes the opportunity of providing greater melodic activity in that measure (compared with the previous ones), which immediately helps to project medial functionality. As soon as stage 2 brings the minor dominant in first inversion (v⁶), the tonic prolongation yields to a sequential progression that fully supports the sense of "being-in-the-middle" of the theme. In short, the lament bass essentially expresses medial and concluding functions, the initiating function being created by the prior presentation phrase.

A similar situation is found in the opening movement of C. P. E. Bach's Sonatina in A minor, Wq. 50 No. 3, H. 138 (Example 15.5). Following an opening presentation, the continuation begins with a diatonic version of the lament bass. Here the sense of medial function is more strongly expressed than in the Corelli example, since the VI⁶ harmony

EXAMPLE 15.5 C. P. E. Bach, Sonatina in A minor, Wq. 50 No. 3, H. 138/i, mm. 1–8.

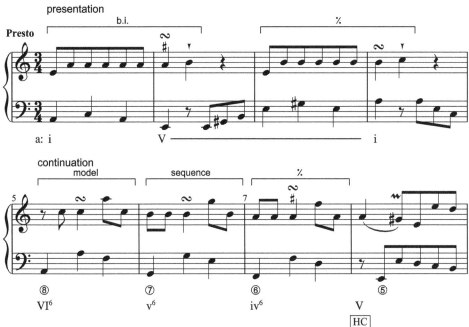

of stage 1 (in m. 5) already signals the onset of the sequential progression. As well, Bach uses this harmonic progression to support a clear model–sequence repetition, which also articulates phrase-structural *fragmentation*, the reduction in the size of the groups, from two-measures in the basic idea and its repetition to a single bar for the model and its sequences.

Example 15.6, from the second minuet of Handel's *Water Music*, Suite No. 3 in G minor, brings greater formal complexities in a context that may, like the previous examples, seem sentential. Here, the lament topic appears at the very opening of the theme to support the basic idea, which is repeated two times over the course of the entire bass-line descent. As a result, the arrival at m. 6 of stage 4 on dominant harmony is not perceived as cadential, since it is still supporting an "opening idea"; as a result, Handel has the bass continue down stepwise all the way back to tonic (①), which moves directly to another dominant, one that is entirely cadential in function, thus creating the half cadence at m. 8. The lament schema itself, therefore, does not participate in any ending function. Returning to the opening of the theme, we might also question the extent to which initiating function is expressed. Note that like the prior Bach example, stage 1 of the lament schema begins with tonic for only two beats, the final beat of the measure bringing a VI⁶; indeed, given the prevailing harmonic rhythm, we are encouraged to hear all of the first measure as VI⁶, thus signaling a sequential progression from the very start of the theme. Moreover, although we might be tempted to speak of an "extended" presentation, one that includes the third statement of the basic idea, we are hard-pressed to recognize a

EXAMPLE 15.6 Handel, *Water Music*, Suite No. 3 in G minor, Minuet II, mm. 1–8.

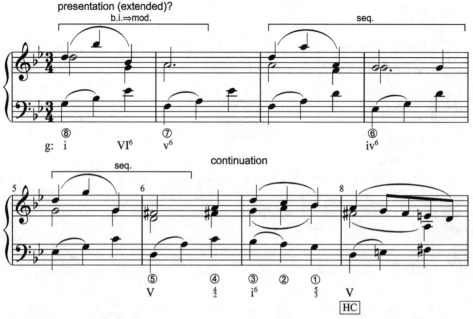

broader tonic prolongation supporting that initiating function. Indeed, the basic idea itself seems to function as a "model" for two sequential repetitions. In other words, a case can be made for recognizing that the theme starts immediately by expressing a medial function, a large-scale continuation. This seemingly paradoxical formal situation can be better understood when we distinguish between *intrinsic* and *contextual* formal functionality (Valières et al. 2009: 18; Caplin 2013: 132–33). The former arises from our perception of the musical content of a given passage irrespective of its actual placement within the broader form; in this case, the intrinsic functionality of the lament bass is effectively *medial*. But coming as it does at the very start of a formal process—the onset of a new "movement" of the work—we contextually interpret the schema as *initiating*, at least for its first couple of stages. The resulting conflict between intrinsic and contextual functions, which we might consider to be a type of *form-functional dissonance* (akin to Krebs' [1999] notion of "metrical dissonance"), creates a palpable sense of instability at the opening, which might seem odd if this movement were fully self-contained. Yet in a performance tradition in which this second minuet is played immediately following the first in the same tempo and without any break in the pulse and then further followed by a complete reprise of minuet I, the lack of a fully functional initiation at this medial location in the larger formal context seems appropriate enough.

Let us turn now to cases where the bass line is chromaticized, a situation that offers greater opportunity for harmonic variety. The opening of the slow movement of J. S. Bach's Concerto in G minor, BWV 975, based on an earlier concerto by Vivaldi, illustrates a fairly typical baroque usage (Example 15.7). Here, the lament bass appears at

EXAMPLE 15.7 J. S. Bach, Concerto in G minor, BWV 975/ii, mm. 1–11.

the very beginning of the work and is used twice to support the first two four-measure phrases. Again, we could recognize the three fundamental formal functions of beginning, middle, and end underlying each phrase. Medial functionality is clearly articulated by the sequential progressions, and ending functions are evident enough with the arrival on dominant harmony at mm. 4 and 8, following cadential pre-dominants (iv⁶ at m. 3; ii₃⁴ at m. 7). But like the prior example of Handel, the sense of functional initiation is rather weakly expressed. The opening idea is supported by tonic harmony for only two beats of the first measure; afterward the shift to VI⁶ moving to V⁶ already suggests sequential activity, which is further reinforced by a model in mm. 2–3 that is repeated as a sequence in mm. 3–4.[4] The use of the lament bass at the very opening of the theme thus creates a degree of form-functional dissonance arising from the intrinsically medial characteristics of the schema and its contextual location as a formal beginning. Note that in the second phrase, Bach varies the harmonies to make the sequence even more prominent through the use of secondary dominants tonicizing v and iv. As a result, the model already arises on the second beat of m. 5, such that only the downbeat tonic brings any hint of initiating function. This harmonic change is appropriate enough, of course, seeing as the phrase is the second one of the movement and thus does not have to articulate an initiating quality as strongly as the first phrase.

Following the opening two phrases, Bach relinquishes the lament bass for a harmonic situation that is more stabilizing in the new key of A minor. If he had continued using the same bass pattern for the entire movement, we could have spoken of the lament schema being used as a ground bass. Indeed, Bach writes a number of such ground-bass movements, perhaps the most famous being the "Crucifixus" from the B-minor Mass, whose opening phrases are shown in Example 15.8. As we have done up to now, we can identify the form-functional elements *within* the complete schema, though here, a sense of formal initiation is largely absent: except for the first bar, whose tonic downbeat initiates the entire movement, the grouping structure throughout the rest of the piece sees all of the phrases starting on the upper E (⑧) and concluding on the lower E (identified here as scale-degree ①). And throughout the piece, this opening moment of the schema is, with only one exception (m. 13), never harmonized with tonic.[5] As a result, an intrinsic sense of formal initiation is, from the harmonic perspective, extremely weak, if not lost altogether. What about the sense of formal end? Inasmuch as the schema concludes with a fifth leap, the potential for authentic cadential closure is strongly projected by the bass line. Indeed, the harmonies of the opening three phrases end with the progression V–I. But with this situation we confront a potentially awkward formal dilemma. If Bach were to realize every final pitch of the schema with a genuine authentic cadence, then it would be difficult to shape a larger-scale formal design for the movement as a whole. To avoid that situation, Bach uses a variety of strategies to foil a sense of closure for most of the schemata and thus to allow for a broader formal plan to emerge.

Let us examine how he accomplishes this result. To be sure, the instrumental opening phrase could be seen to close with an authentic cadence ("imperfect," because the highest instrumental part ends on 3̂). We will come back to the true status of this cadence after we have worked through the rest of the schemata. When the voices enter, they do so

EXAMPLE 15.8 J. S. Bach, Mass in B minor, BWV 232, "Crucifixus," mm. 1–14.

(Continued)

EXAMPLE **15.8** (Continued)

(Continued)

EXAMPLE **15.8** (Continued)

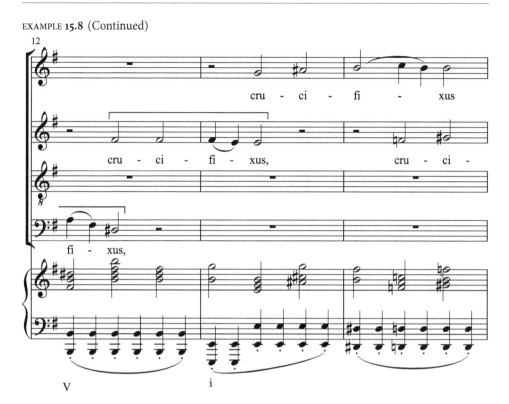

one at a time, sounding the sole word "Crucifixus" for two full phrases, the end of each one of which, at mm. 9 and 13 respectively, could be thought of as articulating an authentic cadence, since the requisite cadential harmonies are present. But we might question whether it makes sense to speak of genuinely functional cadences at these points in the piece, where the text has moved no further than its first word, and where the same opening idea, a descending sigh figure, predominates. In other words, since both the text and the musical ideas are entirely initiatory, the potential cadences at m. 9 and 13 do not seem to bring a genuine sense of formal end to anything larger in scope than the lament bass itself. Moving further into the piece, Bach uses a variety of devices (harmonic, melodic, textural) to avoid projecting a formal ending at those points where the lament bass leaps from ⑤ to ① (Example 15.9a–c). Only first, at m. 29, does Bach write a clearly articulated perfect authentic cadence (Example 15.10), which corresponds to the completion of a full grammatical unit of the text.

Following this cadence, the second full line of the "Crucifixus" text begins ("passus et sepultus est") with a complete change in texture from polyphonic to homophonic. The first full cycle of the lament ground bass ends on the downbeat at m. 33 with an imperfect authentic cadence (IAC). The text is then repeated, but this time Bach concludes the text and the music of the chorus on the downbeat of m. 36, right at the onset of dominant harmony. He thus changes the way in which the lament bass expresses its

EXAMPLE **15.9** J. S. Bach, Mass in B minor, BWV 232, "Crucifixus": (a) mm. 16–17; (b) mm. 20–21; (c) mm. 24–25.

(Continued)

EXAMPLE **15.9** (Continued)

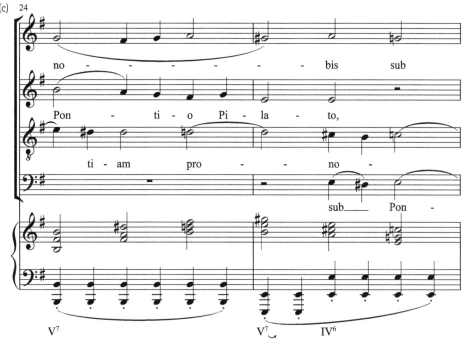

sense of ending function, now having it articulate a half cadence over ⑤ rather than an authentic cadence over ①. The resolution to tonic at the following bar does not create a cadence of any kind, but rather sets up the return of the opening "Crucifixus" text, the pervasively polyphonic texture, and a chromatically embellished version of the sigh motives. The section between the PAC at m. 29 and this recapitulatory onset at m. 37 thus functions as a contrasting middle, one which appropriately enough ends with a weak cadence on dominant harmony in order to set the stage for a return of the opening materials. This third section of the piece, like the first, also finds ways of avoiding the sense of authentic cadence when the lament bass reaches ① at mm. 41 and 45 (Example 15.11a–b). That moment is saved for the end of the complete text at m. 49 (Example 15.12) and the achievement of another perfect authentic cadence. Following this cadence, Bach writes one more cycle of the lament bass, this time altering it so that it modulates to the relative major of the home key, G major, closing there with an IAC. This passage clearly has an "after-the-end" function, one which also prepares for the D-major outburst at the beginning of the following "Et resurrexit."

Having worked our way through the entire "Crucifixus," let us reassess the form-functional implications of closure as expressed by the constant cycling of the lament bass. Although the potential for cadence is offered at the end of each schema, Bach exploits a variety of means for avoiding that sense except in a small number of

EXAMPLE **15.10** J. S. Bach, Mass in B minor, BWV 232, "Crucifixus," mm. 28–38.

(Continued)

EXAMPLE **15.10** (Continued)

EXAMPLE 15.11 J. S. Bach, Mass in B minor, BWV 232, "Crucifixus": (a) mm. 40–41; (b) mm. 44–45.

EXAMPLE **15.12** J. S. Bach, Mass in B minor, BWV 232, "Crucifixus," mm. 48–53.

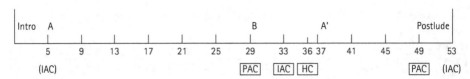

FIGURE 15.1 Form and cadence in the "Crucifixus."

cases. Within this overall ternary form (Figure 15.1), we find unambiguous perfect authentic cadences ending the A and A′ sections at mm. 29 and 49 respectively.[6] As well, we find a weak IAC within the B section at m. 33 and an even weaker half cadence closing that section at m. 36, thus taking advantage of the possibility that the dominant harmony supported by ⑤ can change from being the *penultimate* harmony of an authentic cadential progression to being an *ultimate* harmony of a half-cadential one.[7] Within this scheme, we can now better understand that the IACs closing the first lament bass at m. 5 and the final cycle at m. 53 lie outside the boundaries of the fundamental ternary form; rather they function to end the two framing units of the overall form, the "before-the-beginning" introduction and the "after-the-end" modulating postlude. These cadences thus have what I term a "limited scope," such that they end the schema alone, not any other larger section of the form proper (Caplin 2004: 86).

I turn now to some examples of the lament bass as used by composers of the classical period. But, before looking at specific cases, I want to note one major change in compositional style from earlier eighteenth-century practice to that in the later decades of the century. I am referring here to the organization of the bass line as a melodic part distinct from the structural upper voice. Typical of baroque works is the prominence of descending scalar bass lines, even at the very start of a thematic unit.[8] The bass line of Bach's "Air on the G string," from the third orchestral suite, is exemplary of this practice (Example 15.13). A standard midcentury manifestation of this opening descent has been well described by Gjerdingen (2007: 46–50), who identifies the combination of Romanesca and Prinner schemata that so typically begins a galant movement and that results in a complete octave descent in the bass voice (Example 15.14).[9] By the later decades of the eighteenth century, this preponderance of bass descents, particularly at the very opening of a theme, had largely run its course, and the high classical style sees a marked change in bass line structure, one whose model of a fundamentally ascending bass motion is given in Example 15.15a and specifically illustrated in Example 15.15b (Caplin 2008: 163–65). As a result of this change in practice, the lament topic, with its striking descending bass motion is not so suitable for use at the opening of a thematic unit, unlike the case for earlier styles, where such a bass descent is appropriate to general stylistic norms. Thus in classical themes, the lament tends to appear in a medial formal context, typically as a continuation following a solidly expressed initiating idea or phrase supported by a root-position tonic prolongation.

The opening of Mozart's Overture to *Don Giovanni* illustrates this technique well (Example 15.16). Following a presentation phrase that prolongs tonic, the continuation begins with the lament bass, whose arrival on ⑤ brings a half cadence and standing

EXAMPLE 15.13 J. S. Bach, Orchestral Suite No. 3 in D major, BWV 1068, Air, mm. 1–4.

EXAMPLE 15.14 Gallo, Trio in G major, i, mm. 1–2, from Gjerdingen, *Music in the Galant Style* (2007), 50, ex. 3.9.

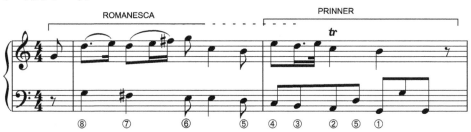

on the dominant. A similar situation occurs at the beginning of the transition in the first movement of Haydn's Piano Sonata in E flat major, Hob. XVI:52 (Example 15.17). Following a two-measure basic idea, the music moves directly into a continuation phrase, one that brings two successive lament bass schemata, the first in the home key, the second in the subordinate key. Note that ⑤ (third beat of m. 13) is not cadential, but rather passes through to ♯④ as pre-dominant of the half-cadential progression that closes this modulating transition. The lament topic thus has an exclusively medial function. Note, by the way, that the chromatic descending bass is used here in a major-mode context, a situation that is rarely, if ever, employed in baroque works but that more readily appears in the classical style, with its greater use of modal mixture in general.[10]

The opening of the minuet of Mozart's String Quartet in D minor, K. 421 (Example 15.18a), illustrates again how the classical composers normally want to set up a secure sense of structural initiation via a firm root-position tonic before embarking on the lament topic. Here, the opening basic idea is supported by tonic, which continues into

EXAMPLE 15.15 Model of classical bass line (a) and its realization in Mozart's Piano Trio in B flat major, K. 502/ii, mm. 1–4 (b).

(a)

① ② ③ ④ ⑤ ①
I (V⁴₃) I⁶ ii⁶ V I

(b)   **Larghetto**

the first bar of a contrasting idea (c.i.). The second bar of that idea sees the appearance of V⁶₅, which in itself maintains the tonic prolongation as support for the full four-measure initiating phrase (a *compound basic idea*).[11] But then Mozart lets the contrasting idea "become" (⇒) a model for sequential repetition as the bass continues its stepwise descent. A second repetition of the sequence begins with the upbeat to m. 7, which is slightly altered to accelerate the harmonic change leading eventually to a perfect authentic cadence to close the theme at m. 10. Like the previous example, the appearance of ⑤ at the downbeat of m. 8 does not yet signal a cadence, as the bass passes further down to ③, which initiates the authentic cadential progression. If the lament topic is not associated here with formal ending, we might wonder if it participates in formal beginning. After all, the complete schema technically begins with ⑧ appearing at the very opening of the theme. Moreover, the next step in the descent, ♮⑦ occurs within the boundaries of the compound basic idea. In other words, the schema embraces both initiating and medial functions within the theme. But now an interesting issue of "in-time" listening is raised by this situation. Inasmuch as the motion from i to V⁶ is so ubiquitous in tonal syntax, we probably would not even think that a lament bass is being projected until we hear ♭⑦, which does not occur until the beginning of the continuation phrase (m. 5). Indeed, it is

EXAMPLE **15.16** Mozart, *Don Giovanni*, Overture, mm. 1–12.

possible to write a more normative eight-measure theme using this same opening and avoiding any reference to the lament topic (see the reconstruction in Example 15.18b). It is questionable, then, whether it makes much sense to speak of the lament topic participating in the formal initiation projected in the opening measures of this theme. Instead, we are more likely to think that the topic is associated here exclusively with medial functionality, along the lines of the previous classical examples we have examined.

This is not to say that there are no cases where we would want to identify the lament bass from the very beginning of a thematic unit. For it seemed appropriate enough in connection with the baroque pieces shown in Example 15.6 and Example 15.7 to do just that, even when ⑧ supports a root-position tonic. In fact, there are some classical examples where we perceive the sense of the lament bass immediately at the opening of a theme. The first movement of the same Mozart quartet starts with a diatonic version of the descending tetrachord that quite readily evokes the lament topic (see Example 15.19). It is instructive, however, to observe how Mozart harmonizes the pattern, namely in a manner that is entirely tonic prolongational, with little hint of its more natural

EXAMPLE 15.17 Haydn, Piano Sonata in E flat major, Hob. XVI:52/i, mm. 9–14.

sequential expression. Note especially how the arrival on ⑤ brings a six-four sonority that is entirely tonic in its function. Following this two-measure basic idea, a contrasting idea brings what seems to be a weak IAC to close an antecedent phrase.[12] The following consequent phrase begins again with the lament bass, but now with greater chromaticism. The harmonization here pulls more quickly away from a secure sense of tonic prolongation via a tonicization of the subdominant; the harmonic destabilization here, though not typical of most periodic forms, is nonetheless logical enough, seeing as the beginning of the consequent stands "in the middle" of the complete theme.[13] Unlike the antecedent, the arrival on ⑤ brings a genuine dominant harmony, but one that is not cadential, in that it returns to tonic prior to the onset of the true authentic cadential progression that arises within m. 8. In short, both phrases of this theme begin with the lament bass, but the topic is harmonically adjusted to project a clear sense of functional initiation at its very opening and a medial function in its middle. In this way, Mozart avoids creating an undue dissonance between intrinsic and contextual formal functionalities that can easily arise when the lament bass is used at the very opening of a thematic unit, such as that already discussed in connection with Examples 15.6 and 15.7 and also to be seen in the passages to be discussed next.

EXAMPLE **15.18** Mozart, String Quartet in D minor, K. 421/iii, mm. 1–10: (a) original version and (b) recomposition.

EXAMPLE **15.19** Mozart, String Quartet in D minor, K. 421/i, mm. 1–8.

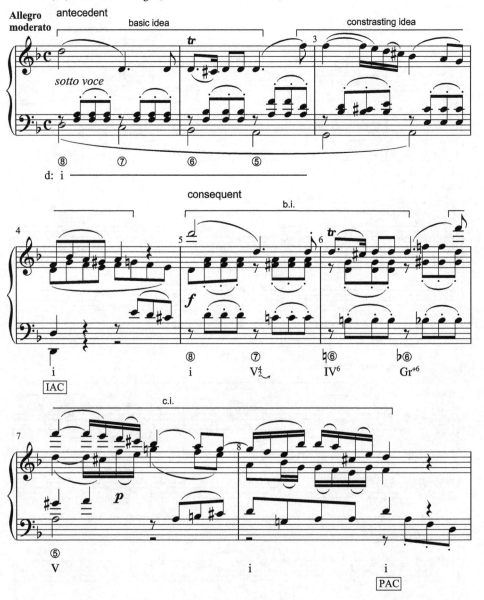

Slow introductions, which are generally destabilizing in preparation for the true beginning of the movement, seem especially suited to the immediate onset of a lament bass, as a number of prominent examples from the classical style attest. Indeed, the chromatic motion of the bass is sometimes complemented by highly chromatic inflections in the upper voices as well, as seen perhaps most strikingly at the opening of Mozart's "Dissonance" Quartet (Example 15.20). Here, the projection of a functional initiation is minimal due to the extreme dissonance created by the various chromatic lines, this despite the broader harmonic motion from i to V⁶ within mm. 1–4. Moreover, these opening bars are then repeated sequentially, further projecting an overall, intrinsically medial functionality.[14] Even more harmonically extreme is the opening of the Introduzione to the finale of Beethoven's "Waldstein" Sonata (Example 15.21a). Here, the arrival on ♮⑦ in m. 2 brings a major triad in root position (VII, or perhaps V/III); the opening two-measure unit is then repeated in a manner that suggests a sequence, though a truly sequential transposition is not effected. For this time, the final harmony of the two-measure unit is a first-inversion B-major triad, which suggests that it may be functioning as a secondary dominant of the leading tone (and thus calling into question

EXAMPLE **15.20** Mozart, String Quartet in C major, K. 465, "Dissonance," i, mm. 1–12.

whether we can even hear the D♯ in the bass as ♭⑦ in F major). The extreme harmonic instability projected from the very beginning of this thematic unit creates a marked conflict between the intrinsic and contextual functions of the lament topic, and this formal dissonance supports well the aesthetic of destabilization that is typical of slow introductions in general. The opening of the Introduzione itself references the beginning of the first movement of the "Waldstein" (Example 15.21b), though the harmonization of the lament bass there, which conforms to the model shown in Example 15.2f, is somewhat less radical than that of the following movement.[15] Yet here, we are not dealing with a slow introduction, but rather already with the main theme, which should normally be quite *tight-knit* in formal expression.[16] So the form-functional dissonance arising here is especially strong, which surely helps in expressing the overall emotional agitation and excitement associated with this most remarkable sonata-form opening.

My last two examples of classical usage involve cases where the composer seems to be making an explicit reference to an earlier musical style. Beethoven's Thirty-Two Variations in C minor, WoO 80, is constructed as a ground bass, whose theme brings the lament topic, as shown in Example 15.22a. The choice of ground-bass technique itself is a throwback to earlier eighteenth-century practice, and the use of the chromaticized lament bass right at the start of the theme further associates it with the High Baroque. Other baroque-like features include the uniform texture and regular harmonic rhythm that prevail until the downbeat of m. 6, whereby each link of the bass regularly appears at the downbeat of the measure. This uniformity breaks down when the bass moves one

EXAMPLE **15.21** Beethoven, Piano Sonata in C major, Op. 53, "Waldstein": (a) ii, mm. 1–9; (b) i, mm. 1–9.

(Continued)

EXAMPLE **15.21** (Continued)

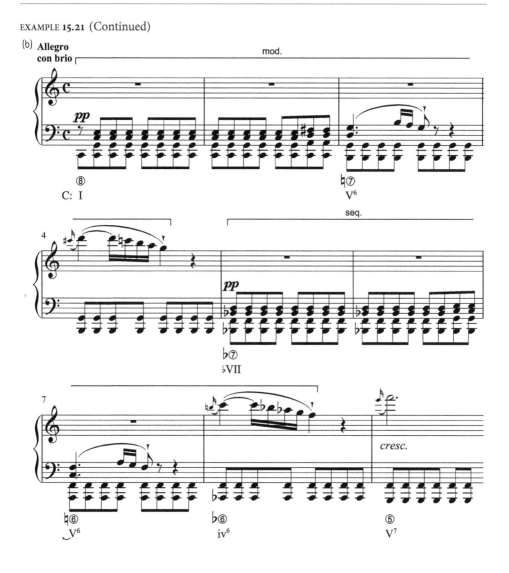

step further to ④ at the second beat of m. 6, thus "too early" in some sense. The full chords in both hands at that point also effect a change from the melody-and-accompaniment texture to a fully homophonic one, which is then changed again by the monophonic texture (with octave doubling) that ends the theme. These dramatic changes in texture and harmonic rhythm (further supported by the various dynamic changes within these measures) situate the theme as more classical in nature. As well, the clearly sententical structure with its manifest fragmentation in mm. 5–6, which also develops motivic material from the initial basic idea, betrays a classical sensibility. As for the form-functional expression associated with the lament bass, we can continue to identify its essential medial functionality. That the arrival on ⑤ is noncadential is evident by its being harmonized as a passing six-four sonority that effects a broader prolongation of the subdominant. As for the schema articulating an initiating function, the situation is a bit cloudy. On the one hand, its use at the very opening of the theme projects a degree of form-functional dissonance of the type we have examined in the last number of examples. But a closer look reveals that the specific harmonies chosen by Beethoven downplay the sequential potential of the schema and even let us recognize that the bass notes ⑧–♮⑦–♭⑦, which bring the progression i–V⁶–V⁴₂/IV, could be seen to prolong tonic for three bars (in that the last chord still has a root C), which provides a fairly substantial harmonic support for a sense of initiating function.[17] Finally, it is instructive to observe the changes Beethoven makes when writing a *maggiore* variation to the theme (Example 15.22b). The first two measures see the bass begin its descent from ⑧ to ♮⑦ supporting again the progression I–V⁶ as at the opening of the theme. But then Beethoven abandons the bass descent entirely and has that voice move upward in stepwise motion. A hint of sequence is offered by the progression V⁶₅/ii–ii, and the following diminished-seventh harmony in m. 101 promises to continue the sequence by functioning as a secondary dominant of iii. Instead, the diminished-seventh undergoes a common-tone resolution to I⁶, which initiates the cadential progression to close the theme with a PAC.[18] The structure of this bass line, with its stepwise ascent from ① to ⑤ conforms much more to classical norms (see again Example 15.15a) than to the descending line of the lament schema, which evokes the world of the Baroque.

My final classical example of the lament topic comes from Mozart's Adagio and Allegro in F minor, a late work that Lawrence Dreyfus has characterized as being "in neo-Baroque high style," which includes "the use of extreme chromaticism, strict part writing and imitation, contrapuntal artifice and, above all, an appeal to nearly extinct gestures from the musical past," the latter being the descending tetrachord of the lament bass (1991: 330–31). Indeed, Mozart highlights the lament topic right at its opening theme (Example 15.23a).[19] To this list of neo-baroque features, at least for this theme, we could add the generally uniform texture and steady harmonic rhythm. Here, the theme consists exclusively of the lament schema, such that the arrival on ⑤ brings a half cadence. The harmonic plan of the very opening resembles the Beethoven variation's theme just discussed, and so a modicum of initiating function is projected by the harmonic dimension. But unlike Beethoven's theme, which was clearly structured as a sentence theme-type, Mozart barely hints at classical phrase structure: the passage does not readily parse into discreet ideas or phrases, and the sense of its constituent formal functions is largely projected by harmony alone, albeit mm. 4–5 bring a modest acceleration in surface rhythm to support a sense of medial functionality. Indeed, a listener hearing the piece for the first time would be unlikely to guess that it was written at the height of the classical period. This backward-looking stance even continues into the opening of the Allegro (Example 15.23b), where Mozart brings a kind of *maggiore* variation on the lament bass (also noted by Dreyfus [1991: 330]), and even continues the stepwise bass descent down a full octave, thus evoking the Romanesca–Prinner combination of the earlier galant style. Compare this, of course, to Beethoven's *maggiore* (Example 15.22b), which transports his baroque-tinged theme fully into the high classical era.

EXAMPLE 15.22 Beethoven, Thirty-Two Variations in C minor, WoO 80: (a) Theme, mm. 1–8;
(b) Variation 12 (*Maggiore*), mm. 97–104.

EXAMPLE 15.23 Mozart, Adagio and Allegro in F minor, K. 594: (a) mm. 1–7; (b) mm. 40–43.

We have seen in the course of this study that the lament topic is highly adaptable to a wide variety of form-functional situations within a thematic unit. Its most natural formal position is that of "being-in-the-middle," since its fundamentally sequential harmonic expression associates itself directly to various medial functions, especially the continuation phrase of a theme. But the schema is also suitable for closing a thematic unit when its concluding pitch ⑤ supports a cadential dominant of some sort (either the ultimate dominant of a half cadence or the penultimate dominant of an authentic cadence). Indeed, when the lament topic is used as a ground bass, the potential for playing with listeners' expectations of closure can especially be engaged, as the Bach "Crucifixus" examples well illustrated. More complicated are the various ways in which the lament schema can project a sense of formal beginning: the various examples discussed here have shown a continuum of possibilities, ranging from the powerful expression of initiation offered at the very opening of Mozart's D-minor quartet (Example 15.19) to the barest hint of a beginning, as with the Introduzione of Beethoven's "Waldstein" (Example 15.21a). We observed as well that, when the lament appears at the very start of a theme, a sense of form-functional dissonance can arise between the schema's intrinsic expression of medial functionality and its contextual position as a formal beginning.

With its stepwise descending bass line, the lament schema assimilates itself well to baroque compositional practice, which tends to emphasize melodic descent in its lowest voice. Despite the many examples of the topic in the classical era and beyond,[20] its use in baroque compositions is ubiquitous, as Williams's survey and Dreyfus's comments on a "nearly extinct gesture" affirm. In the classical style, the descending bass rubs somewhat against the standard practice of ascending bass lines, and so the topic tends to appear most typically in sequential passages, where descending bass-line structures more readily arise within that style. Occurring at the opening of a classical theme, the topic often seems to reference earlier compositional eras.

Finally, the kind of detailed technical discussion that I have brought to bear on the relationship of topic to formal function might seem somewhat out of place in a larger study of musical topics, such as the present volume, which naturally enough tends to focus attention on the aesthetic and historical issues associated with topical reference. We must always be aware, however, that a composer's decision where and how to employ a given topic is not exclusively a matter of his or her desire to express a specific affect or to allude to some extra-musical meaning; a topic cannot simply be thrown into the formal discourse willy-nilly. Rather, the use of a topic must also be grounded in the set of constraints—be they harmonic, melodic, rhythmic, formal, and so forth—that govern all compositional activity. The appearance of any given topic must ultimately be integrated into the compositional fabric in ways that conform to the structural goals intended by the composer.

Notes

1. The designations "natural" and "flat" are made in reference to the key of C minor, whereby in the course of the scalar descent, the seventh and sixth degrees are notated first with a natural sign and then with a flat sign, as shown in Example 15.1b. This designation of the scale-degrees will be retained throughout this study, even in other tonal contexts, where different combinations of natural, flat, and sharp signs might obtain in the actual musical notation.

2. Note that for the sake of consistency, I continue to identify the stages here in reference to the bass notes, even though this creates a conflict with the underlying sequential pattern of descending triads; in the perception of this version, we might alternatively associate each stage with each harmony of the sequential progression.

3. The following description of the sentence follows Caplin (1998: 35–48).

4. That the melodic goal C♯ at m. 4 still seems to be part of the sequence, in fact, diminishes somewhat our sense of half cadence at this moment; moreover, the prominent appearance of the dissonant seventh within the dominant harmony clouds our perception of a genuine half-cadential articulation.

5. Most typically, the initial harmony of the pattern is VI⁶, but other non-tonic chords are found as well (e.g., IV$^6_4$ at m. 25, V⁹/iv at m. 41).

6. Though each PAC is equally strong syntactically, the first one is slightly less "perfect" rhetorically than the second, inasmuch as the structural melodic descent $\hat{3}$–$\hat{2}$–$\hat{1}$ appears in the alto voice (lying above the soprano) in mm. 28–29, while that same descent is restored more appropriately to the soprano in mm. 48–49; on the distinction between *syntactic* and *rhetorical* strength of cadences, see Caplin (2004: 106).

7. On the distinction between an ultimate dominant of a half cadence and a penultimate dominant of an authentic cadence, see Caplin (1998: 29).

8. See, for example, the bass-line reductions in Lester (1999: 27–33, esp. exx. 2–3 and 2–5).

9. Bach's "Air" also opens with a variant of the Romanesca.

10. See also, Mozart, String Quartet in C, K. 465/iv, mm. 55–59; Beethoven, String Quartet in G, Op. 18 No. 2/iii, Trio, mm. 1–8.

11. A compound basic idea consists of a two-measure basic idea followed by a two-measure contrasting idea without cadential closure (Caplin 1998: 61).

12. There are actually some unusual features of mm. 3–4 that challenge the interpretation of an IAC at the end of the opening phrase. In the first place, where we would expect a pre-dominant to appear in the first half of the measure, given the bass support of ④, the harmony is actually more dominant than pre-dominant, the F in the soprano and D in the alto being suspensions from the prior i$^6_4$; but inasmuch as this dominant first appears inverted, then we should be suspicious of interpreting a genuine authentic cadence on the downbeat of m. 4 (see Caplin 2004 for the harmonic requirement that a cadential dominant must remain at all times in root position). Second, we will shortly discuss that the PAC closing the consequent phrase appears in the middle of m. 8. It is very unusual for the cadence of an antecedent to be metrically positioned earlier in the measure than that of the consequent; normally both cadences occur on the same position. Indeed, many of the cadences in the rest of the movement appear in the middle of the measure, thus suggesting that we are dealing with a situation of what eighteenth-century theorists called "compound meter," whereby each notated measure consists of two simple measures. For that reason, we might wonder whether the opening phrase might also be seen to end in the middle of m. 4. In order to find a cadence there, we would have to hear the arrival on the A in the melody as articulating dominant harmony (despite the lack of bass voice), a possible, but not immediately obvious interpretation.

13. We thus must be open to recognizing that whereas we would probably still want to interpret the second phrase as a consequent, inasmuch as there is a clear return of the basic idea in mm. 5–6, these measures nonetheless project a certain "continuational" quality due to the harmonization of the idea.

14. The harmonic pattern is based on that shown in Example 15.2f, except that the subtonic harmony is minor (vii), a most unusual realization of the lament pattern.

15. In both movements, it should be noted, the lament bass is used within a prevailing major-mode context, a classical feature already noted in connection with the Haydn sonata (Example 15.17).

16. On the distinction between *tight-knit* and *loose* formal expression, see Caplin (1998: 13, 17).

17. Compare this to the "Waldstein" first movement, where the tonic prolongation is broken already at the arrival of $\flat\hat{7}$, which supports the sequential repetition beginning on VII.

18. Alternatively, the diminished-seventh chord could be enharmonically interpreted as a secondary dominant of V, and thus the I^6 could be seen as a passing chord within a broader pre-dominant prolongation, just as the i^6_4 functioned in the theme (see Example 15.22a, m. 6).

19. The topical reference here is explicit, in that the work was commissioned to memorialize the recently deceased Field-Marshal Gideon Baron von Laudon, a national war hero (Dreyfus 1991: 330).

20. See Williams (1997) for a survey of the topic as it appears throughout the nineteenth and well into the early decades of the twentieth century.

References

Agawu, V. Kofi. 1991. *Playing with Signs: A Semiotic Interpretation of Classic Music*. Princeton: Princeton University Press.

Bernhard, Christoph. 1648–49. *Tractatus compositionis augmentatus*. Reprinted *as Die Kompositionslehre Heinrich Schützens in der Fassung seines Schülers Christoph Bernhard*, ed. Joseph Müller-Blattau. Leipzig: Breitkopf und Härtel, 1926.

Caplin, William E. 1998. *Classical Form: A Theory of Formal Functions for the Instrumental Music of Haydn, Mozart, and Beethoven*. New York: Oxford University Press.

——. 2004. The Classical Cadence: Conceptions and Misconceptions. *The Journal of the American Musicological Society* 57/1: 51–117.

——. 2005. On the Relation of Musical *Topoi* to Formal Function. *Eighteenth-Century Music* 2/1: 113–24.

——. 2008. Schoenberg's "Second Melody," or, "Meyer-ed" in the Bass. In *Communication in Eighteenth-Century Music*, ed. Danuta Mirka and Kofi Agawu, 160–88. Cambridge: Cambridge University Press.

——. 2013. Teaching Classical Form: Strict Categories versus Flexible Analyses. *Tijdschrift voor Muziektheorie* 18/3: 119–35.

Dreyfus, Lawrence. 1991. The Hermeneutics of Lament: A Neglected Paradigm in a Mozartian *Trauermusik*. *Music Analysis* 10/3: 329–43.

Gjerdingen, Robert O. 2007. *Music in the Galant Style*. New York: Oxford University Press.

Krebs, Harald. 1999. *Fantasy Pieces: Metrical Dissonance in the Music of Robert Schumann*. New York: Oxford University Press.

Lester, Joel. 1999. *Bach's Works for Solo Violin: Style, Structure, Performance*. New York: Oxford University Press.

Monelle, Raymond. 2000. *The Sense of Music: Semiotic Essays*. Princeton: Princeton University Press.

Rosand, Ellen. 1979. The Descending Tetrachord: An Emblem of Lament. *The Musical Quarterly* 65/3: 346–59.

Sanguinetti, Giorgio. 2012. *The Art of Partimento*. New York: Oxford University Press.

Schoenberg, Arnold. 1967. *Fundamentals of Musical Composition*, ed. Gerald Strang and Leonard Stein. London: Faber & Faber.

Vallières, Michel, Daphne Tan, William E. Caplin, and Stephen McAdams. 2009. Perception of Intrinsic Formal Functionality: An Empirical Investigation of Mozart's Materials. *Journal of Interdisciplinary Music Studies* 3/1–2: 17–43.

Williams, Peter. 1997. *The Chromatic Fourth during Four Centuries of Music*. Oxford: Clarendon.

CHAPTER 16

··

TOPICS AND TONAL PROCESSES

··

JOEL GALAND

TOWARD the end of Beethoven's *Missa solemnis*, a bucolic "Dona nobis pacem" emerges in a flowing 6/8, offering a vision of the "outer and inner peace" that could be restored to us, were we ever redeemed from the fallen state figured in the preceding "Agnus Dei." The key is D major, the Mass's overall tonic, but on two occasions, Beethoven abruptly shifts to a military style in B flat major to accommodate repetitions of the phrase "Agnus Dei, qui tollis peccata mundi." The first time (mm. 164–89), Beethoven does not restore D major immediately upon resuming the 6/8 music, turning instead toward F major (mm.190–201), the point of departure for a chromatic sequence based on the ascending 5–6 paradigm (mm. 200–12) and leading to G major for the fugue subject entry at m. 216. Earlier, G major was the key of the "Benedictus," another idyllic movement in a compound triple meter (12/8). For analysts sensitive to topical allusions, the musical style of the "Benedictus" and the "Dona nobis" must surely evoke the pastorale. There is evidence that composers in Beethoven's time associated both F major and G major with this topical field. Could Beethoven's using them here indicate that his choice of tonal plan was connected to his topical allusions?

Beethoven was certainly familiar with Austrian Mass traditions, including the convention of setting off the "Benedictus" from the "Sanctus" and the "Dona nobis" from the "Agnus Dei" through marked affective contrast, even though each text pair expresses a single prayer in the liturgy. He would have encountered the subgenre of the *Missa pastoralis*, even if he did not necessarily know Haydn's *Missa Sancti Nicolai*, whose framing "Kyrie" and "Dona nobis pacem" consist in a G-major pastorale in 6/4 time. In any case, the pastorale associations of the "Dona nobis" were in Beethoven's mind, judging from the annotation "*pacem* pastoralisch" that appears among the sketches for the "Agnus Dei" (Drabkin 1991: 137). We also know that Beethoven associated F major with the pastorale on earlier occasions and not only in the Sixth Symphony.[1]

In short, it is not unreasonable to suppose that topic and tonal plan interact somehow in the final pages of the *Missa solemnis*. My charge in this chapter is to explore how far we may generalize this conclusion for the classical repertoire, and for instrumental music in particular, for which text-setting conventions such as operate in Austrian

Mass cycles do not obtain. If it were possible to correlate topic and tonal process, topic theory might acquire a firmer purchase on mainstream analytical methods. To what extent did the choice of musical topics and tonal plans in a composition mutually condition one another? Might it be possible to "semanticize" the tonal paths taken by eighteenth-century and early nineteenth-century composers on the basis of the keys with which certain topics were associated?

At this point, it may be helpful to distinguish between three categories of topic–key interaction. First, a composition can be in the typical key of its prevailing topic, as is the case in Haydn's *Missa Sancti Nicolai* or Beethoven's Symphony No. 6. This type of interaction is tangential to present study, which is concerned with topic and tonal *process*. Second, the onset of a topic in its typical key might coincide with a modulation that could not have been predicted from generic or formal norms alone. Such is the case with the F-major passage cited from the *Missa solemnis*. To be sure, tonicized chromatic mediants are part of the musical language of Beethoven's time, but they are stylistically marked. We can hypothesize that the topic appropriate to this section of the mass cycle influenced the tonal trajectory, "causing" a swerve into a relatively remote region. I will refer to this type of interaction between topic and key as "deviation" in order to indicate the effect of topic on tonal plan. Third, topics might fit into a conventional tonal plan. The G-major passage cited from the *Missa solemnis* is a case in point; there is nothing unusual in itself about moving to the subdominant key for a contrasting middle section—episode within a rondo, trio within a minuet, or Benedictus within a Sanctus. The fit between the key and the topic can be a matter of coincidence but, in this and other similar cases, we can hypothesize that the tonal plan influenced the choice of topic. I will refer to this interplay between key and topic as "coordination."

On the basis of examining hundreds of instrumental movements by the familiar Viennese classical triumvirate,[2] I find that while there is solid evidence for the first category—topics bearing on the choice of a piece's overall tonic—Haydn, Mozart, and Beethoven have not systematically exploited the second category (deviation). This does not mean that the rare manifestations of deviation are necessarily happenstance. The possibility of topic influencing tonal plan is something, I will conclude, that we should include in our analytical "tool kit." My third category (coordination) is the trickiest of all, because it refers to tonal processes likely to unfold anyway, regardless of the musical topics at hand, but it posits an influence of such processes on selection and succession of topics. While this influence cannot be proven, neither can it be precluded; composers may sometimes have coordinated topics with tonal processes by selecting topics that fit into the tonal plan of a musical form. The complementary categories of "deviation" and "coordination" make clear that, rather than a one-way influence of topics on tonal plan, in this chapter I discuss mutual influences between them. Insofar as I aim at assessing the influence of topics on the structure of Classic music, my study echoes earlier efforts by William Caplin (2005), who, in order to allay the suspicion that applying topic theory to music analysis amounts to little more than sprinkling referential garnishes on a structurally substantial dish, has explored the possibility of correlating musical topics with their formal functions.

In the second section of this chapter, I review those associations between topic and key that have been reasonably well established. While these associations are hardly exclusive—no topic appears in one key only—we can conclude that some topics were more "at home" in some keys than in others. In the third section, I describe the inter-action of topic and tonal plan in specific musical passages, although, necessarily, in an "informal, ad hoc" (Caplin 2005: 124) manner that can be merely suggestive for future analytical work. But first, I address some of the challenges in assessing the relation-ship between topic and formal process, and I establish a few conditions under which an alleged connection between the two might be either dismissed or considered potentially significant.

CONDITIONS

The first condition to speaking sensibly about a connection between topics and tonal plan is a strong connection between a key and a topic. How did certain keys become allied with particular topics? Evidently, eighteenth-century writers associated keys with affects that, in turn, were deemed more appropriate for certain styles or genres than oth-ers. And a style or a genre, for its part, could be used as a topic if it was imported to another context. But a cursory survey of the field reveals that keys are characteristic of comparatively few topics. The most comprehensive "dictionary" of eighteenth-century topics of which I am aware is Kofi Agawu's "Universe of Topics for Classic Music."[3] Several of Agawu's sixty-one topics, such as the "murky bass," are arguably not topics at all, in the sense that they do not imitate other musical styles or genres, although they may appear as *features* or figurae of styles or genres.[4] Other topics, notably dance topics like minuet and gigue—might permeate an entire piece. Voice-leading techniques such as the strictly controlled suspension chains characteristic of the *stile legato* (which in turn is a feature of the "learned style") are part and parcel of the idiom and occur in all sorts of pieces. The chances of such topics sounding in key X are the same as those of the passage housing them being in key X. Nonetheless, there are a handful of topics whose tokens are more typically expressed in some keys than in others. It turns out (as a for-ward glance at Table 16.1 will confirm) that these topics are also the most complex, those that Raymond Monelle describes as "great topical worlds that constitute musical and cultural genres" (2000: 5). They do not have a simple signifier (like the limping rhythm of *alla zoppa*) but rather a network of signifiers, not all of which need be present in the token at hand. Their signifieds are equally complex, encompassing several cultural units and accommodating multiple intellectual interpretants.[5]

Once we grant that certain complex topics have characteristic keys, how do we go from there to making convincing assertions about the influence of topic on tonal pro-cesses in actual pieces? Only some of the twenty-four possible major and minor keys appear frequently in the classical repertoire, among them precisely those keys that carry relatively robust topical associations.[6] It would be much easier to correlate tonal plans with topical syntagma if rare keys alone conventionally indexed topics, but this was evidently not the case. To be sure, a key like C flat minor will be marked in opposition to a relatively common key like B flat major, and we can safely predict that musical passages set in seldom encountered keys will likewise be marked in some way. Consider an extraordinary moment from the finale of Mozart's Piano Concerto in B flat major, K. 456. The finale is cast as a binary rondo, consisting of an exposition (mm. 1–144) followed by an expanded recapitulation (mm. 145–324).[7] Eighteen measures into the recapitulation, Mozart modulates to C flat minor (notated as B minor) and then inserts an eight-measure phrase in that key (mm. 171–78). Wide leaps in the bassoon and rapid arpeggiations in the solo piano point to the *tempesta* topic. When Mozart repeats the phrase in mm. 179–87, however, the leaps and arpeggiations are gone; instead a new, pathetic solo subject, lyrical and yearning, emerges from the implacable tutti background, much like the human figures foregrounded in the landscapes of Caspar David Friedrich. The obvious topical allusion is to *Empfindsamkeit*, an association reinforced by the soloist's repeated *pianto* figure. After a retransitional passage (mm. 185–208), the recapitulation resumes as if nothing had happened. In retrospect, we realize that Mozart interpolated the C-flat-minor passage, temporarily interrupting the recapitulation, with its prevailing hunting gigue topic. Within the topical universe of Mozart's concerto rondos, the B-flat-major hunting gigue is unmarked, while the C-flat-minor *tempesta/Empfindsamkeit* passage *is* marked (unique, in fact). Now, several of the eighteenth-century descriptions of B minor assembled in Steblin (2002: 295–98) are compatible with both *tempesta* and *Empfindsamkeit*.[8] But the same can be said of other rare minor keys, such as B flat minor (mm. 291–93) or G sharp/A flat minor (mm. 280–81). Nor is the Mozart C-flat-minor passage topically unusual in itself—it would be equally at home in a more conventional *tempesta* key like D minor.

Another challenge in discovering significant correlations between topics and tonal processes is that the same broad tonal plans (i.e., those belonging to a Schenkerian middle ground) are shared by a great many movements. This is obviously the case for sonata expositions, but it is also the case to some extent for developments, for which there are a handful of relatively common middle-ground paradigms, as Edward Laufer (1991) has demonstrated. Compounding the difficulty are the correlations, however fragile, that Caplin and other theorists have found between certain topics and formal functions. For example, C major is Haydn's key for ceremonial symphonies with trumpets and drums, and it is a martial key, according to a decisive majority of Steblin's witnesses (2002: 226–30). Military-type themes or those containing fanfares are typically opening gestures—they precede or inaugurate tonal processes. Rarely does the *arrival* of C major as a new key coincide with a sudden shift to a military topic (although I identify one such passage below). Or consider the musette-like pedal point, a pastoral *figura*. As Caplin (2005: 117–18) points out, musettes are especially appropriate for post-cadential formal functions.[9] It is indeed easy to find closing sections combining pedal points with tunes that strike us as rustic or bucolic; Haydn's "popular" closing themes are often of this type. Sometimes, such tunes sound in the pastoral keys of F or G major—almost necessarily so in either the exposition or the recapitulation if the movement is in B flat major, C major, F major, G major, D minor, E minor, F minor, or G minor (assuming that expositional major-mode material remains major in the recapitulation).

In short, if the onset of a topic coincides with a predictable tonal goal (our "coordination" category) and its musical characteristics suit the formal function it articulates, we should be cautious about invoking that event to support the thesis that tonal processes were shaped by the composer's intention to reach tonal centers associated with certain types of musical expression. A hint of D-minor *tempesta* within the development of a pastorale-inflected F-major movement, for example, could be epiphenomenal to what Hepokoski and Darcy (2006) might term "a first-level default" for development sections, namely modulating to the submediant minor.[10] Does the exposition of Haydn's String Quartet in C major, Op. 74 No. 1/iv, which ends with a sixteen-measure musette in G major, significantly correlate topic and tonal plan? In the rondo finale from Mozart's String Quintet in G minor, K. 516, the pastoral amelioration to the slow introduction (not to mention to the first and third movements) certainly completes a significant topical trajectory. But does the G-minor/major modal shift in itself represent a significant mapping of tonal process onto that trajectory, even though G major is a typical pastoral key?

All other things being equal, the more unusual a tonal plan, the more significant the correlation between that plan and the topical surface. That is why the chorus "Hört, hört das laute Getön" from Haydn's *The Seasons* must be so exciting to the topic analyst. It has an unusual, sharply etched tonal plan, moving from the French hunting key of D major to the German hunting key of E flat major and ending there. We have no trouble identifying the musical topic at hand, even if we don't happen to be familiar with the actual hunting tunes that Haydn quotes or paraphrases.[11] It is hard to imagine a more persuasive example of topic influencing tonal plan but most pieces do not conveniently move between two distantly related keys, both of which bear widely agreed on topical associations and both of which unambiguously express these topics in the sense of actually incorporating appropriate repertoire. In order to talk about the influence of topic on tonal processes, we need to identify topics and we need to identify tonal centers, and rarely are those analytical enterprises as straightforward as they are for "Hört, hört das laute Getön."

Problems with identification of topics have been frequently discussed by authors interested in topical analysis.[12] Similar considerations apply to identifying tonal centers. I began by taking a passage from the *Missa solemnis* to exemplify the interaction of topic and tonal process. Originally, however, I had planned to use it as a negative example, because the F major is so transient. The dominant of F resolves twice, the first time to an unstable F-major six-four chord (m. 194) that moves, unusually, to a subdominant triad (the subdominant inflection, of course, reinforces the reference to the pastorale). The second time yields the only authentic $\hat{5}$–$\hat{1}$ bass motion in the passage (mm. 199–200), but this potential cadence is undercut (to borrow a useful concept from Hatten [1994: 99–100]) by several factors: the melody only reaches $\hat{3}$; the bass in m. 199 reaches $\hat{1}$ on a weak eighth, after the other voices have resolved; the subsequent downbeat—the only time in the passage that an F-major five-three chord is metrically stressed—coincides with a *subito pp*; and an E♭ in m. 201 transforms the barely tonicized F into a V⁷, launching the chromatic sequence that will connect to the G-major sixth chord at m. 211, in preparation for the G-major fugue subject. Much depends, obviously, on how high individual analysts set the bar for identifying a tonal center. It is reasonable to argue that Beethoven does not establish F major as a tonal center at all. Nonetheless, he does briefly use the F-major signature. The coordination of pastoral musical traits—of which the fleetingly evoked F major is only one—with a text carrying pastoral imagery finally persuaded me, to offer the passage as a positive example.

After all, just because the "knockdown" argument we can make for Haydn's hunting chorus is rarely possible does not mean we must rule out the possibility that composers sometimes correlated tonal processes and formal functions elsewhere. Even when a tonal process—like a D-minor arrival in the development of an F-major movement—is unexceptionable in itself, the analyst may be able to suggest that the composer has coordinated tonal event and topic in a way that calls itself to our attention. In other words, an unmarked feature can be deployed in a marked manner.

TOPIC AND KEY

Eighteenth-century opera presents ample evidence of composers' sensitivity to the association of key and thematic character or affect. Topical—not just affective—associations come to the fore in Viennese opera buffa. John Platoff (1997) has demonstrated that while there is only limited empirical evidence—from both historical sources and statistical analysis of the repertoire—for the large-scale tonal architectures sometimes imputed to Mozart's operas, there is strong evidence that short-range tonal choices were occasionally governed by convention: "At least some of the time, Mozart and other composers chose keys (perhaps especially for arias) by relying on the conventional association of particular keys with certain character-types, affects, or dramatic situations" (148). He cites Salieri, who claimed in his memoirs that he set about composing an opera by first reading the libretto and "decid[ing] on the key appropriate to the character of each lyric number" (149). Platoff's statistical analysis reveals that G major is associated with "peasant simplicity" (148), that "F is the prime key for what might be called '6/8 maidservant' arias" (154), and that roughly three-quarters of numbers with trumpets and timpani are in C or D major (155). Although Platoff does not mention topics directly here (but see Platoff 1992), he mentions affects associated with them: "martial, noble, or grandiose sentiments, whether serious or comic" for the D-major trumpet-and-drum key, and "naïve sentiments (often amorous longings) or their reverse, cynical reflections on men and the game of love" for the F-major 6/8 arias. These affects are straightforwardly related to topics—march and military for the trumpet-and-drum keys and the pastorale for F and G major. Goehring (2004) does not focus on key relations, but the many examples he cites of pastoral passages and maid servant arias from a variety of eighteenth-century Viennese operas suggest similar conclusions. I would like, by way of example, to review at some length the evidence for our two pastorale key associations and then move more briskly through other topics that may be linked with specific keys: *ombra, tempesta,* hunt, and military.

The association of the pastorale with F and G does not, for the most part, stem directly from eighteenth-century writers. Of the many descriptions of F major that Steblin compiles (2002: 258–62), only one directly associates that key with the pastorale, and it happens to be the only noncontemporaneous passage: Hugo Leichtentritt, writing in 1938. Nonetheless, Steblin's sources do reveal consistent associations between F major and affective states consonant with the topic. It is "peaceful," "calm," or "quietly joyful" for half of the authors writing after about 1780. Vogler mentions that in Gluck's *Orpheus* and his own *Castor and Pollux* "this key appeared to agree especially with a quiet joy in the happy shades of Elysium." (And what is the pastorale, after all, but an attempt through art to recapture a lost paradise?) With the G-major descriptions (270–73), we are on even firmer ground; ten out of thirty descriptions, including those of Vogler, Schubart, Schilling, and Hand, invoke the idyllic or the rustic. Vogler, writing in 1812, asserts that "it was always the favorite key for Pastorals." Others, like Galeazzi, write more generally about simplicity and innocence. Only Grétry's adjective "warlike" flat-out contradicts the topic.

Richard Will (2002) lists seventy-two eighteenth- and early nineteenth-century characteristic symphonies with *pastorale* or some closely related term in the title. Of these, twenty-six (36%) are in D; ten (14%) are in C, nine (12.5%) are in G (12.5%); and only eight (11%) are F (one key is unidentified). It may be significant, however, that at least sixteen of the D-major works date from before 1780, while F major emerges thereafter, in pastoral symphonies by Beethoven, Ott, Roessler, Toeschi, and Touchemoulin. There were others that Will does not cite, like Franz Anton Hoffmeister's Symphony in F (*La primavera*) of 1793.

D major does seem to have been a favorite key for pastorale symphonies and Masses in the middle decades of the eighteenth century. Surveying the Austrian pastoral Mass tradition, Bruce MacIntyre (1996: 117–18) offers a comprehensive listing of pastoral musical traits, including the "use of a pastoral key (G? D? C?)" (his question marks). He cites Mark Germer (1989: 126), who examined sixty-five pastoral Masses and found that a little over 50 percent were in D major, followed by C (17%) and G (15%). The G-major pieces, however, include some of the more celebrated examples, like Vanhal's *Missa pastoralis* and Haydn's Advent Mass *Missa Sancti Nicolai*. By Beethoven's time, G major seems to have been firmly established as the key for pastoral Masses and pastorellas, leading David Wyn Jones (1995) to speculate that "had Beethoven done the unlikely exercise of ascertaining which key was most likely to be associated with pastoral subject matter he would have probably concluded G major" (51). Citing the divergent affects eighteenth-century writers attribute to it, Jones concludes that is "little evidence that F major was widely regarded as a pastoral key," though he believes it *was* one for Beethoven. He credits the influence of Haydn's oratorios, in which several F-major movements have pastoral content. (The two most obvious pastoral numbers in *The Seasons* are the chorus "Komm, holder Lenz!" and Simon's aria "Der munt're

Table 16.1 Some Additional Topical Key Associations (Affective Associations from Eighteenth- and Early Nineteenth-Century Sources Cited in Steblin 2002.)

Topic	Keys	Musical Examples	Some Relevant Contemporaneous Affective Key Associations
hunt	D	Méhul, *La chasse du jeune Henri* Haydn, Symphony No. 73, "La chasse," iv	The association with both keys is based on physical factors (the construction of hunting horns) rather than affective associations.
	E flat	Haydn, Symphony No. 22, "The Philosopher," iv Mozart, String Quintet K. 614/i	
tempesta	d (but also c and other minor keys)	Mozart, Piano Concerto K. 466 Gluck, *Don Juan*, No. 31	Most remarks are more appropriate for slower tempos, accommodating *ombra* or lament, than for *tempesta*.
ombra (overlapping with lament)	c	Mozart, *Idomeneo*, Nos. 5, 17, and 24 (choruses and "the voice")	Plaintive, pathetic, or lamenting (Masson, Schubart, Grétry, Rochlitz, inter alia); tragic and ominous (Galeazzi).
	d (less often f and g)	Mozart, *Don Giovanni*, Overture and Finale	Melancholy (Grétry and most other authors), gloomy (Galeazzi), "ghost must speak in d minor" (Anon), lament (Hand).
ombra (shading into "exalted march")	E	Numerous *ombra* scenes from Jomelli operas Mozart, *Mitridate*, Act 3 Scene 4	Religious character (Schubart, Leseur); majesty and solemnity (Mattheson, Galeazzi, Castil-Blaze, and numerous others).
"exalted march" (Allanbrook 1983)	E flat	Mozart, *Don Giovanni* (much of Donna Elvira's music) Mozart, *Sinfonia concertante* K. 364/i Mozart, *Idomeneo* Quartet Mozart, Wind Serenade K. 375	The above plus heroism (Galeazzi); battle or military key (Andersch, Schilling, Sulzer).
march (This topic can be widened to include the family of military-inflected topics, such as fanfare, as well as ceremonial marches. The latter category can include pieces in triple meter. See Andrew Haringer's chapter, this volume.)	C	The many Haydn C-major symphonies with trumpets and drums (in both triple and duple meter) Mozart, *Le nozze di Figaro*, "Non più andrai"	Military or martial (Charpentier, Galeazzi, Wagner, inter alia).
	D		Warlike or martial (Mattheson, Hawkins, Schubart, Sulzer, many others).
Turkish	A/a, B flat, C/c, D, F, G	Mozart, Piano Sonata K. 331/iii Mozart, Violin Concerto K. 219/iii Beethoven, Symphony No. 9/iv	

Hirt versammelt nun," in G and F, respectively). Krones (2000), too, hears F major as Haydn's pastoral key. Geoffrey Chew, another scholar who has studied pastorale musical traditions in eighteenth-century Austria, has excavated resonances of the Austrian pastorella genre in Mozart's operas. In this context, he refers to Susanna's "Deh vieni" and its "classic F major" (1996: 183). He finds that Papageno's "Der Vogelfänger bin ich ja" "matches many typical strophic *ariae pastorellae* of a generation earlier, in tempo and time (Andante, 2/4) ... [and] in key (G major)" (184).

There is, in short, sufficient scholarly consensus for considering both F major and G major as pastoral keys. Certainly, examples from the repertoire abound. To "Deh vieni" and the Haydn oratorio numbers, we can add the numerous 6/8 pastorales or rustic gigues in both F and G that turn up in Viennese opera buffa. A few familiar examples include the G-major peasant choruses in *Le nozze di Figaro* (No. 8 "Giovani liete" and No. 21 "Ricevete, o padroncino") and *Don Giovanni* (No. 5 "Giovinette che fate all' amore"); Zerlina's F-major first aria ("Batti, batti"); and both of Despina's arias (in F and G, respectively). The convention continues well into the nineteenth century, particularly in operetta—the genre in which eighteenth-century topics most obviously subsist. In *Die Fledermaus*, the chambermaid Adèle's aria "Spiel' ich die Unschuld vom Lande" opens with an ironic pastorale (6/8, G major), while large swathes of Offenbach's pastoral *opera-bouffe, Le chateau à Toto* (1868), sound in F and G.

Of course, the topic appears in other keys as well. Flat keys and pastorale tokens dominate what Allanbrook has dubbed the "private finale" of *Figaro*, the central section of the last number, during which Figaro and Susanna reconcile: "Flat keys are especially suited to the pastorale because of their soft, mellow sound and their slanting relation to the main and public key of the opera, D major" (1983: 146). Thus, Figaro and Susanna's "Pace, pace, mio dolce tesoro," in a flowing 6/8, is in B flat major. So is Dorabella's stylistically similar "È amore un ladroncello" from *Così fan tutte*. Figaro's soliloquy "Tutto è tranquillo e placido" (Finale of Act 4, mm. 109–20) is in E flat major; although this passage is not in a characteristic compound triple meter, the classical poetic imagery, the modulation to the flat key from the preceding G major, and the parallel thirds in the horns all lead Allanbrook to situate this interlude within the pastoral mode (1983:146). Although in opera buffa we do not encounter pastorales in keys beyond three flats, pastorale passages in A flat or D flat major are common enough in instrumental music. For example there are the "purple patches" in A flat and D flat over drone basses in the finale of Beethoven's Cello Sonata in C major, Op. 102 No. 1 (mm. 75–95, 184–212).[13] The topic also emerges in sharp keys beyond D major, such as A major ("Là ci darem la mano") and E major (*Idomeneo*, No. 15 "Placido è il mar"). Finally, there are minor-mode pastorales, like Barberina's F-minor cavatina from *Figaro*. Sicilianos are often cast in minor, as in Mozart's Piano Concerto in A major, K. 488/ii (F sharp minor), or the variation theme of the String Quartet in D Minor, K. 421/iv. Despite such variability, however, this study takes it as established that F major and G major were the most conventional homes for the pastoral topic.

Table 16.1 collates additional topical key associations around which a scholarly consensus has formed.[14] The hunt topic has its characteristic keys—the French hunting key of D and the German key of E flat—by way of the actual construction of hunting horns, not to mention the keys of existing hunting calls, some of which composers imported wholesale into their works (as Leopold Mozart did in his *Jagd-Sinfonie* in D major, Méhul in *La chasse du jeune Henri*, and Haydn in *The Seasons* and the finale of the Symphony No. 72). The associations of the hunt topic with these keys have been convincingly established (Ringer 1953; Pöschl 1990; Monelle 2006).

Birgitte Moyer (1992) and Clive McClelland (2012) have placed the associations of the *ombra* topic with D minor and C minor on similarly sure footing. There is also an elevated style of *ombra* associated with E flat major; the *ombra* scene in Jomelli's *Fetonte* is paradigmatic. This more ceremonial manifestation of the topic shades into the subtopic that Allanbrook (1983: 19) has dubbed the "exalted march," which also seems to have a certain affinity with E flat major.[15] That the *ombra* topic appears in both D minor and E flat major may partially account for why the development of Mozart's D-minor quartet K. 421 opens the way it does. The only keys in which Mozart presents the *ombra*-inflected lament bass of his principal theme, analyzed in the preceding chapter by Caplin, is in D minor and, briefly, E flat major in mm. 42–45 (an instance of our "deviation" category), although in the latter passage, it is immediately deflected back to the minor mode.

C major and D major have been well established as keys appropriate for military and march topics. Recent confirmations include Platoff's statistical surveys of keys in opera buffa (1997) and A. Peter Brown's (1996) documentation of the Viennese trumpet symphony tradition that emerged in the late seventeenth century and flourished during the reign of Charles VI in numerous sinfonias by Caldara, Fux, and Wagenseil. Haydn's several C-major symphonies with trumpets and drums, Mozart's "Linz" and "Jupiter," Beethoven's First and Fifth Symphonies, and his "Consecration of the House" overture continue this tradition. So do the grand C-major and D-major symphonies of Anton and Paul Wranitsky, featuring virtuosic timpani and clarini writing, and graced with programmatic titles like *Grand Characteristic Symphony for Peace with the French Republic* (1797).[16]

At least one other topic—the Turkish style—has characteristic keys. According to Schubart (1806: 330–32), these are F and B flat major, although Germans composing in the Turkish style also adopt C and D major. Locke (2009: 118) observes that A major/minor, C major, B flat, and G major/minor are particularly frequent. Usually, a piece will establish the Turkish style at the outset.[17] A famous instance of the Turkish style emerging *within* a movement is, of course, the solo tenor variation in the Finale of Beethoven's Ninth Symphony; the sudden plunge into B-flat major from the preceding choral variation is one of the many juxtapositions of D and B flat heard throughout the cycle. The sheer number of keys associated with the Turkish style (five different tonics, all very common in the repertoire), however, make this topic less likely than the hunt, for example, to provide support for our hypothesis about the influence of topic on tonal processes.

Applications

In Mozart's opere buffe, there are multisectioned ensemble numbers whose tonal plans partially correlate with topic, even though, to return to Platoff's argument (1997), we must be careful not to go too far in discovering (or inventing) large-scale tonal archi-tectures across entire operas. We have already noted that Allanbrook contrasts the flat keys of the pastoral "private finale" in Act 4 of *Figaro* to the sharp-side "public keys" of the surrounding music. In the Act 1 finale of *Don Giovanni* it may be significant that when the Don attempts a garden seduction of Zerlina, the two sing in F major (mm. 92–138), which is also the key of the contredanse to which they exit with Masetto (mm. 139–69). The key then shifts to D minor with the entrance of the masked conspirators; of course, Donna Anna and Don Ottavio have been associated with this *ombra* key since the Introduzione and subsequent duet ("Fuggi, crudele"). The Act 2 sextet "Sola, sola in buio loco" begins with Elvira singing in E flat major, the key of her "exalted march" ("Ah chi mi dice mai") and of her last aria ("Mi tradì"), but, after a striking enharmonic modulation, Ottavio enters in D major (m. 27), which, owing to its military topical asso-ciation, indexes noble and heroic affects. At m. 45 Donna Anna enters in D minor and modulates to C minor; she is most at home in these *ombra* and *tempesta* keys. In this section, however, I will explore possible interactions of tonal process and topic in instru-mental music, beginning with the easily recognized military topic.

One of Haydn's many celebrated C-major symphonies with trumpets and drums is No. 60, assembled from his incidental music to Jean-François Regnard's *Le distrait*. Here, unlike some of the other C-major symphonies, such as No. 48 ("Maria Theresa") or No. 82 ("L'Ours"), there is nothing particularly martial about the opening sonata-allegro movement. But in the F-major, slow fourth movement—titled Adagio di lamentatione, but somewhat pastoral in mood—the predictable modulation to a C-major is confirmed by a new theme that abruptly introduces the military topic for the first time in the sym-phony, finally exploiting the hitherto underutilized trumpets and drums. F major to C major is unmarked as a tonal process, but I submit that here, the coordination of this process with topical references *is* marked. It is certainly an unusual moment. The belated introduction of the military style may stem from the Chevalier making his appearance only in the third act of the play (the movement would have been used as an entr'acte between the third and fourth acts). Moreover, the Chevalier is a toy soldier of a figure—among other things, he is exceptionally short—so Haydn's unusual shift to a military topic in the middle of this Adagio may be interpreted as a comic effect.[18]

The Symphony No. 82 in C major, "L'Ours," reverses this topical trajectory: this time, we go from military to pastorale. While the first movement includes militarily inflected topics, the finale opens with a musette that later recurs in F major. Restating the prin-cipal theme in the subdominant during the development is fairly common and there-fore generally offers poor evidence for our thesis about the influence of topics on tonal processes, even if the subdominant happens to be tonally appropriate for the theme's topic. In the case of "L'Ours," however, the abrupt opening of this development with the musette in F—the startling drop from dominant to subdominant—borders on our devi-ation technique and suggests a possible topical motivation for the tonal process.

Mozart's String Quartet in B flat major, K. 458, "The Hunt," furnishes another instance of a subdominant restatement with plausible topical relevance.[19] The first movement exploits the close musical relationship between the hunt and pastorale topics, which share their characteristic 6/8 meter, but B flat is not the key most closely associated with either. The principal theme is clearly a hunting gigue. The pastoral topic first emerges in the siciliano-styled closing theme (m. 77) and subsists in the episodic theme that opens the development (mm. 91–106); both of these passages are in F major.[20] For an iteration of the hunting theme in its "home key" of E flat major, however, we must wait until the recapitulation.[21] At m. 167, Mozart restates the principal theme—or more precisely, the variant of it that originally launched the transition at m. 27—in the subdominant. To be sure, subdominant inflections are normally unmarked in the context of recomposed transitions, so this would be a case of coordination rather than deviation.[22] It is rather less common, though, to restate faithfully the principal theme's four-measure incipit at the lower fifth, well after the tonic has been reestablished. The turn to the subdominant in revised transitions usually coincides with later material. The association of the principal theme's hunt topic with the German hunting key of E flat could have been a motivation for Mozart's tonal strategy in this particular recapitulation.

Another movement that combines aspects of both the *chasse* and the 6/8 pastorale is Haydn's String Quartet in D Major, Op. 33, No. 6/i.[23] Haydn touches on F major at the opening of the development for just four bars (mm. 59–63). The recapitulation is unusual. Measures 1–4 recur in the dominant only (mm. 71–74); following a brief interpolation that reestablishes D major, the recapitulation resumes with an almost literal tonic restatement of mm. 5–11 (= mm. 78–84). Measure 85, however, deviates from m. 12 just enough to prepare another interpolation that begins by prolonging E flat major (mm. 86–90); correspondence measures resume at m. 99 (= m. 13). The brief development and the parenthesis within the recapitulated primary theme yield a rapid juxtaposition of three principal hunting and pastorale keys.

Because F major and D minor are relative keys, contrasts within a movement between F-major pastorale topics and D-minor *tempesta* or *ombra*, while lending support to the association of these topics and keys, are not ordinarily to be considered proofs of the influence of topics on tonal processes, since the tonal processes involved would typically happen anyway. There would have to be something particularly striking about the way the composer articulates the F major–D minor pairing to posit a coordination of topic and key. The first movement of Haydn's Symphony No. 80 in D minor presents such an instance. The exposition begins in a *tempesta*-tinged D minor and ends with a rustic *Deutscher* in F major.[24] Less predictable is that when the development reaches A major, Haydn does not introduce standard retransitional rhetoric over a dominant pedal. Rather, he restates the *Deutscher* twice, first in A major at m. 110 and then in F major at m. 120. At the last minute, the F-major iteration casually veers back to D minor via an enharmonically shared diminished-seventh chord on E (VII°7 of F equaling VII°$_5^6$ of D); the recapitulation begins at m. 128. By effecting an unusual retransition (A–F–E–D instead of simply A–D for the bass plan), Haydn directly confronts the movement's two topical worlds together with their characteristic keys, in a way that was not possible in the exposition. He exploits an ordinarily unmarked correlation of topical trajectory and tonal process in a marked manner.

There should probably be a moratorium on using Mozart's Piano Sonata in F major, K. 332 for any further topical analysis, but this movement presents a coordinating strategy similar to the preceding Haydn example, only with a reversed tonal and topical trajectory.[25] As is well known, Mozart's principal theme might be characterized as a minuet inflected by pastorale and hunt. F major is, therefore, an entirely appropriate key, as are D minor and C minor for the *tempesta* eruptions that launch the transition, intrude on the second theme area, and dominate the development. But don't we usually encounter D minor sooner or later in F-major sonata movements? What makes the alliance of topic and tonal process so persuasive in K. 332 is that an unmarked tonal process is deployed in a marked manner. The sudden plunge into the relative D minor *simultaneously* launches the transition and the *tempesta* topic—and not just any transition could have juxtaposed pastorale and *tempesta* topics like this. Had Mozart's famously idiosyncratic and topically pluralistic principal theme been constructed as a more conventional, tight-knit sentence, it might have been placidly followed by a transition departing from the same F-major material, the principal theme and transition together forming a single unit of the type Adolf Bernhard Marx termed the "period with dissolving consequent" (*Periode mit aufgelöstem Nachsatz*).

The development's tonal processes are also marked with respect to what we might call a "first-level default" for major-mode development section during the third quarter or so of the eighteenth century. This default corresponds to Heinrich Christoph Koch's description of the first main period within the second reprise (1983: 200). Koch tells us that composers frequently lead this period to the submediant minor—or perhaps ii or iii—by way of a V-phrase (i.e., a phrase that reaches a half cadence in that key), confirm the key with a cadential phrase, and then return to the tonic by way of an appendix phrase (i.e., the retransition). Any random sonata-allegro movement from the 1760s and 1770s is more likely than not to proceed much as Koch describes. K. 332/i, however, is one of a relatively smaller number of movements that goes only as far as the half-cadential arrival on V/vi or III♯, omitting both the cadential phrase in vi and the retransition (although the composer might touch lightly on an inverted dominant).[26] This type of development permits Mozart to confront at a deep middle ground the keys associated with the minuet-inflected pastoral and *tempesta* topics already treated so paratactically in the exposition. We can hear the same abrupt contrast between A major (as the goal of a D-minor *tempesta* passage) and F major (as the onset of the recapitulation) in the first movement of Beethoven's Violin Sonata in F major, Op. 24, "Spring."

The juxtaposition of III♯ with I often occurs in F-major pieces; I have calculated that nearly 25 percent of Mozart instrumental pieces or movements with this development plan are in this key. It would be interesting if this telescoped developmental type were regularly encountered in combination with both the F/d tonal pairing *and* a topical opposition of pastorale and tempesta. This does not seem to be the case, however. For one thing, the development plan may be combined with this topical confrontation but in a different key. The transition and second group of Haydn's Symphony No. 85 in B flat major, "La Reine," exemplifies what Hepokoski and Darcy (2004: 170–77) have called the *trimodular block*. The transition (m. 42) reaches a "dominant lock" on V/V at

m. 52 and an apparent medial caesura at m. 61. What follows, however, is not yet the second theme but rather a *tempesta* outburst in F minor that soon dissolves into a second dominant lock and caesura (mm. 70–76, with "caesura fill" in mm. 76–77). The second theme proper follows, presenting a lyrically expanded, bucolic version of the principal theme in F major. The development, constructed as a sequential chain of variations on the principal theme, ends by returning to *tempesta* rhetoric in G minor (mm. 172–98) and closing on III♯. Haydn stands on this D-major chord for twenty-one measures; no retransition connects it to the B-flat-major recapitulation at m. 212. The extended false recapitulation in the Symphony No. 71, also in B flat major, is prepared in a similar fashion, with analogous topical and tonal parataxis: lock on III♯ in mm. 111–18, two-measure lead-in, and (provisional) tonic return of the principal theme in mm. 121–34.

Moreover, we cannot make any topical generalizations about this development type, whether or not the F/d pairing is involved. In the Piano Concerto in F major, K. 459, for example, Mozart maintains the prevailing march topic clear through the tonal contrast between D minor and F major. In Haydn's String Quartet in E major, Op. 54 No. 3, the context for the III♯–I succession is as bucolic as can be. The movement's prevailing topic is a pastoral-tinged bourrée; pedal points, mostly in the bass, occupy some 28 percent of the movement and 44 percent of the development, which ends with a drone bass on G♯ supporting III♯ (mm. 98–106). This pedal point connects directly to the recapitulation at m. 107. In this movement, the III♯ does not follow a tonicized vi (C sharp minor). An earlier pedal point had, to be sure, prolonged C♯ (mm. 88–94), but as V⁷/ii. The implied F sharp minor, however, never materializes; a D-major sixth chord at m. 95 replaces what could have been an F-sharp-minor arrival. Very little, in short, counteracts the movement's idyllic ethos, to which the many passages of harmonic stasis contribute. It may not be insignificant that, although the principal theme is in E major, it opens the development section in the pastoral key of ♮III (G major, mm. 59–67), followed shortly thereafter by a leisurely prolongation of D major (mm. 79–85).[27]

Sometimes, a relatively remote modulation to F major coincides with the onset of a pastoral topic. In the finale ("Capriccio") of Haydn's Symphony No. 53 in D major, the D-minor middle section quickly veers into the relative major; the remainder of the first reprise consists of a musette. F major is also a frequently encountered key for flat-side "purple patches" within sonata-form expositions—either en route to or within the secondary theme zone—that may exhibit pastoral indices such as drone basses, simplified textures, and a melodic style that sounds artless in comparison with the immediately surrounding music. Familiar instances include Mozart's String Quartet in A major, K. 464/i, mm. 187–91 (F-major *Ländler* within the recapitulated transition) and String Quartet in D major, K. 499/i, mm. 65–70 (deceptive cadence launches ♭VI interpolation within the secondary-theme zone); and Beethoven's Piano Sonata in A major, Op. 2 No. 2/iv (♭VI tonicized to expand the consequent phrase of the rondo return that launches the coda) and String Quartet in G major, Op. 18 No. 2/iv, mm. 96–104 (tonicized ♭VI within a parenthesis expanding the D-major second theme).

It is sometimes a stretch, however, to invoke the pastorale when such F-major interpolations appear, the characteristic key notwithstanding. Consider Haydn's String Quartet in D major, Op. 50 No. 6/i: Here the "singing allegro" and brilliant styles predominate, and the approach to the perfect authentic cadence that ends the second theme area is particularly concerto-like (mm. 44–48, with cadential trill at m. 47). This cadence fulfills an earlier and less fantastic trill cadence at m. 37 that resolved deceptively to F major (♮VI). Haydn prolongs ♮VI for five-and-one-half measures but, despite the harmonic repose, there is nothing particularly pastoral about this passage, with its *sforzando* attacks on almost every downbeat and the brilliant style of the first violin part.

Another caveat: These sorts of interpolations—which usually arise from phrase expansions within transitions and secondary themes—typically tonicize flattened scale steps.[28] To the extent that we associate the pastorale not only with F major but with flat keys generally, such passages suggest a robust connection between topical reference and tonal process—but not necessarily between topical reference and the intention of reaching *specific* keys. It is easy to find flat-key interpolations with pastorale traits. Several of them happen to appear in D flat major within the corpus of Beethoven's cello sonatas. There is the D♮ pedal point that expands the retransitional dominant at the end of the development in Beethoven's Cello Sonata in F major, Op. 5 No. 1, mm. 205–10. Another D-flat-major idyll expands the second theme (mm. 308–12, originally presented in A flat major at mm. 127–31). In the rondo finale (a 6/8 gigue with imitative opening) similar pastorale reveries built on G flat and D flat major delay the retransitional dominant toward the end of the central episode (mm. 117–28, recalled in the coda at mm. 205–18, this time with successive pedal points in descending thirds expanding D flat major, B flat minor, and G flat minor). In this movement, the pastoral topic emerges not in the tonic F major but almost exclusively in these harmonically static passages further down the flat side from F. Earlier, I mentioned an analogous use of D flat major in the C-major cello sonata Op. 102 No. 1.

Although such moments undoubtedly testify to a mutual dependence of topic and tonal process, we cannot claim that they show a composer striving to reach a particular tonal center associated with a topic. The sudden drop from one major key to another on its modally mixed flat side is what arouses in us the sensation of being cast into a different temporal order, an impression often reinforced by other pastoral traits. Whether such moments sound in F major, G major, or something else, these parentheses within the tonal process give the illusion of "annulling time within time," words with which Schiller characterized aesthetic experience but which also capture so well what postlapsarian man seeks in the pastorale.

CONCLUSION

In order to assert a robust connection between choice of topic and tonal process, the topic needs to carry generally agreed-on key associations. The tonal process in question should either be relatively unusual and not simply an unmarked feature of the genre— for example, a chromatic or distant key relation—or else it should be articulated in a marked or unusual manner. I have identified several passages that meet these criteria. There are, admittedly, no *necessary* connections between topics and tonal process. For example, although remote modulations to F major often coincide with the onset of the pastorale topic, so do remote modulations to more distant flat keys. Some of the associations suggested in this chapter may be epiphenomena of tonal processes that operate anyway across a wide variety of topical references. But such reservations do not preclude out of hand the possibility that composers did sometimes coordinate tonal processes with topical succession. Analysts can propose such a correlation and discuss it, even if they cannot prove it.

Because analytical claims about tonal plans and topics mutually influencing one another are so fragile, it is probably best to make them about passages whose topical references are fairly clear. Thus, this sort of analysis will tend to rely on *ratio facilis*.[29] It may not yield sophisticated hermeneutic readings, such as one encounters in the work of Robert Hatten, but, even if an awareness of the key associations carried by a handful of topics is in itself unlikely to open exciting new vistas for topically informed analysis, it can enhance such analysis, albeit in an informal, ad hoc manner. And there is always the chance that other analysts, more imaginative or more sensitive to topical implications than I, will replicate and widen this research, discovering additional and deeper connections between topic and tonal process.

NOTES

1. David Wyn Jones (1995: 51) finds further evidence in some of Beethoven's songs and in sketches for an abortive operatic project. Hatten (1994: 20) discusses the oppositional associations, pastoral and bellicose, in the "Dona nobis pacem."

2. A word on methodology. For this study, I looked at the following works: Haydn—the traditional 104 symphonies and the piano trios and string quartets composed in the 1780s and '90s; Mozart—most instrumental music composed after he moved to Vienna; Beethoven—the string quartets, cellos sonatas, and violin sonatas. I also drew on my familiarity with several dozen works belonging to other genres. I looked for topical allusions in connection with any non-diatonic modulations and modulations to scale degrees borrowed from the parallel minor. Because of the high degree of subjectivity inherent in tonal and topical identification (see note 12 below and the corresponding main text), mine was necessarily an informal empirical study, and I chose not to present precise statistical data. I feel confident in concluding, however, that while composers sometimes articulated relatively distant tonal goals with topics "at home" in that key, this was not a routine aspect of the classical style.

3. First presented in Agawu (1991: 30) but enlarged from twenty-seven to sixty-one topics in Agawu (2009: 43–44).

4. On figurae, see Rumph (2012: 95–96 and this volume), who adapts this concept from Hjelmslev.

5. On the notion of "cultural unit," see Monelle (2000: 23–26), drawing on the theories of Umberto Eco and David Schneider. In the case of the pastorale topic, for example, the "signified encompasses courtly shepherdesses, sunlit tranquility, peaceful landscapes,

amorous play, and the lyric spirit, not to mention Christmas and Christian heaven" (5). The interpretant, a concept drawn from Peircian semiotics, mediates between sign and object. See Monelle (2000: 23–30) and Rumph (2012: 8, 85) for how this concept applies to topic theory.

6. John Platoff (2007) examines a corpus consisting of twenty-eight opere buffe performed in Vienna between 1783 and 1791 plus all of Mozart's complete and incomplete operatic works, comprising a total of 706 musical numbers. Only eight out of twelve possible tonics appear, and one of the eight, E, in only about 2% of the numbers. Only eighteen numbers "use a minor tonic wholly or in part," and eleven of those are by Mozart. Moreover, minor is used for only five tonics, A, C, D, F, and G. To be sure, instrumental music ranges more widely, but these keys appear far more frequently than the others.

7. This type of rondo is sometimes known as a rondo with reversed recapitulation or an omitted refrain but it is better heard as an expanded binary form. See Daverio (1994), Galand (1996), which presents a Schenkerian view of K. 456/iii, and Hepokoski and Darcy (2006), where a rondo with reversed recapitulation corresponds to their Type $4^{1\text{-exp}}$ Sonata.

8. Mattheson, for instance, writes that "when performed under certain circumstances, it can touch the heart." One J. A. Schrader reports in 1827 that it is a key of "bitter, gloomy lamentation, on account of hard suffering." For Beethoven, it was a "black key." Several authors, apparently all paraphrasing C. F. D. Schubart, mention "submission to one's fate."

9. Allanbrook says much the same thing: "The drone, used as a closing gesture for its stabilizing effect, often bears with it a pastoral affect; a suggestion of Arcadia at the cadence is certainly appropriate to the comedic close" (1992: 180).

10. It is certainly Koch's first-level default, although, of course, he does not put it that way (1983: 200).

11. On French and German hunting keys, see Ringer (1953) and Monelle (2006: 42). Pöschl (1990: 55, citing Clewing 1937) presents a table of the horn calls Haydn used, aligning them with calls from two French hunting manuals (*Almanach du chasseur* of 1773 and *Manuel du Veneur* of circa 1810). Some are nearly exact quotations, while some are loose reminiscences. Monelle (2006: 87) notes that in the finale of the Symphony No. 73, "La chasse," Haydn uses a call entitled *La Sourcillade*, although not exactly as originally published in 1734: "As usual, we must assume that he had heard it in the field, inaccurately recalled by living huntsmen" (89).

12. Elaine Sisman (1993: 69–71) famously raised the question of the reliability of contrapuntal and imitative textures for the identification of the learned style. Melanie Lowe (2007: 25–28) took Sisman's questions for the point of departure in her own thoughtful discussion of the challenge involved in identifying topics, and this challenge lies at the heart of the chapters contained in the second section of this volume. Reading through them, one can understand why "identification in topical analysis can never be 'mere'" (Agawu 2008: 54). Individual tokens of a topic will rarely present every feature of the "ideal type," and scholars can differ over the number of features that suffice for a topical identification, as Bujić's response (2006) to Hatten's (1994) analysis of Beethoven's Op. 101 sonata suggests.

13. For Sisman (2000: 63–66, 72) these moments are "visions" that make "briefly present an absent idyllic *locus amoenus*—the 'pleasant place' of pastoral" (63).

14. In Table 16.1, the right-most column cites representative eighteenth and early-nineteenth-century affective characteristics that support the association of topic and keys in the left-most two columns. Most of these citations can be found in Steblin (2002), to which one can add Sulzer's article on the march (1774: 744) and Schubart's discussion of

Turkish music (1806: 330–32). I thank Danuta Mirka for bringing these last two passages to my attention.

15. Interestingly, Mozart seems to have been the only Viennese composer of his time to use E flat major as a trumpet-and-drum (and hence, potentially martial) key (Platoff: 149 n. 28 and 155 n. 43). This suggests that certain associations between topics and keys were more characteristic of some composers or regions than others.

16. On the Wranitsky brothers, see Jones (2006: 57–97).

17. The typical position of Turkish music references at the beginning of movements or multimovement works and their function as a "noise killer" is discussed by Catherine Mayes (this volume).

18. Sisman (1990: 316) proposes that these fanfares might allude to the messenger in the fifth act.

19. My discussion of the tonal process supplements Melanie Lowe's analysis of K. 458/i (this volume).

20. Lowe describes it as an *Alphorn* melody. Hepokoski and Darcy (2004: 212–14) would say that the episodic theme here "writes over" the principal thematic material that more conventionally opens the developmental "rotation," and this "writing over" points to another possible interaction between tonal plan and topic. The first movement of the D-major quartet K. 575 is another work that introduces a new, episodic theme in a pastoral style and key within the development: the G-major theme with prominent inner-voice drone in mm. 86–94. The use of G major at this point in a D-major piece is in itself unexceptional. But the new theme resembles the principal theme in some respects; they both feature a pedal point and they both begin with an ascending arpeggiation. We can hear the episodic theme as a loose rewriting of the principal theme, one that realizes the governing topic more fully.

21. Danuta Mirka (personal communication) brought this E-flat-major restatement to my attention.

22. "The melody usually shifts to the key of the fourth, but, without making a cadence in it, soon again returns to the main key" (Koch 1983: 201).

23. Also this quartet movement is analyzed by Lowe. As with Mozart's K. 458/i, my remarks can be usefully read in conjunction with her discussion.

24. See Eric McKee's chapter in this volume for an informative discussion of this dance.

25. Here is a small selection of published work that applies topic theory to this movement: Allanbrook (1992), Powers (1995: 24–27), Agawu (2008: 40–43). Elsewhere in this volume Stephen Rumph and Robert Hatten draw on Allanbrook's analysis while Tom Beghin problematizes it further down.

26. This developmental paradigm is theorized from a Schenkerian perspective in David Beach (1983) and discussed more generally in Hepokoski and Darcy (2004: 198–205) as a "lower-level default." The most comprehensive account of the technique in Haydn's works is James Webster's (1991: 133–45).

27. Numerous other pieces juxtapose III♯ and I with very little or no hint of confronting, much less of troping, the *tempesta* and pastoral topics. I offer one more example from the Haydn quartets. In the String Quartet in F major, Op. 74 No. 2/i, the development begins with an A-major statement of the principal theme. A major returns at the end of the development (prolonged in mm. 164–71), now heard as V/vi but approached sequentially from E flat major via an ascending sequence based on the chromatic 5–6 paradigm (mm. 153–64).

There is no unmediated juxtaposition of characteristic minor-mode and major-mode topical references.

28. William Rothstein (1989) interprets such interpolations from a Schenkerian perspective and through the lenses of historical theory. Koch's concept of parenthesis (1983: 53) is most obviously relevant here.

29. Monelle (2000: 16) applies Umberto Eco's distinction between *ratio difficilis* and *ratio facilis* to topic theory.

References

Agawu, V. Kofi. 1991. *Playing with Signs: A Semiotic Interpretation of Classic Music.* Princeton: Princeton University Press.

——. 2008. Topic Theory: Achievement, Critique, Prospects. In *Passagen, IMS Kongress Zürich 2007: Fünf Hauptvorträge, Five Key Note Speeches,* ed. Laurenz Lüttecken and Hans-Joachim Hinrichsen, 38–69. Kassel: Bärenreiter.

——. 2009. *Music as Discourse: Semiotic Adventures in Romantic Music.* New York: Oxford University Press.

Allanbrook, Wye Jamison. 1983. *Rhythmic Gesture in Mozart:* Le nozze di Figaro *and* Don Giovanni. Chicago: University of Chicago Press.

——. 1992. Two Threads through the Labyrinth: Topic and Process in the First Movements of K. 332 and K. 333. In *Convention in Eighteenth and Nineteenth-Century Music: Essays in Honor of Leonard G. Ratner,* ed. Wye J. Allanbrook, Janet M. Levy, and William Mahrt, 125–71. Stuyvesant, NY: Pendragon.

——. 1994. Mozart's Tunes and the Comedy of Closure. In *On Mozart,* ed. James M. Morris, 169–86. New York: Woodrow Wilson Center and Cambridge University Press.

——. 1996. Comic Issues in Mozart's Piano Concertos. In *Mozart's Piano Concertos: Text, Context, Interpretation,* ed. Neal Zaslaw, 75–105. Ann Arbor: University of Michigan Press.

Allanbrook, Wye, and Wendy Hilton. 1992. Dance Rhythms in Mozart's Arias. *Early Music* 20/1: 142–49.

Beach, David. 1983. A Recurring Pattern in Mozart's Music. *Journal of Music Theory* 27/1: 1–29.

Brown, A. Peter. 1996. The Trumpet Overture and Sinfonia in Vienna (1715–1822): Rise, Decline, and Reformulation. In *Music in Eighteenth-Century Austria,* ed. David Wyn Jones, 13–69. Cambridge: Cambridge University Press.

Bujić, Bojan. 2006. When Is a Musette Not a Musette? A Response to Robert Hatten. *Muzikološki zbornik* 42/1: 165–69.

Caplin, William. 2005. On the Relation of Musical *Topoi* to Formal Function. *Eighteenth-Century Music* 2/1: 113–24.

Chew, Geoffrey. 1996. The Austrian *pastorella* and the *stylus rusticanus*: Comic and Pastoral Elements in Austrian Music, 1750–1800. In *Music in Eighteenth-Century Austria,* ed. David Wyn Jones, 133–93. Cambridge: Cambridge University Press.

Clewing, Carl. 1937. *Musik und Jägerei.* Kassel: Bärenreiter.

Daverio, John. 1994. From "Concertante Rondo" to "Lyric Sonata": A Commentary on Brahms's Reception of Mozart. In *Brahms Studies,* ed. David Brodbeck, 111–38. Lincoln: University of Nebraska Press.

Drabkin, William. 1991. The Agnus Dei of Beethoven's *Missa Solemnis*: The Growth of Its Form. In *Beethoven's Compositional Process*, ed. William Kinderman, 131–59. Lincoln: University of Nebraska Press.

Hatten, Robert S. 1994. *Musical Meaning in Beethoven: Markedness, Correlation, and Interpretation*. Bloomington: Indiana University Press.

——. 1995. Metaphor *in* Music. In *Musical Signification: Essays in the Semiotic Theory and Analysis of Music*, ed. Eero Tarasti, 373–91. Berlin and New York: Mouton de Gruyter.

——. 2004. *Interpreting Musical Gestures, Topics, and Tropes: Mozart, Beethoven, Schubert*. Bloomington: Indiana University Press.

Goehring, Edmund J. 2004. *Three Modes of Perception in Mozart: The Philosophical, Pastoral, and Comic in* Così fan tutte. Cambridge: Cambridge University Press.

Hepokoski, James, and Warren Darcy. 2006. *Elements of Sonata Theory: Norms, Types, and Deformations in the Late-Eighteenth-Century Sonata*. New York: Oxford University Press.

Jones, David Wyn. 1995. *Beethoven: Pastoral Symphony*. Cambridge: Cambridge University Press.

——. 2006. *The Symphony in Beethoven's Vienna*. Cambridge: Cambridge University Press.

Koch, Heinrich Christoph. 1983. *Introductory Essay on Composition*. Trans. Nancy Kovaleff Baker. New Haven: Yale University Press.

Krones, Harmut. 2000. Bemerkungen zur Tonartensymbolik bei Joseph Haydn. In *Das symphonische Werk Joseph Haydns*, ed. Gerhard J. Winkler, 27–43. Eisenstadt: Burgenländisches Landesmuseum.

Laufer, Edward. 1991. Voice-Leading Procedures in Development Sections. *Studies in Music from the University of Western Ontario*13: 69–120.

Lowe, Melanie. 2007. *Pleasure and Meaning in the Classical Symphony*. Bloomington: Indiana University Press.

MacIntyre, Bruce. 1996. Johann Baptist Vanhal and the Pastoral Mass Tradition. In *Music in Eighteenth-Century Austria*, ed. David Wyn Jones, 112–32. Cambridge: Cambridge University Press.

McClelland, Clive. 2012. *Ombra: Supernatural Music in the Eighteenth Century*. Lanham, MD: Lexington.

Monelle, Raymond. 1991. Music and the Peircean Trichotomies. *International Review of the Aesthetics and Sociology of Music* 22/1: 99–108.

——. 2000. *The Sense of Music: Semiotic Essays*. Princeton: Princeton University Press.

——. 2006. *The Musical Topic: Hunt, Military and Pastoral*. Bloomington: Indiana University Press.

Moyer, Birgitte. 1992. *Ombra* and Fantasia in Late Eighteenth-Century Theory and Practice. In *Convention in Eighteenth and Nineteenth-Century Music: Essays in Honor of Leonard G. Ratner*, ed. Wye J. Allanbrook, Janet M. Levy, and William Mahrt, 282–306. Stuyvesant, NY: Pendragon.

Platoff, John. 1992. How Original Was Mozart? Evidence from *Opera Buffa*. *Early Music* 20/1: 105–17.

——. 1997. Tonal Organization in the *Opera Buffa* of Mozart's Time. In *Mozart Studies* 2, ed. Cliff Eisen, 145–73. Oxford: Oxford University Press.

Pöschl, Josef. 1990. *Die österreichische Jagdhornbläserbuch*. Graz: Weishaupt.

Powers, Harold S. 1995. Reading Mozart's Music: Text and Topic, Sense and Syntax. *Current Musicology* 57: 5–44.

Ringer, Alexander. 1953. The Chasse as Musical Topic of the Eighteenth Century. *Journal of the American Musicological Society* 6: 148–59.

Rothstein, William. 1989. *Phrase Rhythm in Tonal Music*. New York: Schirmer.

Rumph, Stephen. 2012. *Mozart and Enlightenment Semiotics*. Berkeley: University of California Press.

Sisman, Elaine. 1990. Haydn's Theater Symphonies. *Journal of the American Musicological Society* 43/2: 292–352.

——. 1997. Genre, Gesture, and Meaning in Mozart's 'Prague' Symphony. In *Mozart Studies* 2, ed. Cliff Eisen, 27–84. Oxford: Oxford University Press.

——. 1993. *Mozart: The "Jupiter" Symphony, No. 41 in C major, K. 551*. Cambridge: Cambridge University Press.

——. 2000. Memory and Invention at the Threshold of Beethoven's Late Style. In *Beethoven and His World*, ed. Scott Burnham and Michael Steinberg, 51–87. Princeton: Princeton University Press.

Steblin, Rita. 2002. *A History of Key Characteristics in the Eighteenth and Early Nineteenth Centuries*, 2nd ed. Rochester: University of Rochester Press.

Webster, James. 1991. *Haydn's "Farewell Symphony" and the Idea of the Classical Style*. Cambridge: Cambridge University Press.

Will, Richard. 2002. *The Characteristic Symphony in the Age of Haydn and Beethoven*. Cambridge: Cambridge University Press.

CHAPTER 17

TOPICS AND FORM IN MOZART'S STRING QUINTET IN E FLAT MAJOR, K. 614/i

KOFI AGAWU

ON TOPICS

THE goal of this essay is to identify certain features of the first movement of Mozart's String Quintet in E flat major, K. 614/i, that might enhance understanding and appreciation of the work as a form of wordless discourse (Bonds 1991). My main tool will be the phenomenon of topic, a phenomenon whose modern formulation we owe principally to Leonard Ratner (1980). By now, we can, I believe, take for granted the reality of topics: everywhere one looks within the major genres of the eighteenth century—symphonies, concertos, chamber music, and, especially, operas—one finds them. What to do after finding them remains an issue for analysis, however. In this essay I will suggest ways in which topical awareness yields insight into musical form.[1]

Before embarking on the analysis, I would like to clarify what I understand by "topic," recognize the precarious disposition of topics, and comment on the nature of the topical universe. First, I follow Ratner in defining "topic" not as "a subject for musical discourse" (1980: 9) but as "a subject to be incorporated into a musical discourse" (1991: 615). Crucial here is the phrase "to be incorporated" because it acknowledges a prior level of structure that is independent of topic. Topics typically give profile to tonal process and argument. Although one can sometimes imagine a more fundamental form-generating role for them (as we will see in Example 17.1 below), it is hard to see how topics can trump harmonic, contrapuntal, melodic, or rhythmic elements as the foundations of musical structure. Topics are always already auxiliary in application, and it is precisely in reference to this adjunct capacity that topical analysis achieves its most persuasive results.

Second, as audible configurations, topics assume different degrees of salience. While some are direct, immediate, and palpable, many are subtle and distantly sensed or felt.

Raymond Monelle says that "the odor of topicality permeates our music, extending into every aspect" (2006: 7). A texture may suggest a topic without stating it explicitly; listeners may catch only a whiff of a particular topic. Wye J. Allanbrook uses an equivalent metaphor when she compares the disposition of topics to "flickering images of our own humanity" (2014: 87). Topical analysis requires a gradation of reference and a sensitive set of discovery procedures that will render topics as shadows in dim light rather than fully visible bodies, allusions rather than presences, or conversations overheard rather than heard.

Third, all known topics may in principle be gathered into a universe of topics, portions of which serve as horizons for the analysis of particular compositions. Some scholars have attempted to order the seemingly diverse and heterogeneous collection on the basis of social or historical provenance, internal musical function, or semiotic potential. Yet the size of the universe and the nature of its internal ordering remain contested. Ratner, for example, divided topics into types and styles, and added a group of pictorial signs (1980: 9–30). Robert Hatten, too, sought to construct a universe of expression by reordering Ratner's universe into four categories: codes of feelings and passions; styles based on locale or degree of dignity; topics (either types or styles); and pictorialism (Hatten 1994: 74–82). That such orderings are logical is not in dispute; what is less clear is the extent to which they reflect the priorities of composers in the eighteenth century. Finally, Harold Powers, motivated by a similar need to bring some order to the universe of topic, devised two broad categories subdivided into four and three subcategories respectively (1995: 28). First are musical types: balletic, metric or rhythmic, generic, and stylistic; second are musical textures: amorphous, languishing, and vigorous. Again, although Powers seeks to convey differences in character and to advance reasons for possible use, his scheme lacks historical or even systematic support as a report on composition or on listening habits. None of this is to deny the well-established fact that musical material carried affective freight in the eighteenth century. For composers of operas, for example, the availability of styles with high or low associations provided a helpful tool for musical characterization. But this freight took on a less direct, more complex form in the composition of a wordless sonata, concerto, or string quartet, genres not normally constrained by an external, preexisting text.

It is for this reason that scholars like Allanbrook prefer to think of the universe of topic as something of a grab bag, an unordered collection of "expressive hieroglyphs" to be employed in an hoc way toward various expressive ends (2014: 89). Whereas corroborative elements such as text and drama in opera often allow for a firmer delineation of character through the use, for example, of a spectrum of meters and dances (Allanbrook 1983), the universe of topic for instrumental music is more diffuse, its elements less confined in regard to functional potential. In the articulation of form, the intrinsic properties of topics may be exploited directly, or used to question, enrich, or undermine certain harmonic-functional norms (Caplin 2005). Allanbrook suggests that we think of the universe of topics as irreducibly heterogeneous:

> The list [of topics] as presented here is higgledy-piggledy, not a rational, hierarchical array but an accretion, over a long period of music making, of gestures that vibrated

in a familiar fashion in people's ears and pulses....Jumbled together are characteristic styles, social dances, vocal and instrumental effects, textures, and so on. Some
categories overlap or are even co-extensive. Efforts to organize the list by broader
headings, like the perennial eighteenth-century breakdown into church, theater, and
chamber styles, quickly run into trouble. Where, for instance, does the mechanical
(clockwork) style belong? But attempts at presorting are beside the point. The list
reflects the helter-skelter way in which we meet these topoi in life and in the works
themselves. While such expressive profusion may be difficult to organize and theo-
rize, it is nevertheless what is most immediately palpable to the listener—on the surface, where listening takes place. (Allanbrook 2014: 109)

Motivated by a similar conviction, I presented a provisional universe of topics with
twenty-seven items as an uninterpreted list (1991: 30), and later expanded that universe to some sixty-one items (2009: 43–44). Neither list was subject to internal classification; each was simply presented alphabetically and offered as a series of "stylistic
opportunities" for the composer (Pestelli 1984: 136). Ratner himself did not pursue further categorization of the topical universe beyond types, styles, and pictorial elements.
And even though he was always alert to the eighteenth-century thinker's penchant
for rational categorization, he did not show a particular interest in teasing out a firm
structural potential for individual topics from the writings of various eighteenth- and
nineteenth-century theorists. For him as for Allanbrook and myself, the witty allusions that knowledgeable listeners recognize as dances, styles, or pictorial elements are
ultimately anchored to more fundamental tonal thought and process. Topics have no
independent existence; they are agents of intermittent intertextual signaling. While they
may display parametrical continuities (Rumph 2012), they evince no firm underlying
syntax. Nor are they endowed with self-sustaining capability. Topical analysis, then, is
best carried out under the sign of this ontological hierarchy. In what follows, topics will
be incorporated into a more or less "regular" analysis of the movement. (See also the
approaches of Allanbrook 1992, Sisman 1993, and Sutcliffe 2003.)

OVERALL FORM

The first movement of K. 614 is in a clear sonata form. It unfolds across fifteen distinctly
articulated periods. Most periods are secured by cadences; some adjacent periods
are set apart by rests, a few overlap; many feature contrasts of affect or design. Ratner
accords this movement exemplary status in the course of a chapter on sonata form in
his treatise on Classic music. In addition to identifying the main topics, he invokes
Momigny's (1806) terms—*début, verve, mélodieuse, conjunctionelle*—to characterize the
various parts of the oration (Ratner 1980: 237–46). While my analysis is essentially an
elaboration of Ratner's, I will incorporate more detailed description of the moment-by-
moment unfolding and also emphasize ways in which topical awareness enhances our
experience of form.[2]

Figures 17.1 and 17.2 provide synoptic views of the form of the movement. Figure 17.1 identifies each period by measure number and lists some of the topics that might be heard. This chart simply indicates the lay of the land; it can be taken in quickly by scanning the score and taking note of prominent textural changes, changes that often signal topical activity.

Figure 17.2 outlines the overall form using the numbering of periods in Figure 17.1. Thematic and topical affinities rather than shared constructional bases determine the assignment of paradigms. I seek to convey similarity as well as succession among the work's building blocks. Periods 1, 2, 3, and 4 (the start of the exposition) present a narrative of differentiated periods. Period 5 retards the progress of the narrative by repeating

Figure 17.1 Topical references in Mozart's String Quintet in E flat major, K. 614/i

Period	Measures	Topical references
1	1–19	Hunting fanfare (1–2, 5–6), brilliant style (3–4, 7–8, 16–19), sensibility (9–13)
2	20–38	Hunting fanfare, learned style (20–22), brilliant style (31–38)
3	39–54	Singing style, musette (39–40)
4	54–62	Gigue
5	62–78	Gigue, learned style (62–68), brilliant style (70–78), cadenza (72–78), fanfare (75–76)
6	78–86	Sensibility
7	87–124	Sensibility (87–89, 106–24), *Sturm und Drang* (90–106)
8	125–43	Hunting fanfare (125–26, 129–30), brilliant style (126–28, 130–32, 140–43), sensibility (133–36)
9	144–64	Hunting fanfare, learned style (144–46), brilliant style (157–64)
10	165–80	Singing style, musette (165–66)
11	180–88	Gigue
12	188–204	Gigue, learned style (188–94), brilliant style (196–204), cadenza (198–204), fanfare (201–2)
13	204–14	Sensibility
14	215–24	Hunting fanfare, *Sturm und Drang*
15	224–32	Sensibility, fanfare (230–32)

FIGURE **17.2** Paradigmatic form.

(and expanding) period 4, while 6 (end of exposition) and 7 (development) follow in an additive manner as new paradigmatic units. Then comes a large-scale repeat of the 1–2–3–4 succession as 8–9–10–11, followed as before by a doubling of 11 as 12 before proceeding to 13, the relative of 6 (the recapitulation). Period 14 (beginning of the coda) features a modified return of the paradigm containing units 1 and 8, and the movement ends with 15, the equivalent of 6 and 13.

The rhythm of succession implied by Figure 17.2 tells us something about the movement's narrative posture, the use and reuse of material, and the isolation of a single period, 7, as lacking a paradigmatic companion. This difference has to be understood in relative terms because while the actual materials of period 7 are easily traced to earlier parts of the movement (for example, the sensibility material was hinted at as early as m. 9 and served as the agent of closure at the end of the exposition), their conjunction here in a fantasy-like succession positions unit 7 in a column by itself.

Figures 17.1 and 17.2 rely on simple notions of identity and difference. Modulatory distances, for example, are discounted. As guides to the experience of form, they are necessarily incomplete, and need to be supplemented by an account that privileges the linear or in-time experience of listening to the movement. If musical form is the trace produced by the intersection of experiential-diachronic and reflective-synchronic perspectives, we can see immediately that form is shaped by a variety of tendencies distributed across different dimensions, some of them complementary, others in conflict. That is why form, although a fundamental category for musical analysis (Burnham 2002), is also a notoriously complex resultant quality. Let us return to the beginning and go on to the end. (From here on, readers will need access to a score of the movement.)

ANALYSIS

Period 1 (mm. 1–19)

The purpose of these opening nineteen measures is to establish the premises of this particular discourse by giving the listener a feeling for the home key while indicating character through theme and affect. The initial dialogue between the two violas and the two violins immediately features a contrast of topic: hunt style in the violas (mm. 1–2) and a hint of brilliant style led by the violins (mm. 3–4). In mm. 1–2, the syllabic manner of eighth-note articulation, the rapid 6/8 meter, and the 6–5–6 intervallic succession typical of a horn duet (Ratner 1980: 18–19, citing Koch) or horn motion (Monelle 2006: 83, citing Rupert Thackray) collectively engender a rustic aura. Some listeners may hear simulated horns, a hunting fanfare, or perhaps even the beginnings of a gigue that will eventually dominate the movement. (Hearing topics is sometimes voluntary because topics are not always available as immanent configuration; they are less like pebbles that one picks up on a sandy beach and more like willed identities sanctioned by a functional musical context.) Less explicit but no less pertinent is the brilliant style suggested by the violins' response in mm. 3–4. At home on strings, the brilliant style typically features rapidity and virtuoso display; it will be heard explicitly from m. 31 onward.

Measures 1–4 are framed by a I–V progression; they are repeated gesturally in mm. 5–8, but recast in a complementary V–I frame. From m. 9, an additional level of signification emerges: the opening motive, initially associated with the hunt style, now loses its horn flavor and suggests a new topic. Broken into one-measure segments (mm. 9, 10, 11, which then extends to a half cadence in m. 12), this passage hints at the rhetoric of sensibility style. Like the brilliant style of mm. 3–4, the sensibility style here is no more than a flavor; it will, however, be played out in earnest as the movement unfolds—it will return at the end of the exposition, dominate the development, and appear again in both the recapitulation and coda.

Do topics belong to the foreground or background, surface or deep structure? While they are normally considered elements of the foreground or surface, I would like to suggest that they occasionally flavor backgrounds as well. Consider the first nine measures from a generative point of view (Example 17.1). At origin here is the horn duet with a 6–5–3 succession of intervals (level 1). Each member of this two-voice proto-song is in turn subject to elaboration: 6 becomes 6–5–6, 5 is elaborated as 5–3–5, and 3 becomes 3–3–3 (could also be 3–5–3) (level 2). From here to Mozart's music is but a short step (see mm. 1–2, 5–6 and 9). We could say that the horn duet motivates the first nine measures not only as decorative foreground but as structural background. This particular "background" incorporates a contrapuntal error, however: the middle fifth, arrived at through direct motion, hides indirect fifths. But insofar as topical backgrounds are not subject to the same strictures as strict counterpoint, the forbidden parallelism is not a problem; it does not invalidate a putatively grammatical background.

Before proceeding to period 2, it might be helpful to restate some of the assumptions that lie behind the foregoing description. While the textural changes that we have heard in the opening period may be described neutrally as elements of design, a topical designation by contrast historicizes design, and it does so by locating specific textures within a fund of common eighteenth-century signifying textures. Terms like "hunting fanfare," "brilliant style," "sensibility," and "gigue" refer to topical types, classes, or paradigms. Topics appear in varying degrees of explicitness or salience. Context is everything in topical identification; a later context might provide the answer to an earlier topical identity. Insofar as all topics are underpinned by melodic, harmonic, and rhythmic patterns, aspects of syntax (such as a deceptive cadence) may "generate" topical content. Finally, there is a difference between theme (or motive) and topic; the same theme (or motive) may acquire different topical affiliations, just as the same topic may appear in different thematic guises. Overall unity of theme may thus be offset by a contrast of topic.

Period 2 (mm. 20–38)

If the purpose of period 1 was to establish the movement's premises (tonal, thematic, topical, material, and affective), the purpose of this second period is to advance the narrative

EXAMPLE 17.1 Generating mm. 1–9 from a background of horn fifths.

toward an alternative tonal premise, the key of the dominant. Period 2 is thus directly goal oriented. It starts off with vigorous action using the hunting-gigue material from the opening (but without the horn duet) and incorporates a hint of learned style in the stretto-like entry of the first viola in mm. 21–22. The texture is assembled from low to high, incorporating a palpable back and forth or reciprocal action with a sing-song quality to dramatize the move to the dominant (see violin 2 and violin 1 in alternation in mm. 26–30). At the height of the period (downbeat of m. 31, pedal on F as V/V), the brilliant style becomes the vehicle for highlighting the arrival at the threshold of a new tonal station. This is all in preparation for something new in the third period. The third period will bring a drop in dynamic, both literally in the form of a piano dynamic, and qualitatively in the form of smoother, flowing, less agitated musical material. It will be less marked as labor.

Period 3 (mm. 39–54)

The purpose of this third period is to profile the new key, B flat major, the key of the dominant—a place away from home, but one that is always already in danger of returning us there. The period's main topic is singing style, which is delivered in a nice symmetrical period with two eight-measure halves. The first half (mm. 39–46) is led by first violin and finishes inconclusively on V, while the second half (mm. 47–54) is led by cello and finishes conclusively with a perfect cadence. As often in Mozart, symmetries are not always perfect or mechanically exact. For example, the high–low contrast of registers (violin followed by cello) leaves a residual imbalance at the end of the period; registral disjunction, we might say, is upheld rather than resolved. Contrast *within* period 3 is, however, less marked than contrast between it and period 2. While period 2 featured a vigorous hunting-gigue style that did transitional work, period 3 is devoted to song with a hint of musette at its beginning. Now, the impulse to sing is not missing from period 2; rather, it is given fuller rein under a new topical regime in period 3, one that Momigny would call *mélodieuse*, aptly capturing its character (Ratner 1980: 239).

A comment about the emerging sense of form is necessary at this point. In one respect, the music heard so far enacts a nonlinear trajectory that contrasts with the linearity of the tonal trajectory. If we take a larger, cumulative view of the temporal profile of each of periods 1, 2, and 3, we might place period 3 with its singing style at the slow end of the spectrum, period 2 with its hunting gigue in learned style and brilliant-style culmination at the fast end, and period 1, the declarative hunting fanfare that opened the movement in the middle. This produces a 3–1–2 ordering (from slow through fastest to fast) in contrast to Mozart's actual 1–2–3 ordering. Such successions of temporal states, themselves products of topical activity, tell us something about the experience of form. They suggest, for example, that the trajectories mapped out within a work's constituent parameters do not necessarily proceed in parallel. Thus, from a tonal-harmonic perspective, period 1 is tonally stable; period 2 is directional, agitated, and unstable; and period 3 is harmonically stable. Topically, by contrast, period 1 with its annunciatory opening indexing the outdoors, mornings, and the masculine is varied and earns its stability; period 2 "topicalizes" the musical mode; while period 3 professes a strategic stasis under one main topical regime. We may not be aware of these competing profiles while listening to (or imagining) a performance of K. 614/i, but reflection afterward shows that they collectively shape our experience of form.

Period 4 (mm. 54–62)

If the singing style of period 3 seemed to carve out space for the phenomenal occupation of the new key (B flat major, the dominant), this next period retrieves the spirit of action from period 2 and inscribes a neat eight-measure symmetrical period as affirmation of the new key. The gigue element is back, and the expression is overt and outwardly directed, not reflective or introspective as in the previous period. Not infrequently in

Mozart, this process of confirmation entails a drop in topical register. Elaine Sisman drew attention to just such a stylistic shift in the first movement of the "Jupiter," where a high-style alternation of *coups d'archet*, march, and singing style in the opening measures propels the narrative eventually to a low-style contredanse at the end of the exposition (Sisman 1993: 46–47). Such shifts are never expressively absolute, however. In this movement, sharp interjections by the cello in mm. 56 and 58 tweak the low style, introducing an element of irrationality or anger perhaps that suggests that this is not an untroubled peasant dance. So, although the hunting fanfare of period 1 has morphed into a gigue in period 4, the rhetorical claims of higher styles still lurk in the background.

One more detail about period 4 will suggest another interpretative path made possible by topical awareness. We have noted that this period serves as a first-stage confirmation of the movement's alternative tonal premise. It is however underpinned by a less obvious conventional element that brings an additional topical connotation into view. Level 1 in Example 17.2 cites a familiar conjunct bass pattern consisting of rising fourths and falling thirds followed by stepwise motion. This pattern is incorporated as *melody* by Mozart (levels 2 and 3). Beethoven later used the same pattern as a fugue subject in the finale of his Piano Sonata in A flat major, Op. 110 (the initial subject–answer exchange is quoted in Example 17.3). With the benefit of hindsight, today's listener may well detect a whiff of learnedness in Mozart's otherwise low-style melody.

EXAMPLE **17.2** Generating mm. 54–62 from a bass pattern of rising fourths and falling thirds followed by stepwise motion.

EXAMPLE **17.3** The pattern of rising fourths and falling thirds in Beethoven, Piano Sonata in A flat major, Op. 110/iii, mm. 27–34.

Period 5 (mm. 62–78)

Because period 4 was too brief to do the work necessitated by the accumulated energy of periods 1, 2, and 3, Mozart repeats himself. But he does not do so mechanically. Indeed, the occasion for repetition or restatement in Mozart is often the occasion for imaginative recasting (Ivanovitch 2004). We can see this in the way period 5 recasts the essential tonal-harmonic framework of period 4 by prying open its middle. Specifically, m. 68, the equivalent of m. 60, hesitates before beginning its cadential drive. Mozart had already signaled the expansion by substituting a more mobile harmony in m. 66 for the tonic in m. 58. In period 5, the mere eight measures of period 4 are extended to seventeen, effectively doubling the length of the previous period. The gesture is a frankly grand one, dwarfing everything that came before.

Notice once again how the expansion of the period engenders an expansion of topical content. First comes the gigue in learned style with perhaps an operatic flavor (see the exchange between the violins in mm. 62–68); then things stall harmonically in mm. 68–69, allowing the brilliant style to do some of the gestural work (see the second violin in mm. 68–69). The first violin extends the brilliant style in mm. 70–71 in a manner reminiscent of period 2. Then a cadential six-four chord initiated in m. 72 is profiled by rushing figuration suggesting a cadenza (mm. 72–75). The first violin reaches an apogee in the form of a huge fanfare (mm. 75–76), discharging into a perfect cadence, complete with a trill on $\hat{2}$ leading to $\hat{1}$, all this in the dominant key, B flat major (mm. 77–78). Just as the six-four chord is often used to signal the beginning of a cadenza in a concerto, so it is used here topically to signal an elaborate cadence. The chord's five-measure duration is striking: no other auxiliary dissonance has been given this much space in the movement up to this point.

Period 6 (mm. 78–86)

With the recomposition of period 4 as period 5 the essential long-range tension between a tonic key area, E flat major, and its dominant, B flat major, has not only been successively indicated and established, but the process has been dramatized before our very ears. The tonal business of the exposition is now properly discharged, but a rhetorical necessity leads Mozart to stage a stylized confirmation of the larger tonal dialectic. Period 6 is notable for its low energy and stasis, as if merely echoing what has been stated and affirmed in the two previous periods. The task is discharged with the help of sensibility style, whose brief constituent gestures recommend it for closing work in this instance. To be sure, the sensibility style can be used to support other formal functions, be they developmental, confirmatory, or connecting. When it first appeared in m. 9, the style was incorporated into low-level acts of development in the second half of the nineteen-measure opening period. Sporting a similar call-and-response pattern (this time between first violin and the rest of the ensemble), the sensibility style in period 6 performs a more stable, confirming function. With the repeat of the exposition, we hear its connecting function. Clearly, topics do not have invariant associations with formal functions (Caplin 2005); indeed, it is precisely their mobility that contributes a nuanced perspective on form.

Period 7 (mm. 87–124)

The development section is entered by means of a sudden shift of gears: mm. 84–86 are repeated a third lower as mm. 87–89. Although thematic or motivic continuity is thus maintained, the join between the two passages is disjunct rather than conjunct, as if the seams of the composer's craft were being bared for all to see. Dominated by sensibility style, whose rhetoric and implied fragmentation facilitate both deliberate working out and exploration, the development as a whole unfolds a single extended period that stages a return from a(n imagined) distant key, ending on the home key's dominant-seventh chord in m. 124 and literally reproducing material from the end of the immediately preceding period, 6 (mm. 84–86).

The main topical events in period 7 are as follows. Three measures of sensibility style (carried over from the end of the exposition) enable Mozart to set up an expectation for C minor. Then, by means of a deceptive cadence (mm. 89–90), a vigorous new topic, *Sturm und Drang*, makes a striking appearance. *Sturm und Drang* is typically indexed by instability, dissonant or minor-mode harmonies, fragmented textures, and—depending on the instrumental medium—brilliance or agitation in execution (as in tremolo passages) or even virtuosic figuration.[3] Although the *Sturm und Drang* topic is new at this point, one can find hints of it earlier in the movement, notably in the brilliant-style passages encountered in period 2. Here, in the development, its first proper manifestation in mm. 90–96 does not conclude; it is abandoned after five measures. In m. 96 fragments of sensibility return as placeholders, but they are soon superseded by a second outburst of *Sturm und Drang* (mm. 100–6), now in G minor rather than A flat major. Note that in spite of the feeling of intensification we experience between the two *Sturm und Drang* passages, the second one, in minor, lies a half step *lower* than the first, in major. Intensification comes from immediate repetition and from the juxtaposition of modal opposites, not from the lowering of pitch.

The second *Sturm und Drang* gesture ends on the dominant of C minor (downbeat of m. 106), the moment in the tonal plan of sonata form that Ratner calls the "point of furthest remove," by which he means the point at which the tonal trajectory is reoriented toward home and away from exploration (Ratner 1991: 225–27). Then (mm. 106–23), in the most extended manifestation of the sensibility *topos*, the movement works its way back to the doorstep of the home key, deploying a host of neighbor-note configurations. This "freezing" of topic calls attention to other processes, including motivic play, the charting of a purposeful harmonic trajectory, and a wonderfully evocative inner voice (first viola in mm. 113–17)—a line rather than a melody—that enhances the superlative nature of the moment. The stalling of sensibility figures starting in m. 106 creates an aura of enchantment, producing an almost disembodied form of the topic.

EXAMPLE 17.4 Generating mm. 107–13 from parallel six-threes followed by a six-four.

The relative stability of the sensibility topic from m. 106 onward also sets into relief various subsurface contrapuntal processes. One such process, abstracted in Example 17.4 and encompassing mm. 108–13, originates in a chain of sixth chords—six-threes mostly, but broken by a six-four at the end (level 1). Mozart enlivens this conventional progression by means of chromatic passing notes (level 2) and, less conventionally, by an upper-voice pedal on G (level 3). Arpeggios in the violas (mm. 110–13) further activate the progression at the musical surface. Another process is the familiar bass progression of descending fifths in mm. 114–27 (a prominent earlier usage is in mm. 22–25). Level 1 of Example 17.5 postulates an 8–3–8–3 intervallic pattern as origin while level 2 incorporates passing notes. The two levels of Example 17.6 further suggest a path to the enrichment of the dominant seventh within the V–I progression spanning mm. 116–27.

Period 7 lasts thirty-eight measures, making it exactly twice as long as the longest periods we have heard so far, namely, the two nineteen-measure periods 1 and 2. It is shaped by two antithetical topics: sensibility, which is delicate and sensitive and not interested in long trajectories of musical thought, and *Sturm und Drang*, which is aggressive and disruptive and promotes instability. We might in fact hear the two *Sturm und Drang*

EXAMPLE **17.5** Generating mm. 114–27 from an 8–3–8–3 linear intervallic pattern.

EXAMPLE 17.6 Chromatic enrichment of V–I progression in mm. 116–27.

passages (mm. 90–96 and 100–6) as interruptions of the more stable sensibility-laden development, but this says nothing about the tonal rationale of the development. Again, insofar as it comes across as an emergent or resultant quality, form as mediated by topics and tonal adventure enshrines conflicting tendencies.

Period 8 (mm. 125–43)

With this period, we begin the process of recapitulation, that is, the formal restatement and formalized reconciliation of previously opposed tonal premises. Topically and tonally, period 8 is identical to period 1, a few ornamental details notwithstanding. In general, because the recapitulation is given over to tonal business first and foremost, a topical account often adds little in the way of new information beyond noting obvious returns or decorations. This says nothing about the actual experience of the reprise, however, for details of specific transitions remain to be discovered and savored by the listener. Still, insofar as topics, like the thematic material they embody, tend *not* to change during recapitulation, we can pass over these portions of the movement fairly rapidly.

Period 9 (mm. 144–64)

The equivalent of period 2, this period has the task of effecting a transition, or more appropriately, the *idea of transition from the home key to the home key*. In the exposition, the transition linked the home key, E flat major, to its dominant, B flat major. In the recapitulation, the target key is also the point of origin. Therefore the composer must find a way of staging that which is known in advance, namely, the reattainment of the home key, so that it can acquire, at least initially, the quality of dominant. The logical means are to move toward the subdominant and approach the home key from there. This is exactly what Mozart does in this movement: the first four measures of period 9 (mm. 144–47) veer toward A flat major. Then, with the aid of a circle-of-fifths progression, we cycle back to B flat major as dominant of the home key. Alternative perspectives on the E-flat major triad between mm. 144 and 165 remind us that hearing relations rather than absolute identities is key to appreciating Mozart's tonal strategy.

Regarding topics in period 9, there is no change from the exposition. As in period 2, period 9 begins with the gigue material in learned style, complete with reciprocal action to underline the purposefulness of the music. A plateau is reached in m. 157 with first violin not just playing but *dis*playing in brilliant style.

Period 10 (mm. 165–80)

The dominant chord at the end of period 9 is resolved at the beginning of period 10 as we transition from vigorous, brilliant-style violin figuration to a more relaxed singing style, this time in (indeed beginning *on*) the home key. The parts are now switched so that the viola takes the first strain of the melody (mm. 165–72) while the first violin takes the second strain (mm. 173–80).

Periods 11, 12, 13 (mm. 180–88, 188–204, 204–14)

The recapitulation's crucial tonal adjustment having been accomplished by the beginning of period 10, the rest of the movement sits happily in the home key and distributes its dynamism into the rhyming of thematic material from the exposition. Topically, period 11 retains the gigue style with an inflection of learnedness; it is a trim eight-measure symmetrical period, the equivalent of period 4. Period 12 repeats and expands period 11; it is the equivalent of period 5, whose dramatic six-four chord and culminating fanfare we reencounter. And period 13 (mm. 204–14) starts off with a cadence confirming the tonic in sensibility style; then, freezing the topic, it shifts through the submediant to the dominant, ending inconclusively in order to prepare either a repeat of the development and recapitulation (the first time) or the beginning of the coda (the second time).

Periods 14 and 15 (mm. 215–24 and 224–32)

The last two periods constitute the movement's coda. The first of them (mm. 215–24) is announced by the same hunting fanfare that began the movement and functioned as a lead topic throughout. The main task here is to reinforce a sense of peroration, and, concomitantly, to discourage further tonal exploration except that which can be rationalized immediately. Brilliant-style figures are enlisted to create this sense of peroration; indeed, as they intensify, they recall the sixteenth-note figuration of *Sturm und Drang* that we encountered in the development section.

Perhaps the most striking event in the coda is, alas, not a topical event but a harmonic one (with rhythmic-textural reverberations): the V^4_2 chord in mm. 217, 219, and 221. Its first appearance in m. 217 is strikingly calibrated. It is scored with the seventh in the bass and the root in the treble, and announced by the two violins with acciaccatura shouts (A♮–B♭) in m. 216. The bass A♭ is attacked by a previously silent cello, and, perhaps most important, the V$^4_2$ chord enters not in the normal way as a product of passing motion from a root-position dominant but directly. The chord will eventually delay—in a particularly memorable way—the approach to the final cadence from a first-inversion tonic chord in m. 222 to the decisive perfect authentic cadence in mm. 223–24.

Topically, period 14 features hunting fanfare (or gigue-style hunt) and brilliant style figuration, while period 15 is given over to the poking or pecking figures associated with the sensibility style heard at the end of the exposition (period 6) and again at the beginning, in the middle, and at the end of the development (period 7). A fanfare in the three lowest strings adds to the affirmative sense of closure in the last three measures.

HEARING FORM

We have arrived at the end of the movement. How might we characterize the experience of hearing form? We might begin by acknowledging that the experience has been wide-ranging (on account of Mozart's topical vocabulary) and at the same time directed and orderly (on account of its enactment of a conventional key-area plan). We might report specific adventures in the realms of melody, harmony, phrase rhythm, thematic process, and so on. My interest here has been in the contribution of topics. Although I have emphasized their musical manifestation, a topical perspective exceeds the purely musical. At the connotative level, topics invoke the theater, the chamber, and the outdoors, as well as compositional labor, referential styles, and gestures—in short, material carrying human and social freight. To the extent that these realist invocations have a purpose, it is to delight. Unlike the historian, Mozart is not burdened with a documentary obligation. Rather, like the poet or sculptor, his task is to edify through a play of forms.

Listening to form with help from topics takes on several unexpected features. A topical hearing rejects the smooth trajectories delivered by structuralist analysis, complete with their tonal plots and banal assurances of closure. These tell only a part of the story. For the hearer of topics, the movement's materiality indexes a scarred, variegated landscape, sometimes marked in strange ways, with bits sticking out here and there—unruly objects, we might say. Musical form becomes something more complex than the enactment of a ritual dialectic. As objects that generally refuse generation from prior structures and remain unassimilated into overarching unities, topics complicate and at the same time enrich our experience of form. They compel an intertextual hearing in which one senses—often fleetingly—the connotations of Mozart's materials: fanfare, *Sturm und Drang*, singing style, sensibility style, brilliant style, and gigue. These flavors point listeners to imagined worlds inscribed in Mozart's chamber music.

Postscript: Not Mozart

Sometime presumably in the 1790s, Johann Christian Stumpf (1740–1801), a contemporary of Mozart's, arranged the movement we have been studying here as a serenade for two clarinets, two horns, two bassoons, and double bass.[4] This precious document affords a penetrating insight into the nature of Mozart's imagination. One need only listen to the opening period (Example 17.1) to hear the profound contrasts between Mozart's and Stumpf's worlds. Whereas Mozart's two violas simulate the style of horns, Stumpf restores the material to two horns. The aesthetic distancing so fundamental to topic theory is erased. Mozart captured the style and sound of horns on strings, thus enclosing functional music (the hunt style) in quotation marks, defamiliarizing it, making it at once strange, distant, and yet recognizable. Such acts of "othering" are essential to topical definition and are surely the source of some of what delights us in Mozart. Stumpf, on the other hand, returns the hunt style to its proper home, to instruments that would normally play the hunting calls; in doing so, he erases a crucial part of Mozart's achievement. The timbral intervention that transforms functional music into art music is undermined. Stumpf's hunt approaches the literal, whereas Mozart's hunt remains at one stage removed from the literal.

Such transformations, translations, and reimaginings lie at the heart of Mozart's aesthetic, and they are often highlighted in topical analysis. In a favorable review of Stephen Rumph's study of Mozart in the context of enlightenment semiotics (2012), Patricia Howard has described Ratner's presentation of topic theory as "simplistic"; according to her, "everyone can recognize a march!" (2012:107). But what about the pianto, gavotte, learned style, singing style, Swabian allemande, or indeed the dozens of other signs that make up the thesaurus of characteristic figures bequeathed to Classic composers by their predecessors? What accounts for the apparent indifference to topical articulation in a wide range of writing about eighteenth-century music? Perhaps the ubiquity of topics is deceiving. Perhaps we should learn to re-hear marches rather than merely recognizing them. As nuggets of expressivity, they engender fresh engagement with a work's sounding surfaces. Composers, performers, and listeners are increasingly finding their understanding of style, meaning, and form enriched by the topical approach.

Notes

1. The term "topic theory," first used by Michael Spitzer (1996), refers nowadays to a collective research enterprise centered on the structural, sociocultural, and historical affiliations of musical works as revealed by their topical content. As far as I can tell, the term never appeared in the writings of its founder, Leonard Ratner. Significant recent contributions to topic theory include Hatten (2004), Monelle (2006), Grabócz (2009), Rumph (2012), Tarasti (2012), and McClelland (2012). For appraisals of the field, see McKay (2007) and Agawu (2008).

2. Ratner's printer inadvertently left out three pages (encompassing mm. 131–211) from the annotated score of K. 614/i in his example 18-8 (1980: 237–44).

3. It has been suggested that the application of the topical label *Sturm und Drang* to a work like this originating in 1791 betrays an anachronism. Monelle, for example, thinks that the term should simply be retired: "it is probably no longer OK to speak of a 'Sturm und Drang' topic" (2010: 110). McClelland (this volume) summarizes the debate around this concept. I continue to use it in this essay, however, partly in deference to Ratner's usage, partly because the musical character indexed by the term is often contextually self-evident, and finally because there is a consistency to its usage across many writings in topic theory.

4. For the first recording of Stumpf's Serenade after K. 614, see *?Mozart!* vol. 6: *Nonet KV 428 / Serenade KV 621 / Fragments KV 384* (Consortium Classicum, MDG 301 0499-2).

REFERENCES

Agawu, V. Kofi. 1991. *Playing with Signs: A Semiotic Interpretation of Classic Music*. Princeton, NJ: Princeton University Press.

——. 2008. Topic Theory: Achievement, Critique, Prospects. In *Passagen, IMS Kongress Zürich 2007: Fünf Hauptvorträge, Five Key Note Speeches*, ed. Laurenz Lütteken and Hans-Joachim Hinrichsen, 38–69. Zurich: Bärenreiter.

——. 2009. *Music as Discourse: Semiotic Adventures in Romantic Music*. New York: Oxford University Press.

Allanbrook, Wye Jamison. 1983. *Rhythmic Gesture in Mozart:* Le nozze di Figaro *and* Don Giovanni. Chicago: University of Chicago Press.

——. 1992. Two Threads through the Labyrinth: Topic and Process in the First Movements of K. 332 and K. 333. In *Convention in Eighteenth and Nineteenth-Century Music: Essays in Honor of Leonard G. Ratner*, ed. Wye J. Allanbrook, Janet M. Levy, and William Mahrt, 125–71. Stuyvesant, NY: Pendragon.

——. 2014. *The Secular Commedia: Comic Mimesis in Late Eighteenth-Century Music*, ed. Mary Ann Smart and Richard Taruskin. Berkeley: University of California Press.

Bonds, Mark Evan. 1991. *Wordless Rhetoric: Musical Form and the Metaphor of the Oration*. Cambridge, MA: Harvard University Press.

Burnham, Scott. 2002. Form. In *The Cambridge History of Western Music Theory*, ed. Thomas Christensen, 880–906. Cambridge: Cambridge University Press.

Caplin, William. 2005. On the Relation of Musical *Topoi* to Formal Function. *Eighteenth-Century Music* 2/1: 113–24.

Grabócz, Márta. 2009. *Musique, narrativité, signification*. Paris: L'Harmattan.

Hatten, Robert S. 1994. *Musical Meaning in Beethoven: Markedness, Correlation, and Interpretation*. Bloomington: Indiana University Press.

——. 2004. *Interpreting Musical Gestures, Topics, and Tropes*. Bloomington: Indiana University Press.

Howard, Patricia. 2012. Review of *Mozart and Enlightenment Semiotics* by Stephen Rumph. *The Musical Times* 153/1920: 105–9.

Ivanovitch, Roman. 2004. Mozart and the Environment of Variation. Ph.D. diss., Yale University.

McClelland, Clive. 2012. *Ombra: Supernatural Music in the Eighteenth Century*. Lanham, MD: Lexington.

McKay, Nicholas. 2007. On Topics Today. *Zeitschrift der Gesellschaft für Musiktheorie* 4/1. Available: http://www.gmth.de/zeitschrift/artikel/251.aspx. Accessed 9 December 2013.

Momigny, Jérome-Joseph de. 1806. *Cours complet d'harmonie et de composition*. Paris: Chez l'auteur.

Monelle, Raymond. 2006. *The Musical Topic: Hunt, Military and Pastoral*. Bloomington: Indiana University Press.

——. 2010. Review of *Music as Discourse: Semiotic Adventures in Romantic Music* by V. Kofi Agawu. *Music and Letters* 91/1: 110–11.

Pestelli, Giorgio. 1984. *The Age of Mozart and Beethoven*. Cambridge: Cambridge University Press.

Powers, Harold. 1995. Reading Mozart's Music: Text and Topic, Syntax and Sense. *Current Musicology* 57: 5–44.

Ratner, Leonard G. 1980. *Classic Music: Expression, Form, and Style*. New York: Schirmer.

——. 1991. Topical Content in Mozart's Keyboard Sonatas. *Early Music* 19/4: 615–19.

Rumph, Stephen. 2012. *Mozart and Enlightenment Semiotics*. Berkeley: University of California Press.

Sisman, Elaine. 1993. *Mozart: The "Jupiter" Symphony, No. 41 in C major, K. 551*. Cambridge: Cambridge University Press.

Spitzer, Michael. 1996. Creativity, Life and Music: Three Books about Beethoven (Review article on *Beethoven's Piano Sonata in E, Op. 109* by Nicholas Marston, *Beethoven* by William Kinderman, and *Beethoven Forum*, Vol. 3, edited by Glenn Stanley). *Music Analysis* 15/2–3: 343–66.

Sutcliffe, W. Dean. 2003. *The Keyboard Sonatas of Domenico Scarlatti and Eighteenth-Century Musical Style*. Cambridge: Cambridge University Press.

Tarasti, Eero. 2012. *Semiotics of Classical Music: How Mozart, Brahms and Wagner Talk to Us*. The Hague: De Gruyter Mouton.

CHAPTER 18

....

TOPICAL FIGURAE

The Double Articulation of Topics

....

STEPHEN RUMPH

MUSICAL topics have invited comparison with language ever since Leonard Ratner introduced the rhetorical term *topos*. Wye Allanbrook referred to "an expressive vocabulary" (1983: 2), while Raymond Monelle described the topic as "a kind of musical term or word; it has a conventional meaning, understood by all hearers" (2006: 3). But language has a dual aspect not addressed by writers on topics. While words function as meaningful signs, they are articulated by meaningless elements. This second level of articulation comprises phonemes (the /t/ of *topic*), their distinctive features (unvoiced, alveolar, plosive), and the suprasegmental structures of tone, prosody, and syllabification (the stress on *to-*). This "double articulation" of language, as André Martinet called it, characterizes many sign systems (1963: 17–19). The dot and dash of Morse code, the colors of national flags, and the 0 and 1 of computer code are all meaningless elements that articulate meaningful signs. Do musical topics also have a double articulation?

Consider a classic example of topical semantics, the opening Duettino from *Le nozze di Figaro*.[1] The topical argument seems a direct translation of the stage action: as Susanna persuades Figaro to stop measuring and admire her new bonnet, his heavy-footed bourrée gives way to her delicate gavotte (see Example 18.1). Yet the Duettino contains a third topic. During Figaro's counting music, the cellos sustain *alla breve* suspensions beneath the melody, evoking the churchly *stile antico*. While the *stile antico* does not map readily onto the libretto, it shares a structural feature with Susanna's gavotte. The most distinctive feature of both gavotte and fourth-species counterpoint is a displacement of rhythmic grouping to the second half of the measure. As signs, *stile antico* and gavotte belong to opposing categories—ancient/modern, strict/free, sacred/secular, sung/danced. Yet both are articulated by the same nonsignifying feature.

Such structural features, which articulate multiple topics yet do not themselves signify, suggest a second articulation for topics. Nor do gavotte and fourth-species exhaust the topics articulated by displacement. The same underlying feature produces the offbeat accents of sarabande and mazurka in triple meter, and the syncopations of *alla zoppa* and the *empfindsamer Styl* in duple meter.

Such nonsignifying features suggest an uncharted syntactic level below the topical surface. In the Duettino, for example, the displaced grouping of the alla breve suspensions creates a smooth transition between the bourrée and gavotte. From the beginning of Figaro's theme, the suspensions strongly accent the third beat, preparing the rhythm of Susanna's gavotte. Before Susanna has sung a note, Figaro's phrases have shifted to the third beat, and he even anticipates the exact rhythm of her melody. As signs, *stile antico*,

EXAMPLE **18.1** Mozart, *Le nozze di Figaro*, Act 1 Scene 1, Duettino "Cinque…dieci…venti," mm. 1–38.

(Continued)

EXAMPLE **18.1** (Continued)

(*Continued*)

EXAMPLE **18.1** (Continued)

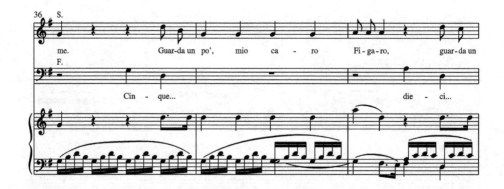

bourrée, and gavotte do not suggest an obvious connection; yet the nonsignifying level reveals an impeccable logic.

The possibility that music might possess a double articulation has met with some resistance. Nicolas Meeùs (2002) has noted formal similarities between musical and linguistic articulation (economy, hierarchy), yet he denied the fundamental distinction between the signifying and nonsignifying level. Likewise, Marshall Brown restricted music to "the lower or systematic articulation," claiming that, "music does not, in general, have words" (1992: 76). Meeùs and Brown rightly distinguished language from music, which does not function primarily as a referential code. Nevertheless, topics do function as conventional signs with stable referential meanings; and, like many other nonlinguistic signs, they are articulated by a smaller number of nonsignifying features. Topics suggest a limited case of musical double articulation that can enrich our understanding of how these signs interact with each other and the musical structure.

In one respect, topical articulation suggests a close analogy with phonological theory. Since the 1960s, phonological grammar has sought to explain the way surface representations are derived from an underlying lexicon.[2] For example, the word *impossible* is derived from the underlying representation *in + possible*; the alveolar /n/ assimilates to the labial /p/, however, surfacing as /m/. In generative phonology, the surface is derived according to ordered and inviolable rules. In the current reigning model, optimality theory (McCarthy 2007), multiple candidates compete according to a hierarchy of violable rules. In the case of topics, the lexicon is the universe of available styles and genres, and the surface representation is their articulation within the musical work. This chapter explores the way in which the topical lexicon is articulated within late eighteenth-century music and how this articulation interacts with the structures of meter, rhythm, pitch organization, and dynamics.

To avoid confusing and inexact parallels with language, I have adopted Louis Hjelmslev's term "figura" for the shared structural features of topics (1961: 45–47). Hjelmslev used the term to encompass all the nonsignifying elements of the expression plane, whether phonemes, distinctive features, or prosody, and semiotic researchers have generalized the term to other sign systems. Topical figurae will be defined as structural features that (1) articulate multiple topics and (2) do not signify topically. The second criterion thus eliminates double upbeats (gavotte), imitative counterpoint (learned style), or triangle timbre (Turkish style), signifying features that belong to the first articulation. Timbre seems to lack a second articulation in late eighteenth-century style: instrumental tone colors signify directly, without nonsignifying figurae. Pedal points present a borderline case. While they belong exclusively to the pastoral genre, they do articulate multiple dances; and while they are indeed signifying features of those topics, they also function as abstract structures, as in the Quiescenza schema or sonata-form retransitions.[3]

Figurae will be notated with slashes, the phonological symbol for the phoneme— hence, /displacement/. The borrowed notation proves somewhat misleading, since figurae actually combine the properties of both phonemes and distinctive features. Like the former, they function as minimal nonsignifying units of difference; like the latter, they usually occur in combination rather than sequentially. The phonological notation can perhaps serve as a reminder that comparisons between music and language, however alluring, always remain inexact.

DELETION AND MARKEDNESS

As iconic signs, topics reproduce some features from their represented objects while omitting others. This process can be compared with the phonological operation of deletion. Examples of linguistic deletion include the silent /d/ of *grandma* or the elided /œ/ in the French phrase *je t'aime*. Topical deletion varies considerably in degree. The theme that emerges in the finale of the "Eroica" Symphony virtually replicates a contredanse Beethoven had previously used as a ballroom dance. Don Giovanni's aria "Fin ch'han dal vino," on the other hand, preserves the rhythmic and metric features of a ballroom contredanse as well as the "quadratic syntax" of this dance (described by Eric McKee, this volume), but deletes its timbre and binary form.

Few rules govern the deletion of topical features. In the case of topics based on bodily movement, meter and tempo cannot be deleted. This means that only dances and marches fall into separate and mutually exclusive movements. While characteristic styles can range freely across different tempos and meters, rhythmic gesture is restricted.

Moreover, we may note an asymmetry in the distribution of these movement-based topics. While duple meter includes both dances and marches, triple meter is restricted to dances. As Allanbrook has shown (1983: 22; see Figure 13.2 on page 361 in this volume), the extremes of the metrical spectrum are similarly unbalanced. While 2/4, 3/4, and 4/4 accommodate a variety of topics, 3/8, 6/8, 9/8, and 12/8, at one extreme, and alla breve, at the other, correlate overwhelmingly with pastoral or ecclesiastical topics.

This asymmetry exemplifies markedness, a linguistic concept Robert Hatten (1994) has applied fruitfully to music semiotics. The marked term in an opposition tends to occur less frequently and with a greater specificity of meaning. For example, *man* can denote either a male human or humanity in general, while *woman* specifies a female human. Marked phonological features include consonantal voicing or vowel rounding. The marked distribution of topics also gives triple meter, alla breve, and compound triple meter a stronger expressive profile than duple or intermediate meters. While 4/4 does not imply any single topic, 6/8 almost inevitably suggests pastoral or rustic dances.

In language, unmarked features tend to undergo deletion while marked features survive. In the English pronunciation of *opera* or *camera*, for example, the unstressed /ə/ sound is deleted. Topics also tend to preserve marked features. The syncopated fourth-species suffices to signify the learned style, while open "horn fifths" alone can evoke hunting music. Double-dotted rhythms are preserved in the French overture topic, while the unmarked phrase and formal structure can be deleted.[4] The preservation of marked features undoubtedly results from their greater salience and specificity of meaning.[5]

All topical figurae are structurally marked, occurring less frequently and with greater specificity than their unmarked opposites. Figurae either depart from or exaggerate a normative stylistic feature. The unmarked opposites of these figurae need not be specified; they belong to the stylistic backdrop against which topics emerge. Indeed, those topics that seem least marked structurally—march, minuet, contredanse—tend to serve as default settings for entire movements.

The only other deletion rule concerns mode. The minor mode invariably survives in representations of the *tempesta* and *ombra* topics. Otherwise, composers freely deleted phrase structure, texture, form, and, most significantly, timbre. Topics show a remarkable independence from timbre—string quartets imitate hunting horns, keyboards imitate cathedral choirs, opera singers imitate trumpets. This indifference to timbre is perhaps the defining feature of topical representation, permitting genres and styles to circulate beyond their traditional performance venues.[6]

The emancipation of topics from timbre runs parallel with the rise of instrumental music. The early canzona, ricercar, and fantasia adapted choral polyphony to the keyboard and instrumental consort, while the toccata and variation set drew on the newer styles of opera and madrigal. The growth of amateur keyboard culture helped composers immeasurably as they abstracted styles and genres from their enclaves in traditional society and commodified them as musical signs; the bourgeois consumer who purchased a Mozart sonata had the whole of musical Europe at her fingertips. Topical representation exemplifies the democratizing tendency that David Wellbery has traced in eighteenth-century theories of the literary sign: "The desacralization of language is the extrication of language from its place within the ceremonies of religious and absolutist authority and its transformation into a medium of communication and debate among equal subjects" (1984: 36).

THE ECONOMY OF FIGURAE

If every unit of meaning corresponded to a unique sound, humans would need thousands of distinct sounds to communicate. Instead, human languages are organized economically, deriving their entire lexicons from a few dozen phonemes. Artificial sign systems favor the same economy; Morse Code, for instance, represents thirty-six letters and numerals with only two figurae. As Hjelmslev put it, "a language is so ordered that with the help of a handful of figurae and through ever new arrangements of them a legion of signs can be constructed" (1961: 46). The same principle of economy governs topical figurae.

Let us consider the sarabande, a slow triple dance with a stressed second beat. The most distinctive sarabande rhythm is the three-note pattern that begins the Andante of Mozart's Piano Concerto in G major, K. 453 (Example 18.2). In an uneconomical system, this rhythm would correspond to only one topic. In fact, it belongs to several, depending on the tempo. In a quicker tempo, the same rhythm can help articulate the polonaise, as in the Rondo alla polacca of Beethoven's Triple Concerto (Example 18.3) or in his Polonaise, Op. 89. The lilting rhythm would also become a fixture of the nineteenth-century waltz.

If we transform the rhythm itself, still more topics appear. Sarabandes in 3/2 regularly augment the motive, while the 3/8 sarabande rhythm in Ferrando's "Un'aura amorosa" from *Così fan tutte* diminishes it (Example 18.4). Shifting the rhythmic grouping one beat to the left relative to bar lines removes the offbeat accent and yields a rhythm common to 6/4 gigues and loures (the gigue-like scherzo of Beethoven's Ninth Symphony relies almost entirely on this rhythmic motive). The rhythm is a staple of early minuets, as well as quick later minuets like Figaro's "Se vuol ballare" (Example 18.5). The metrically aligned version, of course, occurs most often in diminution, within 3/8 or 6/8 meter. In a slow tempo, the *sautillon* rhythm evokes the siciliano; in a quicker tempo, the gigue. In summary, our three-note rhythm functions quite parsimoniously. Diminished, augmented, displaced, and located in quicker tempos, it helps articulate multiple topics—sarabande, polonaise, minuet, waltz, siciliano, and gigue.

This ubiquitous rhythm, which we may dub the "dance motive," might suggest the equivalent of a topical phoneme. Yet it remains a signifying feature, not a figura. In all its transformations, the motive belongs to the signifying surface of the represented dances. To reach the second articulation, we must abstract the nonsignifying structural operations that produce the different versions of the rhythm. In the case of sarabande, the pertinent figura is /displacement/, the same figura that produces Susanna's gavotte. /

EXAMPLE **18.2** Mozart, Piano Concerto in G major, K. 453/ii, mm. 1–5.

EXAMPLE **18.3** Beethoven, Concerto for Violin, Cello, and Piano in C major, Op. 56/iii, Rondo alla polacca, mm. 1–8.

EXAMPLE **18.4** Mozart, *Così fan tutte*, Act 1 Scene 12, "Un'aura amorosa," mm. 24–25.

EXAMPLE **18.5** Mozart, *Le nozze di Figaro*, Act 1 Scene 2, "Se vuol ballare," mm. 1–4.

Displacement/ is clearly marked, in both structure and frequency. The unmarked (metrically aligned) opposites of sarabande and gavotte include siciliano, gigue, pastorale, passepied, *Deutscher*, minuet, contredanse, bourrée, march, French overture—in short, most topics based on rhythmic movement. Structurally marked features are also more easily identified. While listeners might confuse a bourrée with a march or a minuet with a passepied, few will fail to recognize a gavotte or sarabande.

The marked and unmarked versions of the "dance motive" frequently appear together. They alternate in the early sarabande and minuet, often within the same phrase. Both versions appear in the first movement of Mozart's Piano Sonata in A major, K. 331. The theme features a siciliano rhythm (Example 18.6a), which returns displaced in the sarabande-like Variation V (Example 18.6b). The two versions also alternate in the trio of Beethoven's Eighth Symphony and in Figaro's "Se vuol ballare." In K. 331, /displacement/ results in a new topic; in the Eighth Symphony and Figaro's aria, the figura produces a variation within the same topic.

What new insights can this type of analysis provide? Let us revisit the first movement of Beethoven's "Eroica" Symphony, which showcases both versions of the "dance motive." The marked (displaced) version emerges at the beginning of the transition (Example 18.7a), and the unmarked version in the new E-minor theme of the development (Example 18.7b). Moreover, Beethoven has dramatically juxtaposed the two versions. The first half of the development systematically isolates the offbeat rhythm of the transition theme, exploring its displaced accent. After a leisurely rehearsal of the theme, the fugato in mm. 236–46 adds a *sfp* accent to the second beat. The offbeat accent soon dominates the entire texture, leading to a massive syncopated passage (mm. 247–79). The famous dissonant climax (mm. 280–83) projects the metrical conflict into the clashing antiphony between winds and strings, which enter, respectively, on the first and second beats (Example 18.8). The E-minor theme that emerges from this violent catharsis restores the rhythmic motive to its unmarked (metrically aligned) version.

Moreover, the offbeat accent in the transition belongs within a larger pattern of metric displacement that stretches back to the opening measures. The "Eroica" begins with a theme whose trochaic rhythm and triadic melody strongly confirm the notated meter. The chromatic disruption in m. 7, however, sparks an agitated syncopation in the violins.[7] The restatement of the theme leads to an extended hemiola with *sf* accents (mm. 28–35). The transition echoes these offbeat accents, absorbing them into its graceful, dance-like theme. The closing section continues to emphasize the second beat with *sf* accents and enlists the displaced "dance motive" from the transition in a *ff* fanfare (mm. 109–16). In short, the development brings to a boil a metrical conflict that reaches back to the opening measures of the Allegro con brio.

EXAMPLE **18.6** Mozart, Sonata in A major, K. 331/i: (a) Theme, mm. 1–4; (b) Variation V, mm. 1–2.

EXAMPLE **18.7** Beethoven, Symphony No. 3 in E flat major, Op. 55, "Eroica," i: (a) mm. 45–49; (b) mm. 288–92.

EXAMPLE **18.8** Beethoven, Symphony No. 3 in E flat major, Op. 55, "Eroica," i, mm. 276–79.

At this point, our analysis can take two directions. We can view /displacement/ as a purely structural feature, belonging to Beethoven's formal design. Our reading would then treat the two versions of the "dance motive" as abstract motives, the surface expression of an underlying structural conflict. This interpretation, which ignores topical semantics, provides a perfectly self-sufficient account of the Allegro con brio.

Alternatively, we can proceed to explore the semantic implications of /displacement/. Such a reading might begin with a consideration of dance in the "Eroica." The symphony culminates not in a triumphal march, but in a contredanse borrowed from the finale of Beethoven's ballet *Die Geschöpfe des Prometheus*. In this context, Beethoven's dramatic transformation of a motive inextricably associated with dance suggests a program-matic intent. The purging of the marked offbeat might be interpreted as the return to a lost simplicity, a state of innocence before chromaticism and syncopation infected the natural order. The pastoral flavor of the opening motive, with its lazily circling triadic melody, would fit this reading. Moreover, as Charles Rosen has pointed out, the new E-minor theme returns to the outlines of the opening triadic melody (1997: 392–93).

Of course, many other interpretations could account for Beethoven's transformation of the "dance motive." Yet they would all stand on a solid structuralist footing. The her-meneutic reading is not grafted onto the musical surface, but rather emerges from an analysis of structural oppositions spanning the Allegro con brio. Likewise, the semantic interpretation does not rely on a superficial labeling of topics (indeed, we have not iden-tified a single dance), but rests instead on an abstract markedness structure. The topi-cal figura mediates between syntactic and semantic analysis, making possible a holistic interpretation of the topical sign.

ASSIMILATION, NEUTRALIZATION, AND ICONICITY

In phonological analysis, assimilation and neutralization are primary diagnostics for featural markedness. Assimilation occurs when a phoneme adopts the marked feature of an adjacent phoneme. In neutralization, conversely, a particular environment removes a featural contrast by suppressing the marked term. Voicing, a marked feature, demon-strates both processes. In the Italian word *svanire*, the unvoiced sibilant *s* assimilates to the voiced *v*: /s/ → [z]. In the German word *Beweis*, on the other hand, the word-final position neutralizes voicing: /z/ → [s]. In general, assimilation increases markedness, while neutralization reduces it.

The broader phenomenon of markedness assimilation, another concept marshaled by Hatten (1994: 37, 64, 118, 292), has powerful implications for topical analysis. As Edwin Battistella explained, "marked values from different oppositions tend to cluster in a given entity or location, creating or reinforcing larger marked entities" (1996: 64). Battistella adduced the language of official utterances, like "in witness thereof" or "by the power invested in me," in which the marked speech act and diction (illocutionary, formal) assimilate to the marked context (ceremony). Sign and object are thus united by an analogous structure in the expression and content planes—S′:S::O′:O. Markedness assimilation exemplifies Peirce's category of second-order icons, or diagrams, in which the sign replicates the relationship among the parts of its object. The relationship between sign and object thus rests on resemblance, an iconic motivation, rather than mere convention or habit. Markedness assimilation and neutralization provide powerful concepts for analyzing topical syntax and semantics, placing musical meaning on a truly structuralist footing.

Let us explore the implications of markedness assimilation and neutralization, turning from rhythm to texture. A wide range of topics are subsumed by /homorhythm/. This figura comprises octave and chordal textures and helps articulate fanfare, *ombra*, opera buffa, march, fantasia, and hymn, as well as rustic dances.[8] /Homorhythm/ relates closely to the figura /solo/, which can articulate cadenza, recitative, and the imitative counterpoint associated with learned style. While /homorhythm/ might seem overly capacious, its textures are functionally interchangeable: octaves and chords play the same annunciatory role in introductory motives, and they frequently alternate in cadential passages. This figura is clearly marked within late eighteenth-century style, whose unmarked homophonic texture distinguishes melody and accompaniment through different rates of movement.

We may observe markedness assimilation in the relationship between /homorhythm/ and dynamic markings. Octave and chordal passages are almost invariably *p* or *f*, if not *pp* or *ff*. Chordal textures either exploit the massed bombast of the ensemble, as in the Mannheim "hammerblow" and military marches, or they retreat into the hushed interiority of the chorale and chromatic fantasia. Octave passages are either brash and public (the opening of Mozart's "Haffner" Symphony) or mysterious and intriguing (the opening of his Piano Concerto in C minor, K. 491). Only rarely do we find /homorhythm/ paired with a moderate *mf* or *mp*. The dynamics assimilate to the marked texture.

Markedness assimilation occurs frequently within late eighteenth-century style. The second movement of a sonata cycle is typically marked for tempo (slow), key (non-tonic), style (lyrical), and dynamics (soft). Likewise, tonally marked secondary themes often introduce marked textures and instrumentation. This clustering of marked features heightens contrasts and increases the salience of formal events. In the case of homorhythmic textures, which often occur in introductory or cadential positions, the assimilation of dynamics helps signal pivotal events in the form.

Assimilation also spans the two articulations and reinforces the link between signifier and signified. The marked texture of octave and chordal passages, as noted, often serves to call attention to formal events. These "stop-look-and-listen" textures, as Janet Levy called them (1982: 531), function as structural indices or, as Kofi Agawu (1991) referred to them, introversive signs. Yet the same indexicality also motivates their use in topics, or extroversive signs. The slow chordal motion of hymns and fantasias directs attention inward, whether in pious or pathological introspection; the eerie octaves of the *ombra* create a sense of foreboding and anticipation; fanfares call the listener to attention. /Homorhythm/ thus functions both introversively and extroversively, as both formal signpost and topical figura. Both functions rely on the same marked departure from the normative texture.

/Homorhythm/ thus creates an analogue between signifier and signified. For instance, the bare octaves of the basso buffo depart from the normal homophonic texture, but they also segregate these low characters from their social betters. Stylistic marking correlates with social marking. In the opening of *Don Giovanni* ("Notte e giorno faticar"), as Leporello turns his thoughts to his noble master, his lowly octaves give way to a rich homophonic texture. In the same way, the marked rhythms of gavotte, *alla zoppa*, or mazurka correspond to their marked cultural status as feminine, exotic, or nationalist dances. The assimilation of musical and cultural markedness creates an iconic relationship between signifier and signified, a bond that transcends simple one-to-one mapping. Indeed, as Michael Shapiro explained, markedness structure functions as a Peircian interpretant, connecting sign and object (1983: 15–21). The listener registers the sign as syntactically Other, a representation that governs the correlation with the semantically Other object.

The opposite of assimilation, neutralization, occurs when a particular environment removes a featural contrast. Examples include the sonata-form recapitulation, which suppresses the marked secondary key; or the Picardy third, which removes the marked minor mode. /Anacrusis/, a marked rhythmic figura that articulates gavotte, bourrée, and contredanse, provides another example of neutralization. Many concertos and symphonies begin with an upbeat theme, which can create hypermetrical ambiguities, as in the opening themes of Mozart's Symphony in G minor, K. 550, or Haydn's "Surprise" Symphony.[9] The following transition typically begins with an elision, precluding the possibility of /anacrusis/. The new formal environment removes the upbeat/downbeat opposition, thereby settling the hypermetric conflict. In the case of /homorhythm/, any homophonic or polyphonic texture neutralizes the marked texture. Because octave or chordal passages normally stand apart as introductions, interruptions, or cadential punctuation, we might say that the flow of the musical discourse itself neutralizes /homorhythm/.

We can isolate several other marked textures. /Augmentation/, in which the melodic line moves at an unusually slow rate relative to the accompaniment, articulates the singing allegro topic. Yet the same figura also produces the *stylus mixtus*, which pairs the *stile antico* with a modern accompaniment, and trio-sonata textures in which a walking bass supports the slower upper voices.[10] Mozart's "Jupiter" Symphony illustrates how /augmentation/ articulates multiple topics. Both the secondary theme of the first movement and the minuet begin with a leisurely melody floating above a ticking eighth-note accompaniment, examples of singing allegro. The last movement opens with a plainchant motive poised above a similar eighth-note accompaniment, exemplifying the *stylus mixtus*. In the figura /diminution/, conversely, the melodic line moves at an unusually rapid rate relative to the other voices. This figura articulates both the virtuosic passagework of brilliant style and the species counterpoint of the *stile antico*, as well as more vigorous strains of the contredanse.

The fluidity of textural figurae allowed composers to exploit the multivalent potential of their thematic material. Haydn's "Fifths" Quartet begins with a singing allegro, a broad lyrical melody accompanied by eighth notes (Example 18.9a). Yet the head motive, with its ponderous half notes, hints at the sacred style, suggesting a *stylus mixtus* construction similar to the "Jupiter" Symphony finale. The transition realizes this

EXAMPLE **18.9** Haydn, String Quartet in D minor, Op. 76 No. 2, "Fifths," i: (a) mm. 1–2; (b) mm. 13–14.

implication, transforming the motive into a *cantus firmus* with a rapid countersubject above (Example 18.9b). The transition thus inverts the textural figura from /augmentation/ to /diminution/, pivoting around the ambiguous character of the head motive. Haydn has extracted new meaning from his opening theme.

Mozart's Clarinet Quintet also demonstrates the exploratory potential of figurae. The opening theme juxtaposes an alla breve hymn to a brilliant sixteenth-note cadenza, articulated, respectively, by the marked figurae /homorhythm/ and /solo/. A third texture emerges in m. 20, which combines the half notes of the hymn with a melody in steady eighth notes (Example 18.10). This new figura, /diminution/, absorbs the soloist's rapid notes into a strict third-species counterpoint. The texture mediates between the extremes of hymn and cadenza, neutralizing both /homorhythm/ and /solo/. Moreover, it unearths the historical source of both the brilliant style and species counterpoint, the principle of diminution. In this way, we might say that Mozart's play with figurae performs an archaeological exploration of the musical style.

FIGURAE AND MUSICAL DEVELOPMENT

Topical figurae also play a role in musical development, as we shall explore in the opening Allegro of Mozart's Sonata in F major, K. 332. This movement famously abounds in

topics—aria, learned style, minuet, *tempesta*, hunt. But how did Mozart shape this patchwork surface into a coherent discourse? To help answer this question, we shall pursue a melodic figura, /arpeggio/. /Arpeggio/, or melodic writing that arpeggiates the tonic triad, articulates fanfare, hunt, pastorale, *ranz des vaches*, *Deutscher*, and Mannheim rocket. Melodies confined to the notes of the tonic triad are clearly marked within late eighteenth-century style. Semantically, /arpeggio/ originates in the natural wind instruments; syntactically, it interfaces with the most basic harmonic and voice-leading structures. Our analysis will explore both sides of the figura, beginning with its syntactic role.

The opening cantabile melody arpeggiates the tonic triad in two widening loops, arriving on $\hat{8}$ in m. 5 (Example 18.11). The first two measures are purely triadic, while mm. 3–4 include neighbor tones. The circling melodic contour mirrors the Alberti bass; in fact, mm. 1–2 augment the left hand's first four notes. The harmony also traces a circular pattern above the bass pedal, an example of Robert Gjerdingen's Quiescenza schema (2007: 181–95). The contrapuntal motive in mm. 5–8 reverses the $\hat{1}$–$\hat{3}$–$\hat{5}$–$\hat{8}$ arpeggiation of mm. 1–4 in a series of descending loops, inverting the rising sixth of m. 3 and ending with a retrograde of the $\hat{1}$–$\hat{3}$–$\hat{5}$ incipit. The motive also retains the spacious intervals of the opening melody, filling in a pentatonic scale.

The minuet-like idea in mm. 9–12 restores unmarked scalar melody. The melody fills in a descending sixth (the interval opened in mm. 3 and 5) and reaches the cadence through $\hat{4}$ and $\hat{7}$, the two degrees missing from the pentatonic contrapuntal motive. The following hunt motive in mm. 13–20 fills in the tonic triad, retracing the $\hat{5}$–$\hat{3}$–$\hat{1}$ descent of the contrapuntal motive. At the same time, the lower voice preserves triadic melody, resulting in the characteristic "horn fifths."

EXAMPLE **18.11** Mozart, Piano Sonata in F major, K. 332/i, mm. 1–25.

The /arpeggio/ figura dominates the transition, beginning in m. 23. The two-measure head motive consists entirely of triadic tones and leads to a rolled chord. The motive retraces the î–3̂–5̂ ascent from mm. 1–4 (in minor) and restores the Alberti bass; it also echoes the rising sixth of m. 3. The aimless circling of the primary theme, however, has straightened out into a thrusting spiral, reminiscent of both the Mannheim rocket and military fanfare. The secondary theme preserves the triadic emphasis of the transition, even as bends the melody back into a circular shape (Example 18.12). The theme begins with the rolled-chord flourish from the transition and again ascends the tonic triad to 5̂.

Triadic melodies have the property of rapidly opening linear and registral space. In both the primary and secondary themes of K. 332, the initial ascent to 5̂ takes only four beats. In order to fill out the time span with a triadic theme, the composer can either twist the melody into circular loops or open up further registral space. The tonally stable primary and secondary themes take the first path, circling about the tonic triad. The modulatory transition takes the second, releasing the triadic melody into a rocket-like ascent. The closing theme retraces the î–3̂–5̂–8̂ arpeggiation of the primary theme in mm. 86–89, but now with a purposeful drive to the upper octave; even the Alberti bass has straightened out into a î–3̂–5̂–8̂ pattern (Example 18.13). On the other hand, the little minuet that begins the development returns to the looping triadic contour of the primary and secondary themes.

The stormy minor passage in the secondary key area (mm. 60–70), which echoes the violent gestures of the transition, synthesizes both methods of development (Example 18.14). The left-hand melody consists of an ascending triad, which rises sequentially through the octave. Yet the harmonic progression merely rotates through the circle of fifths, looping back to end on a half cadence. The theme may awaken the fire of the transition, but it spends its vigor in futile circles.

In summary, the /arpeggio/ figura provides a major source of musical continuity across the movement. The pervasive triadic melodic writing helps unify the fragmentary thematic surface, while providing a coherent arc to the patchwork primary theme. The alternation between circular and linear contours enhances the tonal argument, sharpening the contrast between the stable and modulatory areas of the form. As David Beach (1994) has shown, the prominent 5̂–3̂–î arpeggiation in the primary area is even reflected in the tonal plan of the development, which descends from C major to A minor before returning abruptly to F major.

Let us now consider the semantic face of the figura, exploring how the topics articulated by /arpeggio/ work together to create meaning. As noted, Mozart's primary and

EXAMPLE **18.12** Mozart, Piano Sonata in F major, K. 332/i, mm. 41–47.

EXAMPLE **18.13** Mozart, Piano Sonata in F major, K. 332/i, mm. 86–100.

EXAMPLE **18.14** Mozart, Piano Sonata in F major, K. 332/i, mm. 60–70.

closing themes share a common melodic shape, arpeggiating the tonic triad from î to 8̂. Yet while the primary theme traces aimless circles both melodically and harmonically, the closing theme thrusts aggressively toward melodic and harmonic closure. These bookends mark out an opposition within the /arpeggio/ topics. The topics share a common origin in the natural wind instruments—the shepherd's pipe, the hunter's horn, the soldier's trumpet. But these instruments enshrine both tranquility and violence, both beauty and sublimity.

The primary thematic group suggests the pastoral mode in its lazy melodic contours, musette pedal, subdominant inflection, hunting horns, and F-major key; even the learned canon has a pentatonic subject! The minuets in the second group and beginning of the development return to this placid state. The violent eruption of the transition, however, corresponds to a move away from this placid realm to the battlefield, from pipes and horns to trumpet calls. With its closing fanfare flourishes, the first movement would seem to decide for the bellicose strain. Yet the last measures of the third movement return to the bucolic womb (Example 18.15). The sonata ends with a theme whose musette pedal, circling melody, and hints of *ranz des vaches* ally it with the opening measures of the first movement. K. 332 begins and ends in the timeless natural realm.[11]

Hatten has described the outlook of the pastoral genre as "integrative, sturdily optimistic assurance, perhaps originating from earlier pastoral associations between nature and the harmonious natural order" (1994: 83). Mozart's natural world indeed proves sturdy enough to weather storms and violence. When the *tempesta* from the transition returns in the secondary key (mm. 60–70), its rocket-like propulsion is captured in the circle-of-fifths orbit. A similar rapprochement occurs within the primary theme. For Allanbrook, this "codetta" reflected the additive, patchwork construction of the opening theme, while also preparing the surprise turn to D minor in the transition (1992: 130–34). I would suggest a further explanation for the tacked-on motive that engages both faces of the /arpeggio/ figura.

Syntactically, the hunt topic is uniquely defined by the combination of scalar and triadic melody, combining the upper and lower segments of the overtone series. Semantically, the hunt reconciles peace and war, animal and human spheres. It unites horse and rider, hunter and prey, and contains warfare within a playful ritual.[12] The hunt thus creates a smooth transition from the placid topics of mm. 1–12 into the violent transition. On this reading, mm. 13–20 encapsulate the semantic vision of K. 332: the sonata portrays a resilient pastoral world that can accommodate the full gamut of human and natural experience.

Not all listeners will agree with this particular reading of Mozart's sonata. But it does not arise from a mere surface labeling of topics. The /arpeggio/ figura allows us to engage the topics of K. 332 as structural entities embedded within fundamental musical processes. With one foot in the musical syntax and the other in the topical code, figurae bestride the gap between formal analysis and cultural hermeneutics. They can lead to a more holistic understanding of how topics create meaning, both musical and extramusical.

EXAMPLE **18.15** Mozart, Piano Sonata in F major, K. 332/iii, mm. 242–45.

NOTES

1. See the contrasting topical readings in Allanbrook (1983: 75–77) and Heartz (1990: 145–47). For a more detailed analysis of the Duettino, which engages prosody and markedness structure, see Rumph (2011: 85–90, 94–107).
2. The classic study for generative phonology is Chomsky and Halle (1968); for optimality theory, Prince and Smolensky (2004).
3. The Quiescenza schema is discussed by Robert Gjerdingen (2007: 181–95). The formal function of pastoral pedals represented by the musette topic is considered by William Caplin (2005: 117–18). Because Caplin associates the musette with a tonic pedal, he links this topic to the post-cadential function exemplified by codettas. Dominant pedals facilitate its link with the retransition.
4. Composers naturally deleted phrase and formal structure, large-scale features, as they tailored their materials to the supple play of contrasting topics.
5. This discussion has implications for the formation of topical tropes, which Robert Hatten discusses in the next chapter. The necessity of preserving marked features limits the possible combinations of topics in tropes.
6. This feature may have contributed to the emergence of topical mixtures in chamber music by way of transcriptions. See Dean Sutcliffe's chapter in this volume.
7. This startling moment provides the point of departure for Vasili Byros's analysis in Chapter 14. While Byros concentrates on the autobiographical contexts of the "Eroica" Symphony, highlighting the *ombra* topic, he also points to the *Ländler* topic of the main theme. My reading, linking the "dance motive" of the first movement to the contredanse Finale, complements his analysis, which links the *ombra* crisis to the Funeral March.
8. In fantasias, chains of chords may turn into arpeggiations. Matthew Head (this volume) finds such textures emblematic of the fantasia topic.
9. The opening theme of K. 550/i forms the subject of Danuta Mirka's analysis in Chapter 13. Hypermetrical ambiguities led to conflicting hypermetrical readings surveyed by Mirka.
10. Fux defined the *stylus mixtus* in *Gradus ad Parnassum* (1725) as "a composition with sometimes one, two, three or even more voices, mixed with a group of instruments, sometimes with full choir, as is the custom today especially, in churches (Wollenberg 1992: 236–37).
11. As Allanbrook put it (1983: 44), the sonata "ends coyly calando with four measures in pastoral style."
12. Schubart's description of the hunt, quoted by Andrew Haringer (this volume, pages 196–97), emphasizes the reconciliation of human and animal realms in the hunt.

REFERENCES

Agawu, V. Kofi. 1991. *Playing with Signs: A Semiotic Interpretation of Classic Music*. Princeton: Princeton University Press.

Allanbrook, Wye Jamison. 1983. *Rhythmic Gesture in Mozart:* Le nozze di Figaro *and* Don Giovanni. Chicago: University of Chicago Press.

——. 1992. Two Threads through the Labyrinth: Topic and Process in the First Movements of K. 332 and 333. In *Convention in Eighteenth- and Nineteenth-Century Music: Essays in Honor of Leonard G. Ratner*, ed. Wye J. Allanbrook, Janet M. Levy, and William P. Mahrt, 125–71. Stuyvesant, NY: Pendragon.

Battistella, Edwin L. 1996. *The Logic of Markedness*. Oxford and New York: Oxford University Press.

Beach, David. 1994. The Initial Movements of Mozart's Piano Sonatas K. 280 and K. 332: Some Striking Similarities. *Intégral* 8: 125–46.

Brown, Marshall. 1992. Origins of Modernism: Musical Structures and Narrative Forms. In *Music and Text: Critical Inquiries*, ed. Steven Paul Scher, 75–92. Cambridge: Cambridge University Press.

Chomsky, Noam, and Morris Halle. 1968. *The Sound Pattern of English*. New York: Harper and Row.

Gjerdingen, Robert O. 2007. *Music in the Galant Style*. New York: Oxford University Press.

Fux, Johann Joseph. 1725. *Gradus ad parnassum*. Vienna: Ghelen.

Hatten, Robert. 1994. *Musical Meaning in Beethoven: Markedness, Correlation, and Interpretation*. Bloomington: Indiana University Press.

Heartz, Daniel. 1990. *Mozart's Operas*. Edited, with contributing essays, by Thomas Bauman. Berkeley: University of California Press.

Hjelmslev, Louis. 1961. *Prolegomena to a Theory of Language*. Trans. Francis J. Whitfield. Madison: University of Wisconsin Press.

Levy, Janet M. 1982. Texture as a Sign in Classic and Early Romantic Music. *Journal of the American Musicological Society* 35/3: 482–531.

Martinet, André. 1963. *Éléments de linguistique générale*. Paris: Armand Colin.

McCarthy, John J. 2007. Derivations and Levels of Representation. In *The Cambridge Handbook of Phonology*, ed. Paul de Lacy, 99–117. Cambridge: Cambridge University Press.

Meeùs, Nicholas. 2002. Musical Articulation. *Music Analysis* 21/2: 161–75.

Monelle, Raymond. 2006. *The Musical Topic: Hunt, Military and Pastoral*. Bloomington: Indiana University Press.

Prince, Alan, and Paul Smolensky. 2004. *Optimality Theory: Constraint Interaction in Generative Grammar*. Malden, MA: Blackwell.

Rosen, Charles. 1997. *The Classical Style: Haydn, Mozart, Beethoven*, expanded ed. New York: Norton.

Shapiro, Michael. 1976. *Asymmetry: An Inquiry into the Linguistic Structure of Poetry*. Amsterdam: North Holland.

Wellbery, David. 1984. *Lessing's Laocoon: Semiotics and Aesthetics in the Age of Reason*. Cambridge: Cambridge University Press.

Wollenberg, Susan. 1992. *Gradus ad Parnassum* (1725): Concluding Chapters. *Music Analysis* 11/2–3: 209–13, 215–43.

CHAPTER 19

THE TROPING OF TOPICS IN MOZART'S INSTRUMENTAL WORKS

ROBERT S. HATTEN

INTRODUCTION

A topic is a *familiar style type with easily recognizable musical features*, ranging in complexity from a simple figure (fanfare, horn call), to a texture (learned style as polyphonic and/or imitative; chorale or hymn style as homophonic), a complete genre (various dance and march types; French overture), a style (*ombra, tempesta, Empfindsamkeit*), or some overlap of these categories.[1] Topics may occur in families with hierarchies of inclusion; for example, larger topical fields or *modes* such as the pastoral, military (heroic), hunt, or ecclesiastical may encompass several topics.[2] A topic's semantic field (and hence its general expressive correlation) is often rather clearly situated oppositionally, which further supports its immediate recognition, and general expressive interpretation, by the listener.[3]

But a familiar style type only becomes topical when it is *imported*, without losing its identity, into different contexts. Recognizing that a musical type has been imported into a new musical context may occur with *any* intertextually appropriated musical element. Non-topical imports may include direct musical quotations from another musical work, or even style types that are unique to a composer. However, *any* distinctly defined musical element that is imported will typically be *marked* as topical by the very fact of its appearance in a new context, and it may well be incorporated into the larger (e.g., classical) style and competently understood as a stylistic topic upon further usage.[4]

The markedness of a topic (or topic in formation) is thus fundamental to that topic's *tropological* potential.[5] Whenever a composer makes an allusion to a topic, we already recognize the trope of *synecdoche* (part for whole; a species of *metonymy*). This kind of troping may occur either through the use of one or more distinctive features of the topic or by fragmentary use of a complete topic. But imported topics then *interact* with their new contexts in significant ways, ranging from a momentary flavoring of the discourse to the assumption of a thematic role in that discourse. *Musical tropes* generate fresh meanings from such interactions. A *merger* of the imported topic with the prevailing style (or with other imported topics) produces a trope akin to *metaphor* in poetic language. The trope of *irony*, on the other hand, typically avoids such a merger; instead, the topic maintains its distinct character and plays a role in *contradistinction to*, or even outright *contradiction of* the prevailing discourse. Thus, in the case of Romantic irony, the unassimilated topic may be interpreted as *commenting on* the prevailing musical discourse. A combination of metaphorical merger and ironic commentary may result in *parody* or *satire*, since the potential merger is subject to critique (as implied by its lack of fit, its exaggeration, or its deliberate distortion by other means; see Sheinberg 2000).

The tropological process is also not exclusive to topics, but it is perhaps most clearly exemplified by them, since topics carry strongly conventionalized meanings (correlations) and thus their contribution to an interaction can be more readily understood.[6] Topical troping involves various axes of relationships between a topic and its new environment, the latter understood to encompass the prevailing genre, style, and thematic discourse as well as any other neighboring topical imports, whether simultaneously superimposed or successively juxtaposed with the given topic. There are several dimensions along which an imported topic and its potential tropological interaction may be marked with respect to its new environment. I will examine four axes with respect to classical eighteenth-century instrumental works, specifically with reference to instrumental works of Mozart. These axes should be understood to apply not only to the topic itself in relation to its new environment but also to the trope(s) it occasions by interacting with that environment or by engaging with other topics in shaping that environment.

1. Degree of *compatibility* between a topic and its new environment, ranging from similarity to complementarity to contradiction (compare Cook 1998).[7]
2. Degree of *dominance* by a topic over other material or topics in its new environment. Dominance may be based on hierarchical weight, temporal precedence, parametric density, completeness, and/or prototypicality.[8]
3. Degree of *creativity* (and a resulting *emergent meaning*) in a topic's interaction with other material or topics in its new environment. A topic is more likely to generate fresh meaning if it is highly novel or striking in its tropological interaction.
4. Degree of *productivity* over the course of a movement, with respect to the ongoing thematic and expressive discourse (including the trope's influence on other movements of a larger work). A topic or trope that productively engages with the motivic or thematic discourse will directly influence the resulting expressive trajectory.

I will review each of these axes in turn.

COMPATIBILITY

A topic may be more or less compatible with a given background or surrounding musical context (which may include other topics). Two or more highly compatible topics may integrate or merge, forming a trope that is so obvious as to escape notice. Incompatible topics, on the other hand, may spark a fusion more akin to creative metaphor. Topics that are not only incompatible with a background discourse but also inassimilable by metaphor may provoke a secondary-level interpretation in terms of irony.

Borrowing terms from Umberto Eco's semiotic theory (1976: 183–84), one may observe cases of *ratio facilis* when a tropological interpretation is easily forthcoming (as directed by stylistic conventions), or *ratio difficilis* when, in the case of more creative tropes, the interpretive process is more challenging and the uniqueness of the combination may require hypotheses that go beyond established stylistic conventions.[9] At times, a trope may serve as a compositional premise whose initially uncertain meaning is clarified through the course of the movement (see "Productivity," later). In the opening theme of Mozart's oft-cited Piano Sonata in F major, K. 332/i (Example 19.1), the combination of two topics, the singing style (characterized by a melody with Alberti-bass accompaniment) and the pastoral (characterized by use of a pedal point and an applied V/IV that emphasizes the more relaxed subdominant) are highly compatible (complementary as well as similar in some aspects). Perhaps for this reason, the pastoral mode is neglected in Allanbrook's (1983: 6) initial interpretation, in which she describes the first four measures merely as being "in a simple singing style." "Simple" is, in fact, one of the defining features of the pastoral, and simplicity as applied to any musical parameter may cue the pastoral (Hatten 2004: 56).

Interestingly, the melody of the first four measures is not stepwise, as would be expected for a *prototypical* example (McKay 2007) of the singing-style topic; instead, the arpeggiated contour suggests an allusion to yet another compatible topic—not a fanfare, in this case, but a topic in formation: the yodel.[10] Finally, the dance meter of 3/4 in the context of the pastoral topic may imply a pastoral dance—here, the *Ländler* is an obvious candidate.[11] That this subtle melding of four topics has escaped notice is, on the one hand, a reminder of the difficulty in reconstructing the style types of a historical style competency, and on the other hand, evidence of the less striking tropological force of their combination here. Even competent listeners may be less aware of such metaphorical fusion when the expressive meaning appears so transparent or unmarked (exemplifying *ratio facilis*). Yet that meaning is nonetheless fresh (creatively new) and emerges from the highly compatible correlations of the participating topics, even if we are unaware of the multiplicity of topics and their tropological fusion. Interpreting the trope's expressive purport in this case is not difficult, and each of the topics makes a contribution. The theme is gentle (pastoral mode), lyrical (singing style), expansive (yodel), and swaying (*Ländler*), all of which adds up to a mood of utter contentment. My designations of the contributions of each topic are obviously too pat, but something of the kind can readily be imagined.

Incompatibility (triggering *ratio difficilis*) is encountered in m. 4 when the melody suddenly breaks off.[12] This disruption of the unmarked flow of the discourse exemplifies what I call a *rhetorical gesture* (Hatten 2004: 135). The disruption is also a synecdoche by virtue of its part-for-whole allusion to the *empfindsamer Styl*: indeed, a choked-off sigh is emblematic of the style. However, the rhythm of this disruption (two eighths on the downbeat, followed by a quarter note) is highly characteristic of the *Ländler*, as is an interruptive stop for clapping or stamping of feet (noted by McKee, this volume). These dance-like effects might be suggested in performance of the sonata by means of a peremptory emphasis on the interruptive rhetorical gesture in the melody at m. 4— shifting interpretation from *empfindsamer* sigh to choreographed stomp. Or perhaps a subtle trope is also at play here, as the choked-off melodic sigh interacts with the dance-like verve of the rhythm.

After the melodic interruption Allanbrook (1983: 6) perceptively interprets the initiation of a four-measure "parody of learned counterpoint" as an "answer" to the opening four measures. Several levels of troping may be unpacked here. First, the topical use of imitation interacts with its new environment (the established topical merger of pastoral/ singing-style/yodel/*Ländler*) by dramatic contrast or contradiction. The incompatibility of a topic with its environment is interpretable as ironic whenever two levels of discourse are suggested and the second appears to comment on the first. In Beethoven, this may lead to Romantic irony; in the Mozart example we are also perplexed, but it is a bit early in the movement to invest so heavily in a Romantic-ironic trope.[13] However, the yodel-related alternating leaps in this compound melody seem rather exaggerated for an imitative (quasi-fugato) subject; its quirky character may thus suggest a parody of the serious, learned style, and hence undermine the learned style's correlation of "authoritativeness" (Hatten 1994: 87, 145; see also Keith Chapin, this volume, who notes that

EXAMPLE **19.1** Mozart, Piano Sonata in F major, K. 332/i, mm. 1–12.

the perceived artificiality or pedantry of the learned style could lead to interpretations tinged with irony or ridicule). Parody may also enter tropologically from the agential implications of this point of imitation, in that we might infer another agent in mm. 5–8 "answering" an initial agent by "mocking" the more straightforward opening gambit in mm. 1–4.[14] Alternatively, the authoritative connotations of the learned style might lead one to interpret its use here as marking a quick recovery from the disruptive sigh's overly sentimentalizing character; under this interpretation the response would assume a corrective rather than a mocking role in the ongoing rhetorical drama.

Given their juxtaposition within a single functional location (the opening theme), we have warrant to combine both of the four-measure units into a higher trope by exploring the possibility of metaphorical interaction between them (Hatten 1994: 170). Beethoven ventures this kind of trope in the eight-measure theme launching the Allegro of the finale to his Piano Sonata in A major, Op. 101 (Hatten 1994: 107, 170). However, in Mozart's theme it is unclear how we might fuse the two passages (and their already tropological aspects) into an emergent expressive meaning. We could begin by considering what these passages have in common—such similar features as tempo, meter (and its dance topic implications), key, mode, and motivic leap of a sixth; and then examine how they differ in texture and melodic contour. The second four-measure unit complements the first by developing (inverting) the melodic-sixth "yodel" element, which becomes the main motive of the imitative subject in mm. 5–6. This developing-variational link assures that the first two parts of the twelve-measure main theme belong to the "same" discourse at a higher level, even as rhetorical contrast threatens to split that discourse into two strands. And, given that shared discourse, one might develop a higher-level trope that somehow integrates, or "blends"—in Zbikowski's (2002) appropriation of Fauconnier (1994, 1997)—the two four-measure topical characters.

Another way past the particular interpretive quandary of these first eight measures might be to default to a more general trope of "aesthetic play" (as characteristic of the "high comic" style), in which the topical contributions are understood more abstractly.[15] From this standpoint, we would forego the interpretation of the theme as a drama of expressive states experienced by an internal agent, and instead simply enjoy the play of surfaces. The abstract use of topics for formal play cannot be discounted in Mozart, especially when a multitude of topics appears with such rapidity and contrast. Under this interpretation, the formal functions that are actually directing the discourse merely receive topical flavoring. One such example is found in the transition section of K. 332/i (Example 19.2), in which a prototypical *tempesta* topic (complete with rocket arpeggiation, lightning flashes, and accelerated activity within the minor mode) enhances the instability of the modulation and dramatizes the irregular phrase structure characteristic of a transitional formal function—all without serious expressive consequences for the movement. However, if one were to interpret the movement in terms of a pastoral expressive genre (Hatten 1994: 82–84), the threat of a storm that is overcome might more readily be interpreted as part of a dramatic trajectory involving an experiencing agent (possibly by *allegorizing* the storm in terms of a human agent's stormy feelings).

EXAMPLE **19.2** Mozart, Piano Sonata in F major, K. 332/i, mm. 23–26.

To summarize, the variety of options in interpreting the incompatibility between mm. 1–4 and 5–8 of Mozart's K. 332/i is indicative of the *ratio difficilis* characteristic of any complex aesthetic text (Eco 1976: 188; see also 261–76), and it requires a higher degree of interpretive abduction—exceeding mere recognition of style types and topics.[16]

DOMINANCE

A topic may be more or less dominant with respect to its context. If less dominant, a topic may function as an inflection (or flavoring) of another topic or the prevailing discourse—illustrating what I have termed the "attribution model" of musical troping; if more dominant, a topic may function as a stronger contributor to any metaphorical interaction—illustrating what I have termed the "speculative model" (Hatten 1994: 169). The potential for a topic to be dominant depends on many factors, including its *hierarchical weight* (and extension) in the style, its *temporal precedence* in the discourse, its *parametric density* (how many musical parameters are controlled by the topic), and—related to density—its *completeness* (as opposed to mere allusiveness) and/or *prototypicality*.

In K. 332/i (Example 19.1), the relatively weak allusion to a yodel suggests that it merely inflects the more dominant singing style of the opening four measures, as well as the more dominant learned style of mm. 4–8. The pastoral and singing style, on the other hand, appear more balanced in the opening four measures, each contributing roughly equally to the trope in terms of parametric density (pastoral pedal point and harmony vs. singing-style melody and Alberti-bass accompaniment). The *Ländler* increases in parametric density if the yodel and the *rhythm* of the choked-off sigh figure are heard as further characterizing features of the dance.

Hierarchically, the pastoral is not merely a topic, but a *mode*, akin to the literary mode of the pastoral (Hatten 2004: 53–67), and thus significant allusion to the pastoral may trigger a larger expressive field characterized by simplicity, leading to such interpretations as "gentle" or "spiritually serene." The singing style (as prototypical melody-and-accompaniment texture) is also part of a larger style, one that is more central to the classical era, namely the galant, which is characterized by proportion and symmetrical resolution. Either of the topics featured in the first four measures of

Mozart's theme could quickly move to a position of hierarchical dominance; however, when first encountered, they are in complementary balance, and the very principle of balance is itself characteristic of the all-embracing galant style.

Another topic appears in the last four measures (mm. 9–12) of the K. 332/i primary theme (Example 19.1), where Allanbrook (1992: 132, 134) notes the emergence of the minuet. This topic becomes, for Allanbrook, the dominant topic for the entire movement—perhaps inevitably, given the parametric weight of a consistent 3/4 (dance) meter and the use of a minuet topic for the second and closing themes (see Example 19.4 below). But more than one dance may be implied by 3/4 meter, and as noted earlier, the opening is more characteristic of a pastoral *Ländler*.

Beginning in m. 13 (Example 19.3) a horn call (a synecdoche for the hunt mode) inflects a more clearly projected minuet, and in addition, the higher register invokes a "music-box" topic. The primary topic here may be minuet, but the attributions of hunt and music-box topics are strongly foregrounded, or *strategically marked* (Hatten 1994: 42). Just as a colorful adjective may draw attention away from the prosaic noun that it enlivens, so may attributive topics appear to overbalance the dominance of the primary topic. Thus, the attributive trope of a "hunt/music-box minuet" leans toward the speculative model in which we not only identify the attributive flavors of "hunt" and "music box," but interrogate their possible synthesis with (or within) a minuet. The significant contrast to the entire preceding theme (with which it shares the tonic key, a shared context that supports an interpretation of dialogical opposition) may also provoke a higher speculative interpretation, stemming from the premise of topical contrast itself. In this interpretation, the emergent meaning may well be as basic as a "play with topics" (as considered in the previous section). Indeed, Agawu's "umbrella notion of play" (1991: 99) would appear to support this very possibility, especially when he urges us "to acknowledge the inadequacy of topics as ontological signs, and replace that formulation with structuralist notions of arbitrary signs" (117), or when he observes that, in contradistinction to Schumann, "Mozart's topics do not command the essence of the narrative" (142).

The emergence of the minuet topic as dominant for the movement becomes more evident with its prototypical appearance in the second and closing themes of the exposition of K. 332/i (Examples 19.4a–b), as noted by Allanbrook (1992: 134). With the repeat of the exposition, however, there is a possibility of reinterpreting the *Ländler* within the context of the preceding emphasis on the minuet. Here, a contradiction between low

EXAMPLE **19.3** Mozart, Piano Sonata in F major, K. 332/i, mm. 13–16.

EXAMPLE **19.4** Mozart, Piano Sonata in F major, K. 332/i: (a) mm. 41–44; (b) mm. 71–76.

(*Ländler*) and high (minuet) stylistic registers would be implied. A possible *metaphorical* trope might be couched in terms of an "all-embracing" acceptance of both stylistic registers (rather than proposing an awkward synthesis or merger of *Ländler* and minuet into a new dance topic). By contrast, a possible *ironic* trope might emerge from the "subversiveness" of one dance operating in the realm of the other. For this interpretation one might usefully reference Allanbrook's (1983: 79–82) compelling analysis of the social registers of dances as used ironically by Mozart in *Le nozze di Figaro*—notably, Figaro's appropriation of the higher class minuet for his threatening of the Count, in "Se vuol ballare."

One last lesson in dominance: we cannot assume that any given *tropological interpretation* is dominant over another, when both metaphorical syntheses and ironic subversions may well be equally possible responses to perceived contradictions. Incompatibility among topics, topical tropes, or their contradiction with their new environments may lead to unpredictable speculative interpretations. Although subsequent events may tilt the interpretation one way or another (see "Productivity," below), the potential for metaphor *or* irony must be kept open. And the theorist must take into account that individual interpreters may fail to recognize tropological situations altogether, or interpret them along lines unwarranted by the subsequent discourse.

CREATIVITY

A topic may be more or less creative in its tropological interaction with a new context, depending on the relative frequency with which similar interactions have appeared in a musical style. Thus, tropes have a life cycle (Shapiro and Shapiro 1988: 39). When strategic juxtapositions or superpositions of even highly contrasting topics have occurred

EXAMPLE **19.5** Mozart, Piano Concerto in C major, K. 415/i, mm. 1–5.

often enough, they may enter into the style as fully troped blends that require no inter-pretive labor. Monelle (2000: 16), following Eco (1976: 189), notes that "there is an irre-sistible interpretive landslip from ratio difficilis toward ratio facilis." Historically, tropes may be absorbed by a style, becoming style types or topics in themselves, and their inter-pretation is then deproblematized into an act of mere recognition. The first time Mozart combined a march topic with imitation, in the opening of the Piano Concerto in C major, K. 415/i (Example 19.5), it may have created a striking trope (at least for the more learned members of his audience).[17] Two or three years later, by the time of the Piano Concerto in C major, K. 467, learned treatment of a march may have become so typical for Mozart's listeners that the trope no longer had as much creative force. In mm. 1–4 (Example 19.6a) an initial march theme is immediately troped, not with the learned style but with the buffa style—quasi-Leporello, according to Agawu (1991: 35). Only in mm. 36–43 (Example 19.6b) does Mozart trope the buffa/march theme with the learned style in a series of *stretto* imitations.[18] In both concerti, the troping of march with imitation suggests parody because of the childlike evocation of the march topic (single voice, key-board timbre). Thus, a tongue-in-cheek interpretation dominates over the heroic/noble connotations of the military march topic. Interestingly, this is the case even though the

EXAMPLE **19.6** Mozart, Piano Concerto in C major, K. 467/i: (a) mm. 1–4 and (b) mm. 36–39.

march, based on its strong identification with the underlying meter, may be understood as the primary topic being inflected.[19]

Marches, fanfare figures, and drum riffs are all associated with the military topic, which, as a broader topical field, may also suggest a *mode*, as comparable in range to the pastoral. Monelle (2006) surveys the development of hunt, military, and pastoral topics, implying their comparable weight. In place of the military topic, however, I would substitute the *heroic mode*, which has two oppositional expressive fields. The *victorious* is marked by major mode and includes triumphant marches, fanfares, and the like, whereas the *tragic* is marked by minor mode and subdivides into two further types, most clearly marked by oppositional tempi, but featuring certain topics and style types, as well: *fast*, featuring *tempesta* rockets and diminished-seventh harmonies, and *slow*, featuring funeral marches and (chromatic) lament basses.

The tragic is often troped with the pastoral, as is familiar from the early history of opera. A contemporaneous theoretical treatment of this trope is found in Guarini's celebrated preface to a later printing of his extended pastoral verse drama *Il pastor fido*

(1580–84), as well as his later, anonymously published essay titled *Il Verato*, in which he defends the "tragicomic" as a new genre (1976: 23, 27). Troping of pastoral and tragic in Mozart may be found in his minor-mode siciliani in 6/8 meter. The F-minor Adagio from the Piano Sonata in F major, K. 280; the F-sharp-minor Adagio of the Piano Concerto in A major, K. 488; and Pamina's G-minor Andante aria, "Ach, ich fühl's" from *Die Zauberflöte* are notable examples.

Other cases of incompatible topics that are juxtaposed often enough to suggest a transparent style type (still productive, but less strikingly new) include the following:

1. *Tempesta* and *empfindsamer Styl* juxtaposed in one theme. See the opening themes of Mozart's Piano Sonata in C minor, K. 457/i, and Piano Quartet in G minor, K. 478/i. This dialogical trope enhances the heroic/tragic mode by opposing its topical extremes: a more heroic rocket figure answered by a more tragic sigh figure. The trope held obvious appeal for Beethoven, as exemplified by the opening themes of his Piano Sonata in C minor, Op. 10 No. 1/i, and Piano Concerto in C minor, Op. 37/i.

2. March (drum riff) and *empfindsamer Styl*, as juxtaposed in the opening theme of Mozart's "Jupiter" Symphony, K. 551/i. The extreme topical and dynamic contrast only begins to be tropologically merged when a countermelody in m. 24 fills the gap between the two topics, which now share a *piano* dynamic level.

3. Various dances and singing style integrated into a single theme (as in K. 332/i). The theme for the variation finale of K. 284/iii is in typical galant singing style, but topically marked by a double upbeat characteristic of the gavotte. This leads to humorous consequences when the contrasting strain expands by two beats, necessitating an awkward insertion of an extra measure before the rounded-binary return.

The power of a creatively fresh trope is in the emergence of new meaning for the listener. But the instability, or indeterminacy, of a listener's interpretation obligates a composer to provide ongoing clues to guide that listener, both in identifying the tropological encounter and in continuously interpreting its consequences. The next section addresses this issue.

PRODUCTIVITY

A topic may be more or less productive in its tropological encounters, either with other topics or the prevailing musical discourse. As a generative event or dramatic premise, a potential trope may require an entire movement or cycle to fully unfold or develop its emergent meaning (with respect to the K. 284/iii finale just mentioned, compare the treatment of mm. 12–13 in the subsequent variations). To the extent that a trope is thematized in this way, its development may provide further clues for interpreting its significance.

Mozart's Sonata in D major, K. 576/i (Example 19.7), begins with a hunting fanfare motto in a 6/8 gigue meter, answered by a chain of galant-style, two-chord, slurred gestures with trills. The potential trope of contrasting styles is forged by the tropological addition of two more topics (or topical flavorings) in mm. 9–12: the horn fanfare is treated to *stretto* imitation (learned style) and a cascade of continuous sixteenths (brilliant style) stitches together the repeated-note finish of the fanfare with the subsequent galant motives as a kind of countersubject. The topical play continues with brilliant sixteenth-note riffs taking the place of a potential singing-style melody over accompanying Alberti-bass broken chords (mm. 16–19), followed by a clockwork perpetual motion over block chords (mm. 20–24) and a culminating sequence leading to the half cadence (mm. 24–27). A preliminary second theme (mm. 28–41) starts in A major, after the medial caesura in m. 27, but soon becomes transitional, leading to a stronger medial caesura in m. 41. The preliminary second theme begins by developing the primary theme's troping of fanfare and learned-style *stretto* (now tightened to the distance of only one eighth-note), and continues with the brilliant-style cascade of sixteenths (but without the galant motives). After a more fully articulated medial caesura in m. 41 (here, a PAC in the dominant), a more definitive (and contrasting) second theme appears. Its *dolce*, singing-style motive (derived from the four-note ascent in the galant gestures) is treated to varied repetition by diminutions: the lyrical line is turned into a brilliant-style series of continuous sixteenths. A closing theme (mm. 53–58) derived from mm. 16–19 ends the exposition.

Of the many topics, and hence potential tropes, available to the listener, which ones will the composer choose to highlight in the development section? Mozart elects *stretto/ canonic* treatment of the fanfare, at temporal distances of a dotted half (m. 63 in B flat major) and a dotted quarter (m. 70 in G minor), perhaps in order to complement the *stretti* at rhythmic distances of a quarter (m. 9) and an eighth (m. 28), as found in the exposition. In between, he opts for brilliant-style diminutions of the galant gestures into continuous sixteenths (mm. 65–69). After the second *stretto*, he introduces a series of *Fortspinnung*-inspired motives (mm. 72–80). His next gambit features two-measure chromatic descending lines in two-part counterpoint, appearing both below and above the Alberti triplets (mm. 83–92), to create triple invertible counterpoint; a fresh trope is achieved by the interaction of the lament topic with the learned and singing styles.[20] A single, ascending chromatic line is extended and intensified climactically between pedal A's, with the Alberti triplets now in the bass (mm. 93–96). Upon reaching V⁷ of the home key, a brilliant, single-line cascade of sixteenths (mm. 97–98) serves to usher in the recapitulation.

The dominant trope of this movement thus appears to be a blend of four topics: (1) *hunting fanfare*, (2) *learned style*, and (3) *brilliant style* are integrated within the 6/8 meter and fast tempo of (4) a *gigue*. What emergent meanings might one discover from the productive development of this trope? Is this a case of relatively abstract, high

EXAMPLE **19.7** Mozart, Piano Sonata in D major, K. 576/i, mm. 1–12.

comic play with virtuosic display? Certainly, the high spirits of the hunting fanfare are made more exhilarating (brilliant style) and authoritative/definitive (learned style) by this topical troping.

Hybrids of genres, such as this enhanced gigue, are an especially clear case of troping, since they involve an entire movement or work that progressively "elaborates the blend."[21] One of the most impressive tropes of this kind is found in the finale of Mozart's String Quartet in G major, K. 387, which features alternating fugal (learned) and galant styles, initially integrated in mm. 31–39.[22] Which style is more dominant in the trope? Are they equally important, or is the trope perhaps an ironic one in which the galant subverts the ponderously fugal, only to be absorbed into learned texture in its turn? Evidence for these interpretive questions, if not conclusive answers, is provided by the productive working out of the fugal versus galant trope in the remainder of the movement.

A trope may also evolve as a culminating, integrative means of achieving thematic and expressive closure among competing themes and their individual topical characters. Here, the finale of Mozart's "Jupiter" Symphony stands supreme, with its culminating fugato serving to integrate all five themes and their contrasting topics. But how might we interpret the tropologically emergent meaning? As a triumphant apotheosis? Or perhaps allegorically, as a transcendent embracing of the cosmos?

TROPOLOGICAL AND MOTIVIC
PRODUCTIVITY

Mozart's String Quartet in D minor, K. 421, offers an interesting case of two nonconsecutive (second and fourth) movements that share a topic (the siciliano) as well as a motivic dialectic between an initial thematic motive and a repeated-note figure.[23] The second movement (Andante, 6/8) is in F major, with the characteristic siciliano figure (dotted-eighth–sixteenth–eighth) occurring for the first time only in the final (cadential) measure of an eight-measure sentence (Example 19.8a). The fourth movement (Allegro ma non troppo, 6/8) is a set of variations in D minor (Example 19.8b). The tempo marking might suggest that this is a gigue, but siciliano rhythmic figures are omnipresent, and the Allegro designation most plausibly applies to an eighth-note pulse level. The typical dotted-quarter beat of 6/8 can hardly approach Allegro for this movement without trivializing the gestures of the theme (and its diminutional first variation, as well).

Both the second and fourth movements touch on topics that enhance the seriousness of the expressive discourse: in the second movement Mozart interpolates a gentle hunting fanfare in imitation that leads to repeated thirds on $\hat{5}$ and $\hat{3}$; in the fourth movement he interpolates a repeated-note (fateful/bird-call) figure in the first violin on $\hat{5}$ above a continuation of the opening thematic material in the other voices. But is the fourth movement's allusion to the second movement an example of expressive productivity by means of *topical troping*, or is this productivity due merely to motivic *developing variation*?

The repeated-note interpolation in the second movement functions as a rhetorical gesture that suspends an otherwise four-measure presentation phase (mm. 1–2, 4–5) for one measure (m. 3).[24] The fanfare's interpolative role is highlighted by the shift in texture (to unison, introducing a point of imitation) and dynamics (from *piano* to *mf*). The productivity of the digressive material introduced in m. 3 is evidenced by its progressive intensification—harmonically, texturally, dynamically, and temporally (here, by expansion)—both in the theme itself (where the fanfare interpolation is subsequently incorporated into the theme and climactically developed in mm. 6–7) and throughout the movement. The legato, three-sixteenth anacrusis (melodically varied from its fanfare-like arpeggiation) is integrated with the siciliano motive already in mm. 7–8, and again in m. 24. If we take the treatment of the motive beginning with the pickup to m. 3 as implying a trope of fanfare (upward arpeggiation) and learned style (imitation), we may ask whether the trope extends beyond these two topics to embrace the siciliano topic hinted by the opening meter and rhythms of mm. 1–2. And if so, is the potential interaction more metaphorical or ironic? The integration of topics in mm. 7–8 may imply a fusion akin to metaphor, but the subsequent intensification of the fanfare motive's interruptive function suggests a dialogical function as response or commentary, perhaps tinged with irony.

The simple diatonicism and the hint of repeated chords in the first measure support an interpretation of the repeated gestures in m. 3 as *attributive* to the opening measures—adding dignity to the pastoral siciliano and foregrounding the two halves of its presentation phase (mm. 1–2 and 4–5). But the development of the repeated-note motive from m. 27 on, and the *forte* outbursts in mm. 31–32 and 47–48 (Examples 19.9a and 19.9b) emphasize the fanfare motive's role as an independent agent in the thematic discourse. And the post-cadential use of the idea for the codetta beginning in m. 77 may

EXAMPLE **19.8** Mozart, String Quartet in D minor, K. 421: (a) ii, mm. 1–8; (b) iv, mm. 1–8.

(*Continued*)

EXAMPLE **19.8** (Continued)

be heard even more clearly as ironic commentary on the preceding discourse. A crescendo to vii°⁷/V in mm. 79–80 suggests that this commentary addresses the tragic element that had threatened the pastoral serenity of the main motive as early as its shift to C *minor* after the double bar (in m. 9). The movement ends with the fanfare gesture's thick-textured cadential echo of F major and *subito piano* release onto the repeated tonic chord (mm. 84–86).

The third movement (Menuetto) provides motivic linkage to the fourth movement by featuring three repeated quarter notes (itself a prototypical minuet motive) in m. 3, and then foregrounding this motive (which also ended the second movement) by sequencing it progressively down by step in mm. 5 and 7 (Example 19.10).

The finale, a set of variations in 6/8, further strengthens the motivic ties to earlier movements. Its repeated notes (in the accompaniment, as well as in the fateful, bird-call-like rejoinder by the first violin on repeated high A's) are well motivated thematically, and hence expressively, as a continued working out of the trope proposed in the second movement (see Examples 19.8a–b). The end of the first strain features the fateful bird call on a high D, resolving down an octave in clear reference to the opening of the *first* movement (Example 19.11). Compare, as well, m. 7 of the second movement, where the minor-seventh drop from the repeated notes anticipates the

EXAMPLE **19.9** Mozart, String Quartet in D minor, K. 421/ii: (a) mm. 31–33 and (b) mm. 47–49.

EXAMPLE **19.10** Mozart, String Quartet in D minor, K. 421/iii, mm. 1–4.

EXAMPLE **19.11** Mozart, String Quartet in D minor, K. 421/i, mm. 1–4.

EXAMPLE **19.12** Mozart, String Quartet in D minor, K. 421/iv: (a) mm. 41–44: (b) mm. 73–76; (c) mm. 130–42.

(Continued)

EXAMPLE **19.12** (Continued)

diminished-seventh drops in m.22 of the theme of the finale, as well as in the finale's reprise (variation 5). We can retrospectively recognize in the first theme of the opening movement the first violin's insistence on D against the cello's lamenting descent as progenitor of these repeated-note motives.[25]

The first variation of the finale features an integration of upward arpeggiation and decorated repeated notes that echoes m. 3 of the second movement—most clearly with the return via F major in the second strain (Example 19.12a). This variant more clearly integrates the responsorial/fateful bird call (at ends of mm. 42 and 43). The

third variation (mm. 73–96) features integration of the repeated notes in a highly varied and rhythmically fragmentary version of the theme in the viola (Example 19.12b).
This variation features a grotesque reduction of the theme, and the repeated-note idea
is appropriately developed as an obsessive echo through the instruments and registers,
approaching textural saturation at the cadences in the second strain.

The fateful repetition is absent from the first strain of the penultimate variation,
which moves to more hopeful D major, but the motive returns in the second strain, and
then in triplet diminution for the Più Allegro reprise of the theme in D minor (variation
5). Here (Example 19.12c), the repeated notes haunt the theme in every register, heightening their foreboding with diminished-seventh drops instead of octaves (mm. 131 and
133), before the ultimate resolution into a Picardy-third close. Note the problematizing
of that Picardy third with an augmentation of the chromatic-lament descent, derived
from chromatic slippage in the theme itself (second violin, mm. 2–4 and 6–7).

CONCLUSION

The play of topics and tropes overlaps with motives and themes in such a way that one
cannot (and should not) give analytical priority to one over the other. Motives, topics,
and tropes tend to interact seamlessly, since they are usually working toward the creation
of a unified expressive discourse. The techniques of thematic integration and developing
variation are clearly relevant to the unfolding of topics and tropes, which may in turn
help clarify the expressive purport of often subtle motivic relationships. Indeed, as demonstrated by the foregoing examples, Mozart's intertwined compositional and expressive strategies both support, and are enhanced by, the troping of topics.[26]

NOTES

1. *Tempesta* is the term Clive McClelland (see his chapter, this volume) recommends to
   replace *Sturm und Drang* as a topical designation for tempestuous minor-mode music
   where, for example, rocket-like arpeggiation of diminished-seventh chords can suggest
   lightning flashes.
2. Hatten (1994: 74–82) illustrates how larger topical fields are coordinated by oppositions
   such as minor–major (mode) and high–middle–low (style). Hatten (1994: 83) also notes
   that "the pastoral as a topical field can serve as an interpretive frame for a movement or
   cycle of movements, prescribing an overall outcome." The resulting dramatic trajectory
   is called an *expressive genre* (Hatten 1994: 74–84), and it need not be restricted to a single
   formal genre (sonata, variations, fugue etc.). Later, Hatten (2004: 53) substitutes the term
   mode for *topical field*, in deference to literary modes such as the pastoral. For a historical
   study of three such topical fields or modes, see Raymond Monelle (2006).
3. Topics are not only familiar due to their common usage; they are also stylistically (and
   thus relatively systematically) organized according to oppositional features, such as

major–minor mode, fast–slow tempo, or duple–triple meter. This oppositional organization of topics into semantic fields helps guarantee that a stylistically competent listener will not only recognize a topic rather easily, but have an immediate if general awareness of its expressive purport—and thus what it brings to an encounter with a unique musical context.

4. Markedness, as theorized for music by Hatten (1994: 34–44), is defined as "the asymmetrical valuation of an opposition (in musical structure, language, culture). For musical meaning, markedness of structural oppositions correlates with markedness of (expressive or other) oppositions among cultural units. Marked entities have a greater (relative) specificity of meaning than do unmarked entities. Marked entities also have a narrower distribution" (291). The marked member of an opposition may be foregrounded (as is typically the case when a topic is introduced into a new context), but markedness is not equivalent to salience. Rather, marked oppositions enter into the style and help coordinate meaning even when the music-structural oppositions are no longer new or striking.

5. Tropes are theorized for music by Hatten (1994: 161–96) primarily in terms of analogues with metaphor and irony. For the concept of a topic in formation, or "prototopic," see Monelle (2000: 17, 80).

6. For a discussion of *syntactic* troping involving an unusual harmonic syntagm in late Beethoven, see Hatten (2012a).

7. An incompatible topic will be marked and carry a narrower or more specified expressive meaning relative to an unmarked background.

8. A dominant topic may thus appear to be strategically unmarked relative to other topics that are foregrounded as more salient in a particular passage, but it may nonetheless provide stylistically marked grounding for any expressive interpretation. For more on the distinctions among salience, strategic markedness, and stylistic markedness, see note 4 and Hatten (1994: 42–43).

9. Both Raymond Monelle (1992: 15–16) and Nicholas McKay (2007) adopt Eco's concepts of *ratio facilis* and *ratio difficilis*: Monelle, to emphasize the conventionality of topics, and McKay, to create a scale of *prototypicality* for topical categorization. My own contribution is to apply these two ratios to tropes—specifically, to distinguish more conventional from more creative troping of topics.

10. The yodel is a pastoral melodic figuration that was clearly stylistic by the time Beethoven wrote the finale of his "Pastoral" Piano Sonata in D major, Op. 28, and as a topic it would be further developed in the nineteenth century by composers from Schubert to Mahler. It is often associated with the *Ländler*, given the dance's rural origins in Austria and southern Germany, as noted by McKee (this volume).

11. See McKee (this volume) for relevant features of the *Ländler*. The dance called the pastorale is another possibility, although the tempo here is perhaps a bit fast. Allanbrook (1983: 43) describes the pastorale as "characterized by a moderately slow tempo"; the example she gives of the *calando* final measures of K. 332/iii is not in 3/4 but in 6/8 meter.

12. This moment is also unremarked by Allanbrook (1983) but later acknowledged—without topical labeling—in her later essay (1992: 132).

13. For the most striking example of Romantic irony in Beethoven, see the buffa addendum to the finale of the tragic String Quartet in F minor, Op. 95, as discussed by Longyear (1970: 147) and Hatten (1994: 186–88).

14. For more on the implications of agency for interpretations of expressive meaning in music, see Hatten (2010); Robinson and Hatten (2012: 77–80).

15. Caplin's (2005) exploration of the way certain topics are associated with clear formal functions may provide further insight into this more abstract mode of interpretation.

16. Abduction is Peirce's term for the kind of inference that requires hypothesizing—speculatively arriving at a generalization that will account for a series of observations. Eco (1976: 295) uses the term "undercoding" for abduction in those cases such as innovative musical works where the code is either not known or does not exist in complete form. See Hatten (1994: 261, 269) for further discussion of abduction in the context of style growth and change, and for more on Eco's concept of undercoding.

17. Ratner (1980: 3) begins his discussion of expression with a quote from Mozart's letter to his father about his three recent piano concerti, K. 413–415, in which he states: "There are passages here and there from which connoisseurs alone can derive satisfaction; but these passages are written in such a way that the less learned cannot fail to be pleased, though not knowing why" (Anderson 1966: 833).

18. Ratner (1980: 391) introduces another topic, the "clockwork" mechanism, for which this passage might be a suitable candidate. A music box is a related mechanical object.

19. Recall my similar conclusion for the hunt/music-box/minuet trope in K. 332, mm. 13–22, discussed above.

20. For a discussion of the lament topic, see William Caplin's chapter in this volume.

21. In Fauconnier's terminology (1994, 1997), adopted for music by Zbikowski (2002).

22. Chapin (this volume) helpfully specifies the distinctive learned and galant features found in mm. 1–31.

23. The relationship of topics to motives in the evolution of a musical discourse is central to Allanbrook's "Two Threads through the Labyrinth" (1992) as well as roughly the last two-thirds of Chapter 3 ("The Comic Surface") of the book manuscript she left behind.

24. I intentionally use the term "phase" instead of "phrase" in adapting Caplin's "presentation phrase" because a tonic prolongation does not constitute a phrase. As defined by William Rothstein (1989: 5), a phrase is best understood as "a directed motion in time from one tonal entity to another." However, I completely agree with Caplin's (1998: 72) analysis of this theme with respect to its use of interpolation.

25. And perhaps, as Danuta Mirka suggested to me, the repeated notes of the siciliano accompaniment, as well. A further motivic link is provided by the lament-type chromatic descents in the inner voices of the finale, as prefigured by the opening of the first movement. The first movement's lament is discussed by Caplin (this volume).

26. For an extended treatment of this argument, see Hatten (2012b).

REFERENCES

Agawu, V. Kofi. 1991. *Playing with Signs: A Semiotic Interpretation of Classic Music.* Princeton: Princeton University Press.

Allanbrook, Wye J. 1983. *Rhythmic Gesture in Mozart:* Le nozze di Figaro *and* Don Giovanni. Chicago: University of Chicago Press.

——. 1992. Two Threads through the Labyrinth: Topic and Process in the First Movements of K. 332 and K. 333. In *Convention in Eighteenth- and Nineteenth-Century Music: Essays in Honor of Leonard G. Ratner,* ed. Wye J. Allanbrook, Janet M. Levy, and William P. Mahrt, 125–71. Stuyvesant, NY: Pendragon.

Anderson, Emily. 1966. *The Letters of Mozart and His Family*, 2nd ed., prepared by A. Hyatt King and Monica Carolan. London: Macmillan.

Caplin, William E. 1998. *Classical Form: A Theory of Formal Functions for the Instrumental Music of Haydn, Mozart, and Beethoven*. New York: Oxford University Press.

———. 2005. On the Relation of Musical Topoi to Formal Function. *Eighteenth-Century Music* 2/1: 113–24.

Cook, Nicholas. 1998. *Analysing Musical Multimedia*. Oxford: Clarendon.

Eco, Umberto. 1976. *A Theory of Semiotics*. Bloomington: Indiana University Press.

Fauconnier, Gilles. 1994. *Mental Spaces: Aspects of Meaning Construction in Natural Language*, 2nd ed., with a foreword by George Lakoff and Eve Sweetser. Cambridge: Cambridge University Press.

———. 1997. *Mappings in Thought and Language*. Cambridge: Cambridge University Press.

Guarini, Battista. 1580–84. *Il pastor fido*. Venice: Pitteri.

———. 1976. *Il pastor fido: The Faithful Shepherd*, ed. John H. Whitfield. Trans. (1647) by Richard Fanshawe. Austin: University of Texas Press.

Hatten, Robert S. 1994. *Musical Meaning in Beethoven: Markedness, Correlation, and Interpretation*. Bloomington: Indiana University Press.

———. 2004. *Interpreting Musical Gestures, Topics, and Tropes: Mozart, Beethoven, Schubert*. Bloomington: Indiana University Press.

———. 2010. Musical Agency as Implied by Gesture and Emotion: Its Consequences for Listeners' Experiencing of Musical Emotion. In *Semiotics 2009: The Semiotics of Time* (Proceedings of the Thirty-Fourth Annual Meeting of the Semiotic Society of America, 15–18 October 2009, Cincinnati), ed. Karen Haworth and Leonard Sbrocchi, 162–69. New York: Legas.

———. 2012a. On Metaphor and Syntactic Troping in Music. In *Music Semiotics: A Network of Significations: In Honour and Memory of Raymond Monelle*, ed. Esti Sheinberg, 87–103. Farnham, UK: Ashgate.

———. 2012b. Enlarging the Musical Discourse: Mozart's Piano Quartet in G Minor, K. 478. In *Mozart's Chamber Music with Keyboard*, ed. Martin Harlow, 182–97. Cambridge: Cambridge University Press.

Longyear, Rey. 1970. Beethoven and Romantic Irony. In *The Creative World of Beethoven*, ed. Paul Henry Lang, 145–62. New York: Norton.

McKay, Nicholas. 2007. On Topics Today. *Zeitschrift der Gesellschaft der Musiktheorie* 4/1–2 Online. Available: http://www.gmth.de/zeitschrift/artikel/251.aspx. Accessed 24 March 2009.

Monelle, Raymond. 2000. *The Sense of Music: Semiotic Essays*. Princeton: Princeton University Press.

———. 2006. *The Musical Topic: Hunt, Military and Pastoral*. Bloomington: Indiana University Press.

Ratner, Leonard. 1980. *Classic Music: Expression, Form, and Style*. New York: Schirmer.

Robinson, Jenefer, and Robert S. Hatten. 2012. Emotions in Music. *Music Theory Spectrum* 34/2: 71–106.

Rothstein, William. 1989. *Phrase Rhythm in Tonal Music*. New York: Schirmer.

Shapiro, Michael, and Marianne Shapiro. 1988. *Figuration in Verbal Art*. Princeton: Princeton University Press.

Sheinberg, Esti. 2000. *Irony, Satire, Parody, and the Grotesque in the Music of Shostakovich: A Theory of Musical Incongruities*. Aldershot, UK: Ashgate Press.

Zbikowski, Lawrence M. 2002. *Conceptualizing Music: Cognitive Structure, Theory, and Analysis*. New York: Oxford University Press, 2002.

SECTION IV

PERFORMING TOPICS

CHAPTER 20

PERFORMING TOPICS IN MOZART'S
CHAMBER MUSIC WITH PIANO

JOHN IRVING

"THE term *topoi* is somewhat difficult to define." Thus Edward S. Forster, in the introduction to his translation of Aristotle's *Topica* (1960: 268–69). Much of Aristotle's treatise outlines strategies by means of which an argument may be examined and either confirmed or rejected. Book IV, for instance, deals at length with the distinct relations of *genus, species,* and *differentia,* providing the would-be orator with seemingly innumerable strategies for distinguishing between these three, with a view to demolishing an opponent's arguments.

Aristotle begins his *Topica* by describing its purpose as being "to discover a method by which we shall be able to reason from generally accepted principles about any problem set before us and shall ourselves, when sustaining an argument, avoid saying anything self-contradictory" (1960: 273).[1] Is *Topica* a methodology, then? In large part, what Aristotle devotes his attention to is presenting *ways of proceeding*; and those ways are rigorously catalogued and examined in minute detail. That is to say, his *raison d'être* is exhaustive enquiry into conceptual quantities, qualities, and relations underlying things, actions, and claims expressed through language. We could be forgiven for regarding Aristotle's *Topica* as an encyclopedia of nitpicking, a thorough mastery of which would allow one to dissect any and every argument with the most razor-sharp of scalpels. What we might miss in our reading of the eight rather dry books that comprise Aristotle's *Topica*[2] is its implied purpose, expressed right at the start: "to discover a method by which we shall *be able to reason* from generally accepted principles" (1960: 273; my italics). In other words, it is a primer, a repository of knowledge to be applied in action at a subsequent stage. *Topica* prepares the student *to act* (in an oration) by forensically dissecting language (both in syntax and semantics), its underlying goal being a thorough conceptual platform from which the student might build practical outcomes.

But this is only a part of the story. Revisiting the writing of the eighteenth-century philosopher and linguist Giambattista Vico, Stephen Rumph has recently mapped out new ground for topics as *vita activa*, invention prior to critical judgment, application of learning in civic use, physical properties inhabiting the world of impulse, gesture, and accent, all of these exhorting us to a stance "attending more closely to the physical artic-ulation of the sign [specifically, the musical sign] and exploring the way in which topics emerge, develop, and interact within the musical syntax" (Rumph 2012: 91–94). In Vico's formulation, language was no mere abstract repository of what lay in the mind; it was a channel of communication that operated in two directions—both the expression of the thought and equally the gathering of the sense impressions that impinged on the mind, integrating conception and action. Vico and Aristotle are not, in fact, mutually exclusive in their view of topics, though the emphasis of each view is markedly different: Aristotle documents and exemplifies reflection; Vico celebrates action first and foremost.

The assumptions underlying this chapter, exploring the potential of topical under-standing to influence performance (specifically, performance of Mozart's chamber music with piano), draw significantly on both strategies.[3] Categorization, analysis, reflection, and—hopefully—understanding each exist a priori as desirables to effective performance and reflect the Aristotelian impulse to establish a repository for action. Doing something with the knowledge thus gained is what preoccupied and enthused Vico, it seems, and it is this *activity*—informed choices enacted physically in real time—that is embodied in a performance. The trace of both authors will be detectable in what follows, but most especially Vico, since it is the motivation for expression of a thought in performance that is at the forefront of my mind in writing this chapter, and also in my work as a fortepianist in Mozart's chamber music. Four mature chamber works are examined as case studies: the Sonata for Violin and Piano K. 454; the Quintet for Piano and Winds K. 452; the Piano Trio K. 548; and the Sonata for Piano Duet K. 521. (Readers are advised to have scores of these works to hand. In what follows, topical references are frequent and wide-ranging, and specific musical examples are not included.)[4]

PEACEFUL COHABITATION: TWO FINALES

Composed for violinist Regina Strinasacchi (1761–1839), the Sonata in B flat major, K. 454,[5] is famous for having been allegedly completed only the day before its first per-formance by Mozart and Strinasacchi, at which Mozart played from an incomplete score.[6] Its finale has typically been regarded as a joyful and ebullient conclusion to the sonata, celebrating the virtuosity of Strinasacchi every bit as much as that of Mozart himself: "The final movement, a bustling and festive Rondo [actually a sonata-rondo], manages to evoke all the *brio* and grandeur of Mozart's most virtuosic orchestral writ-ing."[7] The topical characteristics of this movement are seldom commented on, an excep-tion being Paul Badura-Skoda: "The finale is formed by the *Allegretto* beginning like a gavotte, playful, humorous, of an eternal lightness."[8] It does indeed begin "like a gavotte." In fact, the gavotte topic underlies the entire movement. But closer inspection of the topical basis for K. 454's finale reveals rather more about the organizational power of topics within this Rondo, presenting by the way an interesting challenge to performers.

It is precisely *in performance* that a sophisticated topical landscape emerges in this finale. It could be read off the page, but at least in my own case, it was *felt* first of all in performance as a succession of gestures, and only rationalized subsequently in analysis of the score. That process of rationalization then—happily—fed back into my playing of the Rondo, which now focuses on capturing and expressing a degree of sophistication in form and content hitherto unsuspected.[9] As Badura-Skoda remarks, the Rondo opens "like a gavotte." Or does it? Is it "like a gavotte" or is it actually a gavotte? On the page, it certainly looks like a gavotte, in that it has a ¢ (alla breve) time signature and begins on the midmeasure with the double upbeat characteristic of this topic in Mozart's music.[10] The opening phrase can be read as an antecedent–consequent pair. The consequent arrives halfway through m. 4; following a half cadence, the gavotte idiom continues within a somewhat more vigorous rhythmic spirit, contrasting an actively moving bass line with the static tonic whole note at the very start. This half-measure gavotte upbeat is continued from m. 8, where the piano restates the opening phrase, extending this time through a succession of descending triplet eighth notes in the right hand and leading to the Rondo's first strong perfect cadence (m. 16). From this point, over a firmly "downbeat" tonic pedal repercussion in the piano's left hand and continuous eighth notes in the middle of the texture, the violin opens up a further succession of "gavotte-like" maneuvers, launching always from the midmeasure (mm. 16, 18, 20,[11] 22). Note that, although the half-measure upbeat is retained throughout this passage, the salience of the gavotte topic is attenuated because Mozart departs from the characteristic melodic shape of the double upbeat, stated at the beginning: the gavotte reference is continued through scansion alone.

And so we could go on describing what we see. But in performance, although we do see, we also act: for instance, listening, initiating, responding, recollecting, contrasting, and, above all, expressing *gestures*. And in playing this Rondo it is an expressing of its gavotte gestures that really counts. In each of the cases described above, though visible on the page, it is a physical gesture that is encoded in the notation. It is not so much that the violinist *starts* with a half-measure upbeat (as the notation suggests); rather the violinist *moves toward* the next downbeat. Take, for instance, the antecedent phrase (from m. 4). This involves a subtler succession of shorter bow strokes than are needed for the opening quarters, supported now by a three-step bass figure in which Mozart carefully reminds the pianist that those three quarters are decidedly not of equal weight, but comprise a gesture of two components—a slurred pair (moving strong–weak) followed by a single, separate impulse. In all these cases what the players are doing is *playing the gavotte* (that is, they act its gesture of "movement toward"). Considering things this way, against a topical framework, leads to a potentially odd interpretation of mm. 24–29, taking the Rondo to a dominant cadential close preceding a contrasting secondary area announced at m. 30. On the page, this passage does not look much like a gavotte. Yet it starts halfway through m. 24 with a unison triplet eighth-note figure; and the violin introduces a contrasting figure entering in the middle of m. 26. But again, it is in the act of performance that the potential for this passage to be read and realized as a gavotte comes alive. So far as the performers' gestures are concerned, the impulse here is still always towards the next downbeats, with half-measure upbeats. Strikingly rhythmic and energetic these gestures may be; but they are contained coherently within the repertoire of "moving toward" gestures characterizing the Rondo thus far. What we have, arguably, in its first section (mm. 1–29) is a showcasing of a relatively broad range of related gestures whose particular local impulses are quite varied on a moment-to-moment timeline, but which are members of the same family. This is not how I formerly approached the movement, and it is most gratifying that, by (1) exploring the potential for a scansion that I previously sensed intuitively, (2) filtering this awareness through a specifically topical understanding, and then (3) feeding all this back into my practice as a basis for interpretive action and expression, I now approach the Rondo in a different, and personally more rewarding way.[12]

So much for the opening gavotte. It is from this point in Mozart's Rondo that, taking a topical approach toward its performance, we discover that there is something else going on. The contrasting theme in the dominant sounded at m. 30 escapes immediately from the gesture of the gavotte. Its decidedly downbeat scansion is reinforced immediately in m. 31 by Mozart's unusual texture of rhythmic unison, played out across four octave registers (just in case we missed it first time). From this moment on, the gestural land-scape has been redrawn. Moreover, quarter-note beats, rather than the previous half notes, now become rather important, starting with the violin's trill figure (*piano*) on the upbeat to m. 33, and highlighted further in a succession of suspensions commencing on the upbeat to m. 37. Indeed, the more closely we look into this episode, the more we sense that not only is it an episode characterized by strong downbeats and a vigor stem-ming from concentration on quarter-note beats (contrasting with the half-note beats of the opening refrain), but there is a marked tendency toward quarter upbeats. While eighteenth-century discussions of the gavotte and the bourrée make clear that both dances are in alla breve (thus proceeding in half-note rather than quarter-note beats), within the bourrée there is significantly greater concentration on the quarter notes as active ingredients within the prevailing meter.[13] Is this episode, therefore, "like a bour-rée"? Well, perhaps, as with the opening section, it actually is a bourrée, given that we alter our performance behaviors here in order to enact the physical gestures represent-ing the bourrée, namely another species of "moving toward," this time launching from a quarter upbeat toward the next downbeat. Reading it thus, my violinist partner might well give extra emphasis to the trill figures at the end of mm. 46 and 47 (marked actually as a rapid *forte–piano* alternation in the score). And we will almost certainly character-ize just that little bit more keenly the quarter upbeats in the ensuing passage (from m. 50; and again from m. 56). But more than this, the capturing of the quarter upbeat produces a heightened awareness of the contrast in this whole section between the way in which we move through a measure, and the way we formerly moved in mm. 1–30. The episode offers a much greater variety of ways in which to move through each measure (and, con-sequently, phrase) than had the gavotte.[14]

So has the gavotte been displaced by a bourrée? Not altogether. The gavotte certainly survives the experience, for it returns three more times, beginning with the refrain at m. 90 and again at mm. 150 and 239. I would claim that the gavotte is adapted to the new setting and that, once again, its presence is something felt in the physical gestures of performance action rather than seen on the page. Measures 36–42 are a case in point. They do not look much like a gavotte but, as in previous examples, the gesture encoded here is that of "moving toward" downbeats with half-measure upbeats. With its swirling triplet quarters and ultimately its powerfully sweeping triplet tenths, this is a gavotte "with attitude" for sure, but once again it has a physical manifestation, "tangible" in the literal sense that the player's fingers carve out the rugged terrain for these measures (and metaphorically reflected, perhaps, in the listener's appreciation of the "shape" thus realized in auditory perception). An added dimension here is that, returning to the violin part, there is a tension between this gavotte and the intimation of a bourrée in the tied quarter-note suspensions above, which hint at the learned style of species counterpoint.[15] That combination characterizes the instrumental roles too: the conflicting scansions in the piano and violin appearing as rival protagonists for gavotte and bourrée respectively (is the gavotte trying to shake off its rival here?)? Temporarily, we may feel that the bourrée wins out (though the gavotte manages to insert itself briefly within the violin line in mm. 48–49). As the episode comes to a close, so the scansion tips almost imperceptibly back toward the half-measure upbeat of the gavotte from m. 80, still with a lingering miniature upbeat sixteenth-note accretion at this stage, which could be interpreted as a distant echo of the "short upbeat" character of the bourrée. If we do interpret it thus, then the tied *mfp* chord on the second half-note of m. 89 might be felt as a final neutralization of the bourrée (for the moment), clearing the way for a reprise of the gavotte from m. 90.[16]

Within Mozart's sonata-rondo structure in this finale, the conflicting gavotte/bourrée scansions are replayed in subsequent reprises and episodes. Realization of the possibility of such topical conflict as a basis for an interpretation in performance offers fruitful potential for players of this piece and prompts a final observation here. Mozart's coda (m. 246 to the end) brings the work to a rousing conclusion through displays of virtuosity first from the violin (mm. 251–59) and then the piano (mm. 259–66). Note that the bourrée upbeat motive is shifted by a quarter note to midmeasure (mm. 243–44, 246–47) and incorporated into the gavotte upbeat. Amid such posturing it is easy to overlook some revealing details in the violin part. Against a neutral one-harmony-per-measure background the violin's triplets meander pliably through varied successions of stepwise and arpeggiated shapes in which the precise placement of momentary dissonances, transitions from stepwise movement to arpeggios and back again, and the quite detailed slurrings are all essential to the virtuosic effect. While it looks on the page as if this is a straightforwardly "downbeat" passage, emphasizing movement from the first to the second half-note (and not, therefore, a gavotte), there are certainly moments where the forward movement conveyed in performance gestures could justifiably express a gavotte: for instance, the second half of m. 252, leading toward the dissonant treble G the other side of the bar line; likewise in mm. 253–54 or the second half of m. 254, setting up the beginning of the following measure as a changeover to arpeggiations; or the midpoint of m. 256, returning from arpeggiations to stepwise motion. And then there are the violin's curiously humorous shapes counterpointing the piano sixteenth notes from m. 259, in which the successive slurred pairs (half and quarter notes) might be expressed as a distinctively gavotte-like scansion, gradually climbing in pitch, as if the gavotte is belatedly straining to poke its head once more into view, though acquiring a miniature bourrée-like trilled upbeat along the way, which is now shifted by one more quarter note to the left. Neither gavotte nor bourrée wins out in the end: the closing gestures (mm. 266–67) firmly establish a half-measure (gavotte) upbeat, but fail to shake off the micro-upbeats (bourrée) after all. Something of a reconciliation between the two topics stems from Mozart's incorporation of a bourrée upbeat into the gavotte upbeat, shifted back to its original metrical position.

All these observations of detail that might productively influence our interpretation of the score and our management of representative physical gestures when performing K. 454's Rondo finale flow from a consideration of topical possibilities (and I stress *possibilities*, not definitives). Investigating both the presence of topics per se, and the possibility of their coexistence—even conflict—and (partial) resolution offer, in my view, a fascinating potential for action as a performer. K. 454 is by no means the only work in which this is true. Another illustration of a sonata-rondo finale that may be read as an underlying gavotte topic adapted to contrasts of scansion (though not so overtly as in K. 454's bourrée) is that of the magnificent Quintet for Piano and Winds in E flat major, K. 452 (completed less than one month before K. 454). The straightforward gavotte gesture in its characteristic double upbeat form is slightly inflected quite early on, attracting an additional eighth note on the front from m. 16 soon undermining, through frequent repetition, the gavotte, not simply because of the extra note, but because of the differently charged momentum indicated by Mozart's precise articulations. It makes a reappearance (this time without the double upbeat) as a punctuation to the wind chorus following mm. 51–53 and 55–57 in the midst of an episode strongly foursquare in character. It shares the stage of the central C-minor episode, controlling the scansion of mm. 87–103, before ceding ground to an extended passage whose tread through the measure becomes more and more varied and fragmented in impulse toward the end (mm. 117–30), a characteristic captured again at the conclusion of the movement. Reading these various narratives against the topical background of an established gavotte being usurped, reinstated, and eventually banished without trace offers fresh perspectives to performers, not least in view of the large-scale counterpoint of overarching sonata-rondo form against local topical process (sometimes in alignment, sometimes not). There is also the definition of instrumental roles to consider: while the piano establishes the gavotte at the outset and occasionally reinstates or otherwise represents it, it is not the gavotte *persona*; indeed, neither piano nor winds are especially faithful to a particular scansion, or to the presence, absence, or deformation of the gavotte topic running as a thread throughout the texture. Rather, each instrument moves in and out of contrasting topical roles as the movement unfolds and a reading of K. 452's finale drawing on topical representation helps underline the cooperative character of this ensemble that emerges so clearly in period-instrument performances, in sharp contrast to the confrontational aspect that so frequently characterizes modern-instrument performances, in which the winds are always struggling to be heard against a mighty Steinway.[17]

SOUNDING THE SARABANDE: TWO
ANDANTES

Mozart composed the Piano Trio in C major, K. 548, in July 1788. It has no explicit connection to the violin sonata K. 454, completed a little over four years earlier. Unlike
K. 454, we know nothing whatever of the circumstances of the trio's composition,
nor anything about its early performance history or intended personnel. Yet the central movements of both works (Andante in K. 454, Andante cantabile in K. 548) arguably share some common ground, which only becomes apparent through a topical
interpretation.

The link is the sarabande, though neither movement identifies the sarabande's characteristic short–long scansion as a defining gesture at the opening. Indeed, neither movement could be further from it: K. 548 has an explicit *mfp* stress on the first quarter note of
mm. 1 and 2; by contrast, K. 454 marks the first beats of mm. 2 and 4 with *sf* and *sfp* respectively. And yet the subtle signs of the sarabande soon begin to define the landscape. As
before, the historically informed player, working with instrument technology suited to
the period (a Viennese-action fortepiano; a pre- or early-Tourte bow; a violin or cello
in classical setup) has a distinct advantage over the modern player in that the way the
instruments speak the notation inherently suggests particular modes of discourse that
are clouded by the later technology with its generally much heavier sound (and means of
sound production), uniformity of tone, denser textures, and tendency toward "blend" at
the expense of everything else. Those modes of discourse include heightened attention
toward details of articulation, texture, accent, and register because the overall quality of
sound has much greater clarity. So when, at m. 6 of K. 454's Andante, Mozart scores the
second quarter-note beat for a double-stop on the violin and a left-hand dyad, marked *sf*,
the players tend to give this a quite distinctive profile that combines immediacy of pitch
onset with clarity of voicing within the texture (neither is achievable on modern equip-
ment). And in turn the expression of such detail in performance gestures (a slightly
faster bow stroke, for instance) encourages a search for corresponding levels of detail
elsewhere in the score, each of which makes a subtle impression on the performance,
including the reprise of this idea at mm. 13 and 14, where the moment is enhanced by
transfer of the other element of the texture (rocking sixteenth-note octaves) to a higher
register in the violin. And all of a sudden features such as the left-hand octave descent,
E♭– E♭ (m. 9); the slightly skewed left-hand entry from beat 2 after a quarter rest (mm.
3, 11); even the disposition of particular dynamics (mm. 28, 95); dissonance and resolution (mm. 69, 70); rhythmic patterns across the three beats, as in mm. 35, 39, 67, 88, 90,
92; or the placement of particular harmonies such as the cadential six-four chords on
beat 2 in mm. 58, 63, and 68 seem to tell in sound for rather more than they do visually
on the page. Each time, the expression of these moments in the gestures of performance
(including the cooperative gestures in the unfolding dialogue between the players that
is so fundamental a feature of this movement's narrative progress) reveals more than the

hint of a sarabande as an expressive ingredient within the work. The Andante is far from being an actual sarabande, but the more the player probes its language with appropriate instruments and historical approach, the more the identity of the movement in performance appears to be about the counterpointing of topical emergence with realization and projection of a formal structure.

The same can be said of K. 548's Andante cantabile. Here, the presence of the sarabande within the expressive palette is encoded a little more overtly within Mozart's notation than in K. 454, for instance at mm. 5 and 6 (*mfp* markings on beat 2), or the chromatic ascent in high register to treble A in the piano's right hand (m. 22, reinforced by the slurring). In case there were any need to state the point of his *mfp* marking more firmly, Mozart devotes an ostentatious entry for the cello, sweeping down through two octaves in mm. 64 and 65. As in K. 454, details such as rhythmic patterning (for instance, mm. 3, 23, 31, 37–48), and the placement of melodic dissonance and resolution (for instance, mm. 83–86, incorporating subtle "echo effects" wherein beats 1 and 2 mirror each other in terms of motivic content and metrical weight) begin, in such a context, to cohere as cross-referential features flitting across the surface of the piece in a way made recognizable only through topical awareness by the performers, consequently adding to our appreciation (as listeners and scholars) of the complexity of both Mozart's language and our involvement with it.

PERFORMER-INSPIRED TOPICS

The outer sections from the Andante of the duet sonata in C major, K. 521 (1787), composed for Mozart's talented pupil Franziska von Jacquin, are (in their notation, at least) considerably less sarabande-like than the slow movements of K. 454 or K. 548. Yet like them, this movement exhibits traces of a sarabande's presence. They are quite subtle. For example, one might easily argue that the unusual V^7 chord at the start of m. 3 (a remarkably early arrival of the dominant seventh of the supertonic minor within the home key of F major) is a weakly stressed first-beat chord embodying part of a gesture *leading off* that beat and *toward* beat 2 (supertonic G minor, stretching across two beats). Seen thus, m. 3 appears to behave a bit like a sarabande, though it does not look like one, nor does it necessarily sound like one unless played with a degree of sensitivity toward the scansions and gestures of dance. Performer intervention, in order to make audible a potential topical dimension, is arguably more subtle in kind than in the movements discussed so far in this chapter, suggesting an alignment of topically generated narrative with improvised embellishment. By choosing sensitively to apply embellishment, according to historically informed procedural etiquette, the player can at one and the same time add a layer of decorative and aesthetically pleasing embellishment at structurally significant moments (most notably, repetitions of phrases or sections) and by so doing reveal a dance topic, going beyond what the notation makes plain. That is no doubt true of other movements too, but within the Andante of K. 521 there are several moments at which the physical action and presence of the player can induce something that is "not really there."

The sarabande topic is not simply a matter of emphasis by way of accent on the second beat (and usually also length, emphasizing the imbalance of the scansion within the 3/4 measure: short–long). It can be to do with register (mm. 5, 24 in the *Secondo*); or silence (mm. 16–17 in the *Primo*); or rhythmic pattern (mm. 2, 3, 7, 11 in the *Primo*). In each of these specific cases the performer has an opportunity to add improvised elaborations, when they recur toward the end of the Andante (respectively at mm. 63, 82, 74–75, 60, 61, 65, 69). One can imagine various tasteful ways in which this might be done. If one were to attempt the alignment of embellishment with topic placement, as suggested above, then at each of these later points the player's invention would be designed specifically to highlight that gestural step toward the second beat (and also the separation of beats two and three *as a unit*, from beat 1). By so doing, the subtle hints of Mozart's notation can be translated into a topically inspired reprise, turning this repeat section into something resembling a sarabande and adding an expressive layer in the process.[18] Interrogating the reprise in this way potentially enhances the culminating effect of the Coda, for here, Mozart's notation offers something of a saturation of sarabande gestures (if one looks for them). These include:

- mm. 85–86: rhythmic pattern unites beats 2 and 3 as a unit separate from beat 1 (*Primo*), while *Secondo* introduces quarter-note countermelody from beat 2
- m. 87: a more extreme separation (beats 2 and 3 in thirty-second notes)
- m. 84: separation of linear thirty-second-note pattern (beat 1) from vertical chordal texture (beats 2 and 3, including *Secondo* entry from beat 2)
- mm. 89–90: enhancement of mm. 85–86
- m. 91: beat 2 stressed by attaining the highest pitch in this section, and a change in the articulation
- mm. 92–93: beats 2–3 emphasized by change of rhythmic pattern through gradual scale ascent (m. 92) or sudden cascade through an octave and a half in the space of beat 1 (m. 93), followed by relative stasis
- mm. 94–97: beat 2 emphasized by chromatic dissonances in the *Secondo* with bass line additions from beat 2 in alternate measures

One might question whether the Coda's sudden flowering of sarabande-like gestures is enhanced or diluted by the addition of improvised embellishments seeking to profile the sarabande gesture in the preceding reprise (mm. 59–84). There is no right or wrong answer: that Coda might equally be a revelation or a confirmation. The fact is, it does not have to be the same way each time, and involving musical topics within our performance strategies goes hand in hand with the gloriously provisional role of Mozart's notated scores. Happily, both as players or listeners, we can enjoy the contrasting effects of the embellished reprise differently on different occasions. In each case, consideration of the notated score as a site for potential topical revelation has, at least in my own performances of this movement, opened up novel possibilities for communication both with audiences and with other duettists.

This chapter, which is also an account of my own recent journey as a performer of these works, has focused on three essentials: *feeling* topical content in the gestures of performance; *rationalizing* those physical responses in analytical reflection with the score; and *creatively applying* the potential for topical understanding to enhance our experience of this repertoire. By accepting the concept of *topoi* not only as an Aristotelian abstraction, but, as Vico would have it, as the stimulus for action, it exposes how notation can be read in one of a number of different ways, and how, hence, the Music is not the Score. Rather, notation gains value through its essential continuation in performance. It is not something to be slavishly obeyed in every last detail, but something of which a performance leaves a trace—until the next time.

Notes

1. For instance (Aristotle 1960: 423), showing that "white" is not the genus of "snow," or of "swan" (though both are white), because "white" (a quality) is not in the same relation (substance) as "snow" and "swan" (each of which have substance).
2. "Dusty routines," as Stephen Rumph calls them (2012: 83).
3. I presuppose a sympathy toward performance on period instruments, according to historically informed approaches throughout, though it is not impossible that the insights that might flow from an application of topical understanding to Mozart's chamber works might be satisfactorily realized also on modern instruments.
4. Digitized versions of these scores from the Neue Mozart Ausgabe are available at the NMA Online website maintained by the Internationale Stiftung Mozarteum: http://dme.mozarteum.at/DME/nma/start.php?1=2
5. "Eine Klavier Sonate mit einer Violin" as it is called in Mozart's *Verzeichnüß aller meiner Werke* (entered in his catalogue on 21 April 1784); the first edition was published in Vienna by Christoph Torricella later the same year in TROIS SONATES pour le Clavecin ou Pianoforte, *la troisième est accomp: d'un violon oblg:* (the other works are solo keyboard sonatas in B flat major, K. 333, and D major, K. 284).
6. A possibility supported by the state of the autograph, in fact (Stockholm, Stiftelsen Musikkulturens främjande), which reveals that the violin and piano parts were notated in at least two distinct stages, the piano part being entered somewhat uncomfortably between bar lines already ruled to coincide with the violin part, and in at least two different inks. This suggests that much of the final detail of the notation was added in after the performance. The story of the first performance was recounted only in 1799 by Mozart's widow in the *Allgemeine musikalische Zeitung*, and her claim that Mozart played from entirely blank staves on this occasion is perhaps an exaggeration.
7. Thus Kristian Bezuidenhout in the sleeve note to his excellent recording of this work with Petra Müllejans (*Wolfgang Amadeus Mozart (1756–1791): Sonatas for Fortepiano and Violin*, Harmonia Mundi USA HMU907494).
8. The comment comes from the sleeve note to his and Thomas Albertus Irnberger's recording of Mozart's violin sonatas (*Wolfgang Amadeus Mozart: Violinsonaten*, vol. 3, Gramola 98904).

9. This is the moment at which to consider an important philosophical point. I deliberately avoid claiming (here and elsewhere) that Mozart definitively imparted into his music a particular topical content that, as I believe is the case in this movement, might regulate its narrative or structure somehow. This and other cases considered in this chapter pursue investigations of an interpretational kind in which possible readings of the music (consisting of far more than just the notated values on the page) against topical frameworks are offered as potentially helpful or interesting motivations for performance. In no case is there an attempt to retrace an archaeology of authorial intention. When I claim, for instance, that in the finale of K. 454 there is a counterpoint of Rondo form (concept) against an unfolding topical narrative (process), I am not supposing for a moment that Mozart determined the finale that way in 1784 and that almost 230 years later I have discovered this fact.

10. The gavotte-like "double upbeat" consisting of two equal notes repeating the same pitch occurs, for example, in the Romance from *Eine kleine Nachtmusik*, K. 525, the slow movement of String Quintet in E flat major, K. 614, as well as the gavotte-like themes from K. 575/i (m. 17) and K. 581/i (m. 65). Danuta Mirka (this volume) finds it lurking under the surface of the celebrated theme of K. 550/i.

11. Measure 20 slurs through the whole bar of the rising violin triad, one of those moments of ambiguity where the half note B♭ is simultaneously a conclusion of the preceding phrase and the start of something new. If we are reading this section against the gavotte topic, this measure acquires a delicious "double entendre" that may be missed otherwise. Playing Mozart's notated slurs in mm. 20 and 21 casts m. 22 in a different light from the analogous m. 18, for the half-measure rising fourth, F–B♭ in the violin is no longer answering and balancing a phrase that had started four half-note beats earlier, but cuts instead into a different pattern of two whole measures (20 and 21, each commencing from beat 1) and a surplus half-measure at the beginning of m. 22. A topical reading thus throws into relief an unsuspected asymmetry underlying mm. 16–24.

12. A small illustration: I had always found the left-hand octaves starting at m. 26 difficult to represent otherwise than in an uncomfortably march-like tread that seemed altogether too heavy for this passage. Realizing that a gavotte gesture underlies it prompts two much more satisfying responses in performance: (i) my left hand is immediately lightened by representing the gesture as a "movement toward" the next measure (mm. 26–27, 27–28, 28–29); and (ii) instead of initiating a statement-response between my pounding left hand crotchets on beats 1 and 2, answered by the violin on beats 3 an 4 each time, I now participate in one of Mozart's relatively rare outbreaks of heterophony (from the second half note of m. 26 through to the cadence), moving in time with the violin as a supportive but equal partner, rather than a domineering and ungainly one who has apparently got "out of step." (Alarming though it is to confess, I had not even noticed the heterophony prior to reinterpreting this passage in the light of topical knowledge.)

13. Allanbrook (1983: 48) writes that the bourrée is in 4/4 meter (with quarter-note beats) or in alla breve (with half-note beats) and she suggests that the gavotte is in 4/4 meter (1983: 49), although her examples of this dance are uniformly in alla breve. As a matter of fact, eighteenth-century discussions of the gavotte and the bourrée make clear that both dances are in alla breve (see Sulzer 1792–94, 1: 429, 2: 309; Koch 1802: cols. 271, 630). While quarter notes are more prominent in the bourrée than in the gavotte, they are metrical beats in *neither* dance.

14. This is an observation only, not a value judgment. The contrasting scansions crucially lend a shape to the movement.
15. The hint is due to the fact that the learned style shares a *figura* with the bourrée. For the sense of this term and a similar occurrence in the Duettino from *Le nozze di Figaro*, where the learned-style half-note suspensions intimate the gavotte, see Rumph (2012: 84–89 and this volume).
16. And incidentally, allowing this "neutralizing" chord to disperse will take more time (even on a Viennese fortepiano) than suggested by the quarter rest separating it from the succeeding refrain theme. In any sensible performance, Mozart's quarter rest will not be taken literally as one tick of the metronome, but as a sign of regional separation. Deliberately thinking of the effect of transition from a bourrée idiom back to that of a gavotte at this point has taught me how long to extend this rest. (Given that the gavotte has been presaged somewhat in the preceding phrase—from m. 80—I now think it inadvisable to improvise an *Eingang* at this resting point, despite the obvious temptation. The same is probably true of m. 150, although the temptation is greater here, given the rather special chromatics and the fact that the passage ends up on the bottom note of Mozart's piano; additionally, there has been no strongly conflicting scansion in the middle episode to which the *sfp* maneuvers every alternate half-measure from m. 143 would serve as a retort.)
17. A delightful exception to the general state of affairs on modern instruments being Stephen Hough's recording with members of the Berlin Philharmonic Wind Quintet, an account that embeds an articulate approach to phrasing, local rhetoric, and gesture as firmly as in many a period-instrument account. (*Mozart • Beethoven: Quintets for Piano and Winds*, BIS CD–1552).
18. For instance, at mm. 63 or 82 the players might coordinate a *grupetto* (turn) together in their right hands actually starting from beat 2, shortening the notated dotted crotchet in the process, imparting a dissonance on that beat and drawing attention to it against the low bass, F.

References

Aristotle. 1960. *Topica*. Trans. Edward S. Forster. The Loeb Classical Library 391. Cambridge, MA: Harvard University Press.

Koch, Heinrich Christoph. 1802. *Musikalisches Lexikon*. Frankfurt am Main: August Hermann der Jüngere. Reprint, Kassel: Bärenreiter 2001.

[Mozart, Constanze.] Mozarts Witwe. 1799. Einige Anekdoten aus Mozarts Leben. *Allgemeine musikalische Zeitung* 1 (6 February): cols. 289–91.

Rumph, Stephen. 2012. *Mozart and Enlightenment Semiotics*. Berkeley: University of California Press.

Sulzer, Johann Georg. 1792–94. *Allgemeine Theorie der schönen Künste*, new expanded 2nd ed. Leipzig: Weidmann.

CHAPTER 21

RECOGNIZING MUSICAL TOPICS VERSUS EXECUTING RHETORICAL FIGURES

TOM BEGHIN

LEONARD Ratner (1980) made us familiar with "topics" as "types" or "styles": dances, singing style, French overture, and so forth. Different from the traditional *loci topici*, which in rhetoric are introduced at the level of *inventio*, or the first stage of the five-stage rhetorical process, which deals with the choice of ideas (*res*), Ratnerian topics are defined as directly style-specific, seemingly more at home in *elocutio* or "style," or the third stage of the rhetorical process, where ideas are clothed into words (*verba*). The definition of topics proposed in this handbook—"topics are musical styles and genres taken out of their proper context and used in another one"—furthermore suggests an act of "quotation," where stylistic precision is of utmost importance. Rather than their manifestation in actual "words," one may stress the appropriate *choice* of topics, or of certain groups of topics, which would place them in *inventio* after all, but "appropriateness" as a key-quality of topics is undermined by their often-praised variety and contrast—with *il filo* somehow safeguarding a sense of "unity within variety."[1]

Quantity has been an emphasis in the history of rhetorical *elocutio* as well, where the activity of drawing long lists of *figurae* has been both celebrated and trivialized.[2] In his *De utraque verborum ac rerum copia*, a textbook that enjoyed several centuries of success, the humanist Erasmus advised his readers, while "perus[ing] good authors night and day…, [to] note all figures in them, store up in our memory what we noted, imitate what we have stored up, and by frequent use make it a habit to have them ready at hand" (1963: 17–18). Rhetorical figures are to be recognized, memorized, but ultimately used—in one's own speech. Ratner reportedly applied very much the same method when teaching a university course: "[He] would put on a recording of a Beethoven or a Mozart string quartet and then, as the music played, shout out the topics, stopping occasionally to ask if anyone knew what the topic was at a particular moment" (Agawu 2008: 40).

Topical theorists have not tried very hard to draw meaningful distinctions between figure and topic; for many, the latter simply includes the former. Speaking at a Mozart bicentenary event, Ratner (1991: 615) defined "topic" quite liberally as "a style, a type, a figure, a process *or* a plan of action" (emphasis mine). So, are figure and topic different—and how?

Almost always, rhetorical figures have clear declamatory implications. Calling something the expression of doubt (*dubitatio*) means to really feign it. From a critical perspective, Johann Nikolaus Forkel (1788: 57) cautioned his reader not to confuse *suspensio* (the holding in suspense) with *dubitatio* (the feigning of doubt),[3] but most often the actual difference will show in delivery only—by one's tone, inflection, or timing—hence, all in the doing of the performer–orator, whose *voluntas* or intent ideally remains the same through each stage of the creative process. This consistency extends to the situation where composer and orator are not the same person, in which case it is up to the performer to recognize the figures that have been selected to express certain emotions. When portraying rage or anger, for instance, C. P. E. Bach warns against an "exaggerated violent attack," explaining that the expression of these "violent emotions" should be "rather through harmonic and melodic figures."[4] Almost certainly, Bach had rhetorical figures in mind, even if he appears to use *Figuren* here in an applied-mechanistic sense. His own Sonata in F minor, H. 173, the first movement of which, according to Forkel (1783: 37),[5] features "a man who acts in resentment and rage," starts with a "rocket" figure in dotted rhythm—a combined version of Beethoven's Op. 2 No. 1, also in F minor, and Op. 10 No. 1, in C minor. A figure brings life or emotion. Imagine first a body at rest—of an orator, an actor, or a statue. Then start imagining motion: head turns, neck swivels, hand rises. That is how Quintilian (IX, i, 4) and his colleagues conceived of the effect of a figure, which they defined as the linguistic deviation from "plain" or unadorned speech and which occurs "when we give our language a confirmation other than the obvious or ordinary."[6]

In the context suggested by Bach, recognition leads to execution—and at this level it is all about concealing one's art, and this while honoring Horace's axiom that "if you want me to weep, first you yourself must grieve" (*si vis me flere, dolendum est primum ipsi tibi*). According to Cicero or Quintilian, the mere recognition of a rhetorical figure by a judge may actually cause you to lose your case. "Do not act—at least do not get caught acting," is how Sander Goldberg (2007: 52) summarizes this oratorical paradox. By contrast, when it comes to musical topics, the argument is often made that they should be recognized almost in name of "historically informed listening."

So far, this brief introduction confirms the antithesis announced by this chapter's title: recognizing musical topics *versus* executing rhetorical figures. To any student of rhetoric, including those pre-1800 musicians who embraced rhetoric as their big-sister discipline, this juxtaposition would be strikingly odd. A topic is just as rhetorical as a figure can be musical. Topic, if anything, should have more of a rhetorical ring than figure, which in music is often applied, furthermore, in a mechanical or prerhetorical sense: as the constellation of a small number of notes, that is to say, at the level of a single word rather than a sentence or a group of sentences. But the antithesis is there: it was unwittingly planted with the birth itself of the Ratnerian topic. Thirty years later, in light of topic theory's "success story" (Caplin 2005: 113), we have no choice but to come to terms with it. In order to first rehearse some figurative terminology (the knowledge of which can no longer be taken for granted) and to critically assess the much younger creation of a vocabulary of musical topics (by one of the pioneers of topical theory), I would like to begin by examining two samples of figure- and topic-oriented analysis respectively, both of a Mozart solo keyboard sonata—the one of K. 309 by Friedrich August Kanne in 1821, the other of K. 332 by Wye J. Allanbrook in 1992. Then, I will ask how figure and topic may be compatible within a more widely conceived and socioculturally anchored rhetorical analysis of the first movement of Haydn's Sonata in E flat major, Hob. XVI:52—one of the three culminating case studies in Ratner's book (the two others being a Beethoven string quartet and a Mozart opera, confirming that "Classic" also means "Viennese").

   When it comes to music theory and the subject of topics or figures, I would venture the following hypothesis: that—despite the difference between topics and figures—the former have become for modern-day music theorists what the latter were for their eighteenth-century counterparts—so irresistibly fun to play with![7] I gladly join the playground, but do so from the perspective of a performing keyboardist whose main interest remains in applying rhetoric in a "primary" kind of way.[8] In this spirit, most of my examples may be found as videotaped performances posted at this volume's website, to enhance my broader argument that eighteenth-century "musicking" was just as much visual as it was aural. This website also features a few of my favorite examples of rhetorical figures in Haydn's solo keyboard music, which I offer as a concise appendix: "In Defense of the Rhetorical Figure."

Mozart, Sonata in C major, K. 309, First Movement, Exposition

In early 1821 Friedrich August Kanne took over the general editorship of the *Allgemeine musikalische Zeitung, mit besonderer Rücksicht auf den österreichischen Kaiserstaat*. He marked his new role as No. 1 critic in Vienna by publishing an eighty-four-column-long "Analytical Essay on Mozart's Keyboard Works, with a few Notes on the Performance of Them" (*Versuch einer Analyse der Mozartischen Clavierwerke, mit einigen Bemerkungen über den Vortrag derselben*).[9] Spanning the equivalent of an academic semester (from January to June), these biweekly installments, covering the complete solo keyboard works of Mozart, read like an "open university" type of course. Who would have taken the class? The average subscriber of the journal, one would imagine, also had the financial means to purchase the relatively new six-volume S. A. Steiner & Co. Mozart complete edition of 1818, which provided the incentive for Kanne's survey. She or he, furthermore, would have had either the necessary skill to play these scores themselves or have had the opportunity of hearing someone near them do so.[10] The text of the Viennese edition was based on that of the 1798 Breitkopf & Härtel *Oeuvres complettes*, but the works followed a different order, one that combined criteria of chronology with difficulty. "Difficulty" in this new canonizing effort is not to be understood in technical terms—by 1821 we would already have had Clementi or Beethoven sonatas to practice—but in the capacity to critically engage with the works: "Through a gradual compilation"—welcomed by Kanne as the "best and most natural"—"the player is at once prepared and consecrated by the loveliest and most heartfelt imagery of the first sonatas *so as to receive and absorb the higher ideality of the later ones*" (emphasis mine).[11] In this individualized process of "absorbing," it is the player who acts as critic—the listening is of oneself (as one sits at the piano, eyes alternately on score and hands) or of someone else (whom one would observe perform in close vicinity).

Let us sample Kanne's prose on one of those "first" sonatas, in C major, K. 309, reproduced in Table 21.1. Example 21.1 shows the corresponding score with annotations extracted from Kanne's text. Note the change of agency in the course of the first sentence. "The sonata opens with a pathetic main idea," but "he," that is, Mozart, "instills it on the mind." The process of "instilling" is materialized by the rhetorical figure of "repetition." But, "as a good orator," which is still a compliment in Kanne's writings, "Mozart adds paronomasia." Kanne's naming and definition of *Paronomasie* as "reinforcement" (*Verstärkung*) is an example of why scholars (Schmidt 2006, Krones 1996) have assumed his indebtedness to Forkel, who gives the following definition of this figure: "Repetition receives only then its highest value when it is paired with *paronomasia* (reinforcement), which does not repeat a phrase merely as it already was but with new, forceful additions."[12] Forkel continues by saying that these "additions" do not necessarily have to be understood as "additional tones": sometimes, he writes, these "additions" can be materialized by "a stronger or weakened delivery"[13]—an illustration of the fine line between *elocutio* and *actio*: the figure of *paronomasia* may be applied by mere voice (*vox*), without having to go through words (*verba*).

But to ascribe exclusivity to Forkel as Kanne's source for "musical rhetoric" would be to underestimate someone who has been called "a man of universal education" and, one might add, all those readers of the journal, who, coming from different strands of life, must have perfectly well understood what Kanne was talking about.[14] Kanne's understanding of *dubitatio*—more, in fact, than Forkel's, who defines it as the mere "expression of uncertainty"—resonates with the following definition by Quintilian (IX, ii, 19): "*Dubitatio* offers *a certain faith in truth*, when we pretend to be searching where to begin, where to end" (emphasis mine).[15] Also Mozart's *dubitatio*, as Kanne describes it, has a specific oratorical purpose: "He raises shreds of doubt *so as to* execute the ending of his statement *all the more strongly*" (emphasis mine). The true reward of the two questioning moments in mm. 13 and 14 (each probing different first-inversion subdominant chords) is to end one's opening paragraph with an after-phrase that features fanfare-like octaves and fifths, and in getting away with doing so twice. In m. 17 I do not play a suffix in my trill, deliberately "breaking off" my thought (the applied figure is *aposiopesis*); the second time, now really finishing, I do enjoy the full trill all the more—complete

Table 21.1 Excerpt from Kanne, "Versuch einer Analyse der Mozart'schen Clavierwerke," [Wiener] *Allgemeine musikalische Zeitung* 5/19 (7 March 1821), 147–48, and 5/20 (10 March 1821), 153

His sonata thus opens with a pathetic main idea [*Hauptgedanke*], which he instills on the mind one more time after the aforementioned seven measures by way of repetition [**repetitio**]. As a good orator, he adds **paronomasia**, i.e., reinforcement of the expression, as may be seen in the third and fourth quarter of the eleventh measure and in all of measure twelve.

In the thirteenth measure he himself raises shreds of doubt against this, so as to execute the ending of his main statement [*Hauptsatzes*] all the more strongly [**dubitatio**]…Now, through new periods [*Perioden*] in his language of emotions [*Empfindungssprache*], he leads the soul to his purported middle statement [*Mittelsatz*], specifically through a **gradatio** of a two-measure long, triple-repeated figure, each time breaking off at the top, until he allows the first cadence to enter. The left hand introduces the middle idea [*Mittelgedanke*] or, rather, by the activation of mere movement, lays out a foil on which it is about to shimmer. This [middle idea] is both artfully invented and capable of arousing nice intellectual pleasure because it completely reverses itself [**hypallage**] in the second part of the sonata, the upper voice becoming the lower one while the lower, without change, becomes the upper one.…

Epistrophe or the return of the concluding statement [*Schlusssatz*] is also beautified by **paronomasia**…and is not yet led to a conclusion but first held up by new figures of **dubitatio** until the trill on A finally announces the end of the first part.

Es beginnt also seine Sonate mit einem pathetischen Hauptgedanken, den er durch die Wiederhohlung nach den ersten erwähnten sieben Tacten dem Gemüthe noch ein Mahl einprägt. Aber wie ein guter Redner fügt er dieser Wiederhohlung die Paronomasie, d.h. die Verstärkung des Ausdrucks bey, und zwar ist dieselbe im dritten und vierten Viertel des elften Tactes, und im ganzen zwölften sichtbar.

Er erhebt einige Zweifel selbst dagegen, im dreyzehnten Tacte, um auf eine desto stärkere Weise alsdann den Schluss seines Hauptsatzes auszuführen in folgender Stelle…Nun führt er in neuen Perioden seiner Empfindungssprache die Seele zu seinem geahneten Mittelsatze, und zwar durch eine Gradation in einer zweytactigen, dreymahl wiederhohlten Figur, welche jedes Mahl auf der Höhe abbricht, bis er die erste Cadenz eintreten lässt. Die linke Hand beginnt den Mittelgedanken, oder legt vielmehr durch ihre bloss angeregte Bewegung erst die Folie unter, auf welcher nun dieser schimmern soll. Kunstreich erfunden, und fähig zugleich ein schönes intellectuelles Vergnügen zu erwecken, ist dieser dadurch, dass er sich im zweyten Theile der Sonate alsdann ganz umkehrt, und die Oberstimme zur unteren, diese aber auch unverändert zur oberen wird.…

Die Epistrophe oder Wiederkehr des Schlusssatzes ist gleichfalls durch die Paronomasie verschönert…und wird noch nicht zum Ende geführt, sondern durch neue Figuren der Dubitatio erst aufgehalten, bis der Triller auf a endlich das Ende des ersten Theiles ahnen lässt.

with up-front appoggiatura and a fairly relaxed *Nachschlag*—before yielding to the excitement of what Kanne identifies as a *gradatio* (mm. 21–26). At this point, I invite the reader to assess my video recording of the whole sonata exposition, performed on a Walter fortepiano modeled after Mozart's own of 1782 (Web Example 21.1) ▶.[16]

Kanne names six rhetorical figures. Of these, *Umkehrung* or *hypallage* belongs here only retrospectively and would involve memory: it refers to the reversal of hands at the corresponding point in the recapitulation. Three are figures of repetition: *repetitio*, *paronomasia, epistrophe.* They are "figures of speech" (*figurae elocutionis*), because their identity depends on a certain formula: it does not matter *what* is repeated—only *that* and *how* something is repeated. *Dubitatio*, on the other hand, is a figure of thought (*figura sententiae*), since the idea of doubt may be expressed in any number of ways, as, for example, by one or more questions ("is it? really?"), an affirmative sentence ("I, for one, do not know…"), or with a "but" at the beginning ("But what do I say?" "But no…"). *Gradatio*, Kanne's fifth figure, requires some scrutiny. The Latin equivalent of the Greek

EXAMPLE **21.1** Mozart, Piano Sonata in C major, K. 309/i, exposition, with annotations after Friedrich August Kanne.

(Continued)

EXAMPLE **21.1** (Continued)

klimax, gradatio implies a ladder where one progresses step by step: from a to b, from b to c, from c to d, etc. As such, it is a figure of speech, and, to be more exact, a figure of repetition. Historically, however, and not just in music, the figure was conflated with that of *auxesis* (Greek) or *incrementum* (Latin), where "step-by-step" was also understood to mean "more-and-more," steering the figure away from repetition toward enumeration and the effect of a crescendo. In mm. 21–26, however, any sense of heightening passion is cast in overall step-by-step diatonic descent, where an overall decrescendo may be in order. But over those drum-like repetitions in the left hand Kanne may have perceived something of a three-step ladder in the right hand, its registral shifts resulting in *gradatio*-like anchors from measure to measure—from a to b, from b to c, from c to d.[17]

Kanne's analytic prose is surprisingly active, leaving the agency mostly with the composer–orator. "Until [Mozart] allows the first cadence to enter," is a turn of phrase rarely found in modern-day analysis. We would say: "Until the first cadence enters," or simply, "until the first cadence."[18] Equally clear is the speaker's *voluntas*: he "instills" (on the mind), he "raises doubt" (on purpose), he "leads" (the soul). Ambiguity of the German language, as in "*the* mind" or "*the* soul" implies empathy between composer, performer, and listener: we need not ask *whose* mind—we are in it together.

Playing Mozart's Walter, rather than the bigger Viennese piano that Kanne would have had by 1821 (with a range of six-and-a-half octaves and a *prell*-action that would have accommodated thicker hammers), I wonder about the one and only hint to anything related to *inventio*: "His sonata opens with a *pathetic* main idea" (emphasis mine). I recognize the *exclamatio* in the second measure, reversing the direction of a C-major arpeggio by the skip of a major sixth up to the high E, which, furthermore, is ornamented, whence to be held longer than the two first octaves. These I hold longer than half of their value, somewhere between the ordinary length recommended by C. P. E. Bach (1753: 127) and the three-quarters recommended by Türk (1789: 356). Assertive—yes, but pathetic?

Quite remarkably, when sitting at a piano closer to Kanne's, I easily adjust to his suggested pathos. This may be gauged by comparing two close-up videotaped performances. In the first version (Web Example 21.2, ▶ at the Walter fortepiano), my eyes are wide open, alert, focused on my hands. As my ear reacts to the higher and thinner upper register of the keyboard (the *exclamatio*), also my eyes show increased alertness, but then also immediate relaxation. The silence after my release (which is nice and short: Mozart writes a quarter note) acts as the briefest of transitions to my continuing thoughts in m. 3. This is a *transitio* not in an organic sense (as in "the music continues and I have no choice but to follow") but rhetorically (as in "let *me* continue"). As Forkel's *paronomasia*, my figure of *transitio* is unspoken and occurs by mere force of timing and gesture.

At the later instrument (a replica of an 1808 Nannette Streicher, see Web Example 21.3 ▶), there is more homogeneity but, then, also more contrast. The slower decay of sound also makes me want to linger on every tone: instead of a peak (either spontaneous or unsuspected), the high E becomes the third in a series of "pathetic" tones. I frown my eyebrows all the way and well into the silence. Only at the first tones of the continuation phrase do I light up and give in to what now comes across as an expressive contrast. Whereas in scenario one there are subtle shades of light and shadow throughout, in scenario two first there is shadow, then there is light. But mostly, in scenario one, I am alertly in control as an orator, whereas in scenario two I feel like a player yet also listener of Mozart—driver and passenger at the same time.

MOZART, SONATA IN F MAJOR, K. 332, FIRST MOVEMENT, FIRST GROUP

Sensitivity to instrument is essential also when discussing the opening measures of Mozart's K. 332, the piece where topical theorists have sent "the doubting Thomases" (to use Agawu's [2008: 2] words), and, of course, it was Allanbrook's 1992 analysis that initially elevated it to topical stardom. Table 21.2 reproduces the paragraphs that set up her reading of the movement, with Example 21.2 showing the corresponding score. If K. 332 is an absolute favorite for topical theorists (to convince their colleagues), then it has been for fortepianists too (to make their case among pianists). In a polemical exchange with Charles Rosen, Malcolm Bilson (1990: 2) called the two-note "sighs" under a slur "*the main stuff* of this theme." Drawing his inspiration directly from his keyboard (whether it be a clavichord, a *Tangentenflügel*, Viennese harpsichord, or fortepiano), Mozart exploits the decays of those beginning-of-the-slur attacks, the juxtaposition of these two-note sighs culminating in the *exclamatio* of m. 3 (a major sixth from B♭ to an exposed high G that is actually quite hard to sing) and the precipitated leading-tone *quaestio* or question in m. 4. The effect of this measure-to-measure concatenation is similar to that of *asyndeton* or, as Quintilian calls it, "dissolution…which, owing to the absence of connecting particles…is useful when we are speaking with special vigor" (IX, iii, 50). Here maybe not so much vigor, but certainly excitement—either a tinge of anxiety (or the "emotional disturbance" that Vickers [1988: 304] associates with the figure) within an otherwise beautiful F-major triad, or of an eager, out-of-breath kind of enthusiasm (as Longinus [1998: 165] described the effect).[19]

If there is excitement right from the beginning, then what Allanbrook perceives as a "stranding" and "precipice" (the "unstable leading tone" at the end of the "antecedent phrase"), rather than coming out of the blue, is a result of the overall insinuating opening statement by the keyboardist–orator, so not a "hypothetical soprano" who is being "interrupted." I would in any case question the perception of a generic "singing style" topic, unless singing is conceived to include "speaking" (as eighteenth-century singing did, of course). But what has always puzzled me more is the perception of "learned counterpoint" at the beginning of the "consequent" phrase. After devoting my mental powers to the finer details of Mozart's articulations in the antecedent phrase (including the seemingly contradictory across-the-bar slur in the left hand), there is always a sense of relief as my hands are allowed to glide down on the keyboard, three tones under a

Table 21.2 Excerpt from Allanbrook, "Two Threads through the Labyrinth" (1992), 131–32, 136

The exposition begins with an introductory period in F major, with extensions. The first four measures…are cast in a simple singing style—a "soprano" accompanied by an Alberti bass. Static harmonically, the phrase does not even achieve a full half cadence, moving in leisurely fashion through pre-dominant harmony (I–V^7/IV–IV–vii^6), all over a tonic pedal…. [H]alfway through the phrase, stranded on an expressive precipice, desire unstaunched (the phrase ends on a half cadence, the "singer" on an unstable high E-natural, the leading tone), the hypothetical soprano and her questioning, reflective antecedent phrase are interrupted by a robust and authoritarian consequent gesture—a four-measure parody of learned counterpoint (… mm. 5–8). An angular two-measure subject in the treble is answered by the same in the bass, in strict imitation at the octave; a suspension in the "countersubject" in measure 8 intensifies the learned affect. This is the topic least recognized, either overtly, in analysis, or tacitly, in performance: the treble is frequently taken to be a singing line all through these twelve measures, just unaccountably inarticulate in measures 7–8 (when the second entry takes place in the bass). The subject in itself would have been perfectly suited to the singing style, had the Alberti bass continued; in that case it would probably have come to a comfortable cadence in the eighth measure of the phrase…Instead, although the four-measure fall of the subject is sufficient to answer the four-measure rise of the singer, the lengths imposed by the counterpoint postpone the cadence; in this they are aided by the angular, "abstract" intervals introduced into the subject in the place of a conjunct melody, intervals—especially the perfect fifth followed by the perfect fourth—which are less songlike, more appropriately learned and contrapuntal. Hence four measures of galant minuet style are introduced…to close the period with a solid iambic V–I.

…The performer too must be aware of the progress of these gestures, as few performers are today, and must articulate each one with its proper qualities—lyric legato for the singing style, for example, or strict rhythmic authority, *allegro pomposo*, for the contrapuntal—taking care not to smooth them over into an indistinguishable wash of "melody." If one does not attend to the discreteness of the gestures, the movement becomes tonal and thematic chaos; its unity lies in variety, in the mutations into various kinds.

slur making for quite pleasurable hand positions, their smooth melodic content to be enjoyed first in the right hand, then the left, yes, suggestive of a simple canon, but without the pretense of any learnedness[20]—an emerging middle voice in m. 7 casually giving rise to a 4–3 suspension and the accompanying trill in fact dispelling any possible sense of *gravitas*, so certainly not "intensifying the learned effect," as Allanbrook suggests. This whole consequent phrase, in fact, is much more comfortably "sing-able" than the antecedent one.[21] For my performance, see Web Example 21.4 ▶.

Wondering where such a perception of a "robust and authoritarian consequent gesture" might have come from, I am intrigued by Kanne's analysis of this moment, which is in *some* agreement with Allanbrook's: "The fifth and sixth measures necessarily create expectations that this sonata would distinguish itself by contrapuntal weaving; only, who can ask the genius: why didn't you do so? Most probably, he had his public [*Publicum*] in mind."[22] "Contrapuntal weaving" does not quite have a connotation of "learnedness" but the point of counterpoint sticks nonetheless. When we look at Kanne's

EXAMPLE **21.2** Mozart, Piano Sonata in F major, K. 332/i, mm. 1–25, (a) with annotations after Wye J. Allanbrook and (b) with author's annotations.

ALLGEMEINE

MUSIKALISCHE ZEITUNG,

mit besonderer Rücksicht auf den österreichischen Kaiserstaat.

Den 31ten März.   N^{ro.} 26.   1821.

Versuch einer Analyse der Mozart'schen Clavierwerke, mit einigen Bemerkungen über den Vortrag derselben.

Von

Friedrich August Kanne.

Drittes Heft.

Sonate X. Allegro F-dur.

(Fortsetzung).

Das Thema ist sehr gehaltvoll, und kündigt sich schon im fünften und sechsten Tacte an, als wollte es Empfindungen von besonderer Stärke und Tiefe anregen; doch wird diese Erwartung nicht in dem Maasse erfüllt, weil *M.* sich begnügt, seinen oratorischen Satz in schöner Begeisterung fortzuspinnen, ohne gerade ein so intellectuelles Vergnügen dem Spieler bereiten zu wollen.

Der 5te und 6te Tact erweckt nothwendig Erwartungen, dass diese *Sonate* durch contrapunctische Verwebung sich auszeichnen werde; allein wer kann den Genius fragen: Warum thatest du

Fünfter Jahrgang Nro. 26.

es nicht? das Wahrscheinlichste ist, dass er sein Publicum vor Augen hatte. Bey alledem ist dieser Satz aber so reich und zugleich effectvoll, dass auch der gebildetste Spieler in der Beschauung desselben das innigste Vergnügen empfinden muss; denn der Periodenbau ist trotz seiner fliessenden Natürlichkeit so kunstvoll, und enthält so schöne und geistreiche Gegensätze, dass ein blühendes schönes Bild aus seinem Total-Anblick hervorgeht.

Besonders innig ist der auf die brillantesten Steigerungen folgende Mittelsatz auf der Dominante, und lässt sehr viel Gesang im Vortrag zu, die markirte Stelle mit den nachschlagenden Achteln, welche mehr einem Accompagnement beym ersten Anblick gleich kommt:

wird durch schönen Harmonienwechsel in der Folge gewürzt und dadurch gerechtfertigt.

Das Adagio B-dur ist sehr figurirt und blühend gehalten, die Phantasie des Tonsetzers schwimmt in lyrischer Wonne, und erfreut sich in dem sanften Wogen seiner Empfindung.

Oft lang verhaltene Regungen befreyen sich von ihren Fesseln, in den spät erst zur Beruhigung geführten, und durch lange Suspensionen oder Dubitationen aufgehaltenen Perioden. Die Gegensätze sind gehaltvoll, die Stimmenführung grössten Theils volltönig.

Mit vieler Klugheit hat die Verlagshandlung diese Sonate zum Schluss des Heftes gewählt, denn das Finale ist eines der brillantesten, welches aus *Mozarts* Feder in diesem freyen, höchst poetischen und doch mehr natürlichen als kunstvollen Style geflossen ist.

FIGURE 21.1 Cover page of [Wiener] *Allgemeine musikalische Zeitung* 5/26 (31 March 1821).

musical example, however (see Figure 21.1 for a facsimile from Kanne's journal), we see that Mozart's measure-to-measure slurs are gone, leaving only one single slur for the syncopated note in m. 6. This altered notation encourages a heavier note-by-note execution—one that, from a declamatory point of view, invites the pianist to frown her eyebrows in deep earnestness. I have recorded such a performance on my 1808 Streicher (Web Example 21.5) ▶.[23]

Allanbrook's third topic (mm. 9–12) is that of "galant minuet style…introduced…to close the period with a solid iambic V–I." In a performing culture, however, where dissonances were supposed to be stressed—and instruments built to help you stress them—a V⁷–I closing gesture (or dissonance–consonance) would have been trochaic (long–short) or, as here in triple meter, spondaic (long–long) at most, but certainly not iambic (short–long). The perception of "galant," furthermore, seems at odds with the *crescendo* and *forte* in mm. 9–12, which instead point to a more forceful state of mind. I like to think of the subsequent horn call passage (mm. 13–16) as an *apologia* (apology) or *correctio* (correction) of some sort, its soft-spokenness compensating for my inappropriately forceful tone before. Quintilian's example of self-correction includes both: "I beg you to pardon me, if I have been carried too far" (IX, ii, 17). Now truly "galant," the *paronomasia* in m. 17 is intended to please rather than instill, and the repeated trochaic cadential formulae shed playful doubt—or is it suspense, as in the proverbial silence before the storm (and stress) in m. 23?

My focus on rhetorical figures—admittedly pragmatic—has led me to question almost each of Allanbrook's topics. We have singing style—yet I want to speak. We have learned counterpoint—yet my hands revel in the simplicity of a canon. We have a galant minuet—yet my tone gets forceful and angry. Even the horn calls in mm. 13–16 are not what they seem. Yes, there is an ever so brief "open" C-major fifth in m. 13, between two tonic chords, but in m. 15, when its impurity as a tempered fifth on a well-tempered keyboard risks becoming obvious, Mozart adds a pure C-major third: the anacrusis slur just before literally splits one voice (the top F) into two. (The dotted slur in the bass, as added by the editor of the *Neue Mozart Ausgabe*, would therefore seem misguided.) To facilitate appreciating the various acoustic combinations, Web Example 21.6 ▶ lines up four sound files, each played in a Vallotti well-tempered tuning. First, mm. 13–16 transposed down to E flat major, where we would have a pure fifth (Web Example 21.6a) ▶. Then, with an added third, which only adds unnecessary shrillness (Web Example 21.6b) ▶. Then, back to F major, with the tempered fifth (Web Example 21.6c) ▶. Finally, as Mozart did, restoring the idea of "purity" by adding the third (Web Example 21.6d) ▶.

Topic *and* figure, of course, can coexist. Let us assume we are dealing here with horn calls, sonically achieved by the purity of thirds rather than that of open fifths. If so, then an association of "out-of-doorness" (to be further interpreted as "pastoral" rather than indicative of "warfare" or "hunt")[24] may well have been anticipated by the keyboardist–orator, say, to help him convey a corrective, less emotionally charged message. *Correctio*, after all, is a figure of thought (since one may "correct" in any number of ways), so the *res* component of the figure may exactly be those little horn calls, here acoustically modified to fit one's purpose. But topic and figure must be complementary. If they are not, as in all the other instances we have examined, we may claim to be dealing with something akin to ambiguity, parody, or irony, but in the particular case of K. 332 such interpretations unnecessarily move away from the *voluntas* of a performer.[25] Irony is a good case in point. Rhetorically speaking, when it is not directly clear from the delivery of the speaker that we are dealing with irony, then it does not exist. So, here is the crux of my argument: the speaker–performer I have in mind is someone who is both rhetorically conscious and who plays on an instrument whose technology is similar to Mozart's. Interestingly, but perhaps not surprisingly, when I perform the theme of K. 332 on my 1808-Streicher (see Web Example 21.7) ▶, I find it much easier to produce a version that conforms to Allanbrook's 1992 reading—it may even be close to Kanne's from 1821, but we would still be off from Mozart's by at least thirty years.[26]

For my musical examples I have deliberately directed the reader to videotaped performances to restore a "seeing and hearing" kind of paradigm, as famously expressed by C. P. E. Bach: "Because a musician cannot move others unless he himself is moved, he must of necessity be able to transport himself in all the affects that he wants to arouse in his listeners.... One *sees and hears* it from him" (emphasis mine).[27] The four snapshots in Figure 21.2 constitute an appeal to restore physiognomy in our criticism of classical scores. The first image is of me playing the opening statement: you see a worried look in spite of the beautiful F major triad. By compensation (appeasing myself and my listener), you see an attempt at cheerfulness—raised eyebrows, sparkling eyes: the horn-passage in image 2. Then the "storm-and-stress," much less "out-of-the-blue" than the score might betray, since my look in image 3 is "more so" than the one in image 1, moderate

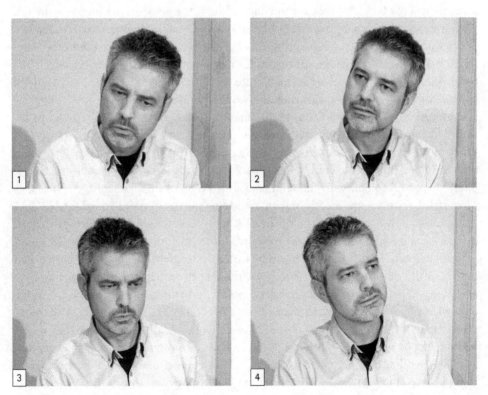

FIGURE **21.2** Four physiognomic poses during author's performance of Mozart's Piano Sonata in F major, K. 332/i, exposition.

anxiety now giving way to utter distress. Finally, at the beginning of the second group (m. 41), we see another attempt at brushing aside problems: image 4 is a gentler version of image 2. (In my interpretation, this is not a "solid and sturdy minuet," as Allanbrook [1992: 137] calls this passage, but a simple German dance, so the trio of a minuet rather than the minuet itself.)[28] This brief physiognomic analysis of four key moments of this sonata exposition suggests that with tweaked, interrelated versions of topics, figures, *and* facial expressions, we can construct a more oratorical, less fragmented, more rhetorically planned and structured version of what Leopold Mozart referred to as *il filo*, or the "thread," in Allanbrook's "labyrinth."

Writing about the same sonata, John Irving (2006: 274–76) has drawn attention to discrepancies similar to the ones we observed, which, as he puts it, "threaten the identity and meaning of a topic." But the "struggle" he observes is one between the "material content of a composition" and "the particular mode of expression," so between the "real" or conceptual topic and the actual manifestation of a topic—as a minuet that does not quite reveal itself in its usual guise, or that "does not behave quite normally." Irving justifies these discrepancies by invoking the Derridean concept of *différance*, a perpetual "'differing' and 'deferring' of an actual encounter with the object of our perception." Derrida aside, this strikes me as essentialist or platonic, and not in line with rhetoric's ultimately pragmatic distinction between *res* and *verba*. When applied to rhetorical figures, the conceptual beauty of *res* is that it need not be relegated to *inventio* but that both—*verba* and *res* together—may combine to define style (*elocutio*):[29] think Erasmus's *On Copiousness of Words and Ideas* rather than Aristotle's *Topics*.

But, by accepting topics alongside figures, is *elocutio* getting overcrowded? A related question would be: what or who is it that we perceive? Is it the musical score or text, in its predelivery stage? Or is it a keyboardist–orator, in the C. P. E. Bach "seeing-and-hearing" kind of way—rather than, say, Beethoven, who would have withdrawn to an adjacent room so no one could see him? Are we even talking about performing? When Ratner (1991: 616) called the fortepiano "a quintessential locale for the play of a topic," he was, by his own clarification, conceiving of the keyboardist as an alternative to an ensemble. If a keyboard sonata is a domestic version of a symphony or an opera buffa, then maybe it is more about listening and imagining than performing and stirring in a direct-oratorical sense.

In this respect, it is interesting to see Kanne in 1821 refer to Haydn's keyboard works as "somehow getting stuck at the level of usefulness, whereas Mozart's keyboard compositions are 'true conversations of the soul.'"[30] If we think about who actually played Haydn's sonatas—pupils, *Liebhaberinnen*, aspiring masters—then what is wrong all of the sudden with "usefulness"? In the name of the "Art" (Kanne uses the terms *Kunst* and *kunstreich*), it seems more gratifying for him to turn Mozart into some kind of a continued virtual presence than to remind his readers of Haydn's erstwhile users of keyboard sonatas. But there is another factor at play here. For all its documentary value of his and his readers' implicit knowledge of classical rhetoric, Kanne's analyses may be used just as well to illustrate a crumbling of the model of oratory. For every use of the term "oratorical," there is another of "organic" (especially in connection with "structure," as in *organischer Bau*), increasingly so toward the end of his survey, as if the very effort of covering a complete oeuvre of a composer forces one to loosen, if not abandon, an oratorical outlook.[31] We can still argue that a "conversation among souls" is to be understood as a rhetorical address—as in Mozart's soul speaking to that of his player–listener—but the emphasis has irrevocably shifted from simply "doing" as an orator–performer to "understanding" the organic beauty of Mozart's compositions.

Haydn, Sonata in E flat major, Hob. XVI:52, First Movement

Historicizing performance, almost by definition, means "to topicalize," or to put quotation marks around ever more aspects of the act of performing. At what point, though, do we end up with so many quotation marks that we might just as well start removing them? This question was centrally on my mind as I prepared myself to record Haydn's complete solo keyboard music on a variety of newly built historical instruments (seven in total), in a variety of digitally packaged historical acoustics (nine in total). In reference

EXAMPLE **21.3** Haydn, Piano Sonata in E flat major, Hob. XVI:52, mm. 1–11, with author's annotations.

to Haydn's well-known last piano Sonata in E flat major, Hob. XVI:52, and its remarkable series of opening chords (Example 21.3), Ratner speculated that Haydn wished "to imitate the harpsichord *as a topic* in this fortepiano sonata" (1980: 413; emphasis mine). Also Tovey (1944: 33), referring to those "unusually grand and broad" opening chords, muses how "very imposing" these would have sounded on a harpsichord. Make it an English harpsichord, and we are closer to reality. But then, by 1794 (the date on Haydn's manuscript), why not simply an English grand piano? Haydn "usefully" wrote the sonata for the twenty-four-year-old Theresa Jansen, who was then a rising star on the London piano scene. The "grand" solo piano sonata—a genre that English pianist–composers were busy developing—would have been new to the sixty-two-year-old composer. So, what about taking "Englishness" as a premise for either performing or analyzing the piece?[32]

A single thick opening chord, as Katalin Komlós (1995: 76–77) has pointed out, is not so uncommon for Haydn: to her examples from the first movements of three piano trios (Hob. XV:12, 14, 17) we may add three more from solo sonatas (Hob. XVI:9, 13, 41). The purpose in each is similar: whether to give the pianist that extra edge to stand her own vis-à-vis her male string-playing partners (her initial roll being the equivalent to their first downward bow) or to muster assertiveness when embarking on a performance on her own. But here we are dealing with something more and something different. More, because we have no single seven-voiced chord, but a whole sequence of them—seven in total. Different, because "assertiveness" has become a topic of its own at this prolonged start of a movement and sonata, to the point of taking over an identification as "theme" altogether. Komlós calls the "main theme," that is, only the two first measures, "Haydn's most robust construction for a keyboard instrument," but in reality they are "just" the beginning to a much larger musical period that stretches all the way to m. 8, or even beyond to m. 10. Is this kind of assertiveness "English"? When we compare Haydn's Hob. XVI:52 with Dussek's Sonata Op. 13 No. 3 (Example 21.4), also dedicated to Theresa Jansen, we cannot but be struck by the similarity in material: apart from the grand chords, there is the emerging melodic content—a rising major third followed by

EXAMPLE **21.4** Dussek, Piano Sonata in G minor, Op. 13 No. 3/i, mm. 1–8.

a minor second, in Haydn's version transferred to the top voice. But equally if not more important during a hypothetical brainstorming session with Theresa (who nota bene was a composer in her own right) would have been the issue of instrument ("This is what a Longman & Broderip or a Broadwood can do really well"), the sociocultural context ("Many people from different strands of upper society flock the concert rooms of this city"), and acoustics ("We'll need something that projects well to the listeners"). All of these factors combine into what, at this point in history and in contrast to the musical scene that Haydn had known in Esterháza and Vienna, we may well call "English"—with or without quotation marks.[33]

Regarding the dotted rhythm, Ratner (1980: 412) and Allanbrook (2002: 208) evoke the topic of a "French overture" or *entrée* which, again, is not a first for Haydn's solo sonatas. The sonatas in E major, Hob. XVI:13, and in F major, Hob. XVI:9, are two examples where dotted rhythms spring from a single assertive chord on the downbeat, whereas the Sonata in C major, Hob. XVI:21—the first of six sonatas dedicated to Prince Nicolaus Esterházy (Hob. XVI:21–26)—features a majestic, dotted pulse immediately as part of the upbeat. The evocation of a princely *entrée* seems particularly fitting for an opus so overtly cast in the sociocultural if not actual architectural context of the Esterházy court. The opening chords of the E-flat-major sonata, however, as I play them on a more resonant, more "orchestral" sounding English piano (my point of reference being the Viennese pianos, which also Haydn would have known much longer and much better), I like to see as the equivalent of the English custom of "rising to speak." Just as, for the first time in his life, Haydn would have heard a performance of a solo piano sonata as part of a larger formal concert, it was also in London that, for the first time, he would have witnessed public soliloquy by officials, lawyers, or politicians.[34] The rhetorical man he was, Haydn would have been fascinated by English displays of public oratory. In early November 1791 he wrote enthusiastically about a luncheon in honor of the Lord Mayor that he had attended, along with some 1,200 other guests. "No toast was more applauded than that of Mr Pitt" (Landon 1976: 106–7). While admitting to feeling "quite silly" (*recht possierlich*) in his gown when he received his honorary doctorate at Oxford (Dies 1962: 135), he received unexpected praise for his oratorical skills from Dr. Burney, who, in a letter to Latrobe, wrote that Haydn "took the opportunity [when seeing the Doctor at a Professional Concert] of making *fine speeches* innumerable, *viva voce*" in thanks for a gift. "By that means," Burney continued, Haydn "saved himself the trouble of writing a letter."[35] Endearingly—but significantly, in terms of our understanding of him as a composer—Haydn started to feel and act "in character," and this barely two months into his first English sojourn.

"Rising to speak" in the British House of Commons is an act as conscious as raising one's arms when sitting down all alone at a keyboard in front of an audience in a specially designated concert room. (Imagine doing so after a symphonic overture or an aria with orchestra by the local band and vocal star.) In the words of the constitutionalist Thomas Erskine May (1844: 191), "proper respect is paid to the assembly, by every member who speaks rising in his place, and standing uncovered." The following spoken example by the Irish statesman Henry Flood is recorded in *The British Cicero*, a historical collection of actual parliamentary speeches, published to enliven the study of rhetoric through real-life English models: "Sir, I rise to propose a reform in the parliamentary representation of the people. . . . But I am told this is not the time. And why? because forsooth there are disturbances in France" (Browne 1810, 1: 315).[36] The speech is dated March 1790, in full awareness of the ongoing French Revolution just across the Channel; and it is nine months before Haydn's first trip to England. The interjection "and why?" is typical for a deliberative oration such as this, where the speaker must establish contact with an as large group of sympathetic listeners as possible. Because the orator proceeds to give his own answer, the applied figure would be *subiectio*, or a mock dialogue with both question and answer integrated in the orator's monologue, "to enliven the line of thought" (Lausberg 1998: 341):

> Now, first I say, that if those disturbances were ten times greater than with every exaggeration they are represented to be [irony and *hyperbole* combined], yet that mass of confusion and ruin [*hyperbole*, now to his own advantage] would only render the argument more completely decisive in favor of a timely and temperate reform here [a nice reversal of argument]. And why? [he asks again] because it is only from want of timely and temperate [literal repeat, allowing the orator to savor the alliteration once more, now perhaps in a *ritardando* delivery] reform there [emphasizing "there" vs. "here" before], that these evils have fallen upon France. (Browne 1810, 1: 315)

These repeated oratorical questions are present also in Haydn's theme—"theme" used here in the conventional sense of a more or less complete opening period. We refer to the repeatedly embellished appoggiatura–release pairs of A♭ and G in mm. 3–5. We call these questioning figures y in distinction to the assertive opening gesture of x ("I rise"). As the pianist ruminates over y, leaving meaningful pauses in between, she has the unique opportunity to explore the surrounding acoustics for any lingering reverb as she leaves sufficient time for the questions to have their proper impact. In oratorical terms, she gives the impression of "consulting" her audience: the applicable rhetorical figure of address is *communicatio*. As the power of the questions ebbs away, the repeated y (extended by a few notes) takes on a transitioning role (*transitio*, m. 5). If Jansen had asked Haydn for thirds—a signature of her teacher Clementi—she got a whole cascade of them. But she got them in a key and of a kind that would have challenged her eloquence just as much as her technical skill.

Picking up on a subdominant harmony—the same that had firmly grounded the "I rise" motive, but now in first rather than second inversion—the ensuing phrase evokes the soundscape of a dulcimer or a pantalon: imagine the left hand's alternating tones being played by two mallets to produce an exotic mixture of sounds, here held together by a smooth but not particularly meaningful 7–6 suspension swing. For this passage, I like to keep my pedal down (or dampers raised) as much as possible, changing with every new bass note, but counting on the inefficient English dampers to sustain a pleasant blur throughout, harmonies leisurely mingling with one another.[37] The function here is not to assert or to consult, but to digress. When I play those two cadential chords in m. 8, nicely understated and short (for optimal effect on an English grand), I keep my listener in suspense (*suspensio*), before launching myself into yet another "I rise" moment, the second of four such moments through the exposition. Technically no longer a "speech act" (since we can "rise" only once), these recurrences confirm a generic stance of "assertiveness." If there was feigned consulting on the orator's part in mm. 3–5, she now answers for herself: a questioning y is replaced by an emphatically answering z (mm. 9–10). Striking is the sheer oratorical force of what in essence is a very direct and simple gesture, from the high B♭ (which with y before had always halted on an inconclusive 3̂) all the way down to E♭, or 1̂—the equivalent of a Member of Parliament flamboyantly pointing down his index finger at an emotional turning point in his speech.[38] Haydn counts on the homogeneity of the English sound in every register to pull off the austere effect.[39] With this massive gesture, have we marked the end of one large opening period or have we progressed into the next period, paragraph, or section? The answer is yes and yes: mm. 9–10 can be considered a gigantic, almost slow-motion elision (ending also being the beginning), designed for grand effect.[40] Indeed, the broad elocutionary strokes—"elocutionary" in the British sense of combining stylistic force with *viva voce* execution—would have been clear to every single listener in the room. The rhetorical strategy emerging from them is as straightforward as it is directly engaging: the pianist–orator moves from "asserting," to "consulting," to "narrating/digressing," and back to "asserting/confirming"—a pattern that she will repeat several times throughout the first movement.

Just as Haydn did when writing the piece back in 1794, when I recorded the piece, also I put myself "in character," playing on a replica of a 1798 Longman, Clementi, & Co. piano in the virtual acoustics of Oxford's historical Holywell Music Room.[41] Once seated at that piano, however, I like to believe that I must remove the quotation marks around my carefully rehearsed formulas, for fear of ending up like the attorney in the following anecdote of Cicero, as retold by Quintilian (VI, iii, 40):

> Caepasius thought he was pleading very cleverly, and produced from the secrets of his stock-in-trade these weighty words: "Look back, gentlemen, upon the lot of mortal man; look back upon its changes and chances; look back upon the old age of Fabricius!" After frequent repetitions of the phrase "Look back," by way of ornamenting his speech [using the figure *anaphora*, i.e., starting consecutive phrases with the same word], he finally looked back himself: and lo! Fabricius had left his seat with hanging head. Thereupon the court burst out laughing; counsel lost his temper, in annoyance that his case was slipping through his fingers, and that he could not complete his stock passage beginning "Look back": and he was as near as possible to pursuing his client and dragging him back to his seat by the scruff of his neck, so that he could conclude his peroration.

In our modern-day classical music world, revolving as it does around the repeated performance of masterworks in highly predictable settings, we cannot but have sympathy for the poor Caepasius, who clearly overprepared his case. When rethinking long-canonized works, one may say that "overpreparing" is all that is left for us to do—performers, musicologists, and theorists alike. When, through the course of this chapter, I made a case for restoring certain particulars of the past (such as instrument technologies or sociocultural realities), I have done so first and foremost with a "primary rhetoric" purpose in mind. At one point, however, one should wonder whether we are entering the realm of acting or role-playing and whether we are turning the performance of, say, a Haydn English sonata into some kind of "historical play," which may well speak to modern-day listeners, but should therefore not lay claim on any absolute artistic authority. On the other hand—and I would insist that this holds true especially in a volume like this—to take seriously those particulars, to metaphorically catch them "by the scruff of their neck" and "drag them back" from the past to the present, may very well contribute to defining what it is that we collectively decide to analyze or perform in the first place. Otherwise, we may end up with a "theory of topics," but it would hardly be a "historical theory of topics." Back in 1794, Haydn wrote an effective English concert sonata. To call it "classical" is only the beginning of a process of reimagination and rediscovery.

NOTES

1. *Il filo* is Leopold Mozart's metaphor from the letter to Wolfgang of 13 August 1778, quoted by Wye Allanbrook, appropriately enough, as the motto of her article "Two Threads through the Labyrinth" (1992: 125).
2. Brian Vickers (1988: 295) retorts: "If all these diatribes [that the study of rhetorical figures be 'tedious,' 'trivial,' or 'mechanistic'] were true, then [this study] would have been one of the most colossal instances of time-wasting in the history of human culture."
3. See Beghin (1996: 151–53).
4. "Damit man ... nicht durch eine übertriebne Gewalt des Angschlages, sonder vielmehr durch harmonische und melodische Figuren, z.E. die Raserey, den Zorn oder andere gewaltigen Affeckte vorzustellen suche" (Bach 1753: 118).
5. For a translation and extensive discussion of this important analytical essay (which Forkel calls "a theory of the sonata *überhaupt*"), see Beghin (1996).
6. On this bodily association of *figura*, see Lausberg (1998: 272).
7. My own interest in rhetorical figures stems from my "classical humanities" high-school years, spent on reading Virgil or Homer in Latin or Greek. It was the work of Elaine Sisman (1993) that inspired me to apply rhetoric to classical music without the detour of "musical rhetoric."
8. I refer here to the distinction drawn by George Kennedy (1980: 4–6) between "primary" and "secondary rhetoric," which was brought to musicological attention by Sisman (2007). "Primary" is the kind of rhetoric enacted in an oral context (say, Cicero delivering a speech, whether or not carefully prepared); "secondary rhetoric" concerns literary genres that emerge in the wake of primary rhetoric and that feature an "apparatus of rhetorical techniques," such as rhetorical figures in literary texts, which are not directly applied to "persuade" the reader, but to beautify or enliven the narration.
9. For a transcription of the complete text and an introduction to the person of Kanne, see Lothar Schmidt (2006); on Kanne's significance in a tradition of rhetorical analysis, see Hartmut Krones (1996). In this essay I rely on the original print of the [Wiener] *Allgemeine musikalische Zeitung* (Kanne 1821).

10. What I am suggesting here is that, in 1820s Vienna, if you were male, music-loving, and financially well-off, you would probably have had someone in the house (your wife or your daughter) who would play Mozart on the piano. On the other hand, if you were female and playing Mozart on the piano yourself, you may have appreciated some help studying Kanne's learned analyses, say, from your music teacher or another music-loving male.

11. "Auch is [die Ausgabe, welche die Herren Kunsthändler *Steiner und Comp.* in Wien verans-taltet] vorzüglich, weil die stufenweise Zusammenstellung der an Tiefe und Inhalt so verschiedenen Tonsätze hier auf die beste und natürlichste Weise veranstaltet ist, durch welche der Spieler von den lieblichsten un innigsten musikalischen Bildern der ersten Sonaten gleichsam vorbereitet und geweiht wird, die höhere Idealität der später folgenden zu empfangen und in sich aufzunehmen" (Kanne 1821: 19).

12. "Die Wiederholung…bekommt nur dann ihren meisten Werth, wenn sie mit der Paronomasie (Verstärkung) verbunden wird, die einen Satz nicht blos so, wie er schon da gewesen, sondern mit neuen kräftigen Zusätzen wiederholt" (Forkel 1788: 57). This passage is discussed in Beghin (1996: 132–38).

13. "Diese Zusätze können theils einzelne Töne betreffen, theils aber auch durch einen stärk-ern oder verminderten Vortrag bewerkstelligt werden" (Forkel 1788: 118).

14. The characterization of Kanne as a "man of universal education" comes from Anton Schindler (1966: 368).

15. "Adfert aliquam fidem veritatis et dubitatio, cum simulamus quaerere nos, unde incipien-dum, ubi desinendum…?" See also Beghin (1996: 109–24).

16. This instrument has an early-Viennese *stoss*-action (as Mozart would have known it) and not the modern *prell*-action that Walter incorporated at some point after Mozart's death. On these changes and their impact on performance, see Beghin (2008).

17. Vickers (1984: 29) blamed "rhetoricians of music" for never "deal[ing] with the more com-plex structure of *gradatio.*" I contend that we here have a counterexample.

18. Kanne here uses *Cadenz* in the sense of "caesura": m. 32 marks the end of the exposition's first paragraph and confirms a modulation to the dominant key.

19. "The words tumble out without connection, in a kind of stream, almost getting ahead of the speaker." This is another example of Longinus's compelling habit of defining a figure while also demonstrating it. The opposite of *asyndeton* is *polysyndeton*: think of the theme of the B-flat-major sonata K. 333, which similarly strings together a single rhythmic pattern, but always with an elaborate upbeat—*and* this, *and* that.

20. As Keith Chapin points out (this volume), canonic imitation need not have learned asso-ciations. His examples of the table top duet, the societal canon, or the visiting book puzzle canon are pertinent here, the two hands perhaps evoking the sheer pleasure of canonizing.

21. This kind of "sing-ability" conforms to the definition of "singing" by Koch (1802: col. 1390) as "that quality of a melody whereby it is made suited to be sung by the human voice with ease." The German original may be found on page 240 of Sarah Day-O'Connell's chapter in this volume.

22. The German original may be found in Figure 21.1. *Publicum* (here in Latin spelling) is to be understood as "clientele" rather than "audience," since Kanne continues: "In any case, this movement is so rich and so full of effect, that also the most skilled player [*der gebildeste Spieler*] must experience deepest pleasure in its assessment." This may well be an early version of the popular truism among performers today that "Mozart's music is so difficult *because* it is so simple."

23. While the reprint of this score fragment may reflect Kanne's own reading, it does not quite correspond with the Steiner Mozart-edition that Kanne would have used. There, we still find Mozart's three-note slur in m. 6, just with an added *sforzando* on C; the same holds for the analogous moment in the bass in m. 8. Two hairpins (*crescendo* and *decrescendo* respectively) in mm. 9 and 10 replace a single written-out *"cresc.,"* leading to the elimination of the *forte* in m. 11. I consulted a copy of the British Library (Hirsch IV.993).

24. The "out-of-doorness" of the opening topics of K. 332 is observed by Allanbrook (1992: 133). The three options refer to Raymond Monelle (2006).

25. We here come to a crossroads between the paradigms of "work as performance" (which would have been the mindset of a C. P. E. Bach or a W. A. Mozart) and "the performance of works" (a modern reality, most often of familiar ones). My insistence (hopefully only deceptively simple) on the keyboardist-orator as primary agent is meant to challenge analytical convention, where techniques at the level of words (*verba*) are often described as agents themselves (as in "this phrase does this" or "that cadence does that") regardless of actual sound (*sonus*) or gesture (*gestus*), let alone the *voluntas* of the composer–performer.

26. This version is perfectly musical and, I dare say, according to circa- or even pre-1800 performance practice, entirely "correct": I respect the slurs, including those that have been removed by Steiner and Kanne. Without the sharper edges of the previous *piano*, however, I give in to the pulse of subsequent measures more readily and deal with developing time in an ever so slightly more "metronomic" way. (Maelzel's new invention, it should be reminded, had been endorsed in Kanne's journal by the great Beethoven in 1817.)

27. "Indem ein Musikus nicht anders rühren kan, er sey dann selbst gerührt; so muß er nothwendig sich selbst in alle Affeckten setzen können, welche er bey seinen Zuhörern erregen will. . . . Man sieht und hört es ihm an" (Bach 1753: 122).

28. For the minuet–trio contrast and the discussion of features that make trios simpler than minuets, see McKee (2005).

29. This observation aligns with Danuta Mirka's discussion on pages 42–43 of this volume's introduction.

30. "Denn selbst des grossen *Haydn* Clavierwerke . . . bleiben öfter noch auf der Stufe der Zweckmässigkeit stehen, indess *Mozart's* Clavier-Compositionen wahre Seelengespräche sind" ([Wiener] *Allgemeine musikalische Zeitung* 5/3 [10 January]: 18).

31. In his assessment of Kanne's essay, while also stressing its traditional rhetorical premise, Mark Evan Bonds (1999) similarly observes a symbiosis of the rhetorical and the organic.

32. The following pages are paraphrased from my *The Virtual Haydn: Paradox of a Twenty-First Century Keyboardist*, forthcoming from The University of Chicago Press. In the spirit of "Englishness," the score of Example 21.3 is transcribed from the Longman, Clementi & Co. edition (1799), as distinct from the earlier Viennese Artaria edition of the same sonata (1798).

33. For more on Theresa Jansen and the Dussek example, see Katelyn Clark (2012).

34. On the first point, see Nicholas Salwey (2001: 51, 203–4); on the second, Thomas Tolley (2001: 53).

35. The gift was of a handsomely bound copy of Burney's *History* and an accompanying poem from his hand. Quoted in Landon (1976: 45).

36. About this particular speech, Lord Byron recalls Fox saying that it was "the best . . . he ever heard upon that subject" (Jennings 1881: 185).

37. I here question an identification of *cantabile* or *stile legato*, as Ratner (1980: 413–14) and Allanbrook (2002: 205) have suggested: anything "sung" would be fragmentary at best.

38. Heinrich Schenker (1922: 4) speaks of an "overwhelming effect" (*Überwältigend ist der Eindruck*).

39. The tendency for English makers was to homogenize the overall "strike-line" of hammers against strings across the keyboard, aiming for a unified ratio of the striking point (in singular) of, say, one ninth of the string. Viennese builders, by contrast, varied the strike-line, deliberately characterizing the different registers. See Robert Winter (1988) and Michael Cole (1998: 138).

40. Schenker's explanation of the elision is more local: "The antecedent actually closes with e♭^{1} as $\hat{1}$ of the full cadence…but through abbreviation [*Synthese*, i.e., a phrase overlap or elision] the consequent begins at once with the $\hat{3}$ $\hat{4}$ $\hat{5}$ ascending formula in the higher octave" (Schenker 1922: 4).

41. See Program Ten ("The London Scene") of my *The Virtual Haydn*, on Blu-ray (Naxos, 2009), CD (Naxos, 2011), or online (Naxos Music Library); the two boxed releases also include a video recording of the complete movement.

References

Agawu, Kofi. 2008. Topic Theory: Achievement, Critique, Prospects. In *Passagen, IMS Kongress Zürich 2007: Fünf Hauptvorträge, Five Key Note Speeches*, ed. Laurenz Lütteken and Hans-Joachim Hinrichsen, 38–69. Kassel: Bärenreiter.

Allanbrook, Wye J. 1992. Two Threads through the Labyrinth: Topic and Process in the First Movements of K. 332 and K. 333. In *Convention in Eighteenth and Nineteenth-Century Music: Essays in Honor of Leonard G. Ratner*, ed. Wye J. Allanbrook, Janet M. Levy, and William Mahrt, 125–71. Stuyvesant, NY: Pendragon.

——. 2002. Theorizing the Comic Surface. In *Music in the Mirror*, ed. Andreas Giger and Thomas J. Mathiesen, 195–216. Lincoln: University of Nebraska Press.

Bach, Carl Philipp Emanuel. 1753. *Versuch über die wahre Art das Clavier zu spielen*. Berlin: Christian Friedrich Henning. Reprint, Kassel: Bärenreiter, 1994.

Beghin, Tom. 1996. Forkel and Haydn: A Rhetorical Framework for the Analysis of Sonata Hob. XVI:42 (D). DMA diss., Cornell University.

——. 2008. Playing Mozart's piano: An Exercise in Reverse-Engineering. *Keyboard Perspectives* 1: 1–36.

Bilson, Malcolm, and Charles Rosen. 1990. Early Music: An Exchange. *The New York Review of Books* 37 (8 November): 58–60.

Bonds, Mark Evan. 1999. Ästhetische Prämissen der musikalischen Analyse im ersten Viertel des 19. Jahrhundert, anhand von Friedrich August Kannes "Versuch einer Analyse der Mozart'schen Clavierwerke" (1821). In *Mozartanalyse im 19. und frühen 20. Jahrhundert: Bericht über die Tagung Salzburg 1996*, ed. Gernot Gruber, 63–80. Laaber: Laaber.

Browne, Thomas. 1810. *The Britisch Orator, or A Selection of the Most Admired Speeches in the English Language*. 3 vols. Philadelphia: Birch and Small.

Caplin, William. 2005. On the Relation of Musical *Topoi* to Formal Function. *Eighteenth-Century Music* 2/1: 113–24.

Clark, Katelyn. 2012. The London Pianist: Theresa Jansen and the English Works of Haydn, Dussek, and Clementi. *Haydn: The Online Journal of the Haydn Society of North*

America 2/1. Available: http://www.rit.edu/affiliate/haydn/london-pianist-theresa-jansen-and-english-works-haydn-dussek-and-clementi. Accessed 15 March 2013.

Cole, Michael. 1998. *The Pianoforte in the Classical Era*. Oxford: Clarendon Press.

Dies, Albert Christoph. 1962. *Biographische Nachrichten von Joseph Haydn*. Berlin: Henschelverlag.

Erasmus of Rotterdam, Desiderius. 1963. *On Copia of Words and Ideas*. Trans. Donald B. King and H. David Rix. Milwaukee, WI: Marquette University Press.

Forkel, Johann Nikolaus. 1783. *Musikalischer Almanach für Deutschland auf das Jahr 1784*. Leipzig: Schwickert. Reprint, Hildesheim: Georg Olms, 1974.

——. 1788. *Allgemeine Geschichte der Musik*. Leipzig: Schwickert. Reprint, Graz: Akademische Druck- u. Verlagsanstalt, 1967.

Goldberg, Sander. 2007. Performing Theory: Variations on a Theme by Quintilian. In *Haydn and the Performance of Rhetoric*, ed. Tom Beghin and Sander Goldberg, 39–60. Chicago: University of Chicago Press.

Irving, John. 2006. Deconstructing Topics: Tracing Their Status in the Allegro of Mozart's Piano Sonata, KV 332. In *Mozart-Studien* 15, ed. Manfred Hermann Schmid, 269–75. Tutzing: Hans Schneider.

Jennings, George H. 1881. *An Anecdotal History of the British Parliament, from the Earliest Periods to the Present Time*. New York: Appleton.

Kanne, Friedrich August. 1821. Versuch einer Analyse der Mozartischen Clavierwerke, mit einigen Bemerkungen über den Vortrag derselben. [Wiener] *Allgemeine musikalische Zeitung* 5/3–8, 19, 20, 22–30, 32, 44–47, 49, 50 (January 10–June 23).

Kennedy, George. 1980. *Classical Rhetoric and Its Christian and Secular Tradition from Ancient to Modern Times*. Chapel Hill: University of North Carolina Press.

Koch, Heinrich Christoph. 1802. *Musikalisches Lexikon*. Frankfurt am Main: August Hermann der Jüngere.

Komlós, Katalin. 1995. *Fortepianos and Their Music: Germany, Austria, and England, 1760–1800*. Oxford: Clarendon.

Krones, Hartmut. 1996. "denn jedes gute Tonstück ist ein Gedicht": "Rhetorische Musikanalyse" von Johann Mattheson bis Friedrich August Kanne. In *Zur Geschichte der musikalischen Analyse*, ed. Gernot Gruber, 45–61. Laaber: Laaber.

Landon, H. C. Robbins. 1976. *Haydn: Chronicle and Works. Vol. 3: Haydn in England 1791–1795*. Bloomington: Indiana University Press.

Lausberg, Heinrich. 1998. *Handbook of Literary Rhetoric: A Foundation for Literary Study*, ed. David E. Orton and R. Dean Anderson. Trans. Matthew T. Bliss, Annemiek Jansen, and David E. Orton. Leiden: Brill.

Longinus. 1998. On Sublimity. In *Classical Literary Criticism*, ed. and trans. Donald Andrew Russell and Michael Winterbottom, 143–87. Oxford: Oxford University Press.

May, Thomas Erskine. 1844. *A Treatise upon the Law, Privileges, Proceedings and Usage of Parliament*. London: Charles Knight.

McKee, Eric. 2005. Mozart in the Ballroom: Minuet–Trio Contrast and the Aristocracy in Self-Portrait. *Music Analysis* 24/3: 383–434.

Monelle, Raymond. 2006. *The Musical Topic: Hunt, Military and Pastoral*. Bloomington: Indiana University Press.

Quintilianus, Marcus Fabius. 1986. *Institutio oratoria*. Trans. Harold Edgeworth Butler. 4 vols. Cambridge, MA: Harvard University Press.

Ratner, Leonard G. 1980. *Classic Music: Expression, Form, and Style*. New York: Schirmer.

——. 1991. Topical Content in Mozart's Keyboard Sonatas. *Early Music* 19/4: 615–19.

Salwey, Nicholas Anthony. 2001. *The Piano in London Concert Life 1750–1800*. Ph.D. diss., St Anne's College.

Schenker, Heinrich. 1922. Haydn: Sonate Es-Dur. *Der Tonwille* 3: 3–21.

Schindler, Anton Felix. 1966. *Beethoven as I Knew Him*, ed. Donald W. MacArdle. Trans. Constance S. Jolly. New York: Norton.

Schmidt, Lothar. 2006. Einleitung zu Friedrich August Kannes *Versuch einer Analyse der Mozartischen Clavierwerke, mit einigen Bemerkungen über den Vortrag derselben*. *Musiktheorie* 21/4: 318–73.

Sisman, Elaine. 1993. *Haydn and the Classical Variation*. Cambridge, MA: Harvard University Press.

——. 2007. Rhetorical Truth in Haydn's Chamber Music. In *Haydn and the Performance of Rhetoric*, ed. Tom Beghin and Sander Goldberg, 281–326. Chicago: University of Chicago Press.

Tolley, Thomas. 2001. *Painting the Cannon's Roar: Music, the Visual Arts and the Rise of an Attentive Public in the Age of Haydn, c. 1750 to c. 1810*. Aldershot: Ashgate.

Tovey, Donald Francis. 1944. *Essays in Musical Analysis: Chamber Music*. London: Oxford University Press.

Türk, Daniel Gottlob. 1789. *Klavierschule oder Anweisung zum Klavierspielen für Lehrer und Lernende, mit kritischen Anmerkungen*. Leipzig: Schwickert; Halle: Hemmerde und Schwetschke. Reprint, Kassel: Bärenreiter, 1997.

Vickers, Brian. 1984. Figures of Rhetoric/Figures of Music? *Rhetorica* 2/1: 1–44.

——. 1988. *In Defence of Rhetoric*. Oxford: Clarendon.

Winter, Robert. 1988. Striking It Rich: The Significance of Striking Points in the Evolution of the Romantic Piano. *The Journal of Musicology* 6/3: 267–92.

CHAPTER **22**

....

ELOQUENT PERFORMANCE

The Pronuntiatio *of Topics*

....

SHEILA GUYMER

PERFORMING CHARACTER

IN her article "Two Threads through the Labyrinth: Topic and Process in the First Movements of K. 332 and K. 333 by Mozart" Wye Jamison Allanbrook advises that, like the music analyst, "the performer too must be aware of the progress of these gestures, as few performers are today, and must articulate each one with its proper qualities—lyric legato for the singing style, for example, or strict rhythmic authority, *allegro pomposo*, for the contrapuntal—taking care not to smooth them over into an indistinguishable wash of 'melody.' If one does not attend to the discreteness of the gestures, the movement becomes tonal and thematic chaos" (1992: 136).

While, as a performer myself, I found this perfectly good advice, the questions I could not help but ask myself as I read Allanbrook's analysis were: What performance practices did she imagine as she analyzed these sonatas? How did she mentally articulate each one with its "proper" qualities? Given that she was writing at the height of the "authenticity debates," was Allanbrook's imagined sound world shaped by research into eighteenth-century performance practices, and the performances of Mozart's sonatas on Viennese fortepianos that were becoming increasingly available at the time? Or does her analysis reveal assumptions about how this music sounds that are more congruent with "mainstream" performances on a Steinway grand? Interestingly, Leonard Ratner taught his students—including Allanbrook—to recognize topics via recordings of professional performers (Agawu 2008: 40). On the one hand, Ratner's teaching technique recognizes the fundamentally performative nature of topics; but, on the other, it underlines how musicological insights may depend on (often tacit) assumptions about performance.

The power of a skilled performer to influence a composition's reception was appreciated by Leopold Mozart, who wrote that

Everything depends on good performance. Daily experience confirms this saying. Many a mediocre composer is transported with delight and has his high opinion of himself renewed whenever he hears his musical gibberish played by good performers who know how to produce the affect (of which he himself had never thought) in the right place, and to distinguish the characters (which had never occurred to him) as much as is possible, and who therefore know how to make the whole miserable scribble bearable to the ears of listeners by means of good delivery. And who does not know that even the best composition is often performed so wretchedly that the composer himself has trouble recognizing his own work?

An der guten Ausführung ist alles gelegen. Diesen Satz bestättiget die tägliche Erfahrniß. Mancher Halbcomponist ist vom Vergnügen entzücket, und hält nun von neuem erst selbst recht viel auf sich, wenn er seinen musikalischen Galimatias von guten Spielern vortragen höret, die den Affect, an den er nicht einmal gedacht hat, am rechten Orte anzubringen, und die Charakters, die ihm niemals eingefallen sind, so viel es möglich ist zu unterscheiden, und folglich die ganze elende Schmiererey den Ohren der Zuhörer durch einen guten Vortrag erträglich zu machen wissen. Und wem ist hingegen unbekannt, daß oft die beste Composition so elend ausgeführet wird, daß der Componist selbst Noth genug hat seine eigene Arbeit zu kennen? (1787: 257)

With these scathing remarks, Mozart echoes both Demosthenes's emphatic assertion that the three most important aspects in the art of oratory are "delivery, delivery, delivery" (Beghin 2007: 131) and Quintilian's observation that a mediocre speech enhanced by good delivery can be more persuasive than a brilliant speech delivered poorly (Harrán 1997: 24). Johann Joachim Quantz considered it a responsibility of the performer to know when and how to adapt delivery so that a composition may fit the context of its performance; for example, instructing orchestral players to moderate any "insolent and bizarre ideas" (*freche und bizarre Gedanken*) to suit a church context, or to bring out the comedy of an opera buffa in the theater (1752: 245).

Yet writers in the field of topic theory have been noticeably silent about the *pronuntiatio* of topics. Most musicologists have focused on topics' semiotic and cultural implications in the communication of meaning, or on their relationships to musical structure. I find this curious, given that there is no lack of relevant information to draw on in the historical treatises, and that modern-day research into historically informed performance practices of eighteenth-century repertoire is now in the capable hands of a second generation of specialist performers.

This chapter explores topics from a performer's perspective. Through examining how performers engage with topics, my aim is to explore some points of difference from standard musicological concepts of what topics are and what they can tell us. I present material collected in interviews I recorded with two professional fortepianists, Robert Levin and Bart van Oort, both of whom specialize in historically informed performance practices. Being a fortepianist myself, I conducted these interviews in the form of lessons. This enabled close engagement with Levin's and van Oort's decision-making: exploring how they analyze a score to determine its topical material, draw on historical performance treatises, and respond to and shape the sounds of a fortepiano.

I found both van Oort and Levin reluctant to specify topical labels, even though I knew both to be familiar with topic theory, and certainly familiar with the dance types and styles from which Ratner drew many of his topical distinctions. Perhaps their reluctance had its source in a distrust that, as a musicologist, I might reduce their interpretive decision-making to a kind of "painting by numbers": identify the "correct" topics, apply the "correct" set of performance practices to each, and *voilà*, an interpretation is formed. As Robert Levin articulated it,

> [while] there are certain basic principles that underpin what he [Mozart] does…there's always a danger that we end up with a set of drawers and that there is a particular character in each one…and you think, 'Mozart is going to write a piece, and so he's going to open up drawers two, six and eighteen, and he's got a sonata.' We have to be careful that, although we can in fact (and should, in fact), understand certain aspects of the typography of the expression, of the conventions (dances—minuets, and German dances, and country dances—and so on) that are animating forces, we do have to be careful to see them as ingredients in the particular flavor, but that they are not the dish. Because…[if] you believe that all you need to do is to recognize these things and then reproduce them phrase by phrase…what you will get is a lamentable kind of two-dimensioned, rather boring thing which celebrates the conventional and manages to overlook everything that is fascinating. (2012: lines 1072–95)

Of course, mere topic-spotting is not enough. Intriguingly, while van Oort and Levin were reluctant to pin topical labels to particular sections, they both talked at length about musical character. This concept is so crucial to their interpretative decision-making that van Oort commented, "You can't decide anything unless you know the character. That's the first thing you need to know, otherwise you will play nonsense" (2012a: lines 664–66). Repeatedly in my lessons, van Oort was careful to distinguish between eighteenth- and nineteenth-century assumptions about musical meaning, and especially assumptions about emotional qualities in music. He commented that "classical style is when you portray an affect. When your music *portrays* Melancholy, or Sadness, or Happiness. You create Sadness or Happiness or Melancholy. You know the tools.…It's a representation…and your audience understands the tools, understands what you are doing, and experiences it like that. Romanticism is where you *are* happiness, when you are sad, and they don't understand it through your affect, but through you" (2012c: lines 851–60).

These pianists' comments suggest that while both recognize specific conventions of musical expression that shape their interpretative decisions within eighteenth-century repertoire, they moderate the conventional with sensitivity to context. Levin raised the dangers of the interpretatively *cliché*, while van Oort scrutinized anachronistic assumptions. Van Oort's claim that he portrays affects using specific "tools" mirrors a comment by Quantz: "Music, then, is an art that must be judged not by personal fancy, but by certain rules, like the other fine arts, and by good taste acquired and refined through extensive experience and practice."[1] What, then, are these tools?

Daniel Gottlob Türk identified three means crucial for "the expression of the prevailing character" in good execution. These are "(1) the suitable degree of loudness and softness of tone, (2) the detaching, sustaining, and slurring of tones, and (3) the correct tempo" (1789: 348; 1982: 338).[2] To Türk, the degree of dynamic, the specific length of notes in performance (as distinct from their notated rhythmic values in the score), and tempo, and how these parameters work in combination, depend on the specific character that the performer wishes to communicate. In practice, the items in Türk's list are closely bound together: perhaps the clearest example is the slur, which, as Leopold Mozart defined it, denotes legato, a slight lengthening of the first note, and a diminuendo (1787: 262). Türk details several combinations of note length and dynamic, which he terms "heavy and light execution." However, it is important to note that "heavy and light execution" refers more to the length of notes in performance than to their dynamic:

> For a *heavy* execution every note must be played firmly (emphatically) and sustained until the full duration of the note has passed. *Light* execution is that in which every note is played with less firmness (emphasis), and the finger lifted from the key somewhat sooner than the actual prescribed duration. In order to avoid a misunderstanding I must also remark that the terms heavy and light in general refer more to the sustaining or detaching of the notes rather than to their softness or loudness. For in certain cases, for example in an *Allegro vivo, scherzando, Vivace con allegrezza, et cetera*, the execution must be rather light (short), but at the same time more or less loud; whereas pieces of a melancholy character, for example an *Adagio mesto, con afflizzione, et cetera*, although played slurred and consequently with a certain heaviness, must nevertheless not be performed too loudly. In most cases, however, heavy and loud are indeed to be combined.
>
> Whether the execution is to be heavy or light may be determined (1) from the character and the purpose of a composition (§ 45); (2) from the designated tempo; (3) from the meter; (4) from the note values used; and (5) from the manner in which the notes progress, et cetera. (Türk 1789: 358–59; 1982: 347–48, translation modified)[3]

Rather than reproduce Türk's wordy prose description, I have summarized in Table 22.1 his examples of how this musical light and shade links both with character and with Italian terms that designate an overarching sentiment in shaping a performer's delivery.[4] Türk adds: "It is understood that in all the aforementioned cases, various degrees of heavy or light execution must be applied" (1789: 359; 1982: 348).

Similarly, Türk's third aspect, tempo, is also closely linked to dynamic and articulation. While some eighteenth-century musicians (such as Joseph Riepel, Friedrich Wilhelm Marpurg, and Heinrich Christoph Koch) chose to separate meter from tempo and affect, and thereby distance themselves from the tradition of the *tempo giusto* (as Danuta Mirka discusses elsewhere in this volume), Johann Philipp Kirnberger's description of the *tempo giusto* of various meters provides useful material for understanding the relationships between concepts of character and performers' decision-making (1776: 106–13; 1982: 376–81). Kirnberger's spectrum of meters is shown in Figure 22.1, moving from the slowest and heaviest on the left, to the fastest and lightest on the right (meters that Kirnberger described as obsolete or useless have been omitted). The lower row lists those meters that Kirnberger describes as being derived from those in the upper row, having a corresponding tempo for the beat (1776: 117–34; 1982: 385–400).

Table 22.1 Türk's Examples for Heavy or Light Articulation

Character	Style of Execution	Designation
exalted serious solemn pathetic	heavy execution fullness and force strongly accented	*grave* *pomposo* *patetico* *maestoso* *sostenuto*
pleasant gentle agreeable	somewhat lighter and markedly softer execution	*compiacevole* *con dolcezza* *glissicato* *lusingando* *pastorale* *piacevole*
lively humorous joyous	quite lightly	*allegro scherzando* *burlesco* *giocoso* *con allegrezza* *risvegliato*
melancholy	slurring and portato [*Tragen der Töne*]	*con afflizzione* *con amerezza* *doloroso* *lagrimoso* *languido* *mesto*

Several meters—12/8, 2/4, and 9/8—occur twice on the spectrum, but Kirnberger explains these as more straightforward ways of writing the rarer meters indicated in brackets: 12/8 as an alternate notation for 24/16, 2/4 for 4/8, and 9/8 for 9/16 (1776: 123, 130; 1982: 391, 397). Kirnberger also distinguishes between a "large" 4/4 which has an "extremely weighty tempo and execution [that] because of its emphatic nature, is suited primarily to church piece, choruses, and fugues," and a much lighter, livelier "small" 4/4, indicated as common time c, appropriate to all styles. Kirnberger adds, "the two meters have nothing in common except for their signatures" (1776: 123; 1982: 391). Thus, the varieties of meter, each with its own *tempo giusto*, provide a gradation from heavy and slow, to light and quick, depending on whether the type of beat is a half, quarter, eighth, or sixteenth note. As Kirnberger explains, "longer note values are always performed

	2/2			C					
	large 4/4 (*grave*)	or alla breve	2/4	or small 4/4	3/4	2/4 (4/8)	3/8	3/16	2/8
3/2									
9/4	12/8 (*grave*)	6/4	6/8		9/8	12/8 (12/16)	9/8 (9/16)		6/16

FIGURE **22.1** Kirnberger's spectrum of meters.

more weightily and emphatically than shorter ones; consequently, a composition that is to be performed with weight and emphasis can only be notated with long note values, and another that is to be performed in an airy and playful manner can only be notated with short note values" (1776: 116; 1982: 384–85, translation modified).

Kirnberger (like Quantz) instructs musicians to acquire a correct feeling for the natural tempo, the *tempo giusto*, of every meter; stating that this is attained by diligent study of all kinds of dance pieces. As he explains, "every dance piece has its definite tempo, determined by the meter and the note values that are employed in it.…dance pieces involving sixteenth and thirty-second notes have a slower tempo than those that tolerate only eighth and at most sixteenth notes as the fastest note values in the same meter. Thus, for example, a sarabande in 3/4 meter has a slower tempo than a minuet, even though both are written in the same meter" (1776: 106–7; 1982: 376–77).

Eighteenth-century treatise writers repeatedly encouraged student musicians to study the dance types to develop their ability to recognize character in music; yet communicating character was vital in composing or performing any type of piece, not only dances. As Kirnberger writes, "every beginner who wants to become thoroughly grounded in composition is advised to become familiar with the dispositions of all genres of dance, because all types of characters and rhythm occur and can be observed most accurately in them. If one has no skill in these character pieces, it is impossible to give a definite character to a piece, which even every fugue must have" (1771: 202 n.78; 1982: 216 n.78, translation modified). Kirnberger's pupil Johann Abraham Peter Schulz explains how the *tempo giusto* of each meter interacts with tempo terms to define precise gradations of tempo and articulation, enhancing the communication of character in performance:

> From this, the advantages of subdividing even and uneven meters into various time signatures of longer or shorter note values [*Noten der Hauptzeiten*] become comprehensible: for in this way each meter receives its own movement, its own weight in performance, and consequently also its own character. Now, if a piece should have both a light execution and a slow tempo, then the composer will select a meter of short (or shorter) values according to the nature of the light (or lighter) execution, and avail himself of the words: *andante*, or *largo*, or *adagio et cetera*, since the slowness of the piece should exceed [be slower than] the natural movement of the meter; and conversely, if a piece should be executed heavily and yet have a fast tempo, then [the composer] will select a heavy meter according to the nature of the execution, and designate it with *vivace*, *allegro* or *presto et cetera*. Now, if an experienced performer looks over the note values of such a piece, then he is in a position to match the execution and the tempo exactly in conformity with the intentions of the composer; at least so accurately that it could not be indicated by other signs or words, no matter how explicit.

> Hieraus werden die Vortheile der Unterabtheilungen der geraden und ungeraden Taktart in verschiedene Takte von längeren oder kürzeren Noten der Hauptzeiten begreiflich: denn dadurch erhält jeder Takt seine ihm eigene Bewegung, sein ihm eigenes Gewicht im Vortrag, folglich auch seinen ihm eigenen Charakter. Soll nun

ein Stück einen leichten Vortrag, zugleich aber eine langsame Bewegung haben, so wird der Tonsezer nach Beschaffenheit des leichten oder leichteren Vortrages einen Takt von kurzen oder kürzeren Zeiten dazu wählen, und sich der Worte: *andante,* oder *largo,* oder *adagio &c.* nachdem die Langsamkeit des Stüks die natürliche Bewegung des Taktes übertreffen soll, bedienen; und umgekehrt: soll ein Stück schwer vorgetragen werden, und zugleich eine geschwinde Bewegung haben, so wird er einen nach Beschaffenheit des Vortrags schweeren Takt wählen, und ihm mit *vivace, allegro* oder *presto &c.* bezeichnen. Uebersieht ein erfahrner Ausführer nun die Notengattungen eines solchen Stüks, so ist er im Stande, den Vortrag und die Bewegung desselben genau mit den Gedanken des Tonsezers übereinstimmend zu treffen; wenigstens so genau, als es durch keine andere Zeichen, durch keine Worte, und wenn sie noch so deutlich wären, angedeutet werden könnte. (Schulz 1774: 1133)

How then does character relate to topic? The answer is implicit in Kirnberger's claim that, "since the different types of principal characters occur in the common dance melodies, aspiring composers can consider the works of the greatest masters in these genres as models that they must always follow" (1771: 202; 1982: 216, translation modified). In other words, it is the stabilizing and categorizing influence of genre that grounded concepts of musical character in the composing *and* performing practices of the dance types. When Ratner first introduced the notion of topics into musicology, he distinguished between "types" and "styles." Ratner's term "type" is synonymous with genre, in that a particular piece may be identified as, say, a minuet or march. But the features of a "type" may be referenced as a "style," and his definition of topic accordingly included examples of when the characteristics that define one musical genre are presented within another. A genre may be defined as "a class, type or category, sanctioned by convention" (Samson 2001: 657). This definition implies two aspects: the features by which a genre is identified; and the repeated use of those features that stabilize genres as socially recognized codes. In Jim Samson's words, genre functions as a "means of ordering, stabilizing and validating the musical materials themselves" (657); and significantly, this included not only the compositional features of each dance type, but *also* (as made explicit in the Kirnberger quotes above) its specific set of performance practices. As Samson points out, genres "are based on the principle of repetition. They codify past repetitions, and they invite future repetitions" (657), and it is this codification and repetition of a set of characteristics that empowers genres' (and therefore topics') communicative role. As Stefano Castelvecchi explains,

genres have time and again been acknowledged as a crucial element in the production and reception of art.... One could go as far as claiming that genre, understood in its broadest sense, is central to communication and interpretation in general: even in everyday life we construe the meaning of a statement in relation to our inferences about its kind.... Like other linguistic and cultural codes shared by authors and publics, genre provides a space in which expression and communication can take place. (2013: 7)

Thus the dance-type topics harness the ordering, stabilizing, and validating power of genre to function as templates for specific characters that eighteenth-century composers and performers recognized, realized, and modified as they chose. But how, then, is character to be determined when (as is often the case, despite the ubiquity of dance types in eighteenth-century music) a piece or passage does not display any obvious dance reference? For example, as Koch explains, "the sonata…has no definite character, but its main sections, namely, its adagio and both allegros, can assume every character, every expression which music is capable of describing" (1793: 315; 1983: 202). Quantz provides some answers:

> I will now indicate some particular features by which, taken together, you can usually, if not always, perceive the dominant sentiment of a piece and in consequence how it should be performed, that is, whether it must be flattering, melancholy, tender, gay, bold, serious, &c. This may be determined by (1) whether the key is major or minor. Generally a major key is used for the expression of what is gay, bold, serious, and sublime, and a minor one for the expression of the flattering, melancholy, and tender.… This rule has its exceptions, however; thus you must also consider the following characteristics. The passion may be discerned by (2) whether the intervals between the notes are great or small, and whether the notes themselves ought to be slurred or articulated. Flattery, melancholy, and tenderness are expressed by slurred and close intervals, gaiety and boldness by brief articulated notes, or those forming distant leaps, as well as by figures in which dots appear regularly after the second note [Quantz means figures with the rhythm of the Lombardian snap, sixteenth note–dotted eighth note]. Dotted and sustained notes express the serious and the pathetic; long notes, such as semibreves or minims, intermingled with quick ones express the majestic and sublime. (3) The passions may be perceived from the dissonances. These are not all the same; they always produce a variety of different effects.… (4) The fourth indication of the dominant sentiment is the word found at the beginning of each piece, such as Allegro, Allegro non tanto, — assai, — di molto, — moderato, Presto, Allegretto, Andante, Andantino, Arioso, Cantabile, Spiritoso, Affettuoso, Grave, Adagio, Adagio assai, Lento, Mesto, and so forth. Each of these words, if carefully prescribed, requires a particular execution in performance. (1752: 108–9; 2001: 125–26)

While the dance types provided models or templates for specific combinations of features, Quantz indicates that mode, interval size, articulation, rhythmic patterns, dissonances, and sentiment term work together in a flexible system that can nuance character, while still communicating which performance practices are to be applied to achieve an appropriate correspondence between music's content and its execution. Performers can use this system of finely calibrated contrasts to create variety in their choices of tempo, dynamic, and articulation, enabling delivery to be persuasive and moving. As an integral part of the decision-making process for historically informed performers, it explains Bart van Oort's claim that if you do not know the character, you will play nonsense. The central claim of this chapter, therefore, is that *eighteenth-century concepts of character function as heuristics for complex sets of performance practices*. As Levin implied in his desire to transcend the interpretatively commonplace, this can be seen most clearly in the dance types that constitute most of Ratner's topics, yet extends beyond them.

Topics in Practice

To explore these ideas in practice, I will focus on the Allegros from Mozart's Piano Sonata in B flat major, K. 333. I will begin by returning to Allanbrook's article, "Two Threads through the Labyrinth," and then contrast her interpretation with an alternate reading drawn from my interviews with Levin and van Oort.

Allanbrook's aim is to examine "the interaction, in Mozart's instrumental music, of process and expression" (1992: 128); in other words, to explore how Mozart's choice and manipulation of topical material shape the movement's developmental thread. She argues that the first movement of K. 333 is "a skillful manipulation of two seemingly contrasting topics—an evocative variant of the singing allegro, and the concerto or soloistic style" (1992: 145). She identifies three commonplace figures in determining her topical analysis: the "lavish decoration of appoggiaturas", especially the "weightier" ones on the downbeats; the Alberti bass; and the sixteenth-note passagework (1992: 145). Not surprisingly, Levin and van Oort also identified these as the essential materials of the movement. But how do Allanbrook and the fortepianists combine these three figures to identify the expressive qualities of this opening?

Allanbrook's labeling of the opening as "singing allegro style" accords with Ratner's definition of this style as "a song-like melody set in quick tempo...accompanied by steadily repeated rapid tones or by broken chord figures" (1980: 19). Allanbrook's

EXAMPLE **22.1** Mozart, Piano Sonata in B flat major, K. 333/i, mm. 1–10.

claim that the opening requires a "lyric legato" in performance (1992: 136) must seem self-evident given that, in the ten-measure excerpt that she presents, almost every note in the first seven measures is marked by a slur (1992: 145, 149). But there are textual issues. Comparing Allanbrook's excerpt (identical to the Henle 1977 edition) to Mozart's autograph shows some relevant differences, and these are marked in Example 22.1.[5]

Of the twenty-four slurs in the first ten measures, seven, almost a third of them, are missing from the autograph (these are marked with lines); yet, without them, how legato, and therefore how much in the "singing," would this opening sound? The absence of those seven slurs brings to mind Türk's instruction that "compositions in which lively, humorous, and joyous feelings are predominant... must be played quite lightly [that is, with more detached articulation] whereas melancholy and similar affects particularly call for the slurring of tones and portato" (1789: 359; 1982: 348). (Recall that Türk's term of "heavy and light execution" has to do with the sustaining or separating of notes in performance, not their loudness or softness.) With a more detached articulation, this line is also reminiscent of Johann Jacob Engel's comment that "representations of joy have a content that is easily grasped, so their movement is sprightly, their leaps not large" (1780: 20–21; 1998: 224). Rather than "singing allegro style," could this opening be more aptly labeled a galant representation of joy?

But perhaps there was another reason for Allanbrook's topical label of "singing style": mid-twentieth-century "mainstream" Mozart performance was typified by a smooth, singing legato, capitalizing on the long resonance of the modern piano. Considered the default touch for modern pianists, this gives rise to precisely the "indistinguishable wash of 'melody'" that, ironically, Allanbrook cautioned against. It is significant that the discrepancies in slurring between the Henle edition and the autograph attracted both van Oort's and Levin's attention. Both pointed out that the last three eighth-notes in the right hand of m. 1 (two skips of a fourth) are slurred in the Henle edition (in this, it follows the first edition published by Torricelli), but are *not* slurred in the autograph. Interestingly, both performers chose to follow the autograph's articulation. When explaining why, Levin made a point of contrasting this detail with the slur over the last three eighth-notes in the right hand of m. 3 (a stepwise ascending figure). He discussed Mozart's expression and imagination, commenting that

> we see the restlessness of that right here, in the fact that, whereas the three quaver upbeats to the second bar are disjointed—that is to say they're skipping—two bars later, what was skipping is now a scale.... everything that can be varied, [is] varied.... it's an associative stream of consciousness that's going on through all of this, and it's *very* witty!...
>
> Once you realize that there's something saucy and a bit naughty about this piece, it means you're much more likely to savour the articulations of the piece. And Mozart, of course, is very, very fond of tiny slurs...and not the big ones. And, as I think you correctly marked in your score, the slur at the end of the first bar, which is added by everybody over the last three quavers, is actually *not* in the manuscript. And it actually makes sense. Yes! It makes a good deal of sense for it [the skips of a fourth] to be separated, because of the leaps. Whereas, when he substitutes for these leaps with the

stepwise motion, at the end of the third bar, then the legato slurs are extremely logical: it is consistent with the character (2012: lines 97–105, 301–3, 320–38).

This quote demonstrates that Levin's analysis is on an exceptionally nuanced level, yet it is consistent with the relationships between character and performance practice described in the historical treatises.

In Allanbrook's analysis, the "singsong repetition" of the downbeat appoggiaturas and "brittle sound of the middle-level register" combine with the "mechanical" Alberti bass to create "an affect that is at once intense and demure—as though the sensitive style were captured on a music box" (1992: 145–46). In Allanbrook's words, the left hand's Alberti bass functions to rein in the passionate expressiveness of the right hand's appoggiaturas (148). But reading the slurs over the left-hand eighth notes as they may have been understood in the eighteenth century could mean to play them with finger-pedaling (van Oort 2012b: lines 437–38). Described by C. P. E. Bach, Türk, and Franz Paul Rigler, this technique is an overholding of notes slurred together in broken-chord bass accompaniments, so that the first, second, and third notes remain down until the fourth has been played (Rosenblum 1988: 157). Does this produce a mechanical ticking as Allanbrook suggests? The legato technique sounds exaggerated with the more pronounced resonance of a modern piano, but on a Viennese fortepiano, the effect, as van Oort points out, is to enrich the comparatively thin sound of the treble register (2012c: lines 438–39).

What Allanbrook describes as an "uneasy marriage of the mechanical with the expressive" of the opening "music-box style" contrasts with the sixteenth-note roulades and runs that begin "rhapsodically," but develop into "virtuoso flights" of a "more brilliant, soloistic mode" (1992: 148–50). Allanbrook's simile of the music box becomes important for her argument later, when she suggests that "the brilliant [concerto] style and the intimate music-box [expressive, singing allegro] style have the mechanical in common" (1992: 150). To suggest a link between the mechanical and the expressive via brilliant virtuosity is a strange *non sequitur* in eighteenth-century terms. While Ratner notes that the term "brilliant" was used by late-eighteenth-century writers to refer to "the use of rapid passages for virtuoso display" (1980: 19), van Oort questions labeling any sections of this movement "virtuosic":

> there is no virtuosity in Mozart in the *modern* sense of the word. Never, not even in the piano concertos.... where the player revels in the craft, so to say. It's not there, because virtuosity in the eighteenth century *was* there, but it meant something else. A six-part fugue is virtuosic: you can be a great virtuoso if you can do these things. A wonderful change in character, or a rapid change in many characters, like C. P. E. Bach does, was considered virtuosic. The great intimacy of clavichord playing was considered virtuosic. The wonderful way to speak a slow movement is virtuosic.... [but] what is happening here, nothing, none of it is virtuosic (although there is brilliance). Or everything is virtuosic, if you look at it in two different ways. And what Mozart is doing here, I believe that even the opening bar is brilliant. It is in the way your eyebrows go up, isn't it? It's in the activity, it's in the *joy* of it... that makes it brilliant. And so, I don't believe that bar seven, or six, or bar eight, are any different

simply because they have more notes. That has absolutely no relevance to it. It's an extremely bleak and unmusical view of music if you say, 'here are the fast notes, well, now we have to see if we can actually play them.' ... I'm sorry, I can't take this seriously! (2012b: lines 662–93)

Türk describes *brillante* as a synonym for "glittering, brilliant, that is to say, spirited, lively" (1789: 115; 1982: 111)[6] and, significantly, Quantz regards brilliance as a necessary feature of any Allegro movement (1752: 304; 2001: 319), adding that "brilliant ideas must always alternate with flattering ideas" (1752: 294; 2001: 311). Quantz explains that flattery (that which is charming, coaxing, or beguiling) "is expressed with slurred notes that ascend or descend by step, and also with syncopated notes" (1752: 116; 2001: 134). Van Oort identifies the right hand's two-note appoggiaturas in K. 333 as *Seufzer* (sighs), which he regards as "the most basic bearer of expressivity... the most basic figure in the classical style, and especially in Mozart," and explains them as conveying an affect of sadness, longing, a tender sweetness, "a little smile" (2012b: lines 236–37, 245). Yet, to Allanbrook, the sixteenth-note "passagework [in mm. 6 and 8] sounds more mechanical and emphatic than rhapsodic" as it alternates with the appoggiaturas in mm. 5 and 7. She argues that "this quick oscillation between the styles [singing style and concerto style] brings out a mechanical quality in the appoggiatura figure, so that when that expressive figure appears in the cadence at measure 9 it has grown bold and assertive in addition, as the result of its pairing with the virtuosic scale." She regards the final cadence in m. 9 as "triumphantly emphatic," its sense of triumph underlined by the two-measure extension and the scale that opens "the texture out to normal (non-music-box) distances between registers" (1992: 150).

Several observations might be made about this. The way Allanbrook describes the sixteenth-note scales as "brilliant," "virtuosic," "rhapsodic," "mechanical," "soloistic," "emphatic," and "concerto style" suggest related ideas within a twentieth-century aesthetic (albeit she was writing for a twentieth-century audience), but seem a strange mixture when considered with the connotations these adjectives have in the eighteenth-century treatises. Is the "mechanical" quality that Allanbrook heard in the sixteenth-note passagework (let alone in the appoggiaturas) in some way indicative of this music's "meaning," or a reflection of the metronomic evenness of tempo that became a norm in Mozart performance practice in the mid-twentieth century? Describing the sixteenth-notes in mm. 6 and 8 as emphatic, bold, and assertive may suit the sound of a performance on a modern Steinway, but do those adjectives fit performance on a Viennese fortepiano? If we follow Leopold Mozart's performance advice, the slur in m. 6 tells us to make not only a smooth legato, but also a diminuendo, which would take away from an emphatic quality. To play the scale in m. 8 with strength, let alone aiming to give a "triumphant" quality to the top F in m. 9, would risk overplaying a fortepiano and creating a strained sound: the high F is the highest note of the fortepiano, and the instrument is delicate in this range. As van Oort points out, "the high notes of this instrument will not allow you to do that [play loudly]. So there's no decrescendo here [in the score] because it's in the piano.... What's more logical than that? You don't have a slur, it's just *leggiero*" (2012b: 511–14). Perhaps the harmonies on the downbeat of m. 9 are not to open "the texture out to normal (non-music box) distances between the registers," as Allanbrook argues (1992: 150), but to throw into relief the right hand's momentary *in extremis* by contrasting it with a fuller texture on the downbeat. As van Oort explains,

> The romantic style tells us to emphasize expressivity. We always get The Best out of expressivity, you know? That's why the high notes are always so loud in Verdi and Puccini, which is kind of awful, and I'm quite sure that they didn't even want that. In the classical style, most of the expressivity … is in the *leggiero* kind of things. You are expressive here [van Oort gestures a graceful, upward movement with his hand, palm up], not here [an emphatic downward movement, palm down]. Simply because the little piano can't do it. … loud, high notes are virtually impossible on the little piano, unless you have a big bass, or a big chord, or both. … Can you just fake for me the way modern pianists would play it? It's possible on the big piano, on the modern piano obviously, namely with the singing high notes. … You'll hear that it's impossible [on a fortepiano]. … You get this very hard and unattractive sound, which doesn't want to sing, even. It just goes bop. … The highest note of Mozart's piano is rarely used on a heavy beat, it just won't work. … Can it still be forte? That's what modern pianists do, but is it possible on Mozart's piano? (2012a: lines 834–71)

Allanbrook's discussions of topics and musical meaning in Mozart were pioneering and insightful in many ways; but in this essay, the fundamental terms out of which she built her interpretation reflect the norms of an instrument that did not come into existence until long after Mozart's death. Her essay illustrates how easily attempts to understand earlier modes of musical thinking may be undermined by unconscious, anachronistic assumptions about how the music sounds in performance.

When I asked Robert Levin to identify the character of the opening of K. 333 (that is, to demonstrate his interpretative decision-making), his answer made a provocative contrast to Allanbrook's analysis. Levin focused first on the Alberti bass, commenting that

> the *most revealing* sense of character, and above all, character change in Mozart, is to be found not necessarily in the melody voice … but by looking at accompaniment figures. Because you can be sure that if Mozart decides to change the accompaniment figure, then there the character is going to change (2012: lines 47–50).

In these opening ten measures, the left-hand figure changes five times (with a two-measure repeat). Levin's comments on these figures merit quotation at length:

> it seems to me the one place in the piece where it is least likely to have a rest at the beginning of the bar [in the left hand Alberti bass accompaniment], is the very *first* bar. And the way energy is generated through the device of that quaver rest … as Malcolm Bilson has so well pointed out, the vivacity of the left hand is something which is completely indigenous to a period parallel-strung piano, and it is almost impossible to achieve on an overstrung piano … because if you give the energy to the left hand that its rhythmic profile would seem to demand, then the result of that is that the right hand is overshadowed. So there is an impoverishment of the texture by the need to present one thing at a time on concert grands (2012: lines 66–83).

And by the time he [Mozart] gets to the fifth bar of the piece, suddenly the first quaver is present whereas it was not before. And the result of that is suddenly that there's a syncopated figure in the right hand, which changes the character completely and it becomes... shall we say, teasing in its quality. It's witty, yes, of course, the dissonance, on the first and the third beats, all of that. But then, he does something that he is extremely fond of doing, which is to suddenly have the left hand stop dead in its tracks. Again, a more normative, competent composer would have kept the quavers running. But what Mozart does is he stops the note after a single crotchet of the left hand, and this is the equivalent of somebody suddenly spilling the red wine all over the white tablecloth at the reception and the hostess says, "Oh dear, oh, James, please!" and the butler has to come and mop it all up, and so on. The right hand goes into this panic of semiquavers, while the left hand just sits there rubbing its hands, and having precipitated this, this tempest in a teapot, because that's really all it is, you know. And, just to make sure that you haven't missed the point... [in] the third bar on, he [Mozart] substitutes for the syncopes in the right hand a series of quavers... and once again the left hand stops and throws the right hand into a flurry of panic, and sends the right hand sailing up to the very, very top of the keyboard, the very top note that's available, the high F. And then the left hand comes in... and again, you notice [there's a rest on the downbeat]. A saucy little rascal is what it [the left hand] is, and you realise that all over this piece is lurking a sense of mischief (2012: lines 105–44).

Mischief. Of course. The left hand's Alberti bass is not to rein in the right hand's expressivity with mechanical regularity, but to add its own touches of vivacious humor by teasingly subverting convention with its unexpected downbeat rests, strong-beat dissonances and sudden silences. Its rhythm brings out the mincingly complaining quality of the "sighing" appoggiaturas before taunting the right hand into an overexcited two-measure extension to the "normal" eight-measure phrase structure. Levin's interpretation suggests that this music is not imitating a music box; nor is it about topical contrast between singing and concerto styles, between lyrical expressivity and mechanical virtuosity. Yes, this music alternates brilliance and flattery (to use Quantz's terms), but it does so with the quicksilver playfulness of a saucy rascal.

Levin's interpretation of the expressive qualities of this piece is particularly convincing when one thinks of it with the sounds of a Viennese fortepiano in mind. Yet the real value of his imaginatively programmatic analysis is not (or not simply) in the creative finesse of his storytelling, but in what that story reveals of Levin's empathic attention to details of both score and sound, counterpointed with his extensive experience of Mozart's repertoire. Using these, Levin pinpoints what is distinctive in *this* work about how Mozart combines three commonplace figures (appoggiaturas, Alberti bass, and scales) in a process of expressive play. Rather than artificially segmenting the movement by categories of (theorist-defined) topics, Levin's analysis explores how three basic building blocks overlap and morph in a far more plastic, mercurial way. It is reminiscent of Quantz's comments that

each piece which has the [overall] character of one of those mentioned previously [that is, flattering, melancholy, tender, jocund, bold, serious, etc.] may have in it diverse mixtures of pathetic, flattering, gay, majestic, or jocular ideas. Hence you must, so to speak, adopt a different sentiment at each bar, so that you can imagine yourself now melancholy, now gay, now serious, &c. Such dissembling is most necessary in music. He who can truly fathom this art is not likely to be wanting in approval from his listeners, and his execution will always be *moving*. (1752: 109; 2001: 126)

My intention, of course, is not to undermine the concept of topics, but to test their foundations and limitations as useful tools in the process of analysis and interpretation. As Kofi Agawu has commented, "identifying topics…is only the first stage of analysis; interpretation must follow" (2009: 50). If a critical interpretation of music incorporates assumptions about what music means and how it sounds in performance, my aim is to encourage analysts who seek historically justifiable interpretations to consider their own, potentially anachronistic, assumptions about performance practices. As Allanbrook herself later pointed out, "failure to consult the historical context at worst falsifies analysis, and at best leaves it unedifyingly incomplete" (2008: 273).

While the relatively coarse categories of topics have their limits in analysis and interpretation, there are times when identifying an overarching generic reference is very much to the point. In discussing the finale of K. 333, both van Oort and Levin alluded to a "dance-like" quality (probably that of a gavotte, though neither named it as such), arguing for a "light," detached execution of the left-hand quarter notes of the opening. However, both placed more importance on a topical reference of a different kind. While topics that reference "types" usually model Baroque dances, Ratner's definition also allowed for topics that reference other genre types. That this movement has features of the piano concerto genre is not unique in Mozart's solo piano sonatas, and Ratner also identified the concerto topic in the first movements of the Piano Sonatas K. 279, K. 309 and K. 457 (1980: 135). Nor was it unusual that a solo keyboard sonata, a chamber piece for the home, could reference the concerto, a genre typical of the public concert hall. As Ratner explains, "the newly evolved fortepiano of the later 18th century was a popular house instrument; it could serve as a surrogate for the large ensembles of the opera house, church, and concert hall. An amateur could recreate scenes from the theatre, battles, dances, arias, processions, Turkish and rustic effects" (1980: 134).

In my lesson with him, van Oort (2012c) used this concept of topic when he asked me to identify indicators of the piano concerto genre in the third movement of Mozart's sonata K. 333. Although, as a piece for solo piano, clearly this movement is not in any literal sense a piano concerto, van Oort identified the texture and features of different passages as "concerto soloist," "orchestral tutti," and "orchestral accompaniment." The defining aspect of the concerto genre is the relationship between soloist and orchestra, of one performer contrasted with a group, and van Oort used this concept to interpret, for example, the *piano* opening (m. 1) with the *forte* repeat of the rondo theme (m. 8); the soloist's cadential trill that introduces an orchestral tutti (mm. 35–36); soloistic brilliance (in the right hand) accompanied by orchestral chords (in the left hand) in mm. 29–33; and dialogic exchange between soloist and orchestra (mm. 15–24). These are marked in Example 22.2. Although van Oort did not mention it, a further, particularly explicit concerto-like feature of this movement is the long, written-out cadenza of measures 171–98.

After identifying these generic markers, van Oort demonstrated how he uses specific performance practices to characterize the various sections. In other words, he makes performance choices that he regards as congruent with the concerto-like features of the score.

EXAMPLE 22.2 Mozart, Piano Sonata in B flat major, K. 333/iii, mm. 1–46.

(*Continued*)

EXAMPLE **22.2** (Continued)

Van Oort's use of timing and dynamic fluctuations to contrast the "soloist" and "orchestra" sections made contrasts in the repetitions of the movement's rondo theme clearly audible. He conveyed the individuality (and, in eighteenth-century terms, the virtuosity—that is, interpretive sensitivity) of the concerto soloist by using larger fluctuations of timing and dynamic in the "soloist" sections; by contrast, he characterized the "orchestral" sections through a more stable tempo and stronger overall volume. In other words, he used concepts of a specific generic, or topical, type to decide on details of dynamic and tempo.

Levin made a similar comment about this movement:

> I find the direction *grazioso* particularly interesting given the fact that the piece is, as I've said, a version for solo keyboard of a concerto. And *grazioso* is something that we imagine as being connected to something more intimate than something which is [as] public and larger-than-life as a concerto (2012: lines 506–13).

He went on to explore this tension between the intimacy of a *grazioso* chamber piece and the larger canvas of a concerto in more detail:

> What's interesting is that . . . [Mozart takes] up the content of the first movement, and reprocesses it. . . . [But] this time he has to trump himself in the energy department,

and so you get these cascades of semiquavers, and this *big* trill, running into the retransition that gets you back to the Rondo. So the energy level is pumped up at this point in a way that I think leaves the *grazioso* idea of the opening. It is a little bit cheeky, actually, this opening tune, which you can see in the spring of the step in the left hand, and in the cuteness of these saucy little appoggiaturas. I mean, he could so very easily have slurred them four plus four, or all eight.... So when he suddenly gets to the minim in the fourth bar (which is inflected, of course, as a dotted crotchet and two semiquavers in the right hand), nonetheless the smile is there and the slight insolence of some of these quavers, he's very aware of the effect he's having on the audience. And then the almost snide way that he sneaks up through the E-flat and the E-natural, back to the original, and he's *already* ornamenting it, with the triplet of semiquavers, which he didn't need to do at all. He could have waited to do that later in the piece. But the fact that he's *already* ornamenting shows the inherent restless- ness in this character, the eagerness to get things going, and so that's, in other words, a way of giving the *lie* to *grazioso* (2012: lines 517–47).

And for Levin this contains the essential clue to the music's character—a character that he defined through a comparison with Beethoven:

So on the one hand, yes, yes it's very gracious, but there is a plot that's going on, and so it's going to explode at a certain point. Now, Beethoven is the expert in this kind of thing. But in Beethoven, the restlessness makes one think that Beethoven has come to the party dressed in clothing that's two sizes too small, and you think that the buttons are going to start to pop. He's speaking the court language but there's something explosive under the surface, and if somebody says the wrong thing, well, a fist is going to go through a window pane. And that kind of tension in Beethoven's early Classic period pieces, it's fascinating and it's absolutely irresistible. You feel it in the C major piano concerto all of the time. Or, for that matter, in Op. 2 No. 3 where constantly the piece is just going through the roof, in the most exuberant kind of way. And Mozart does that, but not quite with that kind of proto-violence that you get in Beethoven. It's not nearly so revolutionary. But there is this kind of restlessness in the invention, which is another reason why saving the slur in the left hand in bar 2, to bar 6.... Takes it again back to the archness. Yes! You see! You see! The figure in the right hand, interestingly enough, although it be unchanged, is transformed by the fact that the left hand is suddenly doing it too. The first time you just don't think about it, it seems normative. But when you suddenly then have [both hands slurred], oh-ho!! Oh-ho, you little rascal!! You see? And this is the thing! One has to look for the clues of character in Mozart in the tiniest details. Because he deploys character in these little slurs and in these rhythmic figures (2012: lines 547–76).

In this quote, Levin touches on a vital dimension of the meaning of character: the way in which clear, albeit subtle, distinctions of character create contrast (for example, the change in character between mm. 2 and 6 by slurring only the right hand in one, but both in the other). It is through creating such contrasts that the music becomes more than "an uneventful series of predictable, stock gestures," as Levin put it, and that the persuasiveness of the delivery is enhanced. The essential value, therefore, of the concept of character (and, consequently, Ratner's concept of topic) is that it *aids the performer in systematically identifying and executing contrasts.* As van Oort put it, "if I may be blunt, contrast is the first and most important thing in classical repertory. Er, not meaning, necessarily, always as loud and as soft as you can, or as fast or as slow as you can. That's not the point. The point is that you create moments" (2012a: lines 404–8). And for Levin, such interpretation amounts to no more, or less, than a sensitive reading of what Mozart composed into his score: "I'm not creating distinctions where none exist. I'm insisting on making distinctions that the composer has supplied.... And if... [my performance] is so restless that it's too much to take in at a single sitting, well, don't blame the messenger!" (2012: lines 710–16)

VIRTUE AND VIRTUOSITY

Van Oort's and Levin's discussions of virtuosity and the concerto genre in K. 333 touch on another dimension of an eighteenth-century conception of "performing character": the ethical implications of virtuosity. *The Chambers Dictionary* (2010: 1746) defines virtue and virtuoso as originating from the same Latin root word, *virtus*, meaning excellence, inherent power, efficacy. In Aristotelian rhetoric, the persuasiveness of a fine orator was considered such a powerful tool that it required virtue to both develop and wield it (Allard-Nelson 2001: 254). Significantly, *ethos* (Greek for "character") is one of the three methods of persuasion in rhetoric (Allard-Nelson 2001: 249). An orator uses the appeal of *ethos*, of credibility, to convince listeners via his or her honor and trustworthiness, and conveys *ethos* through his or her tone and style in using both *pathos* (an appeal to the emotions) and *logos* (an appeal to the intellect) (Ramage and Bean 1998: 81–82).

The notion that performers demonstrate *ethical* character, in the sense of excellence and persuasive efficacy, through their "virtuosic" choices of performance practice, helps explain why words like "must," "should," "always," and "never" occur so often in the historical treatises (for example, I counted the words *muß* or *müssen* fifteen times in just three paragraphs—on pages 106–7—selected entirely at random from Quantz's treatise). With strikingly judgmental language, after his scathing criticism of incompetent composers quoted above, Leopold Mozart attacks the pride and laziness of would-be virtuosi who "reveal their great ignorance and bad judgment in every measure of the piece. They play without system and without expression... and it is evident that the player does not know what to do."[7] In contrast, Mozart reserves his most lavish praise not for soloists, but for orchestral players who "have great insight into all music, into composition technique and all the varieties of Character; indeed, he must possess particular skills to perform his office with honor."[8] Quantz also implies a connection between musicians' performance decisions and their honor, stating that "there must be no partiality, so that the work of one person is poorly performed, and that of another well; each person must seek to perform whatever is placed before him, no matter who has written it, with the same zeal he would show in his own work, at least if he wishes to maintain that *reputation for honesty which is such a laudable characteristic in a musician*" (1752: 245; 2001: 270, emphasis added).

This sense of a performer's virtuosity was overtaken by the *Werktreue* ideal, which simultaneously attempts to deny the existence of performers' rhetorical power, yet appropriates it to the composer through the expectations of *Texttreue*. As Lydia Goehr argues, there developed in the nineteenth century an "effective synonymity in the musical world of *Werktreue* and *Texttreue*: to be true to a work is to be true to its score.... A performance met the *Werktreue* ideal most satisfactorily, it was finally decided, when it achieved complete transparency. For transparency allowed the work to 'shine' through and be heard in and for itself" (1994: 231–32). Although Goehr does not say it, that the potency of *Werktreue* rests on composers claiming (or being ascribed) performers' rhetorical persuasiveness is exemplified in her very next comment: "Such was the idea behind George Bernard Shaw's remark of 1888 that the pianist Sir Charles Hallé is always assured of an audience because he gives 'as little as possible of Hallé and as much as possible of Beethoven. When Beethoven', by contrast, 'is made a mere *cheval de bataille* for a Rubenstein', Shaw concluded, 'the interest is more volatile'" (1994: 231–32).

Perhaps musicologists' reticence to discuss the *pronuntiatio* implied by topics has been to avoid the tensions of the "authenticity" of historically informed performance and its critics on the one hand, and debates about relationships between performers' and musicologists' interpretations of musical texts on the other. Yet this is tantamount to avoiding the ethical resonances of the "musts" and "shoulds." For musicologists to avoid grappling with what skilled performers regard as truly persuasive, and therefore truly meaningful in their art, continues to position performers merely as slaves to the *Werktreue* ideal rather than commanding an eloquence of their own, and inhibits our understanding of music's communicative power as a sounding art.

ACKNOWLEDGMENT

I thank most warmly my interviewees, Bart van Oort and Robert Levin, for sharing their insightful musicianship with such generosity and good humor. I also thank Nicholas Cook, my Ph.D. supervisor at the University of Cambridge, for his support and unstinting feedback on a draft of this chapter; Kofi Agawu, John Rink, and David Trippett for their perceptive comments as readers; and John McKean for his patient assistance with several translations in this chapter.

NOTES

1. "Da nun die Musik eine solche Wissenschaft ist, die nicht nach eigener Phantasey, sondern eben sowohl als andere schöne Wissenschaften, nach einem, durch gewisse Regeln, und durch viele Erfahrung und große Uebung erlangten und gereinigten gute Geschmacke" (Quantz 1752: 278).
2. In Türk's *Klavierschule*, Section 3 of Chapter 6, devoted to execution, is subtitled "Von dem Ausdrucke des herrschenden Charakters" (Concerning the Expression of the

Prevailing Chatacter). The quoted passage follows Türk's discussion of the importance of the performer's experience and sensitive feelings.

3. In paragraph 45, Türk (1789: 360; 1982: 348) groups together fugues, well-worked sonatas, religious odes, and songs as genres requiring a heavier execution than playful divertimentos, humorous songs, and lively dances.
4. This table is modeled on Riggs's (1996: 39). My translation draws on Raymond Haggh's (1982: 348).
5. The Henle Urtext edition (1977) includes some slurs marked in the first edition published by Torricelli in 1784. Comparing the autograph (held in the Staatsbibliothek zu Berlin—Preußischer Kulturbesitz) with the Torricelli edition (a copy is held in the British Library) shows a number of differences in dynamics and articulations.
6. For the etymology of the term *brillante* and a thorough discussion of the brilliant style, see Roman Ivanovitch's chapter (this volume).
7. "Den so lang sie ein Allegro spielen, so gehet es noch gut: wenn es aber zum Adagio kömmt; da verrathen sie ihre grosse Unwissenheit und ihre schlechte Beurtheilungshaft in allen Täcten des ganzen Stückes. Sie spielen ohne Ordnung, und ohne Ausdruck; das Schwache und Starke wird nicht unterschieden...daß der Spielende nicht weiß, was er thun solle" (Mozart 1787: 258).
8. "Ein guter Orchestergeiger aber muß viele Einsicht in die ganze Musik, in die Satzkunst und in die Verschiedenheit der Charakters, ja er muß eine besondere lebhafte Geschicklichkeit haben, um seinem Amte mit Ehren vorzustehen; absonderlich wenn er seiner Zeit den Anführer eines Orchesters abgeben will" (Mozart 1787: 259).

REFERENCES

n.n. 2008. *The Chambers Dictionary*, 11th ed. London: Chambers Harrap.
Agawu, Kofi. 2008. Topic Theory: Achievement, Critique, Prospects. In *Passagen, IMS Kongress Zürich 2007: Fünf Hauptvorträge, Five Key Note Speeches*, ed. Laurenz Lütteken and Hans-Joachim Hinrischen, 38–69. Kassel: Bärenreiter.
——. 2009. *Music as Discourse: Semiotic Adventures in Romantic Music*. New York: Oxford University Press.
Allanbrook, Wye J. 1983. *Rhythmic Gesture in Mozart:* Le nozze di Figaro *and* Don Giovanni. Chicago and London: University of Chicago Press.
——. 1992. Two Threads through the Labyrinth: Topic and Process in the First Movements of K. 332 and K. 333. In *Convention in Eighteenth- and Nineteenth-Century Music: Essays in Honor of Leonard G. Ratner*, ed. Wye J. Allanbrook, Janet M. Levy, and William P. Mahrt, 125–71. Stuyvesant: Pendragon.
——. 2008. Mozart's k331, First Movement: Once More, with Feeling. In *Communication in Eighteenth-Century Music*, ed. Danuta Mirka and Kofi Agawu, 254–82. Cambridge: Cambridge University Press.
Allard-Nelson, Susan K. 2001. Virtue in Aristotle's Rhetoric: A Metaphysical and Ethical Capacity. *Philosophy and Rhetoric* 34/3: 245–59.
Beghin, Tom. "Delivery, Delivery, Delivery!" Crowning the Rhetorical Process of Haydn's Kayboard Sonatas. In *Haydn and the Performance of Rhetoric*, ed. Tom Beghin and Sander M. Goldberg, 131–71. Chicago: University of Chicago Press.

Castelvecchi, Stefano. 2013. *Sentimental Opera: Questions of Genre in the Age of Bourgeois Drama*. Cambridge: Cambridge University Press.

Cook, Nicholas. 2013. *Music as Performance: Changing the Musical Object*. New York: Oxford University Press.

Engel, Johann Jakob. 1780. *Über die musikalische Malerey*. Berlin: Voss.

———. 1998. On Painting in Music. In *Source Readings in Music History*, rev. ed., vol. 5, ed. Wye Jamison Allanbrook, 220–31. New York: Norton.

Goehr, Lydia. 1994. *The Imaginary Museum of Musical Works: An Essay in the Philosophy of Music*. Oxford: Oxford University Press.

Harrán, Don. 1997. Toward a Rhetorical Code of Early Music Performance. *The Journal of Musicology* 15/1: 19–42.

Kirnberger, Johann Philipp. 1771–79. *Die Kunst des reinen Satzes*. 2 vols. Vol. 1, Berlin: Rottmann 1771. Vol. 2, sections 1–3, Berlin and Königsberg: Decker und Hartung 1776, 1777, and 1779.

———. 1982. *The Art of Strict Musical Composition*. Trans. David Beach and Jurgen Thym. New Haven: Yale University Press.

Koch, Heinrich Christoph. 1793. *Versuch einer Anleitung zur Composition*. Vol. 3. Leipzig: Adam Friedrich Böhme. Reprint, Hildesheim: Georg Olms, 1969.

———. 1983. *Introductory Essay on Composition*. Trans. Nancy Kovaleff Baker. New Haven: Yale University Press.

Levin, Robert. 2012. Interview with author. Transcript of audio recording. Cambridge, UK, 29 October 2012.

Mozart, Leopold. 1787. *Gründliche Violinschule*, 3rd ed. Ausburg: Johann Jakob Lotter und Sohn. Reprint, Wiesbaden: Breitkopf und Härtel, 1991.

Oort, Bart van. 2012a. Interview 1 with author. Transcript of audio recording. Utrecht, The Netherlands, 12 August 2012.

———. 2012b. Interview 2 with author. Transcript of audio recording. Utrecht, The Netherlands, 12 August 2012.

———. 2012c. Interview 3 with author. Transcript of audio recording. Utrecht, The Netherlands, 13 August 2012.

Quantz, Johann Joachim. 1752. *Versuch einer Anweisung die Flöte traversiere zu spielen*. Berlin: Voss.

———. 2001. *On Playing the Flute*, 2nd ed. Trans. Edward R. Reilly. London: Faber and Faber.

Ramage, John D., and John C. Bean. 1998. *Writing Arguments*, 4th ed. Needham Heights, MA: Allyn and Bacon.

Ratner, Leonard G. 1980. *Classic Music: Expression, Form, and Style*. New York: Schirmer.

Riggs, Robert. 1996. Authenticity and Subjectivity in Mozart Performance: Türk on Character and Interpretation. *College Music Symposium* 36: 33–58.

Rosenblum, Sandra P. 1988. *Performance Practices in Classic Piano Music: Their Principles and Applications*. Bloomington: Indiana University Press.

Samson, Jim. 2001. Genre. In *The New Grove Dictionary of Music and Musicians*, 2nd ed., ed. Stanley Sadie and John Tyrrell, vol. 9, 657–59. London: Macmillan.

Schulz, Johann Abraham Peter. Takt. In Johann Georg Sulzer, *Allgemeine Theorie der Schönen Kunste*, vol. 2, 1130–38. Leipzig: Weidmann.

Türk, Daniel Gottlob. 1789. *Klavierschule, oder Anweisung zum Klavierspielen für Lehrer und Lernende*. Leipzig and Halle: Hemmerde und Schwetschke.

———. 1982. *School of Clavier Playing*. Trans. Raymond Haggh. Lincoln: University of Nebraska Press.

SECTION V

LISTENING TO TOPICS

CHAPTER 23

....

AMATEUR TOPICAL COMPETENCIES

....

MELANIE LOWE

"IF you have no pupils at the moment, then compose something more, even if you have to let your work go for a smaller sum; for God's sake you have to make yourself known. But let it be something short, easy, popular. Talk with an engraver about what he would most like to have—perhaps easy quartets for two violins, viola, and basso. Do you believe perhaps that you lower yourself in such things?"[1] So a worried and controlling father wrote to a brilliant if somewhat irresponsible son in 1778. Seven years later, said son published six string quartets, works that were hardly short, easy, or popular. In between Leopold Mozart's admonishing advice and the publication of Amadeus Mozart's Opus 10 quartets—the so-called "Haydn" quartets that comprise what we, today, have come to view as the pinnacle of Mozart's quartet composition (if not all quartet composition in the eighteenth-century)—Haydn published his "new and special"[2] Opus 33, and Haydn's former student Ignaz Pleyel brought out two sets of six quartets, his Opuses 1 and 2.

The sales of Mozart's Opus 10 quartets were, of course, famously underwhelming, at least during the composer's lifetime. While there seems to be no financial accounting of the quartets' commercial failure for Artaria, there is an abundance of circumstantial evidence that leads to this conclusion. For one thing, when Dittersdorf was trying to sell his own quartets to the same publisher, the letter he wrote—two years after Opus 10 came out—suggests that Mozart's quartets did not sell well; indeed, he assures Artaria that his will sell better because they are stylistically more accessible than Mozart's.[3] But the "sales-pitchy" words of the competition aside, the publication history of Opus 10 speaks for itself: in Mozart's lifetime, his extraordinary "Haydn" quartets were reissued only three more times by Artaria and published only once, by Sieber, in Paris (Finscher and Seiffert 1993: b/6–7). To be sure, with four issues and evidence that a second set of plates was needed for the later imprints, they were perhaps not quite the commercial disaster they have been made out to be.[4] But still, there can be no doubt that, before the composer's death at least, Mozart's Opus 10 was hardly a commercial success.

Haydn's landmark Opus 33 quartets—his first works composed directly for publication—fared much better in the late eighteenth-century musical marketplace. After their initial 1782 publication by Artaria, Haydn's set enjoyed nine reissues during the following decade with publishers in Amsterdam, Paris, and London. Individual quartets from the set also circulated in an assortment of arrangements, from solo keyboard and keyboard four-hands to winds and strings to piano trio. Four individual movements even received words to become songs (Hoboken 1957: 395–401).

Pleyel, however, should have been absolutely ecstatic at the astonishing commercial triumph of his first two sets of string quartets. In 1783 the first edition of Opus 1 was published in Vienna by Rodolfo Gräffer. They sold well. During Pleyel's lifetime, these six quartets were reissued more than forty times in complete sets by no fewer than fifteen publishers throughout Europe. Individual quartets from the set enjoyed a parallel life as arrangements, over thirty different ones, in fact—from keyboard to winds and strings to full orchestra; like some movements of Haydn's Opus 33, there are several vocal versions, some with words added interlinearly. Pleyel's Opus 2 quartets, published a year later, in 1784, were equally successful, reissued about thirty times by eighteen publishers over the same three decades. And as with his Opus 1, there were dozens of arrangements in the same wide variety of instrumentations and vocal renditions (Benton 1977: 99–111). These data leave no doubt: commercially speaking at least, if Pleyel's first two opuses surpassed Haydn's Opus 33, which they very clearly did, they left Mozart's Opus 10 in the dust.

What was it about Pleyel's quartets that made them so incomparably commercially viable? And what was it about Mozart's quartets that made them so much less so? Alternatively, what is it about Mozart's quartets that have led them to endure, to triumph in the end, so to speak, while Pleyel's quartets are now largely forgotten?[5] A corollary question: What is it about Haydn's quartets that leaves them perennially in the middle—not as successful as Pleyel's at the time but so much more so than Mozart's, and not completely forgotten today like Pleyel's, but hardly the heart of the quartet canon like Mozart's? Of course, these questions have been asked countless times and answered many different ways, to varying degrees of satisfaction. But I shall ask them again here and perhaps answer them somewhat differently.

The vast majority of music published in the late eighteenth century was composed for performance in the home by amateur players for a domestic audience, if there was any audience at all. And it follows logically, then, that the most salable works were also the most technically undemanding—music suitable for amateurs. Generally speaking, Pleyel's works have an "accessible" style and contain relatively few polyphonic textures—both good, important, and frequently made observations about his music.[6] But surely there must be more to commercial viability than music that is merely easy to play and contains no fugues.

Elsewhere I have argued for a high degree of topical competency among the lay listeners that made up the late eighteenth-century public concert audience, and that this competency allowed for an immediate perception and understanding of musical structure and form. Moreover, as interpretive activity is largely dependent on at least some degree of structural intelligibility, I suggested that topical competency was the springboard for the construction of meaning among the musically uninitiated (see Lowe 2007). In this chapter I shall build on this construction of amateur topical competency to consider relationships between patterns of consumption, musical style, and consumer identity. Although the enterprise is undoubtedly speculative by nature (and I would maintain that there is simply no way around this reality),[7] I suggest that we can learn quite a bit about the consumers of string quartets from the quartets themselves, the music these amateur musicians chose to play. And we know just what music these consumers preferred, for the publication history alone speaks directly to that point. In the 1780s, amateur players and their occasional listeners preferred Haydn to Mozart, and Pleyel to either.

In addressing questions of amateur topical competency, my strategy is comparative and therefore, to facilitate—and also to compress—an expansive analytical procedure, my discussion here will be limited to movements governed by clearly defined topics. First, we shall consider three minuet movements, one by Mozart, one by Haydn, and one by Pleyel, all of which incorporate contrapuntal techniques to varying structural and expressive ends. We shall then examine four *chasse* movements, one by Mozart, one by Haydn, and two by Pleyel. In both sets of examples, we shall take up in turn issues of topical content and syntactical function, parametric density and topical dissonance, and then finally the social and cultural associations of the topics themselves to address relationships between topical discourse, amateur topical competency, and consumer identity in the 1780s. As we shall see, the commercial viability of such works in the eighteenth-century musical marketplace was bound up with the topical competency of amateur musicians.

LEARNED/GALANT TROPES IN MINUETS

Of the three minuet movements, the least structurally and expressively sophisticated is also the least well known today, the Grazioso finale of Pleyel's String Quartet in G minor, Op. 2 No. 3. Despite its lack of a minuet title or tempo indication, there is no question as to its topical identity. Indeed, it exhibits almost all of the archetypal musical characteristics of the minuet: 3/4 meter; nearly equal stress on each beat of the measure ensuring a steady rhythmic profile; a slight accent on the first beat of each two-measure group, defining the *pas de menuet*; consistently regular four-square phrase structure; and even the presence of the late eighteenth-century minuet "motto" rhythm—a quarter note followed by four beamed eight notes—in the first violin part of the very first measure (Example 23.1).[8] The large-scale structure is the usual da capo form of eighteenth-century dance movements; the first dance is a clear rounded binary form in minor mode while the second offers a simple eighteen-measure binary-form *maggiore*. The movement's designation Grazioso may also be read as a minuet indicator, as the word is among those most frequently used to describe the dance in its own time. The mid-eighteenth-century dancing master Carl Joseph von Feldtenstein, for one, even remarked that the minuet "appears to have been invented by the Graces themselves" (1767: 36–37; cited in Allanbrook 1983: 33).

EXAMPLE **23.1** Pleyel, String Quartet in G minor, Op. 2 No. 3/iii, mm. 1–20.

With the minuet topic so clearly defined, a passage of imitative counterpoint should provide for some expressive enrichment, if not also a degree of topical dissonance or even topical challenge. And yet in this movement Pleyel integrates the imitation (mm. 9–16) so completely into the dance's phrase and period structure that the tropological force of the combination of learned and galant elements is effectively diffused. The four-voice canon at the interval of two measures generates a perfectly symmetrical eight-measure period (mm. 9–16) to balance the opening eight measures. Moreover, the canon subject is a two-measure segment that repeats itself immediately a third higher, yielding a decidedly homophonic texture. In essence, rather than two lines of interlocking counterpoint, Pleyel gives us a melody in parallel thirds. The impact of the tropological fusion of the minuet and the learned style is thus mitigated to the point of nonexistence, as neither period structure, phrase rhythm, nor texture is disrupted by it.[9] Pleyel's melodically defined *pas de menuet* continues without a single hiccup into the concluding four-measure phrase of the opening strain.

Interpretively speaking, then, Pleyel's Grazioso presents neither player nor listener much challenge. The minuet, whether encountered as a dance in the ballroom or as a topic in vocal and instrumental music, was understood by nearly all music enthusiasts of the time as a noble dance of utmost grace and elegance. In the terms and categories established by eighteenth-century critics and theorists, we may encapsulate its expressive content as the courtly (galant)—as opposed to the ecclesiastical (learned)—variety of the high style.[10] As quartet players in the late eighteenth century were predominately members of the landed nobility and wealthy upper-bourgeois citizens,[11] the patrician character of Pleyel's topically consonant Grazioso easily reflected the high social status of its consumers. Uncomplicated by any other affect, his minuet finale essentially handed *Kenner* and *Liebhaber* alike an unequivocal social and perhaps even political meaning: a tacit endorsement of the stratification of contemporary European societies.[12]

Like Pleyel's Grazioso, the scherzo of Haydn's String Quartet in B minor, Op. 33 No. 1 (Example 23.2), is also governed by a minuet topic, as evidenced by its 3/4 meter, nearly equal stress on each beat of the measure, *pas de menuet* measure groupings, and overall da capo design with a rounded-binary "minuet proper" and a simple binary-form *maggiore* trio. But while Pleyel's minuet movement is of the courtly variety, the allegro tempo, upbeats, and bariolage (first violin, mm. 6–7, 28–29) impart a rustic spirit to Haydn's scherzo minuet. Haydn's scherzo also incorporates imitative counterpoint, but whereas in Pleyel's minuet the canon is confined to its own eight-measure period, here the contrapuntal textures are infused throughout the movement. Already on the upbeat to the fourth measure, the second violin picks up the second motive of the first-violin's opening melody (motive b) and forms a two-measure figure that is then imitated by the viola and cello. Even as the *pas de menuet* is subverted somewhat by the second violin's two-measure phrase (mm. 4–5) and its imitation in the lower voices (mm. 6–7), the phrase rhythm—at least as dictated by the first violin—remains "danceable" throughout. To be sure, while sustaining the second violin's subversive rhythmic move, the viola and cello's imitation in measures 6–7 may also be heard to supply a textural patch over what would otherwise be a more jarring structural seam. At m. 7 the lower two voices, following in imitation, provide an underlying continuity for the surprising and potentially disruptive bariolage effect in the top voice. While the resulting phrase rhythm is asymmetrical, as the archetypal eight-measure strain is expanded to twelve measures by the insertion of a four-measure phrase (mm. 5–8), the imitation provides for an underlying textural logic and seemingly seamless continuity.

In the second strain, Haydn telescopes to one measure the distance between the points of imitation, presenting something of a textural challenge to the underlying *pas*

EXAMPLE 23.2 Haydn, String Quartet in B minor, Op. 33 No. 1/ii, mm 1–24.

de menuet phrase rhythm (mm. 13–22). By opening this intensely contrapuntal passage
with the entrance of the lowest voice and following it with the highest, Haydn shifts
the hypermetrical downbeat to the second measure of each two-measure segment. If
we continue to hear the *pas de menuet* as governing the phrase structure, the result is a
syncopated phrase rhythm in the first six measures of the ten-measure period (Figure
23.1a):

(a)	Phrase structure:	2		2		2		2		2
		1+1		1+1		1+1		1+1		1+1
	Measures:	13 14		15 16		17 18		19 20		21 22

(b)	Phrase structure:	1	8	1
		1	4+4	1
	Measures:	13	14–21	22

FIGURE 23.1 Two alternative ways of hearing the *pas de menuet* in Haydn's String Quartet in B minor, Op. 33 No. 1/ii, mm. 13–22.

On the other hand, we may also hear a shift of the *pas de menuet* one measure forward, generating a symmetrical eight-measure period framed by two single measures (Figure 23.1b). In either hearing of the phrase rhythm in the opening of the second strain, the archetypal two-measure phrase structure of the minuet is disrupted.

Expressively, then, the unmarked nontragic galant style of this minor-mode minuet is challenged simultaneously on two stylistic axes. The tempo, bariolage, and syncopated phrase rhythm compromise the minuet topic's courtly decorum by imposing a marked, low-style affect. Such expressive content would flirt with bathos were it not for the pervasive imitative counterpoint, whose infusion of a marked, high-style texture simultaneously challenges the minuet from the opposite category of pathos.[13] And yet, as the learned style was by the late eighteenth century increasingly ridiculed for its pedantry (see Chapin's chapter in this volume), we may also hear the saturation of imitation in this minuet as ironic, thereby "short-circuiting" the expressive pathway to move directly into the realm of the bathetic. In either interpretation, the impact of the topical trope on the minuet is much higher in Haydn's movement than in Pleyel's, yielding a scherzo with a high degree of topical dissonance. As such, Haydn presents his players and listeners with considerable interpretive challenges—what to make of such expressive contradictions? While the courtly high style of the minuet topic is undermined by the rustic elements, the low style of the countrified elements is simultaneously contradicted by the expressive authority of the imitative counterpoint. In the end, players and listeners must navigate a tricky interpretive course—engage actively with the movement's topical discourse—to arrive at a coherent musical meaning.

The second-movement Minuetto of Mozart's String Quartet in A major, K. 464, likewise displays the usual topical markers of the late eighteenth-century minuet (Example 23.3). Like Pleyel's Grazioso, Mozart's minuet is of the courtly variety: an unqualified minuet tempo, no upbeats, a steady rhythmic profile, and the melodic gesture—three straight quarter notes, all on the same pitch (mm. 5, 7, and so on)—so frequently encountered in contemporary dance minuets composed for the ballroom.[14] Also like Pleyel, Mozart follows an opening homophonic eight-measure period with a passage

EXAMPLE 23.3 Mozart, String Quartet in A major, K. 464/ii, mm. 1–43.

of counterpoint. But unlike Pleyel's, Mozart's extension actually sounds contrapuntal, and from this point on, like Haydn's scherzo, Mozart's minuet is infused with counterpoint, much of it imitative. In m. 9 the primary motives from the opening period's antecedent (motive a) and consequent (motive b) phrases are played against one another, revealing their "more felicitous relationship," as Allanbrook puts it, "as subject and countersubject" (1996: 140). Moreover, this contrapuntal relationship retroactively casts the slower moving, seemingly accompanimental lines in the second violin and viola as a learned-style *cantus firmus* (motive c). These unassuming lines thus receive a new status that will become salient in the repeat. Measures 13–17 then present motive a in *stretto*; motive b receives the same treatment immediately following in mm. 17–21. Motives b and c (represented by single dotted half notes in mm. 30 and 32) are treated to textural inversion in the opening period of the second strain (mm. 29–37), the point of inversion heightened—and the phrase rhythm disrupted—by a full measure of rest (a grand pause, in effect) in m. 33. When the material from the first strain returns to round out the binary form of the minuet proper (Example 23.4), motives a and b are presented not in succession, as in the movement's opening period, but rather in the contrapuntal relationship of the extending second period of the first strain. And here, once again, Mozart ups the contrapuntal ante: in the third measure of the "antecedent" phrase of the return (m. 57) motive a enters in inversion. This leads directly to the "consequent" phrase in which motive b is presented not only in counterpoint with motive a but also in *stretto* with itself (mm. 59–62).

Of these three minuet movements, Mozart's is undeniably the most expansive structurally and harmonically. It is also the most intensely contrapuntal. And while Haydn's infusion of counterpoint into a rustic scherzo presents the player and listener with considerable interpretive challenges, Mozart's contrapuntal combinatorics engages amateur topical competency alongside the interpretive challenge presented by his troping of free and strict styles. Because the counterpoint here reveals the combinatorial possibilities of

EXAMPLE 23.4 Mozart, String Quartet in A major, K. 464/ii, mm. 55–64.

the movement's rather limited musical material (nearly all of the material is derived from motive a, b, or c), the learned/galant trope in this movement may itself be heard as signifying "difficulty," a rhetorical device "whose effect depends on the effort of understanding [it]" (Sisman 1997: 53). When the musical surface throws up such an interpretive challenge, as it undeniably does in this deceptively inaccessible movement, the amateur player and listener may ultimately relinquish control over musical meaning. Such a surrender, along with the inability of leisured and wealthy quartet enthusiasts to enjoy an uninhibited reflection of their high social status, would certainly have contributed to the tempered reception of Mozart's Opus 10 quartets in the late eighteenth-century musical marketplace. Ironically, for *Kenner* and *Liebhaber* alike, the meaning of Mozart's Minuetto may have ultimately been the inability to construct a coherent meaning.

PARAMETRIC DENSITY OF MUSICAL HUNTS

Of the four *chasse* movements to be discussed below, the most familiar is likely the opening Allegro vivace assai of Mozart's String Quartet in B flat major, K. 458, a quartet that acquired the nickname "Hunt" early in its history because of the obvious hunting associations that define the first group (Example 23.5): 6/8 meter, triadic melodies outlining primarily tonic and dominant chords, horn-call *bicinia*, and regular periodicity.[15] Topically speaking, the first movement of Haydn's String Quartet in D major, Op. 33 No. 6, opens exactly the same way (Example 23.6): 6/8 meter, triadic melodies outlining primarily tonic and dominant chords, some horn-call *bicinia*, and regular periodicity. The key, D major, is undoubtedly significant here, for the Marquis of Dampierre chose the

EXAMPLE 23.5 Mozart, String Quartet in B flat major, K. 458/i, mm. 1–8.

EXAMPLE **23.6** Haydn, String Quartet in D major, Op. 33 No. 6/i, mm. 1–8.

EXAMPLE **23.7** Pleyel, String Quartet in A major, Op. 1 No. 3/i, mm. 1–10.

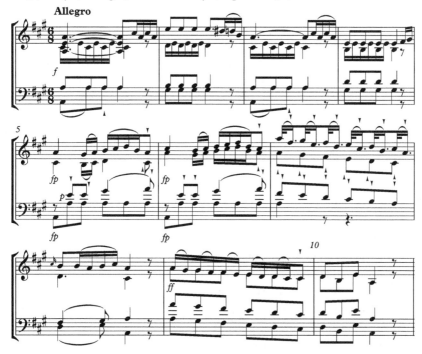

horn in D for his collection of calls, the most famous and widely disseminated collection of hunting calls in the eighteenth century. Simply put, both Mozart and Haydn open their *chasse* movements with a presentational passage defined by a "pure" and conventionalized sign.

Pleyel, too, opens the first-movement *chasse* of his String Quartet in A major, Op. 1 No. 3 with clear markers of the hunt topic: 6/8 meter, triadic melodies outlining primarily tonic and dominant chords, and regular periodicity (Example 23.7). Conspicuously absent, however, are the hunting *bicinia*. It is also worth noticing that a touch of Scotch snap sets up the cadence. Nevertheless, like both Haydn and Mozart, Pleyel opens with a presentational passage that summons the hunt. Following an admittedly long-winded first group,[16] Pleyel's second group introduces a new melody that likewise unfolds in a regular four-square phrase structure (Example 23.8). Scotch snaps once again impart certain rusticity to the expressive field. The overall effect is stasis in the parametric density of the *chasse* and, with its presentational style, a clear alignment of expressive surface and syntactical function.

Haydn continues with a bridge that solidifies the hunt topic with "horn calls" in both textural and thematic "echo" imitation (Example 23.9, mm. 19–22). He then follows with a second group whose running sixteenth notes (mm. 27–33) connect back motivically to the first group while their imitative dialogues connect forward through the presentation of a new triadic melody (mm. 36–43). Even with the imitation, all of this material unfolds over two clearly articulated eight-measure periods. The overall effect is an increase in the parametric density of the hunt topic and a clear alignment of expressive surface and syntactical function.

Mozart, on the other hand, at the same structural point in the movement, introduces a new topic and a new rhythmic element—brilliant-style passage work (Example 23.10, mm. 31–34) and hemiola (mm. 38–41), both of which, as surface expressions of instability, function as conventionalized signs of continuation. While the new thematic material that immediately follows (m. 55) retains many expressive markers of the hunt topic (here, triadic-outline melodic motives, primarily tonic and dominant harmonies, and "echo" imitation), the second group lacks a clear or predictable sense of period structure, a change-up that is all the more striking because it follows a first group in which the phrase units "avoided elision to a degree unusual in Mozart's music" (Irving 1998: 70). Combined with a slippery four-sixteenth-note motive that develops continually through the second group (it starts with a double eighth-note upbeat, then loses it, then gains a triple eighth-note upbeat, the effect of which is to shift continually the rhythmic scansion and to demand more effort in both the projection and perception of meter), Mozart's second group denies us the "double psychic economy" that Haydn's so nicely provides—that subtle sense in which listeners and players alike can relax, because there is no question as to expressive identity or syntactical function.[17] In other words, very little here is presentational, just at the point we would most expect it. To put a fine point on the comparison, then, Haydn's increase in the parametric density of the hunt topic enhances structural intelligibility. Mozart's enriching and troping of the hunt topic diminish structural intelligibility.

Pleyel's development proceeds predictably enough, with the triadic melodies and Scotch snaps from the exposition presented in a regular and clear period structure (Example 23.11a). Following a climactic moment, the retransition (Example 23.11b) chases its way with a touch of more "echo" imitation back to A major for a predictable

EXAMPLE **23.8** Pleyel, String Quartet in A major, Op. 1 No. 3/i mm. 51–62.

recapitulation. In other words, the light parametric density of Pleyel's hunt topic remains static and there is no topical troping, contest, or expressive dissonance of any kind. The climactic moment in Haydn's movement, on the other hand, is the short development, which for twelve measures effectively lowers the parametric density of the hunt topic (Example 23.12). Haydn opens with the horn call motive from the exposition's bridge but

EXAMPLE **23.9** Haydn, String Quartet in D major, Op. 33 No. 6/i, mm. 19–43.

EXAMPLE **23.10** Mozart, String Quartet in B flat major, K. 458/i, mm. 31–77.

(Continued)

EXAMPLE **23.10** (Continued)

EXAMPLE **23.12** Haydn, String Quartet in D major, Op. 33 No. 6/i, mm. 59–70.

EXAMPLE **23.13** Haydn, String Quartet in D major, Op. 33 No. 6/i, mm. 71–78.

without the upper voice of its *bicinium*. Imitative treatment of the bridge material follows (mm. 63–68), now presented in a style more learned than any other passage in the
movement, even if the passage itself is still laid out in a clearly demarcated eight-measure
period. As if to compensate for the very short development, Haydn's recapitulation is quite

developmental (and it starts in the dominant), but the parametric density of the hunt topic returns to just what it was in the exposition: clear articulation of 6/8 meter, triadic melodies outlining tonic and dominant harmonies, horn call *bicinia*, and regular periodicity (Example 23.13). A sixteen-measure coda brings back the horn calls from the bridge, stated one final time in the proper voicing. The movement closes quietly with eight measures that recall the triadic melodic motives from the first group, while the long bass pedal suggests the pastorale, a topic highly compatible with the hunt (Example 23.14).[18]

The second half of Mozart's *chasse* movement could hardly develop more differently than either Pleyel's or Haydn's. To start, he opens with an entirely new melody, an *Alphorn* tune floating over bass pedals that immediately changes the setting and the cast of characters (Example 23.15).[19] The music moves from the woodland to the Alps, from the huntsman to the shepherd. Expressively speaking, we have left the hunt behind

EXAMPLE **23.14** Haydn, String Quartet in D major, Op. 33 No. 6/i, mm. 153–64.

EXAMPLE **23.15** Mozart, String Quartet in B flat major, K. 458/i, mm. 91–98.

and entered the realm of the pastoral. When the sixteenth-note motive from the second group returns, following the *Alphorn* tune, its rhythmic scansion within the 6/8 measure shifts again (Example 23.16). In fact, nearly all parameters of this motive are in motion: the texture shifts continually, gone is the triadic melodic outline, and in its place are chromatic lines and harmonies that hint of *tempesta*. The climax of the development comes when the sixteenth-note motive regains its double eighth-note triadic upbeat, thereby shifting the rhythmic scansion back to its original position. The only moment of "echo" imitation returns as well, but at this point Mozart doubles-down—what was once a polite series of lateral melodic passes (Example 23.10, mm. 42–46) is now a scramble of canonic imitation (Example 23.16, mm. 126–28).

Mozart's recapitulation follows the exposition's structure and topical discourse quite closely, which makes good formal sense, for it is the coda that provides the true culmination of the movement. The opening *chasse* melody is now presented, literally, as a "chase"—in learned-style imitation not unlike that in the much earlier vocal genres of *chace* and *caccia* (Example 23.17).[20] More important, though, is the decidedly learned technique: the *chasse* is in *stretto*. There are certainly other important details to notice here, particularly regarding motivic development (for instance, the return of the sixteenth-note figure in various guises; the shifting of 6/8 scansion in its last appearance just six measures before the end) but for our present purpose, the learned-style *stretto* is most significant. To put fine point on my comparison once again, Haydn follows a developmental recapitulation by reaffirming the hunt topic. At first glance Mozart may appear to do so as well but—even if the imitation can be associated with the hunt—it is too learned for a simple topical reaffirmation. Mozart's enrichment of the hunt topic actually generates considerable expressive dissonance: sacrificed for the sake of the *stretto* are the horn call *bicinia*, the outlining of predominantly tonic and dominant harmonies, and clear periodicity. To be sure, just like at the end of the "Jupiter" finale, the free style triumphs, but to accomplish that return, Mozart sacrifices the *chasse* itself.

The easiest way to see what's so strikingly different about Pleyel's topical discourse is to put the coda of his *chasse* (Example 23.18) in direct dialogue with Mozart's coda. Just like Mozart, Pleyel brings back material from the development and imitative textures. But Pleyel's recalled material still resides firmly within the topical field of the *chasse*, whereas Mozart retrieves the material that is the least *chasse*-like in the whole movement. Moreover, Pleyel's imitation is plainly a chase—it's not learned at all. Mozart's imitation, as we observed earlier, is decidedly strict in style, self-consciously so, in fact.

With these three movements in mind, let us look at one more *chasse* movement by Pleyel, the finale of his String Quartet in D Major, Op. 2 No. 6 (Example 23.19). To be sure, because this movement is a *chasse* finale, a direct comparison to Haydn's and Mozart's *chasse* first movements is not unproblematic, particularly regarding issues of relationships between topical discourse and structural intelligibility. But the differences in topicality here are so striking and clear that a quick analysis reveals once again how a light parametric density is a hallmark of Pleyel's quartet style.

First, like Haydn but unlike Mozart, we never get off our horse in this movement. The defining rhythmic element of the *chasse*—the obstinate eighth notes—gallop

EXAMPLE **23.16** Mozart, String Quartet in B flat major, K. 458/i, mm. 106–37.

(*Continued*)

EXAMPLE **23.16** (Continued)

EXAMPLE **23.17** Mozart, String Quartet in B flat major, K. 458/i, mm. 239–54.

EXAMPLE **23.18** Pleyel, String Quartet in A major, Op. 1 No. 3/i, mm. 199–209.

throughout.[21] But the parametric density of Pleyel's hunt topic is much less either than Haydn's or Mozart's *chasse*, especially at the opening. The topic is defined mostly rhythmically, and also by the French hunting key of D major (Monelle 2006: 42). There are parallel sixths but no hunting *bicinia* in the opening presentation of the primary theme. Its period structure is balanced, 9 + 9, but it is not symmetrical: a phrase structure of 1 + 8 measures is followed by a 4 + 5 measure structure. The melodies are not triadic, and neither do they outline predominately tonic and dominant harmonies. Indeed, already in the third measure Pleyel gives us a hint of the supertonic before retroactively recasting it as a dominant function with the C♯ upbeat to the next measure. The point here is that such low parametric density in topical definition effectively diminishes the possibilities for topical enrichment or dissonance. The *chasse*, residing almost entirely in the galloping eighth notes, can be either present or absent; there is little opportunity for topical shading. To be sure, the tiny bit of "chasing" imitation that enters in the short developmental passage at m. 52 (Example 23.20), and returns just before the end, may bolster the *chasse* a bit, but it is barely topical enrichment and most certainly not learned enough in style to present any topical troping, expressive dissonance, or interpretive challenge. Where Haydn and Mozart trope and challenge topically and structurally, Pleyel presents topics straight-up, unmixed, and crystal clear.

The structure of Pleyel's movement is also exceptionally uncomplicated. Most importantly, though, for the purpose of this chapter, is that the structure is readable entirely

EXAMPLE **23.19** Pleyel, String Quartet in D major, Op. 2 No. 6/iii, mm. 1–18.

through surface expression; no awareness of tonal motion or formal process is necessary for the player or the listener to know where he is in the movement's structural unfolding. One example will suffice to demonstrate the structural implications of Pleyel's surface expression. After the opening eight-measure tune, presented in a melody over *Trommellbass*-like *chasse*-rhythmed accompaniment (see Example 23.19), an abrupt change in texture provides the connective tissue and announces the arrival of the new key. Immediately following this striking unison is another abrupt change in texture and a hint of hunting *bicinia* (m. 22); a player or listener with no knowledge of tonal workings can hear some sense of formal motion, if not formal progress, in the restatement of the primary theme. Indeed, all key structural points in this movement are marked with

EXAMPLE **23.20** Pleyel, String Quartet in D major, Op. 2 No. 6/iii, mm. 51–65.

a conspicuous change in texture to provide the formal signpost. By contrast, in Mozart's *chasse*, the texture, motivic material, and rhythmic scansion are always shifting and in such constant play that even with repeated playings and listenings, the expressive surface provides few formal signposts, and those that might be there are seen only with an intensely focused look through a thick motivic fog.

But the real payoff of the comparison of these four *chasse* movements, especially when considering amateur topical competency in relation to quartet consumer identity, comes with social and cultural readings of their different articulations of the hunt topic. As has been established by Alexander Ringer and, especially, Raymond Monelle in his rich cultural unpacking of the topic, the hunt is always noble and heroic; its indexicalities also encompass manliness, risk, exhilaration, and youth. While the hunt itself, and certainly as practiced in eighteenth-century German lands, was hardly a heroic adventure, the signified of the hunt topic in music, art, and literature was not the tempered and choreographed "sport" of contemporary practice but rather its gallant mythology (Monelle 2006: 70, 95, 65). Socially, as Monelle explains, there was a strong reason for eighteenth-century aristocrats, especially German aristocrats, to hunt:

> Hunting rights were confined to the landed nobility…In a time when wealth was being redistributed in favor of trade and the towns, it seemed vital to the aristocracy to preserve their exclusive right to hunt. This was what distinguished them, what confirmed their continuity with the landed aristocracy of the past. Ferocious penalties

were put in place against hunting by unauthorized persons. It seemed unthinkable that a "noble stag" could be hunted by a peasant or a townsman. Hunting was necessary for the self-identification of the nobility. (Monelle 2006: 64)

When we remember that quartet players were largely members of the aristocracy and that their power and privilege was increasingly under threat in the late eighteenth century, an uncontested musical projection of nobility, manliness, youth, and overcoming would seem considerably more attractive than one in which any of these indexicalities is challenged. In addition to the obvious musical and technical demands of the piece, Mozart's excursions to the Alps and learned flirtations may also have taken quartet players and their listeners expressively too far afield—to an affectation of the pastoral and the marked high style of the ecclesiastical. Such expressive dissonance presents considerable interpretive challenges alongside the technical.

To put it directly, in Mozart's Opus 10, too much control over the construction of meaning is delegated to the players and listeners, and at times, as in the Minuetto of K. 464, amateur topical competency might not be up to the job. Among the *chasse* movements discussed here, the three most commercially viable ones (and for quartets in the late eighteenth century, we must remember that commercially viable means "will sell well among the wealthy")—Haydn's and Pleyel's—offered hunts without topical dissonance, expressive contest, or structural complication. Of those three, only two—Pleyel's—provided a musical experience that was not just technically but also interpretively undemanding. With exceptionally light parametric density and complete avoidance of topical troping and expressive dissonance, Pleyel's quartets relieved the players and their listeners from interpretive responsibility.

Notes

1. Leopold Mozart, letter of 13 August 1778 to his son Wolfgang. The translation here is by Mark Evan Bonds (2007: 221–22).
2. Joseph Haydn, letter of 3 December 1781 to J. C. Lavater, in Landon's (1978: 454) translation.
3. Carl Dittersdorf, letter of 18 August 1788 to Artaria: "und bin sicher, daß Sie sich bey meinen wegen den lucrum cessans der Mozartischen (welche zwar bey mir so wei bey noch größern Theoretiquern alle Hochachtung verdienen, aber wegen der allzugroßen darinen beständig herrschenden Kunst nicht Jedermanns Kauf seyn) erhollen werden" (Eva Badura-Skoda 1988: 47).
4. Bonds interprets this publication record somewhat differently, arguing that "Op. 10 sold reasonably well in its time, particularly in light of its high retail cost" (2007: 222).
5. Dozens of recordings of Mozart's Opus 10 string quartets are commercially available today. At the time of writing, not one recording of a single of Pleyel's Opus 1 quartets is commercially available, and to my knowledge, there is only one recording of the Opus 2 quartets.
6. Bonds, for example, describes Pleyel's Op. 1 quartets as "unassuming" (2007: 202) and "relentlessly homophonic" (210) "with very little in the way of harmonic complexity or counterpoint" (2008: 44).

7. On scholarly discomfort with the speculative nature of musical analysis and interpretation, see Lowe (2007: 14–19).
8. Wye Allanbrook suggests that "the motto seems to be a deliberate attempt to signal 'minuet.' Its percussive repeated notes in thick chordal texture intensify the dance's traditional even movement and restraint, in addition to protecting the dance against the distortion of a rapid and light execution" (1983: 34). Pleyel presents the "motto" rhythm without note repetition and thick chordal texture.
9. On the concept of topical tropes, see Hatten (2004) and his chapter in this volume.
10. For a more complete description of the musical elements and expressive aspects of the classic minuet dance type, along with a discussion of the relevant eighteenth-century sources, see Lowe (2002: 172–78).
11. In the eighteenth-century musical marketplace, string quartet parts were considerably more expensive than other domestic genres. The demand for this music was generated primarily by wealthy amateur players.
12. For a richer investigation of the sociopolitical aspects of the late eighteenth-century minuet, including interpretations of the minuet movements in Haydn's Symphonies Nos. 23, 3, and 99 and in Mozart's Symphony in G minor, K. 550, see Lowe (2007: 99–132).
13. On the opposition of pathos and bathos, see Hatten (1994: 74–82).
14. For discussion of eighteenth-century dance minuets, see Lowe (2002: 182–87).
15. For a detailed description of the musical characteristics of the hunt topic, see Monelle (2006: 35–110).
16. Bonds's (2007: 210) comment on this aspect of Pleyel's style is worth noting (not only for its amusing turn of phrase): "Pleyel's sonata-form movements sound even longer than they are for the simple reason that they suffer from a superabundance of repetition. For Pleyel, anything worth saying once is worth saying twice."
17. Janet Levy suggests that certain presentational passages provide the listener a "double psychic economy," as when, for example, we hear familiar accompanimental patterns in presentational passages: "because there is no question of what the passage *is,* we can relax and simply experience its unfolding" (1982: 489–92).
18. For a detailed description of the musical characteristics of the pastoral topic, see Monelle (2006: 185–271). On topical compatibility, see Hatten's chapter in this volume.
19. On the pastoral horn and *Alphorn* tunes, see Monelle (2006: 100–2).
20. Monelle notes the vocal horn call in Gherardello da Firenze's *caccia* "Tosto che l'alba." For more on hunts in early vocal music, see Monelle (2006: 72–74).
21. On the association of the horse with both hunting and nobility, see Monelle (2000: 41–80).

References

Allanbrook, Wye Jamison. 1983. *Rhythmic Gesture in Mozart:* Le nozze di Figaro *and* Don Giovanni. Chicago: University of Chicago Press.
——. 1996. "To Serve the Private Pleasure": Expression and Form in the String Quartets. In *Wolfgang Amadé Mozart: Essays on His Life and His Music,* ed. Stanley Sadie, 132–60. Oxford: Clarendon.
Badura-Skoda, Eva. 1988. Dittersdorf über Haydns und Mozarts Quartette. In *Collectanea Mozartiana,* ed. Cordula Roleff, 41–50. Tutzing: Schneider.

Benton, Rita. 1977. *Ignace Pleyel: A Thematic Catalogue of His Compositions*. New York: Pendragon.

Bonds, Mark Evan. 2007. Replacing Haydn: Mozart's "Pleyel" Quartets. *Music and Letters* 88/2: 201–25.

——. 2008. Listening to Listeners. In *Communication in Eighteenth-Century Music*, ed. Danuta Mirka and Kofi Agawu, 34–52. Cambridge: Cambridge University Press.

Feldtenstein, Carl Joseph von. 1767. *Die Kunst nach der Choreographie zu tanzen und Tänze zu schreiben*. Braunschweig: Schöder.

Finscher, Ludwig, and Wolf-Dieter Seiffert. 1993. *Neue Mozart-Ausgabe* VIII/20/Abt. 1/2: Streichquartette. Vol. 2. Kritischer Bericht. Kassel: Bärenreiter.

Hatten, Robert. 1994. *Musical Meaning in Beethoven: Markedness, Correlation, and Interpretation*. Bloomington: Indiana University Press.

——. 2004. *Interpreting Musical Gestures, Topics, and Tropes: Mozart, Beethoven, Schubert*. Bloomington: Indiana University Press.

van Hoboken, Anthony. 1957. *Joseph Haydn: Thematisch-bibliographisches Werkverzeichnis*. Vol. 1. Mainz: B. Schott's Söhne.

Irving, John. 1998. *Mozart: The "Haydn" Quartets*. Cambridge: Cambridge University Press.

Landon, H. C. Robbins. 1978. *Haydn: Chronicle and Works*. Vol. 2: *Haydn at Eszterháza 1766–1790*. Bloomington: Indiana University Press.

Levy, Janet. 1982. Texture as a Sign in Classic and Early Romantic Music. *Journal of the American Musicological Society* 35/3: 482–97.

Lowe, Melanie. 2002. Falling from Grace: Irony and Expressive Enrichment in Haydn's Symphonic Minuets. *Journal of Musicology* 19/1: 171–221.

——. 2007. *Pleasure and Meaning in the Classical Symphony*. Bloomington: Indiana University Press.

Monelle, Raymond. 2000. *The Sense of Music: Semiotic Essays*. Princeton: Princeton University Press.

——. 2006. *The Musical Topic: Hunt, Military and Pastoral*. Bloomington: Indiana University Press.

Sisman, Elaine. 1997. Genre, Gesture, and Meaning in Mozart's "Prague" Symphony. In *Mozart Studies* 2, ed. Cliff Eisen, 27–84. Oxford: Clarendon.

CHAPTER 24

EXPECTATION, MUSICAL TOPICS, AND THE PROBLEM OF AFFECTIVE DIFFERENTIATION

ELIZABETH HELLMUTH MARGULIS

SINCE Leonard Meyer (1956), music theorists have looked to expectation as a primary generator of musical affect. Huron and Margulis (2010) argue, in fact, that expectation has held a "privileged place" as a theorized source of music's affective impact. In a report that surveys the state of research on music and emotion, Juslin and Västfjäll (2008) lay out a framework of six basic cognitive mechanisms through which music can elicit an emotional response: expectation, brain stem reflexes, evaluative conditioning, emotional contagion, visual imagery, and episodic memory. Of these proposed mechanisms, only expectation depends essentially on musical structure. The structural elements that contribute to a musical topic's affective connotation, for example, are not well accounted for by the framework unless they are understood to arise through emotional contagion or repeated association with positive or negative stimuli (evaluative conditioning) or through the mediation of some kind of visual imagery. From the perspective of a music theorist, intellectually committed to the importance of structure in musical experience, its limited role in this proposed architecture of affective response is surprising. When it comes to evaluating the relationship between musical syntax and emotion, expectation has been asked to bear much of the burden of explanation.

What is musical expectation? It can be understood as a specific manifestation of a more general cognitive strategy. As documented by recent research in psychology, brains can be understood as organs of prediction (Hawkins and Blakeslee 2004); there is a general biological imperative to use information from the past to generate expectations about the future so that it can be adequately prepared for and effectively dealt with. Priming studies in language demonstrate that people allocate activation to words that are likely to appear in a sentence in advance of their appearance, such that reaction times and accuracy on questions about individual words are better if they have been primed by the preceding context. For example, responses are faster and more accurate for the word "pool" than the word "bathtub" in a sentence beginning "I swam in the" (McNamara 2005; Pickering and Branigan 1999). Many studies have adapted this methodology to music, identifying reaction time and accuracy advantages for harmonic (Bigand et al. 2003) and melodic continuations (Marmel, Tillmann, and Delbé 2010; Margulis and Levine 2006) that have been primed by their contexts. Tillmann and Bigand (2002) review experimental evidence for priming effects in both language and music.

These priming advantages represent evidence of implicit activation. It is not that a listener necessarily thinks "I'm expecting the word 'pool'" or "I think a G will come next." Rather, these expectational mechanisms can operate outside of the reach of consciousness, becoming most noticeable only when they are violated. Meyer's original theory adapted Dewey's conflict theory of emotions (1895) to claim that affect arises when a tendency is blocked. The general claim is that listeners generate expectations without being aware they are doing so. When these implicit expectations are violated, they experience some kind of affect.

But what has remained challengingly unclear is just what kind of affect that might be. The experience of listening to music does not seem merely like a series of smaller and larger surprises. Quite the contrary, music can seem intense, expansive, gloomy, and any of a thousand other qualities. Margulis (2005, 2007a) distinguishes between three types of expectation-based tension—the tension of having a strong expectation, for example, which might register as a sort of forward-directedness in the music, versus the tension of an expectation being violated, which might register as a sort of attention-grabbing intensity—but the range of this taxonomy is insufficiently wide to encompass the diverse affective impressions music elicits. Huron (2006) offers a much broader account, linking expectation to experiences as diverse as musical humor, awe, and chills. But Schubert (2003) identifies forty-six affective adjectives frequently used to describe musical passages. How can the single phenomenon of surprise result in the felt experience of so many different qualities?

This study follows up on an intuition of Danuta Mirka (2009: 303 n. 20) that a separate line of work in music theory on musical topics might be relevant to the diversity of emotional responses evoked by violation of expectation. Although the rest of this volume explores this subject matter in more nuanced ways, a simple definition will suffice for the purposes of this chapter: after Ratner (1980), a musical topic can be defined as a type of music with references to styles and genres familiar from eighteenth-century musical life. It is assumed that eighteenth-century listeners would have recognized such references and grasped the associations of topics with the affects or social and cultural meanings of the styles and genres from which they were derived. In this way topics would have provided expressive context for the aspects of the listening experience determined by musical structure and would have served as important elements in the ongoing musical discourse. Many of these topics continue to carry affective connotations for twenty-first-century listeners. Their associations are underscored by pairings with relevant text in songs and opera, and by their pairing with relevant imagery and events in film, television, and commercials. Moreover, individual topics may exploit various of the mechanisms proposed by Juslin and Västfjäll (such as emotional contagion, where expressive qualities in the music iconically mimic normal properties of emotional expression and induce the associated feeling in the listener) to establish appropriate affective associations.

Given the (over)reliance on expectation as a mechanism connecting musical structure and musical affect, how might the problem of differentiation of affect be addressed? It is possible that it cannot be, except by appealing to some alternative mechanism, something other than expectation. But it is also possible that musical context, such as musical topics, might provide a sort of filter through which syntactic surprises are expressively interpreted.

As shown in Figure 24.1, the same syntactic surprise, when positioned in a different topical context, might be registered phenomenologically as tender or playful or majestic or agitated or something else. The idea is that syntax determines the surprise, but topic determines the way that surprise is felt and experienced.

This claim is related to but distinct from the notion that topics are associated with particular expressive connotations. Previous work on the psychology of musical topics (Krumhansl 1996, 1998) has revealed that topics affect perception even in listeners without special training. Changes in topics are registered as the beginnings of new ideas, and are correlated with openness, memorability, and emotional intensity ratings. The relationship between topics and more static aspects of musical affect seems uncontroversial; specific topics conjure up specific affective worlds, and should influence the perceived expressive character of passages, sections, or pieces featuring them. By way of

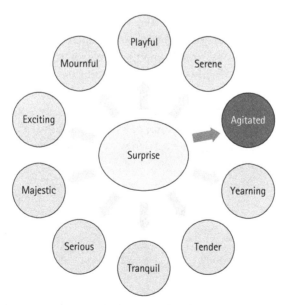

FIGURE 24.1 The same syntactic surprise, positioned within a different topical context, might be registered phenomenologically as playful or agitated or something else. The topical context might be understood to tip the syntactic surprise in a particular interpretive direction (illustrated by the darkened arrow).

contrast to these more static aspects of musical affect, this study aims to delve more into the dynamic, moment-to-moment affective fluctuations characteristic of musical listening, and to understand the way topics might partner with mechanisms of expectation to generate a more differentiated experience than expectational accounts have previously been able to provide. The idea is that particular topics cause syntactic surprises to be experienced variously as moments of increased playfulness or tenderness or excitement or any other affect, depending on the topic within which the surprise is embedded.

To investigate this claim, participants without special musical training were recruited to listen to excerpts from eighteenth-century string quartets (some of which were transcriptions for string quartet from other eighteenth-century genres). The excerpts were prepared so that they could occur in one of two versions: normative or surprising. In the surprising versions, a pause had been inserted after the cadential six-four chord. While the participants listened to these excerpts, they moved a joystick forward or back to indicate fluctuating impressions along a particular affective dimension. On one-fourth of the trials, they continually rated the music's ominousness; on one-fourth of the trials, its playfulness; on one-fourth of the trials, its sublimity; and on the remaining one-fourth of the trials, its tension. Unbeknownst to the participants, each of the excerpts represented one of four musical topics: *tempesta*, the brilliant style, the singing style, and siciliano. The hypothesis was that the surprising event—the general pause—would result in increased ratings along a particular affective dimension only when it occurred in the appropriate topical context. General pauses were selected as the surprising event because they could remain invariant from context to context, and represent a compositional gambit broadly characteristic of eighteenth-century music. The goal was to preserve maximal equivalence of the structural disruption across the excerpts in order to isolate as much as possible the role of the surrounding context (topics). The same musical surprise, in other words, might be interpreted as ominous in one context but playful in another. The hypothesis relevant to this study was not that excerpts included in a particular topical category would be perceived as overall more evocative of one affect than another but, rather, that the surprising event—the pause—would be interpreted as a momentary intensification of a particular kind of affect depending on the context. The phenomenological experience of the surprise itself, in other words, would vary from context to context.

METHOD

Participants

Thirty-two members of the University of Cambridge community were recruited from flyers posted in the Student Union. Their mean age was twenty-four ($SD = 3$). Simply by virtue of the idiosyncrasies of the population that responded to the flyer, eight of the participants were men and twenty-four of the participants were women. Although there

is no particular reason to expect that women and men would perform the task differently, it would be ideal in the future to repeat the study with a more balanced distribution of male and female participants.

The flyer expressly indicated that no musical training was required. The participants
who enrolled varied in background with six reporting no musical training of any sort,
and four participants reporting over ten years of lessons or ensemble participation. The
average participant had two or three years of music lessons as a child. None of the participants were music majors, and debriefing after the experiment revealed that none had
been trained in the theory of musical topics. None of the participants considered themselves expert musicians.

Materials

In an effort to choose musical topics with maximal expressive distance from one
another, a two-dimensional representation of affect, the circumplex model, was consulted (Russell 1980; Posner, Russell, and Peterson 2005). According to this model, affective responses can be organized in a two-dimensional space with arousal (high or low
amount of energy) along the y-axis and valence (negative or positive) along the x-axis.
Anger, for example, can be conceptualized as high arousal and negative valence, whereas
sadness might be understood as low arousal and negative valence. Excitement might be
thought of as high arousal and positive valence, and contentment as low arousal and
positive valence.

As shown in Figure 24.2, four musical topics were selected to represent each of the
four quadrants: *tempesta* for high arousal and negative valence; siciliano for low arousal
and negative valence; brilliant style for high arousal and positive valence; and singing
style for low arousal and positive valence. Although this positioning within the spectrum of affective connotations is not essential to the theory espoused here, it was a useful aid for selecting topics with maximum expressive difference from one another.

Excerpts representative of each topic were chosen, and appropriate opportunities
for insertion of a pause (always following the cadential six-four chord) were identified in close consultation with Danuta Mirka. Many of the excerpts have been expressly

Arousal \ Valence	Negative	Positive
High	*Tempesta* Mozart, Piano Concerto in D minor, K. 466/i, mm. 1–16 Beethoven, String Quartet in C minor, Op. 18 No. 4/i, mm. 1–13	Brilliant style Haydn, String Quartet in G major, Op. 64 No. 4/i, mm. 84–99 Haydn, String Quartet in E flat major, Op. 33 No. 2, "Joke," i, mm. 80–90
Low	Siciliano Mozart, String Quartet in D minor, K. 421/iv, mm. 1–8 Mozart, Piano Sonata in F major, K. 280/ii, mm. 1–8	Singing style Haydn, Symphony No. 64 in A major, "Tempora Mutantur," ii, mm. 1–9 Gluck, *Orfeo ed Euridice*, "Che farò senza Euridice," mm. 1–14

FIGURE 24.2 The selected topics and associated excerpts laid out in the two-dimensional
affective space of the circumplex model.

identified as representative of particular topics in the existing literature. Gluck's aria "Che farò senza Euridice" is treated as a paramount example of the singing style by Ratner (1980: 19), and the first phrases of the slow movement of Haydn's Symphony No. 64 are characterized in terms of this style by Mirka (2012). Mozart's minor-mode sicilianos in Piano Sonata in F major, K. 280/ii, and String Quartet in D minor, K. 421/iv, are discussed by Robert Hatten in this volume, and the latter is shown by Ratner (1980: 16). These excerpts, in both normative and surprising versions, were notated into Finale, and transcribed for string quartet, where necessary, by Haley Beverburg Reale. In the case of the excerpt from Haydn's Symphony No. 64, the original version already featured a grand pause, so the recomposed version eliminated the pause to create a "normative" version. The grand pauses in this piece are given close scrutiny by Sisman (1990) and Mirka (2012).

Performances of these excerpts by the Grantchester String Quartet, a quartet composed of University of Cambridge undergraduates James Wicks, Emma Gait, Alice Cane, and Elizabeth Edwards, were recorded by engineer Daniel Halford in a studio at the Faculty of Music in the University of Cambridge.

The normative excerpts were on average 36 s long ($SD = 6$); the surprising excerpts 38 s ($SD = 6$). The mean length of the surprising event (the pause) was 1.8 s ($SD = .8$).

Procedure

Participants moved a slider forward and back to indicate fluctuating perceptions along a specific affective dimension dynamically, as the music progressed. They were instructed to move the slider gradually, responding to moment-by-moment changes in the music. Affective dimensions were selected to occupy each of the four quadrants on the two-dimensional space in Figure 24.2: tension for high arousal and negative valence (*tempesta*); ominousness for low arousal and negative valence (siciliano); playfulness for high arousal and positive valence (brilliant style); and sublimity for low arousal and positive valence (singing style). The hypothesis was that only surprises in excerpts using the musical topic associated with that quadrant would elevate ratings along that dimension. For example, a pause should elevate impressions of tension in the *tempesta* style, but impressions of playfulness in excerpts in the brilliant style. Clive McClelland and Roman Ivanovitch (this volume) explore, respectively, the connotations that might link *tempesta* with tension and the brilliant style with playfulness. Minor-mode sicilianos have often been linked with melancholy, and melancholy, in turn, with thoughts of death, appearances of ghosts, and hallucinations of visitations from the dead (Wald 2007), thus leading to the proposed association between this topic and ominousness. Although the singing style was not associated with the eighteenth-century notion of the sublime, which implied fear and terror, the meaning of sublimity suggested to the twenty-first century participants—pleasing impressions of great beauty—is consistent with this style's characteristics as described by Sarah Day-O'Connell in this volume.

Experimental sessions lasted one hour. Participants were seated at a computer terminal in a sound-isolated booth and outfitted with Sennheiser headphones. They answered five minutes of questions related to demographics and their musical background before proceeding to the first set of trials. Each block of trials involved rating a particular affective dimension—ominousness, playfulness, sublimity, or tension—but the order of these blocks was randomized. Some participants, in other words, rated all the excerpts first for sublimity; others rated them all first for ominousness, and so forth.

During each of the four blocks, participants started by reading a set of instructions about the task and performing a practice trial. They then proceeded to the experimental trials, in which all sixteen excerpts (eight normative and eight surprising) were presented in random order (subject to the constraint that two versions of a single excerpt could never follow one another immediately in succession) while participants continually rated them along the affective dimension featured in that block. The dimensions were blocked in this way so that rather than jumping from thinking about excerpts in one way to thinking about them in another, participants could concentrate on the particular dimension at hand. Between each of the four blocks, participants were invited to take a short break.

All stimuli were presented and responses collected using MediaLab (Jarvis 2006a) running on Windows XP via Parallels Desktop on a 13" MacBook Pro. The joystick was connected to the machine via a USB port. MediaLab called DirectRT (Jarvis 2006b) during the experimental trials, and that program tracked joystick position every 20 ms.

RESULTS

Although the task required a high degree of concentration, and asked participants to rate music in unfamiliar ways, during post-session debriefing most participants remarked on how much they had enjoyed the session, several even asking for a CD of the recordings that had been used. This positive response suggested that participants had been able to marshal attention and stay engaged throughout the session.

Intersubject correlations assess the degree to which participants' responses are similar to one another. For these data, correlations were on the order of $r(30866) = .35$. As discussed in Krumhansl (1998), these correlations are difficult to interpret for continuous response data because of the high degrees of freedom. However, previous studies including Krumhansl (1998) have identified this level of correlation as sufficient to warrant averaging across subjects. Accordingly, participants' ratings were grouped together to produce a mean response for each moment of each excerpt across all thirty-two participants.

A typical result is shown in Figure 24.3. The solid line indicates mean sublimity ratings across the course of the normative version of the excerpt from the first movement of Haydn's "Joke" quartet; the dotted line indicates mean sublimity ratings across the course of the surprising version of the same excerpt. For such a seemingly difficult and

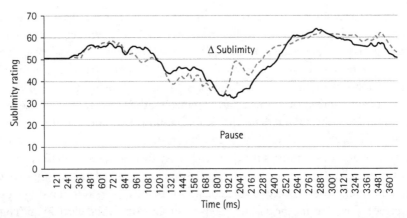

FIGURE **24.3** Mean sublimity ratings across the course of the excerpt from the first movement of Haydn's String Quartet in E flat major, Op. 33 No. 2/i. The solid line indicates ratings for the normative version of the excerpt; the dotted line indicates ratings for the surprising version of the excerpt.

subjective task, the ratings follow one another quite closely across the course of the excerpt, dipping and peaking at roughly the same points; however, at the position where the pause was inserted, the ratings diverge noticeably, with the dotted line jutting suddenly upward, indicating an increase in perceived sublimity.

The change in ratings across the course of the pause (marked Δ Sublimity on the figure) was compared with the change in ratings across the correlated time course in the normative excerpt. Calculating Δ Rating$_{surprise}$–Δ Rating$_{normative}$ (where "rating" could be sublimity, ominousness, playfulness, or tension rating, according to the dimension under consideration) produced a measure of the extra amount of affect along this dimension generated by the surprising event.

A repeated measures ANOVA was carried out using this rating change as a dependent variable, and excerpt category (normative versus surprising) as an independent variable. For the excerpt shown in Figure 24.3, for example, the difference was significant, $F(1,31) = 15.08$, $p = .001$. Associating the affective dimension from each quadrant of the two-dimensional representation with the topic representing that quadrant linked *tempesta* (high arousal, negative valence) with tension; siciliano (low arousal, negative valence) with ominousness; the singing style (low arousal, positive valence) with sublimity; and the brilliant style (high arousal, positive valence) with playfulness. A repeated measures ANOVA examining change in rating across the length of the pause was carried out for each excerpt for each dimension. Significant increases were predicted only along the associated dimension for the topic at hand; the pause should elevate tension ratings, for example, only for excerpts in the *tempesta* style.

Table 24.1 lists the results of the repeated-measures ANOVA for each excerpt where ratings along a particular dimension increased across the course of the surprising pause. The prediction was that, for each dimension, there would be two excerpts where the pause generated a significant increase in ratings: the two excerpts featuring

Table 24.1 The Excerpts for Which Pauses Resulted in Elevations of Ratings Along One of the Four Dimensions, and Associated F-Values for the Difference.

Sublimity

Siciliano–Mozart, String Quartet in D minor, K. 421/iv	$F(1,31) = 12.29$, $p = .001$
Singing–Haydn, Symphony No. 64/ii	$F(1,31) = 6.53$, $p = .016$
Brilliant–Haydn, String Quartet in E flat major, Op. 33 No. 2/i	$F(1,31) = 15.08$, $p = .001$

Ominousness

Siciliano–Mozart, String Quartet in D minor, K. 421/iv	$F(1,31) = 6.97$, $p = .013$
Siciliano–Mozart, Piano Sonata in F major, K. 280/ii	$F(1,31) = 8.03$, $p = .008$

Tension

Tempesta–Beethoven, String Quartet in C minor, Op. 18 No. 4/i	$F(1,31) = 4.92$, $p = .034$

Playfulness

Brilliant–Haydn, String Quartet in E flat major, Op. 33 No. 2/i	$F(1,31) = 7.59$, $p = .01$

the associated topical context. Figure 24.4 compares these predictions with the actual results.

The pause was associated with an increase in tension ratings in one of the predicted *tempesta* examples and none of the excerpts involving other topics. The pause was associated with an increase in ominousness ratings in both of the predicted siciliano excerpts and none of the others. It was associated with an increase in playfulness ratings in one of the predicted excerpts in the brilliant style and none of the others. For sublimity ratings, however, the pause was associated with an increase not only in one of the predicted

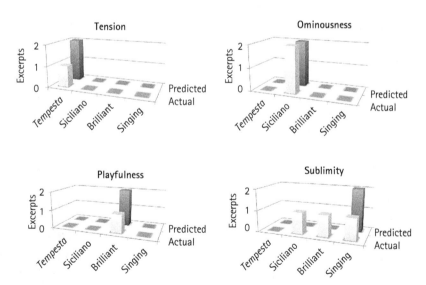

FIGURE 24.4 Predicted (back row) versus actual (front row) statistically significant rating increases for excerpts in each of the four topical categories along each of the four affective dimensions.

excerpts in the singing style but also in one of the excerpts in the brilliant style and one of the excerpts using the siciliano topic.

Discussion

These results are broadly consistent with the notion that musical topics might serve as a kind of funnel through which syntactic surprises are affectively differentiated. They provide preliminary evidence that topical context can influence the way musical surprise *feels*. Although pauses did not consistently elevate tension in the predicted *tempesta* topic, when they did elevate tension, it occurred only within that context. The same held for playfulness: pauses did not consistently elevate perceived playfulness within the brilliant style, but if a pause increased perceptions of playfulness, it was within this topical context. And for excerpts using the siciliano topic, pauses always increased perceptions of ominousness, with no other topical context triggering elevated ratings for this quality.

In the case of sublimity ratings, however, pauses sometimes elevated ratings not only within the expected context of the singing style but also within excerpts using the brilliant style and the siciliano topic. One way of understanding this result implicates the event used as the proxy for syntactic surprise: the pause. It is possible that something about pauses can seem sublime regardless of topical context. Rapid changes in texture and loudness have consistently been shown to correlate with the experience of chills (Grewe et al. 2007; Guhn, Hamm, and Zentner 2007; Panskepp 1995, 1998), and sublimity, in turn, has been associated with chills (Konečni 2005). The sudden reduction of loudness and texture, then, may have been perceived as sublime, independent of any expressly syntactic surprise.

It is also possible that sublimity was a less familiar and more awkward concept to apply to music listening; perhaps listeners were simply less capable of reliably applying this descriptive; however, if this were the case, intersubject correlations for sublimity ratings should be lower than for the other ratings, or correlations between individual subjects' sublimity ratings on the surprise and normative renditions of each excerpt should be lower. Since neither of these happened, the explanation associating pauses, chills, and impressions of sublimity seems more plausible.

It is important to note that this study has several substantial limitations. First, it employed only one kind of syntactic surprise: a pause after the cadential six-four chord. It is possible that such an event is actually more likely, and therefore less surprising, in particular topical contexts. This would introduce a confound—*degree* of surprise—that would vary from trial to trial, making interpretation more difficult than if an event with precisely the same amount of surprise had been inserted into every excerpt. This kind of control, however, is hard to introduce into music with sufficient ecological validity to elicit reportable perceptions of fluctuation along affective dimensions. Pauses were viewed as the best possible token surprise because they are semirealistic—such pauses really *do* happen in eighteenth-century music, as demonstrated by the excerpt from Haydn's Symphony No. 64—yet they are statistically uncommon, and should still count as surprising. Moreover, they could be inserted in the same basic form from excerpt to excerpt, unlike a surprising harmony, for example, which would have to be adjusted to match the surrounding texture and motivic material. And pauses were furthermore selected because studies had already investigated their perceptual ramifications (Margulis 2007b, 2007c) and stylistic properties (Mirka 2009). But since only pauses were examined, it remains possible that topics influence the perception of pauses specifically, not the perception of syntactic surprises more generally. The only way to eliminate this alternative explanation is to run additional studies that use different kinds of surprise than the general pause.

Additionally, this study used only eighteenth-century music written or transcribed for string quartet. To increase confidence about the generalizability of the results, it should be replicated using different kinds of music, different topics, and different affective dimensions. A useful survey of topics in nineteenth- and twentieth-century music can be found in Agawu (2009).

The particular topics and affective dimensions used in this study were chosen in order to gain as wide a spread along the two-dimensional representation of affective responses as possible, in order to have a better chance of establishing an effect. Future studies should sample the range of topics and possible affective responses more thoroughly. It would also be helpful to replicate the results using a measure other than continuous response joystick movements. This methodology was judged easiest to access subtle, dynamic, moment-to-moment impressions, but it would be good to have postexcerpt question responses, for example, to correlate with the continuous response data.

In summary, this study offers preliminary evidence for a potential solution to the differentiation problem for expectation-based theories of musical affect. It has long been a problem for such theories to account for the way that various amounts or kinds of surprise might correlate with all the rich and diverse affective impressions listeners have of music. This study suggests that context, in the form of musical topics, might filter musical surprise such that it is phenomenologically registered as any of a number of affective responses.

This study also serves as an example of the way it might be productive to think about how different strands in music theory might be woven together. In this case, expectancy theory and topic theory, each with its own robust and relatively isolated body of literature, could be profitably understood to relate to one another through the lens of experimental psychology. By examining what topics and expectations might really mean for ordinary listener experience, these two theoretical stances could be brought together. This potential for theoretical exchange may characterize many corners of music theory that generally consider themselves quite independent. Given concerns about fragmentation in music research (see Korsyn 2003), this perspective seems particularly welcome.

Acknowledgment

The author would like to thank Ian Cross, Sarah Hawkins, and all the members of the Centre for Music and Science at the University of Cambridge for their support during this project. The author would also like to thank the Fulbright College of the University of Arkansas for the year of fellowship support, and Danuta Mirka for the many ideas, especially about stimuli.

REFERENCES

Agawu, Kofi. 2009. *Music as Discourse: Semiotic Adventures in Romantic Music*. New York: Oxford University Press.

Bigand, Emmanuel, Bénédicte Poulin, Barbara Tillmann, François Madurell, and Daniel A. D'Adamo. 2003. Sensory versus Cognitive Components in Harmonic Priming. *Journal of Experimental Psychology: Human Perception and Performance* 29: 159–71.

Dewey, John. 1895. The Theory of Emotion. *Psychological Review* 2: 13–32.

Grewe, Oliver, Frederik Nagel, Reinhard Kopiez, and Eckart Altenmüller. 2007. Listening to Music as a Re-Creative Process: Physiological, Psychological, and Psychoacoustical Correlates of Chills and Strong Emotions. *Music Perception* 24: 297–314.

Guhn, Martin, Alfons Hamm, and Marcel Zentner. 2007. Physiological and Musico-Acoustic Correlates of the Chill Response. *Music Perception* 24: 473–83.

Hawkins, Jeff, and Sandra Blakeslee. 2004. *On Intelligence*. New York: Times.

Huron, David. 2006. *Sweet Anticipation: Music and the Psychology of Expectation*. Cambridge, MA: MIT Press.

Huron, David, and Elizabeth H. Margulis. 2010. Musical Expectancy and Thrills. In *Handbook of Music and Emotion: Theory, Research, Applications*, ed. Patrik N. Juslin and John A. Sloboda, 575–604. New York: Oxford University Press.

Jarvis, Blair G. 2006a. *MediaLab*. [Computer Software]. New York: Empirisoft.

———. 2006b. *DirectRT*. [Computer Software]. New York: Empirisoft.

Juslin, Patrik N., and Daniel Västfjäll. 2008. Emotional Responses to Music: The Need to Consider Underlying Mechanisms. *Behavioral and Brain Sciences* 31: 559–621.

Konečni, Vladimir J. 2005. The Aesthetic Trinity: Awe, Being Moved, Thrills. *Bulletin of Psychology and the Arts* 5: 27–44.

Korsyn, Kevin. 2003. *Decentering Music: A Critique of Contemporary Musical Research*. New York: Oxford University Press.

Krumhansl, Carol L. 1996. A Perceptual Analysis of Mozart's Piano Sonata K. 282: Segmentation, Tension, and Musical Ideas. *Music Perception* 13: 401–32.

Margulis, Elizabeth H. 2005. A Model of Melodic Expectation. *Music Perception* 22: 663–714.

———. 2007a. Surprise and Listening Ahead: Analytic Engagements with Musical Tendencies. *Music Theory Spectrum* 29: 197–217.

———. 2007b. Moved by Nothing: Listening to Musical Silence. *Journal of Music Theory* 51: 245–76.

———. 2007c. Silences in Music Are Musical Not Silent: An Exploratory Study of Context Effects on the Experience of Musical Pauses. *Music Perception* 24: 485–506.

Margulis, Elizabeth H., and William Levine. 2006. Timbre Priming Effects and Expectation in Melody. *Journal of New Music Research* 35: 175–82.

Marmel, Frédéric, Barbara Tillmann, and Charles Delbé. 2010. Priming in Melody Perception: Tracking Down the Strength of Cognitive Expectations. *Journal of Experimental Psychology: Human Perception and Performance* 36: 1016–28.

McNamara, Timothy P. 2005. *Semantic Priming: Perspectives from Memory and Word Recognition.* New York: Psychology Press.

Meyer, Leonard B. 1956. *Emotion and Meaning in Music.* Chicago: University of Chicago Press.

Mirka, Danuta. 2009. *Metric Manipulations in Haydn and Mozart.* New York: Oxford University Press.

———. 2012. Absent Cadences. *Eighteenth-Century Music* 9/2: 213–35.

Panksepp, Jaak. 1998. *Affective Neuroscience: The Foundations of Human and Animal Emotions.* Oxford: Oxford University Press.

———. 1995. The Emotional Sources of "Chills" Induced by Music. *Music Perception* 13: 171–207.

Pickering, Martin J., and Holly P. Branigan. 1999. Syntactic Priming in Language Production. *Trends in Cognitive Science* 3/4: 136–41.

Posner, Jonathan, James A. Russell, and Bradley S. Peterson. 2005. The Circumplex Model of Affect: An Integrative Approach to Affective Neuroscience, Cognitive Development, and Psychopathology. *Developmental Psychopathology* 17: 715–34.

Ratner, Leonard. 1980. *Classic Music: Expression, Form, and Style.* New York: Schirmer.

Russell, James A. 1980. A Circumplex Model of Affect. *Journal of Personality and Social Psychology* 39: 1161–78.

Sisman, Elaine. 1990. Haydn's Theater Symphonies. *Journal of the American Musicological Society* 43/2: 292–352.

Tillmann, Barbara, and Emmanuel Bigand. 2002. A Comparative Review of Priming Effects in Language and Music. In *Language, Vision, and Music,* ed. Paul McKevitt, Sean O'Nuallain, and Conn Mullvihill, 231–40. Amsterdam: John Benjamins.

Wald, M. 2007. Melancholie in Mozarts Instrumentalmusik: Biographische Legende oder ästhetische Praxis? *Acta Mozartiana* 54/1–2: 31–53.

CHAPTER 25

LISTENING TO TOPICS IN THE NINETEENTH CENTURY

JULIAN HORTON

HISTORICAL AND THEORETICAL CONTEXTS

Problems of Topical Analysis and Nineteenth-Century Music

TOPIC theory's efficacy as a tool for understanding eighteenth-century music arises in large measure from its ability to bridge the gaps between analysis, hermeneutics, and history. Whereas other approaches fall prey to accusations of hermeticism, topical analysis can speak simultaneously to formal and social concerns—in Kofi Agawu's terms, to music's introversive and extroversive dimensions (Agawu 1991). Leonard Ratner's well-known formulation of the eighteenth-century topical universe as "a thesaurus of *characteristic figures*" (Ratner 1980: 9), drawn from music's various social functions and occurring either as whole-movement types or intramovement styles, captures this productive bifocality: the thesaurus that Ratner describes at once marks out the terrain of eighteenth-century musical style and embodies tangibly the society from which it arose. The theory's credentials are therefore at base historicist: unlike (for example) Schenkerian theory, which in its eighteenth-century applications courts anachronism in its imposition of an organicist mentality on a pre-idealist repertoire, topical approaches coordinate analysis with the music's historical context.

As we enter the nineteenth century, however, these credentials become as problematic as they are advantageous. The critical difficulty is that theory and context no longer align in the way that Ratner describes: topics acquire a conflicted identity in nineteenth-century music, the sense of which is captured in Agawu's remark that, although "there is ... a level of continuity between eighteenth- and nineteenth-century styles that would undermine historical narratives posited on the existence of a categorical distinction between them," it is nevertheless "equally problematic ... to assert a straightforward historical continuity in the way topics are used" (Agawu 2009: 42). On the one hand, the eighteenth-century thesaurus persists, but in changed social circumstances, and this renders attempts to read topical discourse as social commentary irreducibly complex. For the generation of composers born in the first two decades of the nineteenth century, classical topics had themselves become historicized, and were thus received less as markers of social meaning, and more as conventions defining an emerging tradition. On the other hand, nineteenth-century composers also devised fresh topics, which as facets of a new style are conceptually opposed to topics associated with the classical past.

The radical transformation of music's relationship to its social context after 1800 reflects seismic political, social, and cultural upheavals, which necessitate reevaluation of the "contacts with worship, poetry, drama, entertainment, dance, ceremony, the military, the hunt, and the life of the lower classes" that Ratner (1980: 9) nominates. For instance, the musical embodiment of social class in 1750 hardly prevails a hundred years later: we have by this time to account for the expansion of the urban working class and bourgeoisie in the wake of industrialization, as well as the accelerating commodification of music and the transference of high-musical culture's curation from aristocratic to bourgeois hands. Such changes compel reappraisal of apparent continuities. Deployment of the pastoral style in, for example, the "Pifa" from Part I of Handel's *Messiah* and Liszt's *Les préludes* might indicate superficial stylistic affinities (compound meter, major modality, drone bass), but these qualities have to be understood against the backdrop of sharply contrasted social contexts: the "other" of Liszt's pastoral music is an industrialized urban landscape that Handel could scarcely have imagined.

Military music affords particularly clear evidence of these developments. Postclassical continuities are of course manifest: Agawu's observation that marches by Beethoven, Mendelssohn, Berlioz, Schumann, Liszt, and Mahler all express "a mode of utterance that is irreducibly social and communal" is well taken (Agawu 2009: 42; see also Monelle 2006: 113–81). These similarities, however, conceal shifts in social meaning: a march written in 1770 carries very different connotations than one written after the French Revolution and the Napoleonic Wars, or after the revolutions of 1848 or the Franco-Prussian War of 1871. Brief comparison of three examples—the slow movement of Haydn's "Military" Symphony (1793–94), the finale of Beethoven's Fifth Symphony (1808), and the fourth movement of Berlioz's *Symphonie fantastique* (1830)—makes plain the extent and speed of such reorientations. The martial topic of Haydn's slow movement expresses a stylized militarism that resonates with Ratner's terms, drawing from the topical lexicon in order to present war as social convention. The Finale of Beethoven's Fifth, in contrast, reconstrues the march as an agent of utopianism: whereas Haydn reflects a social context through a topical style, Beethoven employs a topical style to imagine a new social context, achieved by locating the march as the goal of a formal narrative. Berlioz's "Marche au supplice" is even more distant from the classical thesaurus. The progress to the scaffold it narrates is inconceivable without the French-revolutionary experience, but its expressive stance is also a negation of Beethoven's idealism. The march becomes a vehicle for a characteristically romantic narrative, which turns the classical objectification of militarism (the march as a figure for "the military" in society) into an expression of subjective experience (the march as the context for an act committed against a protagonist), while also subverting the Beethovenian symphonic trajectory (the march signifies the protagonist's death, not his victory).

If nineteenth-century composers imbued eighteenth-century topics with fresh significance, then they also evolved new topics in response to novel expressive, technological, and social conditions. Various commentators have proposed nineteenth-century topical lexicons: Márta Grabócz and Kofi Agawu have advanced taxonomies for the music of Liszt and Mahler respectively (Grabócz 1996; Agawu 2009: 47); Janice Dickensheets (2003) has offered a more wide-ranging compendium, embracing music from Weber to Mahler.[1] Table 25.1 collates the novel topics suggested by these authors.

One topic that is only implicitly addressed here, but which is pivotal to the evolution of postclassical style, is the nocturne. Although this has characteristics of lied and *bel canto* styles, the circumstances of its development plead for a separate category, which is especially revealing in its combination of cultural and technological motivations. The nocturne's generic features—a piano miniature characterized by a melody and accompaniment division of labor, supporting song-like material often embellished in the *bel canto* manner—are established in the early nineteenth century by John Field and Chopin; but the genre's hallmarks precede Field, and arise notably in music by composers of the London pianoforte school before 1800 (for instance Dussek and Cramer), which in turn harnesses innovations in the design of the sustaining pedal, particularly as introduced by Broadwood, which allowed an arpeggiated or chordal tenor accompaniment to be distinguished registrally from the bass line.[2]

By the mid-nineteenth century, Field's nocturnes had acquired a seminal topical pedigree, notably for Franz Liszt, who considered them the forerunners of all characteristic piano genres "designed to portray subjective and profound emotion." In this respect, we can understand the nocturne as a topic serving a new sensibility, which valued subjectivity, lyricism, and the aesthetics of the fragment over classical generic conventions; as Liszt explained: "Field was the first to introduce a species which belonged to none of

Table 25.1 Nineteenth–Century Topics Collated from Agawu (2009), Grabócz (1996), and Dickensheets (2003)

1. Aria style	12. Folk style	22. Pantheistic style
2. Bardic style	13. *Grandioso*	23. Pathetic
3. *Bel canto* (singing/declaming)	14. *Gypsy music*	24. *Religioso*
4. Bird call	15. Heroic style	25. Scherzo
5. Bolero	16. Indianist style	26. Spanish style
6. *Biedermeier* style	17. Italian style	27. *Style hongrois*
7. Chinoiserie	18. Lamenting (elegiac)	28. *Stile appassionato*
8. Chivalric style	19. *Lied* style	29. Tempest style
9. Declamatory style	20. Lugubrious style (lament/	30. *Totentanz*
10. Demonic style	appassionato)	31. Virtuosic style
11. Fairy music	21. Nature theme	32. Waltz

the established classes, and in which feeling and melody reigned alone, liberated from the fetters and encumbrances of a coercive form" (1859: 5). The conditions enabling this innovation were organological and economic as much as aesthetic: they emerged from the convergence of technological change and the growth of a domestic market for collections of character pieces for piano, as much as in response to new ideals of genre and expression. As a topic, therefore, the nocturne behaves very much as Ratner determines: it functions either as a type (that is, as a whole-movement form), or as a style; it reflects a facet of contemporary cultural life, albeit one having retrospective justification in aesthetics rather than social function; and it embodies a set of textural and rhetorical properties. But as part of a topical universe, it falls on one side of a dialectic, the antithesis of which is the historicized lexicon of classical topics.

Topics, *Formenlehre*, and "Structural Listening"

A substantial account of these developments would need to address the complete gamut of attendant sociocultural factors, from music's emancipation from courtly function, the rise of autonomy, the work concept, and the historicization of past music, to the spread of philosophical idealism and the elite bourgeois culture that gained momentum in the wake of the industrial revolution and the Napoleonic Wars. A more realistic objective for present purposes is to trace the emergence of what Rose Rosengard Subotnik (1996) has dubbed "structural listening": the mode of musical engagement privileging structural cognition, to which shifts of topical practice are formatively indebted. Subotnik tracks this concept to the legacy of Schoenberg and Adorno, but its roots ultimately lay somewhat further back, in late eighteenth-century debates over the relative merits of *Kenner* and *Liebhaber*, or expert and amateur listeners. The progression of musical thought into the nineteenth century evinces a vigorous new estimation of expert listening, driven by an alliance between theory, criticism, and idealist philosophy, which alters fundamentally the conditions under which topics are deployed and comprehended.

As Matthew Riley has elaborated (2003; see also 2004: 87–120), a seminal conception of the *Kenner*'s elevated status was advanced by Johann Nikolaus Forkel. In *Ueber die Theorie der Musik* (1777), Forkel reassessed the value of immediacy: undoing earlier notions of the *Liebhaber* as a listener whose judgment has merit because it represents an immediate response to music's effects, Forkel instead construed *Liebhaber* as incapable of grasping the "most ordinary beauties": a lack of specialized knowledge meant that music's true nature "must remain hidden to anyone not possessing the correct ideas of its essence" (Forkel 1777: 9; Riley 2003: 421, translation modified). The cultivation of this understanding acquired urgency for Forkel, because he regarded it as the key to arresting a perceived decline in the compositional art. Crucially, Forkel (1778–79: v–x; see also Riley 2003: 421–22) placed musical rhetoric at the center of the education that the *Liebhaber* required if this trend was to be reversed.

By the mid-nineteenth century, more-or-less informal variants of Forkel's view had acquired widespread currency, as part of the body of thought that William Weber

(2008) has called "musical idealism." The new idealism had an international reach; as Weber (2008: 87) explains, it "sprang up in almost every major region of western and central Europe—save Italy for the most part—during the first half of the nineteenth century." Critics promulgated notions of informed listening, and promoted the repertoire to which it was appropriate, thereby propelling the establishment of the modern concert repertoire and prevailing conceptions of canon. This mode of thought was especially hostile to the miscellaneous programming of the eighteenth century, which mingled serious instrumental pieces with assemblages of opera arias, popular songs, and virtuoso compositions. Idealists favored instead the symphony concert as the principal public musical institution, and the chamber-music concert as its private counterpart, both underpinned by a canonical repertoire centered on Haydn, Mozart, and Beethoven.

The extent of this shift is exemplified by critical reactions in England, France, and the German lands. Thus in 1842 a critic responding to Henry Blagrove's London quartet concerts opined that they had "done more for the popularization of music in this town than any other. We do not want mobs of musicians, with drums, trumpets and cymbals...The musical quackery of the French School can do us no good: we wish to hear Beethoven, Mozart, Haydn and Handel simply and elegantly treated" (Weber 2008: 114). In Vienna, Ignaz Ritter von Mosel expressed a similar sentiment when he railed in 1818 against the "variations upon popular melodies that are nothing but gutter language" prevailing in contemporary concerts. Mosel also installed Mozart and Beethoven as ideal alternatives, while lamenting their marginal presence (Weber 2008: 117). And, notwithstanding the dominance of opera, an idealism focused on Viennese classicism also took hold in Paris thanks in part to the Conservatoire concerts, which, as Joseph D'Ortique noted, "are not a place to get together and chat, but a sanctuary to which the writer, the painter, all serious artists, flock" (Holoman 2004: 99).

Simultaneously, however, the pedagogy supporting informed listening shifted its focus from rhetoric to form. The early century's emergent *Formenlehre* increasingly valued the cognition of forms arising in a historicized repertoire over the interplay of rhetoric, key succession, and "schemata" (Gjerdingen 2007: 10–16; McCreless 2002; Burnham 2002). This reorientation is apparent in Carl Czerny's widely influential *School of Practical Composition*, first published (in translation) in 1848. Although what Ratner would identify as topics are regular participants in Czerny's theory, rhetoric as such has no independent theoretical status. Instead, Czerny nominates three basic compositional requirements: *originality* (a piece's "ideas and figures must be original, and at the same time also beautiful and effective"); *grammar* (a piece must "observe all the rules of pure composition"); and *form* (a piece "must have the regular form and construction which are stipulated by the species to which it belongs, and which, since the birth of modern music, have been established by the works of all good masters"). The third requirement supplies Czerny's operative concept: the treatise as a whole progresses systematically through the "species" evident in solo, chamber, orchestral, and vocal composition, reflecting the perception that any composition "must...belong to a species already in existence"; and each species is defined above all by its constituent forms, since "in order

Table 25.2 Czerny's Six Categories of Species

Category: Piano Music	Instrumental Music	Solo Vocal Music	Opera	Sacred Music	Semi-Sacred
Species: 1. Sonata allegro	1. Duets, trios etc.	1. Song	1. Overture	1. Mass	1. Oratorio
2. Sonata adagio	2. Other concerted pieces	2. Canzonet	2. Recitative	2. Requiem	2. Cantata
3. Sonata scherzo/ minuet and trio	3. Symphony	3. Romance	3. Song	3. Te Deum	
4. Sonata rondo	4. Overture	4. Grand aria	4. Aria	4. Offertory	
5. Fantasia	5. Ballet music	5. Ballad	5. Duet etc.	5. Gradual	
6. Variations	6. Concerto		6. Grand concert piece	6. Motet	
7. Capriccio			7. Chorus	7. Choral	
8. Étude					
9. Notturno					
10. Short piece					
11. Dance					
12. Military music					
13. Prelude					
14. Fugue					
15. Canon					

to become a regular musical piece, [the composer's] ideas and their development must assume a determinate *form*" (Czerny 1848, 1: 1, italics in original).

Czerny nominates six broad categories of species—solo piano works, instrumental works for multiple instruments, solo vocal works, opera, sacred works, and semisacred compositions—populating each category with species as explained in Table 25.2. The fluidity of defining characteristics is apparent in the fifteen piano species. Having considered the structure of themes themselves, Czerny moves directly to the sonata, explaining its four standard whole-movement forms as separate species. He approaches fantasia and variation in a similar way; subsequently, however, formal and topical typology begins to merge, although there is no attempt to retheorize the species in rhetorical terms. The chapter on dance (1848, 1: 104–8) furnishes a topical lexicon redolent of Ratner, moving through thirteen types, defined by their metrical, rhythmic, and expressive properties (Table 25.3).[3] Military music is treated as a species by itself.[4] Czerny (1848, 1: 109) identifies five subtypes (quick march, defiling march, parade march, solemn march, and funeral march) and three basic march rhythms, attributing their wide generic distribution to the "warlike character which exists in their forms."[5]

Tellingly, Czerny also distinguishes new and old topics. Thus the chapter on the étude explains its popularity in relation to the aging of eighteenth-century forms: "for as we are unfortunately not very rich in variety of musical forms, and as the names sonata, variations, rondo etc. already begin to grow old, we find the title *Study* (Étude) very acceptable" (Czerny 1848, 1: 90). As might be expected, new topics are concentrated in the area of the piano miniature. The nocturne, explained as an outgrowth of the vocal serenade,

Table 25.3 Czerny's Dance Topics

1. Waltz	8. Polka
2. Galop	9. Bolero
3. Minuet	10. Fandango
4. Quadrille	11. Tarantella
5. Polonaise	12. Siciliana
6. Mazurka	13. Russian national dances (2/4 time)
7. Ecossaise	

receives its own chapter, taking John Field as a representative exponent; and the chapter on small forms also introduces the bagatelle, impromptu, romance, ballad, and song without words (Czerny 1848, 1: 97–99). This maneuver sheds light on the treatise's historical orientation. Although Czerny makes no strong distinction between classic and romantic (the forms of the sonata and the nocturne all fall within his general concept of "modern" music), he nevertheless betrays an emergent sense that some species have become reified as a body of practice.

ANALYSIS

Schumann and the Piano Concerto

As a standard-bearer for the strong form of idealism, who was committed more than most to its literary transmission, Schumann constitutes perhaps the clearest example of a composer carving out a postclassical position that acknowledged the new imperative of expert listening. The convergence of criticism and composition in Schumann's case therefore sheds unique light on the postclassical condition of the topic, as a feature of his compositional style, and a more-or-less overt preoccupation of his critical writing.

Schumann's attitude toward the piano concerto offers an instructive case study for several reasons. Of all the genres with which he was concerned during his editorship of the *Neue Zeitschrift für Musik*, the piano concerto provoked perhaps the most consistently enunciated set of ideas, which translated into a compositional mandate ultimately realized in the Piano Concerto Op. 54. The body of concerti with which Schumann engaged, moreover, exhibits a uniquely clear and consistent system of topics, closely aligned with issues of form. Schumann's formal strategies in Op. 54 are in this way intimately related to his reception of the topical postures of the so-called virtuoso concerto.

The reception of the virtuoso concerto in the first half of the nineteenth century exemplifies *in nuce* the critical turn against miscellany mapped out by Weber. This was institutionalized in the founding principles of the London Philharmonic Society, which in 1813 admitted "the best and most approved instrumental music," but specifically excluded

"Concertos, Solos and Duets" (Ehrlich 1995: 4). Idealist critics singled out the concerto as symptomatic of the commercialist dilettantism encouraged by virtuosity, advocating "symphonic" music as a respectable alternative; as Dana Gooley (2006: 76) explains, "when critics described the waning taste for virtuosity, as they did repeatedly...in the 1830s and '40s, they were often enough trying to impose symphonic taste—to give readers the feeling that they should not like virtuosity."[6]

Schumann's own responses are documented in reviews written between 1836 and 1840 of concerti by Field, Hummel, Ries, Moscheles, Kalkbrenner, Chopin, Mendelssohn, Schornstein, Stamaty, Hiller, Döhler, Hertz, Hartknoch, Thalberg, Wieck, Taubert, Lassek, and Sterndale Bennett (Macdonald 2005). Pivotal to Schumann's view is dissatisfaction with the prevailing first-movement solo-orchestral division of labor; and lurking behind this is precisely the tension between structural and casual listening explored above. Composer-pianists had turned the genre into a vehicle for personal display, and this threatened the music's coherence, because it risked converting a unified form into a pot pourri of melodies and virtuosic episodes. In a review of Kalkbrenner's Fourth Concerto, Schumann rebuked "composers of concert-concertos" on the grounds that they habitually "prepared the solos already before the tuttis," surmising that "Herr Kalkbrenner devised his introductory and internal tuttis later, and merely shoved them into place" (Kreisig 1964, 1: 155; translation in Macdonald 2005: 123). Schumann's putative solution is sketched in a review of Moscheles's fifth and sixth concerti, in which he imagined as an alternative to the prevailing form "small concert pieces, in which the virtuoso could unfold the Allegro–Adagio–Rondo sequence in a single movement."[7] In the article "Piano Concertos" (1839), this aspiration is linked to an overcoming of the disparity of soloist and orchestra: the composer who realizes the above idea is also "the genius who will show us...how the orchestra and piano may be combined, how the soloist...may unfold the wealth of his instrument and his art, while the orchestra, no longer a mere spectator, may interweave its manifold facets into the scene" (Pleasants 1965: 146–47).

These arguments have implications for topical analysis, because the way Schumann reconceives the genre bears directly on the relationship between form and topic standardized in the virtuoso concerto by the 1820s, which observed a threefold discourse between bravura, cantabile (or espressivo) and brillant (display) topics, distributed simultaneously at various formal levels. As Table 25.4 explains, this discourse typically maps onto the form as a whole. Often, it also articulates lower formal levels. All three topics, for instance, follow in neat succession in the S1 solo-entry preface and transition of Chopin's Concerto in E minor, Op. 11 (Example 25.1).[8] Chopin begins with a periodic first idea (albeit without a medial cadence), based on the martial 3/4 music of R1's first theme, which clearly enunciates a bravura style (octave and wide chordal textures decorated with rapid figurations). There follows a subsidiary theme (mm. 155–79) drawn from the R1 transition, which shifts to the cantabile posture, referencing Chopin's nocturne and bel canto idioms. This episode is closed with a perfect authentic cadence, ushering in a transition, the continuous sixteenth-note passagework of which emphasizes brillant display.

Table 25.4 Typical Correlation of Topics and Form in the Virtuoso Concerto First–Movement Form

Large-scale functions 1:	Exposition 1				Exposition 2		
Large-scale functions 2:	R1				S1		
Inter-thematic functions:	A	TR	B	C	A	TR	B
Topics:	march	march/brillant/Sturm und Drang	singing style	march/brillant/Sturm und Drang	bravura; espressivo	display (brillant)	singing style

Large-scale functions 1:	Exposition 2 (cont.)		Development			Recapitulation	
Large-scale functions 2:	S1 (cont.)	R2	S2			R3	S3
Inter-thematic functions:	C		Pre-core	Core	RT	A	
Topics:	display (brillant)	march	bravura; espressivo	display (brillant)		march	bravura/espressivo

Large-scale functions 1:	Recapitulation (cont.)			Coda
Large-scale functions 2:	S3 (cont.)			R4
Inter-thematic functions:	TR	B	C	
Topics:	display (brillant)	singing style	display (brillant)	march/brillant/Sturm und Drang

EXAMPLE **25.1** Chopin, Piano Concerto in E minor, Op. 11/i, mm. 139–81.

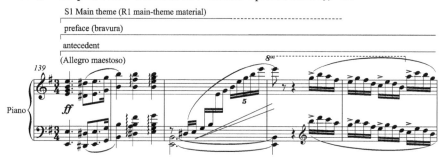

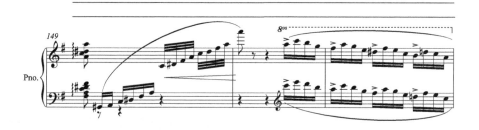

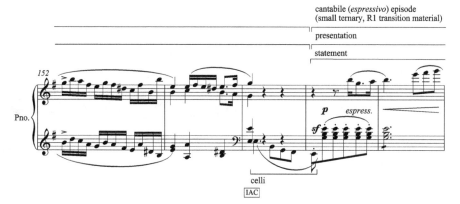

(Continued)

EXAMPLE **25.1** (Continued)

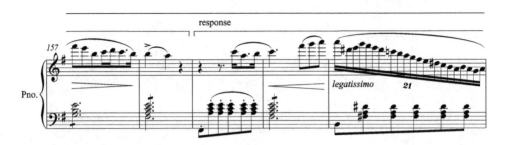

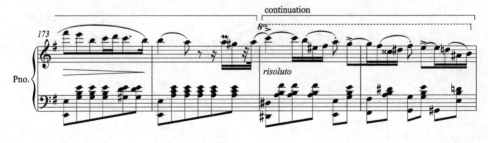

(*Continued*)

EXAMPLE **25.1** (Continued)

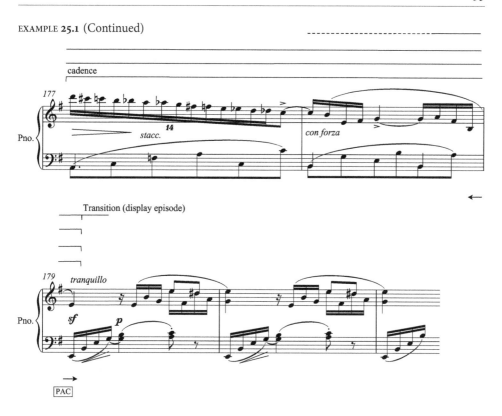

Superficially, Schumann's solutions in Op. 54 seem predominantly formal: the hybrid sonata–ritornello first-movement form is abandoned in favor of a unitary sonata design, which reduces the orchestra's independent contributions to occasional punctuating tutti.[9] Cutting across this, however, is a radical rethinking of the topical rhetoric evident in Chopin's concerto, which works in dialogue with a highly integrated thematic strategy. As consideration of the introduction, first theme, and transition, quoted in Example 25.2, reveals, the elements of virtuoso rhetoric are not jettisoned, but recontextualized. The material is organized as a three-measure chordal flourish and a sixteen-measure period respectively. Two aspects of the virtuoso solo-preface model—the bravura incipit and the *espressivo* continuation—are preserved, but they articulate two formal functions (introduction—main theme) rather than one (solo main theme). Simultaneously, the entire formal dialogue between orchestral ritornello and solo entry is collapsed into the first theme, because the antecedent is orchestral, whereas the consequent is given to the piano: Schumann at once compresses the hybrid model, and also spreads its topical elements across a wider formal area. The introduction and first theme additionally establish a discourse that is revisited later in the movement, which has implications for the disposition of the movement cycle: the incipit posits a scherzando topic, to which the *espressivo* main theme is a response. The dialogue of introduction and theme is therefore

EXAMPLE **25.2** Schumann, Piano Concerto in A minor, Op. 54/i, mm. 1–21.

(Continued)

EXAMPLE **25.2** (Continued)

a dialogue of incipient movement types—scherzo/first movement—as well as functions and topics.

Characteristics of the virtuoso model's display episodes are similarly retained but, in line with Schumann's integrative ambitions, they are made to perform a subthematic rather than thematic function. In the transition, beginning at m. 19, the display character of the virtuoso solo transition is referenced in the piano's rapid sixteenth-note figurations, although this precedent's relationship between figuration and material process is reversed, because the display element of the texture is subordinated to the thematic material in the first violins. The Animato passage beginning at m. 67 retrieves display figuration, and this texture persists until the exposition's concluding tutti enters at m. 134. The analogy with the virtuoso closing-section display episode seems clear, but Schumann problematizes this relationship in two ways. First, the passagework is again subthematic: the piano's figuration is not the material, but its accompaniment; in thematic terms, m. 67 initiates a fresh variant of the main theme. Second, the function of this material is in itself problematic. Although the texture suggests a closing section, from the perspective of the prior material, m. 67 expresses a kind of tonal and thematic stabilization more redolent of the initiation of subordinate-theme function. As with the introduction and first theme, so here also Schumann has dislocated the generic relationship between topic and function; closing-section rhetoric and subordinate-theme function coincide.

Schumann's reconfiguration of the relationship between topic and function appears on the largest scale in the development section, an overview of which is given in Table 25.5. The aspiration to "exploit the Allegro–Adagio–Rondo sequence in a single movement" comes to the fore here; the Andante espressivo episode in mm. 156–84 has the character of an interpolated slow movement, despite its derivation from the first theme (Macdonald 1995: 258; Daverio 1997: 237; Horton 2011: 70–79). More importantly for the present purposes, however, the episode's nocturne character means that it is also an expansion of the *espressivo* posture, so that the development begins by raising one of the three virtuoso styles to the level of a type (the nocturne as movement, not as style). The remainder of the development magnifies the other virtuoso topics in a similar way: the second part retrieves the introduction, and with it the bravura manner;

Table 25.5 Form and topics in the development of Schumann's Piano Concerto in A minor, Op. 54/i

Measures:	156	185	205	251
Movement cycle:	(Slow movement)	(Scherzo)	First movement	
Large-scale functions:		Development		
Inter-thematic functions:	nocturne episode	pre-core	Core	RT
Topics:	nocturne (*espressivo*)	scherzo (bravura)	display/*appassionato*	
Keys:	♭I	♭I →	VII →	standing on V/i

the third part and retransition return to display, albeit once again submerged beneath a development of the first theme.

Bruckner's Topics, Bruckner's Critics

The difficulties of relating topical analysis to social context are in various ways exacerbated as we enter the later nineteenth century. The polarization of critical positions into conservative versus progressive (and particularly "new-German") camps after 1850, enshrined in Franz Brendel's dialectically minded history of music (Brendel 1852), is one facet of a political context characterized by the consolidation of liberal and right-wing attitudes. Simultaneously, the performance conventions and notions of canon that are emergent in the early century become firmly established, and the focus of critical debate moves away from tensions between idealism and older performative or "amateur" cultures, and toward opinions gathering around Wagnerian aesthetics, the strands of formalism embodied in Eduard Hanslick's writings, and varieties of nationalism from *ars gallica* in France to the Kuchkists in Russia. At the same time, the pedagogical culture of the early century begins to feed into compositional practice in more tangible ways: the *Formenlehren* of Adolf Bernhard Marx, Czerny, and others embed a concept of expertise grounded in a conscious recognition of the classical canon and the whole-movement forms it bequeathed, thereby reinforcing the affiliation between structural listening and knowledge of Viennese classicism. The dialectic of classical and postclassical topics gains complexity accordingly: persisting classical topics accrue an additional half-century of sociopolitical baggage; and the novel topics of the early century themselves become reified as markers of tradition.

These factors are nowhere more evident than in Vienna; and in no area of Viennese musical life are they more starkly exposed than in debates about the symphony. Arguments about the coherence of Anton Bruckner's symphonies were central to this discourse. Liberal critics wrestled especially with the problem of explaining bald topical juxtapositions, marrying perceptions of rhetorical discontinuity with complaints that the symphonies offended against the categories of structural listening, especially the apparent absence of thematic and harmonic logic. Thus in response to a performance of the Sixth Symphony's inner movements in 1883, Hanslick noted "the grotesque humour of the Scherzo, which staggers about wearily and moves from one inexplicable contrast to another," while his 1885 review of the String Quintet famously dismissed Bruckner as "an anarchist who pitilessly sacrifices everything that is called logic and clarity of development and structural and tonal unity" (Howie 2002: 381, 443–44). Topical disunity and structural amateurism are similarly conflated in Gustav Dömpke's review of the 1886 Viennese premiere of the Seventh Symphony, the work that did more than any other to establish (belatedly) Bruckner's international reputation. Dömpke dismissed the symphony on the grounds that it was constituted from "the most heterogeneous dregs of Beethoven's and Wagner's music," sourcing this disorder to the absence of "an intellect which is capable of sifting these influences according to their value and essential ingredients." Dömpke traced the Scherzo's rhetorical incoherence to its juxtaposition of high and low styles (the music's "ugly mixture of roughness and over-refinement"), but reserved his strongest judgment for the Finale, which, he complained, "as a whole appears to have been swept together with a broom" (Howie 2002: 508–9).

Hanslick's party line was comparably toed by Max Kalbeck, whose review also highlighted an apparent heterogeneity of old and new and high and low styles, combined without the expertise that is the *Kenner*'s measure of artistic success:

> [The] Seventh Symphony is no more than an impromptu comedy with stock characters which are partly attractive and partly repellent, a picture painted in a variety of colours and modelled on Beethovenian and Wagnerian motives. Ideas coruscate and glimmer in the simmering broth-like mass of orchestral sound, but these ideas are the dead and mutilated remains of an old world doomed to destruction, not the fruitful seeds of a new world struggling to come into being. (Howie 2002: 510)

Kalbeck's view is nuanced by historical value judgments, which are characteristic of their time: combating the progressive claim that Bruckner takes up Beethoven's symphonic challenge, Kalbeck counters that the alliance of Beethoven and Wagner is not progressive, but simply forces together the disjunctive remnants of past styles.

These issues are notably clear in the Finale of the Seventh Symphony. The exposition betrays Bruckner's characteristic preference for three sharply profiled theme groups, central to which is the establishment of topical identities delineated by rhetorically marked caesurae. The first group is a martial variant of the first movement's main theme, organized as an eighteen-measure sentential period and an appended sixteen-measure transition. Any affiliation with classical syntax is, however, belied by the music's tonal organization: the theme begins in the tonic, but the antecedent cadences with an authentic cadence in ♭IV; the consequent sets off in the dominant, but cadences in ♭V. The music's topical clarity erodes as the transition progresses: from m. 27, the rhythm of the first-movement theme returns, displacing the double-dotted rhythms hitherto prevailing (Example 25.3); by m. 31, this has yielded to the chorale-like texture allotted to the horns, which prefigures the second theme.

EXAMPLE **25.3** Bruckner, Symphony No. 7 in E major, iv, mm. 19–38.

Responding to the transition's closing measures, the second group unfolds an unassuming chorale elaborated with a walking bass. Again, the syntax is conventional, contrasting the first group's periodic design with a small ternary form (A section in mm.
35–50; contrasting middle in mm. 51–64; A reprise in mm. 65–88; transition in mm.
89–92), but the harmonic language once more challenges the conventionality of both
topic and form, by dislocating the tonal relationships that frame intrathematic functions. Thus the statement in mm. 35–38 begins in A flat major and concludes with a perfect cadence in B flat; the response that follows opens in B major and cadences at m. 42
in C sharp; the continuation itself exhibits a statement-response pairing, the phrases of
which progress from C sharp to V of E and E flat to V of G flat respectively. Such frac-
turing of the phrase design's diatonic consistency characterizes the entire group, with
a concomitant impact on its tonal stability. The music reaches something like a condition of repose in the latter half of the contrasting middle (mm. 55–64), which stands on

V of F minor; but the reprise sidesteps this preparation, retrieving A flat as a point of departure; and the music's subsequent course gives A flat no security as a possible tonic, instead extending the continuation material into a sequence culminating at the group's end on V of A minor.

Although the first-theme material returns as the basis of the third group from m. 93, its topical identity is quite different. The *lieto-fine* march that the first group promises is transformed into an imposing *fortissimo* theme in octaves, which, in an act of studied archaism, recalls the French-overture style, while also supplying the main theme with a dramatic alter ego that initially tonicizes A minor.[10] The music's Baroque posture is reinforced by its sequential character: the entire group in mm. 93–112 comprises a series of sequences: a four-measure model and its sequence in mm. 93–100; a two-measure model and its sequence in 101–4, which spawns a four-measure linear intervallic pattern in mm. 105–8; and a two-measure model in mm. 109–10, the sequence of which is discontinued in m. 112. Thereafter, the first theme's initial identity is retrieved, and the exposition comes to rest on a tonic pedal in C major from m. 133. This stability heralds another topical shift: the pedal and string trills insinuate the pastoral style; the melodic material has the character of a hunting call or fanfare.

The exposition's topical discourse is tangibly social (extroversive) as well as musical-stylistic (introversive): the first theme and closing group offer opposed formulations of the secular, since an optimistic buffa march is transformed into a dramatized, but stylistically atavistic Baroque pastiche; the second theme is sacred. These topics are at once pointedly historicist and made to do markedly postclassical sociocultural labor: Bruckner's martial secularity is that of an Austria-Hungary in the aftermath of the Austro-Prussian War and the *Ausgleich* of 1868; his sacred style posits Catholicism in the midst of Viennese liberalism (Boyer 1981: 136–37; Horton 2004: 26–63). The tension between eighteenth-century topics and their late-nineteenth-century context is reflected in the conflation of classical syntax and post-Wagnerian harmony: both treat historicized conventions as vessels for modern musical and extra-musical content.

Broadly speaking, the remainder of the movement reorders this discourse so that the buffa march has the last word. The development is conventional up to a point: a precore based on the fanfare material (mm. 145–62) yields to a martial core dwelling on the first theme in mm. 163–90. The closing group returns, beginning in B minor, from m. 191, and appears initially to advance toward a developmental highpoint. This passage, however, comes to a halt over a tonally ambiguous caesura in m. 212, after which the second-theme chorale ensues in C major, bringing with it the emerging possibility that a reversed recapitulation is in progress. This impression is reinforced when the second theme's contrasting middle merges into the first theme's continuation phrase in m. 246, and confirmed with the literal first-theme tonic reprise at m. 275.

If the diagnosis of a reversed recapitulation seems simplistic (the tonic is nowhere implied until m. 275), we might at least argue that the development "becomes" a reversed recapitulation in the sense recently formulated by Janet Schmalfeldt (2011).[11] This process has a fundamental impact on the procession of topics. In the exposition, the juxtaposition of march and chorale leads to a closing section that corrupts the first theme's topical identity. In the recapitulation, retrieval of the closing group leads to a harmonic and expressive impasse (m. 212), after which the music conversely works toward the first theme via the chorale. The reversal of thematic order facilitates continuity between chorale and march, which in the exposition was covert at best; in so doing, it engineers a kind of topical, and therefore social, reconciliation.

Bruckner saves one further event for the coda, which seals this sense of expressive resolution. The recapitulation culminates in mm. 313–15 in an impressive authentic cadence built from an augmentation of the main theme's cadential phrase, which leads into the movement's first sustained use of a post-classical topic. The first theme builds up from m. 315 over a tonic pedal, leading in m. 331 to a grand retrieval of the first movement's main theme. The harmonic stasis here—I and V are conflated over the pedal point—combines with the stratified rhythmic texture to generate an example of the notion of *Klangfläche* developed by Warren Darcy: a rumination on harmonic and instrumental sonority, which suspends the harmony's sense of functionality (Darcy 1997: 276–77; see Dahlhaus 1989: 307–9). We can define this as a topical style, which has its lineage in the openings of Beethoven's Ninth Symphony and above all Wagner's *Das Rheingold*. Its positioning at the movement's end reflects a strikingly modern music-historical attitude: the persistent tension between classical topics and postclassical harmony, manifest in the first theme's inability to cadence in a key related to the tonic, melts away in the wake of the decisive structural cadence, at which point the music is released from its dependence on classical rhetoric and attains a new topical identity.

The subjection of inherited topics to a kind of harmonic and gestural radicalization in this movement amply explains the impression of incoherence expressed in the liberal press, even allowing for partisan political motivations. The narrative implied by the topical discourse and its formal disposition is nevertheless clear: Bruckner creates a rhetorical deadlock in the exposition signified by gestural discontinuities, from which the form is liberated in the recapitulation by reversing the topical and form-functional order. Hermeneutic capital may well be made from the sacred topic's pivotal role in this narrative, mindful of Bruckner's devout faith; yet for the present purposes, it is perhaps more instructive to note the formal logic that the topical discourse articulates. *Pace* Hanslick, Bruckner's music still demands a kind of structural listening, but its detection requires a special sensitivity to the topic's postclassical condition.

CONCLUSION

Agawu's narrative of the topic's evolution from the eighteenth to the twentieth century is worth quoting in full, both as an apposite summary and a starting point for debate:

> To put these developments in a nutshell: in the eighteenth century, topics were figured as stylized conventions and were generally invoked without pathos by individual composers, the intention being always to speak a language whose vocabulary was

essentially public without sacrificing any sort of will to originality. In the nineteenth century, these impulses were retained, but the burgeoning of expressive possibilities brought other kinds of topic into view... Twentieth-century topical practice became, in part, a repository of eighteenth- and nineteenth-century usages even as the universe was expanded to include the products of various strategic denials. (Agawu 2009: 48)[12]

As this synopsis indicates, there should be no impediment to adapting topic theory beyond the confines of the eighteenth century; on the contrary, the development of a substantial view of nineteenth-century musical style is impossible without acknowledging the central role topics play in its construction. It has been the central claim of this chapter, however, that such acknowledgment needs to be nuanced in relation to changing social and cultural circumstances, and this adds a dialectical twist with which eighteenth-century applications of topic theory do not normally have to deal, originating in the fact that postclassical music embodies a dialectic of tradition and innovation, apparent both in the contrast of old and new styles, and in the reframing of eighteenth-century topics, as old means are put to new expressive ends. In both Schumann's concerto and Bruckner's symphony, the topical discourse takes for granted a kind of historicism that is alien to eighteenth-century music, refracting not only isolated topics but an entire lexicon through a historicist prism, while at the same time expecting those topics to support fresh syntactic and harmonic protocols.

These observations suggest, in turn, that if topical approaches to nineteenth-century music are to succeed, then we need to amend our analytical methodology as well as the lexicon it applies. Crucial to this is a willingness to test statements about topical usage against the shifting backdrop of critical, performative, theoretical, aesthetic, and social circumstances, from expert listening and canon formation to revolution and industrialization. Bruckner's topics, like Mozart's, are "subjects for musical discourse," to retrieve Ratner's phrase; but between 1791 and 1896 the nature of that discourse changes irrevocably.

Notes

1. Topic theory serves as a platform for analyzing nineteenth-century music in a rather different sense in the work of Robert Hatten (1994; 2004).
2. On the characteristics of the nocturne as genre, see Jeffrey Kalberg (1988; 1992). On changes in piano technology in this time and the development of the nocturne style, see Rowland (1998: 30–31, 145–47).
3. Czerny's list builds on the discussion of small compositions by Mattheson and Sulzer. See Danuta Mirka's discussion in the introduction to this volume.
4. This reflects Mattheson's suggestion to supplement the church, theatrical, and chamber style with a martial style. See Mirka's introduction (this volume).
5. This typology suggests an ever-growing differentiation of marches in the nineteenth century. For the early stages of this process in the eighteenth century, see Andrew Haringer's chapter (this volume).

6. Gooley examines a variety of perspectives in the writings of Schumann, Hanslick, Wilhelm Triest, Gottfried Fink, Eduard Krüger, August Kahlert, Carl Gollmick, Heinrich Hirschbach, and Ludwig Granzin, in which context Schumann and Fink occupied opposite poles of opinion.

7. "Allerdings fehlt es an kleineren Konzertstücken, in denen der Virtuose den Allegro-Adagio- und Rondo-Vortrag zugleich entfalten könnte" (Kreisig 1964, 1: 163).

8. My abbreviations for components of the sonata form are taken from Hepokoski and Darcy (2006).

9. These formal innovations stand more sharply in relief in the first movement's original conception as a single-movement *Phantasie*, completed in 1841; the remaining two movements were completed in 1845. On the genesis of the *Phantasie*, see Macdonald (1995) and Daverio (1997: 237–38).

10. Mary Hunter's remarks about buffa marches (this volume) provide a useful context for my discussion.

11. The reversed recapitulation is a problematic category. This movement's recapitulation has been interpreted as such by Timothy L. Jackson (1997). On the other hand, the concept of the reversed recapitulation in classical sonata forms is rejected by James Hepokoski and Warren Darcy (2006: 365–69).

12. Agawu (2009: 48–49) cites an unpublished lexicon of twentieth-century musical topics devised by Danuta Mirka.

References

Agawu, V. Kofi. 1991. *Playing with Signs: A Semiotic Interpretation of Classic Music.* Princeton: Princeton University Press.

——. 2009. *Music as Discourse: Semiotic Adventures in Romantic Music.* New York: Oxford University Press.

Boyer, John. 1981. *Political Radicalism in Late Imperial Vienna.* Chicago: University of Chicago Press.

Brendel, Franz. 1852. *Geschichte der Musik in Italien, Deutschland und Frankreich von den ersten christlichen Zeiten bis auf die Gegenwart.* Leipzig: Breitkopf und Härtel.

Burnham, Scott. 2002. Form. In *The Cambridge History of Western Music Theory*, ed. Thomas Christensen, 880–906. Cambridge: Cambridge University Press.

Czerny, Carl. 1848. *School of Practical Composition.* Trans. John Bishop. 3 vols. London: Cocks.

Dahlhaus, Carl. 1989. *Nineteenth-Century Music.* Trans. J. Bradford Robinson. Berkeley: University of California Press.

Darcy, Warren. 1997. Bruckner's Sonata Deformations. In *Bruckner Studies*, ed. Paul Hawkshaw and Timothy L. Jackson, 256–77. Cambridge: Cambridge University Press.

Daverio, John. 1997. *Robert Schumann: Herald of a New Poetic Age.* New York: Oxford University Press.

Dickensheets, Janice. 2003. Nineteenth-Century Topical Analysis: A Lexicon of Romantic Topoi. *Pendragon Review* 2/1: 5–19.

Ehrlich, Cyril. 1995. *First Philharmonic: A History of the Royal Philharmonic Society.* Oxford: Clarendon.

Forkel, Johann Nikolaus. 1777. *Ueber die Theorie der Musik, insofern sie Liebhabern und Kennern nothwendig und nützlich ist*. Göttingen: Wittwe Vandenhöck.

——. 1778–79. *Musikalisch-Kritische Bibliothek*. Gotha: Ettinger.

Gjerdingen, Robert. 2007. *Music in the Galant Style*. New York: Oxford University Press.

Gooley, Dana. 2006. The Battle against Instrumental Virtuosity in the Early Nineteenth Century. In *Franz Liszt and His World*, ed. Christopher H. Gibbs and Dana Gooley, 75–111. Princeton: Princeton University Press.

Grabócz, Márta. 1996. Semiological Terminology in Musical Analysis. In *Musical Semiotics in Growth*, ed. Eero Tarasti, 195–218. Bloomington: Indiana University Press.

Hatten, Robert. 1994. *Musical Meaning in Beethoven: Markedness, Correlation, and Interpretation*. Bloomington: Indiana University Press.

——. 2004. *Interpreting Musical Gestures, Topics, and Tropes*. Bloomington: Indiana University Press.

Hepokoski, James and Warren Darcy. 2006. *Elements of Sonata Theory: Norms, Types, and Deformations in the Late-Eighteenth-Century Sonata*. New York: Oxford University Press.

Holoman, D. Kern. 2004. *Société des Concerts du Conservatoire, 1828–1967*. Berkeley: University of California Press.

Horton, Julian. 2004. *Bruckner's Symphonies: Analysis, Reception and Cultural Politics*. Cambridge: Cambridge University Press.

——. 2011. John Field and the Alternative History of Concerto First-Movement Form. *Music and Letters* 92/1: 43–83.

Howie, Crawford. 2002. *Anton Bruckner: A Documentary Biography*. Vol. 2: *Trial, Tribulation and Triumph in Vienna*. Lampeter: Edwin Mellen.

Jackson, Timothy L. 1997. The Finale of Bruckner's Seventh Symphony and the Tragic Reversed Sonata Form. In *Bruckner Studies*, ed. Timothy L. Jackson and Paul Hawkshaw, 140–20. Cambridge: Cambridge University Press.

Kallberg, Jeffrey. 1988. The Rhetoric of Genre: Chopin's Nocturne in G minor. *19th-Century Music* 11/3: 238–61.

——. 1992. The Harmony of the Tea Table: Gender and Ideology in the Piano Nocturne. *Representations* 39: 102–33.

Kreisig, Martin, ed. 1964. *Robert Schumann: Gesammelte Schriften über Musik und Musiker*. 2 vols. Leipzig: Breitkopf und Härtel.

Liszt, Franz. 1859. Über John Fields Nocturne. Trans. Julius Schuberth. In *John Field: 18 Nocturnes*, ed. Franz Liszt, 2–8. Leipzig: Julius Schuberth.

Macdonald, Claudia. 1995. "Mit einer eigener außerordentlichen Composition": The Genesis of Schumann's *Phantasie* in A minor. *Journal of Musicology* 13/2: 240–59.

——. 2005. *Robert Schumann and the Piano Concerto*. New York and London: Routledge.

McCreless, Patrick. 2002. Rhetoric. In *The Cambridge History of Western Music Theory*, ed. Thomas Christensen, 847–79. Cambridge: Cambridge University Press.

Monelle, Raymond. 2006. *The Musical Topic: Hunt, Military and Pastoral*. Bloomington: Indiana University Press.

Pleasants, Henry, ed. 1965. *Schumann on Music: A Selection from the Writings*. New York: Dover.

Ratner, Leonard G. 1980. *Classic Music: Expression, Form, and Style*. New York: Schirmer.

Riley, Matthew. 2003. Johann Nikolaus Forkel on the Listening Practices of "Kenner" and "Liebhaber." *Music and Letters* 84/3: 414–33.

——. 2004. *Musical Listening in the German Enlightenment: Attention, Wonder and Astonishment*. Aldershot, UK: Ashgate.

Rowlands, David, ed. 1998. *The Cambridge Companion to the Piano*. Cambridge: Cambridge University Press.

Schmalfeldt, Janet. 2011. *In the Process of Becoming: Analytic and Philosophical Perspectives on Form in Early Nineteenth-Century Music*. New York: Oxford University Press.

Subotnik, Rose Rosengard. 1996. Towards a Deconstruction of Structural Listening: A Critique of Schoenberg, Adorno and Stravinsky. In Rose Rosengard Subotnik, *Deconstructive Variations: Music and Reason in Western Society*, 148–76. Minneapolis and London: University of Minnesota Press.

Weber, William. 2008. *The Great Transformation of Musical Taste: Concert Programming from Haydn to Brahms*. Cambridge: Cambridge University Press.

General Index

"f" indicates material in figures. "n" indicates material in notes. "t" indicates material in tables. **Bold** indicates material in examples.

Abblasen, 198, 210n.10

Abert, Hermann, 62, 260, 279, 367, **372**, 373, 376n.20, 377n.26

accompanied recitative, 62, 82, 102, 260, 269, 279, 283

Adorno, Theodor W., 645

affect, 2, 3, 6, 7, 8–9, 10–12, 15, 17, 20, 21–32, 38, 39–42, 46, 48n.9, 48n.17, 49n.20, 51n.46, 100, 264, 309, 357–62, 365, 373–74, 455, 458–59, 578, 579, 580, 588, 629–39. *See also* emotion; character; passion; sentiment

  genre and, 7, 30, 37, 41, 357–58

  style and, 6–7, 30, 37, 48n.9

  sympathy and, 13, 14, 26, 252

  sympathetic vibration and, 13–14

affective signification, 22–30, 31f, 37, 42–43, 52n.52

Affektenlehre, 10, 39, 49n.19, 358. *See also* doctrine of affections

Agawu, Kofi, 1–2, 21–22, 33, 46, 47n.2, 50n.35, 52n.53, 73, 74, 76, 84, 87n.2, 144, 160–61, 195, 212n.39, 474–90, 591, 644, 660–61

  extroversive/introversive semiosis, 79, 88n.9, 381, 383, 504

  Universe of Topic (UT), 2, 22, 62, 415, 455, 468n.3, 475–76

Agricola, Johann Friedrich, 245–48, 255n.7, 255–56n.9, 256n.14

Albrechtsberger, Johann Georg, 304–5, 313, 391

Algarotti, Francesco, 339, 350n.6, 351n.18

Alison, Archibald, 292

alla breve (meter), 88n.16, 211n.32, 359, 365, 377n.35, 498, 542, 549n.13. *See also* meter, 2/2

alla breve (style), 98, 286, 416t, 493, 506

Allanbrook, Wye Jamison, 2, 28–29, 30–31, 33, 39, 46, 48n.16, 50nn.38–39, 52n.53, 61, 84, 88n.16, 90, 120, 121, 157, 211n.30, 221, 294, 331, 349n.1, 372, 377n.35, 377n.38, 469n.9, 475–76, 521, 534n.11, 535n.23, 549n.13, 559–64, 577, 591, 603, 627n.8

  on dances, 144, 157–60

  on expression, 22–23

  on instrumental music, 29–30

  on meter, 357, 360–61

  on imitation (mimesis), 28–29, 100

  on musical and rhetorical topics, 39

alla zoppa, 416t, 455, 494, 505

allemande (Baroque dance), 7, 49n.21, 165t

Allemande (spinning dance), 189n.26, 219. See also *contredanse allemande*

Alphorn, 398–99, 470n.20, 619–20, 627n.19

Altenburg, Johann, 198

Altmann, Wilhelm, 343, **344**

amateur (*Liebhaber*), 47, 71, 72, 206, 602–26, 645

Angiolini, Gasparo, 268

angloise, 7, 11. See also *contredanse anglaise*

aria, 5, 40, 82, 65–66, 79, 86–87, 269, 306–7, 332–35, 416t, 644t, 647t

Aristotle, 39, 539–40, 548n.1

ars combinatoria, 39

Aufzug, 20, 29, 202. *See also* entrée (instrumental music)

authenticity, 2, 577, 596

awe, 287, 297n.12, 630

axial melodies, 397

Bach, Carl Philip Emanuel, 119, 195, 250, 260–62, 268, 269, 272–73, 274, 391, 552, 558, 564, 565, 573n.25

INDEX OF MUSICAL COMPOSITIONS

"f" indicates material in figures. "t" indicates material in tables. **Bold** indicates material in examples.

CPSIA information can be obtained
at www.ICGtesting.com
Printed in the USA
BVHW080956031019
560071BV00003B/6/P